Fiddling Is My Joy

American Made Music Series

American Made Music Series
Advisory Board

David Evans, General Editor
Barry Jean Ancelet
Edward A. Berlin
Joyce J. Bolden
Rob Bowman
Curtis Ellison
William Ferris
John Edward Hasse
Kip Lornell
Bill Malone
Eddie S. Meadows
Manuel H. Peña
Wayne D. Shirley
Robert Walser

Fiddling Is My Joy

The Fiddle in African American Culture

Jacqueline Cogdell DjeDje

University Press of Mississippi / Jackson

The University Press of Mississippi is the scholarly publishing agency of
the Mississippi Institutions of Higher Learning: Alcorn State University,
Delta State University, Jackson State University, Mississippi State University,
Mississippi University for Women, Mississippi Valley State University,
University of Mississippi, and University of Southern Mississippi.

www.upress.state.ms.us

The University Press of Mississippi is a member
of the Association of University Presses.

This book is freely available in an open access edition thanks to TOME
(Toward an Open Monograph Ecosystem)—a collaboration of the Association
of American Universities, the Association of University Presses, and the
Association of Research Libraries—and the generous support of Arcadia,
a charitable fund of Lisbet Rausing and Peter Baldwin, and the UCLA Library.
Learn more at the TOME website, available at: openmonographs.org.

The digital edition of this book may be shared under a Creative Commons
Attribution-NonCommercial 4.0 international license (CC BY-NC 4.0).
For information about this license, see https://creativecommons.org/licenses
/by-nc/4.0/deed.en. This license applies only to content created by the author,
not to separately copyrighted material. To use this book, or parts of this book,
in any way not covered by the license, please contact University Press of Mississippi.

Any discriminatory or derogatory language or hate speech regarding race,
ethnicity, religion, sex, gender, class, national origin, age, or disability that has
been retained or appears in elided form is in no way an endorsement of
the use of such language outside a scholarly context.

Copyright © 2025 by Jacqueline Cogdell DjeDje
All rights reserved
Manufactured in the United States of America
∞

Publisher: University Press of Mississippi, Jackson, USA
Authorised GPSR Safety Representative: Easy Access System Europe -
Mustamäe tee 50, 10621 Tallinn, Estonia, gpsr.requests@easproject.com

Library of Congress Control Number: 2025933330
Hardback ISBN: 9781496856555
Trade paperback ISBN: 9781496856562
Epub single ISBN: 9781496856630
Epub institutional ISBN: 9781496856647
PDF single ISBN: 9781496856661
PDF institutional ISBN: 9781496856654
OA epub ISBN: 9781496857019
OA PDF ISBN: 9781496857026

British Library Cataloging-in-Publication Data available

Contents

Acknowledgments ix

About *Fiddling Is My Joy Companion* **on eScholarship** xiii

Prologue xv

Section 1. Pre-Twentieth Century
The Beginnings and Rise in Popularity of Black Fiddling

Introduction 3

Chapter 1. The Earliest Evidence: Black Fiddling During the 1600s and 1700s 5
- Polydor Gardiner | Rhode Island
- Caesar, Cato, and Robert Prim | Connecticut
- Othello and Sampson | Massachusetts
- Cuffee, Jamaica, and John Marrant | New York
- Peter | Philadelphia
- Derby, Peter, Robert, Sambo, Simeon Gilliat, Devereux Jarratt, and George Walker | Virginia
- Clarinda | South Carolina

Chapter 2. A General Overview: Black Fiddling During the 1800s 39

Chapter 3. A Regional Perspective: Black Fiddling During the 1800s 71
- The Snowden Family Band | Ohio
- James Thomas | Tennessee
- Ben Guyton | Alabama
- George Morris | West Virginia
- Augustus "Gus" Cochran | Alabama
- Solomon Northup | New York, Louisiana

- Gus Rhodes | Alabama
- The Owens Family | Mississippi
- Charles Lipscomb | Texas

Section 2. Early Twentieth Century
The Decline in Prominence of Black Fiddling

Introduction 123

Chapter 4. Black Fiddling and Secular Music in the Rural South 127

Central Appalachian Mountains and Neighboring Regions

Chapter 5. Maryland, Virginia, West Virginia 151
- William Adams Jr. | Maryland
- George Leonard Bowles | Virginia
- Carl Choice Martin | Virginia
- Posey Foddrell | Virginia
- Stephen Tarter | Virginia
- Mert Perkins | West Virginia
- Jilly Grace | West Virginia

Chapter 6. Kentucky 178
- Owen Walker
- James "Jim" D. Booker Jr.
- Arnold Shultz
- Ella Shultz Griffin
- Shell Coffey and Charlie Buster
- William "Bill" Livers

Chapter 7. Tennessee 221
- Frank Patterson Jr.
- John Lusk
- Bennie "Cuje" Bertram
- Walter Greer
- Joel Rice

Chapter 8. North Carolina 254
- Madison Boone Reid
- Joseph Thompson

Southern Appalachian Mountains and Neighboring Regions

Chapter 9. South Carolina, Georgia, Alabama, Mississippi 287
- Henry J. Bryant | South Carolina
- Andrew Baxter | Georgia
- Fort Valley College Music Festival | Georgia
- Elbert J. Freeman | Georgia
- Joe Kinney Rakestraw | Georgia
- Alfred Thomas | Georgia
- George Hollis | Georgia
- Earnest Mostella | Alabama
- Ripley String Band | Mississippi
- Ernest "Boose" Taylor | Mississippi
- Sidney Hemphill | Mississippi
- Robert "Bob" Pratcher | Mississippi
- Thomas Jefferson Dumas | Mississippi

The Ozark Mountains

Chapter 10. Missouri 343
- Ace Donell Sr.
- William "Bill" Katon
- William "Bill" Alexander Driver Jr.

South Atlantic and Gulf Coasts and Neighboring Regions

Chapter 11. Virginia, North Carolina, South Carolina, Georgia, Florida, Alabama, Mississippi, Arkansas 357
- Fred Perry | Florida
- Eddie West | Alabama
- Bo Chatmon [Carter], Harry Chatmon | Mississippi
- Lonnie Chatmon | Mississippi
- Henry "Son" Simms | Mississippi
- Blind Pete | Arkansas

Chapter 12. Louisiana, Texas 393
- James "Butch" Cage | Mississippi/Louisiana
- Morris Chenier | Louisiana
- Douglas Bellard | Louisiana
- Joseph "Bébé" Carrière | Louisiana

- Calvin Carrière | Louisiana
- Canray Fontenot | Louisiana
- Charlie Thomas | Texas
- Oscar William Nelson | Texas
- Teodar Jackson | Texas

Epilogue 440
- Howard Armstrong | Tennessee

References Cited: Print Sources, Interviews,
   Personal/Email Communication 463

References Cited: Discography, Film
   and Video, Radio, Websites 497

Index of Subjects and Names 501

Index of Song Titles and Dance Tunes 521

Acknowledgments

The seeds for *Fiddling Is My Joy: The Fiddle in African American Culture* were planted when I was a panel member for the United States National Endowment for the Arts, Folk Arts Program. Within that context, reading proposals from individuals who were applying for support to organize activities that included Black fiddlers helped me become (somewhat) aware of the breadth and depth of research known and unknown about fiddling in the United States. While Black fiddlers were recognized as important contributors to the cultural experience of individuals in their local communities, I, as a specialist in African American and West African music, knew little about these musicians or the music they performed. Therefore, I want to thank Bess Lomax Hawes, Director of the Folk Arts Program at the time, Daniel Sheehy, Barry Bergey, Mark Puryear, and others who were working on the staff or with whom I came in contact, for providing me with encouragement to pursue research on this project. After the initial seeds of interest in the topic grew, I began to pursue the work in earnest, not realizing the magnitude of what I was planning to do.

Fortunately, several government agencies, academic institutions, and foundations provided funding for travel to interview individuals, visit libraries and research centers to collect material, and hire students for research assistance. Entities in Washington, DC, included the US National Endowment for the Humanities, Fellowship for University Teachers and the Travel to Collections Grant from the Division of Fellowships and Seminars. Financial support from my home institution, the University of California, Los Angeles (UCLA), came from the Academic Senate; Ralph J. Bunche Center for Afro-American Studies and the Institute of American Culture; Afro American Studies Program for Interdisciplinary Research and the Ford Foundation; and UCLA Library to ensure that the project is freely available in an open access edition thanks to TOME (Toward an Open Monograph Ecosystem)—a collaboration of the Association of American Universities, the Association of University Presses, and the Association of Research Libraries—and the generous support of Arcadia, a charitable fund founded by Lisbet Rausing and Peter Baldwin, and the UCLA Library.

Without the assistance of librarians and staff at libraries and research centers, this project would not have been completed. In alphabetical order, these include the Fisk University John Hope and Aurelia E. Franklin Library; Library of Congress American Folklife Center (Judith Gray and Alan Jabbour); Middle Tennessee State University Center for Popular Music; the New York Public Library Schomburg Center for Research in Black Culture; the Rutgers University Institute of Jazz Studies; Smithsonian Institution National Museum of American History; Smithsonian Folkways (Cecille Chen, Will Griffin); Tulane University Hogan Jazz Archive; University of Georgia Richard B. Russell Library for Political Research and Studies (especially ethnomusicology faculty member Jean Kidula and library staff who introduced me to materials collected by faculty member Art Rosenbaum); University of Kentucky Libraries (Louie B. Nunn Center for Oral History); University of North Carolina at Chapel Hill Southern Folklife Center and Wilson Special Collections Library; and UCLA Libraries, including the Ethnomusicology Archive (Maureen Russell, David Martinelli, Aaron Bittel, and Paul Bancel), the Music Library (Bridget Risemberg), and the Charles E. Young Research Library.

My deepest gratitude goes to musicians and their family members, as well as researchers who shared information about fiddling with me in interviews and other communication. Listed alphabetically according to their surnames, these include Barry Jean Ancelet, Howard Armstrong, Etta Reid Baker, Dewey Balfa, John Blake Jr., Leonard Bowles and wife Naomi Bowles, Calvin Carrière and wife Valentine Carrière, Regina Carter, Iris Thompson Chapman, Dwight DeVane, Bill Driver, Dom Flemons, Canray Fontenot, Robert Fulcher, Rhiannon Giddens, John Harrod and wife Jane Harrod, D'Jalma Garnier III, Christian Horton, Scott Linford, Bill Livers and wife Hattie Livers, Kip Lornell, Wayne Martin, Dennis McGee, Cora Phillips, Henrique Prince, Joe and Odell Thompson, Burnham Ware, Claude Williams, and Sule Greg Wilson. Similarly, I want to thank the family members of fiddlers (who have passed), who have given me permission to use materials that enhances the discussion of the topic; these include Eric Caldwell, Iris Thompson Chapman, George W. Foster Jr., Yvette Rowser, and Raffeal Sears. Individuals who assisted in obtaining or making recommendations about individuals who should be interviewed were critical for the success of this project, for without this information it would have been difficult to proceed with the research; these individuals include Barry Jean Ancelet, John Harrod, Kip Lornell, Wayne Martin, and Sule Greg Wilson.

I am greatly indebted to individuals who did musical transcriptions that provided a deeper understanding of features that make Black fiddling distinctive: Brian Eisenberg, Kathleen Hood, Paul Humphreys, David Martinelli, Gigi Rabe, Sam Rabourn, Mackenzie Sato, Danica Stein, and Amy Wooley. In addition, I want to thank individuals for taking the time to read portions of the manuscript and give useful advice and recommendations: Donna Armstrong, Lynne Kostman, Eddie S. Meadows, Deborah Neal, and Ty-Juana Taylor.

Just as faculty and staff in my home department at UCLA and colleagues from other institutions helped by making suggestions about sources and people to contact, UCLA students assisted by conducting library research and transcribing interviews and music examples. These include Ric Alviso, Leonard Brown, Kimasi Browne, Mark DeWitt, Samuel Floyd, Paul Humphreys, Kenneth Igarashi, Cheryl Keyes, Eddie S. Meadows, Daniel W. Patterson, Karin Patterson, Colin Quigley, Anthony Seeger, and Katie Stuffelbeam. While they may not have helped with the scholarly aspects of the research, staff in my home department who assisted me with financial and administrative issues, as well as technology and other matters related to this project, are deeply appreciated. Among these are Jennie Molina, Betty Price, Martha Rider, and others whose names I do not remember.

I am deeply grateful to Craig Gill, the director of the University Press of Mississippi (UPM), his executive assistant Katie Turner, and other members of the UPM staff for their support and encouragement. To the anonymous referees who critically assessed early drafts of the manuscript and offered helpful insights and comments, I thank you.

Finally, enormous thanks go to Kathleen Hood, who assisted me in all matters, especially with technology and permissions; Karin Patterson, whose skills in designing the material for eScholarship make the project visually interesting and user-friendly; David Martinelli for helping to make the audio examples accessible; and Ray Knapp, who shared his experience in using technology in scholarly publications.

To my family (Eddie, Angela, Dominique, Longben, Kaya, and Ndaajiya), I thank you for your support and patience.

About *Fiddling Is My Joy* Companion on eScholarship

fiddlingismyjoycompanion.net

To help the reader understand better the musicking as well as the history and social factors that affected the development of African American fiddling, I have placed various types of materials on eScholarship, an open access publishing platform subsidized by the University of California.[1] While these materials are fundamental and important in understanding a musical tradition, rarely are they presented and made available to readers in a coherent and assembled manner, especially for rural Black America, the primary focus of this discussion.

On eScholarship one will find maps and discussions of land regions and counties, data about demographics (population trends),[2] brief accounts on the history of geographical areas, time periods, and other topics with special focus on African Americans. Audio and video recordings, photos, as well as other material (lyrics, music transcriptions, outlines of the musical form, performance analysis, repertoire, tables, and more) to enhance and provide deeper appreciation for fiddling by African Americans have also been uploaded to eScholarship. To make the materials easily accessible on eScholarship, each item is labeled according to its location in the text and numbered sequentially within each chapter. While audio examples are listed according to the names of performers and tables to specific time periods, other items have been organized according to categories with figure numbers. For example, the following labels are used for items in Chapter 5.

- 🎻 Analysis 5.1
- 🎻 Demographics 5.1
- 🎻 Form (i.e., musical form) 5.1
- 🎻 History 5.1
- 🎻 Land Regions 5.3
- 🎻 Lyrics 5.1
- 🎻 Map 5.1
- 🎻 Repertoire 5.1 (includes songs, recordings, newspaper articles, and other media about or by each fiddler)
- 🎻 Transcription 5.1

Therefore, any material in the endnotes that has the fiddle icon (🎻) next to it, as shown in the above, indicates that it can be found on eScholarship. The following describes how to access these materials.

At the beginning of the endnotes (Notes) of each chapter, the reader will find a link to a web address (URL) [and a QR code] that will take them to the contents page for the eScholarship (Fiddling Is My Joy Companion) material. Once there, the reader can scroll to and click on the corresponding item.

1. For information about eScholarship, please visit https://eScholarship.org/.
2. Although "US" may not always be indicated, it should be noted that all information regarding ancestry and population trends (demographics) have been take from US census records.

In the TOME e-book, the link to the eScholarship (Fiddling Is My Joy Companion) contents will be clickable. The link can also be copied and pasted into a browser's search field. For the printed book, the web address (URL) can be typed into the browser's search field. [Alternatively, a clickable live link to the eScholarship (Fiddling Is My Joy Companion) contents can be accessed by focusing on the provided QR code with cell phone or tablet camera.]

Prologue

For much of my professional career as a music scholar and professor, I have been fascinated with the bowed lute, commonly known as the fiddle or violin in the United States and much of the Western world.[1] This type of instrument is also found in West Africa, which has been the primary focal point of my research, as well as other parts of the globe. In recent years, I have expanded my investigations to include fiddling in African American culture.[2] Yet some may ask: why focus on the fiddle/violin among Black people in the United States when the instrument is rarely identified with African American music? Although the fiddle is not always associated with Blackness and the enslaved are not responsible for introducing the fiddle into North America (Epstein 1977; Southern 1997; Winans 2018b, 204),[3] I believe it is important to explore the degree to which Africans were involved with the tradition after their forced migration to the Americas, particularly since comparable musical practices existed in their homelands. Most people do not realize that bowed lutes have existed in West Africa and other parts of the African continent for centuries (DjeDje 1978a, 2008a; Marcuse 1975). I am also fascinated with the fiddle because of the meanings associated with it and how these features have affected its representation in culture (Himmelman 2019). For example, in spite of its links primarily with the music of white people in the United States, my analyses suggest that the fiddle may be one of the oldest (if not the oldest) uninterrupted instrumental traditions performed by African Americans, excluding percussive instruments such as drums, rattles, and the like.[4] Michael L. Hoffheimer (2002) states: "The violin may not leap to mind as a traditional African-American instrument. But when ex-slave Henry Bedford was interviewed in 1937, he singled out the fiddle as the main instrument used by slaves in his childhood" (1184).

If the fiddle/violin was prominent in African American culture during the earliest years of Black presence in the Americas, what accounts for the ambivalence or sometimes rejection of the instrument by many Black people in later years? Violinist and 2006 MacArthur awardee Regina Carter (2011), who believes the nonacceptance may be related to history, states:

I wonder if it's because, along with our history, the fiddle was something that we didn't want to deal with anymore. Did it not get passed down? Why didn't it get passed down? Has that tradition really continued and we just didn't know about it? Or is this something that died out? And was it a thing that youngsters weren't interested in doing? Or did they associate playing that music with another time, a time that isn't so nice or has some derogatory connotations around it? I'm interested in it because it's part of who we are. I know a group, the [Carolina] Chocolate Drops.[5] It's really beautiful to hear them. When I hear someone playing old-time music now, I say, "Oh yeah. That is a part of my tradition." It's a beautiful part of being an African American. It's something to really be proud of.[6]

Comments by John Blake Jr. (2011), an African American jazz violinist active during the late twentieth century, are also revealing: "I think the violin is an important instrument but I don't know if it has ever got the recognition that it deserved. It didn't get the same type of notoriety as the trumpet or the saxophone. It's still looked at as a novelty instrument. The amplification of the instrument might have also influenced how popular or unpopular it became." As one can surmise from these comments, researching the fiddle/violin raises a variety of questions and issues that can be approached in many ways. However, the issue that most interests me is the contradiction regarding the instrument's simultaneous survival and rejection.

Actually, the question is twofold: (1) why is the fiddle/violin not identified with African American music, and (2) why did Black musicians continue to perform or use it when it was rejected by many within African American culture? Because addressing these two questions will serve as the primary objective of this study, a brief discussion of the history of fiddle/violin as well as the qualities associated with its sound is appropriate. Perhaps this will help us better understand some of the issues that are involved in the contradiction.

History

As noted in the foregoing, Africans are not responsible for introducing the fiddle into the Americas. Rather, I am emphasizing that performing the instrument for Europeans[7] was not the sole and only reason for its prominence among African musicians. The enslaved were aware of bowed lutes before they were forcibly transported across the Atlantic because they had seen or performed them in their African homelands. The earliest evidence of fiddling by Africans in the Americas dates to the late seventeenth century, which is not long after their arrival in 1619[8] (Bruce 1907, 184). There is also documentation that Black people in the United States used gourds to make fiddles similar in construction to those found in West Africa (Work Projects Administration 2006). Before the Civil War, the fiddle and the African-derived banjo[9] were the primary instruments performed by enslaved musicians at nonreligious events for Blacks and whites. However, the most widely used instrument by Africans throughout the slave era was the fiddle, not the banjo. Unlike enslaved drummers who may have been killed or physically harmed for playing drums because these instruments were outlawed, Black people were allowed and even encouraged to perform the fiddle without any negative repercussions (Southern 1997; Epstein 1975, 1977; Winans 1990, 43–53, 2018b). So, what accounts for the prominence of the fiddle? I believe that because fiddling was a tradition admired and valued by Europeans who did not feel threatened by it, enslaved Africans continued performing the instrument. In addition, there was the issue of compatibility. In their homelands, Africans often "played fiddles and other stringed instruments in small ensembles, and could adapt Western equivalents without much effort"[10] (Roberts 1998, 61). Fiddling was also a means to a better life for the earliest enslaved because it allowed for the creation of an identity distinct from other Africans in the Americas.[11]

During the late nineteenth and early twentieth centuries, the fiddle and banjo were the primary instruments used to perform what is now called old-time music, which continued to be important among Black and white people in many parts of the South. When African American secular forms such as blues, jazz, and other styles of popular music were created in the twentieth century, some Black musicians in urban areas of the United States chose the violin to express themselves in performing these genres. During the 1940s, a decline in the performance of Black fiddling occurred in rural areas where it had been the primary form of entertainment for the family and local community. As people in the United States became infatuated with recorded sound and moving images during the early to mid-twentieth century, live performances of fiddle music in rural communities became less important.

Some Black fiddlers found new audiences during the folk music revival of the sixties and seventies. Their participation in festivals, concerts, tours, summer workshops, and seminars helped establish a national and global audience for rural-based fiddlers that was nonexistent in the early twentieth century. Therefore, an inversion had occurred. In earlier years, when the gatekeepers (such as record company executives, researchers, and general audiences) showed little interest in Black fiddling, African Americans kept it alive through live performances. When local Black communities abandoned the tradition, outsiders (or non-Blacks) started to embrace it.

African Americans trained in the performance of Western art music continued to use the violin during the late twentieth and early twenty-first centuries. Jazz—a genre that had a stronger kinship with European art (or classical) music than most Black musicking[12]—was the idiom of choice for many Black violinists with formal training. In later years, some Black fiddlers who played jazz experimented with world music by performing and studying with artists from

Africa, Latin America, and South Asia. Not only were violins a mainstay on the soul music recordings of Motown and other record companies during the 1960s and 1970s, some used the instrument to play other popular music genres such as rhythm and blues, rock, and hip hop.[13] Whenever a new musical genre emerged, musicians experimented with it on the violin (even though they received little recognition). It is also significant that more females began performing the fiddle professionally during the late twentieth and early twenty-first centuries.

As Blake Jr. (2011) notes, "the amplification of the instrument might have also influenced how popular or unpopular it became." Most fiddlers and scholarly references in the twentieth century comment on the violin's low volume. This was not an issue in early North America between the seventeenth and early twentieth centuries because all instruments were acoustic. Furthermore, the fiddle generally performed the high-pitched melodic part with accompanying instruments providing a lower-pitched melody or percussive sound.

The importance of the fiddle is evident in the Black instrumental ensembles popular during the 1920s and 1930s.[14] When Alabama-born W. C. Handy settled in Memphis in 1908, he often organized musical groups that fused the old and new. Coming from a family of fiddlers, Handy knew the importance of fiddle music in the lives of African Americans in the South. Therefore, many of his earliest ensembles in Memphis "always included a violin player, and often as many as three" (Wyatt 2001, 10). As string instruments declined in popularity because other instruments drowned them out, violins in Handy's bands were replaced by clarinetists and saxophonists who perfected legato and glissando once thought to be the province of the violins alone (10). In addition, other types of instruments became more prominent. When Thomas Dorsey performed blues in clubs in Atlanta under the name Georgia Tom, he states that "there'd be maybe three or four piano players there, or five," but not guitarists and fiddlers as "they didn't use them [then]. Only used 'em in the country . . . you didn't see 'em too often in town. There [in the city] they used piano" (Bastin 1986, 88).

After the late 1930s, however, low volume most likely accounts for the limited role of the violin in jazz. Most jazz researchers agree that "the violin was an important part of jazz during its formative years! It was heard in the earliest New Orleans bands and was present in all the new 'dance' bands at the start of the twentieth century. In fact, violin sections continued to be a part of the jazz music scene right on up to the Swing Era" (Blake Jr. 2001). Carter (2011) confirms this trend when she states: "Before bebop, the violin seemed to be playing a more prevalent role in jazz. Once bebop came around, you didn't see that many [violinists]. It seemed like they disappeared from the scene. Then I started to hear . . . [and] see material on Billy Bang, Joe Kennedy Jr., Charles Burnham. But that [was] more experimental music, avant-garde." Most writers indicate that the violin, even with an electronic pickup, was not comparable to musicking by horn players. Black jazz violinist Stuff Smith, who occasionally played with Dizzy Gillespie, made an attempt. But his efforts were not enough to compete with the sounds of saxophonist Charlie Parker and other bebop artists. To continue working professionally, many jazz violinists, like other instrumentalists in big bands, became proficient on several instruments. Kansas City–based Claude Williams was known equally for playing jazz violin and guitar, while New York–based Ray Nance, an exceptional violinist, was probably more well known for his performance of the trumpet than the violin with the Duke Ellington Orchestra.

Volume also became an issue in southwest Louisiana old-time music during the 1930s and 1940s. Most Black Creole ensembles included two fiddles (with one fiddler playing the melody while the second fiddler did the bassing), an accordion, and a triangle. Because of its loud volume, the accordion displaced the fiddle as the dominant instrument in the ensemble. White Louisiana fiddler Dewey Balfa (1987), who is well known for his Cajun fiddling, states: "When you played accordion, everybody heard you a lot better than if you played the fiddle. So, then you were more popular. Still today, ninety percent of the people that plays music in this area wants to play the accordion because it's loud, but it's so limited. The accordionist would attempt to emulate the fiddler's playing style, but only a few accordion players could perform the tone bending performed by fiddlers."

Many Black fiddlers who played old-time music during the late twentieth century believed difficulty in playing the instrument was another reason for the decline (or lack of interest) in fiddling by young musicians.[15] Basically, the lack of frets on the violin makes it more difficult to learn when compared with other instruments. Black Louisiana Creole fiddler Canray Fontenot (1988) explains: "Guitar got frets and . . . the accordion [has] the notes right there. . . . But the fiddle, you got . . . to have the exact touch." Confirming what others have indicated, Joe Thompson (1987), a Black fiddler from North Carolina, clearly states: "This fiddle is a hard instrument to play."

In spite of the low volume and difficulty in playing it, the sound produced on the fiddle/violin is greatly admired by both performers and listeners. When a reporter asked New York–based Noel Pointer (1981), a Black violinist noted for his performance of soul and other styles of popular music, why he played the violin, he stated: "A lot of people ask me why . . . out of all the instruments, why the violin? Well, it's probably the mere fact that the violin is so close to a human voice." Some performers have indicated that violins were included in popular music because they "sweeten the sound," which may account for their use in soul music and other African American popular music styles during the late twentieth and early twenty-first centuries (Patterson 2000). As a result, the sound quality is appreciated in genres not generally associated with the violin. In describing the use of violin in hip hop, music critic Rick Koster (2018) states: "Pondering the sonic and sample-heavy architecture of the average hip hop song, one doesn't immediately think of violin or viola . . . as having a big role. On the other hand, a well-played stringed instrument passage is among the most emotive and distinctive things in all music, so it only makes sense that hip hop could utilize such sounds in a big way."

Literature Review

Fiddling in North America is a topic of research that has received much attention,[16] but the contributions of African Americans constitute only a small portion of findings. Publications about Black fiddling include record compilations, with liner notes, highlighting different musical genres;[17] articles, recordings, and films on select musicians;[18] and historical overviews or studies that focus on specific issues, region, or time period.[19] Except for *Hidden in the Mix*, edited by Diane Pecknold (2013), as well as works providing source material and discussions of performance style,[20] no books, to my knowledge, have been published on the fiddling of African Americans that are comparable to the number of studies on fiddling by Anglo- or Euro-Americans (Beisswenger 2011).[21] To be sure, the authors mention or include information about Black fiddling in their investigations, but details about history, meaning, performance style, and other issues are minimal.

To a degree, the lack of published material on the subject is understandable when one considers factors that worked against the performance and later documentation of the tradition. Although fiddling was prominent during slavery, this did not stop protests from religious leaders. The fiddle's "association with dancing evoked condemnation among the religiously strict, evangelical sects, both black and white. Among some, fiddling was thought to be a skill of which only Satan was capable, hence its playing implied some level of communication with the Devil" (Jenoure 1981, 73). The appropriation and later ridicule and mockery of Black life by minstrel performers of both races during the nineteenth century caused many African Americans to reject the tradition. Having to compete with instruments that duplicated the fiddle's sound became a stumbling block in the instrument's use and popularity, particularly when musicians adopted new musical genres that became popular with Black audiences migrating from rural to urban areas.

Whereas white fiddlers received support and encouragement from government and research organizations as well as the media, by collecting and recording what was taking place, the same forces created obstacles for Black fiddlers.[22] Bolick (2015a) states: "Defining folklore seems to be a scholarly abstraction.... When African American folklore was defined as spirituals or blues, many black fiddlers were passed over" (ix). Similarly, African American fiddlers were underrepresented in the collections of fieldworkers employed by the Works Progress Administration (WPA) during the 1930s.[23] Commenting on research activity in

Mississippi, Bolick (2015a) indicates that "instructions given to the field workers for collecting from African American and Caucasian sources were quite different.... Most pertinently, there was no direction to collect fiddle tunes from African American sources. And yet, there seem to have been eight 1936 African American sources for fiddle tunes" (x). In 1939, WPA workers did not record any fiddle music from African American sources, although many performances by African Americans of other styles of music were documented (x).[24]

When the fiddle/violin became less visible in the performance of vernacular musics and various styles of popular music after World War II, some scholars probably surmised that Black fiddling had disappeared in both rural and urban areas. At that time, individuals conducting investigations tended to be music historians who relied almost totally on print (scores, books, newspapers, periodicals, and so on) or sound (audio recordings) materials for their analyses. Since rural Black musicians who performed secular music rarely had an opportunity to record and little print data were available, sources were seriously lacking.[25] On the rare occasion when the fiddle/violin was performed by Black people, it was regarded as a novelty. This may account for the lack of information on musicians who play the instrument in publications on the history of African American music. In Southern (1971a, 1983a, 1997), information about the fiddle/violin is limited primarily to slavery, early jazz dance bands, and art music; the role of the instrument in blues and other popular music genres is almost nonexistent. Unfortunately, books and texts published in later years continue the same omission. Thus, much of what we know about Black secular music in the early twentieth century is based on musical styles created and performed by African Americans in urban areas. Furthermore, it is these styles that are represented as the musical creations for *all* US Blacks, in spite of the fact that African Americans may have preferred and performed other musical genres. The emphasis on urban culture raises two other issues: the elitism on the part of some African American scholars during the early twentieth century who questioned the worthiness of vernacular secular music when compared to spirituals and art music traditions; and the bias against rural vernacular traditions produced by African Americans because, during the early twentieth century, both Black and white Americans regarded African American culture as primarily urban. Finally, there is the issue of racism—bias against the findings of Black scholars that continues to plague the research on Black music.[26]

Although Black fiddling was prominent during the slave era through the late nineteenth century, the tradition began to decline in many Black communities along or near the South Atlantic and Gulf coasts during the first half of the twentieth century. Yet, fiddling continued to be popular among some African Americans in rural mountain and piedmont areas of the South as well as parts of the Midwest, specifically Missouri. While studies (primarily recordings) have been published on individual musicians in specific states and the activities of rural-based fiddlers who returned to the profession (or started playing the instrument again) during the late twentieth and early twenty-first centuries, rural Black fiddlers have never been examined as a group. For this reason, this book is needed because these developments have not been addressed in scholarship on Black music.

In focusing on Black fiddling in rural areas of the United States before the 1950s, perhaps this will help (1) provide knowledge and material for a more complete understanding of musicking in African American culture, (2) demonstrate other ways in which Black musicking has affected the development of "American" music, and (3) acknowledge and recognize the shared culture that contributed to the development of old-time and what is now called country music. Just as studies about musicking in the Georgia Sea Islands where the communities were majority Black help us understand the degree that African-derived elements were maintained, examining musicking in areas where Blacks were in the minority or isolated from emerging traditions may aid in understanding what happens to these elements in a completely opposite environment. In these contexts, what musical and performance features that have been maintained or appropriated by others are actually African-derived?

Since my research is limited to the previously mentioned topic, there is much that is not included, although cursory mention of certain issues may be cited in the text. Therefore, the following is recommended for further in-depth research: Black fiddling in the urban South and North before World War II;[27] the contributions of Black fiddlers to blues, jazz, and various styles of popular music from the 1950s through the present; the resurgence in interest in old-time music and its performers during the late twentieth century; and an analysis of the activities of newcomers such as the Ebony Hillbillies, Sankofa Strings, and the Carolina Chocolate Drops during the late twentieth and early twenty-first centuries. It is hoped that by combining my research with these and related topics, the end result will be a more complete and inclusive documentation of Black musicking in the United States.

Methodology

To address the two questions raised in the foregoing and gain a deeper understanding of factors that affected the development of the fiddle in African American culture, I believe a comprehensive and in-depth examination of the topic is needed because, as noted above, previous research has focused primarily on select fiddlers and issues. Furthermore, an interdisciplinary approach is required. As Christopher Lornell (1996) explains: "Music should not be viewed only as a historical and musical phenomenon, but also from the perspectives provided to us by scholars in the fields of anthropology, American studies, sociology, and cultural geography, among others" (827). An all-encompassing work that includes an examination of both rural and urban fiddling would have required too much space.[28]

Thus, the purposes of this book are threefold: (1) to focus on fiddling among Black musicians in the southern rural areas of the United States; (2) to provide a thorough analysis of the contributions of these musicians with attention given to factors that may have affected their creativity, particularly physical and social environment, family and community, the media, and interactions with whites; and (3) to produce a companion volume to previous research on West African fiddling.

Since I regard this book as complementary to *Fiddling in West Africa* (DjeDje 2008a), my approach and discussion of issues are similar to those presented in that work: "Scholars who use a multi-sited ethnography focus their studies through several techniques. They may research a people, an object, a metaphor, a plot (story or allegory), a life (or biography), or a conflict. In this book, I am following the fiddle, realizing all the time that the object could not have moved without people" (9). Because duplication of information cannot be avoided in a multisited ethnography (Marcus 1995, 102), similar statements may appear in the discussion about the role of the fiddle and fiddlers in a community: their learning, performance style, and social significance (or importance), as well as other topics.[29]

In this study, questions such as the following are addressed: In what way was fiddling during slavery similar or different from that performed during the early twentieth century? Why did fiddling before World War II continue to be popular in some areas of the United States and not others? What accounts for similarities and differences in the performance style of fiddlers in various parts of the United States, particularly since the media were late in documenting the tradition and making it available to the general public? To what extent has race or interactions between Black and white people affected the history, repertoire, ensemble organization, as well as the general development of Black fiddling?[30]

Thus, this work focuses on four major topics: people (fiddlers, their family and community),[31] creativity (the music, with special focus on repertoire, performance contexts, performance style, and other musical features), time (history), and place (residence of fiddlers as well as the physical and social characteristics of the location). One of the ways this study differs from most investigations on African American music is the amount of attention given to place. Not only are chapters organized according to states within larger geographical regions, but information about the birthplace and residence of fiddlers as well as population trends (demographics) is also provided because I believe these factors affected their musicking and creativity.[32] Even Jeff Todd Titon (2001, 19–21) used demographics to give possible explanations for the dominance, strong presence, and influence of African American performance practices in the fiddle culture of certain regions of Kentucky in the early twentieth century.

I also use geography because I agree with Marilyn Raphael, who states: "Geography underpins everything people look at. The news tells us *what* is happening, ... *where* it is happening, but geography will tell us *how* and *why* it is happening there. Geography helps you understand the whole: all the things on and in the world, and how people interact with everything" (Harlow 2021).[33] Even Bolick (2021a) recognizes the importance of place in examining fiddling when he writes: "This music was created in another time and place, now far distant from our current life experiences. Most of the musicians were farmers or living in rural locations, with their lives rooted in the seasonal cycle of work. Music fit into their communities and their lives in ways that our modern society does not replicate. Most learned their tunes from family or neighbors or made them up. Thus, each tune learned had a personal connection or connections. Sense of place, of family, of community is the current that runs through these tunes" (3).

Organization of Study

The main title for this book, *Fiddling Is My Joy*, is taken from a conversation that Leonard Bowles (1987), a Black fiddler from the Virginia piedmont region, had with his wife after they had been married several years. When she expressed her unhappiness with him spending most of his free time playing the fiddle late at night at house parties and other events, he stated: "But fiddling is my joy." In actuality, his response may explain the importance of the tradition to other fiddlers regardless of race, ethnicity, or cultural background. However, the focus here is on Black fiddling.

This book is organized into two major sections: the pre–twentieth century and the early twentieth century. Presenting substantial information about fiddling on the African continent in Section One (the pre–twentieth century) will help readers to realize that bowed lutes are not unique to Europeans or Western culture. As Robert J. Allison (1999) explains, the "Americanist" approach to writing about slavery often presents enslaved "men, women, and children who arrived in America as blank slates ready to be written on by their new masters." Only a few scholars introduce the material differently by showing "what the people from different African societies brought with them to America, and how they reshaped these local [African] cultures into a distinctive African American identity" (476).[34] In this discussion, the evidence indicates that some enslaved persons who became fiddlers in the Americas were in a position to make contributions because the tradition was not totally foreign to them. Therefore, assessing how differences in slavery in English, French, and Spanish colonies as well as societies in Africa affected fiddling is important in understanding the development of the tradition in the United States.

Section Two, which focuses on Black fiddling in the early twentieth century, is important because of the attention given to Black musicking in rural areas of the United States. Except for discussion of early blues, most published histories on African American music rarely include information on secular musicking in rural America. Just as many rural Blacks during the early decades of the twentieth century continued to perform sacred music traditions, such as hymnody and spirituals from the nineteenth century, the same also occurred with secular musicking. The use of the fiddle for entertainment at occasions only attended by African Americans persisted not only in small, isolated rural communities where there was extensive interaction between Blacks and whites but also in areas where minimal interaction occurred between the races. Simply put, some Black people, similar to slavery times, preferred fiddling for recreation instead of the new types of music that were coming into existence during the early twentieth century. Understanding how this developed in various regions of the United States is included in Section Two.

In the epilogue, I concisely address the two questions raised at the beginning of this study: (1) why is the fiddle/violin not identified with African American musicking, and (2) why did Black musicians continue to perform the fiddle/violin when it had been rejected (or regarded as a novelty) by many within African American culture? For the last word on the subject, I include a profile of Howard Armstrong, one of the most well-known fiddlers in the United States during the twentieth century, who provides his perspective on reasons for the instrument's popularity, decline, and continued use by some African American musicians.

fiddlingismyjoycompanion.net

Notes

1. In the United States, the term *fiddle* is most often associated with vernacular (traditional or folk) culture, whereas *violin* is generally used when discussing urban culture—for example, jazz, rhythm and blues, or art music. In this discussion, I use both terms interchangeably. Because the word *folk* has strong associations with European culture, ideals, and values, which are oftentimes antithetical to African and African American beliefs and practices, this term is rarely used in this discussion, except when included in a published work. Instead, I employ the word, vernacular or traditional, which here refers to the music and culture of common or ordinary people.

2. My publications on African and African American fiddling include the following: DjeDje 1978a, 1978b, 1980, 1982, 1984, 1992, 1999, 2007, 2008a, 2008b, 2016, 2020, n.d.

3. When I use the words *North America* or *America*, I am referring to the area that would become or is the present-day United States. The reader will also notice that the words for race—"black" and "white"—are not spelled consistently throughout this work. I use the small "b" and "w" when a quote from another source includes small letters for the words "black" and" white." However, in my own writing and discussion, I use the capital letter for "Black" and small letter for "white," which is common practice today, particularly since 2020.

4. The widespread use of the fiddle is not unique to the Black experience. Dale Smith (2009) writes: "All in all, the violin is a versatile and occasionally volatile instrument. 'It is a musical instrument welcome in the orchestra pit, the juke joint, the dance hall, parlor, kitchen and chapel.' The violin is, perhaps more than any other instrument, able to fire the emotions and to inculcate solemn repose." Travis Lacy (2014) believes the violin "embodied the elite in European society"; also see Schoenbaum (2013).

5. Organized in November 2005, the Carolina Chocolate Drops was a group that specialized in performing old-time string band music. Their 2010 album, *Genuine Negro Jig*, won the Grammy Award for Best Traditional Folk Album at the 53rd Annual Grammy Awards.

6. When I interviewed Carter, she was touring and promoting *Reverse Thread*, a recording published in 2010 that celebrated the music of West Africa through its inclusion of a Mande harp called *kora*. In 2014, she released *Southern Comfort*, a disk that included several old-time tunes in memory of her father's heritage in rural Alabama, which became one of her best-sellers. According to Burt Feintuch (1983), the "recording industry popularized the term 'old-time,' now frequently used to describe traditional and early hillbilly fiddling" (32). In this study, all interviews have been edited for length and clarity.

7. In this study, various terms will be used for people of European descent who were born in the United States: Euro-Americans, European Americans, white people, whites, Anglo, or Anglo-American.

8. Although Black fiddling in the Americas probably began earlier, the first reference to Black people playing the fiddle in North America dates to the 1690s (Bruce 1907, 184).

9. Documentation of plucked lutes, similar in construction to the banjo, dates to the early seventeenth century for the Caribbean; however, the earliest evidence of the banjo in North America dates to the 1730s (Epstein 1977; Conway 1995; Odell and Winans 2014; Pestcoe and Adams 2018).

10. The size of fiddle ensembles in West Africa varied, but most were small (DjeDje 2008a, 37–42). Thus, it was not difficult for the enslaved to adapt to different performance contexts and ensemble organizations in the Americas.

11. Dominated by males (females rarely played the instrument), enslaved fiddlers were envied for travel opportunities and cash income that came with the job, along with respect as teachers, entertainers, and role models (Cimbala 1995).

12. *Musicking*, a term coined by Christopher Small (1998), refers to all activity that affects or takes place during a musical performance. "It is not just a matter of composers, or even performers, actively doing something to, or for, passive listeners. Whatever it is we are doing, we are all doing it together—performers, listeners (should there be any apart from the performers), composers (should there be one apart from the performers), dancers, ticket collectors, piano movers, roadies, cleaners, and all" (10).

13. Much of the research on the role of the violin in popular music was conducted by Kimasi Browne; see Browne (1995, 1998, 2005, 2019).

14. The violin was included in orchestras and ensembles of early ragtime and blues recordings, but over time violins were excluded and replaced by other instruments; see Southern (1997) for discussion of James Reese Europe, W. C. Handy, Mamie Smith, Ethel Waters, Bessie Smith, and other musicians.

15. The overwhelming majority of both West African and African American fiddlers I interviewed during my field research in the 1970s and 1980s agreed that difficulty in performing the fiddle was the most significant factor contributing to both the small number of people who had chosen to learn to play as well as the instrument's loss of popularity.

16. Demonstrating the wealth of data on the subject, more than 2,600 sources are listed in Beisswenger (2011).

17. Listed alphabetically, several record companies (Arhoolie, Blues Documents, Classic Jazz, Classics Records, Document Records, Flying Fish, Folkways, Library of Congress, Matchbox, Melodeon, Music Maker, Old Hat, Origin Jazz Library, Roots, Rounder, Testament, and Yazoo) and music producers (Bob Carlin, Samuel Charters, R. P. Christeson, David Evans, Bill Givens, Steve Goodman, Alan Lomax, Paul Oliver, Harry Oster, Tony Russell, Chris Strachwitz, Pete Welding, Charles K. Wolfe, and Marshall Wyatt) have published material on Black fiddling. Many of the recordings are reissues or compilations that focus on different time periods, genres, and musicians (Hoffheimer 2002; Durman 2008).

18. See Theresa Jenoure (1981); John Minton (1996a); Fred J. Hay (2003); Paul F. Wells (2003); T. DeWayne Moore (2014, 2018, 2021a, 2021b, 2021c, 2021d); DjeDje (2016, 2020); Montes-Bradley (2021). Some of the fiddlers and violinists noted for performing old-time, blues, jazz, and popular music and who have been the subject of publications include: Howard Armstrong, Billy Bang, Black Violin, John Blake Jr., Karen Briggs, Clarence "Gatemouth" Brown, Regina Carter, "Papa" John Henry Creach, Don "Sugar Cane" Harris, Leroy Jenkins, Bill Livers, John Lusk, Armand Piron, Noel Pointer, Arnold Shultz, Stuff Smith, Virginia "Ginger" Smock, Eddie South, and Joe Thompson.

19. Research on Black fiddling has focused on a variety of topics, including race, slavery, minstrelsy, and the recording industry (Beisswenger 2011; African American Old-time String Band Music n.d.). In recent years, several websites have been created that provide information about Black string band music generally, but also fiddling specifically; see References (Websites).

20. Whereas Pecknold (2013) includes articles examining the role of Black people in country music generally, publications by Anthony Barnett (1995, 1998, 1999) and Durman (2008) provide source material on jazz musicians (Stuff Smith and Eddie South) and string band music. Instructional books on blues fiddling and Black Creole fiddling, with emphasis on pedagogy, performance style, and some biographical and cultural information, have been published by Julie Lyonn Lieberman (1986, 2000) and D'Jamal Garnier III and Robert Wiley (2010), respectively. To my knowledge, only one PhD dissertation by DjeDje (1978a) and one Master's project by Linda L. Henry (2018a) have been concerned with Black fiddling. Other theses and dissertations have focused on related topics; listed according to the date of publication, see Christopher "Kip" Lornell (1976); Nick Spitzer (1986); J. Gary Elliott (1992); Sylvester W. Oliver Jr. (1996); Amy Suzanne Wooley (2003); Mark Y. Miyake (2009); Charles W. Perryman (2013); Mary Tess Barrett (2014); and Kathleen A. Danser (2018).

21. Listed roughly according to date of publication, see books by Charles K. Wolfe (1977b, 1982); Joyce H. Cauthen (1989a); Gerald Milnes (1999); Jeff Todd Titon (2001); Chris Goertzen (2008, 2020); Ron Yule (2009); Howard Wight Marshall (2012); Harry Bolick and Stephen T. Austin (2015); and Bolick and Tony Russell (2021).

22. Several scholars have published articles about the small number of commercial recordings of Black fiddle music as well as other issues; see Wolfe (1987a, 15–18; 1990, 32–35; 2002); Patrick Huber (2013); and Moore (2021a).

23. The Works Progress Administration (WPA), renamed the Work Projects Administration (1939–43), was created in 1935 to provide useful work for millions of victims of the Great Depression (Works Progress Administration 2020).

24. See Bolick (2015b, 12–13) for details on the types of songs collected for Blacks and whites.

25. Southern (1971a, 1983a, 1997) includes much discussion of urban traditions, but minimal information on secular music in rural areas after enslavement. In addition, most research during the early twentieth century focused on religious music, specifically spirituals, and sacred music dominates on the earliest commercial recordings of Black music; see Henry Edward Krehbiel (1962 [1914]); James Weldon Johnson and J. Rosamond Johnson (1969 [1925 and 1926]); John Lovell Jr. (1939); John W. Work III (1940); George Pullen Jackson (1944); Lornell (1989, 2–3); Bastin (1986, 5–10, 345–48); and Wolfe (1989).

26. The issue of racism in scholarship and the academy engendered much discussion in various scholarly music circles following the May 25, 2020, death of George Floyd in Minneapolis.

The primary issue is that, historically, research by people of color tends not to receive the same recognition as that of researchers of European descent (see Brown 2021).

27. However, Danser (2018) includes some of this material in her discussion.

28. Focus on the rural has already required too much space, which is one of the reasons for using *Fiddling Is My Joy Companion* on eScholarship for information on time (history) and place (geography).

29. Acknowledging duplication is important for determining similarities and differences in cultural and musical trends among performers. What African music scholar J. H. Kwabena Nketia (1972, 273) states about the study of African music is applicable for examining African American music: "this duplication should ultimately enable us to get a better picture of the continental or regional characteristics of the music of Africa and their distribution than we have at present." In my opinion, at the heart of the matter is assessing what is distinct about Black fiddling, when it was most prominent as a rural-based tradition, and understanding how it compares with other secular musicking by both Blacks and whites during the same period.

30. Many of these are questions raised by Wolfe (1990, 32–35).

31. In discussions about Black fiddlers, I try to present their full life history with data about family members, family heritage, residences, and community, for these are features that helped shape musicians and their musicking.

32. 𝄞 Therefore, in addition to maps and a description of the physical features of geographical areas, information on population trends and demographics is included throughout the discussion. Due to lack of space in the printed book, most of this information can be found in *Fiddling Is My Joy Companion* 𝄞 on eScholarship.

33. Marilyn Raphael is a professor of geography and director of the UCLA Institute of the Environment and Sustainability (Harlow 2021).

34. The book by Gomez (1998) has been commended by a number of researchers, including McDonald (1999), Miller (1999), and Bedasse (2017), for challenging the norm in examining slavery in the Americas.

Fiddling Is My Joy

SECTION 1

PRE-TWENTIETH CENTURY
The Beginnings and Rise in Popularity of Black Fiddling

Introduction

Africans performed the fiddle in a variety of contexts both for themselves and others almost immediately after they were forcibly transported to the Americas. The fact that fiddling was prominent among Black people in North America before the twentieth century raises several issues. To what extent did fiddling from Africa influence the tradition in the Americas? Are there any similarities or differences in the performance practices (for example, construction of the instrument, ensemble organization, performance occasions, and sound) used by fiddlers in Africa and the Americas?

When music scholars discuss early African American history and slavery in North America to determine their impact on the development of Black music in the United States, the ethnicities and cultural traditions of Africans transported to the Americas are rarely taken into consideration. Instead, Africans are presented as a homogenous group with little differentiation. A similar approach is used when discussing Europeans and their interactions with Africans. In examining this issue in another work, I state: "the richness and diversity of all America's cultural traditions—African, European, African American, and Native American—are overlooked, avoided, or skewed in a misguided effort to show commonalities, similarities and differences" (DjeDje 1998a, 104).

To avoid this error in this study, chapter 1 includes information on history and place as it relates to Africa (the ethnicity and homelands of Africans who were exported along with details about the fiddling on the continent) and the Americas (African presence and the institution of slavery in English, French, and Spanish colonies from the sixteenth through the eighteenth centuries) to provide a background for understanding why fiddling developed as it did. In addition to examining the earliest evidence of Black fiddling in different locations in the Americas (when the number of Africans was small and interactions with Europeans were close), I focus on fiddling during the eighteenth century, a period when the importation of Africans into the Americas was greatest and the separation between the races became more extensive.

Chapters 2 and 3 complement each other because both concern Black fiddling during the nineteenth century when the tradition was at the height of its popularity. Chapter 2 provides a general overview of the topic, including a discussion of history with special focus on the role of the fiddler in the slave community, performance contexts, the organization of fiddle ensembles, repertoire, as well as religion and its impact on social significance within the community. Chapter 3 contains information on place to determine both the degree that geography affected Black fiddling in four regions—northeast, southeast, mountains, and south-central—of the United States, and the extent commonalities and differences exist. Acknowledging geography as an essential component of the discussion not only provides a basis for understanding developments in later years, but it helps in viewing the enslaved as individuals in different locations and not as an amorphous group of people with minimal variations. A regional perspective also allows us to highlight the voices of individuals, particularly fiddlers as well as those who patronized or were critical of their musicking. In presenting the material in this way, some duplication of information is unavoidable. By identifying common elements, however, we should get a better picture of regional characteristics and possibly find out why they exist.

Throughout the investigation, several questions are addressed. What aspects of Black fiddling remained the same or changed from earlier years? What was distinctive about the role of the fiddler, the performance culture, and attitudes toward fiddling? In what ways did nineteenth-century musical practices foreground innovations that would evolve in the twentieth century?

CHAPTER 1

The Earliest Evidence
Black Fiddling during the 1600s and 1700s

The earliest documentation of fiddling by Black people in the Americas can be found in a seventeenth-century diary that Samuel Sewall, a Boston Puritan judge, kept from 1674 to 1729, about fifty-five years (Southern 1997, 28).[1] The diary contains a wealth of information about musicking in the community; however, Sewall's entry on October 14, 1685, is particularly noteworthy for its description of a typical celebration of the King's Birthday that included a parade with fiddling and drumming: "Many Guns fired, and at night a Bonfire on Noodles Island in remembrance of the King's Birthday . . . some marched throw [through] the Streets with Viols and Drums, playing and beating by turns" (Sewall 1878, 154). Although Sewall does not identify the race or ethnicity of the performers, musicologist Eileen Southern (1997) states: "contemporaneous sources attest to the fact that black folk generally joined the boisterous crowds that roamed the streets on holidays, some playing fiddles, drums, and trumpets" (41).

The first specific reference to Black people playing the fiddle in North America dates to the 1690s, when Thomas Teakle, a minister in Accomack (also spelled Accomac or Acomorack) County, Virginia,[2] took legal proceedings against his daughter's friends, who, in his absence, organized a dancing party at his house. According to the case's records, the dance started on a Saturday night and continued until nearly eleven o'clock the following morning. When Teakle returned home, and learned of the desecration of his house with dancing while church services were in progress, he decided to sue the perpetrators (Epstein 1977, 80). Philip Alexander Bruce (1907) believes Teakle's actions demonstrate that dancing in Virginia homes during the seventeenth century frequently occurred, and dancing on a Sunday was not rare even though it never went unpunished (184). Because this incident is important in revealing the early context of Black people participating in fiddling in the Americas, Bruce's comments, although lengthy, are presented in full:

> There were few homes of these times [the seventeenth century] in which there was not a considerable variety of musical instruments, and in one or two instances the number was sufficiently great to form almost a small orchestra. At many of the entertainments some female member of the family giving the dance, no doubt, furnished the music by playing on one of these instruments, but the county records show that, among the servants and slaves, there were some who were especially valued for their skill with the fiddle, and that this skill was called into use on many gay occasions. Attached to the plantation of Captain Richard Bailey, of Accomac county, was a negro slave, who, by his accomplishment in this respect, contributed as much to the diversion of the neighborhood as any person in it. This fiddler is found taking a prominent part in a lively scene which occurred at the Rev. Thomas Teakle's, to the scandal of the whole countryside, though the episode seems innocent enough to modern perceptions. Elizabeth Parker, accompanied by Samuel Doe and his wife, went over to Mr. Teakle's house to visit his daughter while he was away. They carried the negro boy with them, and after their arrival it occurred to the little company that it would be pleasant in the opportune absence of the clergyman to have a dance. The fiddle which had been left behind was sent for, and the dancing began. While it was going on, one James Fairfax came for the boy, but Elizabeth Parker made him abandon his purpose by informing him with some temper that she had borrowed the fiddler of her sister, Ursula Bailey, his owner. She, however, declared that the boy should not go unrewarded for his playing, and she pulled out her purse and gave him a Spanish piece of eight. . . . Margaret Teakle seems to have yielded only too readily to her friend's urgent appeal, and at once fetched the silk with which the fiddler might string his instrument; and as a reward for his playing gave him several yards of ribbon as well as several yards of lace, all of which, no doubt, greatly touched the negro's sense of finery. (181–83; also quoted in Wise 1967, 322–23)

Fiddling by Africans was also commonplace in the West Indies during the seventeenth century. Jean-Baptiste Labat, a French monk, writer, and explorer, who traveled to Martinique as a missionary in 1694, wrote that enslaved Africans had already learned to play the violin well and earned extra money by playing at get-togethers for whites (Epstein 1973, 71; 1977, 30, 80, 112).

While some white people (for instance, Sewall and Teakle) in the Americas during the seventeenth century discussed Black fiddling as if it were a normal activity, comments by others (Labat) suggest they were surprised that Africans could perform the instrument well. Why does this contradiction exist and how have music researchers interpreted the variance? Let us first examine the latter issue (surprise). Like Labat, most whites assumed the violin was of European origin and did not realize that many Africans had similar instruments, indigenous to their culture, in their homelands. Dena Epstein (1977), a music librarian and musicologist, states: "Nothing has been found to indicate that Africans played European instruments in Africa, although it was not impossible for them to have done so. It seems more likely, however, that they acquired that skill in America, as those Africans who went to Europe learned it there" (112). While Epstein leaves open the possibility that Africans may have had access to European instruments before their arrival in the Americas, she takes the position that this was not the case. A few scholars also make the point that Africans' adoption of Western culture began while in transit to the Americas: "when the African was seized and put aboard a slave ship, the exposure to European influences became inevitable" (77). Although she does not link the playing of the violin in the Americas to activities that occurred during the Middle Passage, Epstein refers to Thomas Phillips, the commander of the 1693 voyage of the slave ship *Hannibal* of London, who wrote: "We often at sea in the evening would let the slaves come up into the sun to air themselves, and make them jump and dance for an hour or two to our bagpipes, harp, and fiddle, by which exercise to preserve them in health" (8).[3]

For Sewall and Teakle, the King's Birthday celebration and using the instrument for dancing (among individuals of the opposite sex on a Sunday) seemed to be of greater concern than the race or ethnicity of the performer. To me, this implies that Africans playing the fiddle was a normal activity. If it was commonplace for the "negro slave to contribute to the diversion of the neighborhood," when did Africans begin doing this and why were they chosen to provide the entertainment? In her discussion of musicking during the colonial era, Southern (1997) addresses some of these questions: "the references to slave musicians point out that most often they were violinists and flutists, a phenomenon perhaps to be attributed more to the demands of the white colonists for dance musicians than to mere coincidence or to any preference for these instruments among the black people" (46). While explanations by Epstein and Southern about Africans playing the fiddle in the Americas are plausible, I question if the situation was as straightforward as they surmise. In other words, can other reasons be given for the prominence and familiarity that Africans had with playing the violin? Asked another way, were Africans introduced to fiddling *before* they left Africa? And the answer is yes. Evidence indicates that Africans were well-versed in performing fiddles indigenous to their cultures before the transatlantic slave trade began (DjeDje 2008a, 22–23). Therefore, before discussing African presence in North America, let us examine the role of the fiddle in West Africa.[4]

Chapter 1. The Earliest Evidence: Black Fiddling During the 1600s and 1700s

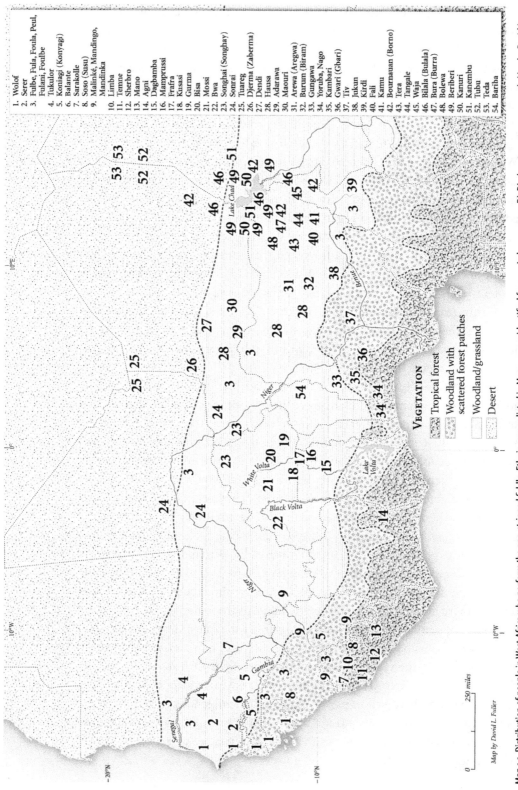

Map 1.1. Distribution of people in West Africa who perform the one-stringed fiddle. Ethnic groups listed in Map 1.1 were identified from varied sources; see DjeDje (2008a, 7, 24–25, 54–56). Map by David L. Fuller. Jacqueline Cogdell DjeDje, *Fiddling in West Africa: Touching the Spirit in Fulbe, Hausa, and Dagbamba Cultures*. Bloomington: Indiana University Press, 2008a, 24.

Fiddling in West Africa

The bowed lute is performed by peoples in several regions of the continent: North Africa, West Africa, East Africa, and portions of Central Africa and Southeast Africa (Nketia 1974; Merriam 1959; Mapoma 2009, 2014, 2016; Sublette and Collinet 2012).[5] In West Africa, bowed lutes are dispersed primarily in the savannah region, an area greatly influenced by North Africa and the Arab world. From Senegal to Lake Chad, these countries include present-day Mauritania, Senegal, The Gambia, Guinea-Bissau, Guinea, Mali, and parts of Sierra Leone, Burkina Faso, Ghana, Togo, Benin, Nigeria, Niger, Cameroon, and Chad (DjeDje 1998b). In some areas of West Africa, the use of one-stringed bowed lutes dates to the eleventh or twelfth century (see Map 1.1 and Photos 1.1 to 1.4).[6]

The location of the fiddle in West Africa is significant because of its relationship to the transatlantic slave trade. Enslaved Africans were taken from eight principal regions: Senegambia (present-day Senegal and The Gambia); Sierra Leone (which extended along the coasts of present-day Guinea, Guinea-Bissau, and portions of Senegal and Sierra Leone); Windward Coast (mainly Liberia and present-day Côte d'Ivoire, but also portions of Sierra Leone); Gold Coast (roughly the same as present-day Ghana); Bight of Benin (present-day Togo, Benin, and Nigeria); Bight of Biafra (from the Niger delta in Nigeria to Cape Lopez in present-day Gabon); and Central and Southeast Africa (Gabon down to the Orange River in present-day Namibia as well as parts of Mozambique and Madagascar) (Curtin 1969, 123–28, 189; Eltis 2001; DjeDje 2024). Ethnic groups whose music traditions included fiddling and the areas from which they were exported are as follows: Fulbe, Mande, Serer, Susu, Temne, Tukulor, and Wolof (Senegambia, Guinea-Bissau, Guinea, and Sierra Leone); Dagbamba (Gold Coast); and Bariba, Gbari, Gurma, Hausa, and Nago or Yoruba (Bights of Benin and Biafra). Since these are peoples who have resided for hundreds of years in West Africa, their musical traditions (including fiddling) were firmly in place before the transatlantic slave trade began.[7]

Although it is impossible to be exact in documenting the history of most musical traditions in precolonial Africa, the available evidence suggests that fiddling among the Fulbe, one of the major groups responsible for the dispersion of the instrument in West Africa, began during the eleventh or twelfth centuries; Hausa speakers, who played a major role in introducing the fiddle to peoples in present-day Nigeria and neighboring areas, began using the fiddle during the sixteenth or seventeenth centuries (DjeDje 2007, 2008a, 22, 66, 132, 2008b, 2008c). The description by Jean-Baptiste Labat[8] (1728) of musicking in Senegambia, which includes information about fiddles and drums, provides documentation that the bowed lute was used in West Africa during the early eighteenth century and possibly earlier:

Photo 1.1. Jelleman of Soolimana [on left playing a harp]. Jelleman of Kooranko [on right playing a fiddle]. Nineteenth century drawings of musicians from the region of present-day Sierra Leone (Laing 1825, 148–49).

Photo 1.2. Tamba Kandeh of The Gambia playing the Fulbe *nyanyeru* (fiddle). Photograph by Jacqueline Cogdell DjeDje, December 1994 (DjeDje 2008a, 89).

Chapter 1. The Earliest Evidence: Black Fiddling During the 1600s and 1700s

Photo 1.3. Musa dan Gado Saminaka of Nigeria playing the Hausa *goge* (fiddle) with resonating hole displayed. Photograph by Jacqueline Cogdell DjeDje, July 2003 (DjeDje 2008a, 30).

Photo 1.4. Salisu Mahama of Ghana, seated and holding the Dagbamba *gondze* (fiddle) with his group. Photograph by Jacqueline Cogdell DjeDje, December 1994 (DjeDje 2008a, 232).

The Women and Girls appeared first, divided into four Parties; having, at the Head of each, a *Guiriot*, or Female Musician, who sung some Verses relative to the Occasion, which the others answered in Chorus. Soon after appeared in another Squadron, all the young Men, divided, like the Women, into Companies with Drums and Fiddles. They made their Procession round the Fire, and quitting this Dress and Weapons, began to wrestle singly with great Agility.... This Exercise was followed by a Sort of Ball to their Violins, both Sexes showing their Skill in Dancing. (also quoted in Astley 1968, 298)

Since its beginnings, fiddling on the African continent has been musically and culturally diverse. West African fiddles have different names[9] "because the term employed to denote the instrument in local languages may most commonly be translated as 'to rub'" (DjeDje 2008a, 28). In terms of construction, most West African fiddles are long-necked with spikes and played horizontally; body resonators are made from a hemispherical gourd or calabash of various sizes. The number of resonator holes varies; some fiddles are constructed with one hole, but two holes are not uncommon.[10] Most often, West African fiddles are constructed with one string, but occasionally two or more strings may be used. While the string for the fiddle and fiddle bow is made with hair from a horse's tail, much variation exists in the material used for the bridge (wood, gourd, or metal ring); neck (wood covered with goat skin or left bare); and fiddle bow (wood covered with goat skin, or wood or metal left bare) (DjeDje 2008a); see photos 1.5–1.8.

Photo 1.5. Front view. Fulbe *nyanyeru* (fiddle) of The Gambia. Photograph by Jacqueline Cogdell DjeDje, August 1990 (DjeDje 2008a, 29).

Photo 1.6. Back view. Fulbe *nyanyeru* (fiddle) of The Gambia. Photograph by Jacqueline Cogdell DjeDje, August 1990.

In terms of gender, West African fiddlers tend to be male. Only among the Tuareg people who have lived for centuries in desert regions of West Africa is the fiddle identified exclusively with women, whereas women in Hausa and Songhai societies only occasionally perform the instrument. In cultures where fiddlers belong to an endogamous group or class, they generally learn from kinsmen, and training begins at an early age. In such instances, fiddlers are attached to a social class (that is, rulers) or a religious group and perform at activities associated with them. Fiddlers not attached or born into a family of fiddlers generally choose the profession and learn to play the instrument as a youth or young adult by observing other fiddlers. Some obtain training by serving as an apprentice with an established musician. As professional musicians who are rewarded for their talents with monies and other services, West African fiddlers have always possessed a social distinction different from nonmusicians; most are recognized and greatly admired for their ability to perform (DjeDje 2008a, 19–20).

The organization of fiddle ensembles in savannah West Africa varies. In addition to percussion (rattle, drum, and/or handclapping), a few societies include other melodic instruments (such as winds and plucked lutes) in ensembles. In performance, fiddlers may (1) accompany their own singing with or without

Chapter 1. The Earliest Evidence: Black Fiddling During the 1600s and 1700s

Photo 1.7. Front view. Dagbamba *gondze* (fiddle) of Ghana. Image shows objects inside resonator. Photograph by Jacqueline Cogdell DjeDje, 1990s.

Photo 1.8. Back view. Dagbamba *gondze* (fiddle) of Ghana. Photograph by Jacqueline Cogdell DjeDje, 1990s.

other performers, (2) accompany solo or group singing with or without other performers, (3) perform instrumental solos, or (4) perform as the lead instrumentalist with the accompaniment of singers and other instruments. Although both the group and percussion are emphasized, the fiddle is the primary and lead instrument, and it plays a central role in the interplay of sounds regardless of the ensemble's size or organization. In other words, both melody and rhythm are important in savannah West African fiddling, which makes the tradition distinct from that in other parts of the continent, such as forest West Africa, where rhythm (percussion) dominates (DjeDje 2008a, 37–40).[11]

The organization of melody in savannah West African fiddling also varies. In most cases, the texture is polyphonic. While some fiddle melodies are florid, others contain minimal ornamentation. Occasionally, the fiddle is played in a percussive manner with little attention given to developing the melody. The bowing in such instances can be described as "sawing" because single strokes are paired with individual pitches. When the same pitches are repeated many times, this produces a percussive sound that corresponds with the syllabic singing. Since a set melodic repetitive pattern (cycle or ostinato) generally serves as the underlying basis for the organization of the music, the form of savannah

West African fiddling is strophic with melodies often performed in a call and response fashion. Furthermore, pentatonicism (melodies based on five different pitches) is prominent throughout the region (DjeDje 2008a, 40–41).

West African fiddling has always been performed in a variety of contexts. In addition to its use as entertainment at life-cycle events, ceremonial, festive, and social occasions, the fiddle serves as a royal court instrument among some people (including the Dagbamba, Gurma, and Korando). Fiddles are also used to accompany work, report on history and current events, as well as perform praise and social comment songs. Among some groups, the fiddle and the sound produced on the instrument have deep spiritual connotations and intimate associations with spirits. When practitioners of the religion call on spirits during religious ceremonies, many feel they are healed immediately or their problems have been dealt with posthaste (DjeDje 2008a, 120–24; Laing 1825, 148).

Since fiddling has been important to Africans for centuries, one might ask: why has this information not been included in the literature on African and African American music history? Actually, the answer is rather straightforward. Because the earliest historical research on slave trading focused on groups living along the Atlantic Coast near ports of embarkation, much of the information about African musicking also emphasized coastal traditions. Not only did this cause groups in the interior, the homeland of many enslaved Africans transported to the Americas, to be ignored, but the omission also led to misconceptions about the music culture of both Africa and African America (Diouf 1998). In fact, the place of exportation did not always reflect the ethnicity of those sold into slavery because Africans were taken from regions in the interior for trade on the Atlantic Coast (Palmer 1995, 224–25; Hutchinson and Smith 1996). Military conflicts between different societies throughout West Africa produced war captives who were enslaved. Therefore, just as people shipped from the Gold Coast may have included groups (such as the Dagbamba) who lived inland, the Bights of Benin and Biafra served as points of embarkation for people (for example, the Gurma and Hausa) who lived in or near the northern parts of present-day Benin and Nigeria.[12]

Another question to be addressed is: what is the instrument's history in West Africa as well as its relationship to the transatlantic slave trade and peoples in North Africa? Instead of abandoning African indigenous religions when Islam was introduced between the eleventh and nineteenth centuries, Senegambians and other savannah West Africans combined these traditions with Islamic elements to form an African Islam distinct from that practiced in North Africa and the Arab world. Although musicking is prevalent in Arab culture, Muslim authorities, like many Christian leaders, have ambivalent attitudes about certain musical practices. As a result, unaccompanied chanting of religious poems and Muslim hymns as well as the playing of certain types of drums are the only performance media allowed in mosques. Not only did many Muslims refer to melodies produced on string instruments as music of the devil, some believed fiddle music caused people to perform immoral acts against their will. In earlier times, string instruments were viewed as signs of the end of the world. In spite of these attitudes on the part of Muslim authorities, West Africans did not abandon indigenous music, just as they did not discard their indigenous religions when faced with the spread of Islam on the continent (Farmer 1929, 24; Ames 1973, 141; Besmer 1983, 34; Erlmann 1986, 10; DjeDje 2008a, 14–17). Sylviane Diouf (1998) explains that when free and enslaved Africans (from the trans-Saharan caravan trade) lived among Arab and Berber (Amazigh) populations of the Maghreb, West African musicians were particularly valued. The music of the Maghreb has thus been influenced by the music of West Africa, and this new type of music in turn was transported south of the Sahara Desert to be absorbed by West African Muslim populations, who transported memories of fiddling with them to the Americas (195).

African Presence in North America
Sixteenth through Eighteenth Centuries

Having established early evidence of fiddling by Africans in the Americas and the widespread distribution of fiddle traditions in the homelands of enslaved West Africans transported to the Americas, we can now focus on reasons for the prominent use of the fiddle by Blacks in the Americas. Many researchers believe Africans played the instrument solely to satisfy whites; thus, it serves as an example of acculturation (the adoption and fusion of European elements into African American culture). However, I propose another argument. Although Africans performed the fiddle for whites, this was not done solely to entertain Europeans. Rather, playing the fiddle not only allowed them an opportunity to maintain their African heritage, but it also was a form of resistance. To determine if these arguments are feasible, let us examine more closely the social history of Africans in North America before the nineteenth century to determine who was involved and how this may have affected fiddling in different parts of the United States in later years.[13]

African presence in the Americas dates to the 1500s. During the early sixteenth century, Africans participated in expeditions led by Spanish explorers on the coasts of the Pacific and areas surrounding the Gulf of Mexico. Some Africans also fought with the Spaniards and French against Indigenous groups on the East Coast and in the Appalachian Mountains in the sixteenth century (Abernethy 1996, 1; Purdue 1985, 23–24; DjeDje and Meadows 1998, 1, 16). Many of the Africans exported during the sixteenth and seventeenth centuries varied in geographical origin. Senegambians (Fulbe, Mande, Serer, Tukulor, and Wolof) constituted the largest group to be sold into slavery during the sixteenth century and were among the earliest African peoples to dominate statistically in the Americas (Curtin 1975, 3; Barry 1997; Diouf 1998, 4, 17–18; Jobson 1932; Roberts

1998, 61; McCartney 2003, 8). When England became a central player in the late seventeenth century, almost half were exported from the Gold and Windward Coasts, while the remaining were from Senegambia and Sierra Leone, Angola, present-day Benin and present-day Nigeria (Curtin 1969, 123–26).

As North America became more involved in the slave trade during the eighteenth century, imports into the Americas became more varied and depended on the requests of the slave owners. In the English colonies, slave owners in South Carolina preferred Senegambians because of their experience as rice planters; slave holders presumed they were in better condition physically for they were transported from the nearest point in Africa and had suffered less during the Middle Passage (Curtin 1969, 162–66; Wax 1973; Creel 1988, 31–33; Perbi 2004; Austin 1984, 29). Before the United States purchased Louisiana in 1803, the territory was controlled by France and Spain; the first ships from Africa did not arrive until 1719, a century after the settlements of Africans in Virginia. Under French control, the majority of Africans forcibly transported into Louisiana were also from Senegambia, but their numbers were small. Also, Louisiana stopped their imports after the late seventeenth century whereas other parts of North America continued through the early nineteenth century (Curtin 1969). Unlike the French who placed little value on Louisiana, Spain loosened trade restrictions to encourage population growth and economic development. Both Acadians (from Canada) and Canary Islanders arrived in the 1770s. It is also noteworthy that, unlike the English, French and Spanish settlers in Louisiana were notable for their openness and tolerance of peoples of other races and cultures.

In summary, much of the increase in the African population in the eighteenth century is derived from extensive African imports. The eighteenth century was the period when the largest and most diverse peoples of African descent entered North American colonies (Creel 1988, 44). The religious practices of Africans imported during the sixteenth and seventeenth centuries were also diverse and similar to what existed in Africa at that time. While societies were adherents of some form of indigenous African religion, those who lived in savannah West Africa tended to be Muslims and a few of the enslaved from Central Africa were Christians (Wills 1997, 14).[14] Africans in northern US colonies also embraced Christianity during the seventeenth century, but the widespread acceptance of European religious practices by Black people in the Americas did not begin until the religious revivals (or Awakenings) of the eighteenth and nineteenth centuries.[15]

Black Fiddling in the Eighteenth Century

As the number of Africans imported into North America during the eighteenth century increased, so did reports about their association with the fiddle during the Middle Passage and in the West Indies and North America.[16] Some of the first encyclopedias (Ephraim Chamber's *Cyclopaedia* published in 1728 and Denis Diderot's *Encyclopédie* published between 1751 and 1765) confirm what had been documented in earlier sources: slave traders often performed music for the enslaved to keep up their spirits during the Middle Passage and any instruments would do, "even a vielle or a musette" (Epstein 1977, 8; Chambers 1728; Diderot 1751–1765).

West Indies

Sources (such as books, journals, and travelogues) describing activity in the West Indies provide information about instruments, organization of instrumental ensembles, contexts for fiddle performances, and learning. The journal of an English soldier who was stationed in Guadeloupe until June 1763, when the Glorious Peace of Paris restored the island to the French, includes an excellent description of Blacks performing the violin and other instruments to accompany singing and dancing:

> Some of the Mulattoes can play indifferently well on the violin; they have likewise a kind of tabor, it hath but one head, and all round the hoop are fixed small pieces of tin; the manner of playing is to hold the instrument with one hand, and beat on the parchment head with the fingers of the other, according to the tune of the violin; others are singing to the tune; and some beat on the boards at the side of the hut in which the ball is kept, and others will clap their hands, all which instrumental and vocal music together makes a most hideous concert. Their chief dances are minuets and jigs,[17] and some of the Creole slaves will dance a minuet tolerably well, after the French mode. The fiddlers get pretty well paid for their scraping, for all that dance, pay the fiddler. The women will dance down two or three men in a jig, and in general there is plenty of rum punch drank at one of these balls. (A Soldier's Journal 1770, 106–7; also quoted in Epstein 1977, 81)

Several comments in the description suggest that the fiddling was African-derived. Most apparent is the fact that the fiddle is combined with percussion, which is typical of fiddle ensembles in savannah and forest West Africa (DjeDje 2008a, 39–42; DjeDje 2008b). When the writer states that the "tabor" is beaten "to the tune of the violin," this indicates that although the two instruments are played together, the fiddler performs the lead, which is also a common performance practice in West African fiddling. Finally, the use of the term "scraping" to describe the playing of the instrument can be interpreted in several ways: (1) to depict the rubbing of the fiddle bow across the strings of the instrument; (2) to suggest that the fiddler's playing technique was not comparable to or different from that used by someone playing in the western (art music) tradition; or (3) to refer to the timbre or sound quality produced on the fiddle. If the latter, perhaps the author did not believe the sound was aesthetically pleasing. In many parts of Africa, producing a rough, raspy, or buzzing quality with an instrument or the voice is intentional because it makes the music sound sweet (DjeDje 2008a, 31; Kubik 2010, 126). Later in the journal, the soldier mentions the fiddle in the context of a wedding:

> When any marriage is to be celebrated, notice is given to all the neighbouring plantations; and on the eve of the Sunday or holiday that the nuptials are to be celebrated, then begin the diversions and joy. Some of the Creole slaves will kill a bullock, or sheep and goats, . . . for every one who comes to the wedding (at which I have seen several hundred) makes a present to the bride, when they dance with her; and which every one does seperately [sic], besides the money which after the dance is put into the violin, and which when the wedding is over, is made a present of also to the bride. (A Soldier's Journal 1770, 108)

Placing the money "into the violin" suggests that the instrument had a hole in the resonator, like many West African fiddles. The description of activities at the wedding and the fact that money is given to the bride all reflect the maintenance of African performance practices (DjeDje 2008a, 45–47).

Eighteenth-century sources from various parts of the Caribbean document the popularity of Black fiddling during Christmas celebrations and at "grand balls" (Epstein 1977, 83). A description in Sir William Young's journal entry on December 26, 1791, of Christmas on St. Vincent is significant for the types of instruments included in the festivities:

> We had a large company to dinner; and in the evening I opened the ball in the great court, with a minuet, with black Phillis, Granny Sarah being indisposed: our music consisted of two excellent fiddle[r]s *Johnny* and *Fisher*, from my Pembroke estate, and *Grandison*, [a] tamborin [player] of the villa; there stood up about eighteen couple. . . . This moment a new party of musicians are arrived with an African *Balafo*, an instrument composed of pieces of hard wood of different diameters, laid on a row over a sort of box; they beat on one or the other so as to strike out a good musical tune. They played two or three African tunes; and about a dozen girls, hearing their sound, came from the huts to the great court, and began a curious and most lascivious dance, with much grace as well as action. (Young 1801, 257–58; also quoted in Epstein 1977, 83)

John Canoe, a Jamaican performance tradition identified with Black Christmas celebrations that originated in the eighteenth century or earlier and continues to the present day, included fiddle, tambourine, *balafon* (xylophone), and drums to accompany costumed dancers who processed through the streets of local communities (Long 1774, 424; Emery 1972, 32). The festivities, instruments, and organization of the ensembles demonstrate that when given the opportunity, the enslaved re-created some of the same performance practices that existed in their African homelands.

A description from Saint-Domingue (Haiti) by Moreau de Saint-Méry (1797) not only provides details about Africans learning to play the violin, confirming the maintenance of African practices in the Americas, but he comments on the instrumental preferences of the enslaved:

> The good ears of the Negroes give them the first qualification of a musician . . . many are good violinists. That is the instrument they prefer. Many certainly play it only by rote, that is, they learn by themselves, imitating the sounds of a tune, or they are taught by another Negro, who explains only the position of the strings and the fingers, with no thought of notes. They learn very quickly, for example, that *Si* is on the third string where the first finger is used, and in hearing a melody, remember what they have learned. This method is used by country fiddlers, and those of France cannot outdo them for volume of sound, capacity for drinking, or the ability to sleep without interrupting their playing. (quoted in Epstein 1977, 116)

New England Colonies

Confirming that dancing and fiddling by the enslaved were favorite forms of entertainment in the New England colonies, several authors include details about occasions and performance contexts; writers also identify fiddlers by name with comments about their social status as heroes and professionals within their communities. Lorenzo Johnston Greene, author of *The Negro in Colonial New England 1620–1776* (1942), writes: "Polydor Gardiner of Narragansett [Rhode Island] was famous as a fiddler and was in demand at parties and balls. So, too was Caesar, the slave fiddler of the Reverend Jonathan Todd of East Guilford, Connecticut, who was such an accomplished performer that the minister used to call in the young people to dance to his playing" (249). Daniel Slade's article (1990), "A New England Country Gentleman in the Last Century," contains comments about Othello, an African who was about nineteen years old when he was transported to the Americas in 1760; he died in 1813 around age seventy-two. While employed by Henry Bromfield, Othello "was known to every man, woman, and child in Harvard, [Massachusetts] and the surrounding country." In describing Othello's musical significance, Slade (1890) writes: "His violin was also a source of great attraction, and many a jig and contradance was incited by its inspiriting strains." When performing in his master's kitchen, "he rapidly drew the bow, and called out the figures for the city nephews, nieces, and cousins, who had assembled for a merry-making" (14). Charles Davis's history of Wallingford, Connecticut, includes mention of Cato and Robert Prim, two Black fiddlers who were popular during the late eighteenth century. Regarding

Cato, Davis (1870) states: "Cato was the name of Col. Barker's negro. He ranked high as a fiddler in the community, and was generally called upon to furnish the music for balls on the nights preceding the annual thanksgiving, and other occasions when dancing was expected" (341). On the subject of Prim, Davis's remarks are brief: "Robert and his violin were indispensable requisites at every party or merry-making" (344). While little is said, enough is given to indicate that Prim, like Cato, was important because of his ability to play the fiddle.

In many ways, Black fiddlers performed functions similar to musicians attached to rulers or minstrels in the courts of European royalty. Some Europeans believed fiddling was not only the slaves' duty, but also an activity fiddlers accepted with pleasure: "In many of the towns, some negro, by his drollery and good nature, was a favorite, affording the people as much amusement as the King's fool, of the olden time, did inmates of a palace" (Fowler 1872, 130–31). Festivals, such as 'Lection Day and Pinkster Day, were some of the most important occasions for musicking by Black and white musicians in New England. On 'Lection Day, a holiday that originated in Connecticut around 1750 and continued in some New England towns through the 1850s, a few whites allowed Africans to elect their own governors similar to the manner in which members of the white community elected their leaders. Thus, 'Lection Day, which paralleled the whites' Election Day, became a holiday unique to northern Blacks. Like their white counterparts, 'Lection Day celebrations included the playing of different musical instruments, even fiddles (Greene 1942, 249–50).

The 'Lection Day celebration in Newport, Rhode Island, in 1756, is noteworthy for the varied languages and instruments Africans used as well as how the response to the election by the enslaved differed from that of slave owners: "On the votes being counted and the election declared, a general shout announced that the struggle was over—and here, contrary to their masters' practice, the vanquished and victors united in innocent and amusing fun and frolic—every voice in its highest key, in all the various languages of Africa, mixed with broken and ludicrous English, filled the air, accompanied with the music of the fiddle, tambourine, the banjo and drum" (Platt 1900, 324; also quoted in Southern 1997, 53). Nathaniel Bouton (1856) comments on a Massachusetts fiddler who attained renown during elections: "Sampson was a famous fiddler, and for many years afforded fine fun for frolicsome fellows in Concord with his fiddle on election days" (252). The description by Isaac William Stuart (1853) of the 'Lection Day parade in Hartford, Connecticut, provides information about participants and instruments: "His [the black elected 'Governor'] parade days were marked by much that was showy.... A troop of blacks, sometimes an hundred in number, marching sometimes two and two on foot, sometimes mounted in true military style and dress on horseback, escorted him through the streets, with drums beating, colors flying, and fifes, fiddles, clarionets, and every 'sonorous metal' that could be found, 'uttering martial sound'" (38–49).

Although 'Lection Day was popular among the enslaved, Greene indicates that white slave owners had conflicting views about Africans participating in celebrations. While a few white people (for example, Mrs. Caulkins of Norwich, Connecticut) believed election festivities "should have been tolerated by the magistrates in a town so rigid in its code of morals," others thought Africans spent too much time (from Wednesday to the end of the week) in amusements, "chiefly in dancing to the fiddle." At the heart of the matter was that some whites believed "'elections'... had a demoralizing effect upon the slaves.... Such holidays were to them as those of Christmas have been to the blacks of our Southern States. The abuse of them led to immoralities which called for frequent admonitions" (Greene 1942, 251).

The earliest description of music making by Africans during Pinkster Day, a Christian religious holiday associated with Pentecost Sunday among the Dutch and Whitsunday in the Anglican Church, does not appear until 1803, but Black participation in this event began during the eighteenth century or earlier (Southern 1997, 53–54). A Pinkster festival in Albany, New York, is noteworthy for elements that are African-derived. Besides the "Guinea dance," King Charles (d. 1824), the leading spirit of the dancing, played master drums and "called" the dances, while others in the festivities played banjo, fiddles, fifes, drums, and the "hollow drum." Commenting on the description, Southern (1997) writes, "The author of the ode leaves no doubt that the festival was African in tone, although his only specific reference to Africa is in a verse about Charles 'leading on the Guinea dance'" (54).

Middle Colonies

Sources that document Black fiddling in the middle colonies during the eighteenth century vary in content. Like references from the West Indies and New England, different occasions are described with writers debating the appropriateness of Africans participating in such activities. Harking back to issues introduced in seventeenth-century writings, observers also question how Black musicians acquired their ability to perform and construct instruments.

The few sources documenting Black fiddling in New York City reference negative aspects of the tradition, in which "black fiddlers were regarded as marginal vagabonds outside the bounds of respectable society" (Epstein 1977, 114). Reports about Black musicians playing the fiddle during New York's 1741 slave revolt led to some whites blaming the incident on Africans' involvement in lewd behavior. Much of the testimony concerned Black people dancing, fiddling, and drumming, as if these activities would lead to serious crimes. One witness stated that he saw one of the accused, Cuffee, "when the flames of the house blazed up very high," and "he huzza'd, danced, whistled and sung...." Jamaica, another accused enslaved person, was described as "fiddling" or "with his fiddle" (114). He was believed to have been enslaved by Ellis, who was "frequently at Hughson's [tavern] with his fiddle" (Southern 1997, 27). In his summation, the attorney general who prosecuted the musicians stated, "This horrid scene of iniquity has been chiefly contrived and promoted at meetings of negroes in great numbers on Sundays," making comparisons to what had occurred in Jamaica and other West Indian islands (Epstein 1977, 114).

While some whites in the middle colonies, similar to white New Englanders, contested Africans playing the fiddle, others took comfort in listening to Black fiddling and depended on it for amusement at various occasions. Michel Guillaume Jean de Crèvecoeur (1925), a French farmer who lived from 1759 to 1780 in Orange County, New York, states that the one pleasure that made living in the colonies bearable was entertainment by Black fiddlers: "If we have not the gorgeous balls, the harmonious concerts, the shrill horn of Europe, yet we dilate our hearts as well with the simple negro fiddle" (96; also quoted in Southern and Wright 1990, 2 Item 9).

Because Africans were not in a position to transport items with them during the Middle Passage, scholars have speculated on how the enslaved acquired the instruments they played. If the instrument was European, researchers surmise that the slave owner purchased it. Others have suggested that Africans constructed their own instruments, basing them on prototypes from Africa. An excerpt from a letter written in 1719 by a Quaker in Philadelphia supports both arguments. After the Quaker learns that Africans can construct and perform their own violins, he decides to purchase one from England: "Thou knowest Negro Peter's Ingenuity In making for himself and playing on a fiddle without any assistance. As the thing in them [the musical impulse] is Innocent and diverting and may keep them from worse Employment, I have to Encourage [him] in my service promist him one from England. Therefore buy and bring a good Strong well-made Violin wth 2 or 3 Sets of spare Gut for the Suitable Strings. Get somebody of skill to Chuse and by [buy] it" (quoted in Turner 1911, 42; Southern 1997, 49).

Southern Colonies (Upper South)

Similar to other parts of the Americas during the eighteenth century, much interaction took place between Black and white people in the context of music making. When Philip Vickers Fithian (a graduate of the College of New Jersey [later Princeton University]) left college, and became a private teacher in the home of Robert Carter in the Tidewater region of Virginia, he documents in his journal the musical interchange that occurred between Africans and Euro-Americans (Southern and Wright 1990, 2 Item 12). The journal entry for Sunday, January 30, 1774, contains comments about an instance when Blacks *and* whites, to his displeasure, gathered together to participate in musicking. "This Evening the Negroes collected themselves into the School-Room [a detached outbuilding], & began to play the *Fiddle*, & dance.... I went among them, *Ben* [Benjamin Carter, the eldest son, a quiet, studious boy of eighteen], & *Harry* [the Councillor's nephew, Harry Willis] were of the company—*Harry* was dancing with his Coat off—I dispersed them however immediately" (Fithian 1957, 62; also quoted in Epstein 1977, 121; Southern 1997, 50–51).

Like other regions, the South had fiddlers who could be considered professional. Samuel Mordecai's *Richmond in By-Gone Days* (1856) includes a description of Simeon "Sy" Gilliat (d. 1820), a Virginia fiddler who was legendary in Richmond for two generations during the late eighteenth and early nineteenth centuries:

> The most prominent member of the black aristocracy of my early years was *Sy. Gilliat*, (probably Simon, or Cyrus,) the leading violinist (fiddler was then the word,) at the balls and dancing parties. He traced his claim to position to the days of vice-royalty, having held office under Lord Botetourt when governor.[18] ...
>
> Sy. Gilliat flourished in Richmond in the first decade of this century, and I know not how many of the last. He was tall, and even in his old age, (if he ever grew old,) erect and dignified. When he appeared officially in the orchestra, his dress was an embroidered silk coat and vest of faded lilac, small clothes, (he would not say breeches,) and silk stockings, which rather betrayed the African prominence of the shin-bone, terminating in shoes fastened or decorated with large buckles.... His manners were as courtly as his dress, and he elbowed himself and his fiddle-stick through the world with great propriety and harmony.
>
> Belonging to the vice-regal family, Sy. belonged of course to the Church of England; ... although strict constructionists might have considered ... that he was "a man of sin rubbing the hair of the horse against the bowels of the cat;" he filled the office for some time, but was impelled to resign it in a fit of unrighteous indignation, excited by hearing that he was suspected of partaking of the wine without the other ceremonies of the sacrament. (355–56)

Gilliat was the star musician of the annual Race Ball, one of the more exciting events for Richmond residents at the end of a week of horse racing, and Mordecai's description (1856) suggests that Gilliat's performances included elements that were both European- and African-derived:

> The ball was opened ... with a *minuet de la Cour*, putting the grace and elegance of the couple to a severe ordeal.... Then commenced the reel, like a storm after a calm—all life and animation. No solemn walking of the figure to a measured step—but pigeon-wings fluttered, and all sorts of capers were cut to the music of Si. Gilliat's fiddle, and the flute or clarionet of his blacker comrade, London Brigs.
>
> Contra dances followed, and sometimes a congo, or a hornpipe; and when "the music grew fast and furious," and the most stately of the company had retired, a jig would wind up the evening, which, by-the-by, commenced about eight o'clock.

Photo 1.9. "The Virginia Reel." [Black Fiddler Playing for white People during the Colonial Period, 1730s–1760s.] Drawn by Howard Helmick, engraved by W. Miller. John Williamson Palmer. "Old Maryland Homes and Ways." *Century Illustrated Monthly Magazine* 1894, Volume 49, Issue 2, 255. https://archive.org/details/sim_century-illustrated-monthly-magazine_1894-12_49_2/page/255/mode/1up?view=theater Accessed October 30, 2023.

The waltz and the polka were as great strangers to the ball-room floor, as were champagne and Perigord pies to the supper-table. (253–54)

During this period, the community's attitudes about the fiddle were both complex and contradictory. While many colonialists viewed the fiddle as both low-class and profane, the violin was believed to be refined because of its association with European art music. These conflicting views can be seen in the manner in which Thomas Jefferson and his brother, Randolph, regarded musicking and the instrument. For Thomas Jefferson, European music was "a delightful recreation for the hours of respite from the cares of the day." Not only did he perform the violin, he stressed music in the education of his daughters and granddaughters. Yet he "seemed not the least bit curious about or interested in the music of the black people who surrounded him throughout his life" (Epstein 1977, 122). In his correspondence and other writings, he mentions the music of Africans only

Photo 1.10. "The Juba Dance." [Black Fiddler Playing for Black People during the Colonial Period, 1730s–1760s.] Drawn by Howard Helmick, engraved by W. Miller. John Williamson Palmer. "Old Maryland Homes and Ways." *Century Illustrated Monthly Magazine* 1894, Volume 49, Issue 2, p. 256. https://archive.org/details/sim_century-illustrated-monthly-magazine_1894-12_49_2/page/256/mode/1up?view=theater. Accessed October 30, 2023.

once.[19] On the other hand, Jefferson's brother, Randolph, was described by Isaac, one of the enslaved at Monticello, as "a mighty simple man [who] used to come out among black people, play the fiddle and dance half the night" (122).

Confirming these complex views, eighteenth-century sources referring to the fiddle's association with the profane and low-class values abound for the Upper South. It is difficult to ascertain from writings which was worse: the instrument, the context in which the instrument was performed, or the behavior of individuals when they played the fiddle. With regard to the latter, religious believers had strong opinions about dancing, which can be seen in the life of Devereux Jarratt, a Black fiddler born in New Kent County, Virginia, near Richmond in 1732 or 1733. After enjoying life as a youth participating in "such diversions as cards, racing, and dancing, he repented and turned to religion." After his conversion, his musical tastes also changed. He writes: "In my younger days, it is true, I learned to play on the violin; yet, after I came to serious reflection, and saw the pernicious use, to which the music of that instrument was generally applied, I conscientiously laid it aside, and to this day, I shut my ears against it. I think I have not heard a tune on the violin, more than once, for near 30 years" (Epstein 1977, 209).

Conservative religious attitudes permeated all facets of society in the eighteenth century. Most educational institutions supported by religious organizations established specific rules that guided students' activities. Although the rules did not prevent the youth from doing what they wanted, they reveal the degree that the social elite disapproved of dancing. And coupled with a Black person playing the fiddle, such behavior by students was considered scandalous. For example, Joseph Marks (1957) indicates that authorities at Harvard and Princeton believed students' dancing both on and off campus hurt the reputation of the college and "was unfriendly to order and good government." Yet, "the students desired to dance, and some later won the right to have an annual ball.... [U]ndergraduates of 1786, danc[ed] up and down the entry as a Negro played upon a violin with 'twenty students hallooing and tearing about'" (56).

Similar to the middle colonies and New England, the enslaved not only performed for white people, the journals of eighteenth century writers indicate that members of both races entertained guests together (Southern and Wright 1990, 1 Item 2). Nicholas Cresswell's description of merrymaking along the banks of Maryland's St. Mary's River in 1774, and Robert Hunter's writings from Baltimore in 1785 mention performance practices typical of the period, even though social mores considered such behavior to be inappropriate. When he was invited to a barbecue by a pilot boat on his way to Barbados aboard the schooner, *John*, Nicholas Cresswell (1924) writes about Black musicians performing fiddle and banjo: "These Barbecues are Hogs, roasted whole. This was under a large Tree. A great number of young people met together with a Fiddle and Banjo played by two Negroes, with Plenty of Toddy.... I believe they have danced and drunk till there are few sober people amongst them" (30; also quoted in Epstein 1977, 115). Hunter (1943) explains just how casual such affairs could be: "We sent for a violin in the evening and had a most agreeable dance.... After the poor Negro's fingers were tired of fiddling, I took the violin and played them the 'Pleasures of Youth' and the 'Savage Dance'" (179–81, 206–7; also quoted in Epstein 1977, 115).

In many parts of the Americas, race and class restricted the behavior of individuals at music events. Amateur and professional musicians who were "gentlemen" rarely performed the fiddle at dances or other casual entertainments because many felt this was the purview of servants, but also community members believed enslaved Black people and white indentured servants were better performers (Epstein 1977, 112–13). However, the genteel did not seem to have qualms about fiddling for their own personal enjoyment or in the presence of Africans. In a journal entry on March 25, 1775, John Harrower (1963), a white indentured servant and schoolmaster who lived in Virginia, wrote: "At noon went to Newpost to see Mr. Martin Heely Schoolmaster for Mr. [Alexander] Spotswood's Children, and after Dinner I spent the afternoon with him in conversation & hearing him play the Fiddle. He also made a Niger come & play on an Instrument call'd a Barrafou [*balafon* or xylophone]. The body of it is an oblong box with the mouth up & stands on four sticks put in bottom, & cross the [top?] is laid 11 lose sticks upon [which?] he beats" (89; also quoted in Epstein 1977, 57).

Harrower's comments are significant for several reasons. One, they document that while Black people performed the West African *balafon* (xylophone), white people played the fiddle, a scenario that probably caused scholars to conclude that fiddling was a tradition identified solely with Europeans. Two, his comments raise the issue of class with regard to Black fiddling because he discusses circumstances when white people participated in activities beneath their social station. Although Harrower was "a plain and simple [white] man in a lowly position," his social status as an indentured servant was clearly below that of the people for whom he worked. "He always waited for an invitation from his master and never took his participation in family affairs for granted" (Riley 1963, xvii, xix).[20] Because of Harrower's lower class, Spotswood, the master, did not appear to have qualms about performing the fiddle in his presence. Harrower's journal entry does not clearly indicate if Spotswood continued fiddling when the enslaved began performing or if he stopped. Since the status of Black people was also lower than that of Spotswood, the master may not have hesitated performing with Africans if he desired to do so. This demonstrates that because the fiddle is a "low-class" instrument, performing it in the presence of low-class people is fine.

While all types of dance music were played on the fiddle, the jig appeared to be the most popular. When Andrew Burnaby, a British clergyman, traveled through North America between 1759 and 1760, he observed whites dancing "jiggs," which he believed was "a practice originally borrowed from the Negroes" (Southern and Wright 1990, 1–2 Item 6). The journal entry by Cresswell (1924) for January 7, 1775, while traveling in Virginia, also mentions the jig accompanied by African fiddling: "Here was about 37 Ladies dressed and powdered to life. All of them fond of dancing.... Betwixt the Country dances they have what I call everlasting jigs. A couple gets up and begins to dance a jig (to some Negro tune).[21] Others come and cut them out, and these dances always last as long as the Fiddler can play" (53; also quoted in Southern 1997, 44). Although "Negro Jig" appears in the dance collection *A Selection of Scotch [sic], English, Irish and Foreign Airs*, published by James Aird in Scotland in 1782, Southern (1997) states: "there is no way of knowing whether this piece was of slave origin, or whether it was composed in imitation of a slave dance tune. The implication is clear, however, that the colonists were developing an awareness of the distinctive qualities of so-called 'Negro music' and using this music for dancing" (44).

Southern Colonies (Lower South)

Religion features prominently in descriptions about fiddling in the Lower South (the Carolinas, Georgia, and Florida), with many of the earliest references associating the fiddle with negative behavior. In many ways, identifying fiddling with the profane in the Americas is no different from attitudes toward fiddling in parts of West Africa where extensive Islamic influence is apparent. Several sources document how some European Protestants regarded dancing and fiddling. On Christmas Day in 1739, the English evangelist George Whitefield wrote from Newborn (New Bern), North Carolina, about his disapproval of dancing. On New Year's Day in 1740, he describes his futile efforts in convincing his hostess of the sinfulness of dancing: "I endeavored to shew the folly of such entertainments, and to convince her how well pleased the devil was at every step she took. For some time she endeavored to outbrave me; neither the fiddler nor she desisted; but at last she gave over, and the musician laid aside his instrument.... Notwithstanding all that had been said, after I had gone to bed, I heard their music and dancing" (Epstein 1977, 208).

In *Narratives of Colored Americans* (1875), Abigail Field Mott includes an account of Clarinda, a South Carolina Black woman who died in 1832 at the age of 102. She was born in 1730, but it is unclear if the birth took place in Africa or the Americas. Clarinda's narrative is important because not only does it include discussion of the role of the fiddle in the conflict with the sacred and secular, it is one of the few references that concerns female fiddlers, for women fiddlers are rare both in African and African American cultures. As a young person, Clarinda "learned to play on the violin, and, usually on the first day of the week, sallied forth with her instrument, in order to draw persons of both sexes together, who, not having the fear of God before their eyes, delighted like herself, in sinful and pernicious amusement." Mott indicates that Clarinda experienced several conversions before giving up her sinful ways. Once while dancing she "was seized with fits, and convulsively fell to the ground. From that moment, she lost her love of dancing, and no more engaged in this vain amusement. She did not however, forsake the evil of her ways, but continued her course of wickedness for about twenty years, when she lost her only child and was confined for several months by severe illness. She remained in a distressed state of mind for about three months, and when a little bodily strength was restored, she sought solitary places, where she poured out her soul unto the Lord, and in His own good time He spoke peace to her wounded spirit." According to Mott, Clarinda became a minister after fully converting to Christianity. Religious meetings were regularly held at her house and she often warned others about their sinful ways. Although these actions caused her much persecution, she never gave up her belief in God. Upon her death, the people who worshipped with her became known as "Clarinda's People" (144, 150).

Like Clarinda, John Marrant, born in New York on June 15, 1755, lived a life of freedom and pleasure as a young person only to change his ways later. The fact that he was able to travel throughout various parts of the South (Georgia, Florida, and South Carolina) suggests that Marrant was a free Black person (Epstein 1977, 116). His decision to become a fiddler is significant: "In Charles-Town, as I was walking one day, I passed a school, and heard music and dancing, which took my fancy very much, and I felt a strong inclination to learn the music. I went home, and informed my sister, that I had rather learn to play upon music than go to a trade" (116). Initially he wanted to play the fiddle at all costs regardless of the social taboos against such a profession. However, after a religious conversion later in life, he decided to give up the fiddle and music making because of its association with the devil. His desire to receive fiddle training from his teacher as an apprentice is similar to the manner in which many West African fiddlers acquire their fiddle skills. Marrant's decision to give up the life of a fiddler could not have been easy, because not only did performing music raise his status in some social circles, it was a financially lucrative profession. The transformation took place at a religious meeting conducted by George Whitefield, the English evangelist who, in 1739, had written about his disapproval of dancing and fiddling (208). Epstein (1977) explains that when "he [Marrant] passed a meeting where George Whitefield was preaching. His friends persuaded him to 'Blow the French horn among them,' but just as Marrant was lifting his horn to his shoulder, Whitefield announced his text, looking directly at him: 'Prepare to meet they [sic] God, O Israel.' Like Clarinda before him, and many sinful fiddlers to come after, Marrant was struck to the ground both speechless and senseless, thus ending his musical career. His conversion adheres to the traditional pattern for such a religious experience, but the description of his musical apprenticeship has no counterpart among black autobiographies of his time" (117).

African-derived music was attacked from all angles in the Lower South during the eighteenth century. Whereas religious enthusiasts criticized fiddling because it promoted sinful living and behavior unbecoming of a Christian, the elite from both races ridiculed the instrument's lowly status. The wider white population (including slave owners, servants, and workers) did not seem to have problems with fiddling but were more concerned about uprisings and how African musicking could cause bodily harm. The first record of Europeans' attempt to prohibit or suppress musicking in the colonies occurred in the seventeenth century with the passage of the Codes Noir of 1685 in the West Indies (Epstein 1973, 69). When slave uprisings became more widespread during the eighteenth century as a result of the rise in the shipping of Africans into the Americas, drums were banned because Europeans believed their performance after dark signaled slave insurrection. For example, in response to the Stono Rebellion of 1739, the South Carolina Slave Act of 1740 contained a ban on loud instruments (drums and horns) that whites believed would call Africans together (Epstein 1977, 144; Southern 1997, 172). Whereas enslaved drummers had to find substitute instruments to satisfy their need for percussive sounds in performances, fiddling by the enslaved flourished. Richard Cullen Rath (2000) states that "drums seem to have been replaced by fiddles . . . , the number of escaped low-country fiddlers reported in the *South Carolina Gazette* steadily increased during the years before the American Revolution and suddenly abruptly disappeared during the war, with the next runaway fiddler not being noted until 1790" (113).

Southern Colonies (Louisiana Territory)

Although the importation of Africans into present-day Louisiana had begun by 1719, sources concerning fiddling in Louisiana do not appear until the late eighteenth century, when Louisiana was under Spanish rule. The lack of sources could be interpreted in several ways: (1) it suggests that Africans imported during those early years did not perform the fiddle; (2) it reflects the degree that the French neglected their holdings on the mainland; or (3) researchers were uninterested because the activity was so commonplace. I assume the latter because, as noted elsewhere, sources on fiddling can be found in French and Spanish territories in the Caribbean (Epstein 1973, 62). In fact, under Spanish rule in the Louisiana Territory, a law was codified allowing the enslaved to perform African music and dance in designated places and situations. "In 1792 Baron de Carondelet, the Spanish governor, proclaimed that Sundays were reserved for the slaves' recreation; in 1795 another ordinance restricted amusements to Sunday, with planters being forbidden to permit 'strange negroes to visit their plantations after dark'" (Epstein 1977, 92). By contrast, the English believed Africans had too much freedom and allowing them to participate in merry-making on Sundays was sacrilegious. The following account by Francis Baily, an English visitor who arrived in New Orleans on June 6, 1797, provides documentation of Sunday musicking by Black people in Louisiana:

> Scarcely had the priest pronounced his benediction, ere the violin or the fife struck up at the door, and the lower classes of people indulged themselves in all the gaiety and mirth of juvenile diversions. Singing, dancing, and all kinds of sports were seen in every street.... The lower sort of people ... look forward with the highest pleasure for Sunday—particularly amongst the negroes, who in *this* country are suffered to refrain from work on that day. Here, arrayed in their best apparel ... they would meet together on the green, and spend the day in mirth and festivity. (Epstein 1977, 92)

Similarly, Fortescue Cuming, a white northerner who traveled by boat from Pittsburgh to New Orleans[22] in 1799, was amazed that "that there is no distinction or difference made by the inhabitants between a Sabbath and any other day in the week." Journal entries describing his observations after walking with companions "around the skirts of the city," provide interesting commentary on Black musicking in New Orleans under Spanish control:

> Sunday, Feb. 24 ... we saw vast numbers of negro slaves, men, women, and children, assembled together on the levee, drumming, fifing, and dancing, in large rings.

Sunday, March 3 . . . we found upwards of one hundred negroes of both sexes assembled on the levee, fiddling, dancing and singing. (Cuming 1810, 333, 336; also quoted in Epstein 1973, 85, 1977, 84; Southern and Wright 1990, 11 Item 87)

Because attitudes toward Africans and African culture by the French and Spaniards differed from those of the British who were the primary slaveholders in other parts of the country, totally different musical traditions evolved in the Louisiana territory, which had far-reaching influences on later musical developments during the nineteenth and early twentieth centuries. Most important is the fact that when left on their own, Blacks performed the fiddle or included fiddling as part of their own recreational activities.

Newspapers

Advertisements describing runaway enslaved musicians in eighteenth-century North American newspapers include much information about Black fiddling, with details on the prominence of the tradition, recruitment, performance contexts, status, and interactions with whites. The majority of references for the southern colonies appear in newspaper advertisements such as the *Virginia Gazette*, but some can also be found in newspapers from Maryland, North and South Carolina, and Georgia. In an effort to identify runaways, ads normally refer to the performance skills of the fiddler, indicating that he is a good, fair, or poor instrumentalist. Some ads report that the person is multitalented with the ability to sing and play several instruments; others mention that the person is a fiddle maker or has another vocation (Southern and Wright 1990, 4 Item 25; Southern 1997, 26–27). The names of fiddlers give some clues to their origins because some maintained their African names in an Anglicized form. Sambo, possibly a corruption of the Senegambian name "Samba," was a runaway Black fiddler from Virginia in 1768 who not only made and played fiddles, he was a carpenter (Southern 1997, 27). Fiddlers also used names given to them by their masters; for example, Derby, Peter, and Robert were names of Virginia fiddlers prominent during the 1760s and 1770s (26–27).

Robert Winans has conducted the most extensive analysis of newspapers as source material for Black musicking during slavery. For his article, "Black Musicians in Eighteenth-Century America: Evidence from Runaway Slave Advertisements," Winans (2018b) perused "more than 300 eighteenth-century newspapers (more than 20,000 individual issues)" and scanned "all the runaway slave advertisements" totaling "over 12,000 advertisements," which led to him identifying information about 761 Black musicians (194). Because ads focused on where the enslaved "ran away from, not the location of the paper where he was advertised, since many runaways were advertised in papers far distant from their homes," Winans discovered the little-known fact that "in the eighteenth-century there were nearly as many black runaway musicians in the North as in the South, with 370 in the North and 391 in the South" (194–95). Also significant is that the overwhelming majority of musicians advertised in the newspapers were fiddlers. Winans (2018b) explains:

> By far, in almost 90 percent of cases, the most common instrument was the fiddle, or violin, the latter term being used in a little more than a third of the instances. Clearly, the fiddle was the almost universal black instrument in the eighteenth century, widely played in all regions of the country at the time. The earliest reference dates from 1711 . . . in the *Boston News-Letter*. . . . All of the references up to the mid-1740s are to fiddle or violin players; after that time a sprinkling of other instruments begins to enter the advertisements (a total of eighteen advertisements for fiddle players before the first advertisement for a non-fiddle playing musician appears in 1748). (196)

Although Winans notes several characteristics identified with fiddlers—how they acquired their instruments; their musical ability, commitment to fiddling, and other music-related skills; craft occupation and status within their local communities; performance contexts and experience as a music or dance teacher—he seems most interested in the degree that Africans were acculturated or had adopted elements from European culture. After noting several factors to confirm his belief that European influence may have been the primary reason the fiddle was prominently used by Black musicians,[23] Winans (2018b) concludes with the following:

> The information on black musicians from the runaway slave advertisements makes clear that, even in the eighteenth century, these are not, except in a very few cases, African musicians; they are already African American musicians. . . . In terms of instruments played . . . the vast majority of eighteenth-century black musicians played the fiddle, which was also the central instrument of the prevailing Anglo-American tradition that surrounded these blacks, although of course bowed instruments similar to fiddles were also known in regions of Africa from which the forebears of these slaves originally came. All of these facts indicate that these were acculturated musicians. They probably played their music as much for whites as for other blacks; in the North they might have played more often for whites. The advertisements do not provide any information on what music they played, but Anglo fiddling and dance would likely have been at least a part of their repertory, along with specifically African American material. (209)

While I do not disagree entirely with Winans's conclusions, I believe the data can be interpreted in different ways; thus, several points need to be made. First, because a substantial increase in the importation of Africans from other parts of West Africa (areas where the fiddle tradition was also prominent) occurred during the eighteenth century, we cannot assume all enslaved fiddlers were born in the Americas. Just as Africans imported into various parts of the Americas during the seventeenth century quickly learned to perform the fiddle in a manner that brought them praise and appreciation from Europeans, a similar process or transition may have occurred among Africans imported during eighteenth century, especially if the enslaved saw the benefits of fiddling as a means of survival. In fact, Othello, the African-born fiddler in Massachusetts who became an important figure in his community because of his prowess on the instrument, demonstrates that such a scenario is plausible (Slade 1890, 14).

Second, if Afro-Creole fiddlers were indeed offspring of Africans who had arrived earlier, some may have been descendants of Senegambians.[24] This is significant because fiddling was prominent in this part of the continent for centuries before the transatlantic slave trade began. While we do not know precisely how many Senegambians were transported into North America, enough were present to influence the life of Africans in the Americas. The fact that Senegambians were not dominant throughout the slave trade is also not an issue, "if one accepts that the early arrivals provided the basis for the enduring elements in many mainstream Afro-American forms, and the last arrivals the basis for the most African (least digested) forms" (Roberts 1998, 61). Paul Oliver (1970) believes that to fully understand the history of African American music, more recognition should be given to influences from Senegambians: "Their culture may have been transplanted to the United States in many forms, including that of music. . . . It does not seem unlikely that the custom of making a fiddle, guitar or banjo from available materials . . . has a history that extends back to enslavement and beyond" (76, 84). In addition, evidence indicating that Africans exported from other parts of the continent performed the fiddle should not be dismissed. In making the point that African traditions in the United States may be older than scholars realize, Harold Courlander (1963) states: "A rustic homemade fiddle, even with a single string, is only a variation of an instrument with a sophisticated history. . . . If we happen to think of brass horns and trumpets as a category of highly developed instruments to which the African was exposed in America during colonial days, it is worth remembering that horns and trumpets of many kinds were widespread in Africa before the first slave cargoes sailed to the New World" (205).

Because of the prominence of fiddling in areas of Africa influenced by the Arab world where Islam is widespread, the religion of Africans transported to the Americas should also be taken into consideration. When Allan D. Austin (1997) published his findings, he estimated that between 5 and 10 percent of all Africans from ports between Senegal and the Bight of Benin were Muslim. If the total number of arrivals in the Americas was roughly 11 million, about forty thousand African Muslims may have resided in the colonial and pre–Civil War territories of the United States before 1860 (22). Today, scholars estimate that approximately 12.5 million enslaved Africans were shipped across the Atlantic over a span of four hundred years.[25] Estimates also indicate that more than half of the entire slave trade took place during the eighteenth century. Slightly more than 305,000 Africans were transported to the United States, a relatively small number compared to those taken to Brazil, the British and French Caribbean, and Spanish territories (Eltis and Richardson 2002, 95; Eltis and Richardson 2010; Franklin and Moss 1994, 43–49).

Like Africans from other regions of the continent, African Muslims made great efforts to retain the religion and language from their homelands: "After years of study in Koranic schools and centers of higher learning, they refused to let enslavement turn them into mere beasts of burden. They kept on reading the Koran and writing in Arabic, and they even established schools. Their literacy not only set them apart from most slaves and many slaveholders but became the basis of their disproportionate influence in slave communities and, in some instances, their key to freedom. In the world of slavery, literacy was a distinction and a danger" (Diouf 1998, 3). If African Muslims in the Americas found ways to maintain their religion, I argue that those who played bowed lutes had the same determination. To be sure, the violins and fiddles that Africans performed were generally introduced or given to them by Europeans, but some enslaved musicians constructed their own instruments that were very much African-derived.[26] Therefore, the reason fiddling among Africans seemed like a "normal activity" is because it was. John Storm Roberts (1998) notes that "the enthusiasm with which New World blacks took to the fiddle, not only in Brazil but in the United States and Cuba as well, is surely related to the occurrence of fiddle-type instruments in parts of Africa" (75).

Finally, the fact that Winans admits that newspaper ads do not provide the entire story about the musical lives of the enslaved fiddlers is significant. In other words, Winans (2018b) can only assume that "Anglo fiddling and dance repertory would likely have been at least a part of their repertory, along with specifically African American material" (209). In the end, we will never know if Black fiddlers' performance for white people was the totality of their experience and involvement with the instrument because no other evidence is available. Epstein's early research on the banjo (revealing that the instrument was not solely a European invention with no contributions from Africa) indicates that what appears most obvious may not be the only explanation.

Summary

Seventeenth- and eighteenth-century accounts about Black fiddling in the Americas raise several issues addressed in *Fiddling in West Africa* (2008a) as well as those to be considered in subsequent chapters of this study. Similar to West Africa, place (or geography) is central to the discussion. Not only did Europeans control and settle in different areas, but the physical environment affected the type of work that could be done and determined the number as well as the cultural features of Africans imported into various regions. Since New Englanders did not feel threatened by Africans (because the number of Blacks was small in comparison to that of whites), Blacks' participation in festivals and parades comparable to activities in Africa was commonplace. Similarly, the tolerant attitude toward African culture by Europeans in French and Spanish territories led to greater resilience of African elements, in addition to the fact that the number of African settlers was large. Although fiddling was prominent in most parts of the Americas by the eighteenth century, differences existed in how the instrument was accepted and used.

Also, important to the discussion is creativity, particularly the degree that African elements were maintained and/or fused with European features as interactions between Blacks and whites increased. In all references, the primary context for Black fiddling in the Americas was entertainment—either for Africans to entertain themselves or as recreation for Europeans. Most likely, interactions between Blacks and whites at performance events led to the sharing of elements. The organization of African fiddle ensembles is particularly significant because of its impact on musical and cultural preferences. The use of percussion (tambourine or drum) and wind instruments within the context of fiddling in the West Indies (Guadeloupe and St. Vincent) and North American colonies (Massachusetts, Rhode Island, and New York) is noteworthy because fiddle ensembles among the Fulbe in Senegambia often included similar instrumentation. Furthermore, almost all groups in West Africa use some type of percussion to accompany the fiddle. Since percussion was not featured prominently in the fiddling of Europeans before their arrival in the Americas, African influence becomes apparent (Rath 2000, 116–17; DjeDje 2008a).

The community's attitudes about fiddling and understanding how these views intersect with religion and other issues (social status/class, gender, and professionalism) are critical to the discussion. The majority of fiddlers were Black males who, if they were not enslaved, would be regarded as professional musicians, similar to most fiddlers in West Africa. Although both Blacks and whites disapproved of Black fiddlers, others valued them for their musical ability. In many cases, the status of Black fiddlers was comparable to that of the enslaved who worked in the master's house. Not only were they treated differently from other enslaved Africans, they had access to knowledge and social activities normally unavailable to other Blacks, which occasionally led to alienation or distance between both groups.[27] Class also was an issue with regard to the performer, the type of music performed as well as for whom and with whom a fiddler was performing. Because the fiddle was considered to be a lower-class instrument, it could be performed by Blacks. Questions only arose when African Americans performed in contexts that some identified solely with the European elite—either the instrument, the performance occasion, or the individuals participating in the event.

As indicated earlier, my central argument in this discussion is not that Africans introduced the fiddle into the Americas, although evidence indicates that some of the enslaved made gourd fiddles similar in construction to bowed lutes in West Africa. Rather, my point is that performing the instrument for white people was not the sole and only reason for its prominence among Black musicians in the Americas nor did this indicate that Blacks had completely divorced themselves from Africa and performance practices that were African-derived. In other words, acculturation did not mean a loss of the tradition. New ideas merely allowed fiddlers greater flexibility, versatility, and opportunity to be creative using performance practices available to them, whether they derived from African, European, or Native American cultures.

Upon arrival in the Americas, African musicians transferred their skills in performing the African bowed lute to the European prototype because fiddling was a tradition admired and valued by Europeans. In addition, there was the issue of compatibility: Senegambians "played fiddles and other stringed instruments in small ensembles, and could adapt Western equivalents without much effort. Therefore, the early arrivals would have been likely to establish a precedent" (Roberts 1998, 61). Because drums were outlawed in the early eighteenth century, musicians who performed string and wind instruments were at an advantage and could continue to exercise their talents openly (Rath 2000, 113; DjeDje 2016, 15). Oftentimes exempt from work in the fields, fiddlers had time and the necessary instruments to continue developing their skills. Drummers and percussionists, in contrast, had few opportunities to practice. Therefore, Islamic-influenced music, through its musicians and their knowledge of string instruments, had a good chance to survive in the South (Diouf 1998, 196–97).

Thomas W. Talley (1922), an African American chemist born and raised in Middle Tennessee who taught at Fisk University but also conducted research on Black music and culture in Tennessee and Alabama, comes to a similar conclusion. He believes the fiddle ensemble was used as a substitute for drumming: "The African on his native heath had his . . . ancestral drum as his leading musical instrument. He sang or shouted his . . . songs consisting of a few words, and of a few notes, then followed them up with the beating of his drum, perhaps for many minutes, or even for hours. In civilization, the banjo, fiddle, 'quills [panpipes],' and 'triangle' largely took the place of his drum"[28] (239).

In some ways, the fiddle or Black fiddling can be compared to the enslaved who spoke Arabic. Diouf (1998) states that when slaveholders offered Bibles in Arabic to African Muslims in an effort not only to portray Allah as a false prophet, but also so Africans might "discover the beauty of the Holy Book and of Christianity," many readily accepted them but not for the reasons intended by their European slave owners. If the words in brackets are used to replace "Muslims," "Bible in Arabic" and "religion" in the following passage, hopefully, what I am attempting to emphasize becomes clearer: "Besides the intellectual interest, the Muslims [African fiddlers] may have had another reason to be eager to receive Bibles in Arabic [fiddles]: to have them was the most efficient way of preserving their literacy. The Muslims [African fiddlers] were looking for an opportunity to maintain important skills, not to exchange their religion [fiddling] for another" (111–12).

fiddlingismyjoycompanion.net

Notes

1. At least two publications refer to fiddling by enslaved Africans during the tenure of Peter Stuyvesant (1592–1672), the director general of New Netherland from 1647 to 1664, when the colony was ceded to the English and renamed New York: Washington Irving (1891, 232) and Edward Robb Ellis (1966, 60). However, the reliability of information in the publications can be questioned because they do not contain source documentation (Pestcoe 2011).

2. Virginia is one of the most important states for the history of both African and European Americans. In 1607, Jamestown, Virginia, became the first permanent settlement for the English, and it is where Europeans, in 1619, deposited the first "parcel" of Africans (Hannah-Jones, Roper, Silverman, and Silverstein 2021).

3. Lynne Fauley Emery (1972) indicates that Europeans encouraged movement on slave ships "for economic reasons," but argues that it was not dancing. Rather, enslaved Africans who "exercised looked better and brought a higher price." Instruments performed by either Africans or Europeans (fiddle, banjo, drum, or an upturned kettle) would have been used to accompany movement (6–9); also see Hanna (1974).

4. Although fiddling has been documented for Central Africa, a region from which many enslaved Africans were transported to the Americas, minimal research has been conducted on this topic (Merriam 1959, 83; Sublette and Collinet 2012). For this reason, the following discussion focuses solely on West Africa.

5. 🎻 See History 1.1 and Video 1.1–1.7d to view images and performances of fiddling by Africans from different regions of the African continent.

6. 🎻 See History 1.2.

7. 🎻 See History 1.3.

8. While Labat's writings about Africa were well received by his peers, some scholars in the twenty-first century argue that his narratives not only promoted Western hegemony and supported the continuation of missionary pursuits but also contributed to the misrepresentation of Blackness as immoral and deviant (Smith 1910; Thompson 2014, 21).

9. See DjeDje (2008a, 28–32).

10. Some fiddlers use the holes in the resonator to store rosin and other materials to decorate the fiddle. When small rocks or pebbles are placed in holes (see photo 1.7), they serve a musical function by providing a rhythmic sound to enhance the musicking played on the fiddle.

11. 🎵 See Video 1.7 to view performances of different West African fiddle ensembles.

12. See Curtin (1969, 186–87, 245); Oliver (1970, 76); Oliver and Fage (1990); Walsh (2001, 158); Perbi (2004); DjeDje (2008a, 2016); and de Barros (2009, 27).

13. 🎵 See History 1.4 and History 1.5 for a more detailed discussion.

14. 🎵 See History 1.6.

15. While different dates may be given for their prominence, the revivals are known as the Great Awakening (1730s–1740s), Second Awakening (1780s–1830s), and Third Awakening (1860s–1900).

16. Because many sources are dated and not readily available, I quote at length from some to provide a full description of musicking by Black fiddlers in the Americas.

17. Although associated here with the enslaved, most researchers identify the jig as a sixteenth-century dance that originated in England and became popular among the Irish and Scots during the seventeenth century (Apel 1970, 448).

18. No documentation can be found that confirms Gilliat's activities at the Governor's Palace; comments about being a court fiddler were his own statements, many years later in Richmond (Epstein 1977, 115).

19. Thomas Jefferson may be the first person in the United States to identify the African American banjo, or what he referred to as the *Banjar*, with Africa (Jefferson 1781, 257; Epstein 1997, 34; Pestcoe and Adams 2018, 8).

20. This relationship between musician and patron is very similar to those in some parts of West Africa. Among the Dagbamba in northern Ghana, fiddlers do not visit or attend activities of the king unless invited (DjeDje 2008a, 199–204).

21. Southern (1997) indicates that "this reference to a 'Negro tune' may well represent the earliest record of the influence of slave music on white colonists" (44).

22. Although the bulk of Cuming's journal includes information about his travels between 1807 and 1809, he adds a postscript at the end of the book about travels from Pittsburgh to New Orleans to "complete the description of the Mississippi" (Cuming 1810, 325).

23. Regarding the issue of literacy, a point that Winans emphasizes in determining whether a person was African- or American-born, Diouf (1998) believes that because literacy was high in Muslim Africa and a concentration of learned Muslims had been forcibly transported to the Americas, the literacy rate among enslaved Muslims was probably higher than it was among slaveholders (108).

24. Rath (2000) uses the *jali* tradition, identified primarily with peoples in Senegambia, to support his arguments about the importance of fiddling in the Americas (113). While his focus is not on fiddling, Michael Coolen (1982, 1984, 1991) is another scholar who has conducted research on connections between Senegambia and the musicking of Blacks in the United States.

25. But the number purchased was considerably higher because millions died during transport to the African coasts for sale to Europeans, during the Middle Passage, upon arrival in the Caribbean, or as a result of slave raids and wars in the Americas (Eltis and Richardson 2002; Franklin and Moss 1994).

26. The narratives of the formerly enslaved include discussion of fiddles that are very similar to those used by West Africans (see chapter 3).

27. Social structure or status on plantations was determined by the proximity of an enslaved person's role to the planter or the Big House (Abrahams 1992, 27).

28. Although his interpretation of the data is excellent, the language that Talley uses in discussing Africans and African culture is pejorative but characteristic of the times in which the work was written and published (Talley 1922, 239).

CHAPTER 2

A General Overview
Black Fiddling During the 1800s

The nineteenth century was a critical period in the history of African American musicking, for this is when ideas unique to the Black experience began to crystallize into a distinct music culture.[1] In spite of abuse, trauma, ridicule, and obstacles, African Americans established an identity, spirit, and musical sensibility admired and emulated by those who most despised them. As interactions and borrowings between Blacks and whites increased, a shared culture developed that included elements from a variety of cultures in Africa, Europe, and the Americas. Although it was often "distorted for mass consumption," this so-called "American" music later served as a basis for creativity by peoples both within and outside the United States (Otto and Burns 1974, 407–17; Sacks and Sacks 1988, 425; Fryer 1998).

The fiddle was at the height of its popularity during the early nineteenth century, or what is also known as the antebellum period. After the Civil War and emancipation, aspects of Black fiddling began to change, but some features remained the same. The most dramatic transformations can be seen in the performer's role in the community as well as the establishment of new performance ensembles and contexts. As more Black and white people converted to Christianity, those who disapproved of fiddling became more vocal, but this did not stop the overwhelming popularity of fiddling among many groups in society.

Understanding Black Fiddling During the Nineteenth Century

Because of the fiddle's continued prominence, references to fiddling during the antebellum period can be found in histories, diaries, newspaper and journal

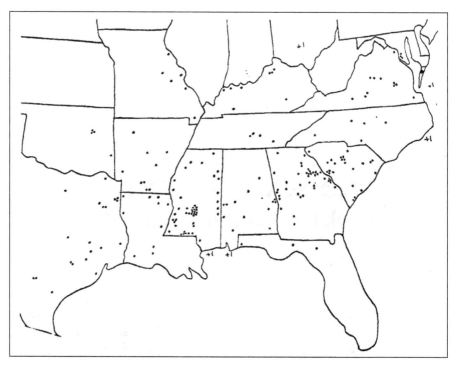

Map 2.1. Ex-slave narrative references to the fiddle, 1840s–1860s. Robert B. Winans, "Black Instrumental Music Traditions in the Ex-Slave Narratives." *Black Music Research Journal* Volume 10, Number 1 (Spring 1990): 47.

articles, fiction, as well as the personal writings of religious and political leaders and slave owners (Epstein 1975, 351; Blaustein 1972). Much of the information about the postbellum period comes from articles in nineteenth-century periodicals that include discussion and descriptions of scenes and occasions not very different from the slave era, confirming that the lifestyle of many Blacks had not changed. Of all the sources, narratives collected from the formerly enslaved (ex-slaves) by the Library of Congress under the Works Progress Administration (WPA) during the 1930s constitute the largest body of data about Black fiddling in the nineteenth-century (Federal Writers' Project 1941).[2] In addition to documenting details about instruments (distribution and popularity, ensemble organization), performance contexts, repertoire (types of songs, song texts and titles, dances), interactions, attitudes, and behavior of Blacks and whites, it is also possible to ascertain if fiddling, as one of many musical traditions performed by African Americans, had deeper or special meaning to Black people (Rawick 1977–1979; Southern and Wright 1990, 208–26). In terms of geography, narratives indicate that fiddle playing by Blacks was the most widespread (see map 2.1),[3] followed by banjo and quills [panpipes]. Percussion—patting (as distinguished from mere clapping), drumlike instruments (tin pans and buckets), bones, actual drums, tambourines, and jawbones—was also prominent. Playing the piano and guitar did not become popular until after emancipation.

When referring to the guitar, most formerly enslaved Blacks commented on its appearance in counties in south-central Mississippi. Mention of the banjo was less strong in Arkansas, Kentucky, and Texas, and even weaker in South Carolina and Mississippi. The use of percussion was strongest in Louisiana, South Carolina, and Georgia, and quill playing was more common in Georgia and South Carolina (Winans 1982, 1990).[4]

Formerly enslaved Africans indicated that the fiddle was often performed without other instrumental accompaniment, which differs from ensemble organizations used during the seventeenth and eighteenth centuries when fiddle and percussion were almost always played together. Also, instead of using the fiddle solely to accompany singing, it was generally performed in the context of dancing that may have included singing. While some indicated that dances rarely took place, others remembered dances taking place every Saturday night at frolics or house parties. Even when slave owners did not permit parties on their property, many allowed the enslaved to visit neighboring plantations to participate in entertainment that may have included musicking by both Blacks and whites (Emery 1972, 105). A few plantations had resident musicians, "who in some cases had been purchased strictly for that purpose, while others had to depend on musicians from neighboring plantations" (Winans 1990, 51). In fact, the purchase of enslaved persons for their musical ability was a public sign of a planter's wealth (Thompson 2014, 82).

Dances Black people performed with fiddle accompaniment changed over time. Not surprisingly, those that were African-derived began disappearing (or going underground)[5] in favor of European prototypes as interactions between the races intensified and Africans adapted to their new environment in the Americas. Contra (partner) dances, including square dances, and specifically named European-derived dances (such as cotillion, quadrille, and waltz)[6] appeared in about equal numbers. The most frequently mentioned African-derived secular dances were "cutting the pigeon wing," followed by "buck dancing," "knocking the back step" as well as various kinds of jubas, shuffles, and jigs. Either Blacks performed these as solo dances, sometimes in a contest situation (for example, cakewalks were mentioned a number of times), or as embellishments to square or contra dancing. The emphasis on European dances was summed up in the comment of one formerly enslaved person: "Some of the men clogged and pidgeoned, but when we had dances they were real cotillions, like the white folks had" (Winans 1990, 46). While it was common for Black fiddlers to perform for dances at all-white and all-Black events, white fiddlers occasionally performed for Black dances as well. The usual situation involved a plantation owner who enjoyed performing the fiddle and regularly played it at dances for the enslaved (Winans 1990, 53; Carlin 2004, 33–34). When Africans performed European dances, they often mocked whites. A seventy-year-old formerly enslaved person explained: "Us slaves watched white folks' parties where the guests danced a minuet and then paraded in a grand march, with the ladies and gentlemen going different ways and then meeting again, arm in arm and marching down the center together. Then we'd do it too, *but we used to mock 'em*, every step. Sometimes the white folks noticed it, but they seemed to like it; I guess they thought we couldn't dance any better" (Stearns and Stearns 1994, 22). The mocking (or masking) is significant because making oblique fun of white folks was "both satisfying and stimulating, since it was risky, and at the same time, called for subtle improvisations" (22).

Black Fiddlers and Their Instruments

Black male fiddlers continued to be important figures in both rural and urban areas during the nineteenth century. As noted above, they were either permanently attached to plantations or hired out by their slave masters to provide entertainment for others. In spite of their high regard and social status on the plantation, fiddlers were severely punished if they did not follow the rules. The remarks by Martha Ann Ratliff (1937), a formerly enslaved person born in Cotton Plant (Tippah County), Mississippi, but was living in Oklahoma City when she was interviewed in 1937 for the WPA project, suggests that fiddling was accepted by whites but only at occasions or contexts they controlled: "My father was a fiddler and some nights he would slip off to play for dances.... He would slip off at other times and as he never would get a pass and when patrollers would git at him, he would outrun them most of de time. They would sometime catch him and whip him. When I would sometime be with him, he would get me on his back and run" (339).

From the seventeenth century through the antebellum period, families of Black musicians rarely existed because they did not have the free time or opportunity to remain together as a family to pass the tradition from one kinsperson to another. When there were no family bonds, many fiddlers were self-taught because they were inspired by the example of older players; others may have learned from more experienced musicians. Those who acquired skills on their own did so because they recognized the importance of passing on songs to a new generation. In that way, they could guarantee that the community would continue to come together at frolics and other events (Cimbala 1995, 18). A few Black fiddlers received formal training; masters taught them personally or arranged for them to take lessons with a music teacher. Until they could purchase their own fiddles, some fiddlers made their own using material (that is, gourds) similar to that employed by musicians in Africa. Other times white masters provided them with violins. Regardless of how it was acquired, the instrument that fiddlers used was special.[7] After the Civil War, Black musicians made a more concerted effort to teach family members how to play many of the instruments needed to make up a string band. Therefore, fiddle ensembles composed of members of one family became more commonplace during the late nineteenth century for social and economic reasons (Armstrong 1987; Sacks and Sacks 1993).

During the nineteenth century, fiddlers continued to be attacked and ridiculed, especially by Protestant Christians who associated fiddling with the profane (Feintuch 1983, 31). When fiddlers encountered problems, many believed they were being punished because of their association with the fiddle. Therefore, reports on slave conversions are common, which some writers account for the decline in Black fiddling toward the end of the nineteenth century. On the other hand, fiddlers were admired and even envied because of their ability to perform the instrument. The fiddler was one of the few persons among the enslaved who had a visible position of authority that most Blacks and whites respected and did not question, to such a degree that some musicians added the title or sobriquet "fiddler" to their names. Not only did this talent allow fiddlers to be members of an elite group or social class, they had access to a world that most enslaved people never experienced (Cimbala 1995, 19).[8]

To understand the issue of class in slave culture, one must realize that the enslaved had few opportunities to develop their intellectual abilities. While some whites were impressed, others either believed Blacks were incapable of learning, or they felt threatened by the slaves' achievements and denied them the opportunity to learn (Diouf 1998, 107–9). Formal training in schools or homes was for whites only, and Black people were severely punished when it became known they were learning to read or develop their minds. The autobiography of Levin Jenkins Coppin (1848–1923), a Black man who became a bishop in the African Methodist Episcopal church, is significant for details about his early life in Frederick Town, Maryland, and how musicians dealt with the limitations of being enslaved: "Those who had musical talent often became 'fiddlers,' and some of them were considered quite expert with the bow. Of course, they knew nothing about the science of music. They played the jingles for the buck dances at corn huskings, parties and the holiday gatherings, of which 'Easter Monday' was the principal" (Coppin 1919, 47–49). Although Coppin acknowledges that fiddlers had special talent, he believed their opportunities were limited due to lack of formal training. Thus, the fiddler had to be satisfied with playing for local community activities. Yet, other individuals in the culture regarded the fiddler as a professional who stood apart from others.

The fiddlers' role as the facilitator of performances placed them at the center of communal gatherings. Similar to preachers, their sacred counterpart, Black fiddlers provided opportunities for the enslaved "to come together to recreate a sense of community in one of the few social outlets available to them—the frolic, the secular counterpart of the Sunday prayer meeting. . . . And like the location of the preachers at the front of their congregations, the position of the musicians at frolics—usually a make-shift stage that allowed them to be heard and seen above the crowd—is suggestive of their central role in the social life of the slave community. Aware of their role as performers, they further attracted attention to themselves by wearing costumes, some cutting impressive figures in bright-hued, long-tailed coats accented with gilt buttons and fancy shirts" (Cimbala 1995, 15, 17). But most important was their ability to perform. In front of energetic dancers, fiddlers did not simply make music—they entertained, understanding that they were the critical element for a successful frolic (Jamison 2015). On these occasions, a role reversal occurred in the relationship of Black and white people participating. For the length of time he played the instrument, the Black fiddler was the person in charge; he could tell whites what they should do and they followed his instructions without question. For an enslaved person to have such authority within the context of slave society was rare. Thus, similar to their counterparts in West Africa, fiddlers were professional musicians whose recognition and role in society went beyond that of providing entertainment; "they were essential performers in the southern black community's efforts to persevere, acting as facilitators of communal recreation, comfort, and identity. . . . [They] eased the troubled minds of their people and reminded them on regular occasions that they could smile. Most importantly, they were central figures at and the facilitators of the occasions that helped keep southern blacks in touch with their sense of being a people" (Cimbala 1995, 25).

Performance Contexts

While some forms of recreation from the seventeenth and eighteenth centuries were maintained (such as festivals, balls, holidays, weddings, weekend dances, barbecues), the contexts for fiddle performances expanded during the nineteenth century with changes in demographics (that is, the increase in native-born Blacks who worked on plantations). Almost nonexistent during the eighteenth century, the corn shucking (a work activity) became an important occasion for recreation for Blacks and whites during the antebellum period but even more so after emancipation; yet, it meant something quite different to both groups. For Black participants, a corn shucking was an opportunity to celebrate mutual participation in working, eating, and dancing—to depart from everyday labor while developing and maintaining their own traditional practices in the face of enslavement. To white observers, the event was entertainment verging on the spectacular built on everyday scenes of work and play in which the enslaved were the featured performers. The corn shucking, according to Roger Abrahams (1992), "turned the system of power relationships of the plantation into a comedy and pastoral romance" that revealed, tested, and reaffirmed the social structure (24–25). In addition to the corn shucking, barbecues, popular among whites with Blacks providing the entertainment, continued as

Photo 2.1. "The Celebrated Negro Melodies," as sung by the Virginia Minstrels [white group in blackface that includes Dan Emmett]. 1843. https://commons.wikimedia.org/wiki/File:Virginia_Minstrels,_1843.jpg. Accessed August 27, 2023.

an important setting for musicking. The newspaper *Harper's Weekly* includes a description of a Black cook who, along with his assistants at the barbecue, doubled as the musician-entertainers: "And when the eating is over, and *Moses* has received many congratulations and many quarters, just as likely as not the old man produces a fiddle, the second assistant cook an accordion, the colored scullions tambourines and bones, and music and a jolly dance will close the barbecue" (A Southern Barbecue 1987, 487).

The freedom to travel and perform within and outside their communities, though limited because of lack of resources, brought new opportunities for Black fiddlers and other musicians to supplement their income. Of particular note were road shows that became important settings for musicking. While some Black shows placed emphasis on concert music and formal theatrical productions, others enticed common people with vernacular music. Here, focus will be placed on new developments that began before and after emancipation (Southern 1997, 253–54, 259–60).

Minstrelsy, a theatrical performance that began in the 1820s by whites in imitation of African American culture, had a major impact on the development of Black fiddling because of the inclusion of African-derived instruments in minstrel ensembles. The fact that the fiddle as performed by Black people became an important source of entertainment in minstrelsy confirms that, prior to the nineteenth century, the instrument was identified with African American culture. In fact, instrumentation (fiddle, banjo, bones, and tambourine) for minstrel shows in the 1840s and 1850s accurately reflected contemporary Black musicking, for the fiddle, banjo, and percussion were the top three instruments mentioned in narratives by the formerly enslaved (see photos 2.1, 2.2, and 2.3). The narratives also provide evidence that southern plantations had built-in minstrel shows; "masters and mistresses, and sometimes their white guests as well, would come down to the slave quarters to witness and to be entertained by a slave dance, and that the slaves played up to this" (Winans 1990, 52–53). Although whites may have been the creators, minstrelsy became one of the most important contexts for Black fiddlers and other artists to maintain a livelihood as professional musicians after emancipation. Charles B. Hicks, the first African American to successfully own and manage a Black minstrel troupe (the Georgia Minstrels), hired several violinists to perform at the beginning of the group's climb to stardom in the 1870s (see photo 2.4).[9] John Thomas Douglass (1847–1886) was a concert violinist, director of a string orchestra, composer, and studio teacher. While some sources indicate that he was self-taught, people close to him state that he was sent abroad by wealthy white patrons to study. Frederick Elliot Lewis (1846–1877) was an accompanist, orchestral conductor, composer, and arranger. George A. Skillings, the troupe's musical director, was not only a violinist but also a teacher of strings (Southern 1989, 157–67).

With the decline in popularity of minstrelsy, the medicine show developed during the late nineteenth and early twentieth centuries as a form of entertainment to attract clients for vendors of patent pills and remedies that were of dubious, if any, merit. Setting up their acts on street corners and vacant lots, medicine show performers entertained audiences who did not pay for the amusement except through the pills and purgatives they were induced to buy. Because musicians had to be able to sing, dance, tell tales, and crack jokes, medicine shows gave employment to innumerable Black musicians, including fiddlers; a few even presented Blacks and whites on the same stage, which continued to be controversial at that time. While some Black musicians performed with a medicine show for only a brief period, others spent most of their careers with one company. Many medicine show acts worked in one or two states or traveled just in the lay-off season, picking up a few local entertainers in Memphis or Birmingham, but others traveled considerable distances (Wyatt 2005, 8–9; Oliver 1972, 55–57, 1984a, 86–87, 263).

The frolic and house party, which evolved into the country picnic, fish fry, juke,[10] cafe, and club, were some of the most important contexts for performing secular music in rural communities during the late nineteenth and early twentieth centuries. Not only were those involved able to entertain themselves without interference from whites or other Blacks, but it was also one of the few

Photo 2.2. "Christy's Melodies as Composed and Sung by Them." 1844 sheet music cover for a collection of songs by Christy's Minstrels [white group in blackface]. E. P. [Edwin Pearce] Christy appears in the circle at top. https://upload.wikimedia.org/wikipedia/commons/4/46/Christy_Minstrels_%28Boston_Public_Library%29.jpg Accessed August 27, 2023.

Photo 2.3. G. W. [Gilbert Ward] Pell's Serenaders, 1848. Courtesy Harvard Theatre Collection. In Eileen Southern, *Music of Black Americans: A History*, 3rd ed. (New York: W. W. Norton, 1848), 95.

Photo 2.4. Original Georgia Minstrels with founder Charles Hicks at center. Harvard Theatre Collection, Harvard University.jpg; https://en.wikipedia.org/wiki/Charles_Hicks#/media/File:Harvard_Theatre_Collection_-_Georgia_Minstrels_TCS_1.440_-_cropped.jpg. Accessed August 27, 2023.

public places African Americans could gather and enjoy socializing with one another outside of the church. This traditional Saturday night gathering generally lasted several hours and included three groups—(1) families, mostly women and children who lived nearby, (2) men, and (3) musicians—with children and adults in their separate spaces and joining together only occasionally. Also, typical of these events were coal-oil lamps that dimly lit the indoor or outdoor area; freshly cooked fish fried in big black belly pots; and homebrew whiskey or moonshine that were sold cheaply, while gambling, flirting, partying, and dancing took place in the largest room in the house or outside the yard, especially during the summer months. The music was performed by local musicians (fiddlers, blues singers, string bands, fifers, quill players, and drummers) who played material familiar and popular with African American audiences. Some musicians were more polished than others, but all were allowed to perform the music they wanted (Oliver 1996, 421; Henry 2020a).

Although frolics and house parties were common occurrences, everyone in the Black community did not sanction them. Just as secular events during the eighteenth century were ridiculed by religious believers, in later years they became the object of criticism because, in the eyes of some, they were profane and evil. Yet, similar to events from earlier periods, the frolic and house party gave solace to those who needed another type of relief than that provided by the church. For both nonbelievers and some believers, frolics and house parties were community events that allowed individuals to deal collectively with the trials and tribulations of living. As Oliver (1996) explains: "Romantic as it may have seemed, the house party was perhaps the only secular activity that rivaled the Sunday church services in respect to displaying home grown music talent" (421–22). For fiddlers, the house party was one of the few events in rural areas where they found support and acceptance to develop their craft.

Performance Ensembles

Black performers, including fiddlers, began experimenting with a variety of instrumental combinations with the emergence of a distinct African American music culture in the nineteenth century. In addition to maintaining practices from the seventeenth and eighteenth centuries, new instrumental fusions, based on earlier forms, came into existence. As Blacks and whites appropriated cultural patterns from each other and new contexts with different audiences emerged, extensive borrowing also occurred. Similar to what happened when Africans were forcibly transported to the Americas, musicians responded to changes by either fusing the old with the new or developing an entirely new creation.

Most seventeenth- and eighteenth-century sources document Africans performing the fiddle in combination with percussion (drums, sticks, triangle, bones, or tambourine) and wind instruments but also as a solo instrument (see chapter 1). The same can be said for the banjo, which was normally performed alone or with percussion accompaniment. The organization of the instrumental ensembles in this manner is similar to what continued to exist in West Africa. Although both bowed and plucked lutes have been used in savannah West Africa for hundreds of years, rarely were the two instruments performed together in an ensemble.[11] In fact, few sources from the eighteenth- and nineteenth-century literature document the fiddle in the Americas being played in an ensemble with the banjo.[12] The lack of information about this instrumental combination for the eighteenth century and earlier suggests that it was not common in the United States before the nineteenth century.

When minstrelsy began in the nineteenth century, white performers combined instruments (fiddle, banjo, and percussion) they associated with African American musicking and performed them together instead of playing each separately. Blacks emulated practices developed by whites when they began participating in minstrelsy rather than performing in the manner they had done centuries earlier. Most likely it was the minstrel show that popularized this performance tradition, although playing the fiddle and banjo together started among Blacks during the eighteenth century (Evans 1978b; DjeDje 2016, 14–16). Comments by Southern (1997) explaining how Black and white ideas were fused to develop the minstrel song are also applicable to the fiddle-banjo combination: "The minstrel songs, originally inspired by genuine slave [Black] songs, were altered and adapted by white minstrels to the taste of white America in the nineteenth century, and then were taken back again by black folk for further adaptation to *their* musical taste. Thus the songs passed back into the folk tradition from which they had come" (96).

To satisfy the tastes of the different audiences in various parts of the country after emancipation, new types of performance ensembles came into existence. Dance orchestras and brass bands were commonplace in cities, continuing a tradition that had begun during the early nineteenth century with society dance orchestras. Doubling as a dance orchestra whenever the occasion arose, the town brass band performed at Sunday afternoon concerts in the town square and for parades on civic occasions and holidays; bands often provided entertainment for events sponsored by Black and white social clubs, fraternal and benevolent societies (Southern 1997, 257, 340). Depending upon the occasion, musicians would alternate between instruments included in the brass band (cornets, trombones, horns, clarinets, and drums) and those used in the string orchestra or string band. Brass bands were composed of seven or eight bandsmen who could double on other instruments. For dances, they added violins, guitars, banjos, mandolins, and basses to a few wind instruments and the drums because of the dance music they played: waltzes, schottisches, polkas, quadrilles, and two-steps. The use of African elements in the bands' performance was minimal. Although musicians may have "ragged" the music, "there was very little improvisation or embellishing of melodies" (Southern 1997, 341).

Although horns and trumpets constructed from different materials were commonplace in parts of Africa from which enslaved Africans were taken, little evidence documents Blacks performing jugs during the slave era. In fact, Winans (1990, 44) cites only two references to jugs in his research. For this reason, most researchers believe jug playing by African Americans dates to the late nineteenth century, when earthenware objects started to be produced and used widely in the United States (Nketia 1974, 92–97, 1979; Brown 1990, 275; Charters 1966; Epstein 1977; Southern 1997). And the jug's prominence as an instrumental accompaniment for the fiddle occurred during the early twentieth century. According to Paul Oliver (2003b), the jug band ensemble "developed among African Americans . . . as a popular novelty entertainment for medicine shows and rural picnics. It takes its name from the use of a jug as a bass instrument, the player making buzzing sounds with the lips and the jug acting as a resonator." Louisville jug bands, using the fiddle as the lead instrument, were among the first to gain popularity. Inspired by street bands, Earl McDonald founded the Louisville Jug Band in 1902 and the first commercial recordings were made during the 1920s with Clifford Hayes playing the fiddle.[13] Although Louisville jug band music developed from the string band tradition, Michael L. Jones explains that "the music McDonald and Hayes made is usually classified as early jazz because of Louisville's close association with New Orleans through riverboat commerce, as opposed to Memphis jug bands, which are more akin to the blues of the Mississippi Delta. The Louisville groups would later use jazz instruments like the saxophone, trumpet and piano on their records" (Jones 2014, 89). It is also noteworthy that jug bands in other parts of the country may or may not have included the fiddle.[14]

Repertoire

Black fiddlers needed to have a large repertoire of tunes because they performed for a variety of occasions (formal balls in the main house as well as dances in the slave quarters). In other words, "the slave musician could not get by with only reels and jigs; he was expected to be able to play minuets and cotillions as well. The demands upon his violin technique, consequently, were almost as great as if he had been a city-slave musician" (Southern 1997, 177). The repertoire (dance tunes and songs) used by African Americans during the nineteenth century provides an excellent way to assess the degree to which Black and white people interacted and were influenced by each other, for the types of dances often determine the music played on instruments. The evidence indicates that not only did African Americans perform tunes that originated in Europe and were introduced to them by whites, but Black fiddlers also created their own songs using elements associated with Africa (see discussion below). In the end, a variety of tunes and song types became a part of the repertoire of both Black and white fiddlers in the United States (see repertoires 2.1 and 2.2).[15] Thus, fiddling in the southern United States is distinct from that in many parts of Europe and North America because African Americans influenced the fiddling of the Scots-Irish, who predominated in many parts of the South (Jabbour 1985).

Repertoire 2.1

List of the most frequently remembered dance tunes and songs played on instruments that appear in the narratives of formerly enslaved Africans in the United States (Winans 1982, 5; 1990, 51–52). The number next to each tune indicates the number of times it was mentioned in the narratives examined by Winans (1990).

10—Turkey in the Straw
6—Run N----r Run (also known as Paterroller'll Catch You)[16]
4—Arkansas Traveller
4—Molly Put the Kettle On
4—Old Dan Tucker
3—Dixie
3—Hop Light Ladies
3—Miss Liza Jane
3—Sally Ann
2—Swanee River
2—Sally Goodin
2—Swing Low, Sweet Chariot
2—Cotton Eyed Joe

A representative selection of songs mentioned once include "Amazing Grace," "Billy in the Low Ground," "Black Eyed Susan," "Buffalo Gals,"[17] "Cackling Hen," "Coffee Grows on White Oak Trees," "Devil's Dream," "Eggnog, Sugar and Beer," "Home Sweet Home," "Natchez Under the Hill," "Tain't Gonna Rain No More," and "Yankee Doodle" (Winans 1990, 51–52; 1982, 5).

Repertoire 2.2

To be included in this list, each song had to be performed (or at least mentioned) by two musicians in this study.

[—] Songs categorized as common stock (Russell 1970, 28).
[++] Songs mentioned in the narratives of formerly enslaved Black people (Winans 1990, 51–52).
[**] Minstrel songs (Winans 1979, 23; Meade, Spottswood, and Meade 2002, 751–65)

Across the Sea [Going Across the Sea]

1. John Lusk (Across the Sea). Central Appalachia (Tennessee)
2. Joel Rice (Going Across the Sea). Central Appalachia (Tennessee)

Arkansas Traveler[18] [++ |—| **]

1. William Adams. Central Appalachia (Maryland)
2. Dock Bertram. Central Appalachia (Tennessee)
3. John Booker (guitar) with Dock Roberts (fiddle). Central Appalachia (Kentucky)
4. Coffey Family (Charlie Buster). Central Appalachia (Kentucky)
5. Walter Greer. Central Appalachia (Tennessee)
6. Sidney Hemphill. Southern Appalachia (Mississippi Hills)
7. William "Bill" Livers. Central Appalachia (Kentucky)
8. Joel Rice. Central Appalachia (Tennessee)
9. Ripley String Band. Southern Appalachia (Mississippi Hills)
10. Various Black fiddlers. Southern Appalachia (Mississippi Hills)

Baby Please Don't Go

1. James "Butch" Cage. Gulf Coast (Southeast Louisiana/Mississippi Capital/River)
2. Calvin Calise Carrière. Gulf Coast (Southwest Louisiana)
3. Joseph "Bébé" Carrière. Gulf Coast (Southwest Louisiana)
4. Morris Chenier. Gulf Coast (Southwest Louisiana)

Barlow Knife

1. Dock Bertram. Central Appalachia (Tennessee)
2. Coffey Family (Andy). Central Appalachia (Kentucky)

Les Barres de la Prison

1. Douglas Bellard [La Valse De La Prison]. Gulf Coast (Southwest Louisiana)

2. Calvin Calise Carrière [Les Barres de la Prison]. Gulf Coast (Southwest Louisiana)
3. Joseph "Bébé" Carrière [Barres de la Prison]. Gulf Coast (Southwest Louisiana)
4. Canray Fontenot [Les Barres de la Prison]. Gulf Coast (Southwest Louisiana)

Big-Eared Mule (Flop-Eared Mule)

1. William Adams (Flop-Eared Mule). Central Appalachia (Maryland)
2. Bennie "Cuje" Bertram (Big Eared Mule). Central Appalachia (Tennessee/Kentucky)

Bile Them Cabbage Down

1. Nathan Frazier and Frank Patterson. Central Appalachia (Tennessee)
2. William "Bill" Livers. Central Appalachia (Kentucky Bluegrass)

Billy in the Low Ground [++] (Sally in the Low Ground)

1. William Adams (Sally in the Low Ground). Central Appalachia (Maryland)
2. Allen Alsop (Billy in the Low Ground). Gulf Coast (Mississippi Delta Region)
3. Bennie "Cuje" Bertram (Billy in the Low Ground). Central Appalachia (Tennessee/Kentucky)
4. Dock Bertram (Billy in the Low Ground). Central Appalachia (Tennessee)
5. Joe Booker (Billy in the Low Ground). Central Appalachia (Kentucky)
6. Ford Britton (Billy in the Low Ground). Central Appalachia (Tennessee)
7. Coffey Family (Shell) (Billy in the Low Ground). Central Appalachia (Kentucky)
8. John Lusk (Billy in the Low Ground). Central Appalachia (Tennessee)
9. Joel Rice (Billy in the Low Ground). Central Appalachia (Tennessee)

Black Eyed Susan [++]

1. Charles Addison (Hogeye). Gulf Coast (Mississippi Capital/River Region)
2. John Booker (Black Eyed Susie). Central Appalachia (Kentucky)
3. Joe Thompson (Black Eyed Daisy). Central Appalachia (North Carolina)

Blues à Bébé (Bébé's Blues)

1. Calvin Calise Carrière. Gulf Coast (Southwest Louisiana)
2. Joseph "Bébé" Carrière. Gulf Coast (Southwest Louisiana)

Boll Weevil

1. Sidney Hemphill. Southern Appalachia (Mississippi Hills)
2. Earnest Mostella. Southern Appalachia (Alabama)
3. Joe Kinney Rakestraw. Southern Appalachia (Georgia)

Buck Creek Gal(s) (Rye Straw)

1. Coffey Family (Charlie Buster). Central Appalachia (Kentucky)
2. William "Bill" Livers (Rye Straw). Central Appalachia (Kentucky)
3. Joel Rice (Buck Creek Gal). Central Appalachia (Tennessee)

Buffalo Gal [++ | **]

1. Various Black fiddlers. Southern Appalachia (Mississippi Hills)
2. John White. Southern Appalachia (Mississippi Hills)

Cacklin' Hen; Cackling Hen; Hen Cackle; Hen Cackled; Hen, She Cackle; Old Hen Cackled; Old Hen Cackled and the Rooster Crowed[19] [++]

1. Adams (Hen, She Cackle). Central Appalachia (Maryland)
2. Howard Armstrong (Cacklin' Hen). Central Appalachia (Tennessee)
3. Bennie "Cuje" Bertram (Old Hen Cackled). Central Appalachia (Tennessee/Kentucky)
4. Black Fiddlers at Train Stations (The Old Hen Cackle). Southern Appalachia (Mississippi Hills)
5. Blind Pete (Cacklin' Hen). Gulf Coast (Arkansas)
6. Jim Booker (Old Hen Cackled and the Rooster Crowed). Central Appalachia (Kentucky)
7. James "Butch" Cage (Hen Cackle). Gulf Coast (Southeast Louisiana/Mississippi Capital/River)
8. Thomas Jefferson Dumas (Old Hen Cackled). Southern Appalachia (Mississippi Pines)
9. Elbert Freeman (Old Hen Cackled). Southern Appalachia (Georgia)
10. Jim Gooch (Old Hen Cackled). Gulf Coast (Mississippi Delta)
11. Walter Greer (Old Hen Cackle). Central Appalachia (Tennessee)
12. John Lusk (Hen Cackled). Central Appalachia (Tennessee)
13. Bob Pratcher (Old Hen Cackle, Run Get the Egg). (Mississippi)

14. Joel Rice (Cackling Hen). Central Appalachia (Tennessee)

Careless Love [—]

1. Bennie "Cuje" Bertram. Central Appalachia (Tennessee/Kentucky)
2. James "Butch" Cage. Gulf Coast (Southeast Louisiana/Mississippi Capital/River)
3. Earnest Mostella. Southern Appalachia (Alabama)
4. Joe Thompson. Central Appalachia (North Carolina)
5. Henry Simms (Be True Be True). Gulf Coast (Mississippi Delta)

Cincinnati/Cincinnati Dancing Pig

1. John Lusk (Cincinnati). Central Appalachia (Tennessee)
2. Joel Rice (Cincinnati Dancing Pig). Central Appalachia (Tennessee)

Cindy (Gal)

1. Thomas Jefferson Dumas (Cindy). Southern Appalachia (Mississippi Pines)
2. Joel Rice (Cindy). Central Appalachia (Tennessee)
3. Ripley String Band (Cindy). Southern Appalachia (Mississippi Hills)
4. Joe Thompson (Cindy Gal). Central Appalachia (North Carolina)

Corrine Corrina/Corrinne/Come Back Corrina [—]

1. James "Butch" Cage (Corrine Corrina). Gulf Coast (Southeast Louisiana/Mississippi Capital/River)
2. Bo Chatmon (Corrine Corrina). Gulf Coast (Mississippi Delta)
3. Earnest Mostella (Corrina, Corrina). Southern Appalachia (Alabama)
4. Joe Kinney Rakestraw (Corinna). Southern Appalachia (Georgia)
5. Henry Simms (Come Back Corrina). Gulf Coast (Mississippi Delta)

Cotton-Eyed Joe [++]

1. Allen Alsop. Gulf Coast (Mississippi Delta)
2. Thomas Jefferson Dumas. Southern Appalachia (Mississippi Pines)

Cripple Creek

1. John Booker. Central Appalachia (Kentucky)
2. Coffey Family (Bled Coffey). Central Appalachia (Kentucky)

Devil's Dream [++]

1. William Adams. Central Appalachia (Maryland)
2. Sidney Hemphill (plays on quills). Central Appalachia (Hills)

Eighth of January, The

1. Bennie "Cuje" Bertram. Central Appalachia (Tennessee/Kentucky)
2. Sidney Hemphill. Southern Appalachia (Mississippi Hills)
3. Teodar Jackson. Gulf Coast (Texas)
4. John Lusk. Southern Appalachia (Tennessee)
5. Frank Patterson. Southern Appalachia (Tennessee
6. Ripley String Band. Southern Appalachia (Mississippi Hills)
7. Various Black Fiddlers. Southern Appalachia (Mississippi Hills)

Eunice Two-Step

1. Calvin Calise Carrière. Gulf Coast (Southwest Louisiana)
2. Canray Fontenot. Gulf Coast (Southwest Louisiana)

Fire on the Mountain/Sambo

1. Dock Bertram (Fire on the Mountain). Central Appalachia (Tennessee)
2. John Lusk (Fire on the Mountain/Sambo). Central Appalachia (Tennessee)

Forked Deer

1. Allen Alsop. Gulf Coast (Mississippi Delta)
2. Jim Booker. Central Appalachia (Kentucky)
3. Coffey Family (Charlie Buster, Shell). Central Appalachia (Kentucky)

Golden Slippers

1. Teodar Jackson. Gulf Coast (Texas)
2. William "Bill" Livers. Central Appalachia (Kentucky)

Grey (Gray) Eagle

1. Jim Booker. Central Appalachia (Kentucky)
2. Joel Rice. Central Appalachia (Tennessee)

Home Sweet Home

1. Joseph "Bébé" Carrière. Gulf Coast (Southwest Louisiana)
2. Canray Fontenot. Gulf Coast (Southwest Louisiana)

It Ain't Gonna Rain No More/Tain't Gonna Rain No More [++]

1. James "Butch" Cage. Gulf Coast (Southeast Louisiana/Mississippi Capital/River)
2. Joe Thompson. Central Appalachia (North Carolina)

Joe Turner [—]

1. James "Butch" Cage. Gulf Coast (Southeast Louisiana/Mississippi Capital/River)
2. Bob Pratcher. (Mississippi)
3. Henry Simms. (Mississippi)

John Henry [—]

1. Coffey Family (Shell Coffey). Central Appalachia (Kentucky)
2. Thomas Jefferson Dumas. Central Appalachia (Mississippi Pines)
3. Elbert Freeman. Southern Appalachia (Georgia Piedmont)
4. Walter Greer. Central Appalachia (Tennessee)
5. Sidney Hemphill. Southern Appalachia (Mississippi Hills)
6. Carl Martin. Central Appalachia (Virginia/Tennessee)
7. Joe Kinney Rakestraw. Southern Appalachia (Georgia)
8. Joe Thompson. Central Appalachia (North Carolina)

Johnny Can't Dance (Johnny Peut Pas Danser)

Joseph "Bébé" Carrière. Gulf Coast (Southwest Louisiana)
Canray Fontenot. Gulf Coast (Southwest Louisiana)

Jolie Catin

Calvin Calise Carrière. Gulf Coast (Southwest Louisiana)
Joseph "Bébé" Carrière. Gulf Coast (Southwest Louisiana)
Canray Fontenot. Gulf Coast (Southwest Louisiana)

Kentucky Waltz

Joseph "Bébé" Carrière. Gulf Coast (Southwest Louisiana)
William "Bill" Livers. Central Appalachia (Kentucky)

Ladies on the Steamboat

1. Dock Bertram. Central Appalachia (Tennessee)
2. Coffey Family (Bled and Shell). Central Appalachia (Kentucky)

La Robe à Parasol

1. Joseph "Bébé" Carrière. Gulf Coast (Southwest Louisiana)
2. Canray Fontenot. Gulf Coast (Southwest Louisiana)

Leather Britches

1. Coffey Family (Charlie Buster, Andy and Shell Coffey). Central Appalachia (Kentucky)
2. Elbert Freeman. Southern Appalachia (Georgia)
3. Sidney Hemphill. Southern Appalachia (Mississippi Hills)
4. Frank Patterson. Central Appalachia (Tennessee)
5. Joel Rice. Central Appalachia (Tennessee)

Madame Faielle

1. Calvin Calise Carrière. Gulf Coast (Southwest Louisiana)
2. Joseph "Bébé" Carrière. Gulf Coast (Southwest Louisiana)

Miss Liza Jane [++]

1. Charles Addison (Liza Jane). Gulf Coast (Mississippi Capital/River)
2. Josephine Compton (Go Long Liza). Gulf Coast (Mississippi Coastal)
3. William "Bill" Livers (Whoop Me Liza Jane). Central Appalachia (Kentucky)
4. Joel Rice (Liza Jane). Central Appalachia (Tennessee)
5. Various Black fiddlers (Little Liza Jane). Southern Appalachia (Mississippi Hills)

Mockingbird, The Mockingbird, Listen to the Mockingbird

1. Earnest Mostella. Southern Appalachia (Alabama)
2. Fred Perry. Atlantic Coast (Florida)

Momma Don't Allow

1. Leonard Bowles. Central Appalachia (North Carolina)
2. Teodar Jackson. Gulf Coast (Texas)

Nearer My God to Thee

1. William "Bill" Livers. Central Appalachia (Kentucky)
2. Earnest Mostella. Southern Appalachia (Alabama)

Oh, You Beautiful Doll

1. James "Butch" Cage. Rural Gulf Coast (Southeast Louisiana/Mississippi Capital/River)
2. William "Bill" Livers. Central Appalachia (Kentucky)

Old Joe Clark

1. Walter Greer. Central Appalachia (Tennessee)
2. Joe Thompson. Central Appalachia (Tennessee)

Po' Black Sheep (Black Sheep)

1. Walter Greer. Central Appalachia (Tennessee)
2. Frank Patterson. Central Appalachia (Tennessee)

Pop Goes the Weasel

1. William Adams. Central Appalachia (Maryland)
2. Bennie "Cuje" Bertram. Central Appalachia (Tennessee/Kentucky)

Rabbit in the Brush/Rabbit in the Log/Rabbit in the Pea Patch

1. Leonard Bowles (Rabbit in the Log). Central Appalachia (Virginia)
2. Walter Greer (Rabbit in the Pea Patch). Central Appalachia (Tennessee)

3. John Lusk (Rabbit in the Brush). Central Appalachia (Tennessee)
4. Joel Rice (Rabbit in the Pea Patch). Central Appalachia (Tennessee)
5. Various Black Mississippi fiddlers (Rabbit in the Ditch). Southern Appalachia (Mississippi Hills)

Run N----r Run (Pateroller'll Catch You) [++ / **]

1. William "Bill" Livers (Run N----r Run). Central Appalachia (Kentucky)
2. John Lusk (Pateroller'll Catch You). Central Appalachia (Tennessee)

Saint Louis Blues (St. Louis Blues)

1. William "Bill" Livers. Central Appalachia (Kentucky)
2. Earnest Mostella. Southern Appalachia (Alabama)
3. Joe Kinney Rakestraw. Southern Appalachia (Georgia)

Sally [Sallie] Goodin (Gordon, Gooden, Goodwin, Goodman) [++]

1. Coffey Family (Shell Coffey). Central Appalachia (Kentucky)
2. Elbert Freeman. Southern Appalachia (Georgia)
3. Walter Greer. Central Appalachia (Tennessee)
4. Fred Perry. Atlantic Coast (Florida)
5. Joel Rice. Central Appalachia (Tennessee)

Sitting on Top of the World

1. Lonnie Chatmon [Mississippi Sheiks] (Sitting on Top of the World). Gulf (Mississippi)
2. Eddie West [Alabama Sheiks] (Sittin' on Top of the World). Gulf (Alabama)

Soldier's Joy

1. William Adams. Central Appalachia (Maryland)
2. Dock Bertram. Central Appalachia (Tennessee)
3. Jim Booker (Soldier Joy). Central Appalachia (Kentucky)
4. Coffey Family (Bled Coffey). Central Appalachia (Kentucky)
5. William "Bill" Livers. Central Appalachia (Kentucky)
6. Joe Thompson (Love Somebody/Soldier's Joy). Central Appalachia (North Carolina)

Sourwood Mountain

1. Jim Booker. Central Appalachia (Kentucky)
2. Coffey Family (Andy and Bled Coffey). Central Appalachia (Kentucky)

Stack O'Lee, Stagolee

1. Blind Pete (no fiddle) (Stagolee). Southern Appalachia (Arkansas)
2. James "Butch" Cage (Stagalee). Gulf Coast (Southeast Louisiana/Mississippi Capital/River)
3. Various Black fiddlers (Stagolee). Southern Appalachia (Mississippi Hills)

Tennessee Wagoner

1. Dock Bertram. Central Appalachia (Tennessee)
2. John Lusk. Central Appalachia (Tennessee)

Tennessee Waltz

1. Elbert Freeman. Southern Appalachia (Georgia)
2. William "Bill" Livers. Central Appalachia (Kentucky)

Traveler (Arkansas Traveler++/Texas Traveler)

1. William Adams. (Arkansas Traveler). Central Appalachia (Maryland)
2. James "Butch" Cage (Arkansas Traveller). Gulf Coast (Southeast Louisiana/Mississippi Capital/River)
3. Coffey Family (Charlie Buster) (Arkansas Traveler). Central Appalachia (Kentucky)
4. Sidney Hemphill (Arkansas Traveler). Southern Appalachia (Mississippi Hills)
5. William "Bill" Livers (Arkansas Traveler). Central Appalachia (Kentucky)
6. Frank Patterson (Texas Traveler). Central Appalachia (Tennessee)
7. Joel Rice (Arkansas Traveler). Central Appalachia (Tennessee)
8. Ripley String Band (Arkansas Travelers). Southern Appalachia (Mississippi Hills)
9. John Booker (guitar) with Dock Roberts (fiddle) (Arkansas Traveler). Central Appalachia (Kentucky)

Turkey in the Straw [** | ++]

1. Eddie Anthony (Turkey Buzzard Blues). Southern Appalachia (Georgia)
2. Black Fiddlers at Mississippi Trains (Turkey in the Pea Patch). Southern Appalachia (Mississippi Hills)
3. Jim Booker (Turkey in the Straw). Central Appalachia (Kentucky)
4. Walter Greer (Turkey in the Straw). Central Appalachia (Tennessee)
5. Ripley String Band (Turkey in the Straw). Southern Appalachia (Mississippi Hills)
6. Various Black fiddlers. Southern Appalachia (Mississippi Hills)

Under the Double Eagle

1. Bennie "Cuje" Bertram. Central Appalachia (Tennessee/Kentucky)
2. Coffey Family (Shell Coffey). Central Appalachia (Kentucky)
3. William "Bill" Livers. Central Appalachia (Kentucky)

Valley (Songs with valley in the title)

1. Bennie "Cuje "Bertram (Red River Valley). Central Appalachia (Tennessee/Kentucky)
2. Jim Booker (Down in the Valley). Central Appalachia (Kentucky)
3. William "Bill" Livers (Peace in the Valley). Central Appalachia (Kentucky)

Waltz (Songs with waltz in the title)

1. William Adams (Fragment of a Waltz, Star Waltz-March). Central Appalachia (Maryland)
2. Allen Alsop (Scrub Waltz). Gulf Coast (Mississippi Delta)
3. Bennie "Cuje" Bertram (Bonnie Blue Waltz, Double Edge Waltz). Central Appalachia (Tennessee/Kentucky)
4. Calvin Calise Carrière (Love Bridge Waltz, Valse à Lawtell, Valse des Mèches). Gulf Coast (Southwest Louisiana)
5. Joseph "Bébé" Carrière (Daddy Carrière's Waltz, Kentucky Waltz, Valse à Cherokee). Gulf Coast (Southwest Louisiana)
6. Lonnie Chatmon (Alma Waltz/Ruby Waltz). Gulf Coast (Mississippi Delta)
7. Morris Chenier (French Town Waltz). Gulf Coast (Southwest Louisiana)

8. Canray Fontenot (Durald Waltz, Love Bridge Waltz, La Valse de Mom et Pop, Old Carpenter's Waltz, Opelousas Waltz, La Valse a Bud, La Valse d'Oberlin, Valse à Canray). Gulf Coast (Southwest Louisiana)
9. Elbert Freeman (Tennessee Waltz). Southern Appalachia (Georgia)
10. William "Bill" Livers (Kentucky Waltz, Wednesday Night Waltz, Tennessee Waltz). Central Appalachia (Kentucky)

Whoa Mule

1. James "Butch" Cage. Gulf Coast (Southeast Louisiana/Mississippi Capital/River)
2. Teodar Jackson. Gulf Coast (Texas)

Worried Blues/Worrying Blues

1. Eddie Anthony (Worrying Blues). Southern Appalachia (Georgia)
2. Elbert Freeman (Worried Blues). Southern Appalachia (Georgia)

Some tunes survived almost intact, while others merely endured name changes from titles, like "Miss McLeod's Reel" to "Hop Light, Ladies." Portions of old tunes were fused into new tunes; for example, "Turkey in the Straw," also known as "Old Zip Coon," came from two Irish hornpipes.[20] Many tunes were composed in the United States bearing the structure of those that came with settlers, with songs consisting of thirty-two measures in 2/4 or 6/8 time, the first eight measures played twice and the second eight, with a different but related melody, repeated. Although Black fiddlers provided music appropriate for the cotillions of their masters, in the slave quarters they added bow shuffles and offbeat phrasing to the same tunes to power the intensely rhythmic, athletic dances done there. The terms *breakdown* and *hoedown* were used to describe vigorous dancing and showy footwork, and soon those words were applied to the type of tunes that inspired such dancing. When performing breakdowns, fiddlers tended to place less emphasis on melody and more on rhythm and the repetition of short phrases. Eventually, hoedown-style fiddling and breakdowns were adopted by whites who visited slave gatherings (Cauthen 1989c, 40–41; Milnes 1999, 97; Wig and Ward 2002–2011).

Interactions between Black and white musicians, which led to both groups adopting tunes from the repertoire of each culture, suggest that Black musicking during the mid-nineteenth century represented an amalgamation of white and Black elements. The fact that most sources indicate Black musicians overwhelmingly incorporated dances and performances practices identified with whites into their performances can be interpreted in several ways. Formerly enslaved Black people interviewed by WPA workers, who were most often white, may have provided them with details they thought whites wanted to hear. The emphasis on European-derived traditions could also mean that, by this period, Black and white musicians had created a shared culture that both groups had participated in and shaped. In other words, by the mid-nineteenth century, many Black people had adopted elements identified with mainstream culture, which was apparent in the widespread conversion to Christianity. In another work, I refer to this transformation as the Americanization of African music (Winans 1990, 53; DjeDje 1998a, 124).

Religion

Although performing, listening, and dancing to fiddle music continued to be a favorite pastime during the antebellum period, the fiddle's popularity began to wane among some African Americans after the Civil War, particularly when Christianity became more prominent and Islamic practices became less apparent.[21] When European and various African religious traditions were fused, many Blacks created a distinct African American religious experience, one that offered a basis for collective identity and an avenue of psychic resistance to oppression (DjeDje 1998a, 126). Calling on spirits to preside over daily life or wearing charms, amulets, and other objects to heal, protect, or harm others continued to be key features of the African American spiritual world. Similar to African practices, Black people also communicated with spirits through musicking. One of the few examples of the fiddle being used for this purpose is revealed in the folktale, "Bur Rabbit in Red Hills Churchyard," collected by Edward C. L. Adams (1928) from a Black person in Richland County, which is located in the South Carolina piedmont.[22]

> I pass 'long one night by Red Hill churchyard an' I hear all kind er chune.... an' I seen a rabbit settin' on top of a grave playin' a fiddle, for God's sake. All kind er little beasts been runnin' 'round dancin' an' callin' numbers....
>
> While I been watch all dese strange guines on, I see de snow on de grave crack an' rise up, an' de grave open an' I see Simon rise up out er dat grave.... An' he look satisfy, an' he look like he taken a great interest in Bur Rabbit an' de little beasts an' birds. An' he set down on de top er he own grave an' carry on a long compensation wid all dem animals....
>
> Atter dey done wored dey self out wid compensation, I see Bur Rabbit take he fiddle an' put it under he chin an' start to playin'. An' while I watch, I see Bur Rabbit step back on de grave an' Simon were gone. (171–73)

In the tale, trickster Rabbit serves not only as the lead fiddler who uses his music to communicate with spirits, but also, he is "the keeper of the faith of the ancestors [and] mediator of their claims on the living" (Stuckey 1987, 18). Realizing the importance of the fiddle to Blacks for both secular occasions and sacred functions, this may be one of the reasons missionaries in Georgia attempted to eradicate its use. As Sterling Stuckey explains, "It is a study in contrasting cultures that missionaries thought the fiddle profane in religious ceremonies and the African thought it divine in that context" (18, 22).

Not all Europeans approved of the enslaved becoming Christians. Slaveholders who opposed Africans' conversion to Christianity not only encouraged fiddling and dancing, but they did not allow Blacks to participate in religious activities; some whites believed "that no good arose" from participating in religious activities and "the most zealous pretenders to religion were the greatest rogues" (Herbemount 1836, 71). After emancipation, changes in Black secular life also affected fiddling and the social status of African American fiddlers. Comparing religious practices before and after the Civil War, LeRoi Jones (1963) indicates that Black churches had almost no competition during the slave era. After Africans worked in the field, there was no place to go for any semblance of social intercourse but the praise houses (48). It was not until well after emancipation that African Americans developed a social life, which gave Black secular musicians, including fiddlers, opportunities to experiment with new musical traditions. "In part, the way of life which grew outside of the church was associated with art, dance, and music, some of which displayed the rudiments of early blues with fiddle, banjo and primitive guitar instrumentation. This music syncretized African and Western influences in a way which was distinctly American, but at the time of its creation was considered 'sinful' by the church. Singers of 'devil songs' and 'jig tunes' were often called to repentance, and children were warned away from the blues by their parents" (Govenar 1985, 6). Charles K. Wolfe (1997) indicates that performers, researchers, and others in the Black and white music community "called the instrument 'the devil's box' because some thought it was sinful to play one. . . . [T]he fiddle was for good times and strong drink. . . . And didn't one take the rattles of a serpent—the rattlesnake—and put them in the fiddle to improve the tone?" (xv–xvi).

Since the fiddle's association with the devil was a common theme in both Black and white culture (from the eighteenth through the early twentieth centuries), a more in-depth analysis is needed to explain possible reasons for this attitude. In my opinion, the basic question is: who associates the fiddle with the devil, the profane, and why? From chapter 1, we learned that practitioners of African or African-derived beliefs do not relate the fiddle to the devil because this figure does not exist in indigenous African religious practices. Rather, individuals who appropriated Islam, Christianity, or a fusion of the two are the ones who regarded the fiddle as profane. Furthermore, differences exist in the views of Protestants, whose criticisms were most pronounced, as opposed to Catholics, who, from the literature, did not discourage participation in secular activities.

Thus, the negative views regarding the fiddle can be placed into three categories: context and behavior, supernatural qualities, and challenges to authority.

Religious leaders were the ones most concerned about contexts—particularly events or occasions when attendees participated in activities that religious authorities considered to be sinful, immoral, or profane—like drinking alcoholic beverages, gambling, or males and females closely interacting (dancing). In the minds of some Protestant white and Black churchgoers, fiddling as well as the lively contortions and movements of all parts of the body not only signified deviant behavior, it also represented difference. Whenever people acted in a way not validated by European practice or values, it had to be something that came from elsewhere. In the case of African Americans, it was Africa, which meant that it was unacceptable. Because it was the fiddle that stimulated this behavior, it symbolized sin and the work of the devil. Also troubling for some religious officials was the ambivalence or contradictions associated with being a musician. When musicians, including fiddlers, participated in nonconventional behavior, the rewards they received—in terms of economics, visibility, and popularity—diminished whatever shortcomings that arose from their disapproval by some churchgoers.

In a few cultures, the exceptional ability or gift to be creative is ascribed to supernatural phenomena. Not only do oral traditions in some West African societies indicate that the talent of their forefathers (or their recruitment into the profession) comes from fairies, spirits, and the unknown, but fiddle music is often used to communicate with sprits at religious ceremonies (DjeDje 2008a, 31, 33–36, 120–24). In the West, the crossroads (when musicians have to decide if they want to be ordinary or special in terms of their talent) is regarded as a place of mystery and power, resulting in the belief that the ability to perform is derived from the supernatural. Similarly, the sound produced on the fiddle is considered to be special or extraordinary.[23] While some regard it as hypnotic and seductive, others believe it expresses deep emotion, unlike sounds produced on other instruments. In some parts of Africa, some individuals believe the sound produced on the fiddle has an unnatural attraction; it can cast a spell that lures people to do things against their will (DjeDje 2010).

Because individuals in the community continued to participate in activities associated with fiddling in spite of the admonitions against it, some religious leaders believed the fiddle was a subversion of authority, like drums and horns that were banned by slaveholders because of their threat to the safety and well-being of white people. Vincent Wimbush, a scholar noted for his research on scriptures, argues that participation in fiddle performances can be regarded "as a kind of gateway to another kind of world [with all types of] sensory and ecstatic experiences. [Religious authorities believed] we can't have all of these people dancing and getting in touch with spirits, and know what they want to do. So, of course, it's 'of the devil' because we can't control it" (Wimbush 2010). Fiddling represented both an alternative pathway to a fulfilled spiritual experience as well as a challenge to religious authority. In this light, it is unsurprising that the instrument accumulated associations with the profane; also see Halpert (1995).

Mary E. Chamberlain (1892) confirms this position in her article, "Folk-lore Scrap-Book," which includes comments by a plantation owner who suggests reasons for the decline in fiddle and banjo playing among rural Blacks:

> [F]or many years, and even long before the war, playing the fiddle and the banjo had been dying out among the negroes, owing to a superstition that "de devil is a fiddler." The master of the mansion says: "In my father's time, and when I was a boy, there were few regular musicians, and at parties, unless it was a very grand affair, a lady played the piano, accompanied by a gentleman on the violin, and monstrous good jigs and reels they played too. But when it got too much like work, almost anybody's carriage driver could be sent for out of the kitchen who could fiddle well enough to dance the Virginia reel by. But when I grew up negro fiddlers were scarce among the plantation hands, except the 'professionals,' who were free negroes. They have been growing scarcer, owing to this superstition about old Pluto.
>
> "Among the city negroes the piano is the favorite instrument, as it is so much easier to acquire a certain proficiency on it than on the violin. In the country, though, it is generally thought unbecoming, at least, for a 'chu'ch member' to play the violin, if not actually an audacious communication with Satan himself. But it involves neither deadly sin nor any spiritual risk whatever to play the accordeon or the 'lap organ,' as they call it. The 'cor'jon,' consequently, is a very popular instrument." (329–30)

In addition to suggesting reasons for the decline in the popularity of the fiddle, the plantation owner reveals subtle details about the sociocultural environment in which he lived. The bias embedded in his description also indicates that he is the product of a society in which people were separated either because of class, gender, profession, race, or place. His comments suggest that fiddling by African Americans was unacceptable at a grand affair, but okay at a lowly dance; also, the violin (not the fiddle) and piano would be more appropriate at entertainment events attended by people of higher social standing. Intuitively, this implies that violin playing was an elite performance tradition not identified with African Americans. When the musician was expected to entertain whites throughout the evening and the activity became more like work, someone lower in status and position ("anybody's carriage driver," a Black person) needed to be summoned to perform these duties. Since the music is performed for dancing, the person also did not need to have a large repertoire of songs or tunes to play. Performing one type of music (the Virginia reel) would be fine, implying that the repertoire of Black fiddlers was limited.

Such comments by the plantation owner that address the question: why is the fiddle/violin not identified with African American musicking? To a degree, the answer is embedded in the issue of class. When white people made clear distinctions between the violin and fiddle during the nineteenth century, Black people were rarely identified with the violin because of its link with the elite. However, the fiddle was identified with Black musicians because of its association with dance music that was regarded as lowly, sinful, and despised by religious leaders and the social elite. Yet it is significant that the larger majority of Black people, which was overwhelmingly rural during this period, had few or any admonitions against fiddling and activities associated with it.

fiddlingismyjoycompanion.net

Notes

1. 🎻 See History 2.1.

2. Some historians question the reliability of narratives because they were collected sometime after slavery, and Blacks may have been reluctant to be completely honest in their remarks about former white masters due to the fact that interviewers were white. Yet, Winans believes these issues have limited relevance for his research. In his opinion, the only problem is that some interviewers did not ask questions about instrumental music traditions during the prewar period (Winans 1990).

3. 🎻 See Map 2.1 and Map 2.2.

4. 🎻 See History 2.2.

5. With the exception of Vodun, a Haitian religion practiced by Africans in Louisiana during the nineteenth century using African-derived instruments, the ring shout (also African-derived and accompanied by percussion) may be the only remnant of sacred dancing by US Blacks (Cable 1886b, 816).

6. All are social dances that were popular in eighteenth- and nineteenth-century Europe and North America. While cotillion (also cotillon) is a courtly version of the English country dance and the forerunner of the square dance, the quadrille is a ballroom dance with an elaborate set of steps and danced by sets of four, six, or eight couples (Lamb 2001; Norton 2014).

7. An article in a nineteenth-century newspaper is noteworthy for its description of what a Black musician considers to be important when deciding to purchase a string instrument (An Artist Selecting an Instrument 1871, 192).

8. The names of some of these fiddlers appear on the contents page of this book (Mordecai 1856, 355–57; Mott 1875, 144–50; Epstein 1977, 116–17; Parramore 1988, 1989).

9. 🎻 See Photo 2.5 for an image of the Georgia Minstrels holding their instruments.

10. Juke (jook) joint referred to an informal establishment operated by Black people that featured musicking, dancing, gambling, and drinking. Set up on the outskirts of a town, juke joints emerged after emancipation and catered to rural workers who needed a place to

relax and socialize after a hard week of working (*Webster's New Collegiate Dictionary* 1974; Strachwitz 1964; Oliver 1984a, 41–42; Palmer and Mugge 1991; Hazzard-Gordon 1990; Hurston 1994; Juke Joint 2019).

11. The use of plucked and bowed lutes within the same ensemble is rare in West Africa. Documentation of this performance practice exists for the Bisa in Burkina Faso and the Gwari in Nigeria (Duvelle1961; DjeDje 2008a, 40; Pestcoe 2011).

12. Sources that document a musical ensemble with fiddle and banjo during the eighteenth century can be found in the following: Platt (1900, 321, 326); Cresswell (1924, 30); Epstein (1977, 115); and Southern (1997, 54). Another source provided by Pestcoe (2011) is "an anonymous hand-colored satirical cartoon print . . . showing five Afro-Jamaican musicians playing cow's horn, 'goombay' (square wooden box drum), jawbone, fiddle, and early gourd banjo." Published in 1803 by William Holland in London, the image can be found at: https://omeka-yale prod.s3.amazonaws.com/original/1e0fe5777892d02c4d18eb3d75d8e54394e0764b.jpg Accessed June 1, 2022.

13. Because of New Orleans's influence on Louisville, Jones (2014, 16–17, 89) believes the history of Louisville jug music begins in New Orleans, where spasm bands (an ensemble similar to a washboard band) first appeared at the end of the nineteenth century. Also, see Ware and O'Neal (1981) and Wright and Cox (1993).

14. Unlike jug bands in Louisville and Memphis that included the fiddle, Alabama jug bands did not (Danser 2018). In some parts of the United States, jugs and jug bands—similar to other instruments, musical types, and song traditions—were part of the shared culture of Blacks and whites and varied in instrumentation (Baklanoff 1991, 136–37; Courlander 1963, 110, 177, 213, 215).

15. Although Winans (1990) does not specify the instrument used to play the tunes, we can assume it was the fiddle because of its prominence in slave culture (51–52).

16. Because of negative associations with the word "n----r," the song "Run N----r Run" was referred to as "Paterroller'll Catch You" in some African American communities (Wolfe 1989).

17. Chris Durman (2008, 806) indicates that modern-day listeners know the tune "Buffalo Gals" as "Maxwell Girl."

18. "The Arkansas Traveler" was first recorded by Alexander Campbell "Eck" Robertson and Henry C. Gilliland as a fiddle duet on Victor Records (unissued) in New York City, on Friday, June 30, 1922 (Russell and Pinson 2004, 757).

19. "Cacklin Hen," which is known by different titles, was first recorded by John Carson as "The Old Hen Cackled and the Rooster's Going to Crow" on OKeh Records in Atlanta, Georgia, on June 14, 1923 (Russell and Pinson 2004, 175).

20. The hornpipe is a dance resembling the jig but distinguished from it by its meter, which may be either 3/2, 2/4, or 4/4. Until the early nineteenth century, the terms jig, hornpipe, and reel were used interchangeably because none was a distinct form in either style or rhythm (Dean-Smith 2001a, 2001b).

21. When African Muslims died, oftentimes their offspring adopted other faiths. In British and French territories, the last African Muslims passed away in the 1880s or 1890s. In the United States as well as Brazil and Cuba, where the slave trade and slavery lasted longer, the last Muslims died between 1920 and 1930 (Diouf 1998, 198).

22. 🎼 See Demographics 2.1 and History 2.3.

23. The "Story of Uncle Dick" in the Kentucky Narratives is excellent for demonstrating how the fiddler's unique sound helped save him from the mouths of hungry wolves (Born in Slavery 2001; Claiborne 1906, 535–38).

CHAPTER 3

A Regional Perspective
Black Fiddling during the 1800s

Winans (1990) hoped that his findings from narratives by formerly enslaved people[1] "would provide a basis for making some regional or state comparisons of usage of particular instruments," but he cautions that problems arise when using the material in this way because "the quantity of data varies considerably from state to state" (45). However, when other sources (diaries, journals, newspaper advertisements and articles, periodical literature, and more) are combined with the narratives (Federal Writers' Project 1941), the amount of material for the nineteenth century becomes substantial, especially when compared with findings for earlier and later periods. Although uneven in terms of time and place (for example, more can be found for the antebellum period and eastern coastal regions than for the postbellum and mountain areas), organizing the material according to regions provides a unique perspective for investigating the activities of fiddlers and their patrons in different parts of the United States. Enough data are available to also determine the degree to which the sociocultural environment may have affected performance practice. More importantly, this information will be useful for examining developments in different parts of the United States during the twentieth century. Therefore, what follows is a discussion of four regions—northeast, southeast, mountains, and south-central—for which documentation exists on African American fiddling in the nineteenth century.[2] For each region, the primary focus is the fiddle with attention given to sources and various socio-musical issues—performance contexts; fiddle construction and ensemble organization; social significance (attitudes toward fiddling by community members); social role and status of fiddler; and performance practice—that may have affected the tradition.[3]

Photo 3.1. "Merrymaking at a Wayside Inn," 1811–13. Attributed to John Lewis Krimmel (1786–1821). Formerly attributed to Pavel Petrovich Svinin (1787/88–1839). Metropolitan Museum of Art. https://www.metmuseum.org/art/collection/search/12728 Accessed August 19, 2023.

The Northeast

Sources with substantial information on Black fiddling in the Northeast during the nineteenth century[4] are limited to Pennsylvania and New York (Bronner 1987). While most references include discussion of the fiddler's role and status, social significance, and performance contexts, it is the latter that is mentioned most prominently and a topic that distinguishes literature about Black fiddling in the Northeast from other parts of the United States.

Performance Contexts. In addition to performances at festivals (such as 'Lection Day and Pinkster), enslaved fiddlers in the Northeast continued to provide entertainment for whites at recreational events as they also worked in other capacities (see photo 3.1). An account from New York in 1846 reports on Caesar, an enslaved man who drove the coach that took the young ladies to the dancing school, played for the dancing, and then served as a waiter during refreshment time (Watson 1846, 212; Southern 1997, 43). Unlike other parts of the country, literature about fiddling among free Blacks is well represented in states in the Northeast, such as the short article in *Harper's Weekly* describing fiddling at the wedding of a "colored solider" in New York, which confirms that African Americans performed fiddle music at both private and public occasions for themselves, not only for whites (Pictures of the South 1866, 411).

In addition, free Black fiddlers constituted the primary entertainment at dance halls in Manhattan's Five Points (Southern 1997, 124). Performing in such contexts is significant not only because few cities in United States during the first half of the nineteenth century had dance halls or other public venues where Blacks could entertain themselves and others, but also a limited number of free Blacks resided in northeastern cities who could patronize such venues. While visiting New York's Five Points in 1842, English author, Charles Dickens, reports that each dance hall in the area had its own fiddler. Of particular interest to Dickens was Almack's, a Black-owned venue (later called Dickens' Place after the English author's visit) that was considered to be "the assembly room of the Five Point fashionables." In describing what he and his traveling partners observed when they entered the establishment, Dickens (1842) writes:

> The corpulent black fiddler, and his friend who plays the tambourine, stamp upon the boarding of the small raised orchestra in which they sit, and play a lively measure.[5] Five or six couple [sic] come upon the floor, marshalled by a lively young negro, who is the wit of the assembly, and the greatest dancer known.... Among the dancers are two young mulatto girls ... who are as shy ... as though they never danced before....
>
> But [when] the dance commences.... Instantly the fiddler grins, and goes at it tooth and nail; there is new energy in the tambourine; new laughter in the dancers; new smiles in the landlady; new confidence in the landlord; new brightness in the very candles. (216-217; also quoted in Dickens 2013, 60–81)[6]

Because of the prominence of percussion and the primary role of the fiddler in the performance, fiddling at Almack's displays many elements found in seventeenth- and eighteenth-century fiddle performances in the West Indies and North America when Blacks were left to perform on their own. Again, these practices raise questions about the degree to which African-derived features had been maintained or disappeared after the enslaved had been transported to the Americas.

A similar performance aesthetic is apparent in an article in the *New-York Tribune* by George G. Foster, who writes about nightlife in Philadelphia. In addition to information about the role of the fiddler (lead musician) and type of music used in dance halls and clubs, Foster (1848) describes the exaggerated behavior of performers and members of the audience. Because some performance practices are similar to those used by groups in West Africa, especially the dancers' movements, physical expressions, and the manner in which the fiddler controls the performance through his fiddling (DjeDje 2008a, 106, 109–13), I quote at length from the article.

> Saturday night is a great time at Dandy Hall; and, although it is but in the beginning of the evening, the house is already swarming with its customers of both sexes. In

the dancing-room, up-stairs, the old negro fiddler has taken his seat on a broken chair in one corner, and a temporary counter made by laying a board across two barrels, in the other, offers the necessaries of brandy and whisky to the company at three cents a glass. The ladies are seated each by the side of her beau. . . . And now the old fiddle strikes up "Cooney in de holler," and the company immediately "cavorts to places." . . . Having taken their places and saluted one another with the most ludicrous exaggeration of ceremony; the dance proceeds for a few minutes in tolerable order; but soon the excitement grows, the dancers begin contorting their bodies and accelerating their movements, accompanied with shouts of laughter, yells of encouragement and applause, until all observance of the figure is forgotten and every one leaps, stamps, screams and hurras on his or her own hook. Affairs are now at their height. The black fiddler increases the momentum of his elbow and calls out the figure in convulsive efforts to be heard, until shining streams of perspiration roll in cascades over his ebony face; the dancers, now wild with excitement, leap frantically about like dervishes, clasp their partners in their arms, and at length conclude the dance in the wildest disorder and confusion. As soon as the parties recover, the fiddler makes his appearance among them and receives from each gentleman a tip as his proportion of the ceremony of "facing the music," and the floor is cleared for a new set: and so goes on the night. (1)

The description by Foster (1850) of the behavior and people who visited New York City's nightclubs also helps us understand why white and Black Protestant Christians protested so strongly against fiddlers and fiddle music: "The walkers in these haunts are mostly sailors, negroes and the worst of loafers and vagabonds, who are enticed and perhaps even dragged in by the painted Jezebels, made to 'treat,' and then invited to the dance—every room being provided with its fiddler, ready to tune up his villainous squeaking for sixpence a piece and a treat at the end of the figure. The liquor is of course of the most abominable description, poison and fire; and by the time the first dance is concluded, the visitor feels his blood on fire—all his brutal appetites are aroused, and he is ready for anything" (54). In summary, the central role of the fiddle at festivals and in dance halls and nightclubs in the northeastern United States demonstrates that fiddling was not only aesthetically pleasing to Black people, African American musicians also used the instrument for entertainment even when they were not performing for whites.

Social Role and Status. Although enslaved Black fiddlers in the Northeast continued to be important figures in all aspects of life during the early nineteenth century, their position did not prevent them from being controlled, manipulated, and exploited by slave masters. Documentation from upstate New York indicates that Black fiddlers often made contracts with their slaveholders. "The document specified, among other things, that the slave was to leave his fiddle with his master and not go fiddling except on holidays or with his master's permission" (Epstein 1977, 148). Controlling the performance activities of fiddlers may have been done for a variety reasons: to ensure that the slaveholder is compensated when his fiddler provided services to others; to regulate the times when members of the Black community participated in activities that gave them pleasure; or to prohibit fiddlers from promoting immoral behavior.

In spite of their freedom, Black fiddlers in the Northeast (similar to their white counterparts) had to work several jobs to maintain a livelihood because they could not survive solely from their musicking. Solomon Northup (1968), a free Black person of Saratoga Springs, New York, writes that before he was kidnapped and sold into slavery in 1841, he worked at the United States Hotel in Saratoga Springs in the summer but relied upon his violin playing in the winter.[7] "In the winter season I had numerous calls to play on the violin. Wherever the young people assembled to dance, I was almost invariably there" (9). In addition, he farmed, performed odd jobs as a lumberman, and worked in construction and other vocations. We know little about Northup's training or how he acquired his skills as a fiddler. Since his father was a farmer and there is no evidence that other family members were musicians, most likely he took lessons or apprenticed with someone in his community for personal enjoyment and his desire to become a learned man with a vocation. About his early life, he writes: "Up to this period I had been principally engaged with my father in the labors of the farm. The leisure hours allowed me were generally either employed over my books, or playing on the violin—an amusement which was the ruling passion of my youth. It has also been the source of consolation." (6)[8]

The Southeast

Surprisingly, the number of sources on Black fiddling in the Upper Southeast is relatively small when compared to the Lower Southeast.[9] In my opinion, at least three reasons account for greater interest in writing about the latter. One factor was the large numbers of Black people in the region that affected interactions between the races.[10] As indicated in the foregoing, the Black population in the Lower Southeast experienced a dramatic increase, which may have startled some whites. Franklin (1980) writes: "What the [white] Carolinians realized all too late was that slaves were not as tractable as they believed and that the danger of having so large a slave population in their midst was more real than fancied" (59). Although whites initiated the increase, many were still learning how to manage the situation. So, these circumstances may have stimulated much writing on all aspects of slavery, including fiddling. Also, differences in the cultural patterns and behavior of Blacks and whites may have been a factor in the amount of information available for the two sub-regions. Because the musicking of African Americans was distinct from that of Europeans visiting or living in the region at the time, cultural differences may have sparked the attention of writers. It has been well documented that difference (exoticism) can be an important stimulant for debate and discussion (Agawu 2003). Finally, since much of the information about Black fiddling in the Carolinas and Georgia during the nineteenth century comes from the narratives of formerly enslaved people, the large number of references for the Lower Southeast could be the result of differences in the types of questions WPA interviewers in the two sub-regions asked interviewees. Perhaps interviewers who collected data in the Lower Southeast asked about musicking whereas interviewers in the Upper Southeast did not (Winans 1990). With regard to content, the available evidence documenting Black fiddling in the Southeast indicates that little had changed from the eighteenth century in terms of the topics and issues.

Fiddle Construction and Ensemble Organization. Sources that include information about fiddle construction and ensemble organization provide the most vivid evidence of African-derived features in the Americas. Although some of the enslaved acquired instruments from whites, many continued to construct their own, employing materials and technology used in West Africa. Isaac D. Williams (1885), a formerly enslaved person from King George County, Virginia, who escaped to Canada in 1855, states: "We generally made our own banjos and fiddles, and I had a fiddle that was manufactured out of a gourd, with horse hair strings and a bow made out of the same material. If you put plenty of rosin on the strings, it would compare very favorably with an ordinary violin and make excellent music" (62). Similarly, reminiscences about performance contexts and fiddle construction by Henry Wright, a 99-year-old formerly enslaved person born during the 1830s in Buckhead (Fulton County), Georgia, show evidence of African-derived elements:

> Even with all the hardships that the slaves had to suffer they still had time to have fun and to enjoy themselves, Mr. Wright continued. At various times Mr. House permitted them to have a frolic. These frolics usually took place on such holidays as the 4th of July, Christmas, or "laying-by time," after the cultivating of the crops was finished and before gathering time. During the day the master provided a big barbecue and at night the singing and dance started. Music was furnished by slaves who were able to play the banjo or the fiddle. The slaves usually bought these instruments themselves and in some cases the master bought them. "In my case," declared Mr. Wright, "I made a fiddle out of a large sized gourd—a long wooden handle was used as a neck, and the hair from a horse's tail was used for the bow. The strings were made of cat-gut. After I learned to play this I bought a better violin." (Wright 1941, 200; also quoted in Minton 1996a, 299)

Chaney Mack, a seventy-four-year-old formerly enslaved African American born and raised in Georgia, provides brief information about fiddle construction

Chapter 3. A Regional Perspective: Black Fiddling During the 1800s

Photo 3.3. "Bob and His Fiddle." Savannah, Georgia. 1876–88. Photograph by O. Pierre Havens (1838–1912). Collection of the Smithsonian National Museum of African American History and Culture. Gift from the Liljenquist Family Collection. https://www.si.edu/object/bob-and-his-fiddle:nmaahc_2016.166.4 Accessed August 20, 2023.

as well as details about music and dancing, which suggest that her father may have been a fiddler in Africa or learned to perform the instrument soon after he arrived in Georgia.

> Yes, my father was a full-blood African. He was about 18 years old when they brought him over. He come from near Liberia. . . .
> He made himself a fiddle outa pine bark and usta play fer us to dance (see photo 3.3).[11] He taught me to dance when I was little like dey did in Africa. Dey dance by derselves or swing each other 'round. Dey didn't know nothing 'bout dese "huggin'" dances.
> I'd be settin' on my daddy's lap and he'd tell me all 'bout when he lived in Africa. He usta play de fiddle and sing 'bout "Africa—Dat Good Ole Land"—and den he would cry, when he thought of his mother back dere.[12]

Although instruments used to accompany the fiddle in ensembles varied, percussion was always prominent. When John Pierpont,[13] a new Yale graduate from Litchfield, Connecticut, arrived in Georgetown District, South Carolina, in 1805, to take up his duties as tutor at Colonel William Allston's Monjetta Plantation, he writes in his journal of musicking by Blacks during Christmas probably because it differed from what he experienced at his home. Important for this discussion are his comments about the use of the drum to accompany the fiddle: "Dec. 25th, Christmas—Throughout the state of South Carolina, Christmas is a holiday, together with 2 of the succeeding days . . . but more especially for the negroes.... On my first waking, the sound of the serenading violin and drum saluted my ears, and for some time continued to prove that no mind is below feeling the powerful effects of music" (Ravitz 1960, 384; Epstein 1977, 84). When Henry Benjamin Whipple, a bishop from Minnesota, visited St. Mary's (Camden County), Georgia, in 1843, on a trip for his health, he recorded the Christmas festivities on the plantation of General Clinch that included a variety of instruments. "Tambourine and fiddle provided music for a dance, and on the twenty-seventh the Negroes had a parade with a band composed of '3 fiddles, 1 tenor & 1 bass drum, 2 triangles & 2 tamborines'" (Epstein 1977, 156). Elizabeth Allen Coxe (1912), who reminiscences about plantation life in South Carolina during the war [1860s], notes how southern Christmas celebrations differed from those in the Northeast probably because of the role of music and the fiddler at holiday festivities: "At Eutaw [in South Carolina] . . . [e]arly in the morning the negro fiddler would go through the house playing and singing.... Every day of Christmas week, in the afternoon, the negroes danced in the broad piazza until late at night, the orchestra consisting of two fiddlers, one man with bones and another had sticks with which he kept time on the floor, and sometimes singing" (188–89; also quoted in Epstein 1977, 144).

C. B. Burton, a formerly enslaved person who lived in Newberry, South Carolina, stated: "we danced and had jigs. Some played de fiddle and some made whistles from canes, having different lengths for different notes, and blowed 'em like mouth organs" (Southern 1971b, 117; also quoted in Lornell 1975, 28). At an open-air dance for young whites in Orange County, North Carolina, in the 1850s, the entertainment was provided by a Black instrumental ensemble including two fiddles, flute, banjo, triangle, and castanets (Lornell 1975, 27). Robert Q. Mallard, a Protestant missionary who grew up in Liberty County, Georgia, not only includes information about all types of sound-producing objects included in the ensemble, but also musical changes that occurred after the enslaved converted to Christianity. Mallard (1892) writes: "I remember that before I became a preacher, I used to hold meetings on my father's plantation, the cotton house affording a convenient place of assemblage. Previously, the plantation resounded with the sounds of jollity—the merry strains of the fiddle, the measured beat of the 'quaw sticks,' and the rhythmical shuffling and patting of the feet in the Ethiopian jig. Now, the fiddle and the quaw sticks were abandoned, and the light, carnal song gave way to psalms and hymns" (163; also quoted in Southern and Wright 1990, 74 Item 646).

Performance Contexts. The literature indicates that performances at balls, dinner parties, and other recreational occasions attended by whites constituted one of the most important functions for Black fiddlers in the Southeast during the nineteenth century, which may partly explain why Southern and Epstein concluded that Black fiddling was primarily performed for whites (Southern 1997, 46; Epstein 1977, 112). Because holidays (such as Christmas and the Fourth of July) were times of much celebration for both Blacks and whites, sources referring to fiddling at these occasions were common. Interestingly, Europeans visiting the South were the ones who most often commented on these and other types of recreational activities. For example, when Bernhard Karl, Duke of Saxe-Weimar-Eisenach, attended a ball on a plantation near Columbia, South Carolina, in December 1825, he notes the uniqueness of the music: "I found there a numerous and splendid society. But the music was of a singular kind; for the blacks who two days ago played very well at the governor's, were now drunk, and could not make their appearance. This was the reason that the whole music consisted of two violins and a tambourine" (Epstein 1977, 147). By comparing the music played by Blacks *at* the governor's ball with that performed *after* the ball, the Duke implies that a performance consisting of violins and tambourine was less acceptable. We do not know if it was the combination of instruments that was unacceptable or the music played on the instruments. Yet, similar to other parts of the South, Black fiddlers also provided entertainment for the enslaved. For example, Betty Jones, a formerly enslaved person from Virginia, recalls performing a dance with water that included the fiddle with other instruments: "Anyhow we'd go to dese dances. Ev'y gal wid her beau, an' sech music! Had two fiddles, two tangerines [tambourines], two banjos, an' two sets of bones.... Dem devilish boys would git out in de middle de flo' an' me . . . and de devil right wid 'em. Set a glass of water on my haid, an' de boys would bet on it. I had a great big wreaf roun' my haid an' a big ribbon bow on each side, an' didn't waste a drop of water on none of 'em" (Writers' Program 1940, 93; also quoted in Emery 1972, 95).

As white slaveholders in the Southeast migrated to different parts of the country, a new context for fiddling—the slave coffle, a group of enslaved people chained together and marched in a line (see photo 3.4)—began to appear in the literature.[14] Planters moving their entire households and workers organized slave coffles, sometimes numbered in the hundreds, while other coffles were led by slave traders transporting groups of the enslaved to better markets. Although the means of travel could be by water, by wagon, or later by railroad, the cheapest was on foot. Black people were handcuffed, two by two, and attached to a long chain that ran down the center of the double file. Men on horseback accompanying the coffles, wielded long whips to "goad the reluctant and weary," and fiddlers among the enslaved were forced to play on their instruments (Southern 1983a, 157). A source from North Carolina contains references to a clergyman who observed a slave coffle where two or three Black males played the violin as they marched "to keep up the appearance of merriment" (Southern 1990, 13 Item 102).

In addition to coffles, the enslaved performed the fiddle on the auction block. Describing his experience after taken into slavery, Northup (1968) writes: "After being fed, in the afternoon, we were again paraded and made to dance. Bob, a colored boy, who had some time belonged to Freeman, played on the violin. Standing near him, I made bold to inquire if he could play the 'Virginia Reel.' He

THE ANTI-SLAVERY RECORD.

VOL. I.   FEBRUARY, 1835.   NO. 2.

HOW SLAVERY HONORS OUR COUNTRY'S FLAG.

[From Rankin's Letters.]

"In the summer of 1822, as I returned with my family from a visit to the Barrens of Kentucky, I witnessed a scene such as I never witnessed before, and such as I hope never to witness again. Having passed through Paris in Bourbon county, Ky. the sound of music (beyond a little rising ground) attracted my attention, I looked forward, and saw the flag of my country waving. Supposing that I was about to meet a military parade, I drove hastily to the side of the road; and having gained the top of the ascent, I discovered (I suppose) about forty black men all chained together after the following manner; each of them was handcuffed, and they were arranged in rank and file. A chain perhaps 40 feet long, the size of a fifth-horse chain, was stretched between the two ranks, to which

Vol. I.   2

Photo 3.4. "How Slavery Honors Our Country's Flag." *The Anti-Slavery Record* Volume 1, Number 2, February 1835, 13.

answered he could not, and asked me if I could play. Replying in the affirmative he handed me the violin. I struck up a tune, and finished it. Freeman ordered me to continue playing, and seemed well pleased, telling Bob that I far excelled him—a remark that seemed to grieve my musical companion very much" (52). The use of music in coffles and on auction blocks was a continuation of activities that had occurred during the Middle Passage. As Southern (1997) explains, "It was common practice to force slaves to sing and dance under the most tragic of circumstances. Just as on the slave ships the captured Africans were made to dance and sing during their 'airings' on deck, so in the slave pens of the States, they often had to sing and dance before being put up for sale on the auction block" (159). Commenting on the deeper meaning of these activities politically and economically, Katrina Thompson (2014) writes: "For many slave owners, it represented a strategic economic decision on commodities, for it also enhanced their feelings of control and domination in the social system; for slave traders, it was a highly profitable business" (131).

During the Civil War, Blacks in the army often performed the fiddle to entertain themselves. On December 11, 1862, Thomas W. Higginson comments on Blacks' participation in both religious and secular activities, and mentions the inclusion of the fiddle in the latter: "By another fire there is an actual dance, red-legged soldiers doing right-and-left, and 'now-lead-de-lady-ober,' to the music of a violin which is rather artistically played, and which may have guided the steps, in other days of Barnwells and Hugers" (Higginson 1870; Southern 1997, 209).

Activities that whites held outdoors were also popular occasions for fiddling by African Americans. In describing his travels in the 1850s to the sulfur springs in Orange County, North Carolina, where a dance took place, native North Carolinian James Battle Avirett (1901) writes: "A quick drive of three miles brings us to the spring, though we stop a few minutes to see if Eli and Sam with their fiddles (colored people did not play the violin in those days, they played the fiddle), Virgil with his flute, Frank with his banjo, Caswell with his triangle and Peter with his castanets had gone on" (99).

Work activities that included Blacks and whites, such as corn shucking and husking or log-rolling, were also occasions at which Black fiddlers were featured. Lewis W. Paine, a white person from Smithville, Rhode Island, who moved to Upson County, Georgia, in 1841, "for the purpose of starting and running some machinery in a factory," wrote an autobiography after serving six years in a Georgia prison for helping an enslaved person escape. His comments about musicking at a corn shucking are insightful for information about (1) the role of the fiddler in performance; (2) how white people perceived the behavior of Black people in performance, including the negative stereotypes that continue to persist in popular culture today; and (3) activities on plantations that may have provided source material for professional minstrel performers.

As soon as the table is cleared the girls give a wink; and in a trice the room is stripped of everything but the bed. Two or three men take hold of this, and set it out of the room. The negro fiddler then walks in; and the dance commences. After they [whites] have enjoyed their sport sufficiently, they give way to the negroes, who have already supplied themselves with torch-lights, and swept the yard. The fiddler walks out, and strikes up a tune; and at it they go in a regular tear-down dance; for here they are at home. The sound of a fiddle makes them crazy; and I do believe that if they were in the height of an insurrection, and any one should go among them, and play on a violin, they would all be dancing in five minutes. (Paine 1851, 183–84; also quoted in Southern 1983b, 91; Southern and Wright 1990, 17 Item 134).

Corn shucking became one of the most important occasions for musicking among Blacks after emancipation, in spite of negative and positive views about the tradition from both Blacks and whites. Although some African Americans attempted to make changes in the event after the Civil War, the element of recreation persisted and even expanded because many Black people appreciated how it led to greater cooperation in work activities. In addition to attendees participating in the popular dances (for example, jig, cotillion, and pigeon-wing) of the day in one of the houses or outdoors on the ground, corn shuckings provided an opportunity for the primary performers at the event (fiddler, straw beater, and caller) to demonstrate their prowess.

In the article "A Georgia Corn-Shucking," David C. Barrow (1882) gives an excellent description of the performers. However, in emphasizing the fiddler's supposed shortcomings, the author demonstrates his obvious bias against the fiddler, who in this context is an authority figure. Barrow writes: "The music is commonly made by a fiddler and a straw-beater, the fiddle being far more common than the banjo, in spite of tradition to the contrary. The fiddler is the man of most importance on the ground. He always comes late, must have an extra share of whisky, is the best-dressed man in the crowd, and unless every honor is shown him he will not play. He will play you a dozen different pieces, which are carefully distinguished by names, but not by tunes. The most skilled judge of music will be unable to detect any difference between 'Run, N----r, Run,' 'Arkansaw Traveler,' 'Forky Deer,' and any other tune. He is never offended at a mistake which you may make as to what piece he is playing; he only feels a trifle contemptuous toward you as a person utterly devoid of musical knowledge" (878). Regarding the straw beater accompanying the fiddler, Barrow focuses on training and playing technique: "The straw-beater is a musician.... No preliminary training is necessary in this branch of music; any one can succeed, with proper caution, the first time he tries. The performer provides himself with a pair of straws about eighteen inches in length, and stout enough to stand a good smart blow. An experienced straw-beater will be very careful in selecting his straws, which he does from the sedge-broom.... The straws are used after the manner of drum-sticks, that portion of the fiddle-strings between the fiddler's bow and his left hand serving as a drum."[15] One of the first sounds which you hear on approaching the dancing party is the *tum tee tum* of the straws, and after the dance begins, when the shuffling of feet destroys the other sounds of the fiddle, this noise can still be heard" (878). Barrow notes that the caller at corn shuckings attained greater recognition and importance as dances became more formalized: "He not only calls out the figures, but explains them at length to the ignorant, sometimes accompanying them, through the performance. He is never at a loss, 'Gemmen to de right!' being a sufficient refuge in case of embarrassment, since this always calls forth a full display of the dancers' agility, and gives much time" (878).

After emancipation, the nightlife and music scene common to New York City's Five Points began appearing in southern cities such as Atlanta, which attracted large Black populations from neighboring rural areas. Instead of performing in dance halls, which was the case in New York, musicians played individually or as a group on street corners in medicine shows and other settings (Ingersoll 1879). Black expressive culture, with various types of performers and performance traditions during the late nineteenth century, was diverse providing the foundation for an urban music scene that included fiddlers and other musicians who were active in the city during the early twentieth century.[16]

Social Significance. The fiddle continued to be viewed negatively by the Protestant Christian community. Because those who participated in the Great Awakening of the mid-eighteenth century were adamant about "dancing, fox-hunting, and card-playing," it is not surprising that these attitudes were pervasive in nineteenth century literature. For the Upper Southeast, criticisms could be found in a variety of sources, including those written by religious leaders, the social elite, as well as novelists. Epstein states that Bishop William Meade of the Protestant Episcopal Church of the Diocese of Virginia wrote with anger about an incident that occurred on February 24, 1811, after he entered the ministry. After officiating at a wedding, he was invited to stay for refreshments but was appalled at what he observed: "At a place where I expected, and had a right to expect, more respect, the fiddle and dances were introduced into the room where I was sitting, without any warning.... As soon as I could, I escaped, and ordering my horse ... went several miles to a neighbor's house. My conduct was well understood, as I wished it to be, and I have never since been thus treated" (Epstein 1977, 208–9).

Some antebellum fictional works included descriptions that weighed in on both sides of the conflict. Richard Hildreth (1836) presents both views in his popular anti-slavery novel, *The Slave: or Memoirs of Archy Moore,* by describing scenes in which fiddle music and dancing are in competition with Methodist psalm singing and preaching (135–36). Yet, as Epstein (1977) explains, "neither side ever won complete dominance and the controversy never really ended" (213). A passage from the pro-slavery novel by John W. Page, *Uncle Robin, in His Cabin in Virginia, and Tom without One in Boston* (1853), depicts fiddling and dancing as so sinful that some of the enslaved refused to interact with those who participated in such activities. In one of the chapters, "The Weddings," Page includes a dialogue between an enslaved person and his master in which the former expresses his disapproval of dancing and fiddling (154–55). Depicting the male, Robin, as a loyal, obedient enslaved person who had appropriated cultural values identified with white people was very much in the character of pro-slavery views of the time (Blassingame 1979).

Interestingly, most of the literature criticizing Black fiddling in the Lower Southeast was written by clergymen. The degree that demographic differences (the population in the Lower Southeast was majority Black, which was not the case in the Upper Southeast) accounts for differences in the number and percentage of sources on the topic is not known, but an issue that should not be entirely dismissed. It would not be farfetched if some whites in the Lower Southeast regarded Blacks' participation in fiddling and dancing as not only anti-Christian and sinful, but an act of resistance.[17]

The thirteenth annual report of the white Association for the Religious Instruction of the Negroes in Liberty County, Georgia, in 1848, reflects the common attitude among some clergy and slaveholders regarding Blacks participating in secular music: "And *the amusements* of the negroes deserve notice. The chief amusement, and that to which they become passionately fond is *dancing*. No one will deny that it is an amusement of the world, and not of the Church. Fiddlers and dancers are not sober and devout persons; neither are those, whatever be their professions, who encourage them. . . . I do not think religion or good morals can flourish on a plantation where this amusement is permitted, and Christian owners should be the last persons to give it countenance" (Epstein 1977, 212–13). Charles Colcock Jones Jr. (1842), a white Presbyterian minister who wrote about his missionary activities in Georgia during the 1840s, believed that if Black people were taught "good" religious music, they would no longer have a desire to sing inappropriate songs, an attitude that corresponded with that of some Black preachers (265–66; also see Southern 1983a, 146).

The response to criticisms was striking in that Black people who joined church gave up dancing, stopped participating in "fiddle-sings," and started performing only psalms and hymns. When the Swedish traveler Fredrika Bremer asked some of the enslaved in South Carolina to sing their songs for her, she was informed that they "'dwelt with the Lord,' and sang only hymns" (Southern 1997, 147). To demonstrate that such undesirable behavior was on the wane, writings about slave conversions were common. The account that appears in the memoirs of John George Clinkscales (1969) about Griffin, an enslaved person who lived in Abbeville County, South Carolina, is noteworthy for revealing how class, occupation, and religious beliefs intersected with Black fiddling:

> Besides being the best muleteer in the district, Griffin was a fiddler whose reputation extended far beyond the boundaries of his master's plantation. Not only did he furnish music for his own people at their annual "cake-walks" but he often helped furnish music at the dances of the white race. That fact, along with his recognized ability as a wagoner, made him an aristocrat. He deigned to associate with men and women of his own color, but for "po' white trash" he had a contempt. When he left home with the load of furniture and provisions for the camp meeting, Griffin was in a jolly, good humor. He called back to one of his fellows: "I don't mind camp meetin', ef dey des let me play my fiddle." In two hours Griffin was picked up at the foot of Crosby's Hill on Rocky River in an unconscious condition and minus one ear. Regaining consciousness, he declared: "Dis is de judgment ob de Lord; I'll nuver tech dat fiddle ag'in." And he didn't. Other things he would do—curse, fight, and drink; but play the fiddle—never. (11–12; also quoted in Epstein 1977, 211–12)

In addition to disapproving of the behavior of Black fiddlers, some white people also did not like the sound Black musicians produced on their fiddles. In Maurice Thompson's reminisces (1884) about plantation music in Georgia and the Carolinas, he states: "Sometimes one would meet with a negro violinist, but the music that he made was wrenched from all four of the strings at once, with little regard for anything but time and noise" (20). When Thompson explains that more emphasis was placed on "time" (rhythm) and "noise" (slurs, slides, and other ornamental elements), this indicates that African performance practices were central to music making by Black musicians.

Although the perspective of white slaveholders who were more tolerant of musicking is not well represented in the literature, sources indicate that it was not uncommon for some whites to participate in music-making with Blacks. Epstein (1977) describes a North Carolina court case from 1849 in which the slave owner, with support from the judge, argues that the enslaved should be free to dance during the Christmas holidays:

> The case of the *State of North Carolina v. Boyce* in December, 1849, illustrated a clash between overzealous patrollers and a more tolerant planter over dancing. A witness, one Roberts, stated that on Christmas night, 1846, "he and other patrollers went to the defendant's plantation between 8 and 9 o'clock . . . [in] the house in which Boyce lived, [they] found therein twelve or fifteen negroes of whom one was fiddling, and the others dancing . . . that Boyce was in the house . . . and several children of the Defendant . . . were enjoying themselves in the dance with the negroes. . . ."

Despite the presence of Boyce and his children, the patrol felt justified in whipping the Negroes—an opinion not shared by the judge, who stated: "It would really be a source of regret, if contrary to common custom it were to be denied to slaves, in the intervals between their toils, to indulge in mirthful pastimes." (159)

Rather than convert the enslaved to Christianity to instill appropriate behavior or maintain discipline, a few slaveholders used musicking as a method of control. In "On the Moral Discipline and Treatment of Slaves," a South Carolina planter, N. Herbemont (1836), states that he often broke up the enslaved's Christian religious meetings and "induced them to occasional meetings for the purposes of merriment. He had fiddles and drums for their use, promoted dancing.... Negroes are naturally prone to gaiety, and I conceive it a duty to ourselves as well as to them, not to change this inclination in them, but rather to promote it by every prudent and allowable means.... [B]y promoting cheerfulness and amusing occupation, the slave would become more honest and much more seldom tempted to rob and pilfer, not only his master's but frequently his neighbour's fields" (71–74; also quoted in Epstein 1977, 194). His comments are significant for the types of instruments he or the enslaved chose for merriment—fiddles and drums, which are common to fiddle ensembles in West Africa (DjeDje 2008a)—but also for the generalizations he makes about people of African descent, views and attitudes that continue in present-day.

Social Role and Status of Fiddler. As noted in the foregoing, almost every rural community or large plantation in the United States had its resident fiddler, with some attached to important officials, and the situation was no different for the Southeast. Having an opportunity to travel (without whites) and gain income, although small amounts because masters often took a portion of whatever was earned, gave fiddlers enormous visibility and much renown (Ball 1837, 283–83; Southern and Wright 1990, 9–10 Item 70). In addition to using newspapers to report on runaway musicians, the majority of whom were fiddlers, ads helped inform others about the availability of musicians for hire as well as recognize them, often by name, for their talents. In the June 27, 1853, issue of the *Richmond Daily Enquirer*, an advertisement about George Walker includes the following about his musical ability and stature in the community: "FOR HIRE, either for the remainder of the year or by the month, week, or job, the celebrated musician and fiddler, GEORGE WALKER. All persons desiring the services of George Walker, are notified that they must contract for them with us, and in no case pay to him or any other person, the amount of his hire, without a written order from us.—George Walker is admitted, by common consent, to be the best leader of a band in all eastern and middle Virginia" (Epstein 1977, 152–53; Southern 1997, 135). In *An Errand to the South in the Summer of 1862*, William Wyndham Malet (1863), an Englishman from Conwayboro (Horry County),[18] in northeast South Carolina, describes a coachman by the name of

Prince, a capital (royal) fiddler who played for country dances; one of his favorite tunes was "Dixie Land" (49).

A few sources about the Southeast include commentary on why Blacks became fiddlers and how they received their training. Some chose the profession because they had a desire to learn the instrument after hearing it performed, which is the case for Andy Brice. Born in Fairfield County, South Carolina, at least five years before the Civil War, Brice lived during a time when fiddling was one of the most popular forms of entertainment in Black and white communities, making him even more determined to learn to play the instrument. The immense joy that Brice felt when he first heard the sound of the fiddle demonstrates the power that the music had over some musicians:

> One day I see Marse Thomas a twistin' de ears on a fiddle and rosinin' de bow. Then he pull dat bow 'cross de belly of dat fiddle. Sumpin' bust loose in me and sing all thru my head and tingle in my fingers. I make up my mind, right then and dere, to save and buy me a fiddle. I got one dat Christmas, bless God! I learn and been playin' de fiddle ever since. I pat one foot while I playin'. I kept on playin' and pattin' dat foot for thirty years. I lose dat foot in a smash up wid a highway accident but I play de old tunes on dat fiddle at night, dat foot seem to be dere at de end of dat leg (indicating) and pats just de same. Sometime I ketch myself lookin' down to see if it have come back and jined itself up to dat leg, from de very charm of de music I makin' wid de fiddle and de bow. (Drago 1998, 106; also, see Brice 1936–38)

Unlike some fiddlers whose family members ostracized or admonished them for participating in music making, playing the fiddle helped Brice woo the woman who became his wife. Because he had extra income from playing at dances for whites and on election days, she saw him as a better catch than her other beaux.[19] Brice states: "I marry Ellen Watson.... How I git her? I never git her; dat fiddle got her. I play for all de white folks dances down at Cedar Shades up at Blackstock. De money roll in when someone pass 'round de hat and say: 'De fiddler?' Ellen had more beaux 'round her than her could shake a stick at but de beau she lak best was de bow dat could draw music out of them five strings, and draw money into dat hat, dat jingle in my pocket de nex' day when I go to see her" (Drago 1998, 106). Belonging to a church was not important to Brice because he had his fiddle. "What church I b'long to? None. Dat fiddle draws down from hebben all de sermons dat I understan'. I sings de hymns in de way I praise and glorify de Lord" (106).

An unpublished letter Dena Epstein discovered at the University of South Carolina is one of the few documents that provides an account on how some Black fiddlers during the nineteenth century learned to play the instrument. In a letter dated November 17, 1856, John Laurence Manning, governor of South Carolina from 1852 to 1854,[20] describes how Robin, one of his enslaved persons, received his training: "Upon a shingle strung, with the hairs of the horse and with a bow made from a twig and horse hairs, Robin first gave evidence of his musical capacity; and I determined at once to cultivate whatever talent . . . he might possess" (Epstein 1977, 153). After his musical talent was recognized, Manning arranged for Robin and his family to receive formal music lessons from two teachers from Germany. Similar to accounts from the seventeenth and eighteenth centuries, the letter reveals that the governor appears surprised that Robin quickly learns to perform the fiddle.

Once a fiddler learned how to play the fiddle, how did they develop the enormous repertoire of tunes most were noted for performing? Was it through listening and imitating what they heard other musicians performing, or did they create their own tunes? Caroline Howard Gilman's *Recollections of a Southern Matron* (1838) about plantation life in Charleston, South Carolina,[21] addresses some of these issues, including how fiddle tunes were learned and passed on within the culture, the behavior of the fiddler and members of her family in the context of a performance, the organization of fiddle ensembles, as well as interactions between rural and urban musicians.

> [W]e possessed the usual plantation luxury of a fiddler. I do not feel bound to say how many tunes Diggory played, nor how well a few visits to town had initiated his quick eye and ear into the tunes and figures of some newly-introduced cotillons. It is amusing to observe how soon a pretty air is appropriated, in Charleston, by the negroes, by their quick musical organs. . . .
>
> Mamma was dragged from her seat like a martyr by one of the boys, and I, as usual, was Lewis's partner. Diggory's air of importance was exceedingly ludicrous; his whole identity seemed changed by the stroke of the fiddle. Poor mamma had never been much of a dancer; all her early associations were connected with the minuet and contra-dance; and when Diggory called out, with the voice of a Stentor,
>
> "Fore and back two, ole missis—ladies change—turn you partiner at de corner—shasha all round," she was nearly beside herself; while Diggory, sometimes stopping short and rolling up his white eyes, exclaimed, "My lor! my ole missis spile eberyting!"
>
> Diggory, alas! in his musical science and dancing oratory was but a specimen of our city ball-room performers. Unacquainted with the science of music, though gifted with decided musical powers, they play antics with the "high heaven of sound," while sawing violins, harsh clarinets, jingling tambarines, crashing triangles, with the occasional climax of a *base* drum, make up in quantity what is deficient in quality; and then overtopping even that climax, comes the shout of a voice with the negro dialect, calling out the figures, which, to a stranger, makes "confusion worse confounded." (76)

In addition to noting his use of percussion, comments about changes in his demeanor when Diggory performs his instrument are significant, especially when they are compared with findings from the eighteenth century. "His whole identity seemed changed by the stroke of the fiddle," causing his relations with whites and position within the social structure of the family to be reversed. Serving as the music leader (fiddler) and caller at the dance placed him in a position of authority wherein he was able to tell whites what to do. Similar to earlier years, the fiddle was a symbol of power. "Eloquence and the ability to perform effectively were talents through which enabled slaves could raise themselves out of the ranks of the field hands, sometimes rising to positions of trust, both on and off the plantation. This possibility was clearer with the other central performers in the corn shucking, the fiddler and dance caller" (Abrahams 1992, 127).

The Mountains and Neighboring Regions

As indicated in chapter 1, Black presence in the mountains, especially Appalachia, dates to the sixteenth century, when Africans fought with Europeans against native groups. By the nineteenth century, even though their numbers were small, Blacks lived in mountain regions that extended from the Southeast to the Midwest.[22] Thus, this discussion is divided into two sections: Appalachia and the Ozarks.

Appalachia

Although the amount of material on Black fiddling in the Appalachian Mountains is small, the sources are more extensive than findings for the Northeast, the Upper Southeast, and the Ozarks.[23] While topics on the subject are similar to writings about Black fiddling in other regions, including details about fiddle construction and ensemble organization, performance context, recruitment, social role and status of fiddlers, information on fiddlers is relatively substantial with material from several states (Alabama, Kentucky, Ohio, Tennessee, and West Virginia). Criticism against fiddling is rare. It is unclear if this is because of lack of interest; the sociocultural environment (that is, the close interaction between Blacks and whites as well as whites allowing Blacks to participate in whatever public gatherings they desired as long as they did not threaten white control); or the fact that whites participated in fiddling as much as Blacks.

Since the fiddle was not threatening to white Appalachians, Blacks could perform it openly without criticism. More importantly, fiddling allowed for the maintenance of African traditions and the construction of a culture that was distinct. According to Dunaway (2003a), "only about 2 percent of the Appalachian ex-slaves reported that they were unable to participate in social gatherings. Weddings, funerals, weekend and holiday gatherings, work parties, and religious meetings were important arenas that made possible the emergence of a counter-hegemonic culture. Through group activities, Appalachian slaves developed their 'collective identification' with a larger community and with a subculture that was more far-reaching than the Southern Mountains" (255). Whereas most plantations in the United States had two distinct cultures, the master's worldview and the enslaved counterculture, something unique occurred in the mountains; Black and white people drew on a performance tradition (fiddling) that had its roots in both West Africa and Western Europe, causing an interesting interchange[24] (Fulcher 1988a, 3). The performance style and repertoire that Black fiddlers used when performing at events for African Americans no doubt differed from those employed when they entertained European Americans, but enough overlap also occurred to reflect borrowing and sharing between the two groups. As Chris Goertzen (2008) explains: "Such occasions constituted the real beginning of the black-white musical interchange that would be so important for American music in general (and specifically for fiddling)" (7).

Fiddle Construction and Ensemble Organization. Many of the instruments used by Black mountaineers were homemade, and constructed from gourds similar to those used by West Africans and Blacks on the East Coast. A formerly enslaved person from Tennessee whose name is unknown told Ophelia Settle Egypt, one of the WPA interviewers, that he learned on a homemade fiddle before switching to a European fiddle: "I used to be a great fiddler. I fust learned how to play on a long gourd with horsehair strings on it. 'Course I couldn't go very high on it, but it done pretty well. That was the fust of my learning to play. After a while I bought me a fiddle for $1.80, and after so long a time I bought me a fiddle sure enough" (Minton 1996a, 229).

As in other parts of the South, sources indicate that Black fiddle ensembles in Appalachian Virginia varied in size and organization. In addition to percussion, the banjo was often included, demonstrating a change from the seventeenth and eighteenth centuries when the plucked lute was rarely combined with the fiddle. While on a trip to Virginia in 1853, Lewis Miller of York, Pennsylvania, sketched a scene, titled "Lynchburg Negro Dance,"[25] depicting three musicians performing a fiddle, a banjo, and a set of bones as they accompanied two Black couples dancing (Miller 1853). Robert Playfair (1856), a British traveler "who wrote from 'Virginia Springs' on Sunday, July 30, 1848 [describes an instrumental ensemble] which consisted of three instruments, a violin, a tambourine ... and the skull of an ass, played upon by a collar-bone of the same animal, sounding not unlike the Spanish castanets" (174; also quoted in Epstein 1977, 146–47; Southern and Wright 1990, 17 Item 137).

Blues musician William Christopher Handy (1873–1958)—who was born in Florence (Lauderdale County), Alabama, on the Tennessee border near the

Appalachian Mountains—recalls how his family members used the knitting needle to accompany the fiddle. Although Handy's enslaved grandfather, Christopher Brewer, was allowed to keep the money earned from playing for dances, he gave up fiddling when he "got religion." Yet, Handy's Uncle Whit continued and was described as "lively and unregenerate at eighty" (Handy 1941, 5–6; Cauthen 1989a, 8, 10; Wyatt 2005, 5).[26] Thus, it was Handy's uncle who taught him how to use a pair of knitting needles to accompany the fiddle. During performances, Handy was told that he should stand behind the fiddler and "reach around the fiddler's left shoulder and beat on the strings in the manner of a snare drummer."

Uncle Whit fiddled and sang while I handled the needles.

Sally got a meat skin laid away
Sally got a meat skin laid away
Sally got a meat skin laid away
To grease her wooden leg every day.

Uncle Whit stomped his feet while singing. A less expert fiddler, I learned, would have stomped both heels simultaneously, but a fancy performer like Uncle Whit could stomp the left heel and the right forefoot and alternate this with the right heel and the left forefoot, making four beats to the bar. This was real stomping. (Handy 1941, 5–6; also quoted in Cauthen 1989a, 8)

Later in life, Handy recognized links between the old and the new when he compared the nineteenth-century fiddling of his grandfather with the performance of an early twentieth-century jazz band: "Country gals and their mirthful suitors got as much enjoyment out of a fiddle at a breakdown or square dance as jitterbugs or rug-cutters get nowadays from a swing band" (Handy 1941, 6; also quoted in Wyatt 2001, 5).

Performance Contexts. In the mountains, not only did Blacks perform at occasions attended by whites, but also whites participated in Black dances, both as musicians and observers. Mrs. Chandler of Guntersville [Marshall County, Alabama] remembered the fiddle tune "Sally Ann" being played by a Black family band that performed for both white and Black dances on her father's plantation. Chandler recalled the amusement of the enslaved when white slaveholders sang with them as verses to the tune were composed to fit the occasion (Cauthen 1989a, 11). In recounting the history of his family in the West Virginia mountains in *Trans-Allegheny Pioneers* (1886), John P. Hale includes information about family members and enslaved Africans performing music at hunting camps and nighttime activities (Milnes 1999, 100).

Black fiddlers also performed at private events and ceremonies such as weddings. Of particular note is Hale's description of Black and white musicians

Photo 3.5. Untitled ["Black fiddler playing for a cotillion"]. *Harper's Weekly: A Journal of Civilization* Volume 18, Number 941, 1875, 44–45.

performing fiddles and banjos at the marriage of his maternal Scots-Irish grandparents, who lived west of the Alleghenies (100). In a letter to his daughter, dated May 26, 1859, William Phineas Browne describes a wedding for an enslaved couple—Sam Browne (the groom) and Livey (the bride)—as it was taking place on his plantation near Montevallo (Shelby County), Alabama: "The yard is full of servants, their guests, and they are having a fine time of it and other white folks also are looking on.... They are now dancing to the music of George's banjo and are in high glee. There are as many as fifty or sixty guests and all seem to be enjoying greatly.... The servants have just sent in for papa's fiddle—there is amongst the guests one or two who play the fiddle and they want, they say, to have some cotillions now" (Cauthen 1989a, 11–12). The manner in which the music was integrated into the event is noteworthy for it reveals attitudes about social status and class and the type of music and instruments Black people wanted for specific activities. Initially, the banjo player provided the entertainment until the wedding party decided to use fiddle music so they could perform more formal dances. The fiddle and the cotillions were no doubt considered "high-brow" because of their association with European culture (see photo 3.5). Furthermore, the fiddle was kept in the "big house," the domain of white people and the enslaved who worked in the house.

Several Appalachian sources focus on the movement of Blacks across country in slave coffles. Perhaps the preponderance of this information for Tennessee and Kentucky is a result of the antislavery sentiments evident in Appalachia at the time. The slave coffle was a sight that even proslavery Southerners found distressing and unpleasant, while abolitionists featured it as a standard item in their propaganda (Epstein 1977, 177). In the summer of 1822 in Paris, Kentucky, James H. Dickey, a white minister who was traveling with his family through Kentucky, observed a slave convoy led by two African American violinists. Because the sight was so startling, Dickey reported his observations in a letter to abolitionist and Presbyterian minister John Rankin (1833, 42), who later published the letter along with others in *Letters on American Slavery* (Southern and Wright 1990, 17 Item 139). Using Dickey's description, several visual images of slave coffles (see photo 3.4) were created and presented in nineteenth century publications.[27] Excerpts from the letter by Dickey are quoted at length below because they provide vivid detail of the bizarre scene as well as the role of the fiddle in the activity.

> In the summer of 1822, as I returned with my family from a visit to the Barrens of Kentucky, I witnessed a scene such as I never witnessed before, and such as I hope never to witness again. Having passed through Paris, in Bourbon county, Ky, the sound of music (beyond a little rising ground) attracted my attention; I looked forward and saw the flag of my country waving.
>
> Supposing that I was about to meet a military parade, I drove hastily to the side of the road, and having gained the top of the ascent [hill], I discovered (I suppose) about forty black men all chained together after the following manner; each of them was handcuffed and they were arranged in rank and file. A chain, perhaps 40 feet long, the size of a fifth-horse-chain, was stretched between the two ranks, to which short chains were joined, which connected with the handcuffs. Behind them were, I suppose, about thirty women, in double rank, the couples tied hand to hand.
>
> A solemn sadness sat on every countenance, and the dismal silence of this march of despair was interrupted only by the sound of two violins; yes, as if to add insult to injury, the foremost couple were furnished with a violin apiece, the second couple were ornamented with cockades, while near the centre waved the Republican flag carried ... [with] a hand literally in chains. (quoted in Rankin 1823–39, 41)

As Black people migrated in all directions after the Civil War, they took their traditions with them into cities and towns. Sounds from rural areas served as the foundation for jug, blues, and jazz bands that evolved in urban areas such as Cincinnati, which sits on the border of Kentucky and Ohio. When white Cincinnati journalist and writer Patrick Lafcadio Hearn visited a workman's hangout on the corner of Culvert and Sixth Streets in Cincinnati, Ohio, in 1876, he saw Black street musicians using a fiddle and banjo to accompany dancing. "The musicians began to sing; the dancers joined in; and the dance terminated with a roar of song, stamping of feet, 'patting juba,' shouting, laughing, reeling" (quoted in Oliver 1972, 53).

Recruitment, Social Role, and Status of Fiddler. Similar to other parts of the United States, whites sometimes encouraged Blacks' interest in the fiddle and subsequently taught them how to play. Such a situation is not surprising in Appalachia where fiddling was prominently supported by both Blacks and whites. Jack Calhoun, a well-known fiddler from Pickens County, South Carolina, born in 1860 or earlier, stated that his master, "John C. Calhoun, learned him to play 'de wyolen' when he was a little." While Jack probably played for Blacks and whites in the community, his primary job was to provide entertainment for the Calhoun family and their guests (Baker n.d.).

Although a variety of instruments (banjo, flageolet, triangle, and jawbones) were used to provide entertainment in Appalachian homes and at community activities, musicians who played the fiddle were the most highly regarded. Writing about Kentucky, James Lane Allen (1887) explains: "The old fiddler, most of all, was held in reverent esteem and met with the gracious treatment of the ancient minstrel in feudal halls. At parties and weddings, at picnics in the summer woods, he was the soul of melody, and with an eye to the high demands upon his art, he widened his range of selections and perfected according to the native standards his inimitable technique. The deep, tender, pure feeling in the song 'Old Kentucky Home' is a true historic interpretation" (865–66). Thus, it is not surprising that several African Americans are noted in various sources for their contributions to fiddling. Because this is significant for Appalachia, especially in comparison to other regions, I discuss four musicians here, chronologically according to their date of birth.

The Snowden Family Band. Thomas Snowden (1802–1866) and Ellen Cooper (1817–1894) were born in Maryland. Like many African Americans from the Southeast in the early nineteenth century, both "traveled to Knox County [Ohio] as members of white households. Ellen was a child of ten, Thomas a young man of twenty-three when they separately left slavery for freedom in Ohio" (Sacks and Sacks 1993, 9). Ellen stayed with the Greers, the white family she traveled with until she married Tom (11–12). The couple settled in the village of Clinton, Ohio, just north of Mount Vernon, where they farmed a small parcel of land and raised a family.[28] Although their primary vocation was farming, the family was best known for performing music as the Snowden Family Band, which started as an ensemble in the 1850s. Thomas, a whistler, provided much of the inspiration for everyone, for all were self-taught musicians. Annie, known as the "infant violinist," played the fiddle as well as Sophia and Ben. Lew played the banjo and Phebe danced, and at least one person also played the guitar. Ben and Lew, who as youth, "performed on the fiddle and banjo from a second-story gable modified into a stage" continued their musicking through the early twentieth century. Because few Blacks lived in the area, the Snowdens were in constant and close contact with their white neighbors, resulting in a significant degree of intimacy. "The Snowdens exchanged song lyrics and gossip and flower seeds through the mails, taught white farmhands how to play the fiddle and sing the most popular songs of the day, and held regular open-air concerts on their farmstead. Just about everybody . . . knew the Snowdens as fine musicians, beyond their everyday activities in the school, the church, and the farming economy" (Sacks and Sacks 1993, 12–13).

Since much of the work of the early settlements required collective labor followed by supper and a dance, the fiddle was the favorite instrument performed by the Snowdens for entertainment. However, when playing for more formal events, they used a variety of instruments that, in many cases, was determined by the audience. "When E. D. Root of Paskala, Ohio, wrote to his Snowden friends with an invitation to visit, he made a point of specifying the instruments he wanted to hear: 'please fetch your violins and dulsimer [dulcimer], and tambereen [tambourine], tryang [triangle], and ben [Ben, the son] fetch his bones" (61–63).

The Snowdens' repertoire was both broad and varied, reflecting the time (the nineteenth century) and the place (Ohio) in which they lived. As Sacks (2003, 323) explains: "satisfying a politically and racially divided audience meant engaging in a complex process of alternately resisting white oppression, accommodating local opinion, and asserting African American musical tradition. Aware of strong anti-black sentiment, the band avoided overtly abolitionist songs, yet they signaled support of Republican values by performing temperance and anti-tobacco songs. Minstrel songs appear in their repertoire, but only relatively benign, parodic ones; they evidently rejected those with demeaning imagery and phony dialect." Their performance of the fiddle and banjo as well as spirituals (such as "There's a Meeting Here Tonight") from early slave culture in Maryland, most likely on occasions when they performed for all-Black audiences, demonstrated that they continued to be grounded in Black vernacular culture with no desire to forget or abandon their roots (Sacks 2003, 323).

As they gained notoriety, the Snowdens' performances became widespread, with regular visits to farming communities within a seventy-five-mile radius. It was not uncommon for them to travel several days for a series of one-night stands in towns and villages every ten miles across the rural countryside. When they reached their destination, supper would be served in the home of a prominent family of the town where they would remain for the night. Because invitations came from friends and acquaintances, who served as local producers for the event, the Snowdens used word of mouth and a simple handbill to gather their audiences at churches, school houses, community halls, family reunions, and picnics. This was distinct from traveling entertainers who advertised in newspapers and performed publicity stunts to attract audiences (Sacks and Sacks 1993, 64–66).

James Thomas. Although born an enslaved person in Nashville, Tennessee, in 1827, Thomas's father was white and of economic means. Though legally enslaved, Thomas's movement and behavior was that of a free person; he attended various religious, political, and cultural functions and regularly visited New Orleans and urban areas in the Northeast. His working conditions were diverse. In addition to performing a variety of chores for his mother, who was the proprietor of a small clothes-cleaning business, he worked as an assistant to a Nashville physician; was hired out as an apprentice barber; and, after five years, opened his own barbershop which catered to clients from Nashville's white upper crust (bankers, merchants, editors, businessmen, ministers, politicians, lawyers). In many ways, his musical life reflected his social environment. Although Thomas could perform European art music, he liked playing the fiddle and preferred participating in music occasions related to Black culture, attending enslaved dances, barbecues, and picnics on nearby plantations. He often played the fiddle with Jordan McGowan, a free person of color who ran a music school (Schweninger 1984, 5–6).

Ben Guyton. Black fiddlers not only taught kinfolk, but their talents, as described earlier, were passed on to whites as a part of a shared culture. The story of Ben Guyton, of Sulligent (Lamar County), Alabama, a small town located near the Appalachian Mountains in the northwest region of the state, demonstrates how elements identified with Africa became a part of the white fiddle tradition. Instead of striking out on his own after the Civil War, Guyton became a servant for his former master, Daniel Hollis. While there, Guyton taught Hollis's son, D. Dix Hollis, how to play the fiddle. No one knew that the son would become the first fiddler in Alabama (Black or white) to make commercial recordings. Thus, the first media representation of Alabama fiddling has Black influence.[29]

George Morris. When Gerald Milnes conducted research in West Virginia during the 1970s, he discovered several white people who remembered family members discussing Black fiddlers who had lived in their communities. One such person was George Morris, or "Black George," a well-known Black fiddler from Braxton County who was born in the nineteenth century and died in 1919. Except for fragments of information and anecdotes, little is known about his life. Everett White, the great grandson of the slave owner, states: "He was a good violin player, Black George was." What is most remembered was the close relationship that existed between Morris and the slave owner's family: "When he [Morris] got his freedom from Grandpa Johnny, my great grandfather, told him he was free to get married and have a family of his own, or whatever he wanted to do. He told Grandpa . . . he'd been treated right and he was as free as he wanted to be. Dad said he laid down across the bed and cried when Grandpa told him he had his freedom" (Milnes 1999, 105). White also recalled an incident with an acquaintance at the family's home, which demonstrated the grandfather's loyalty to Morris: "His [the acquaintance's] name was John McNemar, he was a fiddle player. He was at my grandfather [Nelson] Wine's house one time. A bunch of musicians was there, singers and people that played instruments. Black George was there—He didn't like old Black George, old John didn't. And after while he said, 'Mister Nelson Wines, unless I change my mind, I'll never set my foot in your house no more.' Grandpa set there a little bit and said, 'Unless I change my mind, I don't give a damn'" (105).

Augustus "Gus" Cochran (ca. 1865–1927) of St. Clair County, Alabama, and his partner, guitarist Pomp Montgomery, were well known for making "parties gay and lively with their fiddle and guitar dance tunes" (Cauthen 1989a, 12). Cochran's grandson, Earnest Mostella (ca. 1909–2003), who continued in the profession by becoming a craftsman, specializing in constructing hand-carved fiddles,[30] recalls family stories about "people [who] knew [his grand-father] far and near. They'd go and get him and take him from one place to another to play for 'em; he'd return 'loaded down with gifts'" (12). According to Mostella, his grandmother, a fiddler herself, "didn't always like it when granddaddy went off to play. Sometimes he'd be gone for quite a spell and she'd be good and mad when he did come in . . . But folks would give him money for his playing and he'd turn it over to grand-momma, that'd stop her fussing for a while" (Mathews 2023, 9). According to Mostella, as reported by Mathews (2023), "Cochran was born into slavery and secretly taught himself to play on the fiddle of his enslaver: he whittled a key, the story goes, to open the cabinet where the instrument was kept under lock. In time, he grew into a celebrated musician, playing parties all over St. Clair County for both black and white dancers. . . . [He] created his melodies from everyday experiences" (9-10). "Granddaddy was the true fiddle playing man. Why, he could lay flat on his back, half drunk and still play away—outplay 'em all" (8).

The Ozarks

Although most of the information on nineteenth-century Black fiddling in the Ozarks[31] comes from Oklahoma, there is no evidence that Black musicking in the region is distinct as a result of interactions between African Americans and Native Americans. Like most white mountain slaveholders, Native Americans did not oppose Africans performing the fiddle. Thus, Blacks' participation in music and dancing with whites and Native Americans was common. The instrumentation for performances—fiddle with percussion and sometimes a wind instrument—did not differ from other regions. Lucinda Vann, one of the few Oklahoma natives to comment on the musicking of Blacks in the Oklahoma Cherokee Territory, was born in Webbers Falls (Muskogee County), where she spent most of her life. Lucinda was enslaved by Jim Vann, a Cherokee Indian. About fiddling and other recreational activities on the plantation, Lucinda (1937) states:

> Everybody had a good time on old Jim Vann's plantation. After supper the colored folks would get together and talk, and sing, and dance. Someone maybe would be playin' a fiddle or a banjo. Everybody was happy. Marster never whipped no one. No fusses, no bad words, no nuthin' like that. . . .

There was big parties and dances. In winter white folks danced in the parlor of the big house; in summer they danced on a platform under a great big brush arbor. There was seats all around for folks to watch them dance. Sometimes just white folks danced; sometimes just the black folks.

There was music, fine music. The colored folks did most of the fiddlin'. Someone rattled the bones. There was a bugler and someone called the dances. When martser Jim and missus Jennie went away the slaves would have a big dance in the arbor. When the white folks danced, the slaves would all sit or stand around and watch. They'd clap their hands and holler. Everybody have a good time. *Lord yes, su-er.* (435–41)

Not surprisingly, the majority of Black fiddlers living in Oklahoma during the nineteenth century had learned to play the fiddle before arriving in the Ozarks. For example, Henry Clay,[32] although born in North Carolina, had lived in Louisiana and several other places before settling in Oklahoma. Although Clay began playing the fiddle before the Civil War, his comments about his fiddle performances relate to activities after the war, which suggests that he may not have been able to play the instrument as often as he wanted during slavery. Clay (1973) explains: "On the boat I learned to fiddle, and I can make an old fiddle talk. So, I done pretty good playing for the white dances for a long time after the War, and they sure had some good ones. Everything from a waltz to a Schottische I played. Sometimes some white people didn't like to have me play, but young Master (I always called him that till he died) would say, 'Where I go my boy can go too'" (84). Similarly, Johnson Thompson's father, a native of Oklahoma who had been enslaved by both Cherokee and white slaveholders, probably learned to play the fiddle before emancipation when he and his wife lived in Rusk County, Texas, with their son (Johnson). Thompson (1937), who only remembers his father playing the fiddle in Oklahoma Indian Territory around Fort Gibson (in northeast Muskogee County), states: "Pappy worked around the farms and fiddled for the Cherokee dances" (421).

In Missouri, African American fiddlers were dispersed in various areas, including agricultural regions and counties along the Mississippi River as well as railroad towns and cities, such as St. Louis and Kansas City (Marshall 2012, 111). Most findings focus on performance contexts with some information about specific fiddlers. One source indicates that, in 1837, a slave owner in Jackson, Missouri, gave Bartley, an enslaved seventeen-year-old, a violin believed to have been constructed in 1670. The slaveholder, "Mr. Sanford, had purchased the instrument from a German musician who visited Jackson, paying $30 for it." Obviously, Bartley was noted for his fiddle playing because another slaveholder reports that he accompanied Bartley's fiddling on the piano on "musical evenings" for family members at their home (109).

The South-Central Region

Sources on Black music in the South-Central region include extensive information on fiddling. Joyce Cauthen (for Alabama), Sylvester Oliver (for Mississippi), and John Minton (for east Texas and neighboring areas) provide details on many of the topics discussed in the foregoing, but data about individual fiddlers is not as extensive as that found in other regions (Cauthen 1989a, Oliver 1996, Minton 1996a, 295). In many cases, scholars' findings correlate with the demographics for each state.[33] For example, in Mississippi, where Black people outnumbered white people, musical practices tended to be racially segregated. Even more interesting is that the isolation of African Americans in Mississippi appears to have led to the preservation of older practices (African- and European-derived) for a longer period of time. Minton, one of the few researchers to investigate West African fiddling in the United States, indicates that similar to other Gulf states, enslaved Blacks transported into Texas during the early nineteenth century took their traditions with them.[34] Because many were imported directly from Africa during the clandestine slave trade, some practices were clearly African-derived. Therefore, at least two factors account for the resilience of African culture in Texas: the presence of free Blacks and the continuous trading of the enslaved by Spaniards (Minton 1996a).

One of the most important points about nineteenth century fiddling in the Gulf is its similarity to the East Coast and the mountains. As white and Black people settled in the South-Central region, fiddling not only became an important part of the social life, it sounded like the music of the people who migrated west during and after the Civil War. White fiddlers descended from pioneers who had moved through Virginia, the Carolinas, Georgia, Kentucky, and Tennessee with the enslaved adapted their music to the conditions they found, and adopted what they liked in the fiddling of others they came into contact with, whether African, French, Scandinavian, or British. Fiddle music in Alabama became not just mountain music, but the music of the various regions: Black Belt,[35] Piedmont, Wiregrass, as well as the river communities along the Tennessee and Tombigbee (Cauthen 1989a, 4).

Fiddle Construction and Ensemble Organization. Interestingly, the number of references about the gourd fiddle in the South-Central region surpasses documentation in other parts of the United States, primarily because of Minton's article, "West African Fiddles in Deep East Texas." Most accounts, which are taken from narratives of the formerly enslaved, refer to Texas, but a few document the gourd fiddle in other parts of the United States. Minton believes the prominence of reports on homemade instruments in Texas demonstrates the maintenance of African traditions in the region rather than the imitation of their European counterparts. For example, Minton believes that the music Wash Wilson heard in Texas was obviously African-derived. Born in 1842 in

Louisiana, Wilson was transported to Texas when he was about eighteen years: "Dar wuzn't no money ter buy er muzin insterment. Us 'ud take pieces of sheep's rib, er a cow's jaw, er a piece ob iron wid an old kettle er a piece ob wood, a hollow gourd an' er few horse hairs an' make er drum er things ter make muzic wid. Some times dey 'ud git a piece ob de trunk ob a tree, hollowed out an' stretch er sheep er a goat's skin ober um" (Minton 1996a, 303). While Wilson does not specify whether the "hollow gourd" was bowed or plucked, Minton states that "circumstantial evidence indicates the former. In any case, the instrument is intrinsically suited to an ensemble as typical of West Africa as East Texas or Western Louisiana" (304).

Other examples that support Minton's argument include those by Anderson Edwards, Jack Maddox, and Litt Young. Born March 12, 1844, in Rusk County, Texas, Edwards recalled fiddles constructed from gourds: "On Saturday nights we'd sing and dance.... We made our own instruments, which was gourd fiddles and quill flutes." Born in Georgia in 1849, but transported to Mount Enterprise, Texas, around 1853, Maddox recalled that "Judge Maddox [his enslaver] bought a n----r man who had a three string fiddle. I used to hear him play and sing" (Minton 1996a, 295). Since this was not a four-string European violin, Minton believes the instrument was most likely derived from West Africa, where fiddles are constructed with one or more strings (295; also see DjeDje 2008a). According to Young, who was born in Vicksburg (Warren County), Mississippi, in 1850, but since 1865 had resided in Harrison County, Texas, "We had small dances on Saturday night and play ring plays, and have banjo and fiddle playing and knock bones together.... There was all kinds of fiddles made from gourds and things" (Minton 1996a, 295). Evidence also indicates that Blacks maintained traditions from the slave era after emancipation. When ninety-six-year-old Harre Quarles of Madisonville (Madison County), Texas, spoke with WPA interviewers, he stated that fiddling continued to be an important part of his life after slavery: "Massa tells us we's free June 'teenth.[36] I leaves. I made a fiddle out of a gourd 'fore freedom and larns to play it. I played for dances after I's free" (295).

Sources for the South-Central region provide evidence that the fiddle was prominent in both plantation bands (slave orchestras) and urban dance orchestras (see photo 3.6). Slave orchestras were usually smaller in size, including fiddle, flute, and fife, or two fiddles, flute, triangle, and tambourine. In his interview for the WPA project, Charley Williams (1937), born 1843 on a plantation near Monroe (Ouachita Parish), Louisiana,[37] states that "gourd fiddles and de clapping bones made out'n beef ribs" were used for music making.[38] In Lee County [Alabama], "Lucindy Lawrence Jurdon and Frank Menefee recalled corn-shuckings where 'somebody would clap hands, beat pans, blow quills or pick de banjer strings' to provide music for the 'buck-dance, sixteen-hand reel and cake walk' but, the fiddle was 'the essential requirement for a good-time dance'" (Cauthen 1989a, 7). In December 1853, when two British women (Jane M.

Photo 3.6. "Slave Quarters, Louisiana, 1861–65." *Slavery Images: A Visual Record of the African Slave Trade and Slave Life in the Early African Diaspora*. https://slaveryimages.org/database/image-result.php?objectid=478. Accessed August 20, 2023.

and Marion Turnbull) visited a slave market in Montgomery, Alabama, they reported that they saw "about sixty negroes, all dancing . . . to the music of two violins and a banjo . . . a negro was standing on a chair, calling out what figures were to be performed in the Virginia Reel" (Epstein 1977, 154; Cauthen 1989a, 7).

In urban areas such as New Orleans, Black dance orchestras were commonplace, whether the dances were for the enslaved, free Blacks, or whites.[39] While the instruments included in urban dance orchestras may have differed from those on plantations, the variety was the same—"typically, 'a clarionet, three fiddles, two tambourines, and a bass drum'" (Southern 1983a, 135). "Dance fiddlers were in great demand, and a good one, such as Massa Quamba, could charge as much as three dollars per night for his services" (136). It is also noteworthy that New Orleans was considered to be the capital for violin playing and European art music during the slave era; thus, Black and white musicians often visited the city to learn how to play the instrument (Wolfe 1989).[40]

After emancipation, the prominence of Black fiddle ensembles in the South-Central region did not decline. In describing white dances around Waco, Texas, in the 1870s and 1880s, jazz trumpeter Joe Oliver, who was born in 1847 in Hill County, notes that "If de w'ite folks fiddler did not come den dey has de ole black fiddler whose name wuz Caleb, he plays de fiddle, 'nother plays de jews harp, an' still 'nother one plays de hoe by scrapin' on hit wid a case knife'" (Minton 1996a,

301). Born in 1860, Simp Campbell, another resident from Harrison County, Texas, recalls: "On Saturday night you'd hear them fiddles, banjoes and guitars playing and the darkies singing. All the music gadgets was home-made. The banjoes was made of round pieces of wood, civered (covered) with sheepskin and strung with catgut strings. One of the oldest fiddlers of slavery time teached my brother Flint to play the fiddle" (297).

Rhythmic accompaniment so important to Black fiddle ensembles during the antebellum continued to be prominent after emancipation. Josephine Tippit Compton, born near Waco (McLennan County), Texas, in 1862, remembers that kitchen utensils were sometimes used for accompaniment: "When we had de crowds to come to our house for dances we had a fiddle fur music an' kept time wid skillet lids hit together" (302). Sam Forge, who was born in 1850 in Freestone County, Texas, described the technique of beating straws when he participated in fiddle contests in Texas: "W'en de contest start each man plays his best. . . . An' most of de time he has somebody to accompany him, sometimes wid a straw lookin' piece he put across de strings of de fiddle, den he bounce hit up an' down on de strings an' beat out his accompanyin' de fiddler, de faster de fiddler plays de faster de boy jig his 'companying for him" (302–3). Minton states that because the beating of straws was also widespread among southern whites, it has even been attributed to European tradition, though the evidence for the claim is unconvincing. "More likely, the custom originated in North America, where it is entirely more consistent with black traditions, which routinely exploit the percussive possibilities of melodic instruments (or the melodic possibilities of percussion instruments), often in contrast to white approaches to the same items" (302–3; also see McCormick 1998, 2002).

Performance Contexts. The largest amount of data for the South-Central states concerns performance contexts. Although many of the occasions for musicking (for example, on holidays, special celebrations, and weekends) are similar to those in other parts of the United States, some are distinct to the South-Central region. For example, a few sources provide information on fiddling by the enslaved as they were transported from the East Coast to the Gulf. On a steamboat passage from Mobile to New Orleans, Olmsted (1861) writes: "There was a fiddle or two among them, and they were very merry, dancing and singing. A few, however, refused to join in the amusement, and looked very disconsolate" (287; also quoted in Cauthen 1989a, 7). In 1892, Annie Jefferson Holland writes: "On the long and arduous trek to Texas the tents were stretched at the end of each day's progress. 'Around the camp fires the Negroes would gather with their banjoes and their fiddles and every night was a frolic'" (Govenar and Lornell 2019, 51; also see Holland 1892, 38).

The so-called "high-brow" or formal dances (such as cotillions and minuets) were just as popular as those that were informal (like jigs and reels). A description of entertainment activities at a plantation in western Alabama near

Demopolis demonstrates the use of the fiddle at dances for whites in the "big house" during the antebellum period. In this case, the fiddler, Jim Pritchett, not only played tunes made popular by others, he was also noted for creating improvisations. The ensemble included fiddle, triangle, and banjo, a combination used in other parts of the country.

> Hospitality ruled supreme at the Big House, and kin, friends and strangers found constant welcome and lavish entertainment. At night Jim Pritchett with his fiddle, Mingo with his triangle, and Mose with his banjo, came up from the quarters and made music for the happy belles and beaux. They danced cotillions and the Lancers, winding up with the Virginia Reel. Sundry drams livened old Jim's fiddle, as the "Forked Deer," "Arkansas Traveler" and other old tunes of a like lilt and swing, quickened their flying feet. Jim was a noted mimic, as well as fiddler, and usually wound up with an improvisation of his own, which he called "The Dying Coon," in which his voice added to the witchery of his bow the shouts of the hunters, the baying of the dogs and the snarls and dying wail of the fighting coon. (Benners 1923, 22, 25–56; also quoted in Cauthen 1989a, 10; Epstein 1977, 158)

Since holidays, especially Christmas and the Fourth of July, were the primary times the enslaved were allowed to participate in recreational activities, evidence of fiddling on these occasions abound. A source from Livingston, located in Sumter County in western Alabama, includes a description of Black recreational activities performed by Charlie Johnson on George Whitfield's plantation, who states: "When Christmas come, didn't get no present, just more meat and bread. Christmas and the fourth day of July was the times we was allowed to celebrate. Then we had fiddlin' dances. We had a old slave could fiddle . . . and we do square dances and swing the partners" (Cauthen 1989a, 7). Ruben Laird, from Panola County in northwest Mississippi, told WPA interviewers that he remembered Black people dancing only on holidays. On July fourth, the dance would last all night and day, but during Christmastime, dance activities continued for three days and nights. Laird's physical description of the fiddle and bow used to accompany dancing is similar to those in West Africa: "The music was provided principally by a 'fiddle,' an improvised instrument made by bending a stick in the shape of a bow, holding it in shape with a string and sawing on it with a crude violin bow made of the hair of a horse's mane and tail" (Rawick 1977–79, 1299; Oliver 1996, 123). Thomas Bangs Thorpe, a Massachusetts writer-artist who lived in Louisiana between 1836 and 1854 and wrote journal articles about slave life, often included references to fiddling. Thorpe reports that Christmas festivities on the plantation included singing, instrumental music, and ring dancing to the accompaniment of fiddle, banjo, and bones (Southern and Wright 1990, 19 Items 155 and 157). When two sisters, Jane and Marion Turnbull, toured the United States, Canada, and Cuba between 1852 and 1857, they observed a Christmas ball in New Orleans where a shuffle step was danced to the music of two violins and a banjo (Southern and Wright 1990, 20 Item 160).

The performance of the fiddle at recreational activities in rural Texas continued through the early 1900s. Born in July 1864 in Harrison County, Texas (located northeast on the Texas-Louisiana border close to Shreveport), Bert Strong remained a sharecropper on a 400-acre farm owned by Cavin, his former master, for at least a decade after emancipation. Recalling activities on the farm in the narratives, Strong states: "My old Master give the chil'ren a candy pulling every Saturday night and had them wrestling and knocking each other about. The big fo'ks had dances and parties. They had fiddles but they warn't like these things they have now. The fiddles we had then made music" (Minton 1996a, 291).

Some of the most distinctive contexts for fiddle performances in the South-Central region are found in Louisiana, which is not surprising since slavery there tended to be different from that in English colonies. By 1802, Black fiddlers in New Orleans were an important feature at most public celebrations of Carnaval, one of the few events in the southern states comparable to festivals such as Pinkster Day and 'Lection Day in the Northeast (Southern 1997, 52–58). Describing in his journal Carnaval activities he attended in 1802, Pierre-Louis Berquin-Duvallon, a French planter from Haiti who settled in New Orleans after the Santo Domingo revolt, writes, "In winter, during the Carnaval, there is a public ball open twice a week, one day for grown people, and another for children.... The musicians are half a dozen gypsies, or else people of colour, scraping their fiddles with all their might.... The *ensemble* is so wretched, that every emulation of embellishment would be ridiculous" (Berquin-Duvallon 1806, 26–27; also quoted in Epstein 1977, 92; Southern and Wright 1990, 10 Item 72). From his negative and biased comments, we learn that Berquin-Duvallon had little appreciation for the event partly because the fiddlers' performance was not up to his standards. As noted in earlier chapters, "scraping" alludes to a playing technique that produces a sound, which is not pleasing to many Europeans—perhaps because it was rough and percussive, similar to sounds identified with musicking in Africa. The term "scraping" also belittles the fiddler's playing technique or suggests that it is below par, especially when compared to a performance style identified with European art music. A similar interpretation about Black fiddling is implied when Timothy Flint, a New England minister who visited Mississippi in the early nineteenth century, comments on the cognitive skills of enslaved people: "[T]hey learn easily to read, to sing, and scrape the fiddle. But it would be difficult to teach them arithmetic, or combination of ideas or abstract thinking of any kind" (Flint 1826, 345; Southern and Wright 1990, 12 Item 98).

Although fiddling in New Orleans probably began during the eighteenth century with the first arrival of Africans from the continent, documentation of its performance at Congo Square (or Place Congo), a section of the city where Africans assembled on Sundays and church holy days and danced publicly, does not appear until the nineteenth century. The descriptions of activities at Congo Square are important for at least three reasons. One, they indicate the wide variety of traditions performed by Africans in New Orleans during the nineteenth century. Two, because Senegambians were strongly represented in Louisiana, it is likely that musical elements from savannah West Africa, where the fiddle is prominent, were included in performances. Three, the activities show the performance preferences of Africans. In Congo Square, Blacks entertained themselves, not whites, even though the latter may have been present.

Several accounts document the use of the violin (fiddle) in performances at Congo Square.[41] James Creecy (1860, 20–22), who first traveled to New Orleans in the 1830s, provides a description of activities at the Square, including details about the maintenance of African-derived practices:

> [T]he lower order of colored people and negroes, bond and free, assemble in great numbers in Congo Square, on every Sunday afternoon in good weather, to enjoy themselves in their own peculiar manner. Groups of fifties and hundreds may be seen in different sections of the square, with banjos, tom-toms, violins, jawbones, triangles, and various other instruments from which harsh or dulcet sounds may be extracted; and a variety, indeed, of queer, grotesque, fantastic, strange merry dancers are to be seen, to amuse, astonish, interest and excite.... The dancers most fancifully dressed, with fringes, ribbons, little bells, and shells and balls, jingling and flirting about the performers legs and arms, who sing a second or counter to the music most sweetly.... Young and old join in the sport and dances. One will continue the rapid *jig* till nature is exhausted; then a fresh disciple leaps before him or her and "cuts out" the fatigued one. (also quoted in Epstein 1973, 190, 1977, 134)

In 1886, New Orleans–born novelist George Washington Cable published two articles with visual images that depict the social life and musical activities of enslaved Africans in New Orleans. In "The Dance in Place Congo," Cable not only provides a detailed description of Congo Square, the African groups congregated there, and the musicking performed by Africans, he mentions the different musical instruments used. On the topic of the fiddle and banjo, Cable (1886a, 519–20) writes: "But the grand instrument at last, the first violin, as one might say, was the banjo. It had but four strings, not six; beware of the dictionary. It is not the 'favorite musical instrument of the negroes of the Southern States of America.' Uncle Remus says truly that that is the fiddle."[42]

In "Creole Slave Songs," Cable (1886b) discusses the social structure of New Orleans' residents and explains how it has affected Black musicking. According to Cable, only fiddlers identified as free male quadroons[43] (called *trouloulou*) were allowed to attend quadroon balls: "*Cocodrie* (Spanish, *cocodrilla*, the crocodile or alligator) was the nickname for the unmixed Black man; while *trouloulou* was applied to the free male quadroon, who could find admittance to

Photo 3.7. "The Fiddler." 1886. Drawing by Edward Winsor Kemble. George Washington Cable, "Creole Slave Songs," *Century Illustrated Magazine* Volume 31, Number 6, April 1886, 808.

the quadroon balls only in the capacity, in those days distinctly menial, of musician-fiddler" (808). This passage is important because it indicates that, although fiddling was considered to be menial work, it gave individuals of low status access to events of the upper class, similar to the enslaved who worked in the "big house." In some ways, this is also similar to parts of West Africa where court musicians had greater access to royalty than other people who belong to other socio-occupational groups (DjeDje 2008a, 182–84).

"Creole Slave Songs" is also significant because of the drawings of fiddlers[44] in the article either holding or playing their instrument. The first drawing, entitled "The Fiddler" (Cable 1886b, 808), shows a male fiddler standing straight, but slightly leaning with his back against a wall, holding a fiddle and bow in his hand (see photo 3.7). Most likely the image represents the quadroon fiddler discussed in the article, because the fiddler is standing on an elevated platform (a staged area), dressed in a western-style shirt and pair of pants that appear to be well kept, and holding a fiddle similar in construction to the western violin (Cable 1886b, 808).

The second drawing, entitled "The Voodoo Dance" (see photo 3.8), represents the antithesis of the instrument and fiddler described earlier in the article. Although the description for this drawing is biased, comments by Cable (1886b) are worth repeating because the religious practices, which include fiddling, appear to be African-derived.

> To what extent the Voodoo[45] worship still obtains here would be difficult to say with certainty. The affair of June, 1884 . . . took place at a wild and lonely spot

Photo 3.8. "A Voodoo Dance." 1886. Drawing by Edward Winsor Kemble. George Washington Cable, "Creole Slave Songs," *Century Illustrated Magazine* Volume 31, Number 6, April 1886, 816.

> where the dismal cypress swamp behind New Orleans meets the waters of Lake Pontchartrain in a wilderness of cypress stumps and rushes. It would be hard to find in nature a more painfully desolate region. Here in a fisherman's cabin sat the Voodoo worshipers cross-legged on the floor about an Indian basket of herbs and some beans, some bits of bone, some oddly wrought bunches of feathers, and some saucers of small cakes. The queen presided, sitting on the only chair in the room. There was no king, no snake—at least none visible to the onlookers. Two drummers beat with their thumbs on gourds covered with sheepskin, and a white-wooled old man scraped that hideous combination of banjo and violin, whose head is covered with rattlesnake skin. . . . There was singing . . . and there was frenzy and a circling march. (820)

The fact that fiddle and banjo are mentioned suggests that the use of the fiddle for religious worship (that is, spirit possession) continued in the Americas through the nineteenth century.[46] Kemble's drawing, which accompanies Cable's description of the ceremony, is uncanny because the fiddle is not represented as a western violin similar to the one described earlier in the article (see Cable 1886b, 808). Rather, the playing position of the fiddler in this case—that is, sitting on the floor and holding the instrument in a vertical position—is similar to bowed lutes used by fiddlers in Northeast Africa (Poche 2001).[47] The fact that the fiddle is performed in combination with drums, suggesting elements that are African-derived, also confirms that the performance is not European (DjeDje 2008a, 39–42).

An article by Eugene V. Smalley (1887) also includes interesting comments about musicking in the late nineteenth century. While traveling by boat on the Mississippi River, Smalley and his party docked and went ashore at Belaire, a plantation in Louisiana "celebrated for its careful and systematic field work" (109). The Black people he encounters are obviously sharecroppers whose lives had not changed much from the time of slavery. His description of instruments in the music ensemble (accordion, triangle, and fiddle) and dances performed by Blacks (double-shuffle, and the like) indicates that characteristics associated with modern-day zydeco music date to the nineteenth century:

> The store is usually the center of the business life and of much of the social life of a plantation. It is owned by the planter.... We find a score of negro men and boys in the store listening to the music of an accordion, a fiddle,[48] and a triangle, and with some little coaxing and the promise of a quarter to the best dancer we succeed in getting up an amusing competitive double-shuffle and heel-and-toe dance. The contestants, who have been toiling in the field all day, throw off their coats and get down to the work with evident relish, amid shouts . . . and clapping of hands on knees from the delighted sable spectators. (109)

Social Significance. Like other areas in the United States during the nineteenth century, some slaveholders in the South-Central region believed dancing and fiddling to be sinful; thus, Blacks were urged to give up participation in such activities. David R. Hundley (1860), a Confederate officer who lived in Alabama as well as Kentucky and Virginia, provides insights on the role of Protestant Christianity in the lives of Black people. Most importantly, Hundley's account reveals the perspective of whites who believed participation in Christian activities was one way for Blacks to rid themselves of the desire to engage in deviant behavior. Yet, it is significant that Hundley acknowledges that the enslaved were not the only persons who were sinful:

> On nearly all such plantations, in fact, the negroes unite together without regard to differences of religious beliefs, and hold a common prayer-meeting two nights in every week, at which the master is sometimes present and expounds to them the Word of God. And it is notable what a change for the better Christianity produces in even the most degraded of them. They readily give up their banjos, their fiddles, their double-shuffles, and breakdowns, and are eager to learn what is right and becoming. Of course we speak only of such as are sincere believers of the Gospel; for we have reason to know that they sometimes profess Christianity because *it pays*, and in particular is this true of just about one half the negro preachers. Believe us, amiable Mrs. Stowe, black people are no better than white people the world over. (348–49; also quoted in Epstein 1977, 215)

Although religious enthusiasts were successful in condemning fiddle and banjo playing among whites and some of the enslaved, many Blacks continued to use these instruments, even to accompany sacred singing (Oliver 1996, 130).

A number of accounts from the South-Central states provide the perspective of whites who supported and encouraged Blacks' involvement in secular activities. In situations where varying views existed, both white and Black people were generally punished for participating in musicking. In 1846, John Kalaras of Mobile, Alabama, was arrested, along with the enslaved fiddler, for "entertaining Negroes in a variety of ways, among which was permitting them to assemble in a room to 'trip it on the light fantastic toe'" (Cauthen 1989a, 9). In some situations, slave owners gave Blacks the opportunity to resolve varied opinions about musicking. A letter posted March 22, 1850, from H. W. Poyner, an agent for a Memphis bank and owner of Talla Bena Plantation in Louisiana, to General Giles Harding, the owner of Belle Meade Plantation in Nashville, Tennessee, reveals how some slave owners allowed the enslaved to make decisions about secular and sacred activities. A supporter of slavery, Poyner also indicates (sarcastically) that if northern abolitionists observed the contentment of Blacks when they participated in music making, they would not be making such a fuss about ending slavery. "This is Saturday night, & I hear the fiddle going in the Quarter. We have two parties here among the Negroes. One a dancing party and the other a Praying party. The dancers have it tonight, & the other party will hold forth tomorrow. They are very selfish and never attend each others [*sic*] meeting. I fear that I shall have to break the fiddle or they will break me (or rather the Bank) to keep them shod. I would like to have one of these Northern men here some Saturday night & Sunday to witness their fun and contentment" (Hulan 1969, 14).

Differences in the way Catholics and Protestants dealt with this issue is apparent in an account by a reporter from abroad. When William Howard Russell (1861), a correspondent for the London *Times*, visited Natchez, Mississippi, on June 14, 1861, he described two contexts in which Black fiddlers performed: (1) an informal gathering in front of the slave quarters where children and grown-ups from neighboring plantations congregated to observe and listen to the music and (2) a more formal dance where partner-dancing took place:

> As we passed the house, two or three young women flitted past in snow-white dressed with pink sashes. . . . They were slaves going off to a dance at the sugar-house; but they were indoor servants, and therefore better off, in the way of clothes than their fellow slaves who labor in the field. On approaching a high paling at the rear of the house the scraping of fiddles was audible. It was Sunday, and Mr. Roman informed me that he gave his negroes leave to have a dance on that day. The planters who are not Catholics rarely give any such indulgence to their

slaves.... Two negro fiddlers were working their bows with energy in front of one of the huts, and a crowd of little children were listening to the music, and a few grown-up persons of color—some of them from the adjoining plantations.... The silence which reigned in the huts as soon as the fiddlers had gone off to the sugar-house was profound....

The scraping of the fiddles attracted us to the sugar-house.... In a space of the floor ... some fifteen women and as many men were assembled, and four couples were dancing a kind of Irish jig to the music of the negro musicians—a double shuffle and a thumping ecstasy. (also quoted in Southern and Wright 1990, 18 Item 142; and Epstein 1977, 136)

Represented in the literature from this region are also accounts by slaveholders who were intentional about allowing (or even encouraging) the enslaved to participate in musicking, particularly fiddling, because they believed it helped to increase productivity. Related to this subject, Olmsted (1860, 145) reported on a conversation he had in 1853 with a northern Mississippi slaveholder about the musicking on weekends for the people he had enslaved: "Do your negroes dance much? Yes, they are mighty fond on't. Saturday night they dance all night, and Sunday nights too. Daytime they sleep and rest themselves, and Sunday night we let 'em dance and sing if they want. It does 'em good, you know, to enjoy theirselves.... They dance to the banjo, I suppose? Banjos and violins; some of 'em has got violins" (also quoted in Oliver 1996, 118).

In one of the 1851 issues of *DeBow's Review*, a Mississippi planter explains why he always allowed music and dancing to take place: "I must not omit to mention that I have a good fiddler, and keep him well supplied with catgut [for making strings], and I make it his duty to play for the negroes every Saturday night until 12 o'clock. They are exceedingly punctual in their attendance at the ball, while Charley's fiddle is always accompanied with Ihurod on the triangle, and Sam to 'pat'" (625). A small farmer from Mississippi who also wrote to *DeBow's Review* in 1851 about his methods in managing slaves not only agreed with the Mississippi planter, he gave his views on the behavior of the enslaved when they did and did not participate in music making:

I have a fiddle in my quarters, and though some of my good old brethren in the church would think hard of me, yet I allow dancing; ay, I buy the fiddle and encourage it, by giving the boys occasionally a big supper.... I would build a house large enough, and use it for a dance-house for the young, and those who wished to dance, as well as for prayer meetings, and for church on Sunday—making it a rule to be present myself occasionally at both, and my overseer always. I know the rebuke in store about dancing, but I cannot help it. I believe negroes will be better disposed this way than any other. I would employ a preacher for every Sabbath. One of my negroes can read the Bible, and he has prayer-meeting every Sabbath at four o'clock, P.M.—all the negroes attend regularly, no compulsion being used. (371, 372)

The small planter comes across as a shrewd businessman, for he did not allow his personal beliefs or the views of others to interfere with what he considered to be good business practices. He also found a way to satisfy the different interests of Blacks on his plantation. Those who wanted to dance, have prayer meetings, or do both, were given space and time to participate in the chosen activity. Eli Coleman, a formerly enslaved person from Texas, "recalled that the slaves would dance until their master came to tell them to get ready for Sunday services. And there are examples of slaves, like Ol' Tom, a resident of a Fayette County, Texas plantation, who served their communities as both preacher and musician" (Cimbala 1995, 16).

This method of controlling Black people was not uncommon because several of the formerly enslaved reported to WPA interviewers about slave owners who regularly allowed them to entertain themselves with fiddling on weekends. Prince Johnson, an eighty-five-year-old whose family migrated from Alabama, had interesting reminisces of slave life in Clarksdale (Coahoma County), Mississippi: "Nobody worked after dinner on Saturday. Us took dat time go scrub up and clean de houses so as to be ready for inspectin Sunday mornin'. Some Saturday nights us had dances.... When he [the fiddler] got dat old fiddle out you couldn't keep your foots still" (Epstein 1977, 154; also quoted in Yetman 1970, 190). When Charles Willis (1937), who was born during the 1840s, spoke with the WPA worker about his experiences in Lawrence County (southern Mississippi), he indicated that church and recreational activities generally took place on weekends: "We went to the white folks' church and stayed on the church porch or out under the trees right by so we could hear. We sing old hymns we don't sing now.... We was let off Sadday at noon and could go to the fiddlin's and dance all night. You could hear the n----rs dancin' a mile away. The same man called for us that called fer the white folks. He could sure call 'em too. We did the Back Step and Shuffle. The tunes was 'Egg Nog,' Sugar and Beer and 'Natcha Under the Hill.' I don't recollect none of the words of the tunes" (441). Callie Gray, an enslaved person from northeast Mississippi, did all of her gardening, cooking, and other chores on Saturday so that Sunday would be free for recreation: "They never had to work on Sad'day after twelve o'clock. Sad'day nights they would have fiddle dances or quilting" (Rawick 1977–79, 142; Oliver 1996, 121–22).

Social Role and Status of Fiddler. In some parts of the South-Central regions, not only did Blacks and whites perform together, but they also exchanged tunes while learning from each other. Several whites who contributed to narratives about formerly enslaved people in Texas indicated that they learned to fiddle from Blacks. W. S. Needham Jr., a white fiddler born in Alabama but raised in

Mississippi and Texas, stated that Mance and "Friday," two men who had been enslaved by his father, taught him how to perform the fiddle:

> Mance was a good fiddler. He loved to teach me to play, and I picked it up right away. By rights, a n----r by the name of "Friday" gave me my first lesson, when I wasn't but three years old, but dad gave him to my oldest sister when she married. When I was six, Mance taught me to jig and play such pieces as "Turkey in the Straw," "Molly Put de Kittle On," "Run N----r Run," "Old Dan Tucker," and such pieces, and taught me to go on like they did. I just picked it right up now, and made a many a dollar by playing for dances and such after I got grown. (Minton 1996a, 298)

In Texas, there were also instances of whites teaching Blacks. Born in 1850 in Louisiana but transported to Texas around 1860, Guy Stewart reported that it was whites who taught them how to play the fiddle: "De Marster am a good fiddler.... He larns some ob de n----rs hows to play de fiddle and some de banjo. Lots ob times us all gets tugather, weuns den plays de music, sing and dance" (Minton 1996a, 298).

In addition, some Blacks learned to fiddle on their own, which was probably common but not well documented. Richard Toler, a formerly enslaved person from Virginia who migrated to Texas, explained how he learned his musicking: "After the War I bought a fiddle, and I was a good fiddler. Used to be a fiddler for the white girls to dance. Just picked it up; it was a natural gift.... I used to play at hoedown's, too. Played all those old-time songs—'Soldier's Joy,' 'Jimmy Long Josey,' 'Arkansas Traveler' and 'Black Eye Susie.' Emancipation gave him the opportunity to play, for unlike more fortunate Negroes who worked under less severe taskmasters, he said, 'I never had no good times till I was freed. We was never allowed no parties, and when they had goin's-on at the big house, we had to clear out'" (51; also see Holland 1892, 86).

Similar to other regions, Black fiddlers in the South-Central states were also given special privileges and treated differently from other enslaved persons. For Alabama, Cauthen provides several examples. Jake Green, a fiddler who lived on a plantation near Livingston, Alabama, escaped a great deal of labor because of his talent. Bill, a Black fiddler on Benjamin Fitzpatrick's Oak Grove Plantation in Autauga County, Alabama, was held in high regard by fellow slaves because of his ability. A reporter from the *New York Herald* who interviewed Bill wrote that he was "the musical celebrity and general favorite among the negroes. His musical powers may be overrated, but . . . all say he is the greatest fiddler in Autauga county" (Keller 1976, 224; also quoted in Cauthen 1989a, 10). While Jim Gillard of Opelika (Lee County), Alabama, indicated that his "Martser's brother would fiddle for us," Hattie Clayton recalled, "Lots o' times ole Missus would come to de dances an' look on. An' when a brash n----r boy cut a cute bunch uv steps, de men-folks would give 'im a dime or so" (11).

As performers, the lives of musicians in the South-Central states are not very different from fiddlers in other parts of the country. Where differences exist, it is due to the circumstances of the enslaved and/or the environment in which they lived. Thus, concise details about several individuals and families are presented below to demonstrate the varied experiences of fiddlers in the South-Central states. Except for Solomon Northup who wrote an autobiography about his ordeal in being sold into slavery, most of the material comes from the writings of researchers.

Solomon Northup (ca. 1807–1863). When Northup reached Louisiana in 1841 after being sold into slavery, fiddling provided him with a lifestyle he never would have had if he worked in the fields.[49] Mary Epps, his master's wife, induced her husband, Edwin, to buy a violin for Northup because she was "passionately fond of music." As a consequence, Northup frequently played for the Epps family in the evenings. When Northup obtained his freedom, he writes that "Mistress Epps was actually affected to tears," because she no longer had someone to play the violin for her.

Financially, there were benefits in being a fiddler. Although Epps often took Northup's payment when the fiddler was hired out to perform at events, Northup sometimes personally received money for his performances. "My master often received letters, sometimes from a distance of ten miles, requesting him to send me to play at a ball or festival of the whites. He received his compensation, and usually I also returned with many picayunes jingling in my pockets" (Northup 1968, 165; also quoted in Epstein 1977, 150; Southern 1983a, 99). On one occasion, he collected seventeen dollars in tips (a large sum for a slave to receive at one time).

Northup's role as a fiddler meant that he was known to many people in the surrounding area: "[They] always knew there was a jollification somewhere, whenever Platt Epps [Northup's slave name] was seen passing through the town with his fiddle in his hand. 'Where are you going now Platt?' and 'What is coming off tonight Platt?' would be interrogatories issuing from every door and window, and many a time when there was no special hurry, yielding to pressing importunities, Platt would draw his bow, and sitting astride his mule, perhaps, discourse musically to a crowd of delighted children, gathered around him in the street" (Northup 1968, 165; also quoted in Southern 1983a, 187).

Fiddling gave Northup access to a world foreign to most of the enslaved. "It introduced me to great houses—relieved me of many days' labor in the field—supplied me with conveniences for my cabin—with pipes and tobacco, and extra pairs of shoes. . . . It heralded my name round the country—made me friends, who, otherwise would not have noticed me—gave me an honored seat at the yearly feasts, and secured the loudest and heartiest welcome of them all at the Christmas dance" (Northup 1968, 166). Because the fiddle gives status and is a symbol of great value, fiddlers sometimes regarded the instrument as a friend and referred to it anthropomorphically. Northup writes, "It was my companion—the friend of my bosom" (166). In other words, the instrument was a partner rather than just an accompaniment to dancing or singing (Southern 1983a, 202).

Gus Rhodes. Gus Rhodes, a respected Black fiddler from Alabama's Clarke County who was born in 1853, could play old-time breakdowns by ear as well as European sacred and art music from the written score. Around the time of the 1900 census, Rhodes was living in Thomasville, Clarke's county seat, which had a population of 686 people. In 1897, he was described in the *Thomasville Argus* as "the city's master violinist." A report on "the crowning social fete of the season" notes that "'Gus Rhodes wielded the bow on this occasion in his masterly way, to the tune of ten dollars'" (Cauthen 1989a, 12).

The Owens Family. Oftentimes fiddling was a family tradition, with children learning from parents and becoming well-known artists on their own. Playing for family and friends at local country dances and house parties, or even on the road at distances away from one's home, offered an escape from the burdens of cotton farming (Govenar 1985, 16). In many cases, the music skills learned from performing with family members also provided the source material for new traditions such as the blues that developed in later years. Such is the case for Eli Owens, a Mississippi blues musician who played mouth bow as well as other instruments through the late 1970s. Eli's great grandfather, Andy Owens, born in Marion County, Mississippi, sometime between 1825 and 1833, "was a man of great musical skills and an accomplished craftsman; he played a variety of instruments, including accordion, fiddle, quills (tuned whistles), guitar (as well as beating a straw on a guitar played by someone else), jug, a barrel-shaped drum, a mouth bow, and jews harp." He also constructed many of the instruments—the fiddle, quills, drum, and mouth bow—he performed (Evans 1994, 335). Although Eli's grandfather and father were not musicians, Lucius Pittman, his maternal uncle, was a multi-instrumentalist, playing fiddle and mouth bow. Like the great grandfather, Pittman became well known in southern Mississippi during the late nineteenth century (336).

Charles Lipscomb,[50] the father of well-known blues musician Mance Lipscomb (1895–1976), made his first fiddle out of a cigar box and later played professionally at country dances in the Scots-Irish, Bohemian, and Black American settlements of the Brazos River bottoms in Texas. Because he performed guitar as accompaniment to his father's fiddling, Mance's formative years were greatly influenced by fiddle music (Govenar 1985, 37–38). In a 1961 interview, Mance explained, "Charlie . . . was a professional fiddler and he could play a fiddle just as good as anybody I ever heard. He played way back in olden days. You know he played at breakdowns, waltzes, and schottisches and all things like that. . . . He played waltzes—'Missouri Waltz,' 'Casey Jones'—anything you name he just played it. He was just a self-player until I was big enough to play behind him; then we two played together" (Govenar and Lornell 2019, 51).

Summary

This chapter has addressed the four major topics (history, the individual, creativity, and geography) that are critical in understanding the significance of Black fiddling to African American culture. In addition to affirming that the fiddle was an instrument identified with Black people, much attention has been given to the issue of creativity because the nineteenth century was a critical juncture in the history of Black music in the United States. As noted earlier, it was during this period a distinct musical culture was identified with Black culture that non-Blacks emulated and popularized. Not only were new performance contexts and occasions established, but the latest genres and musical styles for that period were developed fusing old and new material. Because Black people were diverse in their aesthetic preferences, there was not one but a range of cultural expressions that emerged to suit the taste of performers and listeners.

By the early nineteenth century, the fiddle had become firmly entrenched in Black culture and was indispensable at most social events. No one questioned its affinity with African Americans during this period. The fiddle was either performed alone or with accompanying instruments, but percussion continued to be important. When white people began emulating Black culture for personal pleasure and economic gain, they chose two instrumental traditions that, in their minds, symbolized Black creativity: the fiddle and banjo. Whereas most Black people, like their African ancestors, regarded the two instruments as distinct traditions to be performed independently, initially some Blacks and later large numbers of whites began combining the two instruments in performance. Because of the widespread popularity of minstrelsy and the role of these two instruments in the performance, the fiddle-banjo combination became an institution that influenced Black and white creativity in various ways.

Though immensely popular with both Blacks and whites, fiddling had many critics. In addition to some whites thinking that participating in the activity was evil, sinful, and an act of resistance, both Blacks and whites believed fiddling encouraged behavior that was "un-civilized" (or African). Interestingly, the fiddle was never outlawed, like the drum, because of fear of uprisings. Because the fiddle was important to the heritage of European Americans and some whites used musicking to control and increase economic productivity, fiddling among African Americans continued unabated in spite of its association with the profane. For some Black fiddlers, performing the instrument not only gave them a higher social status with some economic gains, fiddling was also used as an act of resistance against white domination.

When the United States is divided into four regions—northeast, southeast, mountains, and south-central—the findings are revealing. As white and Black people migrated and settled in different parts of the country during the early decades of the nineteenth century, they took their traditions with them. The place and with whom they settled affected musicking, but more importantly, the evidence suggests that the number of enslaved Blacks in various areas may have impacted fiddling. Examining the diversity of Black musicking through a regional lens, therefore, yields several insights.

One, not only do publications documenting nineteenth-century musicking in the Northeast contain few references to fiddling, the geographical scope of the sources is also limited to urban areas in New York state and Pennsylvania. This may reflect the small number of African Americans residing in the Northeast during this time period as well as the lack of interest on the part of writers in documenting the role of the fiddle in northern Black culture. African Americans' involvement with European-based concert or art music in the Northeast, even musicking originally created by Africans (which is beyond the scope of this study), may be another reason for the lack of information on Black fiddling during the nineteenth century (Trotter 1881; Southern 1997).[51]

Two, the areas with the largest number of enslaved Africans—the Lower Southeast and South-Central regions—have the largest number of sources on fiddling. In addition to performance context, opposition to fiddling on the part of both Black and white Protestants is another topic well represented in the literature. Catholics who resided in the South-Central regions tended to be more tolerant and placed little constraint on slaves' performance of the instrument. References to the gourd fiddle and Black people constructing their own instruments are more prominent in the Southeast and South-Central regions, suggesting the greater maintenance of Africanisms in areas where large communities of Blacks existed. Finally, using fiddling to control behavior and economic activity is examined more prominently in areas where large numbers of enslaved people resided.

Three, the demographics and social environment in the mountain regions, specifically the Appalachian Mountains, resulted in a shared culture and musical interchange between the races that seemed to be distinct from that in other parts of the South. Similarly, the role and performance of the fiddle in urban areas such as New York City, Cincinnati, and New Orleans, which included a fusion of old and new traditions, provide a basis for understanding developments in the twentieth century, especially in terms of repertoire, performance style, and ensemble organization.

Four, the fiddle was used in all facets of Black life. Fiddling at secular occasions and recreational events (frolics, weekend dances, holiday celebrations, corn shuckings and harvesting, parties, balls, weddings, dance halls, and street corners) for both Black and white people are to be expected. However, the fact that participants in African-derived religions such as Vodun used the fiddle in ceremonies suggests that the instrument's association with the spirit world, which was important for many groups in West Africa, had been maintained. Even folklore about Brer Rabbit playing the fiddle to call spirits and the fable about wolves in the forest being calmed by music performed by a Black fiddler demonstrate the mystical powers of fiddle music.

Finally, the literature indicates that there was something special in the way Black fiddlers performed. The ensemble organization was distinctive in that a variety of instruments or sound sources were used in combination with the fiddle, including those that were melodic (fifes, flute, banjo, clarinet, dulcimer) and percussive (bones, tambourines, triangle, drum sticks, animals' jaw or rib bones, handclapping, and occasionally drums). Writers' comments about playing technique and sound quality are especially interesting (see below).

a. "scraping their fiddle" (Berquin-Duvallon 1806, 26–27).
b. "scrape the fiddle" (Flint 1826, 345).
c. "sawing violins, harsh clarinets, jingling tambarines, crashing triangles, with the occasional climax of a *base* drum, make up in quantity what is deficient in quality" (Gilman 1838, 76–77).
d. "villainous squeaking" (Foster 1850, 54).
e. "scraping of the fiddles attracted us" (Russell 1861, 93–96).
f. "the music that he made was wrenched from all four of the strings at once, with little regard for anything but time and noise" (Thompson 1884, 20).
g. "scraped that hideous combination of banjo and violin" (Cable 1886b, 820)

In total, these findings confirm that although songs and tunes that Black fiddlers played at various music events (for both Black and white audiences) may have been based on music from European culture (Winans 1990), the manner in which African Americans performed the music was no doubt African-derived. In the following chapters, we will examine how these factors affected Black fiddling in different parts of the United States during the twentieth century.

fiddlingismyjoycompanion.net

Notes

1. As noted in chapter 2, I prefer to use the phrase "narratives by formerly enslaved people" or "narratives by the formerly enslaved" instead of "ex-slave narratives."

2. 🎻 See Map 3.1.

3. Instead of summarizing, I include quotes by the enslaved as well as others, which some may regard as extensive, because I believe this is a way to understand more intimately the perspective of those who experienced fiddling and were involved in the development of the tradition.

4. 🎻 See History 3.1.

5. 🎻 See Photo 3.2.

6. Because this is an online edition of Dickens (1913, 60–81), the exact page numbers for this quote are unknown.

7. Southern (1997, 126–27) believes Northup's experiences before his abduction may be typical of Black violinists trying to earn a livelihood from music making in the Northeast. In addition to his autobiography (Northup 1968), Northup's life has been documented in two films—*Solomon Northup's Odyssey* (Parks 1984) and *Twelve Years a Slave* (McQueen 2013)—that include much information about his ordeal as an enslaved person in Louisiana.

8. See Lingold (2013) for an interesting analysis of the musicking Northup may have performed during the time that he lived.

9. Because of differences in demographics and the cultural environment, I divide the Southeast into two sub-regions: Upper (Virginia, Maryland, and Washington, DC) and Lower (the Carolinas and Georgia).

10. 🎻 See History 3.2.

11. Although photo 3.3 dates to the late nineteenth century, it displays features described by Mack, and demonstrates that fiddlers continued to use whatever resources were available to them to construct fiddles; also see chapter 9 for a discussion of Earnest Mostella.

12. Although born in Georgia, Mack's account is included in the Mississippi Slave Narratives, probably because she migrated west after slavery. Later, in the narrative she indicates that in 1884, her father left home and did not return. She and her family members believe he returned to Africa as part of a religious mission (Mississippi Genealogical Web Slave Narrative Project 2006–2008).

13. Although Pierpont later worked as an attorney, merchant, and Unitarian minister, he is probably best known as a poet (Pierpont 1816).

14. One of the earliest descriptions of such a slave coffle comes from the letters of George Tucker (Tucker 1816; Epstein 1977, 177).

15. Although African mouth bow players sometimes produce a melody by beating the string of the mouth bow, "beating the straws" or "fiddlesticks" developed among the enslaved. It is an African American innovation (McCormick 1998).

16. During the early twentieth century, Atlanta not only became an important location for recording sessions by various record companies (including Columbia, OKeh, and Victor), but it was the base for Black fiddlers such as Eddie Anthony (ca. 1889–1936), who released several songs as a member of the group Peg Leg Howell and His Gang. Anthony's earliest recording with Howell took place in Atlanta on April 8, 1927 (Dixon and Godrich 1982, 343–44; Danser 2018).

17. Slave revolts began with enslavement and did not end until slavery was abolished. Although others occurred, the most noted were the Stono Rebellion of 1739 in South Carolina; the planned Denmark Vesey rebellion of 1822 in South Carolina; and Nat Turner's revolt in Virginia in 1831 (Franklin 1980, 153; Smith 2001, 2005).

18. Although Epstein (1977, 159) as well as Southern and Wright (1990, 74 Item 645) indicate that the name of the county is "Norry," the county's name as listed in the *World Book Encyclopedia* is "Horry." As part of South Carolina's Low Country, Horry is located in the northeastern portion of the state on the Atlantic Coast (Kovacik and Rogers 1987, 648).

19. Brice's experience is not very different from the situation among the Dagbamba in northern Ghana, where fiddlers are admired because of their attachment to royalty and access to wealth (DjeDje 2008a, 183–84).

20. Although born in Clarendon County, South Carolina, Manning built Millford Plantation in 1839 near Pinewood, a town in Sumter County where he lived most of his life. The 1860 Slave Census Schedule indicates that John Manning owned 670 enslaved Blacks, making him the sixth largest slaveholder at that time (Geni n.d.).

21. Caroline Howard Gilman was born in Boston. After she and her husband, Samuel Gilman (a Unitarian pastor) married in 1819, they moved to Charleston, South Carolina (Gilman 1838).

22. 🎻 See Map 3.2a, Map 3.2b, Map 3.2c, Map 3.2d, and History 3.3.

23. Minimal research has been conducted on Black fiddling in rural mountain communities west of Appalachia and the Ozarks, most likely because few African Americans lived in these

areas. Southern (1997, 340) comments briefly about George Morrison, a bandleader in Denver, Colorado, who organized a boy's string band for dances in mining camps in mountain towns during the early 1900s. Also, some researchers have investigated Lewis Alexander Southworth (1830–1917) in the Northwest United States, who discovered that he could make more money teaching violin and playing for dance schools rather than mine for gold in Oregon (McLagan 2009; Williams 2009; Baldwin 2021; Meiner 2021). The fact that Southworth was de-churched by members of his community because they believed the violin "was full of wicked things and belonged to the devil" demonstrates that negative attitudes about fiddling continued in different parts of the country (Marshall 2012, 113–14).

24. From his research in the Cumberland Mountains, Fulcher (1988a, 3) learned that the fiddle (normally played without accompaniment) was the most popular instrument in Tennessee before the Civil War and remained so when other instruments appeared.

25. Since the artist titled his sketch "Lynchburg Negro Dance," this implies that he visited the town with this name. Located in Bedford County, Virginia, Lynchburg, according to Dunaway (2003b), is part of the Appalachian Mountains.

26. Handy's father, Charles Barnard Handy (b. ca. 1849), married Elizabeth Brewer (b. ca. 1853) in 1872, which suggests that Handy's relatives on his mother's side of the family—grandfather, Christopher Brewer (b. ca. 1834), and her brother, Whit Brewer—were the musicians involved in fiddling.

27. Visual images using Dickey's description can be found in: Dickey (1835, 13); Dresser (1836, 6–7); Carleton (1864b, 96–97); Epstein (1977, 49); Southern and Wright (1990, 12 Item 92; 10 Item 76; and 57 Item 508); see discussion in Carleton (1864a).

28. The Snowdens had nine children, but only seven survived childhood: Sophia (ca. 1842–1878), Benjamin (1846–1920), Martha (1849–1851), Phebe (b. ca. 1849), Lewis (1853–1923), Annie (1855–1870), and Elsie (1857–1872) (Sacks and Sacks 2002, 11–12).

29. Several sources include evidence of whites crediting Blacks for teaching them how to play the fiddle. Tom Collins, an Ohio River flat boatman who wrote a journal describing his experiences on the rivers in Appalachia between 1849 and 1873, indicates that he learned to play the fiddle "from blacks and heard varied forms of music played by different ethnic and racial groups" (Milnes 1999, 96).

30. To learn more about Ernest Mostella's work as a fiddle maker, see Mathews (2008, 2023).

31. 🎻 See Map 3.3 and History 3.4.

32. In comparing enslavement among Native Americans and white slaveholders, Clay believed life was more bearable with the former because Blacks had more freedom and could worship in whatever manner they liked (Clay 1937, 79–86).

33. 🎻 Go to Tables (see Tables 1–3).

34. 🎻 See History 3.5.

35. 🎻 See Map 3.4. Beyond Alabama, the Black Belt refers to a region in the southern United States that includes more than 600 counties in eleven states. It was once named for the color of its fertile soil and later for the high percentage of African American residents (Black Belt 2017).

36. Although Abraham Lincoln issued the Emancipation Proclamation on September 22, 1862, with the effective date of January 1, 1863, for the enslaved to be free, the order announcing the emancipation of African Americans in Texas did not take place until June 19, 1865. To commemorate this announcement, Black people in Texas began celebrating Independence Day or Freedom Day on Juneteenth (the combining of "June" and "nineteenth"), and in 2021, the US Congress approved legislation that made Juneteenth a federal holiday.

37. The state of Louisiana is divided into parishes just as most states within the United States are divided into counties.

38. Also, see Minton (1996a, 300–301).

39. To have a white dance orchestra provide entertainment for a white-only affair was sometimes a novelty in New Orleans. In 1834, for example, the promoter of a great ball made a special appeal to the New Orleans elite by promising the performance of a new band, fresh from Europe, which obviously was a white group (Southern 1983a, 135).

40. Henry (2018a, 5, 10) indicates that Jeff Lusk, an enslaved person from Middle Tennessee's Warren County, was sent to New Orleans by his slaveholder during the 1840s to learn to play the fiddle.

41. William Wells Brown (1880, 121–22) reports that on Sundays at Congo Square, "different tribes of negroes [Kraels, Minahs, Congos and Mandringas, Gangas, Hiboas, and Foulas], named after the section of the country from which they came," and "not less than two or three thousand people would congregate to see the dusky dancers" (Also, see Southern 1997, 136–37).

42. Although Cable's findings are based on secondary sources, most researchers do not question his interpretation of the data, probably because they found evidence of similar practices or believed his methodology credible. Harold Courlander (1963) agrees "that the banjo was not the favorite musical instrument of Negroes in the region, the favored instrument being the fiddle" (213).

43. *Merriam-Webster* (2014) defines quadroon as "a person of one-quarter Black ancestry," while octoroon refers to "a person of one-eighth Black ancestry." Mulatto has several definitions. However, the two most relevant to this discussion include: (1) "the first-generation offspring of a black person and a white person" or (2) "a person of mixed white and black ancestry."

44. Both drawings were created by Edward Winsor Kemble (1861–1933), a US visual artist. Although Kemble worked for several nineteenth- and early twentieth-century magazines and newspapers, he is probably best known for illustrating later editions of Harriet Beecher Stowe's *Uncle Tom's Cabin* (1852), Mark Twain's *Adventures of Huckleberry Finn* (1884), Washington Irving's *Knickerbocker History of New York* (1891), as well as many of Joel Chandler Harris's *Uncle Remus* stories (1881). Some researchers have been reluctant to use such images in their publications because they are based on the artist's imaginations (Epstein 1977, xviii). At this stage in documenting the history of Black fiddling in the United States, I believe all representations of the fiddle in print (fiction and nonfiction), sound, and visual are important in assessing their meaning and value. In including them, this does not mean they will not be critically evaluated.

45. The term *Voodoo* is a corruption of Vodou (Vodun or Vodoun), the Haitian religion that is based on the beliefs and traditions of the Fon people of Dahomey (present-day Republic of Benin) and other ethnic groups in West and Central Africa. Specifically, Vodou synthesizes African spirits with Catholic saints, resulting in multiple identities for popular religious figures (Brown 2005).

46. However, the description for photo 3.8 is confusing because it indicates that one person (a white-wooled old man) performs a "combination of banjo and fiddle," which is impossible to do if both instruments are performed simultaneously. Therefore, we can only assume that the "old man" plays the two instruments sequentially, rather than simultaneously (Cable 1886b, 820).

47. 🎻 See History 1.1. The resonator used for the bowed lute (*rabab*) in Northeast Africa and West Asia (or the Middle East) varies in shape. While some are quadrangular, others are hemispherical (Poche 2001). Almost all are performed with the fiddle held in a vertical position, similar to the instrument in Cable (1886b, 816). Noteworthy is not so much the accuracy of the image's visualization, but the fact that the author and the artist are clearly making it known that this is not a tradition or an instrument associated with European culture.

48. Kemble's drawing, titled "In the Store," of the instrumental ensemble in Smalley's article is different from those in Cable's "Creole Slave Songs." In Smalley's article, the drawing displays three male instrumentalists—one playing a western cello, one playing the accordion, and another playing the triangle (image of the triangle player is unclear because he is sitting in the background). If one had to rely solely on Kemble's drawing to understand what is stated in the text, the reader would be at a loss, because the instrumental ensemble accompanying the dancer in the drawing includes no fiddle (Smalley 1887, 109).

49. Northup was initially sold "to a Mr. [William Prince] Ford who resided in Rapides Parish, Louisiana, where he was taken and lived a little more than a year, and worked as a carpenter" (Kidnapping Case 1853, 1). Later, Northup was purchased by Mr. [John M.] Tibaut who, in 1843, "sold him to Edwin Eppes [sic] in Bayou Beouf, about one hundred and thirty miles from the mouth of Red River, where he worked on a cotton plantation" (1). When Northup wrote a letter

to friends in New York [in 1852] and informed them of his enslavement, he stated: "I wish you to obtain free papers for me, and forward them to me at Marksville, Louisiana, Parish of Avoyelles" (1). Also see Solomon Northup (2021).

50. In an interview conducted by Mack McCormick on May 5, 1961, in Navasota, Texas, Mance Lipscomb states the following about his father: "Well I used to hear my granddaddy tell them tales of slavery. But my father he wasn't born in slavery, he just missed it—he was Texas born and he lived till he was ninety-year old" (Govenar and Lornell 2019, 72).

51. When researchers began conducting research on Africans in the Americas, many investigated retentions and survivals while others focused on the appropriation of European elements. For the Northeast, interest in the musicking of Black people on Pinkster Day and 'Lection Day reflected interest in the retentions. Examining the musicking of Frank Johnson or Elizabeth Taylor Greenfield (also known as the Black Swan) satisfied the curiosity of those interested in appropriation of European musicking by African Americans. Information on these topics can be found in works by Trotter (1881) and Southern (1997).

SECTION 2

EARLY TWENTIETH CENTURY
The Decline in Prominence of Black Fiddling

Introduction

Fiddling was one of the most prominent instrumental traditions in both rural and urban Black communities in the South at the beginning of the twentieth century. In addition to the fiddle being used in a variety of contexts, those skilled in playing the instrument were expected to have an enormous repertoire. But what fiddlers created and performed also depended on the musical tastes of their audiences, and how these individuals had been affected by time (history) and place (geography). Features identified with the nineteenth century not only remained intact longer in rural areas, but differences between rural and urban environments became more apparent as social changes occurred in the larger society.

Like numerous studies on Anglo-American fiddling that are organized according to geography, partly because of differences in the social history and physical environment of states as well as the cultural background and ethnicity of residents, a similar approach is used here. The only difference is that information for several states is contained in one work. Thus, the material is divided into four parts: (1) Central Appalachia and neighboring regions, (2) Southern Appalachia and neighboring regions, (3) the Ozarks, and (4) the Atlantic and Gulf coasts and neighboring regions. What was presented as one geographical area (the mountains) in the pre–twentieth century has now been divided into three parts—Central Appalachia, Southern Appalachia, and the Ozarks—because the evidence demanded that changes needed to be made in the presentation of the material. In other words, the uniqueness and distinctions of people who lived in various areas needed to be more carefully examined to demonstrate the diversity of the Black experience. In addition to examining diversity, it is important to be aware of what is common, if anything, to all groups and traditions. And this can only be done by digging deeper into the different regions to understand what makes them distinctive and similar. By organizing the material in this way, hopefully, we will be able the address the question: why did some continue to perform the instrument when others abandoned it?

Section Two begins with chapter 4, which includes an overview of Black rural culture to provide a context for discussing issues related to Black fiddling and secular music in the early twentieth century. While chapters 5 through 8 focus on Central Appalachia (Maryland, Virginia, West Virginia, Kentucky, Tennessee, and North Carolina), chapter 9 gives attention to Southern Appalachia (South Carolina, Georgia, Alabama, and Mississippi)[1] and chapter 10 to the Ozarks (Missouri). Fiddling among African American musicians who lived along or near the South Atlantic (Virginia, North Carolina, South Carolina, Georgia) and the Gulf (Florida, Alabama, Mississippi, Arkansas, Louisiana, and Texas) is examined in chapters 11 and 12.

Each chapter is organized similarly. After a brief discussion of the status of research, a profile of selected fiddlers in that particular state is presented with special attention given to socio-musical issues such as family and community, learning, performance contexts, the media, creativity, performance practices, and Black/white interactions. This is done to assess how their life experiences and musicking compare with fiddling locally and in other parts of the United States. Unfortunately, some unevenness exists in the discussion because information on some fiddlers is scant. To assist readers in understanding the significance of time and place, information about the history, demographics, and physical environment of various regions and states can be found in the companion material on eScholarship and is noted in the text with the symbol of a fiddle (🎻).

fiddlingismyjoycompanion.net

Notes

1. The subdivision for the Appalachian Mountains is based on information in the Appalachian Regional Commission; see http://www.arc.gov/appalachian_region/MapofAppalachia.asp. Accessed April 12, 2017. Although I am aware of the work of agriculturalists such as Yarnell (1998), my designation or use of Southern Appalachia as a region is based on the musicking and cultural traditions I have identified in my research on Black fiddling. The neighboring piedmont regions are also included in the discussion.

CHAPTER 4

Black Fiddling and Secular Music in the Rural South

The beginning of the twentieth century was a time of great hope and aspirations for most people in the United States. The country had become one of the major industrialized nations in the world with a productive capacity far beyond its own needs. Like other US citizens, the dreams of African Americans soared because they believed the worst—slavery, Jim Crow laws, and other injustices—was behind them. Many also thought that political changes in Washington, DC, would make a difference. Not until Theodore Roosevelt Jr. (1858–1919) was far into his second term as president of the United States[1] did Black people realize that his friendship was neither systematic nor sustained, that the difficulties they experienced in earlier years would plague them into the twentieth century (Franklin 1980, 308–10).

Similar to the past, racism was the biggest problem. The right to human dignity was just as elusive as it had been in former times, and discrimination in housing, employment, and education was rampant. To survive the hostility and denigration, numerous African Americans made concerted efforts to change their lives and the world around them by migrating from rural to urban areas in the United States.[2] While large numbers in southern states moved to the Northeast, Midwest, and West Coast,[3] those who remained in the South settled in the coal-mining mountain regions or nearby southern cities. A few relocated further south to Florida.[4]

The settlement pattern for rural southern Blacks during the first half of the twentieth century did not change drastically from the nineteenth century. While large numbers lived along the Atlantic and Gulf coasts and some piedmont regions, Black populations were smaller in the Appalachian and Ozark mountains. This is significant because Black people who remained in the South tended to hold on to living patterns, institutions, and traditions from the past much longer—not because they wanted to resign themselves to hardships. Rather, most believed that as long as the situation did not become worse, it was tolerable. Furthermore, independent rural communities provided islands of normalcy, which often protected them from the debilitating persecution they had experienced in earlier years (Foster 2020).

To provide a context for discussing Black fiddling during the early twentieth century, this introductory chapter is divided into two parts: (1) Black life in the rural South and (2) Black fiddling and secular music in the rural South. While the first part focuses on two geographical regions (the mountain/piedmont and the coast), allowing for comparisons with developments in the pre–twentieth century (see chapter 3), issues related to research on Black fiddling and secular music are examined in the second. Because few studies on rural Black secular culture and musicking exist, the information presented is based on limited historical and ethnographic data, specifically materials collected by myself and others, as well as published accounts by folklorists and music enthusiasts with interests in both blues and non-blues traditions.

Black Life in the Rural South

Industrialization and growth in the coal mining industry had a major impact on rural southern culture, particularly in Appalachia. Since Native Americans (the indigenous inhabitants of the region) had been relocated west during the long and arduous Trail of Tears, Appalachia had become primarily white by the late nineteenth century. However, the new coal mining industry needed people to bring coal to the surface, and there were not enough local Appalachian residents to fill the mine shafts, nor could outlying regions of Appalachia provide enough laborers. Therefore, Appalachian coal operators and owners began recruiting millions of workers from Europe to work in the mines (Jackson 2006, 28). In the end, three groups made up the coal mining work force: white people who had lived in the region since the early eighteenth century; newly arrived immigrants from southern and eastern Europe; and recently freed Black people who had lived there previously as well as those who migrated from other parts of the South after slavery ended.[5]

The lifestyle of African Americans in mountain regions often differed from that of Blacks in other parts of the South and the North during the early twentieth century. Similar to the slave era, the small number of Blacks and close contacts with whites resulted in a shared culture. Although each context is distinct, the situation in West Virginia[6] helps to explain reasons for differences. During Reconstruction, many Blacks left Virginia for West Virginia initially to work on the railroad, but remained there to work in the coal mines. While economics was the primary stimulus for settling in the state, better schools as well as greater opportunities for civic and personal liberty, travel, and a desire for new experiences were all reasons Blacks remained in West Virginia during the early twentieth century (Laing 1985, 71–72). Similar explanations can be given for Blacks who settled in the piedmont along the Eastern Seaboard. Bastin (1986) states: "The shifts in population and their attendant lifestyles, seen in the growth of Atlanta and the depletion of smaller communities within easy migration distance, were simply part of the broader pattern of experience within the Piedmont belt" (29).

In the mountains, family ties among Black people were generally strong.[7] In comparison to other southern states where Blacks had little access to education, Black children in mountain areas attended school and remained there through high school. Because recreational facilities were lacking, much of the leisure time was spent with family, friends, and co-workers; music also provided an escape from the mines (Laing 1985, 74–75; Brady 2013, 110). In most cases, Black and white miners worked side by side inside coal mines. Segregation either by occupation or place of work, unlike most factory industries in the South and North, was conspicuously absent in coal mining communities. Since both groups received equal pay in the same positions, this economic togetherness contributed to fewer racial problems (Corbin 1985, 94–96; Laing 1985, 76–77). Because women did not work in the mines, all were housewives and mothers. "Unlike the situation in the northern industrial areas, the black male in the southern West Virginia company town was always the breadwinner"[8] (Corbin 1985, 96–97).

Housing, a major problem for Blacks in the North, was less of an issue in the mountains. Whereas Black northerners were jammed together in the worst houses, forced to pay excessively high rent, and suffered from an inequality of public services, Black migrants in coal mining towns never experienced overcrowding because companies regulated the influx according to the needs of a work force and the availability of houses (Corbin 1985, 97–99).[9] Politically, the situation for southern miners and northerners also differed. After settling in the North, some Black migrants found that politics could serve as a source for protection, prestige, and mobility. Ambitious Blacks became party bosses due to their ability to exploit residential voting blocs in Black neighborhoods. Black Appalachians also used the political system to their advantage, but in a different manner. According to Corbin (1985), "Blacks were elected to state offices and won considerable concessions from the Republicans, including state colleges for blacks, several state orphanages, and the formation of the Bureau of Negro Welfare and Statistics. Blacks were appointed to national as well as state offices. And blacks became political bosses in several commercial towns" (103).

Although race relations in most coal mining towns tended to be intimate and friendly, interaction between the races was not without tensions.[10] In response to the cultural diversity, resentment, prejudices and stereotypes about immigrants became commonplace among white residents. Many of the new arrivals from Europe suffered not only the hardship of working in the coal mines but were also despised, and sometimes cruelly beaten or even slain by white Appalachians (Jackson 2006, 29–30, Straw 2006, 12–15). Racial stereotyping also occurred and some degree of spatial separation was informally enforced. "White and black musicians might jam in one another's homes, but following a jam in a white man's parlor, a black musician would expect to eat alone in the kitchen. Evening and weekend dances featuring black and white performers commonly took place in schoolhouses; during the day, of course, the education system itself was carefully segregated. Dance halls and road houses might accept mixed-race performance ensembles, but even the rough ones . . . would have drawn the line at mixed-race couples" (Brady 2013, 111–12).

Furthermore, interaction, in itself, does not always lead to mutual respect. Although contact occurred, the experience may have been what some scholars refer to as labeled interaction, "the phenomenon where a discriminated group in its relations with the rest of society is expected to act according to a specific label or code"[11] (Kloosterman and Quispel 1990, 152). While aspects of labeled interaction existed among Blacks and whites in most parts of the southern United States during the early twentieth century,[12] the degree to which it affected musicking varied within each community (Otto and Burns 1974). As Sam Phillips, a southern white businessman who "discovered" Elvis Presley stated, "There was still a lot of hatred between the races in the South, but music was the one area where black and white were closer than people realized. The young whites loved [and appropriated] the black music they got to hear" (quoted in Kloosterman and Quispel 1990, 152).

Because many African Americans along the Atlantic and Gulf coasts lived in densely populated Black communities with some areas totally isolated from whites, their response to social conditions often differed from that of Blacks in the mountains.[13] In most cases, the agitation for social change and creation of an identity distinct from the dominant white population were more prominent and intense due to the adverse conditions in which people lived. Not only did the migration outside the South begin much earlier because economic opportunities locally were slow in developing, coastal Blacks moved to nearby urban areas more quickly, particularly if these cities provided greater options for advancement (Starks 1985).

Yet, differences also existed among coastal Blacks, especially among those who lived in the South-Central United States along the Gulf Coast. Besides greater variations in the physical environment and resources, the diversity of culture groups residing on the West Gulf Coastal Plain (Louisiana and Texas) accounted for the differentiation. Country music researcher Bill C. Malone (1979), who draws attention to the cultural diversity, states: "The westernmost portion of the south (Texas, Louisiana, Oklahoma) was peculiarly situated because of its ethnic and racial diversity, the presence of New Orleans there, the emergence of the oil boom, and the sway of the cowboy culture, to produce grass roots music forms of a hybrid nature. The region was heavily rural until World War II, but the presence of alternative cultures and competing economic systems contributed to the breaking down of traditional patterns earlier than in the southeastern states" (81).

Although Black people in all parts of the United States suffered socioeconomically, those in the South-Central states (Alabama, Mississippi, and Louisiana) seemed to have suffered more because little economic development took place in these regions, causing Blacks, who were the majority in their communities, to have little access to wealth.[14] By comparison, Blacks in the Southeast were a little better off financially not only because of the economic opportunities that existed in the states where they lived, but because fewer regions along the Atlantic Coast had majority Black populations (Lornell 1990, 221–22). The Mississippi Delta region is particularly noteworthy because its location along the Mississippi River, in some ways, makes it somewhat comparable to the Gulf Coast.

Black Fiddling and Secular Music in the Rural South

Just as many rural Blacks during the early decades of the twentieth century continued to perform sacred music such as hymnody and spirituals from the nineteenth century, the same was the case with secular musicking. The use of the fiddle for entertainment at occasions attended by African Americans persisted not only in small, isolated rural communities where the interaction between Blacks and whites was extensive, but also in areas where minimal contact occurred between the races. Simply put, some Black people, similar to slavery times, preferred fiddling for recreation instead of the new types of music emerging during the early twentieth century. Thus, the decline in the popularity of the fiddle among Blacks varied in time and location, and several factors motivated changes in taste. Whereas the literature suggests the decline was due to disapproval by those in Protestant religious circles, changes occurred for other reasons as well. When the fiddle-banjo instrumental tradition started to be regarded as old-fashioned and symbolic of white southern culture, many Blacks looked for other musical forms for entertainment and recreation. African Americans who settled in urban areas of the United States to improve their socioeconomic position and create a new identity also did not want representations from slavery (fiddle and banjo) in their new environment (Thomas 2007). The aesthetics of Black culture (such as the emphasis on innovation and experimentation) may have also precluded the survival of the fiddle, particularly in the northern and western United States, where greater emphasis was on change.

In spite of its decline, fiddling continued to be popular among Black people in certain areas of the country; but documentation of this musical tradition does not exist. The fact that minimal research has been conducted on African American non-blues secular music in rural areas of the United States raises several questions. Could the prominence of fiddling by rural Blacks be a reason for the neglect? Was the supposed lack of innovation on the part of Black musicians in the South a factor for the omission? To what extent did developments in the media (radio and recordings) and shared culture, particularly in mountain regions, affect interest in investigations?

Investigators who have conducted research in rural areas of the United States indicate that the fiddle was one of the most popular instruments performed by Black musicians before World War II. For example, Harold Courlander (1963) states: "Large numbers of old tunes that survived through the early twentieth century are called fiddle tunes, even though they were not played on the fiddle, and, in many rural regions, informants testify that the fiddle was once the essential requirement for a good-time dance" (214). The job of the fiddle was to keep the people who came to dance on the floor as long as possible by playing what they wanted to hear, surprising them with something new, and putting both kinds of songs into an order that set the pace for a marathon (Minton 2022, 12). Like the banjo, the fiddle appeared in various makeshift forms, often with a cigar box for a body, sometimes with two strings, or even one. Because of its prominence at secular events that included dancing, the fiddle was also one of the few instruments to be consistently associated with the devil, which may have played a role in some people's reluctance to participate in musical activities regarded as sinful (214).[15]

Mountain culture has always had a special appeal for investigators studying musicking in the United States because many believed the highlands acted as a giant cultural deep freeze, preserving old musical traditions longer than in other parts of the country (Wolfe 1982, 5). Similar to whites, the maintenance of traditions among mountain Blacks was significant. Isolated from new cultural forms that developed in other parts of the country during the early twentieth century, Black mountaineers were among the few to continue performing music that had been popular during the nineteenth century and earlier. What researchers chose to preserve, however, did not reflect the reality and variety of Appalachian culture so much as an image of the culture created and perpetuated by the workers themselves (Straw 2006, 10; Thompson and Hacquard 2009, 126–27). As Karida L. Brown (2018) explains, "African Americans for too long have been made invisible to the regional history of Appalachia. In scholarly works and the popular media alike, Appalachia is represented as poor, backward, and almost always white. However, thousands of African American families migrated during the early 1900s to the coalfields of West Virginia, eastern Kentucky, and eastern Tennessee" (6).

Partly because of larger numbers, more research has been conducted on the secular music of Blacks in coastal rural areas than on those living in the mountain and piedmont regions,[16] which, in my opinion, has affected what we know about Black musicking in the United States generally. Because Blacks on the coast were not physically isolated from innovative trends taking place during the early twentieth century and had greater access to new instruments (guitar) and the media (radio and records), many were motivated to establish a new identity, lifestyle, and music traditions (blues and jazz) that allowed them to be different from whites. This was particularly important in environments in which Jim Crow, racism, and segregation were rampant and on the rise. Traditions signifying old times, unattractive and distasteful to most coastal Blacks, were supported by many Black mountaineers. In other words, the latter appeared to be less resistant to change.

In an environment that emphasized difference, both the fiddle and the music identified with it lost its approval and support. As a result, Black fiddling tended to survive in communities where old-time music played on the fiddle and banjo was used for home entertainment. Black mountaineers also may not have readily discarded the fiddle and the music associated with it because social distancing between the races occurred more slowly. As social distance grew to physical and psychological distance, stereotyping became offensive. And when Blacks began to identify the fiddle and banjo with this stereotyping, the use of these instruments became less tolerable (Bastin 1986, 6, 14).

For individuals (primarily white scholars) conducting much of the research, not only was the new music emerging from Black communities *different* from their own, but many believed it to be exciting. While they may not have been driven by capitalist greed like record company executives, white researchers were interested in the exotic. And in their own backyard, the musicking of Native Americans, African Americans, and possibly rural white Americans, was about as close as they could get to traditions that were different.[17] Thus, it is not surprising that, for Black musicking, many of the investigations on blues and jazz have focused on the Gulf Coast, particularly the South-Central and Mississippi Delta regions, rather than the Atlantic Coast.[18] As noted in the foregoing, blues and jazz, the new music of the twentieth century, flourished initially in the Gulf Coast states because, as some researchers suggest, the history, demographics, and social environment of Blacks in these regions allowed for these creations to come into existence earlier than what occurred in other parts of the United States (Bastin 1986).

Except for Howard W. Odum (1911a, 1911b), Howard W. Odum and Guy B. Johnson (1925, 1926), and Thomas W. Talley (1922), few scholars investigated African American fiddling during the early decades of the twentieth century when it was most popular in rural Black communities. Researchers such as John and Alan Lomax at the Library of Congress as well as John W. Work III, a music scholar and professor at Fisk University, did not begin collecting materials on rural secular music, particularly fiddling, until the 1930s and 1940s. Dwight DeVane (1987) explains:

> Black fiddling is just a tradition that's been overlooked for any number of reasons, mostly because of our own feelings that this is an area that slaps of values that are Uncle Tom-ish. Why would Blacks ever want to deal with that kind of music after the nineteenth century? That's mostly why it hasn't been entertained. But it's been a very biased view on the part of most white folklorists and researchers not to perceive the tradition as something valuable. And there was this rich blues tradition that was flourishing. Why not look at the growth of something vital, changing, and dynamic rather than something that could be construed more as a relic that had been held on with no reason other than it being unnecessary baggage? Perhaps it wasn't ever viewed, by a lot of people, as a legitimate musical genre that had any growth potential or real meaning for Black people.
>
> The people doing the work many times were the liberals of the day, like Stetson Kennedy.[19] He was interested in a lot of Black traditions. But I don't think he was interested in fiddle music. I think he wanted to find the angrier lyrics of the day, which demonstrated the problems that existed in Black society. At that time, all the characters who were writing, literary people too, were trying to come to terms with the upheaval. I think it made sense that people who were attuned to social problems would want to document it.

Although African American scholars had great respect for Black musicians who performed string-band music, which may explain their regret in seeing the decline of the tradition, they did not believe the musicking was as melodically sophisticated as other musical forms created by Black people. These mixed views (or bias) may explain why secular musicking, or "the social song," was rarely investigated. Work III (1940) writes:

> ... the social song is rapidly passing out of existence. Certainly, very few, if any, are being created, and there are few occasions for their performance at all.... The popular dance songs of today, through the modern musical organizations [jazz bands], serve the needs of the revelers much more completely than the old folk song did.
>
> As much regretted as the decline of this body of song is the passing of the musical organization so loosely associated with it—the string bands. The string-band was made of a fiddle (violin), one or two mandolins, one or two guitars, and a double bass fiddle. Each instrument was played by a virtuoso and the original technique these men displayed was amazing. How these men, un-schooled in accepted methods of playing, could achieve such finish, such harmony, and such variety, is baffling....

The social songs can hardly be considered as rich and distinctive in melodic content as the spirituals or the blues, although the improvised accompaniment showed harmonic feeling superior to the spiritual and a development in rhythmic figures comparable only to that shown in the blues. . . . The melodies are not as interesting in structure and design as those of the other types of folk song. . . . This is due, probably, to the fact that they did not spring from deep emotional experience nor, originally, from serious attempts at description of events. Instead, they were created for dance purposes, and that fact explains the highly-developed rhythm of the accompaniment. I have not found a song of this class in waltz time. All of those I have encountered have been in duple and quadruple time, slow and fast, distinguished by rhythmic figures. (44–45)

In spite of the lack of interest by researchers, large numbers of Black fiddlers in rural areas continued to be active because, outside of family activities and the church, their musicking was the only entertainment available during the early twentieth century. Odum (1911a) indicates that rural Black musicians fell into three categories. *Songster* denoted anyone who regularly sang or created songs; *musicianer* referred to individuals who claimed to be expert with the banjo or fiddle; while *music physicianer* denoted a person, who traveled from place to place and possessed a combination of these qualities. Yet, it was the latter who was considered a professional (259). Govenar and Lornell (2019, 71) suggest that rural musicians during the early twentieth century could be divided simply between those who traveled and those who stayed put:

It was the rambler, the wanderer who brought the blues from one district to another, who . . . tended to get on record. . . . In contrast, the singers that remained in their local districts and who depended on their communities for casual employment, who were engaged in plantation or farm work for most of the year and who were available for entertainment at play-parties [house parties] and frolics, country suppers and the occasional camp meeting were the ones most overlooked by the record companies. Often their inaccessibility, the remoteness of their homes and the distance from the few main recording centers were sufficient for them to be omitted. But their greater stability and perhaps, lack of ambition contributed to their neglect.

Curiously, they were often the better singers and musicians, for being the principal source of entertainment for their communities they were subject to the challenge to produce new songs and to change their repertoires. The casual, itinerant musicians needed only to know a handful of songs or a string of blues verses to entertain the people at a casual supper before moving on.

A variety of secular musical idioms could be heard in rural Black communities during the early twentieth century: string band music that included fiddle, banjo, guitar, accordion, and other instruments; fiddle tunes and ballads performed during traveling shows and other occasions; fife and drum music; jug band music; non-blues forms from the nineteenth century; and blues.[20] The idioms were performed in a variety of contexts, which Odum (1911a, 258) divides into several categories: when large or small groups gathered together for a good time; when a lonely Black musician sat on his doorstep or by the fireside, playing and singing a song; when couples stayed out late at night entertaining themselves with love-songs and other lively celebrations; when groups gathered after church to sing light melodies; and when musicianers, music physicianers, and songsters gathered to perform music for special occasions, such as church and private socials, dances, and other social gatherings.

Because blues was one of the most important secular music genres to develop in African American culture around the turn of the twentieth century, its interrelationship with Black fiddling is significant, as will become apparent in this study.[21] In terms of its beginnings, most scholars believe blues first appeared in the South-Central states before developing in other areas. Bastin (1986) writes: "The blues, as a musical form . . . did not emerge everywhere at the same time. In some regions, perhaps in Mississippi, the blues probably emerged in the 1890s. . . . In the southeastern states the blues emerged only in the first decade of the twentieth century. . . . The impetus for this came largely from socio-historical events coinciding . . . with a greater availability of musical instruments, especially the guitar, and with a conscious reaction against certain aspects of black secular music of the nineteenth century" (7–8).

Blues was versatile in its performance and use. In addition to serving as a form of entertainment and music for dancing, it was a way of expressing certain feelings to an understanding audience both on a personal and universal level (Lowry 1977, 88). Blues lyrics allowed Blacks to comment on topics and issues they could never articulate in other public forums; thus, the blues musician was an important spokesperson on Black culture. Daphne Harrison (1993) writes: "The blues artist speaks directly of and to the folk who have suffered pain and assures them that they are not alone. . . . The essence of blues poetry, whether sung by women or men, is life itself—its aches, pains, grievances, pleasure, and brief moments of glory" (6). While many people view blues as a generic style with little differentiation, much diversity exists in the history and performance of the genre. According to Southern (1971a), "country blues represents the earliest type, the singing of one man to the accompaniment of his guitar. Later these men were accompanied by 'string bands' and 'jug bands'—the string bands consisting of fiddles, guitars, banjo, mandolins, and basses; the jug band using ordinary crockery jugs, banjos, harmonicas, mandolins, washboards, and kazoos (toy instruments)" (335–36).

During the genre's beginnings, only a few Black mountaineers performed blues because many believed it was unappealing (see discussion below). When performances of blues became more widespread in mountain and piedmont regions in the early twentieth century, some musicians incorporated the fiddle into the new music, while others only used the guitar for playing blues and reserved the fiddle for old-time music. Although Black audiences may have identified with blues lyrics and their meaning, blues in the early years tended to be a solo performance style, and most Black and white people who lived in the mountains preferred musical activities in which the group or family could participate. In comparing fiddling and blues traditions in early twentieth-century rural culture, DeVane (1987) states: "Fiddling is mostly a family-centered tradition. It is more akin to the dance music tradition whether it be line dance, square dance, flat-foot dancing, or any type of group dancing. And blues is anything but family-centered traditional music."

Younger people who used the guitar to perform the blues became attracted to the instrument because it was symbolic of a new generation and century. Creating something different from their ancestors was a major factor in the change. "Far from emerging mysteriously from the deeply rural areas . . . , it appears to have been associated with the city and urban life," while the fiddle and banjo retained their connotations with the country (Govenar and Lornell 2019, 54). Some researchers also believe that the rise of Pentecostalism in the Black church provided a new role for the guitar. While the fiddle was considered to be the devil's instrument, "the guitar . . . was 'new' and untainted. Its powerful rhythmic possibilities were ideally suited to the fervent singing and holy dancing which the new churches advocated. . . . The new churches . . . played a large part in the popularization of the instrument as well as providing a training ground for many young instrumentalists" (57). However, the guitar was not without its critics within some religious circles because of its association with the blues (Lomax 1993, 360–61). Gussow (2010a, 89) indicates that if the guitar was an emblem of racial modernity for many southern-born bluesmen, the instrument had a different symbolic association for Black southern Christians. For some religious folk, the guitar "was the fiddle all over again, but shiny and store-bought."

The introduction of the guitar had a major impact on the organization of groups that included the fiddle. "A single instrument [the guitar] provided the essentials of the music which the two-man team had previously supplied, the fuller range of the guitar supplying both the fiddle's melody and the banjo's rhythm" (Govenar and Lornell 2019, 56). Many songsters worked in pairs, and the transition from fiddle and banjo musicking to fiddle and guitar, banjo and guitar, two guitars and solo songsters had to be determined by the needs and resources of the communities as well as the capabilities of musicians (57).

In the mountains where the fiddle was most popular during the early twentieth century, geography played a significant role in its development. Since the physical landscape did not permit a lot of travel, influence, or contact with outsiders, there was much interaction among Black and white mountaineers. As Tony Russell (1970) explains: "neither tradition developed independently of the other; the races lived too close together, and each relied upon the other's support too much for any real cultural separation" (9). Thus, the audience for fiddle music was limited. "Often the highest praise a fiddler could receive was 'best in the county,' for in an age of poor roads and rough, hilly country, the width of a county often meant a hard day's journey" (Wolfe 1977b, 20–21).

Because of the close relationship that existed between mountain Blacks and whites during slavery, fiddle tunes and dance forms performed by the two groups were similar, to the degree that songs were oftentimes interchanged.[22] Lornell (1974, 25) states that certain banjo tunes played by whites are considered to be Black originally. Alan Lomax (1999) suggests the same for fiddle music: "The earliest records of slavery in Virginia show the importance of black fiddlers, dance callers, and banjo players in the musical life of the South. They helped to create the square dance music of the Southern frontier, to develop new styles for the fiddle, banjo, and guitar, and to lay the basis for modern country music.... This is the black music that preceded ragtime, jazz, and the blues."[23] In discussing interactions among the races in rural Kentucky, Wolfe (1982) writes: "Both blacks and whites worked in the mines in the area, and partially because of this there was a free interchange of ideas between black and white musicians as well" (110). Comments by Pete Lowry (1977) are significant, except for the fact that he, like many researchers, believes fiddling is a Euro-American tradition instead of one that Blacks and whites have shared since the time of slavery: "What we know . . . is that rags, jigs, and reels were the popular forms of music at the turn of the century. White and black traditions certainly interact, both in musical styles, as well as instruments—Whites borrowed blues and banjos from blacks; blacks borrowed ballads and fiddles from whites. Solo artists, as well as larger entourages, performed at social occasions like picnics, church suppers, and 'frolics.' Pianos were rarely available outside cities or churches, so the focus was on more mobile instruments. Guitars, banjos, fiddles, harmonicas—alone or together—predominated" (94).

Acknowledging the similarities, a few researchers argue that the two traditions should be regarded as one. Winans (1979) states: "Traditional American banjo/fiddle music is unique to neither blacks nor whites, but is shared by them. Perhaps the entire tradition is 'common stock.' I do not mean to imply that the similarities are due merely to blacks having absorbed a white musical tradition. I repeat my belief that the black/white exchange in this tradition has been a two-way street. Traditional American banjo/fiddle music is as much an Afro-American tradition as an Anglo-American one" (27). Actually, Winans is reiterating a point Russell (1970) made several years earlier: "The traditional music of the countryman was a repertoire shared by black and white; a common stock. Some tunes or songs might be associated by some of their users with one race rather than the other, but most would have no racial connotations" (26). The type of group that performed the music was not a factor. It could be a solo singer, with or without instrumental accompaniment, a duet, trio, quartet, or combination of any size brass band, string band, or jazz band. Most important was the function of the music for group entertainment, particularly at dances (26–27).[24]

The repertoire of rural musicians was developed in various ways. Many musicians acquired their repertoire from listening to traveling musicians and the media. Wolfe (1981) explains: "Medicine shows were popular in Tennessee well into the 1930s and were a musical medium which both black and white folk musicians shared; these traveling shows undoubtedly played an important role in black and white interchange of songs, jokes, and stories" (113). Russell (1970) indicates that "while tent shows in some areas may not have played to integrated audiences, broadcasts and records could not be subjected to racist controls, except in so far as many blacks could not afford a radio or phonograph. And in the crowd at a carnival, or before a medicine show platform, though the black man might have to stand at the back, he was still in earshot of the music" (30). Expanding on the media's role in sharing, Patrick Huber (2013) states: "In terms of their actual consumption patterns, southern record buyers of the 1920s were far more omnivorous than record company executives generally seemed to comprehend, and interviews with elderly black and white musicians reveal that many of them purchased records intended specifically for sale in other racial and even foreign-language ethnic groups. Still much of this appears to have been lost on talking-machine firms, which focused their promotional efforts on marketing race records to African Americans and hillbilly records to rural and working-class white southerners" (49–50).

Common stock songs can be organized in a variety of ways. Using lyrics, Russell (1970) suggests several thematic groupings and gives examples of songs for each: (1) ballads of hero or antihero ("John Henry" and "Joe Turner"), gamblers ("Jack O' Diamonds" and "Honey Babe Let the Deal Go Down"), low life ("Salty Dog" and "All Night Long"), and adultery; (2) the locomotive and themes of separation, loneliness, and homesickness ("Going Down That Road Feeling Bad"); and (3) tender songs ("Corrine Corrina"). Instrumental tunes for fiddle and the banjo, based on musical rather than lyric similarities, "draw on a huge collection of couplets and quatrains that are nearly all interchangeable from piece to piece" (28). Although several pieces by jazz composers are now regarded as common stock, the majority of tunes fall into what is known today as country or old-time music—for example, "Arkansas Traveler," "Bile Them Cabbage Down," "Buffalo Gal," "It Ain't Gonna Rain No More," "Leather Britches," "Old Hen Cackle," and "Sourwood Mountain" (28). Yet, Winans believes common stock songs "may be even more extensive than two or three times Russell's list" (28).[25]

The unique characteristics and diverse repertoire of Black fiddling can be seen in tunes performed by William Adams, a Black fiddler Mike Seeger met in 1953 in the Maryland piedmont region. Seeger (1997) states: "He had played for both Anglo- and African-American country dances, and his repertoire was quite broad. He played his own version of Irish tunes as well as other pieces that might be unique to his regional rural African-American culture. He had a distinctive repertoire and had certainly been a really good fiddler" (5). From my analysis of musicking by several Black fiddlers active during the early twentieth century (below), the tunes can be placed into four categories: (1) songs created in the United States that are common stock, most likely developed as a result of interactions between Blacks and whites; (2) songs that are European-derived but performed in a style unique to the Black fiddler; (3) songs derived or originated from African American culture regionally; (4) songs that are original creations by the Black fiddler.

Although both Black and white fiddlers played a role in the development of repertoire, elements identified with their respective cultural heritages are the factors that distinguished performance style. The use of rhythm, particularly offbeat phrasing or syncopation, bent (or blue) notes, and certain melodic ornaments reflect African influence. Jabbour (1985; 1996, 254; 2002, 56) argues that emphasis on rhythm and percussion accounts for the use of syncopation in the bowing styles of both Black and white fiddlers in the Upper South.[26] He rules out the fact that this may have been a phenomenon that came about with the advent of radio and commercial hillbilly recordings around the 1920s. Rather, he believes it began during the revolutionary period of the late eighteenth and early nineteenth centuries. In terms of the construction of the instrument itself, early twentieth-century African American fiddlers are known to have inserted objects into the resonator of their fiddles to produce a percussive sound aesthetic very similar to that used by West African fiddlers[27] (Soileau and Bellard 1993; Tisserand 1998, 74; Marshall 2012, 133; DjeDje 2008a, 31).

Melodies produced from the bowing of both Black and white fiddlers also suggest African influence. Wolfe (1981) writes "Before the late 1920s many fiddlers in the area, especially in the mountains, used a short 'jiggy bow' style in their fiddling. This latter technique yielded a style that was highly rhythmic, driving, and a bit rough; it demanded more action from the bowing hand as opposed to the fingering. Conversely, the long-bow technique . . . involved less drive but produced a smoother, clearer tone; each note was made distinctly, the bow seldom left the strings, and much of the work consisted in noting as opposed to bowing" (115). The words scrape, jiggly, jiggety, jiggy, and sawing to describe the performance style of Blacks are all terms used in nineteenth- and early twentieth-century descriptions to indicate that the bowing used by Black fiddlers was anachronistic or improper. For some Black and white fiddlers, this type of bowing was regarded as crude, rough, and nonprofessional as opposed to the smooth, clearer sound that is considered to be acceptable and expected of Western-trained violinists. In terms of ensemble organization and the role of performers in ensembles, topics that have not been considered by researchers, much of the Black fiddling during the early twentieth century seemed to have included the voice, but this may have varied with the individual. In addition, most Black string bands included only one fiddle, which is different from many of the white string bands that used more than one fiddle (Winans 1979, 23).

Media products published by record companies during the first few decades of the twentieth century greatly affected musicking in Black and white rural communities. The earliest commercial recordings by African Americans that were released during the late nineteenth century document a variety of musical styles and performances by Black artists, but none represent secular music from rural areas and only a few include representation of Blacks in urban areas playing the violin/fiddle.[28] To my knowledge, the earliest commercial recording of Blacks performing secular music (such as ragtime and various types of dance music) on the fiddle/violin are those made by the James Reese Europe's Society Orchestra in New York City in 1913–14 that included a full section of four or five fiddlers. A recording by violinist Joseph Douglass, the grandson of Black freedom fighter Frederick Douglass, who had been trained in the performance of European art music,[29] was made in 1914 but never released (Southern 1997, 309–11). W. C. Handy's first recording (on Columbia Records in 1917) included several African Americans (Edward Alexander, Darnell Howard, and William Tyler) playing fiddle (Rust 1978, 665). The first release of a recording with blues in the title (Mamie Smith singing "Crazy Blues" in 1920) included Black violinist Leroy Parker, who played on many of Smith's recordings.[30] The demand for "Crazy Blues" in Black communities "was so enormous that OKeh realized for the first time the vast potential market among blacks for blues and blues-jazz. In the summer of 1921 the company established its OKeh 'Original Race Records'"[31] (Southern 1997, 370).

The earliest recording of white old-time music that included the fiddle did not occur until 1922 (Lornell 1989, 3–4).[32] Thus, it was not until the early 1920s that the media took an interest in music from rural areas. It was also during this period that record companies began to associate the fiddle and the fiddler with certain characteristics. Wolfe (1997) explains: "As the new music struggled to emerge from its regional bounds . . . , the fiddle became a key instrument in its image. The guitarist was an accompanist, keeping rhythm and backing singers; the banjoist, in those pre-bluegrass days, was a comedian. Only the fiddler was a really serious instrumentalist, the one who kicked off the tune, played the melody, took the breaks, drove the band. It was always assumed that the fiddle was the hardest of the folk instruments to play and that the fiddler was the most serious artist in the classic Southern stringband" (xvi). To market and sell the hillbilly and race series, "mail order was important, since many people living in rural areas found it convenient and often necessary to shop by way of the postal system. Furniture stores were a natural outlet for records because they sold the wind-up Victrola upon which the discs were played" (Lornell 1989, 34).

Even though white musicians made the first recordings of string band music and the media marketed the music primarily to the white community, string bands continued to be popular in "the black community during the early twentieth century, and such entourages existed all over the South. A few interracial groups are remembered in North Carolina, and practically every county had a string band of each race. And although their music was almost totally ignored by the recording industry,[33] it enjoyed a great degree of popularity within the communities" (Lowry 1977, 99). Wolfe (1987a) indicates that there are only about fifty commercial prewar recordings that really reflect Black fiddling, "as opposed to some 20,000 prewar records of blues and gospel music. In the 1930s, when the Library of Congress got into the field, recorders were more open-minded, but their equipment was woefully inadequate for recording a full string band" (17). T. DeWayne Moore (2021d) believes Wolfe's figures are too low, but agrees that "the number of prewar commercial recording of Black string-band music is still small even if we count all fiddle-based bands, including duos, trios, and jug bands. That puts us at five hundred records, and the actual number may be closer to one thousand" (382).[34]

When this music became available on commercial recordings during the 1920s, record company executives used the term "hillbilly" or "old-time" to signify fiddle and string band music performed by whites, while music identified with African Americans (blues, jazz, religious music, and other forms) was marketed as race music. Therefore, when Blacks performed string band music that sounded white, their music was also referred to as hillbilly. In later years, *hillbilly* began to refer to a musical genre or style. By the mid-twentieth century, the labels *country* and *old-time* replaced hillbilly. In the 1960s and 1970s, the terms *pre-blues* and *non-blues* started to be used by researchers to differentiate blues from other secular styles created and performed during the early twentieth century.[35] Yet, Bruce Bastin (1986) believes the term pre-blues is a misnomer because it fails to inform that nineteenth-century music "persisted throughout the period of commercial blues interest and did not simply pre-date it. Popular black secular music did not follow a simple chronological and stylistic path at all" (346).[36]

The misrepresentation of Black music by the media not only affected the development, history, and scholarship on African American music, but also general knowledge about musicking in the United States (DjeDje 2016). Oliver (1984b) indicates that if Black music had been more extensively recorded before 1920, our view of its history might be different, especially on how present-day forms link with traditions from the nineteenth century, how songs were learned and circulated, or "how important was blues before it was vigorously promoted by the record companies on their 'Race records,' issued in segregated lists?" Because rural musicians, including fiddlers, were not commercially recorded, researchers placed greater emphasis on the contributions of professionals instead of ordinary musicians who were the source of most musical activity.

Bastin (1978) states that the "secular music of rural blacks was the talent of the common man and seldom the prerogative of professionals.... This does not mean that the music was inferior because it was not recorded, and the belief that only the very best artists were recorded ought by now to be seen as an understandable but significant blunder" (3).

Radio and recordings affected the development of rural secular music in several ways. One, the lack of media representation affected regional variations. When performers attempted to emulate what they heard on recordings, regional differences declined as the playing styles of musicians began to sound the same. Not only did differences blur and more fusions take place, instrumental and song traditions that were rarely performed fell out of use altogether. This eventually led to certain styles or genres becoming more popular than others in various communities. Two, the media gave a biased picture of Black music, as the recording industry was governed by commercial considerations. It was blues that hit it big, which caused other forms virtually to disappear. With no example of the earlier music preserved on record or in print, it remains a hazy memory (Lowry 1977, 88–89, 92–93). Three, the media accelerated the process of change. As people listened to music on recordings, specific musical styles and individual musicians became more well-known and identifiable. Some musicians liked what they heard and began creating similar music (Rosenbaum 1983, xiv). Four, just as minstrel performers misrepresented Black music and performers by creating an imagined tradition, the same occurred with recorded sound. The type of materials used to promote recordings determined who would buy a particular product. "Whereas promotional materials for old-time music recordings pictured responsible-looking whites playing, dancing, and being jolly in more dignified settings, throughout the latter half of the nineteenth century materials depicting African American musicians were caricatured stereotypes. Watermelon patches and lazy African Americans lounging about, sometimes with banjos and in humorous situations, were often shown.... Blues was the musical expression of blacks, and old-time music became an expression of whites" (Milnes 1999, 106). In the end, "the younger generation of black musicians ignored string and country music and went into jazz, blues, and gospel. White country musicians continued to borrow sounds and songs from blacks well into the rock 'n' roll era.... But, after World War II, steel guitars and Nashville production dropped the string band content from country music" (Pahls 1985).

Social class or socioeconomic standing also affected the fiddle's decline in popularity. Fiddle music, like the blues, tended to be identified with people on the lower rungs of society. Although old-time music and blues were believed to have different heritages, both were considered to be low-class. Old-time music signified a backward mountain lifestyle, while blues was identified with Blacks who were believed to be lazy and unmotivated to work or do for themselves. Because these two musical genres departed from the ideals of European culture, they were both ostracized by Blacks of higher socioeconomic standing; upwardly mobile Blacks, in particular, did not want to participate in either fiddle or blues music activities. In the end, the fiddle, like the banjo, was eventually discarded among the Black populace. Yet, the blues grew in popularity and became the foundation for Black and white commercially popular music, probably because of its association with city life. A similar dynamic occurred with other musical instruments. While some instrumental ensembles were ostracized, others were tolerated. Although considered to be low-class, the jug band was one of the few instrumental ensembles from the nineteenth century that continued to be popular in small Black communities along the Atlantic and Gulf Coasts.[37] The instrumentation of jug bands varied. While some included instruments from the string family (fiddle, banjo, guitar, and/or mandolin), flute, and harmonica along with the jug, other jug bands were only composed of wind, percussion, and sometimes guitar; also see Kent (1997).

In summary, the emergence of new musical genres as well as modern ways in transmitting musicking to listeners not only affected performers and their audiences; the innovations greatly affected the interests of researchers. Almost all parties wanted to be involved in what was new and emerging rather than perform or document what had taken place in earlier years, which some regarded as insignificant or unworthy. As a result, information about Black fiddling and secular music in rural areas of the United States is scarce, which is one of the primary reasons fiddling is not identified with African American culture. Therefore, this study, particularly information presented in the chapters below, is important for providing evidence that will help us better understand the role of the fiddle in the Black community during the early twentieth century. An analysis of the data will also aid in discerning features unique to the tradition in different regions and bring to light factors that led to these trends.

fiddlingismyjoycompanion.net

Notes

1. Theodore Roosevelt Jr. was the twenty-sixth president from 1901 to 1909.
2. Urbanization, the movement of people from rural to urban areas, is often associated with access to greater economic opportunities; most people decide to live in urban areas not because of their climates, landmarks, or cultural attractions but because they offer jobs (Gurda 1999, vii).

3. "The movement of millions of African Americans from rural communities in the South to urban areas in northern, midwestern, and western states during the 20th century" is referred to as the Great Migration. "In 1900, nearly eight million Black people—about 90 percent of all Black Americans—lived in the South. From 1916 to 1970 an estimated six million Black southerners relocated to the North and West in search of economic opportunities and an escape from racial violence" (Great Migration 2024).

4. 🎵 See History 4.1.

5. 🎵 See History 4.2.

6. West Virginia did not become a state until 1863; Black presence in the state dates to the seventeenth century when it was a part of the colony of Virginia. Blacks have been employed in the mines of West Virginia since the early nineteenth century, when coal supplanted wood as the fuel used in salt furnaces.

7. The percentage of Blacks that were married was close to that of whites: 76.0 percent married, and 6.5 percent were either separated, widowed, or divorced (Laing 1985, 74–75).

8. While many Black northerners experienced significant changes in family life after migrating to the North, such was not the case among southern migrants. Not only were northerners without family ties, but also discriminatory and economic policies forced Black women to become breadwinners. As a result, husbands who did not have outside employment and were responsible for the children and house expenses produced unstable family arrangements drastically different from the white model often used for comparison (Corbin 1985, 96–97).

9. This is not to imply that housing and public services in coal mining towns were not bad. Rather, housing for both groups was equally bad and there was no discrepancy in the quality or quantity of public services between Black and white miners (Corbin 1985, 98–99).

10. The growth of Garveyism in the mining fields was concomitant with the growth of the Ku Klux Klan. But generally, the socioeconomic status of Blacks and whites was nearly identical, with an eventual decrease rather than an increase of race prejudice (Laing 1985, 76–77).

11. Many times, the code was imposed by the discriminating group. In other words, the discriminated group and the discriminating group only met within fixed patterns and behaved toward each other according to specific rules. As a result, the two groups had only a limited and very biased knowledge of each other (Kloosterman and Quispel 1990, 152).

12. In her award-winning book *The Warmth of Other Suns* (2010), Isabel Wilkerson provides numerous real-life examples of what can be regarded as labeled interaction among Blacks and whites in the United States.

13. 🎵 See Land Regions 4.1. Blacks who lived on the Sea Islands were often isolated from many whites, which is believed to be the reason African traditions survived much longer on the islands than in other areas of the United States.

14. The economic fallout from the spread of the boll weevil during the early 1920s, the flooding of the Mississippi River in 1927, and other hardships from living in the majority Black cotton-producing Black Belt region are just some of the factors that made Black life in Gulf Coast states different from that of Blacks on the East Coast (History of the Boll Weevil n.d.; Lange, Olmstead, and Rhode 2009). Some Black people developed a begrudging respect for the pest and its abilities to survive, making the boll weevil something of a metaphor for the social, political, and economic situation of the sharecroppers themselves (Steve Leggett n.d.c).

15. In a section of the book *The Land Where the Blues Began* (Lomax 1993) entitled "Fiddling for the Devil," a Black musician who has stopped performing the instrument explains the pros and cons in playing the fiddle (158–62).

16. Some of the first publications on African American music were based on research conducted along the East Coast, particularly studies about the Sea Islands off the coasts of South Carolina and Georgia (see chapter 11).

17. Throughout the early history of ethnomusicology, conducting research on cultures different from that of the researcher was considered the norm, which partly accounts for the large amount of research conducted on Native Americans during the early twentieth century (Myers 1992, 3–18).

18. The few studies on secular music identified with African Americans living on the southeast Atlantic Coast (the South Carolina, Georgia, and Florida sea islands) have focused on Gullah and Geechee culture (see chapter 11).

19. A native of Florida and one of the earliest folklorists to work in the state, William Stetson Kennedy was head of the Florida Writers' Project unit on folklore, oral history, and socio-ethnic studies for the Works Progress Administration between 1937 and 1942. His work resulted in one of the first volumes in the American Folkways Series edited by Erskine Caldwell, and remains a unique and important documentation of the social history of Florida (Banks 2002; Bucuvalas, Bulger, and Kennedy 1987; Stetson Kennedy 1988; Kennedy 2011; Folklorist, Writer, and Activist 2011).

20. Fiddle music has been given several names or labels (for example, dance band music, hillbilly music, country, old-time, pre-blues, and non-blues) by musicians, researchers, and those who work in the media.

21. In spite of the fact that blues influenced and served as the foundation for almost every popular music genre later created in the United States, it faded in popularity in many Black communities during the mid-twentieth century. Yet, blues enjoyed a resurgence of support in the late twentieth century, primarily among white audiences (Hildebrand 1998). During the early twenty-first century, however, a few Black musicians have started performing blues professionally. The PBS television show *David Holt's State of Music* has featured several young blues musicians who are African American.

22. In some areas of the rural South, this close interaction was maintained through the latter part of the twentieth century, which accounts for the continued performance of these forms in Black and white communities in later years (see discussion below).

23. Alan Lomax wrote the introduction to his *Black Appalachia* compilation in 1979, but the work was published in 1999.

24. Wolfe (1991, xxv) believes a common repertoire was shared by both rural whites and Blacks in Tennessee during the nineteenth century, which is what probably existed in other areas in the South. Pauline Norton (2001) states that *breakdown* not only refers to an African American traditional dance characterized by rhythmic patterns with the feet hitting the floor, but also the music accompanying such dances.

25. In addition to similarities, some researchers suggest differences were also apparent in the themes and types of songs created and performed by Black and white musicians during the early twentieth century (Russell 1970, 38).

26. The area that Jabbour refers to as the Upper South is what I identify as the mountain and piedmont regions, where Native Americans, Europeans, and Africans have resided since the sixteenth century (Purdue 1985; Danser 2018, 43–45).

27. As noted in the foregoing, West African fiddlers often attached metal objects to their instruments or placed them inside the resonator to create a buzzing or percussive sound, which, according to most fiddlers, enhanced the sound quality (DjeDje 2008a, 31).

28. Some of the earliest recordings by Black musicians include those by George Johnson, whose 1890 recording made him one of the best-known recordings artists of his time; Bert Williams and George Walker singing popular songs and songs from musicals in 1901; Dinwiddie Colored Quartet singing spirituals and shouts in 1902; Wilbur Sweatman and his band playing Black dance band music in 1903; Fisk Jubilee Male Quartet in 1909; James Reese Europe in 1913 (Southern 1997; Brooks 2004; Graham 2013).

29. For information about Black musicians from the eighteenth century who had been trained in European art/classical music, see LaBrew (1977).

30. Mamie Smith, a vaudeville and cabaret singer from Cincinnati, went into the New York OKeh studio in February 1920 and recorded two songs ("You Can't Keep a Good Man Down" and "This Thing Called Love") composed by her manager, Black songwriter Perry Bradford. Because of the overwhelming public response, OKeh recorded her again in August 10, 1920, singing two more Bradford songs, "Crazy Blues" and "It's Right Here for You." Dixon and Godrich suggest that the songs Smith performed were not blues: "many of this artist's titles are more of a popular

nature, particularly in their style of presentation" (Dixon and Godrich 1982, 679); also, see Southern (1997, 369–70).

31. For information about other Black music groups that included the fiddle or violin during the early twentieth century, see Rye (2010).

32. Vernacular music by white musicians was ignored until the summer of 1922, when Texas fiddlers Eck Robertson and Henry Gilliland recorded for Victor. Their records remained unissued until the spring of 1923. "Robertson's solo fiddling on 'Sallie Goodin' turned out to be a classic performance and should be credited as the first country recordings to be released to the general public" (Lornell 1989, 3–4).

33. Givens (1982) suggests that directors of mobile recording units rejected as too chancy the music of many of the string bands that may have auditioned for them. The overwhelming emphasis on blues precluded the recording of groups that had a large portion of instrumental and vocal dance music and lesser amounts of blues in their repertoire.

34. When recordings were made, Black musicians from rural areas were often taken advantage of like their urban counterparts. It was commonplace for white A&R men to manipulate them with free alcohol and low fee per side; in addition, signatures on legal paperwork were often obtained when the musician was unable to make an informed decision (Barlow 1989, 131–33; Danser 2018, 28).

35. White-owned record companies—including OKeh, Columbia, Victor, and Paramount, which merged with Black Swan, a Black-owned record company—began issuing their race series during the early 1920s. By the end of 1922, race records were being distributed throughout most parts of the United States (Oliver 1984a, 8–9); also, see works by Evans, Lornell, and Wolfe.

36. Since I agree with Bastin's clarification, the term *non-blues* will be used in this discussion and *pre-blues* will appear only when it is part of a quote.

37. Fife and drum bands were also popular in various parts of the south-central United States, specifically Mississippi. But there is no evidence that string instruments were included in these ensembles (Ferris, Evans, and Peiser 1971).

Central Appalachian Mountains and Neighboring Regions

CHAPTER 5

Maryland, Virginia, West Virginia

Maryland

Fiddling among Blacks in Maryland[1] was extremely rare during the early twentieth century, except in the context of minstrelsy, vaudeville, and other traveling shows in rural regions of the state. Could this be due to the early urbanization and higher socio-economic status of Black people in the state, which resulted in many becoming more interested in new and emerging creations? And could the lack of sources reflect the continuation of a trend in some areas—that researchers believed it was more important to document traditions that were believed to be African-derived? Black fiddling in rural Maryland did not fit any of these categories.[2]

The only Black Maryland fiddler from the early twentieth century for which I have found information is William Winfield Adams Jr. (1881–1959), who lived in Ken-Gar, the Black section of Kensington, a small town in Montgomery County in the Maryland piedmont region.[3] Located about nine miles north of Washington, DC, Kensington's surrounding areas were primarily agricultural through the 1870s until the completion of a railroad system that led to people settling in the area and the incorporation of Kensington as a town in 1895. In later years, Kensington developed into a summer retreat for Washington, DC, residents wanting to escape the humid summers (Kensington Historical Society 2022). While little is known about Kensington's Black population during its early history, the US census indicates that there were sixteen Black residents (roughly 1 percent of the town's population) in 1950 and ten Black residents (less than 1 percent of the town's population) in 1960.[4] This is significant because it helps us understand the type of community that nurtured Adams's musical talent. Since Kensington had few Black residents in its early history (1900s–1940s), Adams's audience for fiddle performances probably included family members and close friends. In addition to entertaining whites in his local community, he may have traveled to neighboring areas to perform for both Blacks and whites.

From a 1953 chance meeting with Mike Seeger (1997, 4–5), who recorded Adams playing the fiddle, we have documentation of Black fiddling in rural Maryland.[5] Adams's music provides a window into the repertoire and playing style of one Black fiddler who lived near Appalachia during the early twentieth century. Although scant, comments by Seeger (1997) in the recording's liner notes are revealing:

> Will Adam [William Adams][6] was about 60, was reared in the area, and mentioned having to do laboring work to earn a living.[7] . . . He had played for both Anglo- and African-American country dances, and his repertoire was quite broad. He played his own version of Irish tunes as well as other pieces that might be unique to his regional rural African-American culture. He had a distinctive repertoire and had certainly been a really good fiddler. He was out of practice, didn't own a fiddle, and hadn't played for 25 or so years. On the several times I visited him, he'd play my fiddle, which I had put together from parts I found in a friend's trash barrel. I tuned it a whole tone low for lack of confidence in my glue job on the neck.
>
> Melodically, Will Adams' tunes were unusual, and this one ["Tie Your Dog, Sally Gal"] is full of archaic-sounding double-stops (two-string harmonies). He had a limber bowing wrist, and I'm amazed at his ability to play tunes as difficult and unusual as this, not to mention his feat of simply remembering them after such a long time. I don't recall having heard a tune quite like this one anywhere else and include it in its entirety. I wish I'd spent more time with him. He was a really good fiddler and had a special musical sense. (5)

In 1953, Seeger recorded thirty-nine selections of Adams performing the fiddle with no vocal or instrumental accompaniment, which may have been uncomfortable for him because Adams, like most rural southern musicians, was used to fiddling with other instrumentalists to accompany dancing.[8] Using the categories created by Seeger (1997, 5), twelve of the thirty-nine songs appear to be "unique to his [Adams's] regional rural African-American culture," because little information about them can be found in sources available to me.[9] In other words, these are most likely tunes that Adams or other musicians in his local community personally created or learned from other Blacks.[10] Twenty songs are Adams's "version of Irish tunes" that he possibly learned from commercial recordings by multiple performers who had extensive airplay on radio shows like the Grand Ole Opry[11] during the 1930s. At least four of the twenty Irish tunes—"Devil's Dream," "Arkansas Traveler," "Hen She Cackle," and "Sally in the Low Ground"—were popular among the enslaved during the nineteenth century (Winans 1990, 51–52), and two songs ("Arkansas Traveler" and "Hen She Cackle") are now part of common stock repertoire (Russell 1970, 28). With the exception of the nineteenth-century minstrel tune "Such a-Getting Upstairs I Never Did See," all of Adams's "version of Irish tunes" are listed in Meade, Spottswood, and Meade (2002) and Russell and Pinson (2004), but only eight are included in Dixon, Godrich, and Rye (1997). With such a diverse repertoire acquired from different sources, the evidence confirms Seeger's assessment that Adams "had certainly been a really good fiddler." Also, much of Adams's repertoire is based on songs developed in the shared culture that evolved before emancipation among Blacks and whites in the mountain regions of the United States, but continued after slavery in different parts of the South where Blacks and whites commingled culturally.

Although "Adams' tunes were unusual" (Seeger 1997, 5), the publication of "Tie Your Dog" generated interest from some members of the old-time music community. During an online discussion on several websites and blogs in 2009, visitors, whom I believe were fiddlers, not only were interested in the tune and fiddler, but also the playing technique. In February 2009, David Bragger writes: "Great melody, great bowing." A few months later, in June 2009, Bragger reveals that when he used the tune to teach a workshop, it "went over so well that some of the lesson videos were recorded and posted on the FolkWorks website." In his August 18, 2009, entry on the FolkWorks website, Bragger further explains the reason for his interest in the tune: "'Tie Your Dog, Sally Gal' certainly falls into the category of circular, trance-like fiddle tunes. It has endless potential for melodic and bowing variations."[12]

Upon my introduction to Adams's music, "Smokey Hole" was the song that most interested me. When Sule Greg Wilson played a recording of this tune during my interview with him, my immediate response was: "It sounds so African. It's only when he performs the harmony . . . that it sounds like music produced in the United States. But the other part of the tune sounds very much like the music that Salisu Mahama [a Dagbamba fiddler from northern Ghana in West Africa] would perform without percussion" (Wilson 2013; DjeDje 2008a, 231–41). Because of my initial reaction, I decided to analyze "Smokey Hole" to determine why it sounds "African" to me.[13] My analysis suggests that there are several factors that make Adams's sound African-derived: tuning, melody, as well as form (or structure). Because "Smokey Hole" begins and ends on pitch G, the tuning appears to be in G. Yet, because the seventh note (F#) of the G major scale is rarely played, the music sounds West African to my ears because almost all West African fiddlers use a five-note scale without the seventh note (DjeDje 2008b, 3). In addition, the melody is not at all lyrical or smooth, but is performed in a rough, choppy manner which, to my ears, sounds West African. In terms of form, Adams introduces three themes and varies them extensively by integrating elements from previous themes to unify the piece. Common to all West African fiddling is an emphasis on variation; it could be the rhythm used in the melody or a motive from the melody. In Adams's performance, he unifies the themes by using double-stops. Finally, unlike many old-time tunes, "Smokey Hole" is not based on a set AB melodic pattern that is repeated continuously.[14]

While much of Adams's repertoire includes Irish tunes, he has developed a unique way of playing them. His aesthetic preferences, however, are more apparent in his original creations, especially in terms of melody and form. Thus, when Seeger states that "Tie Your Dog" is "full of archaic-sounding double-stops (two-string harmonies)," which I also found in "Smokey Hole," perhaps this is a playing technique that characterizes Adams's performance style.

Virginia

Musically, Virginia[15] is important to this study because the earliest documentation of Black fiddling in North America comes from this region.[16] Although the fiddle continued to be a prominent aspect of Black culture in both rural and urban areas of the state through the eighteenth and nineteenth centuries, scholars conducting investigations on musicking during this period rarely mention the instrument.[17] In spite of little interest on the part of early twentieth-century researchers, fieldwork conducted by Christopher "Kip" Lornell, Robert Winans, and others during the 1970s indicates that a strong string band tradition continued in several Virginia counties through the mid-twentieth century, but the geographical location of its prominence changed over time (Lornell 1978, 4; Winans 1979, 11). Winans writes that for the early nineteenth century, citations "are mostly from the Tidewater area, and in the latter part of the period some are at the very western edge of the Piedmont" (14). From the late nineteenth to the mid-twentieth century, the tradition continued in several Virginia counties on the border of the piedmont and the Appalachian Mountains (Lornell 1978, 4). During his interview with me, Lornell (1987) elaborated: "Virginia is one of the strongholds for [string band music] in the country. It still is, from the 1880s on up. We're talking about Galax, Carroll County, Grayson County, Patrick County, Henry County, Franklin County; this whole area is really the major lode for interest, among both Blacks and whites, in old-time music."

The degree to which the media influenced the development of Virginia fiddle and string band music is not known. Yet, Lornell (1987) believed the radio played a major role: "When the Grand Ole Opry first went on the air in the mid-twenties, most communities had radio. But it was unusual for individual families to have one. So, a lot of people in rural communities would gather to listen to certain programs on a regular basis. A lot of Blacks listened to it just as much as whites did . . . during the thirties, partly because of the pervasiveness of string band music and old-time music in general." Black fiddler Leonard Bowles (1987), who didn't have a radio when he was growing up, explained: "I used to have to walk five miles every other day to another town to hear a radio sound on the street. I just like the sound of it back then. I never did see it at home. You could buy a radio in the thirties. But we couldn't afford it."

Fiddling continued to be a shared tradition among some Virginians during the thirties and forties. According to Lornell (1978), "Many of Virginia's black banjo players grew up in an era when differences between black and white folk music were less clearly defined. They tended to see their music as 'rural' or 'country' and they did not impose the racial connotations on music that it has today" (4). The instrumental or vocal performance style may have contained typically Afro-American or Anglo-American mannerisms or traits, but the tunes, which researchers now label common stock, were shared by both races (Russell 1970, 25–47; Lornell 1978, 4; Winans 1979, 24). Although Virginia fiddling was popular in a variety of contexts during the early twentieth century, performances at square dances were probably the most prominent. African American fiddling at frolics and Black square dances occurred weekly in some communities (Bowles 1976). Yet, Bowles believes the fiddler's convention, sponsored by a local African American physician, is the primary reason string band music continued to be popular among Virginia Blacks through the 1940s (see discussion below).

All of this suggests that the performance of string band music by Virginia Blacks toward the latter part of the nineteenth century and continuing into the early twentieth century tended to be more widespread in or near mountain regions where the number of Blacks was small in relationship to that of whites. In coastal areas where the Black population was larger, rural performance traditions from earlier years[18] died out and were replaced by the blues and other secular genres much sooner than what occurred in piedmont and mountain regions of the state. Thus, the maintenance of nineteenth-century performance traditions in Virginia raises several questions. To what degree did the physical and psychological isolation or social interaction with other Blacks and whites cause cultural practices to remain intact? In other words, what was distinct about the Virginia piedmont and the people who lived there that caused fiddling to continue as an important tradition through the mid-twentieth century, when it was rejected by other Blacks in the state? Examining the role of fiddling in the lives of several fiddlers (Leonard Bowles, Carl Martin, Posey Foddrell, and Stephen Tarter) in the piedmont and mountain regions of the state will allow us to address these and other issues. Unfortunately, the discussion is uneven. The majority of the attention is given to Bowles because of the availability of data, whereas the discussion of others is limited due to lack of information.

Profiles of Virginia Black Fiddlers

George Leonard Bowles (1919–2004)

Leonard Bowles, the only child of Jo Alzie Bowles (1902–1981), was born in Henry County, Virginia, near Martinsville,[19] the city where he died and had lived much of his adult life. Bowles was a truck driver for the Lester Home

Center in Henry County for forty years before retiring in the 1970s (Wooding 1987, 1A; Bowles 2004). Henry County is significant for this study because of its location in south central Virginia on the border of the mountain and piedmont regions. During the first half of the twentieth century, Henry County's Black population corresponded more closely in terms of numbers with its three neighboring counties in the piedmont that had relatively large Black communities, than with Patrick County, located in the Appalachian Mountains with a smaller number of African American residents. Therefore, because of its location, Henry County's Black residents had an opportunity to fuse cultural practices and behavior patterns from two worlds: the isolated mountains where a shared Black and white culture may have existed and counties in the piedmont where interactions between the races were probably more limited.[20]

In terms of employment, many in Henry County were farmers, probably because over one-half of the county was farmland, with tobacco and livestock constituting the main agricultural products. Large numbers of Blacks also worked in factories. Sawmilling and the manufacture of wood products stimulated the growth of related industries to such a degree that Henry County became a national furniture center during much of the twentieth century. Other important industries in the county included the manufacture of textiles and chemical products (Bowles 1987). Because of the lack of work opportunities that provided enough wages for a growing family, most young people left Martinsville when they became adults, like Bowles's children,[21] who moved to New Jersey and New York: "Whenever they get old enough, about thirteen or fourteen, you see 'em this year. When they fourteen, next year you don't see 'em. They're gone. No work for 'em except in the cotton fields. Most people had to sharecrop. And they worked in the furniture factories and saw mills" (Bowles 1987). Race relations in Henry County were similar to other parts of the South during the first half of the twentieth century. Bowles (1987) stated that before integration, the situation in his hometown was rough: "They had a Black rest room and all that, and a white rest room. A Black [water] fountain over there and a white fountain. They didn't have no Black fountain mostly. White only." In spite of racism, however, Bowles remained in the South: "I never did give no intention of wanting to go North. We had an opportunity, but didn't want to go till after I got married. But what it is, I just settled down for the last fifteen years. I used to be wild, not wild over ladies, just wild with this thing, the fiddle, right here."

Bowles started playing the fiddle around the age of twelve or thirteen. An uncle, who was a musician, gave him his first fiddle. When asked how or from whom he learned to play the instrument, Bowles (1976, 1987) stated:

> Back then, we started working in corn fields to make a living. I come home that day at noon for dinner, and the fiddle's laying there. My uncle had it there, and I picked it up and started to play. And I never did go back to the corn field that day

or the next day. And music just comes from me like that. But no one teach me how to play this. No one. I was just gifted. The fiddle was around my two uncles—Thomas Bowles (1906–1998) and Odell Bowles (1908–1970). Odell could play the fiddle; Tom couldn't play nothin' but the banjo. And he was the most important breakdown[22] dancer there was. My mother, she played guitar or banjo, and my aunt could play the banjo. My grandfather never did play none [no instruments]. My grandfather didn't want no kind of music. I was raised with my grandfather. My mother and father separated.[23]

Unlike some fiddlers who hold the instrument so the resonator is near their chest or on their shoulder, Bowles played the fiddle with the resonator next to his abdomen;[24] he explained that "he started doing it this way so he could look around while he played . . . and look at everybody dancing; see all the pretty girls right there, how they went around in those big dresses; and see which one had on the biggest dress" (Wooding 1987, 2A).

Life in a musical family obviously helped Bowles become more proficient on the fiddle. For encouragement, Bowles (1987) indicated that he was allowed to play with family members during performances even though he had had no formal lessons with anyone:

> They would take me around to parties, and I would play with all the people. They would start. Then I would try to catch what they were saying and get it. And they said, "That's it." And that's the way it went. We'd rest each other. But I could play longer than they could play cause they're old. They're all dead and gone. There were three fiddle players. Monk Gravely played the fiddle, Harry Koger played the fiddle. Jesse Deshago also was a fiddler that played with us some time. But we was all together. And I was the youngest one in the whole bunch. I was the kid. Wasn't no band; nothing but a banjo and a fiddle. It went on like that for years on down up into the fifties. Then the guitar came in. Then from the guitar, the people at the dances we used to have, the ladies, most of 'em, didn't want to hear the banjo and the fiddle. The guitar began taking it over; the guitar by itself.

Although rhythmic accompaniment was included during performances, the type of instruments used varied. According to Bowles (1987), some musicians "used to play with the wash pans [or] old time wash bowls," but he states that he never used percussion accompaniment: "I never did nothing like that. I used to keep time with my feet. If I can't pat my feet, I can't do nothing. What it is I don't know. Sometimes I think my feet is bowing first. When I first met Kip Lornell, Kip used to try to get a pillow and put it at our feet. But I can't help from patting my feet to save my life."

Although extensive documentation exists on Black fiddling during slavery and listening to fiddle music was a favorite pastime for Blacks in Virginia around the turn of the twentieth century, Bowles was surprised to learn that African Americans had played the fiddle when they were enslaved. When I asked if he had heard his parents or anyone talk about Black fiddling during slavery, Bowles (1987) stated: "Fiddle made then? I don't think it was made back in slavery. People is most ashamed to talk about slavery. Most Black peoples 'shamed to talk about that. They mostly got so important, they don't want to talk about the way they was raised neither." Because he alluded to shame as a factor for Blacks in his community not wanting to talk about the fiddle, I asked if this may have also been a reason old-time music was no longer popular. In response, Bowles (1987) explained: "It could be. But I knows right here in this little town where I'm at, we got a lot of Black people ashamed to tell how they come here. They ashamed to tell their children. I don't know why they don't want to tell it. But I tell my children. I tell them where I come along with and where I came from. And they're well blessed for it today. And sometime I think that they don't understand. None of you all understand we come up on the hard way."

During the thirties and forties, Bowles (1987) stated that Black musicians performed in a variety of contexts—in people's homes for birthday parties as well as at school closings as "entertainment when little kids would dance." Musicking at family and community events, such as Virginia breakdowns and square dances, would start on Saturday nights and last until dawn on Sunday mornings: "When we get ready to have a party, they moved everything out this room and put it outdoors. And we'd dance at that house that night. And the next morning, we'd put the things back, sweep the dust, and everything. Some of them had mud floors. And [when] most people go home, we [the musicians] wouldn't go home. They'd cook breakfast. We'd eat up the rest of chicken they'd left from Saturday night. We would eat it and go home. Them were the days I come up with." According to Bowles (1976), musicians rarely received monetary payment for their performances: "I never got a nickel in my life." The food, drink, and the occasional gift of chewing gum from some of the ladies were enough for them to continue their frolics on a weekly basis throughout the year.

Bowles (1987) explained that he always performed his best when participants become actively involved in the musicking: "When we're having a party or something like that, I would watch everybody's movement. I would watch their feet. If they start patting their feet or start moving around, that's when I get happy on my fiddle and get up and walk the floor and playing. I can sit down with a bunch of people. Let 'em listen to what I do. But if it's one or two of us, that's where a hard one comes in. I'm bashful. I can't get myself together. If there had been more people, I wouldn't have been bashful. If they sit down there and won't say nothing, like deacons in the church won't say anything, it's a dull day."

As noted earlier, one of the most interesting and unique performance contexts for African American fiddling in the Virginia piedmont was the Black fiddle convention. While fiddle contests were common among whites in various parts of the United States, with the occasional participation of Blacks, a contest organized and attended only by Blacks was unusual. Lornell (1978) writes: "Even more surprising was the black-only fiddlers' contest held in the auditorium of the hospital of Dr. Dana Baldwin, a prominent Martinsville physician and entrepreneur. This yearly event was held between approximately 1928 and 1945. . . . As far as I know, this was the only all-black fiddler's contest in America.[25] It shows, I believe, the cohesiveness of the black community in Henry County and demonstrates the importance of stringband music for local blacks" (4). Regarding the fiddle contest, Bowles stated the following during his 1976 interview with Lornell:

> They held it in . . . what the black people used to call the gymtorium [on Baldwin's Block, near Fayette and Barton Streets in Martinsville]. It was owned by Dr. [Dana] Baldwin. He's dead now but he was the only doctor black people used to have around here. He used to give what they called the fiddlers' convention. That was a great thing! It was something that people looked for once a year. People from Danville,[26] what we used to call far away—thirty, forty miles away—would come and stay all night. It was held after Christmas, sometime around February or the last part of January. Hundreds of people would come. Black people would look forward to the fiddlers' convention every year. They had harp [harmonica] players, piano players, the best buck timing, straight fiddle, and the best banjo. We had little prize money, win a dollar; two dollars for the winner. It wasn't much money, but it was good for that time. They'd judge the winner by the applause you'd get. They'd start around 8:30 or 9:00 in the evening and wouldn't stop until they finished around 2:00 or 3:00 in the morning. There was a little admission charge at the door, 50 cents, and all the money would go for the musician. (Lornell 1978, 4)

During his interview with me, Bowles (1987) added the following about the all-Black fiddlers' convention.

> He [Dana Baldwin] started that to give the Black people somewhere to go. We didn't have nowhere to go. He just wanted to give us all that. It lasted till he, Dr. Baldwin, died. We just had gotten married when we stopped going to them. I say it lasted until about '43 or '45. We used to look forward to that particular time—the fiddler convention—like when you was a kid looking for Christmas. When it started, I was not grown. But I couldn't wait for that time to come. Go up there and play. Used to win a lot of prizes, only about two dollars, a dollar. Best prize you get was but three dollars. And you'd play the fool of yourself to win that two dollars. It started at seven in the evening and last to about one or two on Sunday morning. One day, once a year; it used to be June or August.[27] I don't know how they worked it [how organizers informed musicians about the convention]. When I know about it and go in there, I see all of them in there. We was well

known here cause we was from this county. The other fiddlers who played with me was Jessie Deshazo and Odell Bowles, my uncle. And I think Harry Koger played with us during that time. And that was it.

And you had two fiddles against two fiddles. A banjo against a banjo. Others was a combination banjo and a fiddle, or a fiddle and a guitar, a banjo, and washboards. There was three of them. We had the best guitar along with the fiddle and banjo. The other people [judges who were not musicians] would sit back like President Reagan . . . and look like big shots and yell: "Well, I think he win." The musicians would get claps and cheers. The one that gets the most cheers would be the winner.

Although square dancing was still a favorite form of recreation for some in Bowles's community during the 1930s, it was not primary as it had been during the late nineteenth and early twentieth centuries. By the thirties, the new media (radio and recordings) that had been introduced into the community gave young people an opportunity to learn and appreciate other African American artists and music-dance genres such as swing, big band jazz, boogie-woogie, and the Lindy hop (Bowles 1976). For example, although Bowles's wife, Naomi, was born and raised in Henry County, she indicated that she had not seen the fiddle or heard fiddle music before she met her husband. In fact, the fiddle created problems in their relationship when they first got married. Bowles (1987) explained:

> She never seen nobody play the fiddle until she married me. We got married and she went out. She never had did no square dance before she met me. Then she learned how to do the square dances, tap dancing, whatever. And she went on, she liked it alright. But back when we was coming on together, she didn't like the girls wiping the sweat off of me. Didn't like the girls fanning me. But some of them she didn't care. Depending on how they look.
>
> I used to go away at nights and stay all night long for good times—having no money, spent no money. Didn't have none to spend at these parties. So, one particular night I went away and I come in that next morning, just about day break, while she was cooking breakfast on a wood stove. And she said, that's before she begin to like the fiddle, "That's got to go. That fiddle got to go." So, she takin my bow and broke it half in two. Kept breakin' it. I go to the fiddle. I hit it down on the side of the stove and broke it up. We cooked breakfast by a fiddle like this and eat.
>
> Her sister find out what happened. Sooner or later, another fiddle came back to town. She got it, she bought me that fiddle. Ain't never do that no more. Then that's when she began to really loved me to be playing the fiddle. She'd seen that was my pride. That's my joy. It's a song dedicated to me, nobody can take it away. It's the same. That's a joy they gave to me, nobody can take it away. (Bowles 1987)

During my interview with Bowles, his wife, Naomi (1987), explained why she did not want her husband to perform the fiddle:

> When we first got married, I thought maybe he would stop playing. I really didn't want him to play cause he'd stay gone all the time. It was me left alone with the children and he being gone. You take so much and you can't take anymore. But after we was married a long time, I didn't mind. I noticed that's what he liked. I see that he wasn't going to stop, so you just got another fiddle. And he just been playing it ever since. And I learned to like it. Like he used to have hunting dogs. I used to hate dogs. He was determined he was going to have hunting dogs, and I began to love those dogs. I don't know why. The things he liked, I likes.
>
> I used to didn't like those things because I just wasn't brought up with those things. When I was growing up, you didn't hear any fiddle and banjo. We went to see Count Basie, Cab Calloway. All these big bands would come to Martinsville. I always went to them. That was before we got married. I heard about fiddle house parties, but I didn't go to them. People called it kind of country. They just didn't go for these kinds of things. I really didn't until I met him.

When asked about the instrument she preferred (fiddle or banjo), Naomi (1987) stated: "I like the fiddle. It sounds better. He really can't play the banjo as good as he can fiddle." Bowles (1987) indicated that he had performed the banjo for about twenty years, and started playing the instrument because:

> the banjo sounds better than the fiddle. Grandpa Jones, on *Hee Haw*,[28] I wanted to represent him. I wanted to be like him. Country man, that's what he plays and that's what I want cause that's what I started from, fiddle and the banjo. Well, a banjo's easier. All you do there is sit down on that fret. You don't be doing all this [Bowles makes physical gestures that would be used in playing a fiddle]. You just hold down this fret and watch other people's feet. They start moving their feet, you just keep playing with the "bom bo bo." Fiddle is hard. Now it is hard. It's not hard to me but it's really for someone. Now you take me right now. If I was to keep this up, what I'm trying to do today, tomorrow, and the next day, probably the next day would just be as easy. But it's hard.

Although family members and many in the community appreciated his music, churchgoers at the Missionary Baptist church where he was a member, not surprisingly, were ambivalent. Bowles (1987) explained: "I have one friend in that church. Cival Williams. He plays the harmonica, or harp, whatever you call it, and he likes all this. But he's about the onliest one. The rest of 'em, I'm gonna tell you the truth, try to sit up and look pretty." While most church members believed the music to be inappropriate or too lowly, Bowles (1987) stated that some churchgoers would "slip" and attend events where fiddling was performed:

"They'd go to 'em frolics on Saturday night, and next Sunday morning they said they didn't go. They got religion on Sunday. On Saturday night, they don't have it. It's in my heart. Nobody don't know what I got inside me, regardless of what I do. I don't try to harm nobody. All the harm I do, I do to myself. But we got a lot of people go to church, and they are saints. They are this and that, and they are a lot worse off than I is. In other words, they declare they didn't go to this dance on Saturday night. Yet, they still sit up in church looking pretty on Sunday morning." Yet, Bowles (1987) believed the Holy Church (the Pentecostal Church) would accept his fiddle music. "They got no fiddle, they have a band. I could carry my fiddle and play with them. Everybody shout cause it's music. You find music anywhere you go. You'll find music in heaven and anywhere, you'll find it. It didn't say what kind of music. Singing don't have to be music. It could be from some kind of instruments."

Regarding race relations, Bowles (1987) indicated there was little interaction between Black and white musicians when he grew up. White farmers who were his employers and lived next door to where he lived may have attended Black fiddle events to observe, but none performed. Also, he was never invited to perform or attend white fiddling events. When asked if he had seen white fiddlers in the town where he was raised, he responded: "To tell you the truth about it, I ain't never heard a white man play fiddle until about twenty years ago. That's the truth because I didn't have the opportunity. I couldn't go to the parties with them. I couldn't go to no kind of entertainment in there, and I didn't know. When I see them play, it was on TV or something like that when the TV first started up." When I inquired if he had heard whites playing the fiddle on WMBA, the local radio station, his remarks are noteworthy: "But you wouldn't know if it's white. You wouldn't know."[29]

Bowles (1987) indicated that his first interaction with whites in a musical setting occurred when he was invited to the Blue Ridge Institute at Ferrum College during the 1970s. While the Ferrum College experience was fine, he indicated that when he played at the Henry County Fair in his community, he experienced racism: "I remember one time we played at the swimming pool up here. We played over there and everybody said we winned it, but we didn't. The organizers said we didn't. They give us a raw deal cause we was the only two Blacks playing. It was a contest at a big carnival [county fair]. My wife square-danced. They hadn't ever seen a Black person square dance. We did not get the award because we had no business there. 'Cause we was Black. That was back before integration come in, and all that was there."

Bowles (1987) believed Black fiddling had declined in popularity because African American fiddle players had died and there were no contexts to perform. For about twenty-five years, from the early 1950s to the late 1970s, he stated that he had not played the fiddle: "I didn't have nowhere to play it. What was I going to do with it? There was nowhere to go to play. People got so they didn't like the

Photo 5.1. Leonard Bowles (fiddle) and Irvin Cook (banjo) performing at Fiddlers' Convention, Martinsville (Henry County), Virginia, October 1976. Blue Ridge Heritage Archives of the Blue Ridge Institute and Museum.

dance. I'd play for my children when they come home. We'd have a time. We'd play it like that." Yet, he believed a resurgence of interest was going to occur: "I'm looking for it to come back. I'm looking for Black people to come back and play this music again. Black people will start buck dancing too. I believe it."[30] Through the urging of Lornell, Bowles returned to fiddling in the late 1970s and began performing in local and national festivals. As a result of renewed interest, "Wish to the Lord I'd Never Been Born," a field recording he made with his music partner, William Irvin Cook (1924–1989), the banjo player/singer who had performed with Bowles since the forties (see photos 5.1 and 5.2), was included on *Virginia Traditions: Non-Blues Secular Black Music* (Lornell 1978).

In explaining how renewed interest in Black fiddling had personally affected him, Bowles (1987) stated: "I believe Kip Lornell spared my life about five more years long. I feel like now I'm back almost in my teens. I was glad that somebody's interested in what we Black people, what me, a Black fiddler is still doing." When I asked how he wanted to be remembered, particularly when I shared my findings with others, he responded: "That I'm still playing. I don't know where I got it from, but I just got a gift to play. I still hold on to my old-timey childhood fiddling. I still know it, I'll never forget it. I'll die with it. Nobody gonna take it away from me." Naomi (1987), Bowles's wife, added: "His wife and his three children and his seven grandchildren are very proud of him 'cause he's still playing the fiddle."

Similar to Adams, Bowles's repertoire is diverse with songs derived from African American and Euro-American culture that have been passed down from

Photo 5.2. Leonard Bowles (fiddle) and Irvin Cook (banjo) performing for dancers at Fiddlers' Convention, Martinsville (Henry County), Virginia, October 1976. Blue Ridge Heritage Archives of the Blue Ridge Institute and Museum.

ancestors and learned from the media. When I recorded Bowles's fiddling during his interview in 1987, he performed six tunes common to old-time fiddlers of his generation: "Richmond," "John Henry," "Possum Up Persimmon Tree," "Old Joe Clark," "Brother Bill Had a Still on the Hill [Mountain Dew]," and "Take This Ring I Give You." The last song, "Take This Ring I Give You,"[31] is memorable because Bowles (1987) stated that he gave it to his wife as a wedding gift: "We got married, me and her, in '41. I didn't have but four dollars. She had eighty cents. I had to pay the preacher three dollars to get married. I didn't have nothing to give her, no kind of wedding ring, or nothing fine at all. So, I told her I would give her that song. 'Just take this ring I give you and wear it on the right hand.'"[32]

When Lornell interviewed Bowles, and recorded his musicking during the late 1970s, many more songs were performed probably because the recordings occurred during several sessions over one year's time.[33] Nine are selections of him performing the banjo with no accompaniment, while the remaining are examples of Bowles playing the fiddle with Cook on banjo. Because both Bowles and Cook learned their music from family members or musicians in their local community, the repertoire of both sessions provides a sample of tunes popular among African Americans in the Virginia piedmont region during the nineteenth and early twentieth centuries. Several songs in Bowles's repertoire are what researchers now refer to as common stock—"John Henry," "Old Joe Clark," and "Going Down the Road Feeling Bad" (Russell 1970). Tunes that seem be unique to Bowles and/or Cook include "Leonard's March" and "Old Rooster

Crowed in the Pine Tree Top."[34] "Wish to the Lord I'd Never Been Born" is noteworthy because the provenance is unclear and cannot be identified with a specific cultural heritage (see discussion below). To understand more fully some of the features that characterize Bowles's performance style, I have analyzed "Wish to the Lord I'd Never Been Born," with attention given to lyrics, form, and melody; the song was initially recorded by Lornell at Bowles's home in Martinsville on October 10, 1976. While Cook sings and plays banjo, Bowles performs the fiddle. As noted above, the performance was later released as part of an audio recording of Virginia non-blues secular music (Lornell 1978).

Most likely "Wish to the Lord I'd Never Been Born" is the type of music Bowles performed for dancing at frolics or house parties that were the most common occasions for fiddling by African Americans in the Virginia piedmont region in the early twentieth century. The context for the performance is significant because the length of the tune on the field recording, three minutes and seventeen seconds, does not represent what would have occurred—that is, a longer performance—at an actual event. Lornell's discussion in the recording's liner notes for this tune focuses on lyrics possibly because of the varied meanings associated with them. Lornell (1978) writes: "There are several recordings from the mid-1920s that incorporate the themes found in this rendition ('The Longest Train I Ever Saw' by the Tenneva Ramblers and 'Been to the East, Been to the West' by the Leake County Revelers) but Cook and Bowles said they learned this tune from local blacks during the 1940s. The reference to 'old Black Annie'[35] in stanza [verse] four is unique and may stem from local black sources" (7). Lornell also lists, in the recording's selected discography, another song with the title, "I Wish to the Lord I'd Never Been Born"—a 1926 Columbia Records recording by vocalist Luther B. Clarke accompanied by a string band (fiddle, banjo, and guitar) called the Blue Ridge Highballers (Russell and Pinson 2004, 214). Significant for this discussion is that Clarke and his accompanists are from the Martinsville and Danville, Virginia, area. Whereas the lyrics by Cook deal with several themes—male-female relationships, loneliness, travel, separation, the locomotive—those by Clarke are concerned primarily with a tobacco business transaction gone bad (Matteson 2008).[36]

Interestingly, the first line of the lyrics—"I wish to the Lord [I'd] never been born or died when I was young"—has been included in love songs by a variety of musicians who recorded the tune during the early twentieth century.[37] Although the lyrics of most of the recordings focus on female-male relationships, the manner in which performers use this theme is distinct. When Sule Greg Wilson (2013), a performer of old-time music who is both a percussionist and dancer, listened to the lyrics by Cook and those recorded by Ted and Gertrude Gossett ("All the Good Times Are Past and Gone"), he noted differences: "They [Cook and Bowles] are talking about people getting on each other's nerves in the lyrics. 'Wish to the Lord, I'd never been born' [signifies] 'Girl, you got too much mouth. I'm just tired of this mess.' So, it's a friendly contention. It tells you where they are, it tells you what they seeing, it tells you the images they want to put in their audience's mind. You can tell when he [Cook, the vocalist] speaks at the end of the song, 'Great day in the morning.' He's laughing at himself or what some in African American culture would say, 'I'm just talking smack.'" Wilson believes a totally different feeling is presented in the lyrics by the Gossetts: "I wish to the Lord I'd never been born or died when I was young / I never would have seen your sparkling blue eyes or heard your lying tongue." "These lyrics," according to Wilson (2013), "are from the other side of the tracks—from Euro-American culture. It's very romantic, lyrical, pining. I mean turtledove, you can get turtledove everywhere. So, the story is totally different from what Cook and Bowles are talking about." Furthermore, Wilson suspects the lyrics from the Bowles-Cook rendition relate to dance movements of people in the audience. "These are also cues when you dance with somebody. You're in their face. That's a cue. Then you look at them. And they look at you and say, 'What are you doing? Are you looking at me?'"

Typical of most old-time music, Bowles and Cook use an AB form for their version of "Wish to the Lord That I'd Never Been Born."[38] Throughout the song, Cook is the person who sings and performs the melodies on the banjo. Bowles accompanies him by playing the melody on the fiddle in unison with Cook while also maintaining a drone and emphasizing the rhythm. In a two-beat bar form, the A and B themes are each eight measures in length, and the entire performance can be divided into ten sections. In section 1 (the opening), which does not include any singing, A and B are performed twice.[39] Even in section 7, both Bowles and Cook perform B twice followed by A and B, which are also performed twice. Thus, the song's form is fairly symmetrical except for section 7, which includes the regular B instrumental melody in response to verse 3 (see section 6), and an instrumental performance of A and B (without the vocal). Perhaps section 7 is included as a variation or an opportunity for Cook to rest from his singing or to think of new text. Since he is the primary melody person, this also allows him the opportunity to perform A more fully with variations rather than slightly hinting at the melody when he sings.[40]

Although Bowles's and Cook's repertoire is culturally diverse, with tunes identified with African American and Euro-American culture as well as recordings made by both Black and white artists before the mid-1940s, their performance style is more African-derived than European. In addition to the extensive off-beat phrasing (syncopation) in Cook's singing and banjo playing, Bowles's fiddling is distinctive for its percussive, buzzing, brassy sound. Instead of playing a distinct melody, Bowles performs the D as a drone throughout the song and only hints at the melody as he uses a sawing technique with his bow. The sound quality of his fiddling is probably what writers in the eighteenth and nineteenth centuries would have referred to as scraping (see earlier chapters). The fact that his audience in eastern Henry County consisted of African Americans who enjoyed the music for dancing, perhaps it is not surprising that his playing style is distinguished for its shuffling. In other words, it is Bowles's fiddling that provides the rhythm or groove that is so important for dancing. Whether this is characteristic of other musicians in Virginia is not known. However, comments by Lornell (1987) regarding Bowles's performance style are revealing: "To use very subjective terms, it's more strident. It's less melodically interesting. It's much more rhythmic than a lot of the other fiddlers. Also, I don't personally think it's quite as fluid in terms of his technique. I don't know if it's an individual thing or a style of Black fiddle playing around here. My sense is that Leonard is quite a utilitarian musician who happened to be an outstanding musician himself."

The insights of other researchers and performers who are knowledgeable about old-time music are also noteworthy. Wilson (2013) states:

> Now this is shuffling, dance music. And the fiddle is just shuffling. Where is the melody that the fiddle would be playing? Even in the break . . . barely. This is house party music—not big barn music. This is a couple dance, a frolic, square dance tune. You got your partner and you're going. The fiddler is totally subservient to keeping the groove going. The fiddler's part is like music played on a mandolin. It's doing the chuck, chuck-a-chuck, chuck-a-chuck. It's a rhythm instrument. It's staying very tight within the rhythm. And the singer is going the whole time. They're not playing for a while, then a verse, playing for a while, and a verse. The way that they play together does not have space.

Comments by Scott Linford (2013b), a performer of old-time music who plays both the banjo and fiddle, are significant for distinguishing what is distinctive about Bowles and Cook as a group and the role of the two instrumentalists in the ensemble: "The performance includes heterophony between the fiddle and the banjo. The tune is being played by two people who have definitely played together before, and know what each one is going to do and how to play together really well. That rough, scratchy timbre on the fiddle really accentuates the rhythmic bowing style more so than an elaborate melody. His voice is great; it has a rough timbre that matches what they are going for with the fiddle and banjo duet. The interaction of the fiddle and banjo gives a really clear sense of how the two instruments are working together to produce this one sound together."

Regarding the performers' roles, Linford (2013b) states: "It's hard to say. It's not like one is the lead and one is the follower. It really sounds like they are playing together. They have a sense of the sound they want to produce. It's produced by the two of them playing together. The thing about the banjo that I like is that you're always responsible for providing the rhythmic drive and some elements of the melody. That also seems to be the role of the fiddle in this recording; it's providing the rhythmic drive and some elements of the melody." Linford also suggests that the performance is reflective of other African American fiddlers:

I've heard some recording by Leonard Bowles before. In my own experience, that style—the Joe Thompson and Odell Thompson's style—that's what I think of as being the African American old-time style. That really, really rough timbre. That kind of sawing where you are really focusing on the bowing aspect of it—not complex, ornate melody.

Also, the fiddling seems to be extremely influenced by interaction with the banjo. That pairing, the heterophony is a really strong awareness of what the other person is going to do to produce a single sound between the two instruments. They are both playing the same melody. But the fiddle is so scratchy and the drone string is so loud that you can barely hear the actual melody part he is playing. I think a couple of times the drone string might have been higher. But it would be like an open string that you'd just keep playing. And then you'd play the melody on the adjacent string. (Linford 2013b)

In summary, Bowles and his fiddling[41] represent a tradition steeped in the African American experience. His background and training come from descendants of African and African American fiddlers who provided entertainment for the enslaved. Since Bowles rarely interacted with whites as a musician during his lifetime, the string band music he performed with family members and in later years with Cook was a Black tradition that remained popular among a segment of the Black population that supported it through the mid-1940s. Their musicking was central and integral to African American culture—not a tradition they participated in solely to entertain or emulate Euro-Americans. Although some of the repertoire may be derived from European American culture, much of it is also African American. Most important, however, is that his performance style includes features (for example, shuffling rhythm and rough sound quality) that clearly demonstrate a performance tradition rooted in the African American experience. As he stated in his 1987 interview, "fiddling is my joy." The only reason the tradition declined or discontinued is because those around him no longer supported this type of musicking for entertainment for they preferred something new and different.

Carl Choice Martin (1906–1979)

Before World War II, many musicians who played fiddle were multi-instrumentalists because, like earlier years, they were born into families in which almost everyone played an instrument. One of the most commercially successful Virginia-born musicians of the early twentieth century was Carl Martin, who "played mandolin, guitar, violin, and string bass all with equal proficiency" (Welding 1979). Although he never made a recording in Virginia nor did he regularly perform the fiddle as an adult, Martin lived there until his family relocated to Tennessee when he was twelve years old. Because he was nurtured as a musician in a part of the state where fiddling and string band music were commonplace, documenting his early life in the Virginia piedmont is important to demonstrate how these experiences possibly contributed to his musicking.[42]

Born in Big Stone Gap, Carl Martin's birthplace is the narrow triangle of the extreme western tip of Virginia, bounded by Kentucky in the north and Tennessee in the south, in which Kingsport and Bristol, Tennessee, were the nearest urban centers (Bastin 1986, 303). Not only was Big Stone Gap relatively small in size in terms of the total population during Martin's time there, the number of Black people was also limited. With a small Black population, the interaction between Blacks and whites, particularly musicians, was probably substantial. Thus, the social environment provided a unique opportunity for the sharing of a culture that had been maintained from earlier years.[43]

Carl's father, Frank Martin (1855–1930), was a stone mason born in the South Carolina piedmont region where he had been well known as a local musician. According to Carl, his father "played violin and guitar. He played a violin all the time, mostly played at parties around there; he'd get out with the fellows and play. They used to call him Fiddlin' Martin. He never did make any records; way back then there wasn't any recording" (Carl Martin 1979). Carl indicates that he learned to play different instruments by watching men from the coal-mining region where they lived come by their house and perform. Big Stone Gap "was a coal-mining region. Fellows would come through there with a guitar—mining men—and they'd stop over at our house and I'd watch them play. I was just a little boy, and I learned to pick up a piece or two" (Carl Martin 1979; Bastin 1986, 301). At least one of his siblings was also involved in musicking: "My brother was a musician too. He was a wizard—played violin, all string instruments—named Roland Martin. He was older than me. He was my daddy's first wife's son. He was born in Spartanburg, South Carolina" (Joyce and Rusch 1977; Bastin 1986, 301; Welding 1992, 96).[44] The Martin family provides further evidence of the role of African Americans in the dispersion and development of musicking in rural mountain culture. As Bastin (1986) explains: "Numerous accounts by both black and white musicians testify to the part played by itinerant black workers in disseminating music in the mountain region" (301).

It was not until Carl's family left Virginia and moved to Knoxville, Tennessee, around 1918, that "he first met his brother Roland, some 30 years older than Carl. Roland had lost his sight to glaucoma while working as a barber, and by the time Carl met him he had taken up the fiddle and formed a string band. Carl played guitar and bowed bass with Roland's band" (Martin, Bogan and Armstrong 1974). Although Carl did not begin playing the violin until several years later, Roland's fiddling had a strong influence on him, particularly in playing fiddle tunes like "Sourwood Mountain," "Downfall of Paris," "Cumberland Gap," and "Cacklin' Hen," as well as blues tunes such as "Hesitation Blues," "Railroad Blues," "St. Louis Blues" and "Wang Wang Blues." While performing with Roland's band, Carl met

Howard Armstrong, who was fourteen years old and playing mandolin, violin, and guitar. Eventually the two started playing together. Martin and Armstrong broadcast over radio station WNOX in Knoxville for a while, and they traveled on the road with a medicine show. When they returned to Knoxville, they met Ted Bogan, formed a group and went to Bristol, Virginia, where they broadcast over radio station WOPI. After performing in Bristol for several months, they played many towns in North Carolina, Virginia, and West Virginia before forming a group called the Four Keys (Martin, Bogan and Armstrong 2014).

Because of his diverse and varied experiences in cities in the South and Midwest, Martin's music career can be considered urban. The basics that he learned during his formative years in the rural Virginia piedmont region provided him with the musical skills to play for parties and dances on street corners and in bars, as well as on radio and in stadiums (Kaplan 1979). When he "teamed up with the two men who were to remain his musical partners, guitarist Ted Bogan and violinist/multi-instrumentalist Howard Armstrong,"[45] they migrated with "many stops from West Michigan to Chicago, where they continued to play, adding songs in German, French, Spanish, Polish, Yiddish, and even Chinese to appeal to people of all the different neighborhoods where they would play" (Kaplan 1979). His life is an example of what can happen to the rural when it meets and interacts with the urban.

Posey Lester Foddrell (1898–1985)

Posey Foddrell was born in Stokes County, North Carolina, but lived the majority of his adult life in Stuart, Virginia, the seat for Patrick County, which is located west of Henry County.[46] Foddrell is another Black musician from the Virginia mountains who was a multi-instrumentalist. In addition to the fiddle, he performed banjo, guitar, piano, organ, and mandolin with both Blacks and whites. Foddrell passed his gift of playing music on to his children, but none chose the fiddle. His wife, Allie Sheppard Edwards (1899–1984), and their children[47] all preferred gospel, blues, and dance music that they performed in varied contexts.

For Foddrell, performing at occasions similar to events from earlier years gave him pleasure. Foddrell worked as a farmer; therefore, it was not uncommon for him and his sons to walk for miles to play at a neighbor's farm during the tobacco-curing season. Since curing a crop took two or three nights and required the help of a lot of people, large gatherings would congregate each night. Food and drink as well as music and dance were part of the evening festivities. When one person's curing was done, the party went to another's farm and begin again. During the winter, neighbors held dances at homes with the Foddrells often providing music for entertainment. When there was no reason to play outside the home, someone in the Foddrell family would perform music in the evening at home, for there was nothing else to do to entertain themselves. Although family members played together, there was always diversity even within the family; every person had an individual style, which allowed them to complement each other (Lornell 1978, 9–10; 2013, 178).

Stephen M. Tarter (ca. 1887–1935)

Stephen Tarter was born in Gate City, Scott County, Virginia, just south of Wise County, which is Carl Martin's birthplace (Bastin 1986, 303–4). Both counties are located in the Appalachian Plateau, the southwestern region of Virginia. Although born in Virginia, US census records indicate that Tarter lived in various locations—for example, the cities of Kingsport and Bristol—in the Tri-Cities region of Tennessee[48] working as a laborer in garages and different odd jobs. However, he died in Scott County.[49]

Like Carl Martin, Tarter was proficient on a variety of string instruments, including the fiddle. As a performer, he learned from his father and became highly regarded among his peers. Lesley Riddle,[50] a Black musician in the area who worked with Tarter, stated: "Steve was one of the finest instrumentalists that I ever heard. . . . Anything that he heard sung or played he could go home and play it. He could play guitar, banjo, mandolin, fiddle, anything that had strings on" (Bastin 1986, 303–4). Although he used guitar instead of fiddle for his instrumentation, it is noteworthy that Tarter recorded two tunes—"Brownie Blues" and "Unknown Blues"—with guitarist Harry Gay for Victor Records in Bristol, Tennessee, in 1928 (Dixon and Godrich 1982, 731). Also, similar to Martin, Tarter did not limit his musicking to the material from his childhood in the Virginia mountains. As a member of the Gate City String Band,[51] he used his skills to master new genres emerging during the 1920s and 1930s.

West Virginia

With so few African Americans residing in West Virginia, it is not surprising that sources on Black musicking are limited.[52] The little that we do know comes from works by Bruce Bastin (1986), Gerald Milnes (1999), and Erynn Marshall (2006).[53] Milnes argues that due to West Virginia's location in the heart of Appalachia, music making in the state has generally been multiracial. Cultural, ethnic, regional, and racial groups have borrowed from one another "using African and European rhythmic, melodic and vocal traditions" with "melodic forms that display Celtic, Anglo, Germanic, and African influence." Thus, West Virginia music "is associated more with place and circumstance than with ethnicity" (Milnes 1999, 7).

Milnes also indicates that Black fiddling and banjo playing during the early part of the twentieth century was popular in the select counties: Hardy and Pendleton in the east (near Virginia), Harrison in the north central part of the state, and areas that had slave populations.[54] In his opinion, most Black fiddlers during this period "were of the rambling hobo variety." As entertainers, they used music to obtain food and lodging. "Some stayed for long periods of time at first one house and then the next, 'working out' their board" (Milnes 1999, 99). Two of these individuals lived in the Burnsville area of Braxton County.[55] One fiddler, Mert Perkins, was well known because he always had a fiddle with him in an old wooden case with a wire wrapped around it, even when riding his horse. In that way, he could stop beside the road and play a fiddle tune upon request. Although some whites regarded him as a jokester, others have stated that they learned some of the older musical practices from him—for example, "how to play in the old cross tunings of (high to low) EAEA, C#AEA, and DADD." Thus, Perkins was important because he was one of the few musicians in the area who could teach others, including whites, how to play European-based old-time music, but he communicated the music using a fiddle style greatly influenced by African practices (Milnes 1999, 98). Jilly Grace, another fiddler, occasionally played for old-style horse-drawn merry-go-rounds. Melvin Wine, a white West Virginian fiddler, indicated that he learned a tune that Grace played for his father called "Tippy Get Your Hair Cut"[56] (Milnes 1999, 99). Other Black fiddlers living in Braxton County during the early twentieth century include George Bailes and a female, Jessie Rhea, but no information is available on them. Yet, Milnes notes that "considering the small size of the African American community in the county [Braxton], a considerable group of African American fiddlers are remembered for their musical talent" (Milnes 1999, 105).

Clarence Tross, a Black musician from Hardy County, remembers that Blacks dominated the music scene during the early twentieth century, playing fiddle, banjo, and accordion for dances, an instrumentation that was common for the "string band tradition before the advent of the guitar" (Bastin 1986, 309). Like African Americans in other mountain areas, Black musicians in West Virginia held on to the old ways of performing even into the 1970s because it was part of family traditions. Tross, who was born into a family of musicians, made his own banjo that he performed with his uncle, Moses Tross, a fiddler who also made his own instrument. Another relative, Andy Tross, played beef bones as an accompaniment to dancing; "beating the bones" was probably popular because it paralleled the function of drums (Bastin 1986, 309).

Finally, several well-known white West Virginia musicians indicated that Black music had a significant impact on their playing and attribute some of their fiddle and banjo tunes to African American sources. Sherman Lawson, a white fiddler from Logan County who recorded with white guitarist and recording artist Frank Hutchison, "learned from a crippled black musician named Bill Hunt, who had moved into the area some time before 1910. He taught Hutchison 'Worried Blues' which he twice recorded for OKeh" (Bastin 1986, 308). Blacks have also had an impact on well-known white musical families such as the Hammonses of Pocahontas County as well as the Wines and the Carpenters of Braxton County. For example, Grafton Lacy (identified in the Library of

Congress Hammons Family recording project as Lacy Grafton), a Black fiddler, is believed to have taught Hammons family members some tunes. Therefore, in addition to Burl Hammons playing "age-old fiddle tunes of British and Irish origin, his repertoire contained many fiddle tunes influenced by African American and minstrel tradition" (Milnes 1999, 97).

Summary

In summary, this examination of Black fiddling in the easternmost portion of Central Appalachia provides evidence that although fiddling was popular among some Black people during the early twentieth century, performance of the tradition among African Americans varied. In some of the more remote, isolated areas of various states, Black musicians continued to participate in events and activities from earlier times. Changes in the local community and interests of younger members of families, such as the case with Tarter and Foddrell, contributed to the decline of fiddling in many rural communities. Therefore, when musicians such as Leonard Bowles performed the instrument, they did it for themselves and not necessarily for the wider Black community. Fiddling was the one thing that belonged to him that nobody could take away; it made him proud and gave him joy, especially during times and situations when many aspects of life were negative, which was often the norm within African American culture.

Therefore, as we examine fiddling among Black musicians in other rural parts of the country, perhaps we will learn if the musicking and experiences of fiddlers in this region reflect the attitude and sensibilities of others. Although the information is minimal and uneven, what is available provides a foundation and beginning for understanding not only fiddling but also aspects of musicking in rural Black culture in other parts of the United States.

fiddlingismyjoycompanion.net

Notes

1. 🎻 See Map 5.1, Map 5.2, Land Regions 5.1, and History 5.1.
2. Minimal research has been conducted on the musicking of African Americans in Maryland except for investigations on Baltimore and brief references to music making on slave plantations (Southern 1997).

3. US census records indicate that both parents—William Winfield Adams Sr. (ca. 1849–1928) and Carolina Lula Hood (1853–1936)—were born in Maryland, and William Jr. was the eldest of four children.

4. 🎵 See Demographics 5.1. For information on Ken-Gar's history and its Black residents, see Gaddy (2020) and Mangin (2022)

5. Before Seeger's death in 2009, he shared the collection with Sule Greg Wilson who gave copies of Adams's recordings to me in October 2013. Seeger included one of the tunes, "Tie Your Dog, Sally Gal," on the Smithsonian Folkways recording (Seeger 1997).

6. Although Seeger (1997, 4–5) uses the name "Will Adam," US census records indicate that his name is William Adams.

7. Mangin (2022) states that Adams Jr. worked on farms and did odd jobs: "On his World War II draft card, he said he was employed by William A. Wagner, who owned a plumbing company in Kensington."

8. 🎵 See Repertoire 5.1 and Analysis 5.1 for a list and discussion of the songs in each category.

9. To determine if the provenance of a tune is African American, European, or Euro-American, I reviewed several discographies—Dixon, Godrich, and Rye (1997); Meade, Spottswood, and Meade (2002); Russell and Pinson (2004); as well as Fancourt and McGrath (2006)—to assess the type of music record companies targeted to various communities before the mid-twentieth century. Whereas Dixon, Godrich, and Rye (1997) includes primarily commercial recordings aimed at the Black community or field recordings performed by African Americans, items in Meade, Spottswood, and Meade (2002) and Russell and Pinson (2004) seem to be intended for white communities. Because the *Discography of American Historical Recordings* (2008–2024) is a database of most recordings made in the US during the 78rpm era, it is a useful source for all communities and categories of musics.

10. One of the songs in Adams's repertoire is "Altamont," a tune identified with John Lusk (see discussion below).

11. The Grand Ole Opry is a weekly country-music stage concert founded in 1925 in Nashville, Tennessee, as a one-hour radio barn dance that broadcast throughout much of North America (Malone and Stimeling 2012).

12. To review the full discussion, go to the Fiddle Hangout discussion forum.

13. 🎵 Go to Audio Examples to listen to "Smokey Hole" by Adams.

14. 🎵 See Form 5.1, Transcription 5.1, and Analysis 5.2.

15. 🎵 See Map 5.3, Map 5.4, Land Regions 5.2, and History 5.2.

16. One of the earliest references documenting seventeenth-century Black fiddling in North America includes a description of musicking in Accomack County, Virginia (see chapter 1), which is located in the eastern edge of the state roughly three hundred miles from the piedmont and mountain regions. Today, Accomack and Northampton counties form the Eastern Shore of Virginia, bordered by the Chesapeake Bay and the Atlantic Ocean.

17. In publications and programs produced by the Hampton Institute, one of the first Black institutions of higher learning to be established in Virginia and the only Black college in the state to collect data on African American music, attention is given to tales and stories, religious music, cradle songs, labor songs, and dance and game songs (Lornell 1978, 3).

18. In addition to string band music, the playing of fife and drum, quills, dulcimer, accordion, harmonica, and rhythmic instruments (triangle, jawbones) were commonplace in Black Virginia communities during the late nineteenth and early twentieth centuries (Lornell 1978).

19. Martinsville was established as a town in 1791. After becoming an independent city in 1928, Martinsville continued to serve as the seat for Henry County through the twentieth century; yet both the city and the county are separate jurisdictions.

20. 🎵 See Demographics 5.2.

21. US census records indicate that Bowles and his wife Naomi Pettie Bowles (1917–2006) had three children, two sons and one daughter.

22. Although the same music would be used in performance, Bowles (1976) stated that the Virginia breakdown performed by African Americans in his community is different from the

square dance. "A square dance has a set caller with called sets. He's not singing, he's there with the band, while people out there are dancing. But in the Virginia breakdown, the set caller is right amongst the dancers. He is in the middle of them, and he's kind of a teacher." With regard to dance movements or step work, the breakdown differs from buck dancing and flat footing performed at square dances. Naomi (1976) explains: "The plain flat foot, you are dancing flat on your feet, and the Virginia breakdown you are dancing on your toes. With the square dance, you're doing more of the flat foot. So that's the difference between the Virginia breakdown and the square dance."

23. US census records indicate that Bowles's grandparents—Josiah (Joseph) Bowles (ca. 1865–1955) and Georgianna Johnson Bowles (ca. 1870–1948)—were also born in Henry County.

24. As noted in chapter 1, fiddlers in different parts of West Africa hold the fiddle in a similar position (DjeDje 2008a). Wolfe (1982, 11–12) indicates that fiddlers in eastern Kentucky held the instrument on the chest rather than under the chin, making it easier to sing but more difficult to maneuver the bow.

25. If the dates 1928 to 1945 are accurate, this means that the Black fiddle convention in Henry County predates the Old Fiddlers' Convention which began in 1935 in Galax, and attended primarily by whites (Old Fiddlers' Convention 2015). Bob Carlin (2004, 38) provides evidence of a Black fiddlers' contest that took place in Iredell County, North Carolina, around 1909. Yet it is unknown when it began and ended.

26. Danville is an independent city bounded by Pittsylvania County, Virginia, and Caswell County, North Carolina.

27. Details regarding the month, year, and time of day the convention took place vary in the two interviews, probably because of memory lapses by Bowles and the fact that these particulars may have fluctuated over the almost twenty-year time period the convention was held (Lornell 1978, 4; Bowles 1987).

28. *Hee Haw* was a US television variety show featuring country music and humor in a rural southern setting that aired on CBS television from 1969 to 1971 before its twenty-year run in local syndication (Television in the United States n.d.).

29. Both Winans (1979) and Lornell (1987) indicated that Virginia Blacks and whites performed with each other during the early twentieth centuries. In the interview, Lornell (1987) elaborated: "I've interviewed other Black banjo and fiddler players from south central Virginia, which is what I would consider this area here [Henry County] to be, who did play for whites and who did play in integrated string bands. In most cases, a few Black musicians were playing with whites for white dances. But I can think of a couple instances where you would get white musicians occasionally playing with Blacks at Black dances. Now the crowds themselves, from what I can tell, were generally pretty much segregated. But the musicians themselves were not always segregated. So, for Bowles's experience that may be true. But within fifty miles of here, that wasn't necessarily always true."

30. Considering that several Black string bands specializing in old-time music and other genres—including the Carolina Chocolate Drops, Ebony Hillbillies [Black fiddler, Henrique Prince, director], and Sankofa Strings from the late twentieth and early twenty-first centuries—became established artists with performances, recordings, and tours in various parts of the United States and abroad during the early twenty-first century, Bowles's comments are significant.

31. Cook, the banjo player who had performed with Bowles since the 1940s, indicated that he learned "Take This Ring I Give You" from his grandfather, Sylvester Cook (1893–1965), who was also born and raised in Henry County. It was the first song Cook and Bowles performed together when they became musical partners (Cook 1976). It is unknown if a song with a similar title, "Take This Ring with You," recorded on Vocalion Records by the gospel quartet, Bessemer Sunset Four, in 1929 is the same song.

32. 🎵 See Repertoire 5.2.

33. 🎵 See Repertoire 5.2, Parts A and B. The Digital Library of Appalachia records indicate that Lornell recorded twenty-one tunes by Bowles between 1976 and 1977.

34. None of these titles appear in discographies, nor can I find information about them in sources available to me.

35. See the Mudcat Café listserv for an insightful discussion on the "Origin of Black Annie."

36. 🎵 See Lyrics 5.1.

37. At least two songs include these lyrics: "I Truly Understand, You Love Another Man," recorded on Victor Records in 1928 by George "Shortbuckle" Roark and Family of Pineville, Kentucky (Lofgren 2001), and "All the Good Times Are Past and Gone," recorded by Ted and Gertrude Gossett in 1930 on Columbia Records and the Monroe Brothers in 1936 on Bluebird Records (ToneWay Project 2003–15). A conversation on Mudcat.org indicates that "John Lomax recorded Fields Ward in 1936 in Galax, Virginia, singing 'Long Lonesome Road,' which has stanzas expressing similar sentiments—'Oh I wish to the Lord I had never been born, or died when I was a baby'" (Mudcat Café n.d.; Ward, Dunford, Ward, and Lomax 1937).

38. 🎵 Go to Audio Examples to listen to "Wish to the Lord I'd Never Been Born" as it appears in Lornell (1978).

39. Probably because of editing for the commercial recording (Lornell 1978), the opening (or section 1) includes one performance of the A melody and two performances of the B melody. On the field recording, which can be heard on the Digital Library of Appalachia website (http://dla.acaweb.org/), both AB melodies are played twice.

40. 🎵 See Form 5.2.

41. When I listened to Bowles performing other tunes from his recording session with Lornell, the same bowing and brassy performance style are used.

42. For recordings of Carl Martin playing the fiddle, see Martin (1966, 1972) in the Discography. The New Mississippi Sheiks is an updated configuration of the well-known string band that was popular during the early twentieth century (Joyce and Rusch 1977).

43. 🎵 See Demographics 5.3.

44. US census records indicate that Frank Martin (1855–1930) was married twice. With his first wife, Harriet Martin (b. ca. 1858), Frank had four children, and Roland (b. ca. 1875) was the eldest of the four. With his second wife, Mary McMann Martin (b. ca. 1879), Frank had seven children, and Carl was the eldest.

45. In 1930, the Tennessee Chocolate Drops recorded "Knox County Stomp" and "Vine Street Drag" for Vocalion in Knoxville. The personnel for this session is unclear. While some sources indicate that the group was composed of brothers Howard Armstrong (fiddle) and Roland Armstrong (string bass) with Carl Martin (guitar), other sources cite the personnel as Howard Armstrong (fiddle), Roland Martin (guitar), and Carl Martin (string bass); see Dixon, Godrich, and Rye (1997, 86, 908); Wyatt (2001); Rodgers (2022).

46. 🎵 See Demographics 5.4. US census records indicate that Foddrell's parents—Pleasant Ewell Foddrell (1842–1925) and Sarah Jane Martin (1857–1925)—were both born in North Carolina. They had ten children (four females and six males) and Posey was the eighth born.

47. US census records indicate that Foddrell and his wife had nine children, four females and five males.

48. The Tri-Cities region comprises the cities of Kingsport, Johnson City, and Bristol. All three cities are located in northeast Tennessee, while Bristol has a twin city (with the same name) in Virginia.

49. 🎵 See Demographics 5.5.

50. Lesley T. Riddle (1905–1979), a Black musician born in North Carolina but raised in Kingsport, was a multi-instrumentalist who played guitar, mandolin, and piano. He collaborated with Black guitarist Brownie McGhee (1915–1996), as well as the Carter Family, a white group that became well known for performing vernacular music (Bastin 1986, 256, 258).

51. See Tarter's obituary, *Roanoke Times*, Roanoke, Virginia, March 20, 1935.

52. 🎵 See Map 5.5, Map 5.6, Land Regions 5.3, and History 5.3.

53. While Bastin (1986) had an opportunity to speak with musicians personally, much of the information in Milnes (1999) and Marshall (2006) about African American music comes from interviews with whites who remembered family members discussing their interactions with Black musicians in their local communities.

54. Counties that had slave populations include Braxton in the central part of the state as well as several in the east: Randolph, Greenbrier, and Pocahontas—the first, second, and third largest county, respectively, by area.

55. 🎻 See Demographics 5.6.

56. In addition to discussing interactions between Blacks and whites, Marshall (2006) comments on Melvin Wine's memories of his grandfather and a Black fiddler known as "Black George" (see chapter 3); she also mentions Woody Simmons, who could trace his first fiddle to a Black person.

CHAPTER 6

Kentucky

Little is known about the musicking of African Americans who lived in rural areas of Kentucky during the early twentieth century.[1] The information I have been able to obtain is based on data collected by folklorists and music researchers,[2] liner notes from recordings, and literature that include brief mention of African American music within the discussion of Anglo-American music. With the exception of fiddle contests in which Blacks were prohibited or not encouraged to participate, the performance contexts (house parties, country dances, courthouses) and ensembles (string band, including fiddle, banjo, and guitar) for Blacks and whites in Kentucky were similar.

Using information from commercial and personal field recordings as well as interviews with local musicians, Titon (2001, 18–19) divides Kentucky fiddling into three regions: (1) the southeastern tradition in the Cumberland Plateau, which is influenced by the musicking of Appalachian settlers, specifically, the Scots, Irish, English, and Germans; (2) the northeastern tradition, which is based on "a cosmopolitan combination of southeastern breakdowns" with northern tunes found along the busy Ohio River; and (3) the third tradition in the south-central (or Pennyroyal/Pennyrile) and Bluegrass region, which is noted for "strong African American influence in melody types, playing styles, and tunes." Although Titon does not include extensive details about the northern part of Kentucky's Bluegrass Region, John Harrod (1987) states that the area has several musical characteristics that distinguish it from musicking in other parts of the state:

> Most people up here can sing while they're fiddling. While they're singing, they aren't really playing the melody note for note. They'll go over on the bass string and keep the roll going with their bow in whatever key they are in. So, they are playing rhythms with themselves while they're singing. When they stop singing,

they'll play the full-fledged tune. So, what I think the fiddlers do is kind of like the equivalent of strumming the guitar. [Also,] northern fiddling is more similar to white fiddling without Black influence. Northern fiddlers tend to be smooth, notey, but real even-timed. Intonation is very clear and smooth. The further south you move, the fiddling gets kind of slurred and syncopated in unique personal ways. The approach to time gets more playful and individual and bluesy.

Kentucky tunes linked to African American culture include: "The Grand Old Jubilee," a song "about a big party blacks had when they learned about their freedom"; "Nero the Slave," supposedly named for a Black fiddler named Nero; "Down South Rag," a bluesy piece; and "Old Master's Horn." "Shippingport," a tune believed to have originated in central Kentucky (the southern part of the Bluegrass Region), is interesting because of its association with the history of Louisville and a Black fiddler named Cato Watts (see below). Two other tunes identified with central Kentucky—"New Money" and "Martha Campbell"—are both bluesy and syncopated, but the twelve-bar blues[3] is not always used (Harrod 1987). An African American provenance is also associated with "Hog-Eyed Man," "Ida Red," "Rat's Gone to Rest," and "Sugar in the Gourd" (Titon 2001).

Profiles of Kentucky Black Fiddlers

From analysis of the available data, several African American musicians were active in Kentucky's fiddling community from the late eighteenth to the early twentieth centuries; yet, information about their contributions is uneven. Not much is known about Cato Watts except that he was an enslaved fiddler owned by Captain John Donne, who was among the early white slaveholders to settle in the region during the eighteenth century. Thus, Watts was not only the first African American resident, he was also the first musician in Louisville (Jones 2014, 34–35; Watts n.d.; Foster 2020). At present, we know that Monk Estill (d. 1835), who was transported from Virginia in 1779, making him possibly the first free Black person in Kentucky, "was a fiddler who played for all the parties and celebrations" (Gibson 2018, 227). Black fiddler Christopher Columbus "Uncle Lum" Martin (b. 1842) "was a fixture of the court square in Greenville" in Muhlenberg County in southwest Kentucky (Brady 2013, 112); Will Christian (b. 1872) was an outstanding African American fiddler from Knott County who played for dances in southeastern Kentucky;[4] Bill Trumbo (b. 1892) was a Black sharecropper from Bath County, who taught the tune, "Rat's Gone to Rest," to eleven- or twelve-year-old white fiddler George Hawkins of northeast Kentucky around 1915,[5] and Hawkins is believed to be the first person to make recordings of the song.[6]

My main discussion of Kentucky Black fiddling focuses on seven Black fiddlers for which information exists—Bennie "Cuje" Bertram,[7] James "Jim"

Booker, Charlie Buster, Shell Coffey, William "Bill" Livers, Arnold Shultz, and Owen Walker—who were active in rural parts of the state during the early twentieth century. Except for Shultz, who resided in southwestern Kentucky, all fiddlers were born, raised, and spent much of their performance career in regions located either within or close to the Appalachian mountain system. In addition to living in different regions, the fiddlers' birth dates, extending from roughly 1857 to 1911, represent different time periods. Therefore, in spite of the unevenness, enough has been found about the lives and musical worlds of fiddlers to form a picture of the Black fiddle tradition in Kentucky. The discussion is organized chronologically according to fiddlers' date of birth, with special attention given to family and community, learning, performance contexts, the media, creativity, performance practices, and Black/white interactions.

Owen Walker (1857–1944)

Gibson (2018) believes "the fiddle tradition established by Cato Watts and Monk Estill in the eighteenth century persisted through the nineteenth century" (227). Particularly important to Kentucky's fiddling community was Owen Walker, who resided in central Kentucky; he was born in Richmond, the seat for Madison County, and died in Winchester, the seat for Clark County.[8] Walker's importance is partly related to the fact that he was the musical mentor to white fiddler Dock "Doc" Philipine Roberts (1897–1978), who also lived in Richmond. Not only did Roberts make "more commercial recordings of fiddle tunes (on 78 rpm records) during the 1920s and 1930s than any other Kentucky fiddler" (Wolfe 1997, 67), music researcher Gus Meade (1980, 1) estimated that as much as 70 percent of Roberts's recorded repertory came from Walker.[9]

Because Richmond had a large population of African Americans during the time he lived there, Walker's audiences were probably diverse and preferred a certain type of repertoire and performance aesthetic. This may explain why he became a well-known entertainer during the World War I era and was much in demand at social events for playing blues, waltzes, and old-time music, similar to Black fiddlers in urban areas (Wolfe 1982, 29). "His band flourished about 1915, and he traveled as far away as Louisville playing for wealthy white patrons as well as black audiences" (Wolfe 1997, 69). In his performances of old-time music and blues (the new genre gaining popularity in different parts of the United States), he probably used musical features identified with African American culture, which helped both him and his mentee, Dock Roberts, gain prominence.

Unlike other Black Kentucky fiddlers during this period, Walker did not choose farming as his livelihood after emancipation. In 1870, US census data indicate "at school" as his occupation, and for 1880, "shoemaker" is noted. His occupation is listed as "restaurant keeper" in 1900, and "pool room" with "own account" is recorded for 1920.[10] Walker's surroundings and the support he received from the Black community obviously nurtured his talents. The fact that he did not have to depend entirely on whites as patrons for his musicking may have encouraged him to compose new songs and use a performance style that appealed to both Blacks and whites. As Roberts and his older brother Levert (also spelled Lebert and Liebert) learned to the play the fiddle, researchers believe they listened a lot to Walker, who passed on much of his repertoire to them, including such tunes as "Old Buzzard," "Brickyard Joe," "Waynesborough," "Martha Campbell," and "All I Got's Gone," all of which Roberts later recorded. In interviews later in life, Roberts acknowledged his mentor's influence, noting that it was Walker who gave him the idea that professional musicians had to dress in white suits with bow ties; "he helped me every way in the world. He was the fiddlingest colored man that was ever around Kentucky. He played like a white man, only he could beat a white man" (Wolfe 1982, 29; 1997, 69; Titon 2001, 22; Keith 2013, 63). If Walker was as great as his admirers have indicated, one wonders why he never recorded when the opportunities became available. Was it because of old age, ill health, or lack of interest on the part of record companies? Did a record company executive surmise—why use the source (a Black fiddler) when a copy (a white fiddler) could be more easily marketed?[11]

James "Jim" D. Booker Jr. (1872–1940)

Although little is known about his life, Jim Booker Jr. is important to the history of African American fiddling because he is not only the first rural Black fiddler to make a commercial recording, but he was also the first to record as part of an interracial group. Booker's recording session with Taylor's Kentucky Boys (a predominantly white string band formed by talent scout Dennis Woodson Taylor) on Gennett and several other record labels took place on April 26, 1927, in Richmond, Indiana. This was almost four months before Andrew Baxter, a Black fiddler from northwest Georgia, and several white musicians known as the Georgia Yellow Hammers, made their recording on Victor Records in Charlotte, North Carolina, on August 9, 1927 (see chapter 9).[12] On August 27, 1927, the Gennett record label also recorded two blues numbers with Booker playing fiddle as a member of the Booker Orchestra, an all-Black group that included his two youngest brothers, Joe (1890–1966) and John (1892–1986), and a neighbor, Robert Steele (1882–1962); see photos 6.1. and 6.2.

Although some members of the Booker family were born in Camp Nelson,[13] an historically important town for Blacks in the state located in the southern part of Jessamine County (Wolfe 1982, 28),[14] census records indicate that Jim Booker Jr. was born in Jessamine County [no town is given] and died in Lexington, Kentucky.[15] During the early twentieth century, the Bookers—father, Jim Booker Sr. (ca. 1837–1903), mother, Sarah Million Booker (1846–1930), and the couple's ten children (five females and five males)—lived a short distance from the

Photo 6.1. John Booker playing guitar. Camp Nelson, Kentucky. 1980. Courtesy of Eric Lon Caldwell.

Photo 6.2. John Booker's fiddle inside case with packet containing Black Diamond Strings in background. Camp Nelson, Kentucky. 1980. Courtesy of Eric Lon Caldwell.

Kentucky River in the southern extreme of Jessamine County.[16] In terms of work, census records indicate that Jim Sr. and his sons were farm laborers, while the mother worked in the home. Interestingly, Jessamine County is not part of the Appalachian mountain system, but is adjacent to it; Garrard and Madison counties, located south and southeast of Jessamine, respectively, are in Appalachia. Unlike some parts of Central Appalachia in which Blacks comprised less than 5 percent of the total population during the early decades of the twentieth century, the number of Black residents in Jessamine County was substantial, probably because of the history of African Americans in central Kentucky.[17]

Like many performers in rural southern communities, Jim Jr. was raised in a family of musicians. In addition to his brothers, Joe and John, who both played fiddle and guitar, Jim Sr. was a fiddler; many of the tunes performed by musicians in Jessamine, Garrard, Madison, and surrounding counties may very well be attributed to Jim Sr. (Meade 1980). Musically, the Booker family is a product of the shared culture that developed between Blacks and whites during the slave era in (or near) mountain areas of the United States. Commenting on the shared music culture that existed among Blacks and whites in central Kentucky during the early twentieth century, John Booker's daughter, Helen Booker Stewart (1994), states:

> Well, Camp Nelson Band is what they called themselves—my father, John Booker, [played], and I had uncles [that played]. Then, Robert Steele was one of them. There weren't more than about three or four. They had the guitar, the violin.... They had one or two more [musicians or groups] that used to follow

them around. Pop knew a lot of white guys too that did that string music. They would all get together some time and go together. They would have barn dances at different places throughout the county.[18] In different little cities, they would go on the weekends, playing for dances and things.

Local newspapers also reported on occasions when the string band performed. In 1928, for example, the following appeared in the *Lexington Herald*: "On last Tuesday evening, Miss Pullen gave us an evening of joy with her pupils. . . . The Camp Nelson string band made music for the occasion. These boys are hard to beat" (Fee Memorial Institute Notes 1928). Not only were the Bookers excellent performers, the fact that their repertoire and performance style were comparable to that of whites may be one of the main reasons Taylor invited them to participate in the recording sessions with Gennett and other record labels (see below).

Because media representation of Black fiddlers playing old-time music was miniscule during the twenties and thirties, Jim Booker's recordings with white musicians were extraordinary, but few details about these records exist except for comments by Wolfe (1997):

> Taylor had brought up a black stringband from Jessamine County, the Booker Family, lead [sic] by fifty-five-year-old fiddler Jim Booker. The family had been known for generations in the central Kentucky area, and shared much of the repertoire of Owen Walker. In [April] 1927 Taylor had brought Jim Booker up for an earlier session with a pick-up band that include[d] white banjoist Marion Underwood and white singer Aulton Ray, with the titles being released as the Taylor's Kentucky Boys. The result was some splendid music, and what was probably the first integrated recording session in the annals of country music. However, when it came time to make a band photo for the Gennett catalogue, Jim Booker was not invited and in his place Dennis Taylor posed, holding a fiddle he didn't know how to play; the image the catalogue presented was that of an all-white stringband. (71)[19]

When Jim Booker recorded with Taylor's Kentucky Boys, the Starr Piano Company released the recordings on its flagship label, Gennett, and advertised them in its 1928 *Gennett Records of Old Time Tunes* catalogue as "Old time Playin'" and "Old Time Singin' and Playin'" (Huber 2013, 28) because the tunes were performed in the style of nineteenth century old-time music that commercial record companies identified with whites.[20] After his April 1927 recording sessions, Booker participated in two other sessions with Taylor's Kentucky Boys in August 1927.[21] Unlike Roberts, who had a successful recording career through 1934, Booker's ended after several months. We do not know if it was Booker's decision or whether extenuating circumstances (illness or old age) caused him to stop making recordings. Furthermore, we cannot dismiss the fact that the

Photo 6.4. Advertisement for the 1927 recording of Taylor's Kentucky Boys: Dennis Taylor (holding fiddle), Marion Underwood (banjo), and Willie Young (guitar). Black fiddler Jim Booker's image does not appear, even though he recorded with the group. Courtesy of Patrick Huber.

issue of race, which was becoming more apparent and institutionalized in the media (that is, hillbilly versus race record series), may have been a factor that brought Booker's recording career to a halt (Huber 2013, 48–49; DjeDje 2016). In the end, Booker was never acknowledged for his talent as a Black fiddler nor did he have the opportunities afforded white fiddlers.

Considering the biases that existed in the record industry, we can only speculate on why Taylor recruited Booker to participate in the recordings. As the local talent scout for Gennett and, for a brief time, Roberts's manager,[22] there is no doubt that Taylor knew much about the music scene and the best performers in the area (Russell 2021, 54). In other words, he could have invited any of the many white fiddlers in the region to participate. Could Booker have been chosen for convenience (Booker and Taylor were neighbors); could the amount of monies Booker agreed to accept have been less than what Taylor would have paid another (perhaps a white) performer; or was Booker simply the best fiddler for the job?[23] I believe Booker was invited because Taylor wanted a product that would be commercially successful (musically and financially), particularly since several record labels (Challenge, Champion, Herwin, Silvertone, Supertone) were involved in the final product, and Taylor was using his name for the group. Although some researchers argue differently (Huber 2013, 50–52), the emphasis on finance may also be a reason Taylor's Kentucky Boys, visually (see photo 6.4), needed to be represented as a white string band performing hillbilly music; thus, a photo of Booker as a member of the group would have been unacceptable.[24] Comments by Salsburg (2017) also help explain the situation: "Gennett was one of the only companies of the era not to issue specialized records for black and 'hillbilly' audiences in separate catalogs, and when the Taylor's Kentucky Boys and Booker Orchestra records were released, they were marketed with the label 'Old Time Playin'.' This was no mistake: the company files flatly state 'made for Hillbilly.' Only those who had had the pleasure of seeing them play—at a square dance, tent show, or society function; in a cornfield—knew the Bookers as Kentucky's preeminent black string band."

When researchers discuss musicking by Jim Booker Jr., emphasis is placed on the fact that he was the first rural Black fiddler to make a commercial recording with a multiracial group playing old-time music, and he recorded blues with an all-Black group, the Booker Orchestra, which included his brothers and a neighbor. Except for Huber (2013, 28–29), few scholars mention that, in addition to these sessions, Booker, his two brothers, and Steele participated in several interracial recording sessions in August 1927. When we consider the songs and musicians who participated in these sessions, not only do we have evidence of the repertoire of the Booker family and other musicians in the Bluegrass Region during the 1920s and 1930s, but we are also able to examine more closely the musicians who performed, the songs they performed and ascertain reasons why the sessions proceeded in this manner.[25]

Since less is known about Booker's participation in the August 1927 sessions, emphasis here will be placed on these recordings; a musical analysis of musicking in April 1927 will be presented later. In August 1927, Jim Booker and his brothers participated in two sessions as members of the newly configured Taylor's Kentucky Boys.[26] At the second session on Saturday, August 27, 1927, Booker and Roberts both played fiddle, while Booker's brother performed guitar.[27] On that same day, another configuration of Taylor's Kentucky Boys included members of the Booker Orchestra (Jim, John or Joe Booker, and Robert Steele) and Roberts accompanying Marion Underwood (the only performer, except for Jim Booker, who was a returnee from April 1927 sessions) on vocal and banjo.[28] Interestingly, the three songs performed at this session—"Turkey in the Straw," "Old Hen Cackled and the Rooster Crowed," and "Down in the Valley"—were unissued (rejected), while the one song licensed by Silvertone ("Sourwood Mountain") and the two by Challenge ("Little Old Log Cabin in the Lane" and "That's What the Old Bachelor's Made of") were released. Why would Gennett not want to release recordings with both Booker and Roberts playing together? Was it because of the sound or were concerns about how the music would be represented to record buyers also taken into consideration?[29] Although business agreements between the record companies may have been factors in the decisions made (Wolfe 1997, 72), could race have been a variable? Releasing a commercial recording by a multiracial group dominated by African

Americans (four Blacks and two whites) playing old-time music, a genre identified by the media as white, was extremely rare in the 1920s, in spite of the fact that the racial mix of the group was probably not unusual in many parts of rural Kentucky at that time.

Furthermore, except for Wolfe (1997) and Huber (2013), rarely do scholars mention that Booker's two brothers each performed guitar as accompaniment to Roberts's fiddling on two different sessions.[30] The fact that several record labels were involved in the production of the music performed at the two sessions suggests that record executives believed there was a strong likelihood that the recordings would be financially successful. With Roberts as the sole fiddler and John and Joe performing in an accompanying role, it was probably easy to represent Roberts as the primary instrumentalist with little to no mention of the accompanying Black artists.

Although limited, the twenty songs that members of the Booker family recorded in 1927 provide evidence of the repertoire used by both Black and white fiddlers in the southern half of Kentucky's Bluegrass Region.[31] This is significant for several reasons. (1) Since most sources heretofore focused on the musicking of whites (Wolfe 1982, Titon 2001), we can only assume that Blacks performed similar music, but now we know for certainty. (2) By comparing the repertoire of the Booker family with that of fiddlers in other parts of the United States (specifically Appalachia), we can determine if overlaps exist. (3) We have some idea of the musical preferences of both record company executives and performers because both parties probably had input regarding songs included on the recordings (Wolfe 1997, 70–71; Huber 2013, 52–53). In the case of the Booker Orchestra, most likely executives decided that the songs should be blues (or a genre that the media identified with Blacks), and allowed members of the Booker family to choose whatever they wanted within these parameters. Record company executives may have also been responsible for attaching the word "orchestra" to the family's name. During that period, "string band" was generally reserved for white groups performing a specific style and genre of music, and "orchestra" was flexible or open. For example, it was not uncommon for "orchestra" to be identified with African Americans performing symphonic music or jazz, such as James Reese Europe and His Clef Club Orchestra or William "Bill" Johnson's Original Creole Orchestra, which became popular during the 1910s (Southern 1997).[32] (4) Finally, dismissing the fact that Booker is performing with whites, these may be the earliest commercial recordings, as noted above, by a rural Black fiddler.[33]

Interestingly, the song categories that folklorist Mike Seeger (1997) proposed for Black fiddler William Adams in Maryland—(1) Adams's version of various Anglo-American tunes and (2) songs unique to Adams's regional rural African American culture—are appropriate for the Bookers in Kentucky. With the exception of "Old Buzzard," which Roberts is believed to have learned from his African American mentor, Owen Walker (Titon 2001, 141), seventeen of the tunes appear to be derived from Euro-American culture (meaning Irish tunes).[34] During the early twentieth century, most Kentucky fiddlers, regardless of their race or ethnicity, probably knew these songs because they were passed down from ancestors or learned from listening to the media. In fact, five song titles—"Arkansas Traveler," "Billy in the Low Ground," "Black-Eyed Susie," "Old Hen Cackled and the Rooster Crowed," "Turkey in the Straw"—are mentioned in the narratives of formerly enslaved Blacks (see chapter 2).[35] The provenance of three song titles—"Old Buzzard," "Salty Dog," and "Camp Nelson Blues"—is African American, and the latter, "Camp Nelson Blues," may have been composed by Jim Booker Sr. (Meade 1980) or other Blacks in the area to honor and remember the history of African Americans in Kentucky's Bluegrass Region. It is also noteworthy that at least five of the songs recorded by Blacks—"Arkansas Traveler," "Old Hen Cackled and the Rooster Crowed," "Salty Dog," "Sourwood Mountain," and "Turkey in the Straw"—are now part of the common stock repertoire (Russell 1970, 28), while nine—"Billy in the Low Ground," "Black-Eyed Susie," "Cripple Creek," "Forked Deer," "Gray Eagle," "Ragtime Annie," "Soldier [sic] Joy," "Sourwood Mountain," "Turkey in the Straw"—are among the most popular tunes recorded by Kentucky fiddlers since the 1920s (Titon 2001, 23).

To provide some insight about features that characterize Booker's fiddling, I focus on two songs: "Forked Deer" and "Salty Dog." Regarding the first song, Alan Jabbour (1966a), a fiddler and well known researcher of old-time music, writes:

> "Forked Deer" is a quintessential fiddle tune of the old frontier. It is old and widely distributed, yet it cannot be traced to the Old World or the northern United States. "Forked Deer" begins with and gives greatest emphasis to the high strain of the tune. And it is fiddled with a fluid bowing style using slurs to create complicated rhythmic patterns, in the manner of the old Upper South. Its title both evokes the forest and (though few fiddlers in the Appalachians realize this) names a river in West Tennessee. An 1839 printed set from Southside Virginia (Knauff, Virginia Reels, vol. 1, #4 "Forked Deer")[36] establishes the tune's longevity under that title in Virginia. It found its way onto the nineteenth-century stage and into tune collections as a "jig": . . . But that did not give it circulation beyond its home region in the Upper South, where it turned up in many twentieth-century sets.

Although Jabbour references many sources in documenting the tune's provenance, no mention is made of the 1927 recording by Taylor's Kentucky Boys. The omission is unfortunate because "Forked Deer," probably due to its wide popularity in the general public, was one of the first old-time or country music tunes to be commercially recorded, and the version by Taylor's Kentucky Boys is the second recording of this tune to be released. In fact, sources indicate that three commercial recordings of "Forked Deer" had been made before the

1927 recording session by Gennett and its partners,[37] but only one—Victor's 1924 recording of "Forki Deer" by Ambrose Gaines "Uncle Am" Stuart on fiddle and Gene Austin on banjo—had been released (Russell and Pinson 2004, 881). Therefore, if fiddlers during the 1920s were avid listeners of the media, the recordings of "Forked Deer" by these two groups may have influenced their interpretations of the song. In explaining the significance of the 1927 performance by Taylor's Kentucky Boys, Tony Russell (2021, 51) states: "'Gray Eagle' and 'Forked Deer' . . . are among the most exhilarating recordings of their era: intricate melodies, flawlessly executed, yet with an energy that elevates them above mere skillful demonstrations of tunes. . . . Alan Lomax, entering it in his *List of American Folk Songs on Commercial Records* in 1942, described it as a "fine piece of square dance music."

To understand the uniqueness of the Taylor's Kentucky Boys performance, comparing it with the first release by Stuart and Austin would be helpful.[38] When compared, the two recordings are similar in that each instrumentalist contributes integrally to the performance in a unique way.[39] In Taylor's Kentucky Boys' performance, this is done collectively. While the guitarist performs a repetitive part that serves as the foundation for the piece, the fiddler and banjo player perform the main melodies. But their parts are highlighted at different points. While one is being featured, the other performs an accompanying role. In the case of Stuart-Austin, there is more opportunity for solo improvisation wherein each musician is given a part to perform alone without any accompaniment. Whereas the Stuart-Austin performance seems appropriate for a contest situation, the simpler form, faster tempo, more intricate rhythms, and Booker's intense fiddle playing make the performance by Taylor's Kentucky Boys, as noted above, more inviting for dancing. Interestingly, the releases by Stuart-Austin and Taylor's Kentucky Boys seemed to have influenced later releases. The Kessinger Brothers' recording on February 10, 1928, is obviously modeled on that of Taylor's Kentucky Boys. In addition to the fast tempo (quarter note = 132 bpm), the tune begins with the high-pitched theme. There is also no doubt that the performance is intended for dancing because a vocalist calls out movements for dancers as part of the recording. The only difference is that the fiddler dominates throughout the performance, while the guitarist plays a simple pattern on the down beat of each note with minimal melodic passages. To some degree, the 1928 recording by Setters-Robison is similar to the 1924 release by Stuart-Austin. Not only is the Setters-Robison version divided into more than three themes, the performers also begin with the low-pitched theme. Unlike Stuart-Austin, however, the fiddler dominates throughout the performance while the guitarist merely plays chords as accompaniment.

Most discussions about the Booker Orchestra's performance of "Salty Dog" make note of the fact that it is a blues song performed by a family of Black string musicians, and the lyrics, when used, are often risqué.[40] For example, in the liner notes to *Violin, Sing the Blues for Me: African American Fiddlers 1926–1949*, record producer Marshall Wyatt (1999) writes: "Jim Booker also recorded two sides with his family string band.... They recorded 'Salty Dog,' known among black songsters for its bawdy lyrics, although here the Bookers render an instrumental version. The three brothers display a fluid style with bluesy accents, and Steele adds a hokum touch with his kazoo.[41] These recordings were labeled 'made for Hillbilly' in the Gennett files, and marketed to a white audience" (17–18).

Although "Salty Dog" (also known as "Salty Dog Blues") is now common stock and has been recorded by many musicians, with each using elements from blues, jazz, or country (such as old-time and bluegrass) music to make it their own, the song's roots are African American. In his 1938 interview with Alan Lomax for the Library of Congress, jazz pianist Jelly Roll Morton (1890–1941) states that he recalls a three-piece band led by Bill Johnson (1874–1972) playing the number to great acclaim, probably before 1910 (Morton and Lomax 1938). Demonstrating the song's popularity, sources indicate that fifteen commercial recordings were made of "Salty Dog" by various artists before World War II, including three by the Allen Brothers, but only fourteen were actually released. It is also noteworthy that five recordings of the tune had been released prior to Gennett's August 27, 1927, session with the Booker Orchestra,[42] which is significant, for an analysis of the earliest records may help in understanding possible reasons for the performance style that the Bookers use in their recording.

Several interesting points can be made about the earliest commercial recordings of "Salty Dog." One, the first three releases were recorded by African Americans who had established careers performing blues and jazz—Charlie Jackson (1924), Clara Smith (1926), and Freddie Keppard's Jazz Cardinals (1926)—while the next two were made by European Americans known for their performance of old-time music: the Allen Brothers (1927) and the McGee Brothers (1927). Two, except for Smith, who began recording in 1923, "Salty Dog" was the first song (or one of the first songs) to be released by the other musicians. In other words, although many of these artists were well known locally in their communities or as traveling musicians, few had been involved in the media when they made their "Salty Dog" recording (Otto and Burns 1974, 414).[43] All of this suggests that because of its popularity, "Salty Dog" was an excellent tune to help an unknown artist become more well known. And three, when Jackson made his 1924 recording, he included the word, "blues," in the title, which is the case for all four songs he made with Paramount in August and September 1924. Yet, only the white musicians (the Allen and McGee brothers) followed suit by using "Salty Dog Blues" as the title of their recordings of the tune; the releases by Smith, Keppard, and the Booker Orchestra (the three Black groups) are titled "Salty Dog."

In my opinion, the features that most distinguish "Salty Dog Blues" are the melody, lyrics, and chord progression. The song is based on two different four-beat, eight-bar melodic patterns with variants (ABA¹). While the lyrics and melody used in the first half (bars 1–4) of the eight bars tend to be varied, those in the second half (bars 5–8) are not, except for minor variations when alternating every other verse.[44] Although blues is included in Jackson's title, the chord progression often identified with the blues—the twelve-bar blues (I-IV-I-I | IV-IV-I-I | V-IV-I-I)—is not used.[45] Rather, a chord progression that I refer to as a cycle of fifths in reverse (VI-II-V-I) is repeated throughout Jackson's performance, except for the first verse. Each chord is held for two bars of each eight-bar pattern. This harmony is significant because the first five recordings of "Salty Dog," regardless of the genre or changes in the lyrics or melody, include the same chord progression.[46]

So how is the Booker Orchestra's recording on August 27, 1927, similar to and/or different from the five releases that preceded it? Before addressing this question, several points should be made. (1) While there is no way of knowing, I have no doubt that Gennett played a major role in deciding on the songs performed by the Booker Orchestra on that day.[47] As noted above, the Booker Orchestra recorded two songs as a group: "Salty Dog" and "Camp Nelson Blues." Whereas the "Camp Nelson" tune[48] employs a twelve-bar blues chord progression, the Bookers' version of "Salty Dog"[49] is based on the cycle of fifths chord progression used in Jackson's 1924 recording. (2) We also do not know if the Bookers realized their musicking would be marketed as hillbilly music, which implied that a performance style representing this tradition needed to be used. Yet, this may not have been an issue for them, because old-time music or performing music identified with rural Appalachia expressed their identity as musicians. Attempting to perform differently would not only have been difficult, but would not reflect their true art as musicians from rural central Kentucky. (3) Raising these issues demonstrates some of the decisions that record company executives probably had to make when deciding how to represent and market the musicians who recorded for them.

Also, as noted above, the Bookers' recording, which is roughly two minutes and forty-three seconds in length, is the first instrumental performance of "Salty Dog." Without risqué lyrics, one might ask, what are the features that identify the song by the Booker Orchestra as "Salty Dog"? Most obvious is the performance of the four-chord cycle of fifths, which is one of the song's most identifying features.[50] In addition, the fiddle melodies have been organized and performed in the style of what a vocalist might sing. Like previous performances, the Bookers' version is based on two (AB) melodies or themes. The A (or first) melody is similar to the Allen Brothers' cover of Jackson's A melody. Performed in a higher register, the B melody, in my opinion, is unique to the Booker Orchestra but created in the style of melodies that might be included in "Salty Dog," if new lyrics had been added. So, in a way, the Bookers have created two melodies—a low-pitched A melody and a high-pitched B melody—that do not exist in any of the previous performances. Also distinct is the fact that the two melodies are organized in a specific pattern (AABBBB), which is repeated three times during the performance as the music's tempo gradually increases. The first time the pattern is performed, the music has a moderate tempo (quarter note equals 104 bpm) with the fiddle and kazoo playing the A melody in unison, and the guitar accompanying by using the root of the chord on the down beat and strummed chords on the off beats, very much in the style of ragtime.[51] When the AABBBB pattern is played a second time (0:59), the tempo increases (quarter note equals 120 bpm) as the fiddler, without the kazoo, improvises on the melody with bent notes and off-beat phrasing; but the same ragtime guitar accompaniment is used. By the time the pattern is repeated the third time (1:49), the tempo has increased even more (quarter note = 126 bpm). Although the fiddle and kazoo perform in unison as before, there is much more variation and driving intensity in the performance of both musicians during the performance of the third pattern. Contributing to the intensity is a second fiddler performing a more elaborate version (counter melody) of B. In many ways, the collective improvisation by all performers (of the Booker Orchestra) in the final repeat of the pattern is similar to that used by Keppard's Jazz Cardinals. Commenting on the performance style used by the Booker Orchestra, Scott Linford (2013b) states: "I hear more sliding into notes, more flatted sevenths, and a half-flatted third. That harmonic progression sounds more like jazz or ragtime. With the kazoo, it sounds more like a jug band. This would have been music for dancing. So, you wouldn't want to speed up too much. Then having played with a lot of old-time bands, I know that you always do have a tendency to speed up, just because you get carried away with the energy. It may mean that they got really into what they were doing and started speeding up."

From this analysis, some general conclusions can be made until additional tunes are examined. The performance by the Booker Orchestra is distinct for fusing elements that have been historically identified with African American culture. Although elements—instrumentation (banjo, kazoo) and performance techniques (off-beat phrasing, bent notes)—associated with African Americans and adopted by European Americans are apparent, the record companies market it as a hillbilly recording, most likely because of the fiddle. This is an excellent example of misrepresentation, for if similar characteristics had been included in a performance of saxophone, cornet, and clarinet, the recording would have been placed in the race series and marketed to a Black audience. What seems to be apparent about Booker as a fiddler is that his musicking is intense. In his performance of "Forked Deer" and "Salty Dog," he performs as if he is in context—that is, performing music for dancing. In both cases, the music is straightforward in terms of form, but the melody and rhythm are more involved. As the leader, he gives opportunities for others to be featured and seems to encourage collective variation, which suggests that he does not mind sharing the musical spotlight.

Photo 6.5. Pendleton "Uncle Pen" Vandiver (Bill Monroe's uncle) with baton, Arnold Shultz (fiddle), unidentified man (guitar), and Luther Shultz, bull bass fiddle. Courtesy of Roger Givens.

Arnold Shultz (ca. 1886–1931)

In southwest Kentucky lived a Black guitarist and fiddler named Arnold Shultz (also incorrectly spelled Schultz) who was a major influence, according to some music historians, "in shaping the music direction of an Ohio County boy named Bill Monroe—the man who created the bluegrass sound more than a dozen years after Shultz died in Butler County. That, some say, makes him [Shultz] a godfather of bluegrass—a musical style he never heard" (Lawrence 1980, E1).[52] In spite of his talent and popularity among whites, Shultz was never recorded. Yet, Forrest "Boots" Faught, a white country and Dixieland bandleader in whose band Shultz performed in the early 1920s, believes that "if Schultz had ever made his way to Nashville or Chicago in those days of the late '20s, he might have become one of the greats of country music . . . because he shattered all the racial taboos in Ohio County. . . . From the roadhouses and barn dances of the farmers and miners to the black community picnics to the homes of the well-to-do whites, Shultz was always welcome. He was Ohio County's No. 1 music man" (Lawrence 1980, E1); see photo 6.5.

Shultz was born in Ohio County near the town of Cromwell in Kentucky's western coal fields region. Although Ohio County's population is relatively large when compared to other counties where Black fiddlers in Kentucky have lived,

Photo 6.6. Ella Shultz Griffin (Arnold Shultz's cousin) playing fiddle. *Messenger-Inquirer*, Owensboro, Kentucky, 1980. Courtesy of Keith Lawrence.

actually Shultz spent most of his time in several small communities within a ten- to twenty-five-mile radius, east and southeast of the town of Hartford, the seat for Ohio County. Therefore, similar to the environments of some Black fiddlers, the number of African Americans in the towns where Shultz resided was small.[53]

Shultz was the eldest son of David Shultz (1844–1918) and Elizabeth Smith Shultz (ca. 1870–1920s). Born into a musical family, he was a multi-instrumentalist. In addition to the fiddle, he could play guitar, banjo, mandolin, and piano (Jackson and Richey 2016, 27). Ella Shultz Griffin,[54] his younger cousin (see photo 6.6), states that by the time Arnold was fourteen years old, he had already learned how to play the guitar and fiddle from observing his musical relatives. When he was not playing music, Shultz worked near the town of McHenry as a coal miner and later as a coal loader around Rosine and Horton in Ohio County. During his early years as a musician, he traveled much, which some researchers believe is the reason for his musical talent (Brady 2013, 102). "One day in late autumn he might play a tune on a relative's porch, then without a word walk down the road, then sit and play another tune. His relations would hear Shultz and his music fade away into the distance. He apparently made it to the Mississippi [River], worked his way south on riverboats as a deck hand then wintered in New Orleans where he absorbed that city's musical influences" (Smith 2000, 23). If he heard that Jelly Roll Morton was going to be in New

Orleans, he would time his trips to hear him. His favorite "'hangout' was wherever 'Jelly Roll Morton' and his band members congregated.... [He wanted to listen very closely to their music because] as noted musician, John Hartford, explained . . . he was very adept at hearing and catching new chords and infusing them into his own musical offerings" (Jackson and Richey 2016, 26–27).

Music was an important part of the Shultz family, but, also similar to other musical families, no one took formal music lessons. Family gatherings to play music were often and informal; the repertoire included nineteenth-century old-time music that had been passed down from ancestors or learned from listening to the radio or musician friends.[55] In 1911, Griffin states that the family's music group, which included bull bass fiddle, banjo, guitar, and fiddle, would perform around Ohio County. "In those days, Shultz would visit his cousin and jam for weeks at a time. 'He was living at Williams Mines (near McHenry) then but he would come [about nine miles southeast] to Prentiss. Sometimes he would stay two weeks at a time. We'd just stay there and make music and the neighbors would all come in'" (Lawrence 1980, E2). Jackson and Richey (2016) indicate that "he played all five instruments in his journeys around the Upper South and Midwestern areas. Besides New Orleans, Shultz's favorite performing places were Louisville and Henderson, Kentucky, Evansville, Indiana, and St. Louis, Missouri; additionally, in numerous little towns and big city suburbs, 'gathering new songs and singing the old ones.' It was told through the grapevine that he also played with W.C. Handy in Henderson" (27)

Although music historians emphasize Shultz's guitar playing, he was also considered to be an outstanding fiddler. When he performed with Faught's all-white group during the early 1920s, he alternated between fiddle and guitar. In fact, Birch Monroe, the eldest of the musical Monroe brothers, remembers Shultz's fiddling, not his guitar playing: "He played a good old-time fiddle. I can tell you that" (Lawrence 1980, E1; also quoted in Brady 2013, 106). Although Shultz never had a formal working relationship with the Monroe brothers, he played at square dances around Rosine and Horton where they were based (Lawrence 1980, E1; Otto and Burns 1974, 412).[56] Tex Atchison, the lead fiddler for the Prairie Ramblers (the most popular country music ensemble of the 1930s and a fixture on Chicago station WLS for twenty years) states that Shultz, who was known for playing "a more blues/swing [type] of fiddle" (Harrod 2002), greatly influenced his fiddling. Atchison even credits Shultz with teaching him how to play the long bow style of swing fiddle as opposed to the short jiggly bow style he had learned from his father (Wolfe 1982, 57, 112).

Shultz had a very close relationship with white musicians in spite of the racial barriers of the times. Faught indicates that he often ignored racists who made remarks about Shultz: "Back then we would go to play for a dance and somebody would say, 'Hey, you've got a colored fiddler. We don't want that.' I'd say, 'The reason I've got the man is because he's a good musician. The color doesn't mean anything. You don't hear color. You hear music'" (Lawrence 1980, E2). In spite of his acceptance among some whites, Shultz and his talent suffered because of discrimination, which is not surprising for "the most contentious places for conflict involving black and white musicians were the occasional contests" (Brady 2013, 112). Regarding the incident with Shultz, Faught explains: "We entered a contest open to anybody in Kentucky, over at Central City at the Selba Theatre. Arnold wasn't with me then. There was bands there from everywhere. I guess there must have been 20 bands that night. We tied up with a band from Powderly.[57] We fought out there til midnight. We finally came out second best. The prize was $50 and expenses paid to Hopkinsville[58] to be on the radio. I'm pretty sure Arnold Shultz was there that night with an all-colored band. They was the best band there. If they had been white, they would have won that contest. They all had calf-skin instruments—mandolin, guitar, tenor banjo and banjo guitar" (Lawrence 1980, E2).

In addition to working with Faught, Shultz performed with Walter Taylor, an Ohio County Black musician who played mandolin. Griffin states that "Walter and Arnold would come to McHenry on payday and make a hat full of money just sitting on the street playing. They weren't bumming. They were just playing and people would automatically walk up and throw them money" (E1). Although Shultz worked with Walter Taylor's Black band through the late twenties, it was during the mid-1920s, when he began playing on his own, that he influenced Bill Monroe, a self-taught musician. As a twelve-year old in 1924, Monroe began following Shultz around to country dances in Rosine. Therefore, "Bill Monroe's earliest paid music work was thanks to Shultz, who asked Bill to 'second him' on guitar when he fiddled for square dances. Bill was thrilled by the invitation—and proud of his stamina when the sun came up and they would still be playing. With his growing sense of life as a competitive event, Bill was awed by how Arnold won a music contest by following up his blues numbers with a beautiful waltz" (Smith 2000, 24). Bluegrass historian Steven Price notes that Monroe was also impressed by Shultz's smooth transition between chords as well as his blues playing (Lawrence 1980, E2). In an interview with Wolfe during the 1970s, Monroe comments on his early musical influences and experiences with Shultz. Although Monroe indicates that he learned a large repertoire of fiddle tunes from his uncle, Pendleton Vandiver (see photo 6.5), it was Shultz who also influenced his playing when he transferred to the mandolin. In explaining further about the relationship between the two musicians, Wolfe (1982) states: "some fans of Monroe have jumped to the conclusion that since Shultz was black, he was responsible for the 'blues' element in Monroe's later music. Monroe is careful to note, though, that he listened to Schultz [sic] play in a conventional black string band, featuring numbers like 'Sally Goodin.' 'There's things in my music, you know, that come from Arnold Schultz—runs that I use in a lot of my music'" (99).

When the repercussions of his interactions with various musicians are discussed collectively, Shultz's influence is far-reaching.[59] For example, Shultz's impact on guitarist Kennedy Jones is important because it was Jones who taught Mose Rager, a well-known country musician from Drakesboro, Kentucky, how to perform guitar.[60] Rager, who played on the Grand Ole Opry in 1946 and toured with Grandpa Jones and Ernest Tubb, taught Merle Travis (who, like Monroe, became a member of the Country Music Hall of Fame) how to play the thumb-pick style on a guitar. Travis later passed the style on to Chet Atkins and millions of others around the world (Brady 2013, 104). Furthermore, Shultz's influence on Monroe can be heard in 1950s rock and roll, for "both Elvis Presley and Buddy Holly list Monroe's music as an early influence on their careers" (Lawrence 1980, E2). Rager believes that musicians of different races learned from each other because there was a free interchange between everyone. Commenting on this issue, Wolfe (1982) includes some of Rager's comments on the role of Blacks in Kentucky country music:

> The whole tradition of secular non-blues black music, which was widespread across the South in the nineteenth century, was especially strong in the western Kentucky area, where it survived well into the twentieth century and was a major influence on much white string band music. Richard Nevins, a leading authority on the development of fiddle music, has written about the area: "Nowhere else in America did the black population take to white fiddle music so immediately, and nowhere else did an almost separate black fiddling tradition grow to such eminent stature as to then greatly influence the very tradition its roots came from. In addition to numerous fiddlers who influenced people like Doc Roberts and Dick Burnett, black guitarists and banjoists emerged as influential soloists, as well." (110–11)

While it is commendable that researchers acknowledge the contributions of Blacks to the development of country music, the only problem is that they refer to the tradition as "white fiddle music," which implies that it is not part of Black heritage or a shared culture with contributions from African Americans, European Americans, and possibly others.

Although Shultz continued to perform at dances for whites and Blacks in Ohio County through the twenties, he began spending more time in Butler County (a neighboring county southeast of Ohio County) in the early 1930s where he lived with the family of an African American butcher (Beecher Carson).[61] Most researchers indicate that Shultz died of a heart problem (Wolfe 1982, 114; Cantwell 2003, 31), but family members think differently. His cousin Griffin believes clashes among band members were factors that led to his death:

> Members of his band were jealous because he was getting all the attention. People would say how good Arnold played. In April 1931, he returned to Prentiss [a small community in Ohio County] to visit relatives. He stayed at our house a week and then he went to Morgantown [in Butler County]. Then he came back

down there [to Ohio County] one Saturday with three boys and they stayed til just about night. Then they left for Morgantown to play for a dance. That's the night they said he got some poison in his whiskey. I think he was (murdered). He drank whiskey all the time before that and he never got sick over it. He drank that and he took sick and died. They gave him poison in his whiskey. People were bragging on Arnold for playing better than they (other musicians) did. So they thought they'd fix Arnold and put him out of the way—and they did. He drank that whiskey and died. (Lawrence 1980, E2)

Shultz's life is another example of a multitalented African American musician who experienced many challenges because of his race. During his life, he refused to allow the biases of others to affect his creativity. Traveling to different parts of the country and performing with a variety of musicians (using different instruments in varying contexts) allowed him to be free to experiment without the limitations of what was expected of him. Just as he was an outstanding performer of all types of music, including genres and styles associated with Blacks and whites, he could play the guitar and fiddle equally well. In the end, he is most well-known for performing the former, probably because of misrepresentation; the guitar is the instrument identified with Black musicians, not the fiddle.

The Coffey Family: Shell Coffey (1894–1985) and Charlie Buster (1895–1993)

When Richard Burnett (1883–1977), a white singer, guitarist, and banjoist from Wayne County in southern Kentucky, was ninety years old, Wolfe conducted an interview with him in which he discussed his early years and experiences with two Black fiddlers—Bledsoe "Bled" Coffey [also spelled Coffee] (1872–1943) and Cuje Bertram (1894–1993)—who were active in the rural Kentucky music scene during the late nineteenth and early twentieth centuries. Burnett stated: "Oh yeah. Bled Coffee here in town, he was a fiddler . . . and . . . Cooge Bertram was a good fiddler. . . ."[62] Yes sir, there were a lot of black men playing old-time music. Bled Coffee was the best fiddler in the county. Been dead for years. I played many a tune with him—[he] used to play with me, oh, sixty years ago. He'd play any of the old songs that I did. The old-fashioned tunes, like 'Cripple Creek,' 'Sourwood Mountain,' 'Soldier's Joy,' 'Fire on the Mountain'—them old fashioned tunes is about all he played" (Wolfe 1973, 7). To learn more about the musicking that Burnett remembered so positively and vividly from his early days, attention is given to two Black fiddlers—Shell Coffey and Charlie Buster—who were influenced by Bled (see photos 6.7 and 6.8). Much of the information comes from interviews that Robert Fulcher conducted with the Shell and Charlie[63] in 1979. I found the interviews useful for several reasons: One, they expand our understanding of the environment

Photo 6.7. Shell Coffey with fiddle. Lexington, Kentucky. March 1979. Photo by Robert J. Fulcher.

that helped nurture Black fiddling in south-central Kentucky. Two, they provide details on how traditions were retained and passed on among rural Black performers during the early twentieth century. Finally, they supply insight on how and when the music culture of African Americans in some parts of the mountain regions began to change.

In addition to being related to each other by marriage, Shell and Charlie were neighbors who were born in Wayne County on December 24, 1894, and October 10, 1895, respectively (Coffey 1979; Buster 1979). Located in south central Kentucky on the Kentucky-Tennessee state line, Wayne was similar to other counties in Appalachia; the number of Black residents was small but stable.[64] Because they were enslaved by the same white master, Coffey is the surname of the three families of Black musicians who were active in Wayne County during the nineteenth and early twentieth centuries. Shell, the offspring of one of the three families, explains the family's musical heritage:

> We used to have a white fella here that was a fiddler. They called him C. C. Coffey, but his name was Coal Coffey. And Coal Coffey's father owned my daddy's people in the time of slaves. Well, there was an old fella that come out of the south after the war broke that they call Mike Coffey. He was [a] great fiddler. And he had a son, Andy. And Bled, he learnt his'n after his cousin, Andy. Andy could

Photo 6.8. Charlie Buster with fiddle. Lexington, Kentucky. April 1979. Photo by Robert J. Fulcher.

play but I believe that's the only one in the family that could do it. Now Bled Coffey, he's a different set of Coffey. His father was named Green [1847–1919].[65] He played violin; he could play a little on the banjo. (Coffey 1979)

Graphically, the musical genealogy of the Coffey family looks like the following:

Mike Coffey
|
Andy Coffey > > Bledsoe "Bled" Coffey
\ /
Charlie Buster > > > Shell Coffey

Shell remembered little about his parents' ancestry,[66] but knew that his father worked as a teamster, hauling oil-well equipment, from about 1900 until his death. US census records indicate that his father also worked as a farmer, which was the case for other males in the family; however, in the mid-1930s, Shell started working as a stonemason. Unlike some mountaineers, Shell's parents did not perform any musical instruments. He only heard them sing in the Baptist church built for freed Blacks on Kendrick Mountain, which had a traveling minister. He stated that his parents sang "old-time" songs: "Away in the Kingdom, Plenty of Good Room, Away in the Kingdom," "These Bones Shall Rise Again," "God's Gonna Trouble the Water," and "I'm Gonna Work till My Work on Earth Is Done." Some songs were sad and mournful ("These Bones Shall Rise Again" and "I'm Gonna Work till My Work on Earth Is Done"), while others, such as "Camped in Some Strange Land," would "put some life in you because it's a pretty fast song." Shell did not begin to attend church regularly until the early 1900s, when he was in his teens. As an adult, he played old-time sacred music on the guitar, while his daughter, a minister, sang and performed the accordion (Coffey 1979).[67]

Charlie also knew little about his family's heritage.[68] He served in the army during World War I, but did not go overseas. Yet, he had traveled both to Detroit, where he stayed for three years, and Cincinnati. Like his in-laws, Charlie worked as a farmer during the early part of his life, but became a stonemason during the 1930s. Unlike Shell, some of Charlie's family were instrumentalists. Charlie's father played the fiddle and a store-bought banjo that had five strings. Charlie stated that his father's fiddle playing was jiggly, which was different from the style that he used. And he did not know where or from whom his father acquired his music skills.

Shell became interested in music when he was nine or ten years old. Since string band music performed on the fiddle, banjo, and four-string guitar was popular during his childhood, these were the instruments he wanted to play. His first banjo was made from an old tin sifter and some screen wire. An old man in the area, called Uncle Grand Macbeth, helped him tune the banjo. After learning to perform the banjo and guitar, Shell stated that the next instrument he wanted to play was the fiddle. "I had a cousin [Charlie] that somebody learned him to play the violin and I got to where I could play. My daddy's first cousin [Bled]—he was a violin player. He'd buy a violin and I kept [it] until I could play a violin" (Coffey 1979). When asked if anyone in his community or family used gourd instruments, Shell stated:

That's all. Gourd guitar, fiddle. You have a gourd with straight neck in it. You cut a hole in one side to hold that sound there. We used to use them [gourds] for dippers. They used to make [grow] great big ones with a crooked neck. I guess it hold nearly half a bushel. Put salt in that to feed the cattle. You don't see no more of them though.

Wasn't raised straight every time. Sometimes you'd raise a bigger one with a great long neck. A great big hole. Just cut a hole inside and fix 'em a bridge and run them strings up and down the neck. They use wires [for strings]. They finally got to where they call the strings gut, cat gut. It wasn't [cat gut]. But that's what they'd call it. (Coffey 1979)

Although Shell never used gourds to make his instruments, he stated that he and other musicians often used substitute materials to construct an instrument when necessary: "An old man come to me and wanted me to go make some music for him. I didn't have no fiddle bow. I couldn't borrow one. And I took a chair arm and rosined [it] up and made as good as with a bow. You can do that" Coffey (1979). Charlie indicated that gourds were used to make fiddles and banjos but added: "I never seen none made out of a guitar" (Buster 1979).[69]

After learning the basic skills, Shell stated that his first performance was with his cousin Charlie on fiddle, while he played banjo (Coffey 1979). Charlie indicates that he acquired his first fiddle when he was seven or eight years old: "I dragged one around and tried to play. It was a little bitty thing, the first" (Buster 1979). Although Mike was the patriarch in the family for music making, Shell and Charlie never performed with him. Rather, they learned their fiddle tunes from Andy and Bled (Coffey 1979; Buster 1979). Shell's comments suggest that Mike was also highly regarded as a fiddler: "Uncle Mike. I never did see him. He was a great fiddler. He had a son, Andy was [a] fiddler. [When] Andy Coffey died, I helped put him away. That's fifty-five to sixty years ago" (Coffey 1979). Although Shell did not know how to play the fiddle that well during Andy's heyday, he remembered some of the tunes that Andy used to perform: "Forked Deer," "Billy in the Low Ground," "Leather Britches," "Sally Goodin," "Lost John," "John Henry," and "Barlow Knife" (Coffey 1979).

In their region, the manner in which musical knowledge was learned and transmitted from one generation to another is noteworthy. Since musicians rarely sang, it was the instrumental tunes that were passed on and identified with individuals. Tunes that Shell learned from Bled include "Chicken Reel," "The Forked Deer," "Ladies on the Steamboat," and "Ladies in the Ballroom," while "Little Rabbit Hare" is a tune he learned from "an old fellow in Lexington" (Coffey 1979). Shell did not remember learning any specific tunes from Andy, but stated that "Andy performed pretty near anything—'Sourwood Mountain,' 'Cumberland Gap,' 'Jane Wallace,' 'Leather Britches.' 'Red Bird,' that was one of the favorites [and] there's one they called 'Heel Up the Hall'" (Coffey 1979).

Even though musicians lived in neighboring communities, they did not always perform with each other. Some may have stayed to themselves because of varying performance styles or repertoire. For example, although Shell knew and performed with Bertram, Charlie rarely played with Bertram. Shell explained: "Bertram never did play with Charlie. He ain't as good a fiddler as Charlie. Charlie was a good, smooth fiddler. About the same as Leonard Rutherford. But Charlie played mostly dance songs and he did not sing. Well, sometimes he'd alto after me. Anything I'd sing, he'd try to alto it" (Coffey 1979).

In Wayne County, house parties and dances held in the homes of people in the community were especially popular for the performance of string band music. Shell explained: "I used to have dances. You'd have a house full.

Sometimes more than you could fit in a house. Some be out in the yard. Back then you didn't have what you have today. That went on till they got to where they wanted to be coming drunk and everything and I just quit. I was a man, forty or fifty years old, had a family [when I had those dances]. We'd have gatherings at Christmas. We'd have two or three days and nights at a time. That's all we'd have at Christmas time. Nothing else to go to" (Coffey 1979). In addition to house dances and providing entertainment at holiday events, both Fulcher and Harrod have noted that Black musicians performed in a variety of contexts during the early twentieth century. Fulcher (1988a) writes: "Andy Coffey . . . and Bled Coffey entertained Wayne County's black and white communities with fiddle and banjo. White people often paid their way with food purchases to see the black dances, featuring fancy buck-dancing steps like 'sifting sand,' 'the dog scratch,' 'heading the steer,' 'rocking the cradle,' and 'counting the crossties'" (3–4). The courthouse yard was a favorite "hang out" for fiddlers and other musicians. According to Harrod (1987), "Court dates [were] the big fair days in the middle of town. Everybody comes to trade things." Fiddlers from all parts of Kentucky would travel to participate in music making on fair days. Many Kentucky fiddlers obtained their music education each Saturday at the Wayne County courthouse in Monticello.

Although many of the musicians in Wayne County lived distances from each other and were somewhat detached from new trends evolving in other parts of the country, they were not cut off completely from outside influences. Like musicians in urban areas, the media had a dramatic impact on the musical world of some rural musicians during the early twentieth century. Shell explained: "My oldest brother—long back after 1902 or 1903, after the oil boom come in this country, when he worked in the oil fields—got enough money to get him a talking machine when it was first put out. Thomas Edison. He got one and it had a big horn on it. When he got one of them, that's where I got my start singing" (Coffey 1979).

After his brother purchased an Edison machine, Shell stated that they regularly made cylinder recordings:[70] "That time, it wasn't disc records. They first come out [with] this roller. They [were] about this long. You slip 'em on. That's what they had then. And when you were going to make a record, we'd take a fiddle and banjo and go and make million of them." When asked if he purchased and listened to cylinder recordings by others, Shell stated: "Oh no. We just [had] tunes we'd make ourselves we'd put on the records" (Coffey 1979).

When the Coffey family listened to disc recordings, it was always the music of other musicians, especially records by Richard Burnett (on guitar or banjo) and Leonard Rutherford (on fiddle).[71] Shell stated: "That's all [the] disc records they sold. . . . After the talking machine came out. That's where I learned the most of what I got." When asked if he remembered the names of songs from old disc records, he stated: "Well, it would take me a long time to go to names.

There's one [called] 'Mamma's Return.' That's a mighty sad song. And another one, 'As We Parted at the Gate.' That's a military song. It's an awful sad one:

> In a gambler's hall one day in a town so far away
> Where the gamblers they were comin' to and fro.
> I was leaving on a train that would bring me back again
> To my sweetheart that was waiting there for me." (Coffey 1979)

Shell's and Charlie's introduction to the blues also occurred through the media. Songs by Blind Lemon Jefferson, "Chock House Blues" (1926), and Jimmie Rodgers, "T.B. Blues" (1931), were among the first blues songs Shell heard on records. And when they performed the blues, most often they used the guitar and not the fiddle (Coffey 1979; Buster 1979).

In spite of the physical isolation and emphasis on retaining cultural practices from the nineteenth century, creativity continued to be an important aspect of the performance tradition of Black mountain musicians; but it varied. Charlie indicated that he had not composed any songs. Rather, he remembered and played tunes from earlier years; most were waltzes and breakdowns—for example, "Rock Creek Girls," "Leather Britches," "Fire on the Mountain," and "Arkansas Traveler."[72] On the other hand, Shell stated that he composed new tunes, in addition to playing the standard repertoire (including "Ladies in the Ballroom," "Jane Wallace," "Red Bird," and "Five Miles to Town"). During his interview, he played a tune titled "Wild Goose Chase." When Fulcher inquired about the origin of the tune, Shell stated: "It's a homemade tune. We just make 'em up ourselves. Going to be a musician, you've got to make some tunes, just the same as you would with anything else"[73] (Coffey 1979). "The Devil at the Crossroads" is a dance tune that Shell stated that he had composed with Charlie's brother [Jay Buster]: "Me and Charlie's brother figured that tune up. We'd go to play for dances; we figured out something for them to dance by" (Coffey 1979).[74] Shell later taught the tune to Bertram: "If you've ever heard Cuje Bertram play it ["The Devil at the Crossroads"]. "I learnt him that tune. I sit down several times with him [and] help him pick it up. We used to live with the road between us. [He] sit right there at breakfast the next morning [and played it]" (Coffey 1979). When asked about the meaning of "The Devil at the Crossroads," Shell stated: "We just made an old funny name for it."

As noted earlier, mountain music culture, particularly during the nineteenth and early twentieth centuries, tended to be more interracial than that in other parts of the United States, partly because of differences in demographics. But the relationships between Blacks and whites in these circumstances have not always been discussed or viewed from the perspective of African Americans. For this reason, Shell's comments about well-known white musicians in Kentucky are significant because they provide insight not only about the interactions of

Blacks and whites during the early twentieth century, but also how Blacks in the region regarded the performance style and behavior of white musicians. In his interview with Fulcher, Shell stated:

> I remember when Rutherford come here; he was just a little boy wearing knee pants. I don't know [where he learned his fiddling]. He's a sociable man. He was a good [fiddler]. Smooth. Yeah, he could make a fiddle just talk. Sing with it. He was pretty smooth.[75] Now he could play good music to listen at, but he couldn't play no ballroom music. I mean music played to dance by. Now neither one of them could play good dancing music. Just play good music to listen, to sing by.
>
> Dick Burnett could play any kind of song with a banjo, guitar or fiddle. He'd sing with his'n. But he [is] sort of like me. He's kind of jiggly. He did funny stuff while he played. He'd shake all over, just like jelly. As the old folks said, "he's a real monkey." That's where he'd get his money at. Sit up there with a cup on his knee. I was helping make that music. And sometimes when he and Leonard Rutherford was playing, I'd get him to play "St. Paul" with me. Of course, I really love that tune. "St. Paul" [is] a military song. I can't play it too good. It's a band piece played when the people went across the sea in the time of war. And "Under the Double Eagle." That's another one. I used to play that pretty good. They played pretty near anything. One piece they'd play and sing was "Flowers for the Fields of Alabama." They could really get something out of that. They played "Ladies on the Steamboat" [recorded on Columbia in 1927]. They would travel. They played here in the courthouse yard.[76] (Coffey 1979)

Wayne Martin (1987), a North Carolina folklorist who has written much on fiddling in the southern United States, believes that the interaction between Black and white musicians in Wayne County affected Rutherford's playing: "In Wayne County, these guys were really playing a lot of slides, a lot of what I think of as blues-influenced music. And they [Wayne County Black musicians] influenced this guy named Leonard Rutherford, a white musician who was recorded. He's a real great fiddler from the twenties and thirties. . . . He recorded a lot for Columbia, 78s. His style is very fluid and there are a lot of sliding notes in it and blues. There's a touch of blues that you know he was influenced by some Black musicians somewhere along the line."

William "Bill" Livers (1911–1988)

Bill Livers is one of the few African American fiddlers active in northern Kentucky during the early twentieth century to live through the late twentieth century (see photo 6.9). In addition to working as a tenant farmer, Livers was known in his community as "a good storyteller who plays the fiddle; an unbelievable fiddler who cooks; [and] an incredible cook who philosophizes"

Photo 6.9. William "Bill" Livers. Monterey, Kentucky. August 1976. Matthew Kaplan Photography.

(Andrews and Larson 1977, 16). As an entertainer who was as much an actor as a musician, Livers's performances were events to be remembered. John Harrod (1997), who performed with Livers during the 1970s and 1980s, writes: "He would play risqué blues numbers and wiggle his hips; and he liked to kiss the women. His stories and tall tales delivered with a convincing display of sincerity . . . were as much a part of his performances as his music. . . . At times, it seemed that his local reputation as a showman obscured his abilities on the fiddle, but when he would get around other good musicians, he knew how to make their heads turn with his music." Similar to other early twentieth-century Black fiddlers in different parts of the South, not until the latter part of his career did Livers become known outside his local community. In addition to recording, he traveled widely in Kentucky and neighboring states with several young white musicians (the Progress Red Hot String Band, later known as the Bill Livers String Ensemble) performing at festivals, universities, and other cultural events (see photos 6.10 and 6.11),[77] including the Folklore Society of Greater Washington, DC (January 19, 1979); the 1982 World's Fair in Knoxville Tennessee, at which he performed for former President Jimmy Carter; the Indiana Folklore Society in Bloomington; and the John Henry Music Festival in Charleston, West Virginia

Photo 6.10. William "Bill" Livers playing fiddle. Franklin, Kentucky. 1980s. Courtesy of Tacy Groves.

Photo 6.11. Eric Larsen (bass), William "Bill" Livers (fiddle), and Ben Griffith (guitar). Franklin, Kentucky. 1980s. Courtesy of Tacy Groves.

(Ware 1981; "Groundhog is Good Eatin" 1986; Harrod 1997; Keith 2013). "In the late 1970s he performed a concert on the grounds of the Kentucky governor's estate and afterward he and Governor Julian Carroll enjoyed a drink together inside the mansion" (Keith 2013, 132). This notoriety is perhaps one of the reasons the life and musicking of Bill Livers has been better documented than Kentucky Black fiddlers discussed in the foregoing. In addition to interviews and field recordings, information about him can be found in scholarly articles, reference works, and archives.[78]

Although Livers was born in Owen County, about three miles south of Owenton (the county seat) in the north-central part of the Bluegrass Region, he spent much of his life in Long Ridge, a small community about four miles north of Owenton.[79] Like many rural-based performers, Livers was born into a family of musicians. Virge Livers, a great-grandfather on his father's side, was a fiddler known throughout Owen and Grant, two neighboring counties in the northern part of the Bluegrass Region.[80] According to Bill, Virge was "one of the best [fiddlers] . . . and an awful good banjo picker. . . . He had two boys, Albert and Claude Livers. Albert, he was on the banjo. And Claude, he was on the mandolin and violin, too" (Andrews and Larson 1977, 17; Harrod 1987). An uncle, Hood Livers, was also a fiddler in the area. "Old Flanagan," one of his songs, was not only popular at square dances, it was "the signature tune in the northern Kentucky area, and an elaborate tune [that] fiddlers played to show off their skills or win a contest" (Ware 1981, 31). However, Bill (1987) indicated that none of his immediate family members (father, mother, or three sisters) performed music:

> They never did try. I'm the only one. If I didn't live with this white family [as a tenant farmer], I never would've done it either. But he [Clarence Orr, the son of his employer] kept aggravating me. I got so where I wanted to play. Soon I kept on learning. I worked for them almost 40 years. We had a lot of fiddlers in the county then. Most of them was white fiddlers. We all get together and have a big chicken soup and corn-cutting with the fiddle. Alfred Carter was another Black fiddler, but he played mostly for white dances. All of those old pieces, I learnt from him. "Old Virge" was one. "Chicken Reel" was another. The only song I can sing, "Boil Them Cabbage Down." I learnt all them pieces from him. Henry Gale was a fiddler. He's old. We used to work together.

Bill's first instrument was the harmonica, which he began playing when he was fourteen or fifteen years old, primarily because this is what he most often heard in live performances and on recordings: "All the music that I hear[d] is a French harp [harmonica] on one of those little old round records with the horn on it, Edison put them out. . . . Oh, I tell you, the real kind of music was played on that thing. I never will forget it. 'Oh, You Beautiful Doll, You Great Big Beautiful Doll.' And the next thing that I heard on that thing was 'Yes, We Have No Bananas Today.' And the next one was 'Casey Jones.' A friend boy of mine was playing the harp and he played right along with that Edison Victrola" (Ware 1981, 31). Bill states that he experimented with all types of music on the French harp: "Oh, I'd play 'Down Yonder,' 'Yes Sir, That's My Baby,' and all that kind of stuff. The first blues I played was the 'St. Louis Blues' and that was back in 1942 or '43. Learned it from . . . a colored guy [who] come through here. . . . He'd sing a while and then he'd blow that comb . . . and just moan. . . . He came here with the carnival and he didn't stay here about three days. And [I] try to play a few blues, but never could get them blues straightened out on that French harp" (Ware 1981, 32–33).

It was not until 1937, around age twenty-seven, that Bill started playing the fiddle. When asked the question, "Did you teach yourself, or did someone [else teach you]," Bill (1987) responded: "The man I worked with. He used to say after I got my work all done, I could go in the house there. Sometimes she'd [his employer's wife] play the piano, it was according to how she feel. I learnt by myself. When he come in, he played violin too. He and I both get together. The first piece I ever played [was] 'Old Kentucky Home.' When you get that one down, you can do the rest of them. It's easy. It's like falling off a ladder if you ever learn it. Then the next one, 'Jesus Lover of My Soul.' I played it on my French harp before I played it on my violin." According to Bill, the fiddle he learned on was 200 years old: "The first fiddle I played on, . . . the man I come from today workin' down there give it to me. He play left-handed. And I played left-handed too, had to, because it was strung up left-handed and there wasn't no other way for me to learn. And I learned left-handed, [but I was right-handed]" (Ware 1981, 32). When he obtained a fiddle that was strung for a right-handed person, it took him about a year to relearn how to play the instrument (Riley 2010).

Like other musicians in the rural areas of northern Kentucky, Bill played for house parties, after-church socials, fish fries, barbecues, and festivals in Long Ridge and neighboring towns. Livers remembers that Virge Livers and his two sons sometimes walked or rode mules three or four miles from their home in Owenton to play for dances and parties (Andrews and Larson 1977, 17; Ware 1981, 33). "We used to go to Frankfort [about twenty-five miles south of Owen County]. Played for a dance there every Saturday night" (Livers 1987). Rarely did fiddlers receive enough payment for performances to make musicking a profession, but the pay was helpful in supplementing their income. "I didn't make any money during the week time but I played for a big round or square dance. You could pick up maybe five, six, or seven dollars. You could buy cigarettes or cigar or chewing tobacco, whatever you wanted" (Livers 1987).

Besides recreation in homes, taverns, and other venues that Blacks and whites would have attended for recreation, the courthouse was a favorite location for performances during the early decades of the twentieth century. Musicians traveling in carnivals and medicine shows would set up in the courthouse yard in the middle of town and entertain whoever wanted to listen. Oftentimes, the guitar and French harp were combined. Other times, it was washboard, twelve-string guitar, and drums that served as instrumentation. Livers, along with local artists (Navy Pitts, Sylvester Carl, and Chester Morton), performed at the courthouse once every two months in addition to playing for all the tap dances and concerts around New Liberty[81] (Ware 1981, 31; Keith 2013).

During the 1940s, Bill Livers also performed with an all-white band called the Owen County Idiots. After playing together several years, the name was changed to Bill Livers and the Holbrook Idiots. Performing for white audiences was not uncommon for Black fiddlers during this period, but Livers's situation was unique, and his role in the group was precarious probably because he was more well known in the community for his antics as an entertainer than his ability in playing the instrument. Jeffrey A. Keith (2013) elaborates: "At these events he likely had to conform to audience expectations about the behavior of African Americans.... According to one secondhand report, he donned blackface while performing at a local dance.... The band's stage name set up Livers as the leader of a white group of 'idiots.' Yet this belies the fact that he might have been the butt of the joke. In retrospect, many people, white and black, have wondered whether Livers was taken advantage of by his fellow musicians. One white friend even speculated that the Idiots' show was akin to 'minstrelsy' and that Livers was 'the comic'" (124–25).

When performances at house parties, courthouses, and recreational venues began to fall out of fashion in the 1950s, Livers started having his own fish fry at his home, which, during the early 1970s, became a big event in the community with anywhere from 100 to 140 people attending (Ware 1981, 33). "He would clean out the tobacco barn and put up some lights and there would be fish, hushpuppies, coleslaw, beer and whiskey, and music and dancing till the sun came up" (Harrod 1987). Although he rarely attended church, Livers (1987) stated that there were no prohibitions against him playing the fiddle in a religious context: "They let me play in my wife's church anytime, but I just wouldn't go." Although his wife, Hattie, did not care for fiddle music (because of the lifestyle associated with fiddlers), she indicated that she liked listening to recordings: "I like the music but I don't care for it. I never like country music. I like it on the radio. Also, I don't like the blues. He was going to play one Sunday. He was going to bring his fiddle, but he never did play in any of the churches. I like any kind of music except the violin" (H. Livers 1987).

After learning how to play the fiddle, Livers expanded his repertoire by picking up tunes from the radio as well as movies, parties, and circuses he attended.[82] Livers would show up alone at white country square dances and sit in with the band or buck dance. At the fish fries at his home, he often played "Old Virge," a song composed by his grandfather. Another favorite was "Carroll County Blues," a tune he learned from a local musician (Andrews and Larson 1977, 17; Ware 1981, 33).[83] In addition to songs by others, Livers also composed two tunes: "Rainbow's End" (see lyrics below) and "Taft Highway."[84] Regarding the former, Livers (1987) explained: "I heard part of it over the television, but I never did get it finished up. But I wrote the rest of it."

> Oh, I've traveled this whole world over, looking.
> I'm going down to the Rainbow's End.
> I've got no place, I've got no home.
> I've been traveling all alone.
> I'm going down to the Rainbow's End.
> There is someone who's waiting there alone.
> I'm going down to the Rainbow's End.
> I've got no place, I've got no home.
> I've been traveling all alone.
> Till I reach at the Rainbow's End.

"Taft Highway," according to Harrod (1987), is about Livers's wife, Hattie, leaving him one time: "She went walking down the Taft Highway."

Unlike some musicians who resisted new ideas, Livers continued to add new material to his performances. By the late 1970s, his repertoire was eclectic.[85] Although songs from the white country music tradition predominated, a mixture of Black and white influences could be heard, including blues, rag, swing, popular, and old-time dance tunes (Andrews and Larson 1977, 17; Ware 1981, 31). Livers and his friend, Charlie William Payne, a piano player who sometimes accompanied him, were known for their performance of "Running Around Blues," a blues song they composed together. Yet, Livers (1987) stated: "whites didn't like the blues too much. They like that hard music."[86]

In my interview with him, Livers (1987) commented on his interest in both sacred and secular music. "I played church or religious songs on the fiddle [for example, 'Have Thine Own Way Lord,' 'Nearer My God to Thee,' 'Jesus Lover of My Soul,' 'Peace in the Valley'][87] and Cab Calloway tunes ['Underneath the Harlem Moon']. I sang and played it too." The newer styles were learned from young friends he met in the seventies. Harrod (1987) stated: "The longer we played together, the more we were doing the blues. Less breakdowns and more blues and the old pop tunes. Cab Calloway, Lena Horne, 'Stormy Weather.'" Ajay Kalra (2006b), who closely examined Livers's musicking as well as that of other African American performers who performed at Berea College's annual Celebration of Traditional Music as part of a fellowship program at the college, explains:

> Perhaps more than standard old-time fiddle tunes, Livers seemed to enjoy playing Tin Pan Alley and early jazz standards such as James Bland's "In the Evening by the Moonlight," Ted Koehler and Harold Arlen's "Stormy Weather," Walter Donaldson and Gus Kahn's "Yes Sir, That's My Baby," and Fats Waller's "Ain't Misbehavin'" and "Honeysuckle Rose"; country standards such as the Skillet Lickers' favorite "Sweet Bunch of Daisies," Jimmie Davis's "Nobody's Darling But Mine," Pee Wee King's "Tennessee Waltz" and Leon McAuliffe's "Steel Guitar Rag." He also did pieces that reflected variously on black-white relationships through different periods of history including "Run, N----r, Run" ("The Pateroller Song"), minstrel songs including James Bland's "Oh Dem Golden Slippers," and even outright derogatory songs from the late nineteenth century coon song genre such as "Big Fat Coon."

When Virge Livers performed during the early years, Bill stated that a variety of instruments were included in the ensemble: "They had banjo, guitar, mandolin, and piano. It was string band, all string music. Charlie William Payne was piano player. He used to live right over hear about two miles down the road. He played them old-fashioned music, and I stick right after him" (Livers 1987). The instrumentation Livers included in his groups was similar to those used by other Kentucky string bands. Instead of percussion, melodic instruments were performed in a percussive manner. On the role of percussion instruments in Kentucky fiddling, Harrod (1987) explained: "Never have [seen percussion], except sometimes in some of those old string band recordings. There is really not much going on with the guitar except the person is beating it like a drum. And they might even just be playing one chord, hitting all of the strings at once.

But the rhythm that they're hitting is about the same. The effect is like somebody playing the drum more so than the way you would think of a guitar now. I got some of that with [the] John Lusk recordings.[88] The banjo and the guitar are mainly just used as percussive instruments. The banjo is not playing a melody; it's more or less playing a rhythm. The fiddle is playing the melody." In explaining his experiences performing with Livers, Harrod (1987) provides further insight on musical features unique to the fiddler:

> There was six of us at one time. I played mandolin. Sometimes Eric would play guitar. We had bass a player. Sometimes we had a banjo. This band went through several changes. So, these instruments got switched. We didn't always have a banjo, but we always had a mandolin, guitar, and bass. And the bass player could play piano. So as far as instruments go, we were probably closer to what they used to play around here. I don't think the banjo was ever as big up here in northern Kentucky as it was in the mountains. Most of the banjo players you meet up here played plectrum style, strummed it, or played the four-string banjo. I've never run into a claw hammer banjo player in this part of Kentucky.
>
> On some of his [Livers's] tunes, different ones of us would take leads. And we'd communicate by eye signals, kicks, or the best way we could. Bill would keep playing; he'd just play a little quieter. Mostly when he was playing, we kept other people's breaks to a minimum. On some of the songs, one person would play a break if they really had something good. But mostly when we were playing with Bill, since he was singing, he'd play his own breaks. And that would be enough. By him fiddling and singing, you really didn't have room for everyone in the band to take a break.

Regardless of the type of fiddle music played, dancing always took place. Livers (1987) stated that people used to perform "the old-fashioned round, square dance; some called it off. On the blues, they did two step. If somebody played the guitar and play a piece [and] I didn't have to play the guitar with him, I'd dance every once in a while." According to Harrod (1987), "Some of it was square dancing. But just as much of it was round dancing and couple dancing. Long time ago, we played down at the Monterey Jamboree in an old schoolhouse. And there were a couple of guys in there—mostly old timers [who] came there to dance and Bill would play for 'em. So, different sets might be doing different things. They'd want you to do maybe one square dance and one round dance; they'd be about half and half. Then you'd do a big circle whistle dance.[89] That's just what the people around here wanted us to do. They wanted a little bit of all kinds of music and dancing to go with it. So, it seemed kind of all mixed up."

Burnham Ware (1987), blues researcher and one of Livers's distant cousins, stated that Livers's playing represents a rural, early Black fiddle style that is different from the smooth fiddling heard in the playing of some blues and jazz performers: "Bill was a primitive fiddle player in terms of his technique, and the times I heard him, he was quite screechy.[90] He played at that John Henry Folk Festival one year.... [He was] nowhere near someone like Howard Armstrong.[91] Bill was a very primitive, rural musician. Attempted to learn on his own, but never really was able to. Just didn't have the talent to develop a higher technique, and really didn't know where to go with it; that would be one of the problems you would have with the fiddle. You can develop a technique and learn pretty much on your own, at least playing country blues, or rural blues." Obviously, Ware's comments are biased and do not reflect the tastes of all Kentuckians. According to Harrod (1987), "Bill's bowing is jerky. To some people, jerky is bad. To me, if that jerky is syncopated right, that's the kind of fiddling I like. There's a kind of syncopated bow lick that Doc Roberts had. Bill Livers doesn't have the same bow lick, but he's got a jerky syncopation in his bowing that probably didn't come from white people. Also, I wouldn't call Jim Booker jerky; his bowing was smooth and precise, kind of like Doc Roberts." In a personal communication, Harrod (2002) stated: "His fiddling is primitive, maybe, but when Livers wanted to and had the right audience, he played with great rhythm and feeling." Both Harrod and Keith believe Livers's idiosyncratic behavior affected his fiddling: "Livers disingenuously downplayed his skills so that he would not threaten someone who historically stood in a higher station on account of his race" (Keith 2013, 133). In other words, Livers "was never able to overcome the racial expectations that were ingrained in him during the Jim Crow segregation. In those years, Livers was faced with the burden of crafting his image to suit his surroundings.... As a result, his social demeanor was as variable as his fiddle playing" (132–33).

Even though the fiddle tradition had not completely died out among Kentucky Blacks in northern Kentucky during the early twentieth century, Livers was "a fly in a bowl of milk." In other words, few Blacks performed string band music, and fiddling had begun to decline in popularity even among whites. When I asked, during my interview with him, why fiddle music was no longer popular, Livers (1987) stated: "For some people, it's [playing the fiddle is] a little high. It's hard to play. You know how you play by note, but the violin is so hard to play when you play by ear. All I learnt, I learnt by ear, the little that I know. When you leave that, you've got to change all over again. They don't play [because] they don't take time. I'm the only person who plays anything around here. My old violin, nobody plays but me." Although Livers did not know other Black fiddlers in Kentucky, he was aware of those in other parts of the country. In fact, on a visit to Cincinnati, he stated that he played with string band musicians Howard Armstrong and Carl Martin, who became well known as the Tennessee Chocolate Drops during the 1930s (Harrod 1987).

For Livers, the fiddle was more than an instrument to be used for entertainment; he believed in its association with the devil. Commenting at length on this subject, he stated: "I tell you one thing. You know that the devil is in that fiddle. He just control[s] it. I take my fiddle down and start trying to play something and I couldn't play. I put it back up and go off and forget it. I go back two or three days and get it down and it sounds natural. You know in the Bible when Rome burnt up, this guy watched Rome. Sometimes he played [the violin] while Rome was burning. The violin, it ain't made for everybody to play it. A violin is a master of all music. A violinist, he's the master of all of it." When asked if he could tell when the devil is in the violin, Livers (1987) responded: "It tells you about the devil is in it. That's the reason there is so many tunes. It's been tunes played on the violin you don't hear on nothing else. It's different songs. You heard, 'The Devil's Dream.' There's one called 'Plucking Out the Devil's Eye Ball.' Yes sir." Interjecting his opinions during my conversation with Livers, Harrod (1987) stated, "You sort of get possessed." And Livers (1987) added: "Sometime you be playing and then go out of tune. And you can't tune that thing to save your life. He's contrary. He ain't going to let you master him either. The violin, it's always been a master. He's the master of all music, all the harps, the bands, the prettiest tunes."

Summary

This chapter demonstrates that Kentucky fiddling continued to be a shared tradition through the mid-twentieth century. Not only did Black and white fiddlers perform similar tunes passed on from earlier times, but Blacks created new songs that became a part of the canon of Kentucky fiddlers. It is significant that "Martha Campbell," which has an African American provenance, is one of the most popular tunes played by Kentucky fiddlers (Titon 2001, 23). In addition, performance practices identified with Black musicking—such as the use of slurs, slides, and bent notes as well as rhythms that are off-beat (syncopated)—are common to both Black and white fiddlers. Harrod (1987), who has been aware of these issues for some time, explained: "When I first started seriously recording these old white fiddlers [for example, Doc Roberts, Darley Fulks,[92] and Columbus Williams], the first thing that struck me is that all of these old guys played a lot of blues pieces. It wasn't all twelve-bar blues. It had a bluesy quality—more sliding notes, and there was syncopation timing. They approached the time differently in every piece." Research conducted by other investigators confirms these findings. Milnes (1999) writes: "Kentucky fiddler, Doc Roberts, whose commercial recordings made him widely influential, traced most of his best tunes to African-American fiddler Owen Walker. These included 'Waynesboro' ['Waynesborough,' 'Waynesburgh'], a tune that found favor with West Virginia fiddlers. Roberts is regarded as an important conduit, bringing black fiddling traditions to white audiences" (97).

Similar to other states in the Appalachian Mountains, the similarities and borrowings among fiddlers in Kentucky most likely occurred because of close interactions between Blacks and whites over the years. Again, Harrod (1987) explained: "There was mixing at Black and white dances—white musicians at Black dances, Black musicians at white dances, and white and Blacks playing together. So, there was evidently a lot of contact at least in central Kentucky between Black and white musicians. . . . Also, with fiddling, you can't figure out the bowing just from listening to the music. You really got to watch the bow arm. . . . It would be real hard to learn to be a good traditional fiddler if all you had was records."

Environment and demographics are additional factors that affected fiddling. In counties with small Black populations, the performances by Black fiddlers (in terms of context, music played, and audience) were probably similar to nineteenth-century practices. Although Blacks in these areas knew through the media about the new musical genres being created by African Americans in other parts of the country, the performance of this new music was limited because their audiences had different preferences. However, the experience of fiddlers living in communities with substantial Black populations (including Owen Walker and members of the Booker family in central Kentucky) was different. Black fiddlers in these communities had opportunities to perform for varied audiences: all Black, all white, and mixed. What is noteworthy is that when performing both old songs and new creations, many used a performance style that was African-derived (probably because this is what their audiences wanted to hear), which helped to distinguish their fiddling from other regions in the state. Obviously, these practices were so appealing that they influenced white musicians who shared their ideas with others.

Similar to the past, African Americans have been major innovators and contributors to the development of fiddling in Kentucky as well as other parts of the United States, but this fact is not well known because of misrepresentation (DjeDje 2016). It is also significant that the fiddle tradition was never completely "rejected" by Kentucky Black fiddlers; rather, support from both the Black and white community allowed them to continue performing what existed in the past but also contribute to new creations emerging in other parts of the country. Presenting a fuller discussion of fiddling in African American culture, hopefully, will help eliminate many of the distortions and inaccuracies that now exist about the complex role of the instrument in both Black and white communities.

fiddlingismyjoycompanion.net

Notes

1. 🎻 See Map 6.1, Map 6.2, Land Regions 6.1, and History 6.1.

2. In the 1970s, Robert Fulcher interviewed several Black musicians—Shell Coffey, Charlie Buster, and Bennie "Cuje" Bertram—who had been well-known fiddlers in Kentucky and Tennessee during the early twentieth century (see Fulcher 1987, 1988a, 1988b). John Harrod, a white fiddler and mandolin player born in Shelby County in northern Kentucky who also collected fiddle tunes, has produced recordings of Kentucky fiddle music (see Meade, Harrod, and Wilson 1997a, 1997b). In addition, see publications by the following: Brady (2013), Gibson (2018), Russell (2021), Salsburg (2017), Titon (2001), and Wolfe (1982).

3. The twelve-bar blues, one of the most important chord progressions in popular music, has a distinctive form especially in terms of lyrics and chord structure. The length of sections may also vary to include eight-bar or sixteen-bar blues (see discussion below).

4. 🎻 See Demographics 6.1.

5. 🎻 See Demographics 6.2.

6. A discussion on Banjo Hangout on November 22, 2013, indicates that Barbra Kunkle recorded Hawkins on March 23, 1974, and Mark Wilson and Gus Meade recorded him again on April 6, 1974. http://www.banjohangout.org/archive/274550. Accessed April 25, 2017.

7. Although he interacted with several Black and white fiddlers in Kentucky, Bertram is only briefly discussed in this chapter; a more extensive examination of his life and career appears in the following chapter on Tennessee, where he was born and raised (Fulcher 1987; Titon 2001, 22, 198).

8. 🎻 See Demographics 6.3. US census records indicate that Walker's parents, Squire Walker (b. ca. 1830) and Betsy Elizabeth Parrish Walker (1835–1917), were both born in Kentucky—most likely in Madison County. They had three children (one female and two males), and Owen was the eldest. After slavery, Owen's father worked as a farmer, while his mother spent her time in the home.

9. 🎻 See History 6.2. Doc Roberts began his recording career in 1925, when local talent scout Dennis W. Taylor recruited him to make recordings for Gennett. In 1927, Roberts recorded several sides with members of the Booker family; also see Green (1971, 199); Otto and Burns (1974, 411, 413); Wolfe (1982, 29, 1992, 69, 1997, 67); and Titon (2001, 22).

10. Because I have been unable to locate the 1910 census record for Walker, his occupation for 1910 is unknown.

11. Two tunes Roberts learned from Walker—"Old Buzzard" and Waynesburgh"—were performed at the August 26, 1927, recording session with guitarist John Booker (see below). While the borrowing of tunes by musicians was commonplace in US traditional and popular culture of the eighteenth and nineteenth century, the use of covers (new performances or reinterpretations of an existing recording) became a financial boom with the release of commercial recordings in the early twentieth century (Huber 2013, 27).

12. Taylor was a farmer who lived three miles from Richmond, Kentucky. After becoming a talent scout for the Starr Piano Company, he came up with Taylor's Kentucky Boys as the name for his band. Although not a musician, Taylor liked old-time music and began managing the band in the mid-1920s. The group played for local dances, at school houses, and social events until Taylor eventually got them a recording contract with Gennett (Wolfe 1982, 27–28; Russell 2021, 54). Victor Records, originally known as Victor Talking Machine, was founded in 1901 in Camden, New Jersey, but was absorbed by the Radio Corporation of America (RCA) in 1929.

13. 🎵 See Photos 6.3a and 6.3b for other members of the Booker family.

14. Established in 1863, Camp Nelson is located about twenty miles south of Lexington (the second most populous city in the state), roughly forty miles southeast of Frankfort (the state capitol), and seven miles south of Nicholasville (the seat for Jessamine County). Named in honor of Major General William Nelson, Camp Nelson is significant because, by August 1863, thousands of enslaved Black people from central Kentucky, impounded to build railroads for the Union Army, were stationed there. When Blacks started to be drafted into the army in 1864, Camp Nelson became the most important recruiting station and training camp. Although there were many deaths, many Blacks considered Camp Nelson to be the cradle of freedom because it became the chief center for issuing emancipation papers to the formerly enslaved (Sears 1992, 158; Bogert 1995).

15. Regarding Booker's last days, Wyatt (2018) states: "On April 7, 1939, Booker was admitted to the Negro ward of the Eastern State Hospital, Kentucky's antiquated mental institution in Lexington, and he died there on February 5, 1940, of heart disease 'with psychosis.'"

16. 🎵 See Photo 6.3b. Census records indicate that Booker's parents were born in Kentucky—the father in Washington County, about fifty miles southwest of Jessamine; the county birth place for Booker's mother is unknown. However, all of their children were born in Jessamine County.

17. 🎵 See Map 6.2 and Demographics 6.4.

18. Bogert (1995, 18) indicates that they started playing in the Benevolence Hall and later played at Saturday night bar dances for both Black and white audiences in neighborhood counties.

19. The distance (by car) between Nicholasville, Jessamine's county seat, and Richmond, Indiana, is about 165 miles. Thus, it was a long trek north for Jessamine County musicians participating in recording sessions. Dixon and Godrich (1982) incorrectly indicate that the recording took place in May 1927, but Dixon, Godrich, and Rye (1997) and Russell and Pinson (2004) give April 26, 1927, as the date of Booker's recording with Taylor's Kentucky Boys. Huber indicates that some researchers suggest another reason for Booker's absence: "the portrait [of Booker] may not have been taken at the time of the band's recording sessions and that when it was actually taken Booker was not included in the photo because he was unavailable to sit for the photograph with his two band mates" (Huber 2013, 50; also see Nevins 2003).

20. Unlike other record companies of the era, Starr did not create a race or hillbilly record series (Salsburg 2017); also see below.

21. 🎵 See Repertoire 6.1 for details, including the number of sessions that took place, song titles, names of performers, and record labels.

22. Dennis Taylor usually paid all expenses incurred in developing tunes and making the trip to Richmond, and then paid the artists a flat fee of so much a side. In exchange, the artists usually agreed to give Taylor all royalties that accrued from the record. "This later occasionally led to bitterness between Taylor and his musicians, who often felt that their records sold more than they actually did, and that Taylor was enriching himself at their expense. During his peak years, in 1926 and 1927, Taylor would collect as much as $800 to $900 a month from Gennett, but this would represent royalties from dozens of records by a variety of musicians" (Wolfe 1982, 28).

23. Musicians performing in various capacities (banjo, guitar, harmonica, and vocal) participated in five recordings sessions on April 26 and 27, 1927, as members of Taylor's Kentucky Boys. Booker, the only fiddler and Black person involved in the recordings (to my knowledge), recorded on two of the five sessions (Russell and Pinson 2004, 894–95).

24. Gennett was the company that made the recordings with Champion as its subsidiary. The other companies licensed recordings from Gennett.

25. 🎵 See Repertoire 6.1.

26. I use the term *newly configured* because the persons performing as Taylor's Kentucky Boys in August 1927 are different from the musicians who recorded in April 1927.

27. 🎵 See Repertoire 6.1, section E.

28. 🎵 See Repertoire 6.1, section F.

29. Sears, Roebuck and Company owned both Challenge and Silvertone record labels. The records produced by Gennett and licensed to Challenge generally sold for less than Silvertone

ones because the former seldom used songs requiring royalty payments and the label generally assigned pseudonyms to the artists (Hoffmann 2004, 176). According to Wolfe (1997, 72), both Roberts and record company executives were not pleased with the test pressings and made a decision not to release them. "It is unclear whether Roberts requested this because he didn't think they were all that good or because he didn't want to be associated with Taylor's name" because of previous disagreements.

30. See Repertoire 6.1, sections C and D.

31. See Repertoire 6.1.

32. William "Bill" Manuel Johnson (1872–1972) was founder and leader of the Original Creole Orchestra, the first jazz band to leave New Orleans and tour California as well as other parts of the United States in the 1910s (Hazeldine 2003). Also, because of its identification with European art music, some African American musicians used the word *orchestra* to elevate not only the stature of the group but also the music they were playing (Meadows 2017).

33. In this case, Booker's 1927 recordings complement Victor's 1922 recordings by white fiddlers Alexander "Eck" Robertson (1887–1975) and Henry Gilliland (1845–1924). The four fiddle duets that Robertson and Gilliland recorded on Friday, June 30, 1922, represent the first commercial recordings of rural-based musicians performing old-time music. Two tunes, "Arkansaw Traveler" and "Turkey in the Straw," were released by Victor, but "Forked Deer" and "Apple Blossom" were never issued.

34. See Repertoire 6.1, sections A–F.

35. It is uncertain if "Old Hen Cackled and the Rooster Crowed" is the same or related to "Cackling Hen" that was popular among the enslaved (Winans 1990, 51–52). But when musicking by Black fiddler Elbert Freeman (1967b) is compared with that of white fiddler John Carson (1923), who made the first recording of the tune, some similarities are apparent (see chapter 9).

36. See Knauff (1839).

37. Between 1922 and 1930, a total of seven commercial recordings were made of "Forked Deer"—three before and three after the 1927 recording by Taylor's Kentucky Boys. The three sessions that preceded the 1927 recording include: Robertson and Gilliland (1922), Stuart and Austin (1924), and Daniel (1926). After 1927, two recording sessions took place in 1928 and one in 1930: Kessinger and Kessinger (1928); Setters and Robison (1928); and the Fox Chasers (1930) (Russell and Pinson 2004).

38. Go to Audio Examples to listen to "Forki Deer" by Stuart and Austin (1924) and "Forked Deer" by Booker and Taylor's Kentucky Boys (1927).

39. See Analysis 6.1.

40. See Lyrics 6.1. Although the 1927 recording by the Booker Orchestra is instrumental with no singing, the first release by Charlie Jackson included singing with lyrics that served as the basis for song texts used by subsequent performers, both Black and white.

41. *Hokum* refers to a creative work (movie, play, or piece of writing) that is nonsensical, trite, sentimental, or unrealistic. In the context of music, hokum's origins date to nineteenth-century Blackface minstrelsy, when it referred to a style of comedic farce, spoken, sung and spoofed, while masked in both risqué innuendo and "tomfoolery." In blues and country music, the term refers to songs with lyrics that make sexual innuendos (Oliver 2003a).

42. Go to Audio Examples to listen to the first five releases of "Salty Dog Blues"/"Salty Dog": Charlie Jackson (1924); Clara Smith (1926); Freddie Keppard's Jazz Cardinals (1926); the Allen Brothers (1927); and the McGee Brothers (1927).

43. See Biography 6.1.

44. See Lyrics 6.1 for the first four verses of Jackson's performance with time markers indicating the beginning of each melody. However, Jackson's entire performance includes sixteen verses. In most cases, a specific melody is identified with certain lyrics. Jackson alternates in using the melody for the second half of verses that include the word "Mama," which is different from the melody used for the ending of other verses.

45. See Form 6.1.

46. 🎵 See Analysis 6.2 for a description of "Salty Dog" as performed in the first five recordings.

47. Wolfe (1997, 70) states that Taylor's "general method was to take musicians to his farmhouse, board and rehearse them, drive them up to Richmond [Indiana], to record and negotiate with the record company. In exchange, he would get part of the royalties."

48. 🎵 Go to Audio Examples to listen to "Camp Nelson Blues" by the Booker Orchestra.

49. 🎵 Go to Audio Examples to listen to "Salty Dog" by the Booker Orchestra.

50. 🎵 Go to Audio Examples to again listen to "Salty Dog" by the Booker Orchestra. When the performance begins, the first cycle of fifths starts at 0:01, the second at 0:11, the third at 0:21, and so forth throughout the remaining of the song.

51. Ragtime, a musical genre known for its off-beat (syncopated) rhythms that developed in African American communities during the late nineteenth and early twentieth centuries, is most often associated with the piano. But guitarists were also known for using a ragged performance style (Berlin 2001).

52. William Smith "Bill" Monroe (1911–1996), a white mandolinist, singer, songwriter, and bandleader, was born in Rosine, a small community in Ohio County, Kentucky. Bluegrass, the musical genre, takes its name from Monroe's band, the Blue Grass Boys, the nickname for the state of Kentucky.

53. 🎵 See Demographics 6.5.

54. US census records indicate that Shultz's parents had eleven children: five males and six females. Griffin indicates that she was the only female in the band. Similar to Shultz, who played several musical instruments, she eventually learned to play the fiddle, mandolin, bass, guitar, and banjo that she continued to perform until her brothers moved away from home (Lawrence 1980, E1).

55. Unfortunately, I have no information about fiddle tunes in Shultz's repertoire. But for additional information about his musicking, see Lightfoot (1988, 1990); Lawrence (1981, 2020a, 2020b).

56. Although Otto and Burns do not identify the fiddler who played with Monroe by name, most likely it was Shultz (see Otto and Burns 1974, 412).

57. 🎵 See Demographics 6.6.

58. 🎵 See Demographics 6.7.

59. For details on musicians who were influenced by Shultz, see Jackson and Richey (2016, 27–29). In addition, numerous articles about Shultz (including his relationship to Monroe and noteworthy causes that have been established in his memory) can be found in local Kentucky newspapers that date from the 1970s to the present; see Lawrence (1980, 1981, 2020a, 2020b) as well as material in other regional newspapers: the *Courier Journal, Hartford Herald, Lexington Herald Leader, McLean County News, Messenger Inquirer, News Democrat and Leader, Park City Daily News*.

60. 🎵 See Demographics 6.8.

61. 🎵 See Demographics 6.9.

62. As noted above, a more extensive discussion of Bertram appears in chapter 7 on Tennessee, where he was born and his formative years as a fiddler took place.

63. US census records indicate that Charlie Buster, Bledsoe and Shell Coffey are related to each other by marriage. Bledsoe and Charlie each married two of Shell's sisters. Bledsoe married Shell's older sister, Georgia (b. ca. 1888), while Charlie married Shell's younger sister, Zona (1899–1992). Because Shell's and Charlie's lives are closely intertwined musically and through kinship, they will be discussed together. In addition, the first names of musicians in the family will be used to avoid confusion.

64. 🎵 See Demographics 6.10.

65. Various print sources for Green Coffey—US Colored Troops Military Service Records (he enlisted at Camp Nelson) and US Freedman's bank records—indicate that he was born in Wayne County, Kentucky.

66. US census data indicate that Shell's parents, George W. Coffey (1860–1937) and Lucinda Williams Coffey (1863–1937), were both born in Wayne County, Kentucky, and had twelve children (five females and seven males). Shell was fourth eldest.

67. 🎵 See Repertoire 6.2 for a list of both sacred and secular songs that Buster and Coffey mentioned in interviews with Fulcher.

68. US census data indicates that Charlie's parents, Jack Buster (1870–1948) and Buntie [Brattie] Buster (b. ca. 1880), were both born in Wayne County, Kentucky. They had three children (two males and one female), and Charlie was the second eldest.

69. Fulcher (1988a, 4) indicates that "the guitar made its first appearance in Wayne County just before 1900. . . . Mail-order guitars overtook the black and white musicians' world by 1920, and ensembles soon included it."

70. Invented by Thomas A. Edison in 1877, the cylinder recording was the earliest form of phonograph record (Cylinder Recording 2023).

71. Richard Daniel "Dick" Burnett (1883–1977) and Leonard Rutherford (ca. 1900–1954) began their famous partnership in 1914, when Rutherford was still a young boy. As a blind man, Burnett used Rutherford as his sighted companion and fiddle partner as they traveled around the country. They began their recording career in the 1920s, with Burnett on guitar or banjo and Rutherford on fiddle, when they recorded six sides on Columbia Records.

72. 🎵 See Repertoire 6.2.

73. Because some of the earliest recordings of "Wild Goose Chase" were made in the 1920s (for example, Kessinger Brothers in 1929), Coffey is probably referring to the fact that he had created his own arrangement of the tune (Meade, Spottswood, Meade 2002, 711; Russell and Pinson 2004, 480).

74. "The Devil at the Crossroads" appears to be an original creation by Shell and Jay (Charlie Buster's brother), because no information about a song with this title can be found in sources available to me.

75. Fulcher (1988a, 4) indicates that "smooth fiddling became entrenched as the ideal with the spread of Leonard Rutherford's fame," starting probably in the late 1920s and 1930s.

76. When Burnett lost his sight in 1907 and turned to music for his sole income, he would strap a cup around his knee and play and sing all day with any musician who wanted to join him. After Burnett and Rutherford formed their partnership in 1914, "for the next 35 years, they reigned over the courthouse gatherings, and every other place they appeared" (Fulcher 1988a, 4).

77. Announcements and articles about Livers's performances can be found in the local Kentucky newspapers—for example, the *Courier Journal* and the *Lexington Herald*—during the 1970s and 1980s.

78. 🎵 Go to Audio Examples to listen to selected field recordings performed by Livers. Eddie Chipman, a producer in northern Kentucky, recorded Livers in a local hotel (Sparta Hotel) and overdubbed an electric band (drum, electric bass, and electric guitar) with it (Harrod 1987). Harrod also recorded many of Livers's performances when they performed together as part of the Bill Livers String Ensemble. For select sources documenting the life and contributions of Livers, see Andrews and Larson (1977), Ware (1981), Meade, Harrod, and Wilson (1997b), Kalra (2006a, 2006b), Riley (2010), and Keith (2013).

79. Bill Livers's parents, David Livers (b. ca. 1869) and Lula Thurston Livers (ca. 1889–1976), had four children; Bill was the second oldest and only son (Riley 2010, 558). In this discussion, the first names of family members may sometimes be used to avoid confusion.

80. 🎵 See Demographics 6.11.

81. Burnham Ware's great uncle, Claud Livers, played mandolin in a New Liberty, Kentucky, string/jug band during the twenties and thirties; "the band included Ware's grandfather, Albert Livers, on guitar, Navy Pitts on jug, and Wes Stafford on fiddle" (Ware 1981, 33).

82. 🎵 See Repertoire 6.3.

83. Although there is Carroll County in northern Kentucky, located just northwest of Owen, Livers's home county, the song, "Carroll County Blues," was first recorded in March 1929 on OKeh Records by William T. Narmour (fiddle) and Shell W. Smith (guitar) by musicians from Carroll County, Mississippi (Stanton 1980, 80; Meade, Spottswood, and Meade 2002, 882; Russell and Pinson 2004, 649).

84. 🎻 See Video 6.1.

85. 🎻 See Repertoire 6.3.

86. Harrod (2002) indicates that "Running Around Blues" was a tune that Bill Livers and Charlie William Payne composed together. To describe what he meant by "hard" music, Livers sang an old-time country song with a yodel.

87. "Peace in the Valley," also known as "(There'll Be) Peace in the Valley," was written in 1939 by gospel composer Thomas A. Dorsey, who, in the 1920s, was well known as blues pianist and singer Georgia Tom (Harris 1992a and 1992b). "Peace in the Valley" became a standard with country singers after white country singer Red Foley recorded it. "It was even recorded in later years by Elvis Presley" (Wolfe 1982, 136).

88. John Lusk is a Black Tennessee fiddler from the early twentieth century; see chapter 7 of this study for a discussion of his fiddling.

89. Harrod (1987) states that the whistle dance "is just one of those big circle dances where somebody has a whistle and you change partners. You do the same figures. But you're in a big circle. And then you promenade. And then the caller whistles and you change partners."

90. Some fiddlers perform in this manner because they believe it is aesthetically pleasing. From documentation of Black fiddlers from the slave era, the abrasive sound appears to be intentional and preferred. Researchers have indicated that these are African-derived aspects of Black musicking, not only in fiddling but in the manner in which Black people perform on other European instruments (Brown 1992, 129; DjeDje 2008a).

91. Armstrong is a Black fiddler who was also active in his local community during the early twentieth century, and became more well known in later years; see Epilogue.

92. Darley Fulks (1895–1990) was a white Kentucky fiddler from Wolfe County who had many interactions with Blacks. According to Harrod (1997), Fulks played different kinds of tunes, not your standard breakdowns.

CHAPTER 7

Tennessee

Tennessee's varied geography and history have greatly affected Black fiddling in the state.[1] Whereas African American fiddlers in West Tennessee show influences from the Mississippi Delta with majority Black populations, those who lived in or near Middle and East Tennessee reflect characteristics identified with mountain culture (Stanfield 1985, 134–35). In the introduction to a special issue of the *Tennessee Folklore Society Bulletin* "on traditional black fiddle and string music in the state," Wolfe (1987b) explains:

> Black string band music existed throughout Tennessee, not just in obvious areas like the Memphis delta [in West Tennessee]. The Franklin community, south of Nashville [in Middle Tennessee], was home to a dozen well-known black fiddlers, whose work influenced people like [white] Grand Ole Opry star Kirk McGee..., the [black] harmonica virtuoso DeFord Bailey [1899–1982], for years an Opry star, and a fine banjoist and guitarist who spoke proudly of the "black hillbilly" music his family grew up with. Fisk University[2] scholar John Work [III], perhaps the first black scholar to see the significance of string band music, recorded rare fiddle and banjo music in Nashville.... From East Tennessee came one of the most famous Tennessee string bands, Martin-Bogan-Armstrong, who began their career playing in Knoxville.... On the Cumberland plateau [in the Appalachian Mountains], musicians like Bled Coffey, Shell Coffey, Charlie Buster, and Cuge [Cuje] Bertram were fixtures at dances and courthouse squares, though they never recorded any of their work. (42)

Acknowledging the importance of Black fiddling in Tennessee, Alan Lomax (1999) states in the introduction to the recording *Deep River of Song: Black Appalachia*: "The center of gravity of this collection is the state of Tennessee, where black mountaineers formed orchestras that outdid the best of white mountain string bands. This is the music that preceded ragtime, jazz, and the blues." With such large numbers of Tennessee Black fiddlers actively performing during the early twentieth century, this begs the question: why did Black fiddling in the Tennessee-Kentucky region continue as a living tradition for so long? Although physical and cultural isolation, similar to other mountain areas, may have contributed to the maintenance of the fiddle's popularity, DeVane (1987) suggests another reason is the Grand Ole Opry, which broadcast throughout much of North America:

> A lot of Black fiddling, strangely enough, is based on the popularity of the Grand Ole Opry among both Blacks and whites in the region. That whole music tradition was reinforced and given another deep breath that perhaps musicians didn't get in other areas. Just like Henry Ford's interest in fiddle traditions spawned a whole new interest in fiddle playing when he had this big contest that he put his money behind. And it's no small coincidence that some of these same people showed up on the Grand Ole Opry later on. When I was conducting research in that region [Middle Tennessee], every time I asked any Black musician about fiddling, they said: "Grand Ole Opry, Grand Ole Opry, Grand Opry."[3]

Unlike other southern states where research on Black fiddling is almost nonexistent, a wealth of information has been documented for Tennessee. Most significant is the fact that primary data on rural Black culture, including Black fiddling, was collected by African American scholars in Tennessee—Thomas Washington Talley (ca. 1868–1952) and John Wesley Work III (1901–1967)—starting in the early 1920s,[4] at least twenty or more years before European Americans.[5] Works by Talley (1922) and Work III (2005) are also noteworthy because they include discussion of the creative aspects of Black fiddling, with details about musical characteristics and their relationship to African American music generally. This not only allows for a more in-depth discussion of fiddling in Tennessee but also provides material to compare with fiddlers in other parts of the country. My examination of Black fiddling in Tennessee proceeds chronologically, focusing first on scholarship by Talley and Work III and second on fiddlers for which information is available: Frank Patterson, John Lusk, Bennie "Cuje" Bertram, Walter Greer, and Joel Rice. Similar to other chapters, the discussion is organized chronologically according to each musician's date of birth.

Talley, a professor at Fisk University who was academically trained as a scientist (chemistry), began collecting material on rural Black culture immediately after World War I.[6] This information led to the publication of a book, *Negro Folk Rhymes (Wise and Otherwise)*, in 1922, and a two-part article, "The Origin of Negro Traditions" (1942/1943) in *Phylon,* a journal founded in 1940 at Atlanta University by W. E. B. Du Bois. Talley initiated his research because he was concerned about the attitudes and biases of African American scholars such as John

W. Work II (1873–1925), the father of Work III and a colleague at Fisk also noted for his contributions to the study of African American music, who espoused that secular Black music was worthless and "Negro folk music is wholly religious" (Wolfe 1991, xiii). From growing up in Bedford County during the late nineteenth century, Talley personally knew secular songs from the rural Black tradition that rivaled religious songs in their history and complexity. Therefore, the first place he collected data was his birthplace. Former students of colleges where he had worked in different parts of the South also helped him find material. As a result of his efforts, Talley became "the first scholar, white or black, to do any serious collecting of folksongs in Tennessee" (Wolfe 1991:ix). In addition, *Negro Folk Rhymes* was "the first collection of secular folksongs by a black scholar and the first by a black scholar born into and raised in the traditional culture studied" (ix).

The research by Talley (1922) is important for Black fiddling because, in addition to introducing the thesis that many fiddle tunes were derived from rhymes, he discusses the relationship of instrumental music to the lyrics, or, in his words, "the relation between the Negro Folk Rhyme and the Negro's banjo and fiddle music" (236). According to Talley (1922), two classes (or types) of rhymes exist, with the fiddle and banjo employed differently in each. In one class, the fiddle and banjo are used simply to accompany rhymes sung. In the second, instrumentalists repeat, improvise, and reinterpret the rhymes. In other words, the four-line rhyme in the second class is used not only to introduce the song, it also serves as the theme for variations by instrumentalists who are given the opportunity to elaborately express their proficiency on their instrument. As noted in chapter 1 of this study, Talley (1922) believes the performance of the banjo, fiddle, panpipes, and triangle replaced African drumming. "Thus, the singing of opening strains and following them with the main body of the instrumental composition, is in keeping with the Negro's inherited law for instrumental compositions.... The rattling, distinct tones of the banjo, recalling unconsciously his inherited love for the rattle of the African ancestral drum, is probably the thing which caused that instrument to become a favorite among Negro slaves" (239).

Much of the music included in Talley's work are tunes that grew out of the shared culture of Blacks and whites. He points out that versions of "Liza Jane," "Shortening Bread," "Cotton Eyed Joe," "Here Rattler Here," and other fiddle tunes now widespread among whites were initially identified with African American culture (Talley 1922; Milnes 1999, 97–98). In fact, both Wolfe and Bastin indicate that white banjo player, singer, songwriter, and comedian Uncle Dave Macon, born David Harrison Macon (1870–1952) and one of the early stars of the Grand Ole Opry, was greatly influenced by Blacks although acknowledgment is rarely given (Wolfe 1987c, 108; Bastin 1986, 310). What the overlap in traditions suggests, according to Wolfe (1987c), is that Blacks and whites in Middle Tennessee shared a common song repertoire in pre–World War I, but "it was segregated in years after the war, as both song collectors and commercial merchandizers (record companies and publishers) attempted to divide southern traditional music into Anglo and Afro categories" (109). Thus, Talley's collection remains perhaps our most potent evidence of this complex body of music. After realizing what was happening to "his" music, Talley made several efforts to counter the misrepresentation. In addition to actively supporting, in 1940, the festival at Fort Valley, Georgia (one of the few Black music festivals of its kind), and encouraging Black musicians to participate, he persuaded a younger colleague at Fisk, Work III, to take note of the importance of Black fiddle and banjo music to African American culture—something Work II had never been able to see (Wolfe 1991, viii, xiii).[7]

Work III and other members of the Work family are well known for their research on African American music as well as their affiliation with Fisk University.[8] Not only was Work II one of the first Black collectors of vernacular music, "his enthusiasm for folk music led him to organize Fisk student singing groups about 1898 and take them on tour to raise money for the college in emulation of the original Fisk Jubilee Singers back in the 1870s" (Southern 1997, 282). During the thirties and forties, his son, Work III, was one of three college-educated Blacks actively involved in the collection of African American music.[9] The research of these individuals is significant for many Black intellectuals during the early twentieth century ignored, disapproved, or did not want to have anything to do with traditions that represented working-class Blacks. Yet, it was this culture that fascinated Work III and led to "his pioneering but largely unheralded research in the late 1930s" (Nemerov 1987, 82). Also important was Work III's approach to the study of Black musicking. His sole purpose was not in saving musical traditions before they disappeared, as was the case with many researchers during that period. Rather, he was interested in musical transformations. "Work [III] knew that each form of music served a specific function in its culture. A particular form might fade but would be replaced by something more agreeable to current cultural taste" (Nemerov 2008, 9). In addition, Work III allowed musicians to perform the music they preferred, which was not always the case with record company executives and researchers: "Instead of pigeonholing musicians in terms of what he wanted them to play, Work [III] acted as a fly on the wall and recorded what was there at the moment. . . . He accepted what was indicative of the culture, as opposed to only going after what he expected or thought should be there" (Friskics-Warren 2007, 2).

Profiles of Tennessee Black Fiddlers

During his research in Middle Tennessee in the thirties and forties, Work III came into contact with at least three rural Black fiddlers who had migrated to Nashville from neighboring rural areas: Ford Britton, Thomas S. King, and

Frank Patterson. Because Work III, as a composer, tended to focus on musical style and performance, little data exist on the life history of musicians. All that we know about Britton is that Work III recorded several songs—"Old Joe," "Billy in the Low Ground," and a blues—with him playing fiddle and Dave Merritt performing guitar that were deposited into the Library of Congress in August 1942. The only information I have found on King is that he was born in Nolensville, a small town that was the seat for Williamson County in Middle Tennessee, located about twenty-four miles southeast of Nashville.[10] Not only did King play banjo, he had performed the fiddle (an instrument he taught himself) for forty-one years before he met Work (Nemerov 1987, 88, 95).

Frank Patterson Jr. (1872–1950)

From research conducted by Wolfe and Nemerov in the 1980s, US census data, and my email communication with Patterson's family members, we know that Frank Patterson was born in Walter Hill, a small community in Rutherford County in Middle Tennessee. Sometime between 1900 and 1910, US census records indicate that he settled in Nashville, where he also died.[11] His parents—Frank Patterson Sr. (1841–1921) and Emma Sue Matthews (1854–1943)—had six children (two females and four males); Patterson was the second born and eldest male. No information is available on whether his parents or siblings were musicians. However, family members state that, although Patterson was most well-known for his fiddling, he also played the banjo. His first wife, Elnora Jordan (1881–1942), and three sons were also instrumentalists, who played guitar, piano, mandolin, and banjo, but there is no evidence they played together as a family group (Rowser 2018);[12] see photo 7.1.

Work III's files indicate that Patterson, recalled by musician friends and admirers as a tall, dignified man with a small mustache, learned most of his fiddle repertoire from an older Black fiddler in the 1900s. Around 1916, Patterson, who worked as a sharecropper, moved to a farm near the community of Rencrow in an area that is now a south Nashville suburb. Soon after this, Patterson began leading his own band and playing breakdowns primarily at local dances with banjoist Polk Copeland, and, starting about 1918, Copeland's son, Wesley, on guitar. Wesley, who worked with his family at a neighboring farm, states that the band often played together at house dances.[13] "They'd move all the furniture out of one room. They had a caller. We would play about three minutes and stop and they'd eat, drink, carry on, and come back again. Every now and then they'd stop and carry the hat around. We'd make pretty good" (quoted in Wolfe 1989). In the 1920s and 1930s, the band's territory centered on Antioch, another farm country about thirteen miles southeast of Nashville. Sometime in the 1920s, Patterson moved to Nashville, where he worked as a laborer in addition to performing his music (Wolfe 1989, Rowser 2018).[14]

Photo 7.1. Frank Patterson with first wife, Elnora Jordan, and two of their three sons. Used by permission.

Because Work III spent much of his time collecting data, he rarely had an opportunity to present his findings in articles or books. As a result, there is minimal documentation on how he interpreted the material he found. The only information about Patterson comes from Work III's notes, when the fiddler participated in the seventy-fifth anniversary celebration of Fisk's founding in April 1941. Because Fisk administrators knew of Work III's interest and research in African American culture, he was given the responsibility for organizing a Friday afternoon program featuring the music of local artists.[15] Work III's introductory remarks at the concert provide evidence of not only his understanding and appreciation of vernacular culture but also the importance of documenting such music:

> We are very happy here at Fisk University to present to you an instrumental ensemble which plays the music of forty or more years ago. The tunes you will hear played by these men are those Mister Frank Patterson learned from the man who taught him more than forty years ago. When listening to a folk instrumentalist, do not demand or expect a sweet, vibrant tone. If he is a good performer, he offers you instead a driving rhythm and astounding melodic patterns and ornaments, most of which he inherited from the tradition.
>
> The fiddle is the principal carrier of the melody with its many possible variants, which are always idiomatic. The banjo has several subordinate functions; it may reinforce the melody; it may embellish the harmony; it may accentuate the rhythm, or it may perform all three, as you will observe in the playing of Mister Nathan Frazier, banjoist deluxe. (quoted in Nemerov 1987, 93–94; Wolfe 1989)

Wolfe's research indicates that Patterson and Frazier, who were both established musicians in the Nashville area during that period, had played together before their performance at Fisk, most often for square dances with white dancers and white callers. In addition, Frazier "was well known to the black community in the town for his antics as a street corner musician and 'busker.' 'Ned acted the monkey all the time,' recalled Wesley Copeland. He often played alone—'nobody could keep up with him,' says Copeland—and did tricks with the banjo à la Uncle Dave Macon'" (quoted in Wolfe 1989).

Although documentation about the group's history is scant, the performance at Fisk must have been successful, for in 1941-42, Work III recorded several tunes of Patterson and Frazier performing together that were deposited into the Library of Congress. No doubt the recorded songs do not include the musicians' entire repertoire, but represent what they thought was appropriate for the occasion.[16] Nevertheless, the provenance of the tunes reveals a diverse repertoire of Black string band musicking popular among musicians during the early twentieth century. Among the songs were "I Would If I Could" (titled "I Would but I Couldn't" in Work's notes); "My Journey Home"; "Old Cow Died"; and "Po Black Sheep." Because different versions of "I Would If I Could" had been recorded by both Black and white musicians prior to Work III's 1942 recordings, it seems doubtful that it is identified solely with Patterson.[17] "Old Cow Died" is based on a play-party song, because as a title, it appears in several Black songbook collections, though seldom with this melody. "Po Black Sheep," a tune popular for Patterson's band during the 1920s, was well known to former band member Wesley Copeland, who recalled: "That's what folks used to dance to. That's way back, partner. 'Po Little Black Sheep.' In my comin' up days, people would run over you to get [to] something like that. Get out there in the country and here [hear] that, man, they gone" (quoted in Wolfe 1989).[18]

While "Bile Them Cabbage Down" and "Dan Tucker" were created as minstrel tunes, "Corrina, Corrina" is a country blues first recorded by Mississippi Black fiddler/guitarist Bo Chatmon (also known as Bo Carter) in 1928.[19] The remaining songs ("Arkansas Traveller," "Bill Cheatham," "The Eighth of January," "Fisher's Hornpipe," "Indian and the Woodchuck," "Leather Britches," "Sally Gooden," "Texas Traveler," and "Waggoner") are Patterson's and Frazier's versions of Euro-American tunes that date to the nineteenth century. Nemerov suggests that the performers' version of "Texas Traveler" has the same melody as the nineteenth-century "Old Dubuque," but Frazier's idiosyncratic delivery of the lyric makes this version unique. Folklorist Colin Quigley (1986), on the other hand, believes their "Texas Traveler" "seems to be the same as 'Cumberland Gap,'" another nineteenth-century tune. "The Eighth of January," also from the nineteenth century, is one of the Patterson's best-known tunes (Nemerov 1987, 94–95; Wolfe 1989).[20] To understand more fully some of the features that distinguish Patterson's performance style from that of other fiddlers in this study, two songs—"The Eighth of January" and "Po Black Sheep," chosen because both were popular among Patterson's admirers during his heyday—are analyzed with attention given to form, melody, and rhythm. Although Wolfe (1989) believes Patterson and Frazier's music is "more intricate, showy, closer to display music than the functional music of the Lusk band," I believe this is relative, especially when compared to the musicking of other fiddlers.[21]

Approximately two minutes and twenty-eight seconds (2:28) in length, Patterson's version of "The Eighth of January" is based on three melodies or themes (ABC) organized into three sections that begin and end at the following times: section 1 (0:00–0:47), section 2 (0:48–1:36), and section 3 (1:37–2:28).[22] Unlike other Black musicians included in this study who tend to increase the tempo as they progress through the performance, probably in reaction to the dancers' movements or their personal response to the musicking, the duple rhythm and tempo (quarter note = roughly 132 beats per minute) performed by Patterson and Frazier remain steady throughout. From my analysis, the three melodies have different functions in the performance. The most distinctive is the sixteen-beat A melody played in a high-pitch register, organized with large intervals and descending melodic lines; it serves as the introduction and marker that divides the song into three sections. Melody B, consisting of eight beats, is performed in a lower pitch range (about an octave below A), and used as a transition to the melody that follows it. Melody C's simple construction (also in a low pitch register), with lots of repeated notes and melodic motives with small intervals, is the place where singing and more extensive melodic variation occurs. Because B and C are melodically similar, one could argue that C is simply a variant of B. Although Patterson is the leader, for he seems to be the one who decides when to change to a different section or melody, his performance is more reserved than the intense, more vibrant playing style used by Frazier. Overall the performance is contained, with minimal variation in form, melody, or rhythm.

Comments by Linford (2013a) provide additional insight about the performance style Patterson used in "The Eighth of January": "That's a great recording that sounds like classical old-time music. It's not about the chord progression; it's about the way the melody of the A part and melody of the B part fit together—the melodic contrast from the higher A part and the lower B part. Also, there is heterophonic interplay between the fiddle and the banjo. The fiddling could have been a white fiddler or a Black fiddler. There was nothing cultural or racially distinctive about it. There was a little bit cleaner fiddling, not too many double stops, moderate amount of ornamentation in terms of the melody." In spite of its containment, Sule Wilson (2013) was struck by Patterson's use of short bows to perform the melody, stating that "they're [Patterson and Frazier are] shuffling" as they would do for dance music.

At three minutes and sixteen seconds (3:16) in length, "Po Black Sheep" is based on two melodies (AB) with variations that can be divided into four sections.²³ Similar to "The Eighth of January," the sixteen-beat A melody is the most stable and melodically complex theme. Performed in a higher pitch range with large intervals and descending melodic lines, A stands out from B, which is about one octave lower. While A may be interesting for its soaring lyrical melody, B is noteworthy for its varying structure and singing by Frazier, the banjo player. Although based on eight beats, the B melody is not set, but is composed of different four-beat melodic units that are combined and developed in various ways. While the first part of B (the call) is often varied, the second part (the response) tends to be more fixed, especially on beat 4 (see discussion below). For example, in the first appearance of the B melody in section 1, which is repeated three times (measures 9, 11, and 13), what stands out is the performance of an intricate melodic passage that includes the sixth note of the scale. However, in the second and third performance of B, the call consists of the fiddler playing a sustained note (measure 15) and then repeating an octave of another note several times (measure 17). In the fourth performance of the B melody (measures 19 and 21), the call consists of the fiddler repeating the melody twice with minimal variation.²⁴ It is also significant that although the response for each of the calls for the B melody may vary somewhat in the beginning, the response always ends with an eighth note motive consisting of a major third (A flat and C). In my opinion, the eighth note is a marker that Patterson uses to close both the A melody as well as different versions of the B melody. In addition to employing a more flexible structure throughout the performance, several features—the changes in volume (for example, melody B tends to be softer than melody A), the use of off-beat rhythms, polyphony, and call and response (see both A and B melodies)—gives the performance greater intensity, energy, and excitement.

When performances of the two songs ("The Eighth of January" and "Po Black Sheep") are compared, a much freer performance style is used in Patterson's "Po Black Sheep."²⁵ Instead of the performers playing melodies in unison or heterophonically, polyphony is emphasized and more dialogue (call and response) occurs between the fiddle and banjo. In addition, changes in volume and the use of off-beat rhythms in developing melodies give the performance greater intensity, energy, and excitement. Listening to Patterson play "Po Black Sheep" in this manner helps one understand why his admirers liked this piece.

John Martin Lusk (ca. 1889–1969)

Music collectors Margot Mayo, Robert Stuart Jamieson, and Freyda Simon²⁶ provide another example of Black fiddling in Middle Tennessee when, during the 1940s, they made field recordings of a string band in Campaign, a small town in Warren County about eighty miles southeast of Nashville and sixty miles northeast of Shelbyville in Bedford County, Talley's hometown.²⁷ A short distance from the Cumberland Plateau in East Tennessee, not only was the area bustling with activity during the early decades of the twentieth century, it was rich in music. In the 1920s, Campaign was a stop on the Louisville and Nashville railway line, and home to a sizeable Black population attracted in part by the operations of the Rocky River Coal and Lumber Company. And a few miles to the south, Smartt, a small community in Warren County, was the birthplace of Uncle Dave Macon (Wolfe 1989).

Through contacts with Jamieson's great aunt, Oneida Petit, three Black musicians—fiddler John Lusk, banjoist Murphy Gribble (1892–1950), and guitarist Albert York (1884–1953)—were identified as the last handful of survivors in Campaign who performed a musical tradition rooted in colonial and antebellum America (Jamieson 1987, 56). Born in an area of Campaign called Turkey Scratch where he spent much of his life, Lusk, who had formed his string band a few years before World War I, was also a subsistence farmer who occasionally worked at a nearby lime quarry; his home, according to Jamieson (1987), was comparable to that of other Blacks in the region: "It was the usual faded wooden sharecroppers shack seen all over the South—a box about 16 by 24, set on four knee-high corner posts, peaked tin roof running fore-and-aft, little veranda across the front" (51). The Lusks were well known in the community for their musicking; like many families of musicians, most in the family knew about their ancestors but were not always able to document everyone's involvement in fiddling from their earliest history. For this reason, Linda Henry's research (2018a)[28] about the Lusk family is extremely important:

> I have been able to trace the young musicians back to white slave owners, William Lusk, Thomas Gribble, and Uriah York, who lived on neighboring farms in Warren County. The first "musicianer," Jeff Lusk, was born into slavery, most likely around 1820 on the farm of William Lusk. Joe "Lewis" Lusk and Mary Mollie Lusk were two of Jeff's seven known children. "Lewis" was the father of the next generation of musicians John Lusk and Albert York. Mary Mollie Lusk was the mother of their musical partner, Murphy Gribble.... These musicians and their string band music were part of the McMinnville musical culture throughout the first half of the twentieth century. However, the history of this group . . . first began when their enslaved grandfather Jeff Lusk was sent to New Orleans to learn to play fiddle.
>
> Jeff's grandchildren, Gribble, Lusk, and York, played their distinctive form of square dance music every Saturday for close to thirty years on the same street-corner, busking for white passersby in front of the First National Bank in downtown McMinnville. Some of their street corner repertoire was recorded by Margot Mayo and Stuart Jamieson in 1946 for the Library of Congress. (5–6)

After Gribble and York died, John Lusk continued to play for square dances on Saturdays with his son, Duncan, a guitarist.[29] When Wolfe interviewed Lusk's family and community members in 1977, one neighbor stated: "The whole family,

John, and [his siblings] Floyd and Bud and Mary and Bell, the whole bunch of 'em,[30] could play a musical instrument. The girls wasn't left out—all of 'em could play something. Some of them played banjo, some guitar, some fiddle—they just kept on playing through the years. One would die, but another would replace him, and they'd go right along" (Wolfe 1989). In 1977, Duncan revealed that his "daddy" John was also a "trick fiddler," "he'd put the fiddle up over his head and play as good as an'thing right there, put it behind him and play it like that. I never seen nothin' like it." In addition, Duncan indicated that his father played a variety of instruments—fiddle, banjo and guitar, and his uncle Murph played both fiddle and banjo. Recalling the earlier years, Duncan stated: "When one got tired of playing fiddle, they would switch off" (Henry 2020, 16).

The fact that Lusk performed the fiddle owned by his grandfather, who was sent to New Orleans in the 1840s to learn to play the instrument, is significant, for musicians like Lusk's grandfather became proficient in several repertoires—tunes designed for white dances as well as songs to accompany "sukey jumps" or "kitchen dances" at events organized by Blacks[31]—that was passed on to their children as demonstrated in tunes included in Lusk's repertoire (Wolfe 1989).[32] Wolfe (1989) states that the songs Lusk and his band performed for researchers in 1946 and 1949 can be categorized into three groups. The first group includes well-known fiddle tunes, many of which are derived from nineteenth-century songs shared by Blacks and whites in the South: "The Eighth of January"; "Billy in the Low Ground," the band's most popular piece; "Fire on the Mountain," also called "Sambo" by the band; and "Pateroller'll Catch You."[33] The second group consists of regional tunes known by fiddlers in Tennessee's Cumberland Plateau: "Cincinnati," "Apple Blossom," "Rolling River," "Smoke Behind the Clouds," and "Altamont." The third group includes tunes identified with African American culture: "Christmas Eve," a variant of "Old Joe" familiar to most Black Tennessee string bands; "Rabbit in the Brush," a tune that demonstrates the forceful bowing strokes characteristic of many Black fiddlers; and "Old Sage Friend," a signature piece by Lusk's grandfather.[34]

Jamieson's Aunt Oneida described the group that played in the 1946 recording session as "the best square dance band in that part of the state" (Jamieson 1987, 45). After their test performance, the response from the mostly white audience attending the recording was overwhelmingly positive. Even the researchers were amazed with what they had experienced. Jamieson (1987) states: "As I heard the playback, for the first time really hearing the music, I was thunderstruck.... We had never heard music like that, nor anything even approaching it. We had struck pure gold again, another mother lode! The onlookers burst into yips and Rebel yells; one shuffled his feet around in the improvised sliding patterns of a buck dance. I recall grinning like a jackass eating briars, and calling out happy congratulations to the band—who sat quietly, looking around at all the faces, smiling broadly" (49).

But what was special about the music? In what way was the sound produced by Lusk and his band members distinct from that of white musicians in the area? Jamieson (1987) explains by describing the features he identified with string band music in the United States at that time:

> The fiddle had come first, playing all alone for dances. It concentrated on playing the tune, adding sliding two-note "double-stop" sounds and often intricate embroiderings of vocal-style decorations. The banjo joined later, constrained by its right-hand patterns to playing the strong melody notes, hinting at the others with its off-beat clang chunk-a chords, rhythmically reiterated thumb string notes, gratuitous non-melodic notes filling in the spaces. But it followed the melody, and stayed with it; the melody was its guideline. Later, when guitars joined in they used bass note-chord patterns too, sometimes playing a run of bass notes to change from one chord to another, but they too stayed strictly on the beat. In this tradition, the tune was the twin rails that led the bands around the tracks; the crossties of the beat were spaced evenly. (49)

Jamieson believes Lusk's string band music was also distinct because the musicians used a performance style that emphasized freedom and flexibility; the performers did not seem to be bound by form or how the rhythm and melody should be played. Again, Jamieson (1987) explains:

> What we heard this time was so different it was almost disorienting. The fiddle did not always lead the melody, but passed it to the banjo, like runners passing the baton. Half the time the melody was played by the banjo, the fiddle moaning low rhythmic chords, over and over. Suddenly, at the second part of the tune, the fiddle would leap into an upper octave, with a wide cry, and take over the burden of the tune. The banjo would then play a loose and free polyphonic obbligato around a rudimentary suggestion of the melody, ranging far away melodically, omitting strong downbeats, dancing a different step rhythmically—and this was most radical of all for banjo—not hitting all the upbeats and downbeats, with sudden startling gaps and hesitations. Even when the banjo took over the lower-octave half of the tune, and its wildness was somewhat subdued by the demands of melody, it produced a rolling syncopation like a jazz beat. Down below all, the guitar produced a steady deep heartbeat, like the throb of a great engine in the bowels of a ship, laying down the full chords that defined the threshing floor upon which fiddle and banjo leaped and soared. It was far and away the most sophisticated square dance music we had ever heard—Bach himself would have listened with delight to its wide freedom. (49)

From my analysis of three songs by Lusk from the three groups proposed by Wolfe—"Pateroller'll Catch You" (first group, songs shared by Black and whites);

"Apple Blossom" (second group, songs from Tennessee's Cumberland Plateau region); and "Old Sage Friend" (third group, songs created by Blacks)—and compared them to songs by Patterson, there is no question that the performance style used by the two fiddlers is similar but also different. The form is the same for both performers (that is, songs by Lusk and Patterson are based on two or more contrasting melodies or themes), which is not surprising since this organization characterizes most old-time music. In performances by both fiddlers, a lyrical theme with intricate descending melodic passages (and sometimes large intervals), performed in a high pitch register, is normally used to begin songs. Because A is the melody that identifies the tune and marks different sections of the song, fiddlers rarely change it even when repeated in performance. In performances by Lusk and Patterson, the second or contrasting B theme is played in a lower register and includes more extensive variation in melody, rhythm, and form. For example, in Lusk's performance of "Apple Blossom," the length of the sixteen-beat A melody (0:00–0:15) is never varied.[35] Yet, his eight-beat B melody is always changed; it is performed four times when it first appears (0:15–0:30), and as many as six or seven times, with many melodic variations, later in the performance. Also significant is Lusk's use of double stops. During the second performance of the B melody in "Apple Blossom" (0:45–1:04), he plays double stops using perfect fifths and a flatted seventh to produce diminished fifths.[36] Double stops are also used in "Old Sage Friend," yet more prominently in the B melody as opposed to A.[37] Therefore, when Jamieson states that "half the time the melody was played by the banjo, the fiddle moaning low rhythmic chords," this most often occurs during B and not A.

In other aspects of their performance styles, differences are especially apparent in the use of texture. Whereas Patterson (on fiddle) and Frazier (on banjo) often play both the A and B melodies in unison (monophony) or with one musician slightly varying from the other to produce heterophony, Lusk and his band members use polyphony. Instead of accompanying Lusk's fiddling with the same melody (in unison), Lusk's banjo player performs melodies that complement or contrast with what the fiddle is playing. For example, when Lusk begins "Pateroller'll Catch You" by performing the lyrical A melody (0:00–0:09), the banjo performs a two- or three-note melody that is distinct from A.[38] And during the B melody (0:10–0:22), the banjo performs a slightly more developed melodic passage, while the fiddle accompanies him by repeating a minor third chord using double stops. When the fiddle and banjo play B a second time (0:30–0:45), they each perform their version of the melody, creating a heterophonic texture, instead of playing contrasting parts as they did earlier. In some instances, Lusk and his band members do not even attempt to perform the same melody as is the case in "Old Sage Friend." As Lusk performs the high A melody, the banjo basically repeats the same chord in a rough manner. With the guitar providing a pedal point by performing the same note, the intention seems not to create melody, but rather to produce a scratchy, percussive sound quality to accompany dancing. Yet, the performance aesthetics used here vary only slightly from that of other Black musicians. Linford (2013b) explains: "The big difference is the slightly cleaner, smoother, timbre used by Lusk. His fiddling is not as smooth as Tennessee fiddler Howard Armstrong [see discussion below]. But it is not rough like Leonard Bowles [in Virginia] either. Lusk is also articulating more of the ornate melodic passages than Leonard Bowles or Joe Thompson [in North Carolina]."

This limited analysis of songs performed by Lusk and Patterson demonstrates that their performance styles are similar when it comes to form, one of the features that helps to distinguish old-time music from other genres, but differs in ways that define the personal, regional, or cultural aspects of a tradition. Wolfe (1989) explains the difference by suggesting that musicking by Patterson and Frazier is "closer to display music than the functional music of the Lusk band." While this may be true, what is most obvious in my opinion is the degree to which the two fiddlers employ features identified with African American musicking—polyphony, off-beat phrasing (syncopation), bent notes, and a percussive sound quality. Whereas these characteristics are prominent in the three tunes by Lusk presented in this discussion, they are only apparent in Patterson's "Po Black Sheep," the song that was especially popular among his admirers.

Bennie Esterd "Cuje" Bertram (1894–1993)

In many ways, the life and musical career of Bennie Esterd "Cuje" (also spelled Cuge or Cooge) Bertram (see photo 7.2) are similar to that of Black Kentucky fiddlers (Shell Coffey and Charlie Buster) who were discussed in the previous chapter. In addition to having birthdates only months apart from each other, the three fiddlers had some of the same experiences as musicians. As noted in chapter 6, Bertram, along with another member of the Coffey family, sometimes performed with Richard Burnett (1883–1977), a well-known white banjo and guitar player from Kentucky (Wolfe 1973, 7). Yet, Bertram's life is also distinct and departs from his fellow musicians in several ways. (1) Whereas members of the Coffey family spent much of their time in south-central Kentucky with little involvement with musicking in Tennessee or other parts of Kentucky, Bertram's birth and family ties in Tennessee as well as his move to Kentucky gave him greater exposure to audiences and musicians in both states. (2) Bertram was born into a family of musicians who performed as a group on a regular basis, which was distinct from the experiences of Coffey and Buster who did not have many family members who were musicians. Therefore, while some overlaps exist with his counterparts in Kentucky, Bertram's profile demonstrates how life experiences in both Kentucky and Tennessee affected his fiddling, which helps to expand our knowledge and understanding of Black fiddling in the Appalachian Mountains generally.

Photo 7.2. Cuje Bertram with fiddle. Indianapolis, Indiana. February 1980. Photo by Robert J. Fulcher.

Bertram was born in a section of Fentress County called Three Forks of the Wolf River near the town of Pall Mall, in the Cumberland Plateau region, about five miles from the Kentucky-Tennessee border.[39] Cuje's father, Dock Bertram (1855–1908), was born in Oneida, a small town in Scott County in the Cumberland Plateau about forty miles east of Pall Mall, while Cuje's mother, Telitha A. Crouch Bertram (1854–1939), was also born in Fentress County (Fulcher 1987, 59). Bertram's parents had ten children (two females and eight males), and Cuje was the second youngest. By mountain culture standards, Cuje's father was considered to be wealthy. Not only was he one of two blacksmiths in his community, he "had a big farm over at Three Forks of the Wolf and had horses, mules, and everything"[40] (Fulcher 1987, 60). After his father's death, Cuje and his brothers became laborers on the family farm, but some took up other occupations (carpentry, horse saddlery, wagon drivers) when they left Fentress.

Upon the completion of his World War I military service in 1918 and marriage to Nova Hatcher (1904–1975) in 1920, Cuje Bertram moved to Kentucky with his wife and the first of their nine children. Initially, the couple settled in Wayne County, the home of several older siblings as well as members of the Coffey family, his musician friends. During the 1930s, Bertram and his family (wife, children, and mother) resided in Somerset, the seat for Pulaski County, Kentucky, which is adjacent and northeast of Wayne County. In the early 1940s, he migrated from Somerset to Indianapolis to join relatives who had settled there during the 1910s and 1920s.[41]

Migration, both short and long distances, appears to be a theme in Bertram's life. Before he moved to Indiana to join family members in the 1940s,[42] census records documenting the birth of his children indicate that he was constantly moving between Kentucky and Tennessee, probably because family members resided in both states. But this may have also been characteristic of the lifestyle of residents in the region. What is noteworthy, however, is that his homes in both states tended to be in communities with small Black populations located near or within the Appalachian Mountains.[43] While living in Tennessee, Bertram stated that "the closest Black community was Albany, Kentucky, about twenty-five miles away. We went there to buy things—it was a bigger town than Jamestown" [the seat for Fentress County] (Fulcher 1987, 59). Furthermore, the issue of race, according to Bertram, was never a problem in the communities where he lived. In his interview with Fulcher, he elaborated:

FULCHER: Now, did you ever feel any friction between the white people that were at dances or around?
BERTRAM: No! No! What are you talking about? All was one.
FULCHER: Now, that's what I've heard. Tell me some more about that.
BERTRAM: Wasn't no colored. Wasn't no white. All was one. Me and them white girls, white boys get together.... Sometimes I'd have them over [and we would ride horses]. "Wait, I'm gonna ride behind Cuje." "Yeah, come on." And they'd get their self up there. And [I'd] leave home with 'em. We take 'em to the dance. Have a big time, go back. Cause I was nice. Decent. None of this foolishness. We didn't have that. And no drinking....
FULCHER: Was there ever an instance when people ever gave you trouble or tried to bother you?
BERTRAM: Oh no. I don't know what that is.... The only way I knowed I was colored was to have to go to the lookin' glass. (Bertram 1980; Fulcher 1987, 67–68)

The Bertrams were a family of musicians who regularly performed together for entertainment at home and surrounding areas. Not only did Bertram's father play fiddle and banjo, many of his children could play banjo, fiddle, or guitar. In describing his father's fiddling, Bertram stated: "He was a good smooth fiddler. He didn't jig the bow. That jigging ain't no good." After his father died, members of the family continued the family tradition and regularly played together (Bertram 1980). Similar to other performers in small communities, rarely did anyone in the family receive formal lessons; rather, everyone learned from kin by observing and/or imitating a well-known musician. Bertram explained: "We just caught on. When I was eight years old, Pap would hand me the fiddle and I'd stand at the foot of the stairs and fiddle. He never showed me anything. I just took it in the head up here. I couldn't note but just one finger at a time and directly I got so I could double note and when it come a year or two later, he wouldn't play; I done the fiddling. Had him skinned. It's a gift" (Fulcher 1987, 59–60).

When asked how Dock, his father, learned to play the fiddle, Bertram's response suggested that he acquired his musical skills from performing with whites: "I can't tell you for sure. Jimmy Copely, a white man of Three Forks, he was a wonderful fiddler. They'd go to dances, he'd play the fiddle and my dad would play the banjo" (Fulcher 1987, 60). The repertoire for musicians in the region was the same. Bertram indicated that his father's favorites[44] included old-time tunes that had been played by Black and white people for generations: "Fire on the Mountain," "Billy on the Low Ground," "Tennessee Wagoner," "Cheathem," "Arkansas Traveller," "Downfall of Paris," "Soldier's Joy," "Barlow Knife," "Ladies on the Steamboat," and "Five Miles Out of Town" (60).

Because the fiddle and banjo were the primary musical instruments his family played, Bertram stated that it was not until he was eight or nine years old before he saw others: "A couple of colored fellers came from New River, Tennessee" [near Oneida in Scott County] with a guitar and a mandolin. "Hays Smith, I think, and Shorty . . . came down to the store and Hays took his guitar on the outside of the porch . . . and he played it alright. A mandolin and guitar. The first one ever I saw. Now Daddy always played fiddle and banjer. That's all we had" (Fulcher 1987, 66; Bertram 1980).

For accompaniment to his fiddling, Bertram preferred the guitar: "I like the guitar to second [accompany] me better than I do anything" (Fulcher 1987, 66; Bertram 1980). Yet, Bertram admitted that during the early days: "There wasn't many guitar players in that day and time . . . mostly banjos. Guitar men were scattered. Weren't many playing" (Bertram 1980). When asked about the sound of the banjo and fiddle together, Bertram (1980) stated: "Oh they're alright. A guitar's got more harmony about it. Got more strings. If you know how to handle them, there's just something to it. Sweet music."

In all of the communities where he lived, there was little variety in the instruments used; in fact, Bertram stated that he knew only one Black man who played accordion: "Sometimes John Redman—he played accordion. He was blind, too. He bought it [in] Somerset. He was at the courthouse once in awhile. All through the week John would play that accordion. It sure was pretty. He played it good" (Fulcher 1987, 65–66). Although Bertram appreciated Redman's musicking, it is significant that he did not pay much attention to the type of music Redman played, only stating that it was "kind of waltzy music" and not breakdowns (66).

The media did not play a strong role in influencing the performance style or genres that Bertram played, because he did not acquire a Victrola until later in life and he rarely listened to fiddle music on radio: "I had a Victrola; me and my [older] brother Cooney had one. It had a horn on it. Dogs sitting up on it. An old timer. We'd go up on Wolf River Mountain. Just crank it up. Instead of a record, it was glass, a glass record. . . . I don't think there was any fiddling music in it. Just old funny, foolish talk and laughin' goin' on" (Bertram 1980).

Living so close to the border, Bertram often traveled from Kentucky to Tennessee and performed in small town theaters with family and musician friends. By the 1920s, Bertram and his brothers had established reputations for their musicking in both states. "The Bertrams farmed through the week and on weekends hauled moonshine to the backwoods logging camps, sponsoring a square dance when the last of their whiskey was sold" (Fulcher 1988a, 4). Although they performed in a variety of contexts (house parties, fairs, etc.), one of their favorite places was the town courthouse where musicians met each Saturday and played from morning till night. In his interview with Fulcher, Bertram provided details about courthouse performances in Monticello after his move to Kentucky:

> Well, it was an old-time courthouse. Big shade trees by it. Had a big fine yard in it, a stone fence around it, a big wide walkway, you could walk right in the courthouse.... Somebody played there all the time. Them fellows up there in Wayne County knowed Dick [Burnett], Sonny Parnell, Stonewall Bell, they all played there. That was the old stomping grounds. That was the only pleasure we had. Every Saturday. Just as quick as they'd get their breakfast and get on their horses, or ride their buggy, or what they'd do to get there. Sometimes eight or nine o'clock, but they was there every Saturday. Some days we'd go down at 8:30 and stay till it would get dark.... [T]hey'd step out there and dance, the old timers would [be] back stepping, doing everything. (Fulcher 1987, 64)

On the matter of payment for performances, the issue varied among performers and contexts. When asked if he performed for money, Bertram (1980) responded: "No. No. Always had fun out of it." However, when he and his white musician friends played for dances at schoolhouses in Kentucky's coal mining communities, such as Whitley City and London, he stated that people paid to hear the music: "They paid us in coal mine chips. That's all but the same as gold.... Ronnie [one his music partners] had an uncle in Monticello that had a big store there and we'd take the chips there and he'd give us a dollar for a dollar in chips" (Fulcher 1987, 68). Bertram (1980) also remembered playing at a theater in Stearns, [Kentucky,][45] with the Carter boys for pay: "Why, I never saw such a crowd in my life. [When] we walked down that aisle, me and two boys did, I never heard such hollerin and screamin' all the days in my life. [They] said: 'Why you fellers [are] better than Clayton McMichen.'"[46] Bertram (1980) indicated that they received payment because the show was more formal and organized in the style of a minstrel or variety show, with fiddling, singing, and some stories presented. In addition to whites, Bertram stated that he often performed with Black Kentucky musicians Andy and Bled Coffey: "They had fairs. We used to go from Fentress County [Tennessee] ... and stay a week with 'em and go to the fair, and we'd play and dance together up there."

Not only did Bertram's repertoire include old-time fiddle tunes, he also played waltzes, schottisches, polkas (music that his father never played), ballads ("Barbara Allen" and "Fair Ellenor and Lord Thomas"), and love songs ("Short

Life of Trouble"); but it was rare for him to perform love songs (Fulcher 1987, 60, 64).[47] Interestingly, Bertram's attitude about Black musicking appeared to be similar to that of some Blacks and whites who did not approve of certain genres. Bertram (1980) stated that he did not hear blues until he was a grown man living in Somerset, Kentucky: "'St. Louis Blues' was the first one to ever come out like that and I despised it." He maintained a distaste for blues for most of his adult life and stated that he and his brothers never played blues. In fact, when his Black Kentucky fiddler friend Shell Coffey was asked if the Bertram brothers played the blues, Coffey (1979) stated: "No, they [do] not play nothing, only ball room music. Dancing music. Now I heard him saying, 'I think I learn one or two of them.' But I never heard them play, like 'Lonesome Road.' I think I learned him that.'" For Bertram (1980), it was the blues lyrics that were most distasteful: "Well, it's kinda how they handle the words. It's kinda mixed up blackguardin'. Ugly, ugly words that goes with blues and I don't like it."[48] Yet, Bertram did play a tune called "Trouble" which he stated that he taught to Virgil Anderson, a white banjo player who also lived in Wayne County.[49] Bertram (1980) explained: "'Trouble. I'm so glad that trouble, trouble don't last always.' I know it. I learnt him that song. And I'm glad."[50]

According to Bertram, musicians (especially whites) in his community often learned tunes from him: "I played for 'em all the time; they'd catch on to every move I made. But I was the best. I had more class. I was smoother. I didn't cut it up" (Fulcher 1987, 61). A fiddler who considered himself to be good had to have a specific playing style. Therefore, during the interview, Fulcher asked Bertram about his playing technique:

FULCHER: "Cut it up." What you mean by that?
BERTRAM: Jigging along, you know. Get up there and saw.... People talk about the noting they're doing; most of the playing is done by this hand (*indicating the bowing hand*). If you ain't a good bowman, you ain't no fiddler. Some just jig along, and some just saw; but you can work your wrist and make that tune go. You've got to be limber and you've got to know what you're doing. You got to know when to move it and when not to move it, and when to shake it.
FULCHER: Did you ever move your fingers on your left hand to vibrate a note and make the note waver?
BERTRAM: Yeah: a good many fiddlers did that. We called it distinct note.
FULCHER: Did your father do that?
BERTRAM: Yeah, he was an old-time fiddler.... (Fulcher 1987, 61)

Continuing a practice that began during slavery, Black and white musicians in the Kentucky-Tennessee Appalachian Mountains closely interacted. Fulcher writes: "Cuje Bertram became tight friends with many white musicians, particularly [banjo player] Virgil Anderson and [fiddler] Leonard Rutherford, and was the source of their tunes. Cuje's performances (documented on a ca. 1972 home recording) shared much with Rutherford's rich vibrato, triplets, smooth, sliding notes, and singing in unison with the fiddle" (Fulcher 1988a, 4).

Anderson was eighteen years old in 1920 when he first came in contact with Bertram's music. At the time, Anderson's family was moving between the Kentucky-Tennessee border to different logging or stave camps every six months trying to find work. Recalling his first encounter with the music that influenced his playing, Anderson stated:

> The first time I ever heard 'em, me and my dad was going through the camp. Big, long band mill camp. And we kept walking down there and directly he said, "I believe I hear music." Got a little piece further and they was playin' at the band mill, where the lumber come down on the shoots. And such a crowd; looked like the whole company was there. We just crowded right on through 'em, and got close to 'em. See'd that they was colored people. Boys I'm atellin' you they was singing. They's gettin' that alto. Just almost make you cry. That guitar and banjer. Then they'd lay the guitar down and take the banjer and fiddle. Oh, just so handy as a goose goin' barefooted, you know. Well, I just tied right in with 'em. . . . I remember I bought an old guitar but I didn't know much about it. But when I see'd them agrabbin' them chords just like that, I knowed to get with it. Just grab 'em all at once. . . . Naturally, it was awkward for two or three times tryin' it, but I see'd what had to be done. If I done it, I was gonna do it; if I didn't I was out of it. (Fulcher 1988b, 3)

After that first encounter, Anderson stated that he started playing with Cuje and his brothers, Cooney and Andy Bertram: "They played the fiddle and banjer some by note, but they played a whole lot by chord. I picked up a lot of that. . . . You get into playin' music, you naturally like each other" (Russell 1999). Fulcher (1988b) believes these interactions led Anderson to perform "a fuller, more sophisticated music, with a blues touch, and he was no longer satisfied with just 'noting out' the simple dance tunes his father played. The blues and the Bertrams' chord music, represented by a wide variety of songs and tunes of both black and white origin, became Virgil's love: 'It's the drive, and the time, and the beat that they have. They don't get too fast or too slow. . . . They look like they're gonna get plumb off of it, but they'll never lose their time.' . . . A black man travelling through Monticello one day in the early 1930s left Virgil with the words to 'Bye, Bye Blues.' The chording technique was learned from the Bertrams, but the tuning (gDGCD) and chord arrangement are Virgil's ideas" (3). Russell (1999) indicates that "almost 60 years later, Anderson recorded several of the Bertrams' 'chording pieces, such as 'Station House Blues,' 'Trouble' and 'Cincinnati Blues.'"

In addition to Anderson, Bertram had interactions with other white musicians, particularly Richard Burnett and Leonard Rutherford:

I was 35–40 years old. He [Burnett] played many a time right in the courthouse yard there. And sometimes Leonard Rutherford (Burnett's partner and fiddler . . .) wouldn't be with him. Leonard might be on a big drunk. Or some fellow would get him to smoke a cigarette and there'd be somebody out there with that pint, and Leonard wouldn't be back at all. I'd get sorry for Dick, and I'd say, Dick, I'll help you out; I'll take the fiddle and you play the guitar or banjo. He had a cup tied around his knee and you'd drop a coin in. And I'd go home sometimes and eat dinner at Dick's. He had a fine wife, and he lived just a little piece from the courthouse in Monticello. He was a good man. He was an easy man to get along with, good natured. (Fulcher 1987, 62)

Bertram stated that Rutherford also learned several tunes from him: "He'd [Rutherford would] come to my house and spend days and days if you'd keep him sober. He learned 'Billy in the Low Ground' from me, and that 'All Night Long.' I never did like that 'All Night Long.' And they played one called 'Easy Rider.' Such stuff as that" (Fulcher 1987, 64). Because of the shared culture, it was common for Black and white fiddlers, as noted in the foregoing, to perform tunes from various cultural traditions. The Bertrams' repertoire[51] includes several songs recorded by Burnett and Rutherford: "Billy in the Low Ground," "Cumberland Gap," "She's a Flower from the Field of Alabama," and "Ladies on the Steamboat." They also performed tunes identified with Black culture. For example, when pressed about how he learned songs such as "All Night Long," Bertram stated: "Rabbit's daddy. . . . That's where we all got it from. Rabbit.[52] He played 'All Night Long' and pat both feet at the same time playing the guitar. . . . Me and Rabbit got together, played together a lot"[53] (Bertram 1980).

To summarize, the discussion about Cuje Bertram provides another perspective on the life and musicking of rural Black fiddlers in the Appalachian Mountains. Because of his activity along the Kentucky-Tennessee border during the early twentieth century, Bertram's musical world, geographically, was both interstate and interregional; his movements between states allowed him greater access to different audiences and performance venues. Yet, the constant movement between states seems to not have affected his musicking in any dramatic way. While Bertram's performance style (rhythmically and harmonically) may have included some elements identified with African American culture, which is one of the reasons some white musicians found his musicking appealing, the songs in Bertram's repertoire tended to be those shared among Blacks and whites from earlier years as well as genres (waltzes, ballads, polkas, and schottisches) most often identified with Euro-American culture. When he stated in his interview with Fulcher (1987, 61) that "I had more class. I was smoother. I didn't cut it up [i.e., jig or saw]," Bertram appeared to be proud of the fact that his performance style could be identified as white. Considering the fact that he lived in environments that were overwhelmingly white, his musical preferences and sensibilities are not surprising. Bertram's experiences in Kentucky-Tennessee were different from Kentucky Black fiddlers Jim Booker and Owen Walker in central Kentucky. The evidence suggests that audiences in the latter were more diverse and in some cases predominantly African American, which encouraged Booker and Walker to develop a performance style and create new songs that were more obviously African-influenced, but also appealing to a broad audience of both Blacks and whites.

Walter Greer (ca. 1898–1976)

Although information about Walter Greer (also spelled Grier) is not widespread, he is important because his contributions help us understand more fully the history of Black fiddling in Tennessee during the early twentieth century. Tiffany Minton (2022, 15), who produced a recording of Greer's musicking and wrote an accompanying essay (as liner notes for the recording), explains: "Greer is part of a long-standing legacy of African American musicians from Rutherford County, whose vernacular music traditions and work have significantly contributed to twentieth century American popular music. By the time of Greer's death in a Nashville infirmary on November 1, 1976, he had been keeping the legacy of string bands and old-time music alive in the region for over seven decades." Not only have Greer's musical activities been documented by several scholars, his name is mentioned alongside Tennessee's regional stars in an article published in *Billboard* (Country Music 1969).[54] In many ways, Greer's life history is similar to that of others in this study—musicians "whose legacies were either totally ignored by scholars or scattered and underdeveloped across scholarship" (Minton 2022, 9). Only a few researchers such as Robert Cogswell,[55] "whose intrigue with string band music, helped renew interest in the subject of African American musicians who played old-time music. . . . Cogswell understood that Black string band musicians were still commonplace in the early twentieth century and saw a need to document what players he could before they died" (9).

Although Greer, like Patterson, was born in Rutherford County in the small town of Walter Hill, US census records indicate that his family moved back and forth between his birthplace and Nashville during his early childhood.[56] Before and after he served in the army during World War I, he worked as a farmer and in other occupations. Greer acquired his first instrument, a fiddle, which was made from a cigar box in 1911. "He earned the money to acquire his cigar box fiddle by selling twenty-four packages of bluing powder" (Minton 2022, 2).[57] How he learned to play the fiddle is unknown, but his repertoire[58] "includes regional, popular and slightly obscure and possibly unidentified tunes" (7). The fact that a few songs, such as "Black Sheep" (also known as "Po Black Sheep"), overlap with the specific town and county where another Black fiddler was born and lived (see Patterson discussed in the foregoing), suggests that learning of new material varied. In addition to sharing and acquiring songs from local community members, musicking from the wider community, especially the media, was beginning to have a greater role in the learning process. Although the living patterns of musicians in some mountain communities changed slowly during the early twentieth century, this did not prevent some from being introduced to the wider world through radio and recordings. Therefore, it seems that fiddlers in these communities had a choice—they could learn new songs within the same (old-time) musical tradition with which they were familiar or they could adopt a completely new tradition (the blues) that was also being introduced through the media. Thus far, we have learned that it was generally local audiences that influenced their decisions, because it was individuals on the local level they needed to satisfy (Minton 2022, 12). Furthermore, as Mark Puryear (2003, 16) notes in his discussion of Texas blues, the tastes of local community members often related to their historic experiences, regardless of popular music trends outside those communities.

Similar to other Black fiddlers, Greer performed for Black and white audiences at square dances, picnics, and fairs as well as clubs, theaters, and amphitheaters, such as the Rutherford County's Snail Shell Cave (Minton 2022, 11). He also traveled to perform in small communities in Middle and West Tennessee.[59] For accompaniment, Greer performed with banjo players (Mr. Porterfield) and guitarists (Robert Wood and Walter Gilliam). It is with Gilliam that "Greer began playing in a predominantly Black string band scene located near Shelby Avenue . . . in Nashville. Gilliam is noted as being part of this community"[60] (12).

As part of his master's thesis, Russeltaze Crowder (1969), the first person to document Greer's musicking, made two recommendations: "One, a follow-up study that contributes more extensive research to the role of African Americans in country, folk, and allied genres. Two, that the study of these genres be integrated into public education so that due credit can be given to Black people for their contributions" (Minton 2022, 17). Since few of these recommendations have been acted on, it is hoped the material presented here will help change this trajectory. As more information becomes available, perhaps researchers will be inspired to use the material for producing other publications.

Joel Rice (1922–2001)

While studying for his master's degree in folklore at Western Kentucky University, Dwight DeVane[61] conducted research on Joel Rice, a Black fiddler born in Hartsville, a small town in Trousdale County in Middle Tennessee's Highland Rim region, which is about twenty miles south of the Kentucky-Tennessee state line and forty-nine miles east of Nashville. Rice resided in Tennessee until 1957 when, at the age of thirty-five, he permanently settled in Franklin, the seat for Simpson County in Kentucky, which is located about forty miles north of Hartsville.[62] Instead of examining Rice's musicking after his move to Kentucky, DeVane focused on Rice's early life in Tennessee and how Protestant Christian ideology affected his fiddling. Although fiddling was never highly regarded in the Rice family, Joel's father, Jacob "Jake" Rice (1891–1957), had been a fiddler in his youth. Furthermore, it was Jake who introduced his son to the fiddle in spite of the fact that most Blacks in his community regarded the tradition negatively. Why the father encouraged the son to play the fiddle and how the family reconciled this decision constitute the primary focus of this discussion, for these are issues significant to our understanding of fiddling in early twentieth-century African American culture. This profile also demonstrates that the secular-sacred motif, which played a major role in the development of Black fiddling in earlier years, continued to be a central aspect of the tradition in the early twentieth-century rural South.

Joel Rice was born into a family that had different ideologies about fiddle music. While Jake, his father, embraced fiddling, his mother, Minnie Lee Franklin Rice (1896–1947), did not approve of the tradition because of its association with anti-Christian behavior (frolicking, drinking, and dancing) that she believed was sinful. The following discussion of Rice's family history by DeVane (1979) provides reasons for the family's perspectives on musicking:

> Joel's father, Jake Rice, was born in Alabama. As a young boy, Jake learned to play the fiddle, and was an active musician, playing for black and white square dance occasions and in informal gatherings with other black musicians. Jake was a Baptist preacher's son, yet he played the fiddle until he married in 1913.[63] Joel does not know if his grandfather George Rice [1914–1975], the preacher, opposed Jake's fiddle playing. While only speculation, the church-sanctioned marriage could have symbolized a time for giving up the activities that fiddle playing represented.... Regardless of religious sanctions... the combination of fiddling and religion were present within the same household. Jake must have felt fiddling could exist within a "Christian home," for he bought Joel a fiddle, while knowing his wife objected to fiddling and dancing. At the age of ten, Joel was ready to try and fiddle. (14–15)

Just as enslaved Africans found ingenious ways to participate in traditions important to them, Blacks of the early twentieth century did the same. While Joel did not have to perform his music in secret as the enslaved had to do, he explains that, as a compromise, he physically separated himself from those who opposed fiddling. In addition, he developed a fiddle repertoire that those who disapproved of fiddling would approve:

> When we [one of Joel's brothers played harmonica] found time to practice music, on days when we couldn't do nothing [on the farm in bad weather]...

we'd go down to the barn ... [because] my momma would run us out of the house.... "Ya'll have to get away from the house with that mess"—she didn't go for it. Evidently, a compromise was made, Joel's mother did not try and stop Joel from playing, she just felt the house was not the place for fiddle music. So, his father felt it necessary to go along with her feelings—and her religion.

Joel's father also encouraged Joel to play Christian songs. Joel's mother accepted these tunes and the fiddle into the home.... Within the home setting then, Joel learned a dual repertoire—one set of tunes for the house, and one set for the barn. Joel adapted to this arrangement, and learned to manipulate the co-existence of a double set of values.... He played hymns in the house and cackled in the lot.

Youthful days as a fiddle playing Baptist preacher's son must have enabled him [Joel's father] to find solutions to the social problem that the fiddle and pulpit suggests. Jake must have been a mediator. It is evident that he helped define the boundaries of Joel's home playing. Joel does not know what justifications, if any, his father offered to Joel's mother about buying the fiddle for Joel, or teaching him to play. Joel suggests playing in the barn might have been his father's idea. (DeVane 1979, 15–17, 19)

In addition to associating the fiddle with anti-Christian behavior, many Black and white people during the early twentieth century, like their ancestors from the slave era, continued to identify the fiddle and fiddle music with the devil. In fact, Jake advised his son that in order to become an accomplished fiddler, he had to learn from the devil. Joel explained: "[My father] told me the best way to learn is to wait till night and get out on the road ... by yourself and sit down there and play. Said, the devil would meet me there.... I don't know whether it's true or not. He said go to some crossroads. He always told me that. He really did. He said that's how he learned. But I never did go" (DeVane 1979, 17).

Although raised in a Protestant Christian home, Jake may have introduced the fiddle to his son because he did not see any harm in performing the instrument. In fact, Joel indicated that his father helped him learn how to play the fiddle: "At night, he [Joel's father] could be laying in bed. I be back there [in the barn] playing, trying to get some tune going—it ain't going right—he'd come in and show me how to do it. And then, like any other musician, he [Joel] became obsessed with the instrument and learning to be a musician, and put in the necessary time to do it. This was reinforced by his father who would teach him tunes and sing words to them, by his brother who played another instrument, a harmonica; and by some other white boy in the neighborhood who played fiddle" (DeVane 17).

In spite of the opposing views, fiddling was a family tradition in the Rices' home. DeVane (1987) explained: "As a family, they would play musical religious songs for his mother on the instruments, but not any of the dance songs. So, they could practice sacred music in the house, but the other secular music had to be played in the barn. I know a lot of white fiddlers who play hymns on the fiddle and many of them use what they call an organ style of separating the bow. They'd put the bow in the middle of all four strings and play all four notes at the same time in chords. Beautiful sound." By using a different performance style (playing chords on the fiddle to emulate the sound of an organ), this was another way fiddlers, according to DeVane, attempted to address the ambivalence on the part of Protestant Christians.

When members of the Rice family performed together as a group, their ensemble normally included fiddle, guitar, and banjo. The mandolin and percussion instruments were rarely used. DeVane (1987) explained:

> The rhythm instrument was a guitar. And the banjo, of course, was rhythm and melody. Mandolin, I don't know. I've seen it as a blues instrument more than as a dance instrument in Black culture. It didn't have the qualities of a guitar and it probably was more expensive. Therefore, I don't think it was a big part of this tradition....
>
> Joel mentioned playing straws on the fiddle. This is when a child would take straws and beat time on the fiddle as it was being played by someone. So, you get a quality of sound. And the beating on straws became a percussion instrument. I've never seen any dance music with fiddle and guitar and banjo without the beat [DeVane hits on table to create the sound of the "beat"]. Good musicians play to the sound of the beat. They'll start, but then they attune their playing to what the dancers are doing. And they really use that as percussion. Outside of straws, sometimes the banjo has a percussive aspect to it.

Not only did Joel perform with his family at home, he played at house parties with whites and at other events when he was an active musician during the 1930s and 1940s. "In his school, there were spring pageants they played in, and talent shows they put on in grammar school, which traditionally took place in the fall of the year. People got together for whatever purpose, whether it be for harvesting or something else. And Christmas was a time of playing music" (DeVane 1987). Since dancing was not sanctioned and he and his musician friends had no money or transportation to go anyplace, musical gatherings with only males in attendance were the most frequent occasions for fiddling. In addition to providing a performance context to play music, learn tunes, sing, make songs, and drink, the gatherings of males became a Friday and Saturday night ritual for most of his teenage and adult years. According to Joel, "Saturday nights we would go out and get us some whiskey and sit out and play . . . get on the roadside we would play all night long. That old music sounded good out like that" (DeVane 1979, 20).

As a father, Jake believed that youth should experience life to its fullest, even if it meant participating in acts considered sinful by others or consorting with the devil. When DeVane (1979) asked Joel what his father thought about him playing the fiddle, he replied, "My father was proud for me to take interest in it" (18). Because of Jake's personal experience with the instrument, he associated fiddling with youth culture—the teenage years when the young are not only trying to define their identity, it is a time when challenging authority, social mores, and values of society have greater importance than following the rules. Jake also realized that the frivolities of youth gave way to adult responsibility. DeVane (1987), who believed this turning point in a person's life was an important aspect of fiddling and musicking generally, explained:

> Regardless of race, there seemed to be patterns of times in which musicians played the fiddle; early teens through early twenties was the most active time for many fiddlers—from the frivolity and coming-of-age behavior that just happens, becoming an adult and mixing with the opposite sex, and getting drunk for the first time. All these sorts of things were also associated with music. I think fiddling and fiddlers have been lumped together with all of these activities. But then there's the thirty years of their married life when musicians don't perform too much. And then when they retire or get much older, they reflect and pick it up again. The fiddle was an instrument and a type of music in the 1940s and late 1930s; a gathering place for young people to meet, to party, or to express themselves as opposed to playing for events. The musicians gathered for themselves to make music. Regardless of Black or white tradition, those time frames seem to have been constant.

The issue that DeVane raises regarding the role of the fiddle in the lives of youth is important for understanding reasons that the parents of Black fiddlers disapproved of their children learning to play the instrument. In addition, this perception may be another reason fiddling as a profession was associated with childish, deviant behavior, and regarded negatively by many Protestant Christians as well as others in the United States during the early twentieth century.[64]

When Joel performed regularly during the thirties and forties, the fiddle's prominence had begun to decline in many Black communities. Therefore, it is difficult to assess Joel's popularity as a musician. Yet, DeVane indicated that he was well known and respected in the contexts he performed, which in his case, was among musician friends: "Performing with other musicians, I think, was his strongest tradition. Because of the vast number of songs that he knew, he must have been respected within his circle of friends. You wouldn't know or have friends if you didn't have the opportunity to play with them. When we talked, he would get the biggest kick out of remembering one after another and go on non-stop talking about them" (DeVane 1987).

According to DeVane (1987), Joel Rice had a large repertoire of songs[65] because the contexts of his performances were varied; the music he played with his musician friends was different from that performed with and for family members. "Joel knew a great deal of songs that were acceptable in any context.

He knew a lot of vaudeville songs that probably weren't sung on any occasion. He also knew a lot of ballad and play-party songs that were accepted by his mother. But he couldn't play dance songs and the breakdowns for her because those weren't allowed. Jigs were never really that popular, but reels and breakdowns stuck a lot for many were interchangeable." The titles of Rice's tunes are similar to those performed by Black and white fiddlers in other mountain communities, which not only demonstrates sharing but also the maintenance of performance practices from earlier generations. Like many Black and white musicians in rural communities, old-time music and even play party songs were more acceptable because blues was regarded "as an anti-church and family form of music" (DeVane 1979, 19).

When lyrics were used with tunes, DeVane (1987) indicates that the words and themes reflected the age of the performers as well as the subjects and issues important to them:[66]

> The lyrics reflect that time period of their lives when they're first dealing with sexuality and themes that arise from those contexts. For the most part, [the lyrics are] just great improvisations that are spontaneously put to whatever the ditties the fiddler produces. Most of the fiddle tunes aren't very complex at all—more rhythmic—and lend themselves to words really easy.... And a great many of them dealt with sexual behavior and with their perceived idea of naughty. He would also talk about joke telling with other musicians, and how they would each try to out do each other. It's like telling lies. And I think a lot of them were created in that context as well. He told me about exchanging lyrics, like toasts. In a way, it's a similar dynamic.

Summary

Because research on Black fiddling in Tennessee has been extensive, the information provides us with some inkling on why fiddling continued to be a living tradition in certain communities within the United States, when it was abandoned in others. Factors that seem to be most relevant for Tennessee include isolation, population trends, and support from family and community. In other words, small numbers of Blacks who resided in majority white communities and were sometimes isolated from cultural trends emerging in areas that were majority Black tended to maintain traditions from the past, including fiddling, because of the support they received from family and others in their community. Yet, some researchers (Black and white) who were in a position to document what was taking place did not always do so because they did not believe fiddling was the best representation, culturally and creatively, of musicking by Black people; thus, rejection of the tradition came from both the media and scholars.

Similar to earlier times, performances at homes for recreation and other informal gatherings constituted the primary contexts for fiddling. In addition, Black fiddlers in rural areas near East Tennessee maintained performance practices from the nineteenth century to a greater degree than fiddlers who resided in Middle Tennessee. Like fiddling in Kentucky, traditions that were part of the shared culture of Blacks and whites continued to be important to the musicking of both groups. Yet, differences existed in the manner in which Black fiddlers performed. Although some elements associated with African American music (off-beat phrasing, polyphony, bent notes, more extensive variation) may have been used in tunes derived from white people, these characteristics were more prominent in tunes identified with Black culture. Not surprisingly, the sharing and appropriation of repertoire and performance practices were common among Blacks and whites. While the adoption of these characteristics helped many white fiddlers to become distinguished in their careers, particularly through the release of recordings, the impact on Black fiddlers is difficult to discern. On a local level, perhaps the appropriation of these ideas led to greater opportunities for performances among both Blacks and whites.

fiddlingismyjoycompanion.net

Notes

1. ✣ See Map 7.1, Map 7.2, Land Regions 7.1, and History 7.1.

2. Fisk is a Historically Black University that was founded in Nashville in 1866.

3. Although interest in fiddling by US car manufacturer Henry Ford encouraged owners of some Ford car dealerships around the country to organize fiddlers' contests during the mid-1920s, Ford himself did not sponsor the contests (Gifford 2010, 326–27). Yet, DeVane's comments are significant because Black fiddler Leonard Bowles believes the annual Black fiddlers' contest sponsored by a local Black physician in Henry County, Virginia, contributed to the continued popularity of Black fiddling in that area during the 1930s and 1940s when the tradition had declined among Blacks in neighboring counties (see chapter 5).

4. Details about their findings have only recently received attention from the wider scholarly community for several reasons: (1) lack of knowledge about rural vernacular traditions produced by African Americans in the early twentieth century and (2) the tendency of many scholars to ignore or dismiss the findings of Black researchers. Similar to present-day, investigations by people of color tend not to receive the same recognition as those from Western culture (Horne 2017, 6). Courses on the history of ethnomusicology rarely include information about the Work family and Talley, so their scholarship is not given the same credibility as researchers such as Francis James Child (1825–1896); George Herzog (1901–1983); father and son, John Lomax (1867–1948) and Alan Lomax (1915–2002); Margaret Mead (1901–1978); or Helen Roberts (1888–1985).

5. While Wolfe (1987b, 1989, 1991), Nemerov (1987, 2008), and Gordon and Nemerov (2005) produced recordings of select fiddlers as well as unearthed little known publications and archival material by Talley (1991, 1993) and Work III (2005), researchers such as Mayo, Jamieson, and Simon (1946); DeVane (1979); Fulcher (1987); Jamieson (1987); Cogswell (see Greer and Cogswell 2005, 2022); Henry (2018a, 2018b, 2020, 2024); and Kiely (2018) collected data (photos and recordings) and conducted interviews with fiddlers, family, and community members. Except for a presentation by Kiely (2018) at the annual meeting of the Tennessee Folklore Society, which was based on material collected by Jim Brown and Kiely, I am unaware of other information on Black fiddlers John T. Roberts (b. 1836) and Willis Huddleston Roberts (b. 1842), who resided in Overton County in Middle Tennessee.

6. 🎻 See Demographics 7.1 and Biography 7.1. Born in Bedford County, Middle Tennessee, Talley was the second youngest of six children born to Charles Washington Talley (1827–1913) and Lucinda Talley (ca. 1831–1911).

7. 🎻 See History 7.2 to view and listen to material Work III recorded of the folk festival at Fort Valley State College during the 1940s. No fiddling is included because fiddlers did not start participating until the 1950s (see Elbert Freeman in chapter 9).

8. 🎻 See Demographics 7.2 and Biography 7.2. Work III's parents, Work II (1873–1925) and Agnes M. Haynes (1876–1927), had six children (three females and three males); Work III was the eldest. Unlike his father, Work II, and uncle, Frederick Jerome Work (1879–1942), who were both born and raised in the city of Nashville, Work III was born in Tullahoma, a small rural town in Coffee County in Middle Tennessee, about seventy-five miles southeast of Nashville.

9. In addition to Talley and members of the Work family, other college-educated Black music researchers documenting African-derived traditions during the early decades of the twentieth century include Camille Nickerson (1888–1982), a professor at Howard University between 1926 and 1962, who was interested in the Creole songs of her native Louisiana, and Willis Lawrence James (1900–1966), who started collecting songs in Louisiana in the early 1920s where he first began teaching (Southern 1997, 238). Except for Work III, none to my knowledge researched Black fiddling.

10. As noted in chapter 6, the McGee Brothers, the white country musicians who made an early recording of "Salty Dog Blues," were born in Williamson County. Because of its small size, the US Census provides no data for Nolenville's population between 1890 and 1980; in 1880, however, the town's total population was 145.

11. From email communication with Yvette Rowser, one of Patterson's in-laws, I was able to acquire information about Patterson's personal and musical life beyond what is contained in the literature.

12. Patterson was married twice. With his first wife, Elnora Jordan, he had three sons. On the 1930 census, his marital status is listed as divorced, but on the 1940 census, married is indicated and the wife's name is Fannye. Both were living in Nashville with no children.

13. Wolfe (1989) states that Wesley used the term *breakdown* to describe the musicking his father and Frank Patterson played. Although Wesley, like many young Blacks of his generation, became fascinated with the blues in the 1920s and quit the string band, Wolfe indicates that he did not lose his appreciation for older genres.

14. 🎻 See Demographics 7.3. It is significant that Patterson lived in areas with substantial Black populations, which is different from Black fiddlers in or near East Tennessee.

15. 🎻 See History 7.3.

16. 🎻 See Repertoire 7.1.

17. Dixon, Godrich, and Rye (1997, 634) list one recording of "I Would If I Could" (Miller and Rodgers on Paramount in 1928), and Russell and Pinson (2004, 151, 655, 959) list three recordings: the Callahan Brothers on American Record Corporation (rejected) in 1934; New Dixie Demons on Decca in 1936; and Zeke Williams and His Rambling Cowboys on American Record Corporation in 1937.

18. From his research, Dom Flemons (2011c) learned that Frazier and Patterson were known in Nashville during the 1940s for being fast and tireless players. In addition, Flemons (2015) refers to "Po' Black Sheep" as being a rocker's dream for old-time music, which is the reason he had to learn the song.

19. "Bile Them Cabbage Down" and "Corrina, Corrina" (also known as "Corinne") are performed solo by Frazier on banjo with no fiddling by Patterson.

20. 🎵 See Repertoire 7.1 for publications (or recordings) that have been made of Patterson's and Frazier's musicking.

21. 🎵 Go to Audio Examples to listen to "The Eighth of January" and "Po Black Sheep" by Patterson and Frazier.

22. 🎵 See Form 7.1.

23. 🎵 See Form 7.2 and Transcription 7.1.

24. The first performance of the B melody starts at 0:15, while the second, third, and fourth performances begin at roughly 0:27, 0:31, and 0:34, respectively.

25. Also see Wells (1993).

26. 🎵 See Biography 7.3.

27. 🎵 See Demographics 7.4.

28. Since she completed her master's project in 2018, Henry has produced several publications on Black fiddling, with special focus on the Lusk family; see Henry (2018b, 2020, 2024) and Hobbs (2018).

29. John Lusk was married twice and had seven children: three daughters and four sons. Frank Duncan (1915–1993) was the eldest son and third oldest child. Because he oftentimes played with his father and his musical partners (Gribble and York), Duncan's guitar style was similar to that of York's. Therefore, it is not surprising that when Duncan and his father played together, most often they performed the old repertoire (Henry 2020, 38).

30. The US census indicates that John Lusk's parents—Joe Lewis Lusk (1854–1937) and Mary Malissa (Lizzie) Wood (1858–1920)—had four children: Lenora (Lena) Belle (1876–1942), William Thomas "Bud" (1878–1946), Allen Floyd (1883–1939), and Beulah Etta (1884–1941). According to Henry (2018a), Albert York was a stepson.

31. In New Orleans, Black fiddlers learned how to play quadrilles and reels that were popular at plantation dances. Later, they developed their own styles, "based on the white fiddle tunes but with a more forceful bowing style and a sense of dynamics" (Wolfe 2002). During slavery, *sukey jump* referred to a dance in the slave quarters; after slavery, the term was used for a house dance (Wolfe and Lornell 1992).

32. 🎵 See Repertoire 7.2 and go to Audio Examples to listen to music in Lusk's repertoire.

33. As noted in the foregoing, most Black people use the title "Pateroller'll Catch You," while others, particularly white people, often employ "Run, N----r, Run" (Wolfe 1989).

34. Like most rural Black fiddlers, Lusk never recorded commercially. Several field recordings were made. The first occurred in 1946 when Mayo, Jamieson, and Simon made their initial contact with the group. Subsequent recordings took place in 1949, when Stu Jamieson returned to Campaign with a wire recorder, and in the 1960s when folklorist Charles Faulkner Bryan brought a new magnetic tape recorder to record Lusk and his son Duncan in some fiddle-guitar duets—tapes that have not been recovered (Wolfe 1989).

35. 🎵 Go to Audio Examples to listen to John Lusk playing fiddle on "Apple Blossom." Also see Transcription 7.2, measures 1–8 for the first appearance of the A melody.

36. 🎵 See Transcription 7.2, measures 31 and 33.

37. 🎵 Go to Audio Examples to listen to John Lusk playing fiddle on "Old Sage Friend." After performing the A melody (0:00), the B melody begins at (0:15).

38. 🎵 Go to Audio Examples to listen to John Lusk playing fiddle on "Pateroller'll Catch You."

39. 🎵 See Map 7.1 and Map 7.2. The Wolf River in Fentress County is part of the Cumberland River, and flows primarily through Middle Tennessee and southern Kentucky. It should not to be confused with the Wolf River of West Tennessee that flows into the Mississippi River at Memphis.

40. In describing his father, Bertram (1980) stated: "He was a faith doctor—an awful religious man. When he wasn't at work, he was sitting and reading his Bible. He believed in Christ the Lord. When a man was bleeding to death, Dock read a verse in the Bible. He made the blood stop. Sometimes he'd rub them [people]. Put his hand on them. He had been doing this for as long as I knowed him." Although Bertram didn't remember the name of the church, he stated that his father was baptized at a church in Three Forks of the Wolf River.

41. US census records indicate that Bertram was roughly twenty-nine years old when he settled in Monticello (Wayne County), Kentucky; forty-one years old when he moved to Somerset (Pulaski County), Kentucky; and forty-seven years old when he migrated to Indianapolis, Indiana.

42. Census records indicate that Garfield (1884–1967), one of Cuje's older brothers, took up residence in Indianapolis between 1910 and 1920, while Herbert Cooney (1889–1945), another brother, settled in Indiana during the 1920s. The three siblings who migrated to Kentucky did so between 1910 and 1920.

43. 🎵 See Demographics 7.5.

44. 🎵 See Repertoire 7.3.

45. 🎵 See Demographics 7.6.

46. Born in the northwest or mountain regions of Georgia, Clayton McMichen (1900–1970) was a white fiddler who, along with white fiddler James Gideon "Gid" Tanner (1985–1960), became one of the most successful country music performers of the early twentieth century.

47. 🎵 See Repertoire 7.3.

48. This section of Bertram's interview is unclear. He may be referring to *blackguard*, a term for a scoundrel or a man who behaves in a dishonorable way. As a verb, blackguard or *blackguarding* means to abuse verbally. Because blues were not included in the songs he recorded for Fulcher and later released on the recording *Black Fiddlers* (1999), Russell suggests the omission was because of Bertram's religious beliefs "rather than an intrinsic dislike for the form" (Russell 1999).

49. Virgil Anderson (1902–1997) was born in Palace, Kentucky, a part of Wayne County bordering the Cumberland River. His musicking is featured on both audio and video recordings (Anderson 1980, 1983, 2011; Fulcher 1988b, 2).

50. Although there is no way to know for certain, this may be Bertram's arrangement of the African American spiritual, "Nobody Knows the Trouble I've Seen."

51. 🎵 See Repertoire 7.3.

52. Willie Taylor (nicknamed "Rabbit"), a well-known Black guitarist in the area, was about four or five years older than Bertram. According to Bertram, Taylor was born and raised in Somerset, while his father was from Virginia. When Rutherford was not performing with Burnett, he and Taylor would sometimes play together (Fulcher 1987, 63).

53. There are many songs with the title "All Night Long" or have the phrase "all night long" as part of the song title; in most cases both the melody and lyrics of all of these songs differ. Burnett's and Rutherford's version of "All Night Long Blues" and "Billy in the Low Ground" were recorded by Columbia Records on November 3, 1927, in Atlanta, Georgia (Russell and Pinson 2004, 144). Although the recording took place about four or five years after Bertram had moved to Wayne County (where Burnett and Rutherford also lived), there is no way to document if these are the songs Bertram taught Rutherford.

54. 🎵 See Repertoire 7.4 for a listing of Greer's recordings. For information on Greer's life and musicking, see Crowder (1969), Greer and Cogswell (1975, 2022), Foster (1998), Wells (2003), and Minton (2022).

55. Cogswell was a graduate student when he began his research on Greer. His interview and field recording of fiddling by Greer, while serving as director of the Folklife Program for the Tennessee Arts Commission, was in some ways a return to his roots (Minton 2022, 9).

56. 🎵 See Demographics 7.3. Greer's biological parents, Willie Greer (b. ca. 1865) and Ella Owens (b. ca. 1885), were both born in Tennessee. For a discussion of Greer's life history, see Minton (2022, 3–5).

57. Bluing powder is used in laundering to "improve the appearance of whiteness by counteracting the effects of graying or yellowing" (Minton 2022, 2).

58. 🎵 See Repertoire 7.4.

59. 🎵 See Demographics 7.7 and Map 7.2.

60. According to Minton (2022, 12), Blind James Campbell's Nashville Washboard Band, which recorded for Arhoolie in 1962, was active in the same Nashville neighborhood during this period. Because their repertoires were similar, it is likely that Greer and Campbell were familiar with each other's music.

61. Except for the demographic data and my interview with DeVane in summer 1987, all materials on Rice, which have been deposited into the Western Kentucky University Folklore Archives, were collected between June and October 1979.

62. 🎻 See Map 7.1, Map 7.2, and Demographics 7.8.

63. US census records indicate that Minnie Lee Franklin Rice, who was born in Trousdale County, Tennessee, and Jake married in 1913. They had eight children (two females and six males). Joel was the fifth oldest child, but fourth oldest son.

64. This issue is important for understanding factors that led to the conversation between Bowles and his wife regarding him playing the fiddle (see chapter 5).

65. 🎻 See Repertoire 7.5.

66. 🎻 See Lyrics 7.1–7.4. DeVane (1987) stated that during interviews, Rice performed lyrics to several old-time fiddle and play-party songs; the lyrics presented here were taken from transcriptions of interviews.

CHAPTER 8

North Carolina

Although information about Black secular music in the Carolinas has been available for some time, little, if any discussion, has been concerned with the musicking of Blacks in rural piedmont or mountain regions.[1] Similar to Talley (1922) in Tennessee, several scholars (Odum and Johnson 1925, 1926) collected secular songs while conducting field work in rural areas of the southeast United States and published them in folksong collections.[2] Not surprisingly, most of the early research focused on developments along the Atlantic Coast where large numbers of African Americans resided. Starting in the 1970s, however, several researchers began to address this gap in the literature as it relates to North Carolina.[3]

Yet, African American old-time or country music was not the primary concern of researchers when they began their investigations. Like scholars in other parts of the United States, most were intrigued by the blues, while some were interested in the banjo. Only in the process of investigating different types of secular musicking did researchers discover that the music preference for some Blacks in North Carolina's rural areas was not new creations such as the blues; rather, many preferred the nineteenth-century string band music, including banjo and fiddle, of their ancestors. Comments by Lornell (2013), who writes about the beginnings of his research journey in his home state of New York, help explain missteps he made during his earliest investigations: "I recall knocking on the door of an elderly gentleman living on Clinton Avenue, whom I politely dismissed after a pleasant half-hour conversation. This genial man didn't really interest me because he wasn't a 'blues man' who played in juke joints; rather he played fiddle and used to perform with medicine shows. Given the research that lay before me, this example of youthful indiscretion (I was nineteen at the time) now appears eerily prescient" (174). When questions about the roots of the banjo and its links to Africa were also being considered in scholarly circles during the early 1970s (Epstein 1975, 1977), some researchers believed issues regarding the instrument's history in the United States might be addressed while considering developments in North Carolina. Explaining her initial thoughts when pursuing research on the banjo, Conway (1998) states: "[I]n my early writings I found that before I could address my interest, I had to reconstruct the important African American history of the banjo that had remained unwritten. We could hardly begin to appreciate Dink's artistry[4] without this history" (xxiii). Fiddling by African Americans may not have been the primary focus of scholars when they began their research on secular genres in North Carolina (because most assumed that fiddling was a tradition that Blacks borrowed from whites and European culture with little historical relevance to Africa), but the results of their studies on blues and banjo have resulted in a wealth of data about the fiddle that is extremely valuable for this discussion.[5]

Like other parts of Appalachia, few communities in North Carolina's mountain region have had substantial Black populations; over the years, African Americans have been either a minority or effectively nonexistent (Bastin 1986, 287). Yet, the small numbers did not inhibit the involvement of mountain Blacks in musicking. When Glenn Hinson conducted research in the mountains during the 1970s, he found several musicians who performed traditions from earlier years. The musicking had been maintained not only because mountain Blacks felt less alienated from whites, but also because of the respect they had for old-time music. For many, fiddle and banjo served as a common meeting ground for both races (Bastin 1990, 74). Although the fiddle was regularly used for entertainment among Blacks and whites in different parts of North Carolina's mountain and piedmont regions during the nineteenth century, the performance of the instrument had declined among mountain Blacks by the early twentieth century (Baker 1987; Carlin 2004, 33). Most researchers believe the socio-cultural environment, specifically race and demographics, played a major role in not only the continued popularity of fiddling and old-time music among some Blacks, but also the growing prominence of the blues. Hinson (1978) writes: "In 1900 blacks in North Carolina lost the right to vote; this act was accompanied and followed by a number of laws further restricting black political and social rights. As the culture changed in response to this repression, and as increased industrialization brought about the growth of new urban areas, the music evolved to reflect the altered life-styles of working class blacks" (1).

Most research on non-blues music in the North Carolina piedmont region has been concerned with activity in Orange County, but some information about string band music has been documented for several other counties in the piedmont, specifically Randolph and Iredell in the central and western parts of the region, respectively, as well as Granville and Warren in the northeast. Although unevenness exists in the amount of information available, I believe it is important to examine each county not only to note the contributions of Black fiddlers but also to assess whether similarities and/or differences exist in musical activity.

Black populations in communities in the North Carolina piedmont region were larger than those in the mountains. For Randolph County,[6] Carlin (2004) provides the names of two Black fiddlers who were active during the early twentieth century: Marion Jordan (or Trogdon), a left-handed fiddler whose band included two sons on guitar; and Marshall Fred Davis (1884–1948), who not only performed for white functions as many Blacks had done in earlier years, but he also "worked with white musicians at public dances" (37). Unlike other parts of Appalachia and even western North Carolina where mixed-race performing groups were commonplace (see Kentucky and below), Carlin suggests that this was not the case for certain parts of North Carolina's piedmont region. White guitarist Gurney Peace, who persuaded Davis to perform with his group at local public dances in the city of High Point,[7] comments on the unusualness and difficulties of working with an integrated band during the 1930s: "Back then, segregation wasn't like it is now. And I'd always have to pick where I'd take him, and see if it was alright. I couldn't take him everywhere to play. . . . But he was about as good a fiddler as I ever heard"[8] (Carlin 2004, 37).

Black fiddling in Iredell County[9] during the first decade of the twentieth century is important because of the participation of Black fiddlers in what Carlin (2004) calls "two highly unusual events" in Statesville, Iredell's county seat (38). One event, a fundraiser held in honor of local Black firefighters, was "anchored by an African American fiddlers' convention. As reported by the local newspaper, the *Statesville Landmark*, 'A Meeting of Old-Time Colored Fiddlers' took place on Easter Monday, [April 12,] 1909. . . . What made this event even less common was the integrated audience, which was assisted by ushers of both races. Attendance was good and the event well received" (38). In a newspaper article announcing the event, several fiddlers are mentioned, possibly as an enticement to encourage members of the community to attend: "Such famous old-time fiddlers as Baldy Gaither, Albert Gray, the Bailey brothers, Pink Keaton, Jo. Sallie and others will perform and prizes will be given [to] the three best performers. A dance will be the feature of the afternoon and the old fiddlers will perform at night" (38). In giving reasons he believed the event was unusual, Carlin (2004) states: "There were other communities with enough African American musicians to stage such an evening. . . . They, however, didn't sponsor fiddlers' conventions. African American musicians . . . were known and played for events held by the Anglo-American population in other piedmont areas. But black fiddlers from other communities didn't appear in white contests [see below]" (38).

The second "unusual event" involves the participation of Black fiddler Baldy Gaither[10] in the 1908 white fiddlers' convention that took place a year before the firefighter fundraiser. An article in another local newspaper, the *Western Sentinel*, reports: "After the conclusion [of the Statesville Fiddlers Convention] there were many calls for Baldy Gaither, an old-time colored fiddler from north Iredell, who, after the regular program was finished, appeared and gave some of the old tunes with a vim that pleased everybody. As the audience went out, Baldy, who is 78 years old, gave an exhibition of his proficiency as a dancer" (38). Carlin's description of this event, like the integrated group (see above), implies that these gatherings (a Black fiddlers' convention and a Black performer playing in a white fiddler's convention) were uncommon in most North Carolina communities. Carlin (2004) writes: "By all evidence, these were two highly unusual events, even for Statesville. I've found no evidence of either convention recurring" (38). Although no documentation exists to support an opposing argument, is it possible that these events, even though they occurred only once, were not as uncommon as Carlin surmises?[11] Considering the contrasting views of whites on the issue of slavery during North Carolina's early history (see foregoing), perhaps it is not farfetched that differences also existed regarding the interaction of Blacks and whites during music activities. Furthermore, it was not uncommon during slavery for whites to attend Black events because many considered them to be spectacles that they wanted to observe and participate in. Finally, could the Black fiddlers' convention in Statesville, North Carolina, have been an impetus for a comparable convention that became popular in Martinsville, Virginia, during the 1930s and 1940s? Since the distance between Statesville and Martinsville is only about 110 miles, it would not be farfetched for Blacks to have known about the conventions in the two states even if they were not able to travel and participate in them.

Yet, it is noteworthy that Harvey Gaither (1884–1970), Baldy's son, also became a fiddler, and "was the first black musician to appear at the Union Grove Fiddlers' Convention" (Carlin 2004, 39), one of North Carolina's most famous fiddling events of the late twentieth (125). In explaining the inspiration for inviting Harvey Gaither to perform at Union Grove, the son of the convention's founder, Harper Van Hoy, states: "Harve Gaither, a black fiddler, lit the fire under [me]. Gaither was a novelty in northern Iredell County, a fiddling black man who played 'Pop Goes the Weasel' in an unforgettable way: 'He would end up playing while lying on his back jumping up from flat on his back and land on his feet . . . still playing 'Pop Goes the Weasel'" (Carlin 2004, 39). Van Hoy's remarks raise several issues. It indicates that Harvey was invited to be a spectacle or novelty act, very much in the performance style of Bill Livers, who was the life of the party at some of his performances in Kentucky attended primarily by whites (see chapter 6), as opposed to a musician who might seriously compete in the contest alongside white fiddlers. Furthermore, to what extent was Harvey following in the tradition of his father, who had been asked to perform "at the end" of the white 1908 Statesville fiddlers convention?

Evidence of Black fiddling in other North Carolina piedmont communities is minimal but useful for comparative purposes. Robert House, a former chancellor of the University of North Carolina at Chapel Hill, "recalled black string bands, characteristically with a fiddle-guitar-banjo format although sometimes with a harmonica, which played for country dances, both black and white, in both Warren and Halifax counties. They played square dances and old-style quadrilles, with the specific dance etiquette of the period" (Bastin 1986, 281). Following in the footsteps of his father who played accordion and called figures for set dances, Thomas Burt (b. 1900) of Granville County began playing banjo on a friend's homemade instrument when he was about fourteen years old. After learning to perform the guitar and later mastering the fiddle and autoharp, he and family members (two brothers and a sister on guitar and another brother on ukulele) started performing first for barn dances and parties in and around Durham during the early decades of the twentieth century (Bastin 1986, 287). Also, the Hinton family of Johnston County in the inland coastal region "was part of the early string band tradition, and its roots have been traced even further . . . into Moore County [in the piedmont region] . . . [where] well into the 1940s there was an active black string band so well known that other black musicians traveled to the area to participate" (Bastin 1986, 287).[12]

As noted above, most music research in the North Carolina piedmont region has focused on Orange County, particularly the township of Cedar Grove in the northwest portion of the county.[13] Researchers believe music making among Blacks and whites in Cedar Grove was similar to the nineteenth and early twentieth centuries partly because of demographics and social conditions.[14] In terms of work, both Blacks and whites relied on farming as a major source of income. Since piedmont farms were generally small, Black and white farmers experienced similar economic struggles, unlike the cotton-producing plantations along the Mississippi River (Lornell 1990, 221–22; Lornell 2000).

Much of Cedar Grove's secular music centered around small two- or three-piece string bands that played at house parties in the homes of various community members during the quieter, cooler months, when the demands of farm work (often related to the tobacco industry) were reduced. Dancing, eating, and camaraderie often characterized the events. Although bands performed a repertoire of tunes common to Blacks and whites, Black audiences were diverse in their musical tastes. Not only did African American musicians use the fiddle to play old-time music when the occasion arose, many would perform the blues but used the guitar to do so. By the early twentieth century, several musicians had begun to replace banjos, fiddles, and accordions with guitars as their favorite instruments, especially when guitars became available at low prices, due to the developing mail-order sales market (Lornell 2000; Hinson 1978, 1).

Bastin (1986) explains the diversity of musical genres by suggesting that Orange County had "distinct and separate 'cells' of musicians, including both the string band tradition in Cedar Grove and a blues tradition in and around Chapel Hill, more closely identified with that of Durham" (272). During the 1930s, there were blues performers in their fifties and sixties, as well as musicians who performed instrumental traditions from earlier years with few changes. Among the latter were John Arch Thompson, his brothers Jake and Walter, and friend Charlie White, who were the most important Black musicians around Cedar Grove during the early twentieth century. Not only were they equally adept at playing both fiddle and banjo because they had learned from older relatives or members of the communities who were musically active in the late nineteenth century when the fiddle or banjo were widely used, they could double on other instruments as well (Bastin 1986, 275; Lornell 1974, 25).[15] In terms of context, the Thompsons played at small gatherings such as picnics on weekends, and they provided entertainment at gatherings in various homes in the community, including their own. One of their most important roles at these events was to accompany set dances, square dances, or barn dances. No one knows when this type of entertainment began in Cedar Grove, but residents suggest that the square dance tradition dates to the 1880s and possibly earlier (Lornell 1990, 222).

From this brief overview of Black fiddling in rural North Carolina, the evidence confirms that the fiddle continued to be played in Black communities in the state during the early twentieth century even though it may not have been the most popular instrumental tradition. Also, Black fiddlers (for example, Emp [Imp] Wright, Rufe Atwater, and Bruin Moses) in various areas of the state were regarded as established artists. Unfortunately, minimal information exists on them because most had died by the time researchers began collecting data. For this reason, my discussion is limited to two fiddlers: Madison Boone Reid and Joe Thompson. Both are important not only because they were the last persons in their families to perform the fiddle, but also, they represent two regions of the state, the mountains and the piedmont, where African Americans' performance of old-time music continued to be pronounced during the early twentieth century. Each fiddler is presented chronologically according to his date of birth.

Profiles of North Carolina Black Fiddlers

Madison Boone Reid (1876–1964)

Members of the Reid family have always been multitalented with varied musical interests.[16] Although several of their ancestors played the fiddle in the nineteenth century, the performance of the instrument by those born during the early twentieth century declined, serving as a marker of the diminishing role of the fiddle in African American music culture. When I interviewed members of the family in August 1987, the only person readily acknowledged as a fiddler was Madison Boone Reid, who had learned to play the fiddle from his father, Washington Alexander Reid (1845–1920). The brother and sister duo—Boone Reid picking guitar and banjo as well as fiddling, and Martha Reid Moore (also called Mattie) on banjo—were remembered by family and community members in the early twentieth century as being among the area's finest musicians (Hinson 1978, 4).

Boone Reid and his family were born and raised in Johns River, a township in the mountains of Caldwell County about thirteen miles northwest of Lenoir, the county seat.[17] Typical of many mountain Blacks in North Carolina, the Reids' ancestors had intermarried with Europeans and Native Americans (Bastin 1986, 288). Etta Baker (1987) explained, "We're so mixed up, it's hard to tell if we're Black or white. I have an Irish grandmother and an Indian grandmother. Daddy's family is Irish and mother's Indian." Her sister, Cora Phillips (1987), added: "We had just as many white neighbors as we did Blacks. And we'd go and visit them and play for them." Baker (1987) also remembered that Blacks and whites often performed together: "In my growing up there was white players and Black players that played together. Being out of the same settlement and everything, everybody just learned each other's music."

Although the Reids spent most of their lives in North Carolina, some members of the family had lived in other parts of the South. Baker (1987) recalled that as a child, her family lived in Virginia for several years while her father worked in different locations: "While I was maybe two years old, we moved to East Virginia—Chase City, Virginia. Daddy heard of more work that he could do in Virginia, and a lot of his friends was going there too. When we was in Virginia, he decided he wanted to travel. So, he went to York, Pennsylvania, and he went to Rankin, Pennsylvania. He worked in the wire mill, and he also worked on the shipyard in Baltimore. Then when he came back to Virginia, he brought the family back to North Carolina. I don't know if he played music when he was away working in the steel plants. But he played after he came back to Virginia."

Since the nineteenth century, music played a major role in the family. Phillips (1987) provided details: "They kept a banjo at home all the time. Boone's older brother, Joe (Joseph Monroe Reid [1875–1945]), could play a banjo. Mattie, the baby sister, was a good banjo player. Daddy learned old-timey country music: 'Sourwood Mountain,' 'Going Down the Road Feeling Bad,' 'Crow Jane,' 'Shortening Bread,' 'Going Around the Mountain.' Well, just a lot of them songs that I have forgot. He played music at home and anywhere 'round with his neighbors. They was raised on a farm. They'd have corn shuckings, and everybody would come to that corn shucking. And then they'd have their music and the dancing." Families would get together almost every weekend, "playing songs from both the white and black musical traditions on fiddle, banjos, and guitars" (Hinson 1978, 4).

Adding to what Phillips had stated, Baker (1987) explained that her father also "was a real good dancer.... People loved all his music because he was real good with all the instruments that he played. He played in Lenoir [in Caldwell County] in his older days, but he never did play in Burke County. He made some recordings. The persons who recorded him came to my sister's house, and they had tapes. And it was transferred from tapes to records. One of them records was made back in 1956."[18] When asked if there was anything distinctive about her father's fiddling, Baker (1987) stated, "Well, he was real talented with his fiddle playing. My father learned to play from his father, Alec Reid. With that many years between then and now, the style of playing is altogether different. Daddy didn't play blues on the violin. I think everybody has a different way of playing. He would always put the violin high under his chin. But most people just holds the violin, but he didn't. He was real neat. He played banjo longer than any other instrument."

The contexts in which Boone Reid performed varied. Baker (1987) indicated that he provided "entertainments at different people's homes, square dances," but he did not perform with a band. "It was just different ones. Whoever wanted to bring their instruments and play. His brothers played banjo, violin, and guitar, mostly. My mother played harmonica." Regarding their mother, Phillips (1987) stated, "Mama could play guitar and sing. She had her own tunes. She'd get several of Papa's tunes, and she'd just go on and play, just like we'd come along and done it." When I asked Baker if percussive instruments were ever used when they performed their music, she replied, "no" (Baker 1987).

All of Boone Reid's children learned to perform an instrument when they were young. Phillips (1987) explained that she was five years old when her father began teaching her his way of playing, but Baker began at a much younger age:

> There was four girls.... The ones older than me, they both could play. The second girl, she has left home, but she was a guitar player like Etta.[19] And my older sister was a guitar player. My brothers played fiddle, guitar. My oldest brother, he played a French harp [harmonica]. Oh, he was good!
>
> After we grew up in our early teens, we began to play together. My father would play the banjo, I played the guitar, and Etta played the fiddle. We just kept growing with our music. We never did take music lessons. But whenever we would hear a tune and get it on our mind, then we could start, catch it. Well it was 1918 when we first began to play off of the records, round Edison records. We'd hear the tunes on that, and we'd just catch it, and just go on and play that.[20]
>
> He [Boone] played the fiddle by himself until we began. All the older ones moved out, left home. And then it was just us three. That was a happy time. Played for all the shucking. If you play [at] a corn shucking, they'd have a big supper. Ate that supper. The nights didn't get too long. We traveled. We went around to different places. Neighbors. And we would walk. We didn't have any way to travel then except for buggy. And then we'd get ready to go make our music. We'd just get out and walk sometimes four miles. There was a traveler coming through. And we made an album once.
>
> We didn't play in church. But we'd sing our sacred songs and play right along. But Etta, she plays at her church. I go over there and play with her at her church. I'm a Baptist and member of the church down here. I sing in the choir. We have a singing choir.

Although Baker began her music training with the guitar, an instrument she became noted for playing, her father also taught her how to play the fiddle and banjo. When asked if she still played the fiddle or knew of other fiddlers in the area, she responded: "No. I just quit, but I'm gonna take it up again. I just loved my guitar better than I did the violin. I don't know of anyone [fiddlers] around here now."

Like their parents, the Reid women kept their love for music in their families. Boone's daughter and niece both married musicians who came from musical families (Bastin 1986, 288). While Cora wed Theophilus "Theo" Lacey Phillips (1899–1977), Elizabeth Moore Reid (Mattie's daughter) married Fred William Reid (1903–1986); both men played banjo, guitar, and harmonica. Writing in 1978, Hinson stated, "Babe [Elizabeth] and Fred, Cora and Theo, and one of Cora's sisters, Etta Baker, continued playing together through the years, picking primarily for friends and family. Recently Fred laid down his instruments and Theo passed away" (Hinson 1978, 4). Commenting on her husband's musical family and the times everyone played together, it becomes apparent that musicking played a major role in the lives of both families. Phillips (1987) explained: "There was his mother. He had a sister. And he had three brothers, and they all could play. Theo would travel and go around and find the tunes, and he'd play here. Then we'd catch it and play it like he played. We'd have to practice, and we got to where we could play it. In Papa's [Boone Reid's] days, Theo would come here and we'd make music."[21] Demonstrating that the transmission of musical knowledge continued to be generational, Baker (1987) stated, "One of my sons was a drummer in a band, and they was called the Youngest Band of the South. This other one, John, he plays bass and lead guitar. And the older son, he plays lead guitar. And the girls play piano."

Although the fiddle had been important in the Reid family during the nineteenth and early twentieth centuries, its prominence had declined in the mid-twentieth century. When I asked Phillips about the popularity of the fiddle, she (1987) stated: "My husband, Theo, he had a fiddle. His daddy was a fiddler. I couldn't play. I tried anyway. My husband's family, they were good with a fiddle. And they could play. My husband also had a autoharp, a mandolin guitar-harp." Concerning the decline in popularity of the fiddle, her answer was very different from Baker's: "It's harder for some people, well it was for me. It's harder to study and to figure out to play real fiddle. Now a real fiddler can play. But I can tune anything that I ever picked up. But I can play tunes on a fiddle. But I don't call myself a fiddler. The fiddle is harder than the guitar. It's much harder than the banjo."

Few females in the different families had learned to play the fiddle, suggesting that it was not an instrument women commonly performed. Responding to a question concerning the decline in popularity of the fiddle, Baker (1987) stated: "The fiddle is mostly a lead instrument. But for a guitar, you can lead or you can play whatever. You can either lead with the guitar and second with the bass going. But you can't do it with a violin. You don't get all that sound from the violin. There are a lot of people that can play blues and anything on a violin, like Howard Armstrong [see Epilogue]. I've played at places with him. But for me, I don't think fiddles sound real good alone. They're good with other music instruments. And you're not around with other people when you'd want to play it."

Baker's response to my question is noteworthy for several reasons. She provides a reason for the decline in Black fiddling that relates to her music preferences, and possibly that of others, in terms of sound. The fact that Baker and Phillips did not know any Black fiddlers in the North Carolina piedmont region who may have been active in the early twentieth century confirms that one of the primary functions of rural musicians was to provide entertainment at home and local gatherings. Unless they were invited to perform at other locations within the state, their fame did not spread beyond their local area.

Joseph Aquilla Thompson (1918–2012)

The amount of data on Joe Thompson's role and contributions to Black fiddling is substantial and a tribute to his life history as a performer of the fiddle and old-time music, particularly when he is compared to other Black fiddlers who were born or were active during the early twentieth century (see photo 8.1). Keith Summers (2000) writes: "After World War II musical tastes changed and Joe's music might have been lost forever had not folklorist Kip Lornell located him and his cousin Odell (also a banjo player) in [1973] and encouraged them to perform again" (see photo 8.2).[22] When both the performance and interest in fiddling by African Americans had declined to its lowest, who could have imagined the enormous change in attitude about the tradition that would occur a few decades later? In my opinion, much of this change is due to musicians like Joe Thompson, who is examined below.[23]

Thompson spent much of his life in small towns. After his birth in a small community in Orange County's Cheeks Township just north of Mebane, he moved to the Mebane area of Alamance County in 1948 where he resided the remainder of his life (Lavender 2012). Thompson's ancestors came from Leasburg in Caswell County, which is northwest of Orange County.[24] In recounting his family history, Joe stated: "A man called Walter Thompson had so many slaves, . . . he give them his name, that's where we got the Thompson's [name] from.[25] And he had so much land and stuff, he gave them all a place up the road and right now it's called Thompson Road . . . there in Leesburg [sic]. That's where they [my family] came from" (Martin 1989, 4). Joe's father (John Arch) and uncles worked as farmers who grew "tobacco, corn, wheat, and other crops that brought some income to the family. However, by the turn of the century they were sharecropping for white farmers" (4). While Joe may have spent some of his youth on the farm with family members, his primary job as an adult

Photo 8.1. Joe Thompson playing the fiddle. Mebane, North Carolina. Early 2000s. The Joe and Odell Thompson Families.

was working for thirty-eight years as a rig-saw operator with White Furniture Company in downtown Mebane.[26]

Unlike some family members who played several instruments, Joe only played the fiddle; he was about five years old when he acquired his first fiddle from one of his mother's cousins.[27] The fact that the instrument did not have enough strings when he received it did not deter him from wanting to learn to play. He explains: "I did what I saw my brothers and all of them grown, big boys, do. They pulled strings out of the screen door to put on the guitar, banjos, and things so they could play. So, I pulled me two strings out of that screen door and put it on my fiddle. And when my daddy see I done got me a fiddle, he said, 'This boy, he's trying to play, ain't he?' And my mother said, 'Yeah, he's trying to do like you all doing.' So, he put him some new strings on his fiddle and give me them old basics. So, I got the message, and I finally learned how to play one tune, 'Hook and Line.' When you learn one tune, then it's not hard to learn another one" (J. Thompson 1987).

Joe stated that he learned to play the fiddle by observing and imitating his ancestors and siblings: "This thing [fiddling] come from . . . [what] my granddaddy started, then my daddy; it comes from the 1700s all the way down to here" (Chapman 2004). Although Joe's family learned fiddle tunes from both

Photo 8.2. Odell Thompson (banjo) and Joe Thompson (fiddle). North Carolina. Photo by Wayne Martin, 1990–91. The Joe and Odell Thompson Families.

Blacks and whites in their communities, some musicians stand out from others. For example, Emp Wright,[28] an African American whom musicians in the community considered to be an exceptional fiddler, traveled the area extensively; he lived for some time in Little Texas, a mulatto community near Burlington, North Carolina. In fact, John Arch is remembered saying, "That man [was] something else on the fiddle. He could make it whistle." Joe believed his father learned fiddle tunes from Wright when the family lived near Leasburg (J. Thompson 1987; Conway 1990, 76). "After they got learned, then they started taking them to dances. . . . That was when my daddy was young, around eighteen or nineteen years old" (Bastin 1986, 275–76). Chapman (2011) believes most of Robert Thompson's older sons were involved in musicking, but "the very best of them were Uncle John Arch and Uncle Walter. They are the names that would come up all the time in conversations."

Similar to many areas of West Africa and other rural Black communities in the United States, females rarely played the fiddle. When I asked Odell and Joe if females in their families played instruments, Odell (1987) replied, "No. My sisters, they danced on the set when they were running the set." Joe (1987) added: "When they were dancing, they could dance nice, my sisters and his sisters could really put it on nice. Yes sir." When asked why their sisters did not play instruments such as the guitar, banjo, or the fiddle, Joe (1987) stated: "I had a sister could play the piano a little bit but after she married she quit." They also both agreed their fathers would have allowed their sisters to play an instrument. "If they had wanted to play, they wouldn't mind it" (J. Thompson). Therefore, women probably did not play the instrument because, by tradition, this was not something they did.

Joe and Odell Thompson, along with other relatives, continued to perform at dances through the early forties. Martin (1987) believed they held on to the tradition as long as they did because it was important to their families: "They have a real sense of family. Family history and their fathers doing it, it's very important to them. Not only the fiddling, but Joe talks about his father's religion—the Black Primitive Baptist Church and its importance to him." But everything changed after World War II. Odell (1987) explained: "Well, we went into the service. When we come out of the service, we were young and everybody had their own music. All they had to do was hit a button, and they grab the music. Radio and TV. Just be on your own.... A few years ago, they had a fellow named Kip Lornell who come through, and talked us into some notion of playing this old-time music." Joe (1987) added: "The young people are going to the horn, they're going to the rock 'n' roll; these new instruments and styles are taking over. This young bunch, they don't believe in this old-timey stuff. That's too far back for them." But the Thompsons recognized from personal experience that interest in old-time music was changing. Odell (1987) stated: "It brings joy to the people now; they enjoy this old-timey music better than they do this rock 'n' roll." Agreeing with Odell, Joe (1987) indicated that "It's coming back. This type of music is coming back."

When I asked why there appeared to be greater interest in playing the banjo than the fiddle, Joe's response (1987) not only revealed the reasons he believed the fiddle was not more popular but also his concern about the future of Black fiddling: "I think I know what the problem is. This fiddle is a hard instrument to play. You really got to be cut out for it. There is so much to do, you got to get this thing right, keep the rosin on it, and you can get too much on it or you can have not enough. It makes a mess, you got to have it right. So, it's a hard instrument to play. But I tell you what, if you play the fiddle and play it good, people likes it. I guess I'm the last Black fiddler. There is one Black fiddle player in South Carolina, but he plays the blues. I can't think of his name right now, but he was in Charleston, West Virginia. I remember he played so rough that he'd break the hair out of his bow. He teared his bow up."[29] Chapman's response (2011) to the lack of interest in fiddling by Joe's family members is significant for its implication regarding the future of fiddling beyond North Carolina:

> It's got to be the young people who are going to continue and save it, because Joe's nephews who were very good at it have not kept it up. Nobody in the family is keeping it up. So, unless we can find people like the Chocolate Drops[30] who really see the need and want to salvage that kind of music that Joe played, I don't think

it's going to [last]. I think it's a dying art, unless we can find a way that our young people can take hold and go with it.

I think the older ones who are my age, between 60 and 65, probably did not tamper with it because it's not city music. So, when they went to Philadelphia, those from John Arch's line is the only [family] line that kept it up. When they came to the family reunions, they would have a Saturday night [gathering]. And they would get out there and do it. I don't think it's something that you do in the big city, evidently—not being around each other. The one or two who did learn how to pick the banjo or play the fiddle, they are not together enough to keep the dream alive. That's why I say that. The dancing, you don't ever see that kind of dancing any more. I would suspect that has a lot to do with it, even within his own immediate family. And the rest of us, you can forget it.

With regard to ensemble organization and performance contexts, Joe (1987) remembered that the string band that his father and siblings performed in generally included at least two banjos, one fiddle, and one mandolin. When asked if there was anything special about the sound of the fiddle that caused it to be the lead instrument, Joe (1987) explained that it was tradition: "I always has had the fiddle with the leading instrument. You get them all together, banjo, fiddle, guitar, and the fiddler is supposed to lead." Also, when I asked if a fiddler ever played alone, Joe stated "no" and explained why:

Well it's not too good for one fiddler to play by our self. Sometimes it takes . . . working too hard. You got about eight or ten people out there jumpin' and makin' a racket and it's best for fiddle and banjo to play. Sometimes we get a guitar to give us a bass sound; you know the second and bass come in to help us out. It takes like thirty to forty minutes to dance a set out. And you gotta play good; you got to play a nice speed.

When we played for a dance over in Seattle, Washington, we had about 200 people dancing. And we had the set caller standing right here with the music [instruments]. . . . But we had the loud speakers on. And he has his banjo and we had a bass fiddle and we had a guitar helping us out. We did a good job at it out there.

Odell (1987) added: "If you have several of them fiddlers playing, the other one can slack off a little bit and . . . the audience and dancers would never know the difference."

While working as sharecroppers during the early twentieth century, "the Thompson brothers came into frequent contact with white farm workers who played string band music" (Martin 1989, 4). So, John Arch used to play the fiddle for house parties as far away as Burlington in Alamance County during the 1930s and 1940s because he had been invited by Black and white neighbors to provide entertainment for dances. "As banjo player Dink Roberts, their slightly younger contemporary, remembers, 'John Arch often played with the banjo-picker George (Charley) White—sometimes as often as six nights a week'" (Conway 1990, 76). Conway adds: "It's interesting that the music crossed racial borders, even back in Jim Crow times, around the tobacco barns and other places where blacks and whites would play together. And I believe I've heard Joe say that John Arch and them played for dances—three nights for whites [square dances] and three nights for blacks [frolics and corn shuckings]" (Chapman 2004). As a teenager playing the fiddle at events, Joe (1987) remembered how music was used to accompany dancing:

> We'd call it frolicking back in our day. Like we'd have a big corn-shucking. See, I had three brothers above me and one under. My daddy had corn piled high as my head, long thin rows. And we just shucked corn. That night we'd have a big frolic. You know how boys need to have a can of whiskey. 'Course everybody'd behave themselves all right. We'd call sets. This one call a set, and that one call a set. But I never did get to do much 'cause I always had to play at the dance. And one thing that's kind of important to this type of music we play. It is dance-type music. We never do much singing. We'd be playing for sets. I guess white folks call it square dance.

In an interview with folklorist Michael Casey (1983), Joe gives further details about frolics: "It was square dance. Six and twelve and, eight, twelve and sixteen hand.... I played for a lot of square dancing" (8). Normally, frolics were held two or three months during the winter on a regular basis until the spring farm work began in February or early March. "Chopping time"[31] signaled the end of winter. Generally held at people's houses, dances were family oriented, beginning at approximately 8:00 P.M. and lasting until about midnight. All ages attended barn dances to talk, relax, and of course dance. The night's host supplied a small amount of food and drink. Alcohol was consumed by many, but rarely did drinking get out of hand. If some drunk caused problems, he or she would be quietly removed from the premises. Recalling the spirit of these evenings, Odell stated, "The black people, why they just did it for fun, the enjoyment, the kick they all got out of it. They weren't out for no money, they were just out for fun. [They] cut up, carry on, and dance and go on" (Lornell 1990, 224).[32]

When Joe and Odell started playing old-time music during the 1970s, the context for performances had changed because there were few opportunities to play at dance events. When asked if he played for frolics and square dances, Joe (1987) stated: "It's not many. I think there's white people doing it, but we hadn't played for the white folk lately. We used to. Now we go play at a festival, but not for dancing." As a result of this new context, Martin (1987) made the point that fiddling had become a performance art: "Joe and Odell started out playing for dances; that was the context. They played on the back porch, front porch, and living rooms, but their community importance was attached to their being at dances a lot and mainly at picnics. Now, when people don't care for fiddling as much, don't want it around, they've lost their reason for being. So, it's fallen back to being a kind of performance art. You're not going to find people in the community who are attuned to fiddling. They come and experience it in the context of a good time. Then, it was great. But to sit down and listen to somebody play "Forked Deer" and "Grey Eagle." To a lot of people, that may be great. But if you're thirteen. [The youth are going to say], 'Let's hear a [real] song.'" Therefore, when they returned to playing old-time music, not only did they play at different venues, but their audiences changed.

Black fiddling has struggled to be accepted by various communities throughout its history in the United States. Although popular among many of the enslaved and free Blacks during the eighteenth and nineteenth centuries, Black and white religious authorities, especially those who were Protestants, criticized the tradition and wanted to have it banned. Acceptance became an issue when Blacks migrated to urban areas during the first half of the twentieth century, because as city dwellers, many associated the fiddle with the country. Yet, its popularity in certain rural Black communities continued until old-timers died out, and the young chose other genres for entertainment. In terms of race, the majority of whites supported fiddling during slavery because it was not threatening. Not only was the fiddle part of their European cultural heritage, but also Blacks had learned to perform tunes and dances that gave whites pleasure. By the early twentieth century, however, researchers and those who controlled media, the majority of whom were white, did not promote Black fiddling because it did not represent what they regarded as Black music. Acceptance did not occur until the late twentieth century when a few young white researchers began to acknowledge the role and contributions of African Americans to the development of fiddling and old-time music. Yet, many in the Black community continued to resist identifying fiddling with African American culture.

Members of the Thompson family not only experienced many of the transformations that have taken place in the tradition's history, but they played a major role in affecting change. In essence, Joe encountered both the challenges and rewards of being a Black fiddler. For example, since both Black and white Protestant churchgoers in the southeast United States strongly disapproved of fiddling during slavery, I wondered if attitudes had changed in later years. When asked if the fiddle was accepted in church during the early twentieth century and present-day,[33] Joe and Odell had conflicting views. Excerpts from my 1987 interview with them help explain their different perspectives:

JCD: Would you play your fiddle in church?
JT: Well I could do it, but really, we hadn't done it. In fact, I don't think my church would approve of it.

JCD: Why not?

JT: I don't know.

OT: Yes, they would too. See, they already have string music in there. Well this fiddling ain't any different. Now, on TV, he carries his fiddle, he's a preacher![34]

JT: See we got some deacons that think it is all right and some that don't.

OT: It's kind of mixed up!

JT: They don't want to ruin anything.

JCD: What would you ruin by playing the fiddle? What's wrong?

JT: They figure it may not be Christianity.

OT: Well I can tell you too; they wouldn't say nothing, but you may hear them think it. (Joe and Odell Thompson 1987)

When I asked Chapman (2011), Joe's cousin, if he had spoken to her about his acceptance among members of his community, her response revealed the different attitudes, music preferences, and generational differences among some Blacks:

> He has talked to me about that. I do remember that it wasn't always hunky-dory or fine. The fiddle somehow is less impressive to people, perhaps Black people ... than the violin. Blacks considered fiddling as the devil's music. Some people in the family did. I remember saying, "Ya'll, let's get together and create this dance." And people thought, and a lot of them said, "Oh no. I wouldn't be associated with that." That was even after the 1970s. There are people who don't look at fiddle music as being something to be lauded. They don't embrace it as a part of Black culture. But when we did the film on Joe, there were people that came from all around. We filled up the Mebane Art Center.[35] We may have had 200 chairs on the floor. Before the evening was over, every chair was filled. I think Joe got a standing ovation at his church.... That may have been the first time that something like that happened within his community. Maybe it could be elderly persons who believed that this music was not worth hearing in the church—people who played the fiddle were not as good as those who played the piano.... I think the notion of that maybe moving away with the younger.

Probably because of the ambivalence regarding fiddling and old-time music that existed within their community, both Joe and Odell were surprised and pleased with the response they received from music enthusiasts during their travels. Joe's comments (1987) about their first visit to the northwest United States helped explain his reaction: "I was really surprised when me and Odell went to Seattle [Port Townsend], Washington, in 1987, and we played this type music. On a Monday night, when we played the first tune, they just stood up; I didn't know what was wrong. But they were just listening. When we quit the very first tune, they just applaud. And we played the second tune, and there were lights flashing all up and down the stage. We played the same old-time music we play in Mebane."

Soon after they began performing outside their home community, Joe and Odell became regular participants at workshops and festivals regionally, nationally, and internationally.[36] They were invited to perform at major venues in the United States, including Carnegie Hall (New York City); the Henry Ford Museum at Greenfield Village (Dearborn, Michigan); the John F. Kennedy Center for the Performing Arts (Washington, DC); and the World Fiddle and Banjo Convention. In addition, they received awards and honors: 1990 Brown-Hudson Award from the North Carolina Folklore Society; 1991 North Carolina Folk Heritage Award (now known as the North Carolina Heritage Award) and 2007 Folk Heritage Award from the National Endowment for the Arts (NEA). They were also featured in audio and video recordings: the 1989 film documentary, *Step It Up and Go: Blues in the Carolinas*; *Appalachian Journey*, one of five films Alan Lomax produced for the 1991 PBS American Patchwork series[37]; British television's 1991 documentary on the banjo, *Echoes of America*; Mike Seeger's 1994 video, *Old-Time Banjo Styles*; and Iris Chapman's 2004 film documentary, *The Life and Times of Joe Thompson*.

After Odell's death, the victim of a car accident at Merlefest in 1994, Joe was remorseful. Without family to accompany his fiddling, he considered stopping. But friends encouraged and helped him continue performing at events; Joe explained: "Everybody was always ready. They just kept me busy. A lot of time, I probably wouldn't have went, but they wanted to go. So, we just got started. So, we never stopped going" (Chapman 2004). The continuous activity led to additional awards, including the 2004 City of Mebane Joe Thompson Day; the 2006 Charlotte Folk Society Folk Heritage Award; and the 2007 NEA National Heritage Fellowship. To celebrate his 2007 award from NEA, a black-tie event, "Honoring the Man and His Music," was organized and sponsored by Mebane's Prince Hall Yadkin Lodge #799. On July 19, 2007, the General Assembly of North Carolina Session 2007 "issued a joint resolution honoring accomplishments of Joe Thompson and the late Odell Thompson, legendary North Carolina musicians" (Chapman 2011). In addition to articles in books, scholarly journals, and newspapers documenting him, family members, and North Carolina's Black fiddle tradition, several recordings were released that feature musicking with Odell, the Carolina Chocolate Drops, and other musician friends.[38]

The issue of race among Black fiddlers is complicated. Most researchers applaud the fact that the Thompsons were actively performing string band music during the height of Jim Crow, which many believed may have helped in dismantling laws that discriminated against Blacks. However, others believe that the situation had not changed from earlier years. Using an interview conducted with Joe and Odell, music critic Art Menius makes his argument:

> "We used to go around and play for a lot of white folks at times. We'd go to their house and they'd have dances. Put you in the doorway and they'd be dancing

in each room. They'd had a time back then, too," Odell remembers. Dance sets would often last a half hour or more. Not that the black musicians were treated as equals, however, even if their white neighbors considered them the best square dance band around. The few contemporary accounts suggest that their status at white dances was closer to servile than celebrity. "The caller would tell you what he wanted and we'd commence playing," explains Joe. . . .

The Thompsons recall only a handful of white pickers, mostly neighbors, with whom they played music in the old days. And while they believe their fathers learned music from whites, the same held true for them. "They played for white people. They didn't play with 'em; they played for them," Odell explains. "We all played for them way back then, a whole lot of times." (Menius 1992, 33–34)

While equality did not exist, Chapman believed it was significant that leaders of organizations invited her to include a discussion of race during the showing of her film. While preparing for a presentation in Tennessee, Chapman (2011) stated that she reflected on her task and issues regarding race:

So, I went back and really studied the film to see what was there. You really do see how music was crossing racial lines. Fiddle players were crossing racial lines. They were building the bonds, the steps for integration long before the civil rights movement. And I can truly say that when you start looking at these people who would pull up beside Joe or Joe would pull up beside them, down in the sharecropping fields and all around, because they were great players.[39] People wanted to play with them. So, they didn't care whether there was a law, whatever it was. They just loved the good music. So, it didn't matter. But I was able to take that film and talk about Joe in that way. Just start a conversation about race and race relations. So, it was really apropos for me to go there and talk about Joe.

When Joe Thompson died on February 20, 2012, fans and admirers in the United States, the United Kingdom, Australia, and other parts of the world mourned his death. More than twenty-five publications (newspapers, social media, television, and radio programs) acknowledged his passing with articles, photos, video footage, and audio recordings that paid tribute to him and his contributions. Because of his longevity, Thompson had acquired several titles. Before his death, many who played old-time music, referred to him as "the last family tradition Black fiddler."[40] After his death, other titles appeared, including "nationally renowned old-time fiddler and folk musician" (Fiddler Joe Thompson 2012); the "last of a generation of African American string band musicians in North Carolina" (Brower 2012); the "last black traditional string band player left" (McCray 2012); and "master fiddler and musician"[41] (Field Trip South). Family members and close friends who knew Thompson as a person of few words commented on his humility. His cousin Iris Thompson Chapman stated: "He was the most humble person that I have ever met" (Wilder 2012), and close friend Larry Vellani, who played banjo with him in his later years, added: "Nobody was too big or too little for Joe to sit down and pick with" . . . he was "a gentleman, and a gentle man" (Menconi 2012). Obviously, these attributes were apparent in his music and public performances; individuals at the North Carolina Arts Council reported that Thompson was "a singular person and a singular musician" . . . "he was more than a great musician; he was a great man" (Wilder 2012).

One of his major achievements, according to many writers, was his role in preserving old-time music and the Black string band tradition. A guest on the Mudcat Café online discussion group stated: "He was a great inspirational player and singer of African American Old Time music, with a big influence here on the East side of the pond as well" (Banjo Ray 2012). Terence McArdle (2012), music critic with the *Washington Post,* affirmed this point by indicating that Thompson was "a much-honored fiddler whose music offered a link to an almost-vanished tradition of African American string bands that predated the blues and even the Civil War . . . [he was] among the last of a generation of black musicians who performed at square dances before World War II." Comments by Douglas Martin (2012) in the *New York Times* sum up what many believe was his most lasting legacy: "He planted a seed for the future. In 2005, three young musicians [Dom Flemons, Rhiannon Giddens, and Justin Robinson] started coming to his house every Thursday to learn the old ways. They formed a band, the Carolina Chocolate Drops, 'mostly as a tribute to Joe,' they said. Their 2010 album, *Genuine Negro Jig,* won a Grammy for best traditional folk album."[42] Reflecting on the group's beginnings, Flemons (2012) stated: "When I first met him in 2005, I had no idea that I would be so heavily involved in making music with him and then making a group that has helped get his name out there further than he might have by himself. . . . It has been a constantly humbling journey to be able to have said I worked with him and that my music has forever been affected by his guidance and willingness to share his music with me."

When I asked Joe and Odell about the type of music they performed, Joe (1987) stated: "We play the same thing my father played when I was little seeing him play. Most everything we play comes from my daddy and his daddy." Similar to other southern, rural-based African American fiddlers who lived during the nineteenth and early twentieth centuries, songs that Thompson performed were diverse.[43] Except for "Dona's Got a Rambling Mind," which may be an original creation by someone in the Thompson family, the songs Joe performed consisted of selections shared by Blacks and whites (Lornell 1975, 31; Conway 1990, 76; Carlin 1999). Two songs—"It Ain't Gonna Rain No More" and "Molly Put the Kettle On"—are mentioned in the narratives of formerly enslaved Blacks; three ("Careless Love," "It Ain't Gonna Rain No More," "John Henry") are now common stock; and several—"Black Eyed Daisy," "Oil in My Vessel," and "Ryro's House"—possibly evolved from the music culture of African Americans in the

Southeast. Commenting on the uniqueness of some of the tunes, Martin (1987) stated: "I don't know anybody else who knows 'Ryro' except Joe and Odell. That was the first time I ever heard it. Joe said Ryro is the name of a woman in a bawdy house; a rough house or something like that. Her name was Ryro. And 'That Old Corn Liquor' is great; they sing some when they play too."

Although the repertoire of Black musicians in the North Carolina piedmont region during the early twentieth century is derived from a variety of sources, Lornell (1990) identified two that were common. One source was stage music of medicine and minstrel shows that crisscrossed the South, employing Black entertainers as comedians and musicians. Medicine shows not only toured the area through the early 1970s, but the shows featured traditional performers who played the fiddle and banjo tunes piedmont musicians knew. A second source was music rooted in the British Isles, a tradition that remained strong in Appalachia and certain sections of the south. Because of the close interaction of the races and the slow changes that occurred in the social environment in the area, the music "became part of a shared repertoire from which black and white musicians equally drew" (225).

Although popular in nearby urban areas, blues was virtually absent among local musicians where the Thompsons lived (Lornell 1990, 226).[44] As noted in the foregoing, the prominence of fiddle tunes in the area is most likely a reflection of the social environment. Lornell (1975) believes that because Blacks and whites in the North Carolina piedmont region were never "stratified as in other parts of the South" nor were Blacks alienated from the white community, respect for music played on fiddle and banjo served as a common meeting ground for both races. Furthermore, Black musicians who played for both Black and white dances drew from the same repertoire, for dancing by both groups was almost identical. Although blues became an important medium to comment and protest injustices, the genre did not predominate in North Carolina. "The atmosphere was more relaxed, allowing the blacks to relate to the older musical forms. Even the indigenous blues styles reflect this outlook. There is not the tautness nor the overt emotionalism found in the blues of the Delta or Texas. Instead, the Piedmont style is much more gentle and melodic in nature" (31).

It is doubtful that Joe's performance style changed when he returned to fiddling in the early 1970s because his primary interest was in preserving what his ancestors had performed and taught him. Since fiddle music was used to accompany dances, and the sets often extended as long as fifteen to thirty minutes, the size of a musician's repertoire was less important than his stamina. Although Black and white musicians used the same repertoire when they played for dances, their performance styles differed. For example, Jabbour (1985) learned from research in the area that Black fiddling in the North Carolina piedmont region tended to be abrasive, vigorous, with an energetic quality. In explaining how his father taught him to play the fiddle, Joe Thompson affirms this point:

"My daddy, he said I was always light, he couldn't half hear me. Said I would need a heavy bow. Most white people like to hear that bow [softly] shuffle. But black people, it don't bother them. To hear it [loud], that's what they want" (Conway 1990, 77, 1998, 6). From observing them in performance on many occasions, Martin (1987) believed Joe and Odell Thompson's sound quality was due to several factors: the physical position they used when playing together, their repertoire and tuning, as well as Joe's distinct performance style:

> With Joe and Odell Thompson, it's one sound. They get very close to each other. In fact, their legs are sort of intertwined. They sit facing each other.[45] And the banjo is much louder than the fiddle. But the sound they get is so hard to describe. It's hypnotic. I think they're fantastic.
>
> Joe Thompson does a lot of neat things. Their repertoire's not huge, but he does some of these pieces using regular tuning. And then he tunes up the bass strings, [he] cross-sets the fiddle. A lot of people call it cross-setting. I'm not sure exactly the term he uses for it. It's kind of an archaic thing, I think. And then he plays those others, like A-E-A-E, the tuning of the fiddle. And it's really neat.
>
> The bowing, it's a shuffle, but he also mixes it in with other things. With blues fiddling, obviously, those slides and double-stops are real important. But the bowing is really the heart of it. And Joe's bowing is pretty interesting. The whole sound is. While not bluesy at all, it's very compelling. I guess it's the banjo, but not only the banjo—but just the way they work together to get this insistent rhythm. It's not melodic. He falls in the rhythmic class of fiddlers. I know a guy down on the coast who has the same sort of almost insistent rhythm—a white man—but there is a difference. Some of the lines that you play on the banjo that accompany him was just different than Joe's.
>
> A lot of fiddlers know a guitar gives them a certain amount of leeway than a banjo. 'Cause a banjo, especially claw hammers, is playing notes, melody notes. When you have melody notes, it's like putting more of something into a limited space. And you have to work around that or with a person. And with a guitar, there's no other melody notes. You can do whatever you want to, or within certain confines of the aesthetic.
>
> Joe has an interesting left-hand technique. What you would normally note with the ring finger, he notes with his little finger, which is normally thought of as more difficult. The little, the pinky's a hard finger to note with, but he notes his [that way]. It's just amazing. It's all [a] very individual thing in a way. And I'm amazed by that.

In some ways, aspects of Joe's playing are no different from characteristics used in other African American musical forms. In the film *The Life and Times of Joe Thompson* (Chapman 2004), Martin explained: "Before they [Joe and Odell] would play, they would be tuning up. . . . You tune the strings and as you get closer to the point that you think you are in tune, you start.... I guess modern musicians would call it running the scale. We were doing that one day and I noticed that every time he [Joe] did it, he'd play the third note of the scale and flattened it, unlike the white musicians that I play with. And a lot of the tunes they [Joe and Odell] play, that note is flattened. A lot of people think of that as a characteristic of blues. But in fact, it's probably older than blues."

Since fiddling during the nineteenth century was used primarily for dancing, tunes were often performed with no words or included lyrical content that was unimportant. In addition, most tunes had simple melodies organized in an AB pattern, which the fiddle had the lead role in performing. Generally, the banjo player used a claw hammer or frailing style, which meant that "no picks are used and the thumb keeps a steady bass line going on the fifth string, while the other two or more fingers stroke the other strings in a downward fashion" (Lornell 1974, 26). To highlight some of the characteristics of Joe's performance style, I focus on two songs—"Old Joe Clark" and "Georgia Buck"—performed by Joe and Odell and analyze them in terms of form, melody, and rhythm.[46] Similar to "Soldier's Joy," "Old Joe Clark" is one of the most widely known southern fiddle tunes in the United States. Not only is it popular among those who play bluegrass music, it can be heard at old-time fiddle sessions and country dances. Although researchers believe "Old Joe Clark" dates to the nineteenth century, Jabbour (1966b) states that "one cannot find sets older than the turn of the century. It is possible that it circulated first in children's tradition and in play-parties—which might account for its playful and sometimes outlandish verses—then erupted into the fiddle and banjo world."

With a performance time of roughly two minutes and fifteen seconds, Joe and Odell's playing of "Old Joe Clark" is typical of most old-time music tunes. After Joe sings the lyrics, "Old Joe Clark killed a man, buried him in the sand," twice in a slow free rhythm and no instrumental accompaniment, Joe (on fiddle) and Odell (on banjo) quickly begin playing at a brisk pace (quarter note = 132 bpm) that is maintained through the song's ending. During their performance, Joe and Odell vary the AB structure typically used by old-time musicians.[47] Instead of repeating the AB pattern twice with equal attention given to both melodies, as performed by many musicians (see Jabbour 1966b), Joe and Odell's performance allows for the low-pitched A melody to dominate. Not only do they sometimes play the A melody three times before moving to B, they end the song with A and no performance of B. Thus, the form of their performance is: AABB | AAABB | AAABB | AA. Wilson (2013) explained that Joe played the tune in a manner typical of many musicians, especially those who are African Americans. When some musicians "get into a groove with the dancers, they prefer not to switch back to the other part until it feels right." Joe uses a shuffling rhythm in playing the fiddle melody heterophonically with the banjo, and only once in the performance (at 1:34) does he use double stops. Although Joe occasionally includes some off-beat phrasing (syncopation) and bends the third note of the scale as he plays the melody, these characteristics are only occasionally used in this performance.

"Georgia Buck" was popular in both Black and white traditions in the North Carolina piedmont region and other parts of the south (Conway 1998, 13; Carlin 1999; Bass 1931).[48] The fact that Joe included it on all of the original recordings he made[49] suggests that it was regularly performed by members of the Thompson family. Joe and Odell's performance of "Georgia Buck" differs from "Old Joe Clark" in several ways. At three minutes and fifteen seconds in length, "Georgia Buck" is longer, and singing is more prominent—first by Joe who, during the first fourteen seconds, introduces the song with the lyrics: "Oh, the Georgia Buck is dead. Um, last word he said, 'Don't you let a woman have her way.' Georgia Buck is dead." Starting at (0:21), Odell begins singing the lyrics intermittently throughout the rest of the song.[50]

Unlike "Old Joe Clark," which is based on two distinct melodies or themes (AB), "Georgia Buck" is composed of one sixteen-beat (four-beat, four bar) melody that is repeated throughout the piece with variations. In this performance, the use of bent notes, especially thirds and sevenths, as well as off-beat phrasing (syncopation) is prominent. Although Joe's fiddle melody is performed heterophonically with the banjo, polyphony sometimes occurs (see 1:26–1:56) when Joe uses thirty-second notes instead of playing the melody with quarter, eighth, or sixteenth notes to create greater intensity. The performance reaches a climax toward the end (3:03) when both performers increase the tempo to 138bpm and develop the melody with more improvisation, which results in a more highly involved polyphonic sound.

Interestingly, Joe and Odell also use volume as an element for variation. During the first part of the performance, Joe performs softly to such a degree that his fiddling is barely heard above Odell's singing and banjo playing (see 0:21–0:45 and 1:02–1:26). It is during these parts that it sounds as if the banjo is leading with the fiddle playing a more supporting role. During the interludes or sections when there is no singing (see 0:46–1:01), Joe performs more loudly, but still without a lot of intensity. However, when the singing ends at 2:11, Joe begins improvising by playing the melody more intricately and with a louder volume. As he performs with greater intensity, the tempo also increases to 138 bpm at 3:01. At this point, Joe uses harmonics to produce a high-pitched screechy (or scratchy) sound; they also perform the last four beats of the sixteen-beat melody three times. Either this was a way to indicate to each other that the song is about to come to an end, or it is a climactic moment before the entire melody is played one last time.

Although performances of only two tunes have been examined, it is apparent that Joe's performance style varies and appears to be dependent on context, the tune, and the musician(s) with whom he is performing. Because these two examples were made early his recording career with a family member who knew the tradition of his ancestors, we can conclude that the musicking is similar to what was done during the early twentieth century. Also significant is how Joe's fiddling compares with that of other Black fiddlers included in this study. From the cursory analysis of two songs, we find that commonalities exist. Not only is Joe's use of flatted thirds and sevenths similar to that of other fiddlers, his shuffling, percussive style in performing the melody is comparable to that used by Leonard Bowles in Virginia. In fact, Linford (2013b) states: "Bowles's style and Joe Thompson and Odell Thompson's style, that's what I think of as being the African American old-time style. The rougher timbre, that sawing, where the fiddler is focusing on the bowing aspect of it; not a complex, ornate melody and a lot of pentatonic sort of melodies. I would even add that the interaction between the fiddle and banjo is similar. That pairing, the heterophony is a really strong awareness of what the other person is going to do to produce a single sound between the two instruments."

While additional listening would need to be done, these two examples also demonstrate that Joe employs a more reserved performance style when playing "Old Joe Clark," a piece identified with Euro-American culture, probably because the song's structure fits this aesthetic. However, a more involved and African-derived improvisatory performance style is used in "Georgia Buck," probably because the simple, straightforward formal structure allows for greater freedom and variation. In addition to Joe's extensive use of bent thirds and sevenths, off-beat phrasing occurs more frequently in "Georgia Buck" than "Old Joe Clark."

Summary

Research on Black fiddling in North Carolina stands apart for several reasons. The information collected by researchers confirms what has been discovered for other states. Fiddling was an important and thriving tradition among Blacks and whites in the southern United States; the shared tradition that began during the nineteenth century and earlier continued in rural communities in the state through the mid-twentieth century. Furthermore, documentation of musicking by Joe Thompson, one of the last surviving Black fiddlers, not only allows us to pay tribute to a musician who represents those who were actively performing before him, but his life experiences provide a window for understanding what existed heretofore. More importantly, his mentoring of younger performers who developed careers of their own demonstrates that these traditions do not (and should not be allowed to) die, which is all the more reason why the lives and musicking of *all* performers (Black, white, and others) need to be documented. When fiddling during the late nineteenth and early twentieth centuries was a living art form among African Americans, those who were in a position to document its history and development ignored and dismissed it—whether because of lack of knowledge or researchers regarded it as irrelevant. Only after fiddling became a performance tradition admired by whites did the tradition generate interest on the part of researchers. It is fortunate that Thompson lived long enough to see what could happen to the tradition with support from entities within the larger society.

This case study also reveals some interesting issues regarding the relationship of demographics to fiddling. In North Carolina, fiddling did not survive solely in rural areas where Blacks were outnumbered by whites. Fiddling continued in parts of the piedmont regions where African Americans were in the majority, but declined in the mountains where the number of Blacks was small. Because North Carolina Blacks (and the state) remained predominantly rural longer than other southeastern states, African Americans were slow in adopting new genres identified with Black culture that came into existence during the twentieth century. Bastin explains: "Blues was a musical response to the degradations of black life in America at the turn of the century" (1990, 75). This is perhaps one reason "blues, as a musical form . . . did not emerge everywhere at the same time. In some regions, perhaps in Mississippi, the blues probably emerged in the 1890s. It is far more probable that in the southeastern states the blues emerged only in the first decade of the twentieth century. . . . The impetus for this came largely from socio-historical events coinciding . . . with greater availability of musical instruments, especially the guitar, and with a conscious reaction against certain aspects of black secular music of the nineteenth century" (Bastin 1986, 7–8). Lornell's views on this subject are also noteworthy: "After World War II, with the rise of independent record companies, there were many more opportunities for Black Americans to play emerging popular Black music, particularly rhythm and blues. The independent record companies, the emergence of rhythm and blues . . . [and] Black radio stations are all factors that led to the development of rock and roll and the movement away from that kind of (i.e., fiddle and banjo music) entertainment" (Chapman 2004). With additional research, perhaps we can determine if other factors played a role in the maintenance and/or decline of fiddling among African Americans during the early twentieth century.

fiddlingismyjoycompanion.net

Notes

1. 🎻 See Map 8.1, Map 8.2, Land Regions 8.1, and History 8.1.

2. Both *The Negro and His Songs* (Odum and Johnson 1925) and *Negro Workaday Songs* (Odum and Johnson 1926) include songs performed in areas of North Carolina, South Carolina, Tennessee, and Georgia during the years 1924–25 (Odum and Johnson 1926, x).

3. See Lornell (1974, 1975, 1981, 1990); Bastin (1975b, 1986); Hinson (1978); Casey (1983); Martin (1989); Conway (1990, 1995, 1998); Carlin (1994, 1999, 2004, 2016); and Chapman (2004).

4. Dink Roberts, whom Conway worked closely with during her research, is a North Carolina Black banjo player and songster who lived in Alamance County's Haw River Township, located west or adjacent to Orange County in the piedmont region.

5. I also gained a broad perspective about North Carolina's Black fiddle tradition from personal interviews with two musician families—(1) Etta Reid Baker (1987) and Cora Reid Phillips (1987), who lived in the mountains, and (2) Joe Thompson (1987) and Odell Thompson (1987) from the piedmont region—as well as Wayne Martin (1987), a fiddler who was director of the Folklife section of the North Carolina Arts Council.

6. 🎻 See Demographics 8.1.

7. 🎻 See Demographics 8.2.

8. The 1900 US census indicates that Marshall Davis (1884–1948), the youngest of eight siblings, resided in Randolph County with his father, Cain Davis (b. 1842), and mother, Randy [Rendy] Davis (b. 1853). By 1913 (when he was around nineteen years old), Marshall was living in the city of High Point, where he worked as a fireman (Carlin 2004, 37).

9. 🎻 See Demographics 8.3.

10. US census records indicate that Archibald "Baldy" Gaither (b. 1838) and Rena Howard Gaither (b. 1843) had one son, Harvey Gaither (1884–1970), who was born in Iredell County.

11. From personal experience (I was born and raised in a small town in southeast Georgia), events organized by Blacks were rarely reported in white-owned/controlled community newspapers, unless whites were involved in some way. Thus, Black fiddlers' conventions may have been held in Statesville without acknowledgment or recognition by the white press.

12. 🎻 See Demographics 8.4.

13. 🎻 See Demographics 8.5 and Map 8.3d.

14. 🎻 See Demographics 8.6.

15. The US census indicates that John Arch's parents, Robert A. Thompson (b. ca. 1849) and Katie Nelson Thompson (b. ca. 1858), had eleven children: ten males and one female. While Jacob Arthur (1876–1950) was the eldest, John Arch (1878–1968) and Walter Eugene (1882–1949) were the third and fourth oldest (also see below). Seven miles from the Thompsons' Cedar Grove home, in Alamance County between Mebane and Greensboro, lived another cell of banjo and fiddle players. Central to this group was Dink Roberts, a banjoist who played guitar with a slide, which was unusual for banjo players in the region (Bastin 1986, 275).

16. Boone Reid's parents, Washington Alexander Reid (1845–1920) and Sarah Jane Scott Reid (1838–1931), had eleven children: five females and six males. Boone was the seventh born, while his sister, Martha Reid Moore (1882–1952), was the tenth child and youngest daughter. Boone and his wife, Sallie Scott Reid (1879–1967), had eight children: four females and four males. Cora

Geneva Reid Philips (1907–2000) and Etta Lucille Reid Baker (1913–2006) were the two youngest daughters and the sixth and eighth of the Boones' children, respectively. My interview in August 1987 was conducted with Philips and Baker.

17. 🎻 See Map 8.2, Map 8.3b, and Demographics 8.7.

18. See recording produced by Diana Hamilton, Liam Clancy, and Paul Clayton (1956).

19. 🎻 See Biography 8.1.

20. When I inquired about the type of music she heard on records, Phillips (1987) stated, "It was an orchestra. Bessie Smith. She was playing 'St. Louis Blues.' As far as I remember, that was a guitar. Then we would just catch it. It was on our mind and we'd make a tune. We could just find the notes and then just go on and make it sound like we had heard it."

21. Phillips also performed on the recording compiled by Hamilton, Clancy, and Clayton (1956), but no cuts by her, to my knowledge, have been released. In addition to Etta, all family members, including Cora and her husband, Theophilus, as well as Elizabeth and her husband, Fred, are featured on *Music from the Hills of Caldwell County* (1975). However, none of the performances include the fiddle.

22. Lornell was a student at Guilford College in Greensboro, North Carolina, when he visited the Thompsons' home in fall 1973 to learn about Joe and Odell's role in performing old-time music (see Lornell 1976, 2013).

23. My discussion of Thompson is more extensive than others not only because he is one of the few Black fiddlers to live and experience changes that took place in the tradition over several decades, but also much information is available from personal interviews with him, his family, admirers, researchers, and musicians.

24. 🎻 See Demographics 8.8 as well as Map 8.2, Map 8.3a, Map 8.3c, Map 8.3d, and Map 8.3e.

25. The 1880 US census indicates that the family patriarch, Robert Thompson (b. ca. 1849), and his wife, Katie [Catie] Nelson Thompson (b. ca. 1858), resided in Bushy Fork Township in Person County and in 1900 their residence was Cedar Grove Township in Orange County. This suggests that many, if not all of the couple's eleven children, were born in Person County. Joe's parents, John Arch (1878–1968) and Rosa Crisp Thompson (1882–1960), moved from Cedar Grove to Mebane in Cheeks Township sometime between 1910 and 1920. During this period, the couple had seven children: two females—Effie Elizabeth (1908–1994) and Katie Mae (b. 1909)—who were the eldest, and five males: Chesley Arch (1911–1993), Ervin Jethro (1913–2004), Nathaniel (1916–1997), Joseph Aquilla (1918–2012), and Robert Albert (1923–2009).

26. Founded by the White Brothers of Mebane in 1881, White Furniture Company was a major producer of handcrafted fine furniture for over a century before closing in 1993. The company was awarded the title "best manufacturer of American furniture" in the early 1900s (Marquez-Frees and Sumner 1982).

27. Also, see Lornell (1975, 31); Conway (1990, 76–77); Chapman (2004); Carlin (2004, 41–42); and Bower (2009).

28. Joe Thompson remembered that Emp Wright was light-skinned in color, inferring that he was an African American whose parents were either Native American or white.

29. I am not sure if he is referring to someone in the Martin family; Carl Martin's father migrated from South Carolina to Virginia during the early twentieth century (see foregoing discussion).

30. As noted in the foregoing, the Carolina Chocolate Drops was a music group that specialized in performing old-time string band music. Two of the founding members (Justin Robinson and Rhiannon Giddens) were born and raised in North Carolina. Dom Flemons, the third member, was from Arizona. Much of the group's initial training came from performing with Thompson at his home in Mebane (Flemons 2011a, Flemons 2011b; Giddens 2011a, Giddens 2011b).

31. In an interview (Lornell 1990, 224), Joe indicated that chopping time referred to: "Going out into the woods and cutting wood to burn in the tobacco flue. . . . Back then [in earlier years] . . . a bunch of hands from the neighborhood would go out and help this man cut today and that man cut tomorrow. They went from one neighborhood to the other—that's the way they got their wood cut."

32. For more details about frolics and dance parties, see Fulmer (1995).

33. When I interviewed him in 1987, Joe stated that he was a member of Kimes Chapel Missionary Baptist Church in Mebane.

34. Unfortunately, I do not know to whom Odell is referring when he states that he has seen someone (perhaps a minister) using the fiddle in church services that have been broadcast on television.

35. The showing of Chapman's video at different venues in the local community helped make Thompson's contributions accessible to the local community. The first showing took place in 2005 at the Ebenezer Center for Performing Arts, Ebenezer United Church of Christ (Chapman 2011). For a review of Chapman's film by a local newspaper, see Killian (2004).

36. The various festivals where they performed include: the Augusta Heritage Festival (Davis and Elkins College in Elkins, West Virginia); Dogwood Festival (Mebane, North Carolina); Eno River Festival (Durham, North Carolina); the Merle Watson Memorial Festival (Merlefest) (Wilkesboro, North Carolina); National Folk Festival (Lowell, Massachusetts); Festival of American Fiddle Tunes (Port Townsend, Washington); Smithsonian Institution Folk Life Festival (Washington, DC); Brisbane Biennial International Music Festival (Brisbane, Australia, May 30, 1993); Tennessee Banjo Institute (Murfreesboro, Tennessee); and the University of Chicago Folk Festival.

37. In the film *Appalachian Journey* (1991), the Thompsons are misidentified; the subtitles indicate James Thomas (for Joe Thompson) and Odell Thomas (for Odell Thompson).

38. 🎵 See Repertoire 8.1, which includes information about media.

39. After Odell's death in 1994, several white musician friends (Bob Carlin, Clyde Davis, Alan Julich, Paul and Deborah Mitchell, Jamey Tippens, Lawrence Vellani, and Mark Weems) encouraged and helped Joe continue performing in festivals, concerts, and other events to which he was invited (Chapman 2011).

40. 🎵 See History 8.2.

41. The "master fiddler" title is noteworthy because of its similarity to those given to African musicians to acknowledge both their talents and high regard within their communities.

42. Rhiannon Giddens, one of the founding members of Carolina Chocolate Drops, was not only the recipient of the 2017 McArthur Foundation Fellowship, she has also won and been nominated for several other awards, including the 2023 Pulitzer Prize for Music for *Omar*, an opera co-written by Giddens and Michael Abels (Rhiannon Giddens 2024).

43. 🎵 See Repertoire 8.1.

44. 🎵 Only one, "Careless Love," which is now a common stock song, is included in Thompson's repertoire. See Repertoire 2.2 for other Black fiddlers in this study who include this song in their repertoire.

45. Like their ancestors, Joe and Odell often played face to face so each could motion or touch the knee of the other player with his knee to anticipate a shift in the music (Conway 1998, 18; Wilson 2013).

46. 🎵 Go to Audio Examples to listen to Joe and Odell Thompson perform "Old Joe Clark" and "Georgia Buck." Recorded between 1974 and 1976 by Lornell, these are the first recordings made by members of the Thompson family. Thus, their performance style and sound are probably close to that of their ancestors and other Black fiddlers who were active in rural areas during the early twentieth century.

47. The A melody is based on a four-beat, four-bar melody that equals a total of sixteen quarter-note beats. Played at a higher range, the B melody also is based on a four-beat, four-bar melody that totals sixteen quarter notes.

48. Similar to other songs identified with certain regions of the country, "Georgia Buck" may have been originally created by Blacks but was adopted by whites as a result of the shared culture (Bass 1931, 418–19, 434). In fact, Aaron Washington, a Black guitarist born in 1902 in Williston, a small town in Barnwell County in the southwest portion of the South Carolina piedmont region, indicates that the first tune he learned as a child was "Georgie Buck Is Dead" (Bastin 1986, 339). Although performed by Black and white musicians in earlier years, the first recording of "Georgia

Buck" was made by Al Hopkins and His Buckle Busters on Vocalion in 1927 in New York City (Russell and Pinson 2004, 423; Meade, Spottswood, and Meade 2002, 479).

49. 🎻 See Repertoire 8.1 for a list of recordings of the Thompsons' musicking.

50. 🎻 See Form 8.1.

Southern Appalachian Mountains and Neighboring Regions

CHAPTER 9

South Carolina, Georgia, Alabama, Mississippi

South Carolina

Although numerous sources document fiddling in various parts of South Carolina before 1900,[1] the degree to which the tradition flourished during the early twentieth century is unknown because minimal research has been done on South Carolina's piedmont and mountain regions (or Up Country). In my opinion, differences in the geography and demographics of the Low Country (coastal region) and Up Country affected the degree to which Black fiddling was maintained and developed, but also the type of research investigators conducted.[2] The little that we know about fiddling in the state during the early 1900s comes from interviews conducted with Abbeville County resident Louella Walker, whose father, Henry J. Bryant (ca. 1877–1957), played the fiddle in their community during this period (Kane and Keeton 1994);[3] see photos 9.1 and 9.2. Abbeville County is located on the Georgia/South Carolina state line as well as the border that divides South Carolina's piedmont and mountain regions.[4]

When Louella Walker was interviewed in the early 1980s at age eighty, she stated that her father had been a well-known fiddler in their community. Walker explained that, with little encouragement and lots of opposition from family members who thought fiddling was sinful, her father taught himself how to perform: "He just made his fiddle out of a sardine box and took his thread and made him a bow. They run him out of the house and he learned to play his self. But when I knowed anything, he had 'em, violins. . . . He'd have two. I used to play on one. I learned to play a little bit, but I put it down after I got up good size and started to school and things. When I knowed anything, my daddy was playing it [the fiddle]. And he'd play 'Fox in the Wall' for me. And 'Billy in the

Photo 9.1. Louella Walker holding the fiddle that belonged to Henry Bryant, her father.

Photo 9.2. The Fiddle that Henry Bryant played.

Low Ground' and 'Are you from Dixie?' Used to play all that for me when I was a girl" (Kane and Keeton 1994, 67).

Although Walker indicated that her father performed at a variety of occasions, including funerals in churches, dances (called hot suppers or plays) for Black and white people, as well as cockfights organized by white males, the dances were most popular among African Americans. Similar to other rural areas of the South, hot suppers could last all night on weekends, which is when they most often took place. Held in a tenant farmhouse, cooking and eating food were the most important activities during the festivities. Recollections by Abbeville's Black residents whose family members participated in such events during the late nineteenth and early twentieth centuries provide insight on the music culture during those times. Phoebe Turman stated that the timing of hot suppers was important to the community's social life: "Didn't have 'em in the summertime . . . [because the church] revival was in the summertime. The hot supper was when the weather get cold. That's when they [the men] . . . started to sell their cotton [and] had a little [money] to treat the girls. Boys paid the girls to dance with 'em . . . and he would pay that partner . . . maybe a quarter or something like that. Enough to buy a custard, pie, or cake. As time passed, the gatherings became known as plays, 'cause they played at night" (Kane and Keeton 1994, 65–66). Jim Pressley added: "Saturday night, they had all kinds of things cooking, beef, fried fish, things like that. During much of the evening, men paid for the privilege of dancing with the ladies of their choice" (66).

According to Walker, her father did not allow her to attend many hot suppers because people would "cuss and things like that. . . . When he'd go to play for white people, he'd let me go. And we'd just set and look. And the white people, they didn't mostly dance. They'd be at their homes" (68). Walker remembered attending one hot supper on Christmas Eve, even though her mother did not want her to go because she believed Walker, a small child, might fall asleep: "He was gonna play all night long! Gonna play till 12 and then he go and rest awhile. And [then at] daylight, he'd be playing again for them to dance. And so I went on over there [to the hot supper] and I stood up there and they [her father with his fiddle and another man with a guitar] played and they [the dancers] were just catching one another like you see 'em do on television. . . . 'You swing your partner. I swing mine. You swing your partner, I swing mine.' That's the way they would do. So that was my first time being at a dance. He'd play them songs and they'd dance by 'em. But I never did. I never could dance" (68–69).

The only other documentation of Black fiddling in South Carolina comes from someone who also lived in the western part of the state, but later moved to North Carolina where fiddling was more prominent. Born in 1902 in Williston, Barnwell County, which is located on the South Carolina/Georgia state line close to the South Carolina piedmont region,[5] Aaron Washington performed guitar; he had learned to play the instrument from his uncle, Matt Washington. He stated that when he was about nine years old, the fiddle was very popular: "'Back then you could hear the old people play fiddles, guitars, banjos and accordion too. Mostly it was string music . . . you see the blues, the regular blues, didn't start until quite a few years after I was a kid. I don't know exactly what year, but I would say it was the '20s at least. I don't remember no blues singers before I was 20 years old.' About 1912 Washington moved to Asheville, North Carolina, where he was a member of a string band by 1919. He worked there . . . playing blues by the time he left in 1926, settling in Catskill, New York" (Bastin 1986, 339; also see Lornell 1973, 25–26).

Until additional research is conducted on musicking in all parts of South Carolina, we have no way of knowing how long fiddling continued in the early twentieth century. Yet, it is doubtful that South Carolina's fiddling tradition was as prominent as those in North Carolina, Virginia, and Tennessee. As noted earlier, Black fiddling in the early twentieth century tended to flourish in areas where Black and white people were in close contact with each other. Since African Americans outnumbered European Americans by large majorities in South Carolina, social interaction between the races was probably minimal. But it appears that some South Carolina Blacks enjoyed fiddling because it was a favorite pastime that had become a part of their tradition. In the South Carolina piedmont region, Black fiddlers may have left the state because of other interests or lack of support due to the fact that some believed fiddling was sinful. Coupled with his desire to find work in the coal mining industry, these factors may account for the relocation of Frank Martin, Carl Martin's father, to Virginia early in the twentieth century (see chapter 5).

Georgia

Scholarly research on African American music in Georgia did not begin until the mid-twentieth century.[6] And most investigations focused on religious music, especially activities taking place on or near the Georgia Sea Islands, where the maintenance of African practices was strongest.[7] Studies on Georgia's Black secular music was concerned with the blues, with a few references focusing on musicking in Atlanta and vernacular traditions in select communities in the state.[8] Bastin's investigations on the blues are noteworthy because in addition to identifying several sources on Black fiddling, we also now know more about the history of Black jug bands, the role of Black musicians in the early recording industry, and Black music festivals.[9] Ethnographic research by John Burrison and Art Rosenbaum is particularly useful for documenting the last vestiges of Black fiddling in small towns in northern Georgia during the early twentieth century, which complements the activities of fiddlers in other parts of Appalachia and the piedmont.[10] Black fiddling in Georgia's mountain and piedmont regions is important because it demonstrates the development of the tradition in locations where Black populations were not in the majority, but they were large.

The earliest evidence of fiddling by rural Blacks in Georgia during the late nineteenth and early twentieth centuries appears in the writings of Europeans, fascinated by the virgin territory and so-called strange ways of doing things in the United States. The interest of the British in barbecues, for example, resulted in the publication of several articles around 1900 that include photos of Black fiddling in Richmond County.[11] Commenting on the articles and photo, Bastin and Green (1989) write: "a photograph of 'A Barbecue Orchestra at Work' shows four black men neatly dressed in seemingly matching suits, high collars, and ties, playing a violin, two guitars, and a jug. . . . The 1902 article mentions that six thousand were fed at the barbecue near Augusta, Georgia. . . ."[12] The events lasted three hours, which leads us to conclude that the black quartet had a repertoire both extensive and varied and that they had rehearsed and almost certainly played in public before Howe [the photographer] snapped them" (2). Not only does the photograph document Black fiddling in Georgia around the early 1900s, it provides evidence of the types of instruments (fiddle, guitar, and jug) included in fiddle ensembles.[13]

So far, information on Black Georgia fiddling during the early decades of the twentieth century is limited to three musicians: Andrew Baxter, Elbert Freeman, and Joe Rakestraw. While much has been written about Baxter because he is one of the first Black fiddlers to record commercially in a mixed-race group, little is known about Freeman and Rakestraw, for whom some field recordings, as noted above, were made between the 1970s and 1980s. Similar to the the foregoing, all Black fiddlers in Georgia lived in either the mountains (Baxter) or piedmont regions (Freeman and Rakestraw). Thus, questions raised in previous chapters will be addressed here. To what extent did the media and social interaction between Black and white people affect musical and cultural practices? Is there anything unique or distinctive about Black fiddling in Georgia, and if yes, what factors contributed to these features? Like the foregoing chapters, the discussion is organized chronologically according to the fiddlers' birth dates, with attention given to family and community, learning, performance contexts, the media, creativity, performance style, and race.

Profiles of Georgia Black Fiddlers

Andrew Baxter (1869–1955)

Andrew Baxter and his son, James "Jim" Baxter (1898–1950), who accompanied him on guitar, are among the earliest Black musicians from Georgia to make commercial recordings.[14] Both father and son were born in Calhoun, the seat for Gordon County, which is located in the Appalachian Mountains. Andrew lived his entire life in Gordon County, except for a short time around the 1900s when he, Nancy (his first wife), and their children[15] resided in Hamilton County, which is located in the southern part of East Tennessee on the Georgia/Tennessee state line.[16] When not performing music, Andrew worked as a farmer and by 1920 had become a homeowner in Gordon County.

Andrew started playing the fiddle as a youngster and was considered by many in his community to be proficient by the age of nine. Like other Black fiddlers in the piedmont and mountain areas, his repertoire was diverse; thus, it was common for him and his son to participate in most activities that white old-time musicians were involved in. Gus Chitwood, a founding member of the Chitwood family of musicians who were well known in Calhoun, stated: "They [the Baxters] could play breakdowns; they could play blues; they could play church music; they could play *anything*" (Wiggins and Russell 1977, 13). William "Bill" Shores, a white fiddler who recorded commercially and was active in north Georgia's music community during the early twentieth century, stated in a 1975 interview that Andrew could play some blues, but preferred the old-time stuff like "Katy Hill."[17] They were cotton farmers, but when white people wanted to give a dance or something, Andrew and Jim would nine times out of ten get the job. "One time in Calhoun at the courthouse old Andrew Baxter came down and entered a fiddling contest. Don't remember how he did. There was another group of Negroes that played old time style, somewhere in the north Georgia

Photo 9.3. Andrew Baxter holding fiddle. 1950s. Collection of Marshall Wyatt.

area here; I heard of them, but never knew them, and don't know what they called themselves" (Wolfe 1977a, 8).[18]

The courthouse, which attracted listeners from outlying areas, was a popular site for performances by Black and white musicians in Calhoun. Performing at fiddle contests and on radio was also common. Some of the larger contests were held on the fourth of July, but many took place on other occasions when sponsored by an organization. Documentation by Wiggins and Russell (1977) of a 1927 contest that possibly included a performance by Andrew Baxter is significant, for Black musicians were rarely given opportunities to participate in such events: "1927 saw two fiddlers' conventions in Calhoun, both sponsored by the American Legion, the first to help erect a marker for the Confederate dead and the other to help build a new gymnasium. The former was held on March 11–12. Earl Johnson placed first and A. A. Gray second, a 'Mr. Andrews' was third, and Bill and Bud came in fourth and fifth" (12). Although Mr. Andrews's full name is not given, Gus Chitwood believes this was Andrew Baxter (13).[19]

When record company executives set up studios in various parts of the South to look for talent in the area, the Baxters were among the musicians from Calhoun asked to record (Wolfe 1977a, 4).[20] Between August 1927 and

Photo 9.4. Andrew Baxter and Jim Baxter at a Rotary Club fish fry in Gordon County, Georgia, ca. 1935. [Date on photo is incorrect.] Courtesy of Gordon County Historical Society.

November 1929, the father-son duo participated in three recording sessions with Victor Records.[21] The first session took place in Charlotte, North Carolina, about three hundred miles northeast of Calhoun (Hanchett 1985, 2014). At the time, the Baxters were under a management contract with Phil Reeve, who owned a record store in Calhoun and was the steel guitarist with the Yellow Hammers, an all-white music group from Gordon County that also recorded at the Victor session in Charlotte. While the Yellow Hammers cut eight titles, the Baxters recorded only three tunes: two blues—"Bamalong Blues" and "K. C. [Kansas City] Railroad Blues"—and a train song titled "The Moore Girl." One of the tunes by the Yellow Hammers and the only strictly instrumental selection was "G Rag." Interestingly, Baxter took over the fiddling from Bud Landress, a member of the Yellow Hammers, who instead performed the humorous spoken introduction (Wiggins and Russell 1977, 13; Bastin 1986, 39).[22] Commenting on the 1927 recording session, Wyatt (1999, 18) writes: "Andrew and Jim Baxter recorded 'K. C. Railroad Blues,' the first version of that song ever committed to wax, and one whose graceful lyricism has never been matched.[23] Next, father and son performed 'The Moore Girl,' also inspired by a train, with fiddle and guitar creating the vivid sound of rolling wheels and lonesome whistle. The title 'Moore Girl' is most likely a misnomer for 'mogul,' a type of freight locomotive."

Although all tunes recorded by the Baxters in 1927 were issued,[24] it was not until more than a year later (October 1928) before they had another recording session with Victor, this time in Atlanta. Only two of the eight recordings ("Forty Drops" and "Georgia Stomp") from the 1928 session were coupled for release. Both tunes, recorded in a 4/4 rhythm instead of the 6/8 rhythm often performed for British square dances, were most likely used for set dances in the style of the eight-hand dance sets of Blacks in North Carolina (Bastin 1986, 39); see foregoing discussion. Yet, Victor must have been satisfied with their performances because in November 1929, the Baxters returned to Atlanta with the Yellow Hammers for what was to be the final session by the father-son duo. They recorded seven tunes: four on Wednesday and three on the next day; all, except one from the Wednesday session, were released but on a very rare series (Bastin 1986, 39–40). No evidence indicates how long the Baxters were active as performers after their recording career ended in 1929. In an article in *Old Time Music* (1977, 13), Wiggins and Russell include a 1935 photo of the two musicians seated on a bench, holding their instruments in a playing position, at a Rotary Club fish fry attended by whites (Wyatt 2021); see photo 9.4.

When discussing the Baxters, most researchers' comments have focused not only on the group's notoriety in recording with an interracial group, but many seem to be genuinely impressed with their playing. In 2006, Frankie, the editor of the music blog donegone.net, writes: "Andrew Baxter's fiddling is inventive and poignant, not without rough edges and always exciting. James Baxter's guitar playing is a perfect foil for his father's fiddling. Together, they never appear to be on auto-pilot, but continually shift their phrasing underneath the song. They are one of the real gems in both old-time and country blues—a wonderful example of how deep the art can be."

Because Baxter and fiddler Jim Booker (from Kentucky) are the first African Americans known to have recorded old-time music with mixed-race groups, it is useful to compare their backgrounds, the circumstances surrounding their recordings, as well as their musicking to determine if specific factors contributed to their notoriety. In reviewing their early lives and formative years, several similarities are apparent. Born roughly three years apart (Baxter in 1869 and Booker in 1872) in small rural towns with relatively few Blacks, they are of the same generation and come from similar environments. The fact that they performed in a musical group primarily composed of relatives is significant, because occasions to perform for family, friends, and members of the community probably occurred often. No doubt exposure from these activities allowed others, outside their immediate family and circle of friends, to learn of their talent and ability to perform a diverse repertoire. The fact that both were under contract with white males who also managed the group with whom they recorded suggests that if Baxter and Booker had not been affiliated with these individuals, the opportunity to record would not have occurred.[25] Considering the racial climate in the United States during the early 1920s, it is also remarkable the recordings took place at all. Gadaya (2010) reports: "Due to segregation, they [the Baxters] had to be separated on their train ride to Charlotte and recorded in separate sessions. But for one track, 'G rag,' Andrew Baxter played fiddle with The Georgia Yellow Hammers, a very rare example of an 'integrated' band during the 1920s." Although performances by musicians of different races was commonplace in many Appalachian communities, to have the two races represented on a recording as one group was new. Because the recording industry was still in its infancy (that is, this was virgin territory and the rules were still being written on what should and should not be done in making recordings), perhaps record company executives were willing to experiment with all types of scenarios (in terms of ensemble organization, performers, and repertoire) to determine the type of product that would appeal to buyers.

In terms of musicking, Booker and Baxter recorded roughly the same number of songs essentially with one company (Booker with Gennett and Baxter with Victor). However, there are differences in what they actually recorded and how songs were represented in the media. While members of the Booker family participated in seven recording sessions over a four-month period (April to August 1927), Jim Booker, the fiddler, only participated in five sessions.[26] During the seven sessions, members of the Booker family (as individual artists or together within a group) recorded a total of twenty-four songs, of which four ("Forked Deer," "Gray Eagle," "Maxwell Girl," and "Sourwood Mountain") were recorded twice by Jim Booker. Except for "Camp Nelson Blues," a song probably composed by someone in the Booker family or Kentucky's Black community where they lived, the overwhelming majority of recordings by the Bookers were targeted to white record buyers, in spite of the fact that five songs are noted in the narratives of the formerly enslaved (indicating that many of the songs were popular and possibly had shared origins within Black and white culture).[27] Possibly because of marketing and repertoire, however, musicking by Jim Booker is identified with whiteness, but he, as a Black fiddler, is not represented as a performer of hillbilly music. The fact that Booker's image (see photo 6.1) does not appear in the marketing materials for Taylor's Kentucky Boys suggests that record company executives did not believe the record-buying public would support an African American performing this type of music (see foregoing discussion).

Unlike the Booker family, the Baxters' recording career extended over a two-year period (1927 to 1929). Although Andrew made nineteen commercial recordings, four songs—"Done Wrong Blues," "It Tickles Me," "Treat Him Right," and "Goodbye Blues"—were recorded two or three times and seven songs were unissued.[28] All songs recorded by the Baxters, except "G Rag," were as an all-Black group, and this began during their first recording session (August 9, 1927), not their last. By comparison, the Booker Orchestra had only one recording session as an all-Black group (releasing two songs "Salty Dog" and "Camp Nelson Blues"), and this did not occur until their second and final recording session (on August 27, 1927).

Although the repertoire of the father-son duo was diverse, none of the recorded tunes, except "G Rag," were associated with the shared culture of Black and white performers. Commenting on this fact, the editor of the music blog *Never Yet Melted*, writes: "Many white musicians testified to have learned the banjo or the fiddle in their youth watching black musicians and some of these influential musicians were recorded by phonograph companies or on field recordings. Their repertoire was sometimes very similar to white string-bands but included tunes that were typically African-American in style. Some were able to play in more than one style to please their public, whether it was a white or a black audience" (JDZ 2013). In spite of the diversity of the Baxters' repertoire (see comments by Shores in Wolfe 1977a, 8), most of Victor's recordings by the Baxters were targeted to Black record buyers, perhaps for the following reasons: (1) The titles, themes, and lyrical content of songs concerned issues important to Black people. For African Americans, the Great Migration had begun, and the common mode of transportation was the train, which may explain the Baxters' use of travel and trains as themes in their compositions—see "K. C. Railroad Blues," "The Moore Girl," and "Operator Blues."[29] (2) Andrew's performance style includes African-derived features that are appealing to Black listeners. (3) The Baxters performed new musical forms (like blues and rags) that had become popular among many African Americans residing in urban areas, especially those migrating to cities.[30] For example, six tunes include the word blues in the title—"Bamalong Blues," "K. C. Railroad Blues," "Done Wrong Blues," "East 9th Street Blues," "Goodbye Blues," "Operator Blues"—even though structurally, many researchers today would not categorize these songs as blues. One tune, "It Tickles Me," is a twelve-bar blues, although the term blues is not included in the title. In addition, some songs are actually rags. While they differ from the ragtime piano works of Scott Joplin, they are similar to Black dance music performed at frolics in the rural South during the postbellum era. The Baxters' most interesting performances are "Forty Drops" and "Dance the Georgia Poss" because, according to Lynn Abbott and Doug Seroff (2002), these tunes were derived from rags that date to at least the 1890s (447, 449).[31] The driving rhythms in "Moore Girl" and "Georgia Stomp" were obviously intended for square dancing that continued to be popular among some Blacks in the South. In fact, Jim's calling out instructions can be heard on the latter track.

To highlight some of the elements that characterize Andrew's fiddling, two recordings are analyzed: "G Rag" and "K. C. Railroad Blues." Each song provides an example of the type of music the Baxters not only recorded, but were known for performing in Gordon County. Similar to musical analyses in earlier chapters, focus is placed on form, rhythm, and melody. "G Rag" performed by Andrew Baxter and the Georgia Yellow Hammers is based on "Hamilton's Special Breakdown," a tune recorded by Wyzee Hamilton playing fiddle with banjo and guitar accompaniment on Paramount Records in Chicago in January 1927, about seven months before Victor's recording session in Charlotte (Russell and Pinson 2004, 393; Wyatt 2001, 23).[32] Since performances by Hamilton and the Georgia Yellow Hammers are the only pre–World War II recordings of this song (Russell and Pinson 2004), it may be useful to compare them musically. From my analysis, Hamilton's performance, which is two minutes and fifty-nine seconds in length (2:59), includes three themes roughly organized as follows: AAA | BBA | BCB | ABC. Each theme is based on a four-beat, eight-bar melody, and the quarter note = 120–26 bpm (beats per minute). While the fiddler plays the A theme in a middle range (in terms of pitch), the B theme is more intricately organized in terms of melody and performed in a higher pitch range. The C theme differs from A and B in that it is more rhythmically focused, with emphasis placed on an off-beat rhythm that the fiddler plays using chords or double-stops. The texture is polyphonic. While the banjo and guitar play a repetitive eighth-note pattern (one-and, two-and, three-and, four-and, and so on), the fiddle leads all themes except for the fourth performance of B (at 1:55). At this point, the banjo plays the theme, while the guitar continues performing the repetitive eighth-note pattern, and the fiddler interjects a short melodic phrase as an accompaniment. Throughout the performance, Hamilton generally uses a light touch in playing the fiddle and tends to be precise when attacking notes. In addition, his melodies are more intricately organized, especially when compared with musicking by Baxter (see below).

The performance of "G Rag" by Andrew Baxter and the Georgia Yellow Hammers differs from Hamilton's version in several ways.[33] Most noticeable is the length—roughly three minutes, eleven seconds (3:11)—and a two-part introductory section, about twenty-five seconds long, that includes the performance of the A theme by all instrumentalists and speaking (with no musical accompaniment) by Bud Landress introducing the group.[34] These initial remarks set the stage for Landress's callouts to members of the group and listening audience during the remaining part of the performance. Another difference is the overall organization of the performance. Whereas Hamilton uses three different themes (ABC), Baxter limits his playing to two. The C theme in Hamilton's version becomes the B theme in Baxter's performance. In both cases, each theme is based on a four-beat, eight-bar melody. Without the inclusion of a C theme, the formal organization of the Georgia Yellow Hammers' performance is more straightforward: AA | BB | AA | BB | AA. The tempo is almost the same. In the case of Baxter, the quarter note = roughly 116 bpm. The most significant difference is Baxter's fiddling. Using a firmer touch, which makes his fiddling sound fuller (or louder), Baxter slides into notes as if he's shuffling in playing the melody. Baxter's use of bent notes is prominent, especially during the B section when he uses the flatted third (B-flat) of the G chord (see 1:10 and 2:16) as a sustained note. For some listeners, Baxter's fiddling may sound out-of-tune. But similar to other Black fiddlers, the intonation used is intentional "because of the emotional impact and increased range of expression created by these sounds" (Brown 1992, 129). Similar to Hamilton, the playing of double-stops (or chords) on off-beats gives Baxter's B theme (see C theme for Hamilton) rhythmic interest that helps make it distinct from other themes used. However, Baxter creates more interest in B by including additive rhythms (see 1:22, 2:10, 2:26) during specific points in the performance. When the two Black fiddlers are compared, Baxter's playing is not as intense as Booker's, probably because Baxter is not performing in context (for a square dance or frolic), which is the type of energy Booker employs as lead fiddler during his performance with Taylor's Kentucky Boys. Yet, like Booker, Baxter's form is simpler and more straightforward when compared with Hamilton's version of "G Rag." Whereas Hamilton varied the melody by making it more intricate, Baxter's focus is on the tone quality—inserting bent notes, sliding into notes, or modifying the intonation. Similar to Booker, Baxter also develops the rhythm by playing in a shuffling manner, and inserting additive rhythms along with off-beats.

Although white musicians George Walburn (fiddle), Emmett Hethcox (guitar), and an unknown fiddler may have been the first to use "K. C. Railroad" as the title for a song,[35] Odum's research indicates that a song with a similar title, "Thought I Heard That K. C. Whistle Blow," was popular among Black musicians during the early twentieth century (Odum 1911a, 287; 1911b, 360–61; Odum and Johnson 1925, 225–26).[36] In addition, the Baxters are the first to employ a slightly different title, "K. C. Railroad Blues," as the melody for the sixteen-bar blues that was recorded by Victor Records in Charlotte on August 9, 1927, which became a classic with covers by a variety of musicians in later years (see Dixon, Godrich, and Rye 1997; Russell and Pinson 2004). Since Walburn and Hethcox did not record their version of "K. C. Railroad Blues" on OKeh until October 8, 1927, about three months after the Baxters' release on Victor, we can only assume that the Baxters' version is based on the song that was popular during the early 1900s.[37]

Unlike their other train songs that are performed so the sound produced on the fiddle emulates the movement of a locomotive on railway tracks,[38] it is the lyrics of "K. C. Railroad Blues" that relate to travel; the longing or pining for a loved one who is distant and possibly a train ride away suggests the desire to travel.[39] Both the sixteen-bar chord progression (I-I-I-I | IV-IV-I-I | IV-IV-I-I | V-IV-I-I) and the expanded lyrics (AAAB) that the Baxters use for their performance of "K. C. Railroad Blues" are variations on the standard twelve-bar progression (I-I-I-I | IV-IV-I-I | V-IV-I-I) and AAB text.[40] In the Baxters' performance, the middle section (IV-IV-I-I), normally performed once in a twelve-bar blues, is performed twice. And the lyrics, which are normally presented as AAB, are performed as AAAB. Andrew's playing also includes a variety of characteristics identified with Black musicking, which probably made the record appealing to Black record buyers. In addition to off-beat phrasing and bent notes, Andrew anticipates the melody by performing it before the actual beat or sliding on to the pitch without attacking it precisely. Basically, he plays the fiddle as if he is emulating the voice, especially during the opening and when accompanying the vocal. Only during interludes does he include improvisatory material by playing in a higher register, including some melodic ornaments, or varying the melody. By comparison, however, Andrew's fiddling is not as driving or intense as that performed by Jim Booker (see earlier discussion of "Salty Dog"), even when performing music targeted to Black record buyers.

Fort Valley State College Music Festival

Fiddling by African Americans continued to be performed in Georgia's piedmont region through the 1950s and 1960s.[41] The fact that Fort Valley State College—specifically, administrators at a Black teachers' college in Peach County—decided to sponsor a music festival celebrating the vernacular demonstrates that some Black people found musicking in rural areas of the state appealing.[42] The decision to organize a festival highlighting vernacular culture also supported the college's mission to promote agricultural pursuits of the local community. Since 1915, the college had been organizing the Ham and Egg Show but, in 1937, added an annual arts festival component to the event. The idea to have a music festival came from Horace Mann Bond, president of the college, who was inspired by the singing in a local church. The music festival began in 1940 and continued through 1955. The changing attitude of college students and some members of the community is the primary reason the festival ceased operation in the mid-fifties; "students so ridiculed folk artists that they refused to attend" (Bastin 1986, 82).

Although Fort Valley's music festival lasted only fifteen years, its importance to the history of African American music and culture is considerable. The festival was one of the few events organized by a Black college that promoted both sacred and secular music from rural areas.[43] The festival demonstrated that "change did not necessarily register with everyone, and . . . older black secular music styles persisted after critics blandly assumed them to have disappeared" (Bastin 1986, 85). The festival also caught the attention of Black intellectuals of the time; several nationally known performers, academics, and folklorists (including William L. Dawson, W. C. Handy, Langston Hughes, Zora Neale Hurston, Willis Lawrence James, Guy Johnson, Howard Odum, Louise Pound, William Grant Still, Thomas W. Talley, and John W. Work III) attended and/or participated in the festival as judges and researchers (72–86). The fact that Work III conducted fieldwork at the second festival (March 1941)[44] is significant, for the recordings provide us with the only examples of music performed by Black musicians in rural Georgia during the mid-twentieth century.[45] Thus, the support that the festival received from the Black and white scholarly community suggests that there was strong interest in learning how and why this music was created and performed.

Information from the festival program and Work's recordings do not provide much material on Black fiddling. However, this was not the fault of the organizers, because their 1940 invitation letter encouraged the participation of all musicians (Bastin 1974/75, 12, 1986, 72). In fact, an announcement in the *Atlanta Constitution* newspaper included the following: "Think you could play a musical instrument consisting of a rope, weighted at both ends, and a soda pop bottle? A 12-year-old Negro lad will prove that it can be done at the Fort Valley State College Music Festival at 7:30 o'clock Monday night. The festival will begin at 4:30 o'clock tomorrow afternoon and will include Negro religious and folk music" (Fort Valley State College 1940). Interestingly, fiddlers did not become involved until the early fifties. In 1951, a fiddler named J. D. Smith from Oglethorpe (the seat for Macon County) participated in his second festival; he played "'mainly from sheet music' and one of his two performances was 'The Mocking Bird.' However, his accompanying guitarist, Willie C. Towns, played 'John Henry' as a solo piece" (Bastin 1986, 75). An undated festival lists Clifton Smith's string ensemble, but the instruments are not specified (76). Elbert Freeman, a fiddler from Monticello,[46] participated in the festival in 1952 and 1953 (75). Because he may have been one of the few Black fiddlers active in the Georgia piedmont region during the early twentieth century, examining him more closely will help us better understand the fiddle tradition in this part of state.

Elbert J. Freeman (1901–1970)

Researchers know little about Freeman's life as a musician except for information contained in the 1952 and 1953 Fort Valley music festival's program notes; data collected in 1967 by folklorist John Burrison; and follow-up research by Pete Lowry and Bruce Bastin (Lowry and Bastin 1974/75; Bastin and Lowry 1975a, 1975b). US census records indicate that Freeman spent his entire life in the Georgia piedmont region, where his ancestors had lived since the 1840s.[47] Specifically, he was born in Monticello (Jasper County) and died in Morgan County (about twenty-eight miles northeast of Monticello).[48] As an adult, he worked as a carpenter.

Since Jasper County continued to be majority Black throughout the first half of twentieth century, in spite of the infestation of the boll weevil,[49] these statistics confirm what college administrators discovered when they started the Fort Valley music festival in 1940. Black people in rural communities, even when they were in the majority, appreciated vernacular culture; performance traditions created during the nineteenth century had not been completely abandoned for the new musicking that was becoming popular in some Black southern communities. Thus, Freeman is an example of a musician who satisfied the changing audience. While his repertoire included fiddle tunes from the nineteenth century, he also became well-known for performing blues and modern-day country tunes, which is evident in his performances at the region's music festival.[50]

During Freeman's first performance at the Fort Valley music festival on March 27 and 28, 1952, guitarists dominated the awards. Guitarist Buz Ezell, the oldest participant who had never missed a festival, won twenty dollars, while guitarists Ausby Alexander, with Mose Smith on spoons, and David Lockette won ten and five dollars, respectively. Another guitarist, Major Vance, from Perry, a town about twelve miles southeast of Fort Valley, won six dollars. Freeman's Monticello two-piece string band, with Freeman on fiddle and Ortis Ford on guitar, won twenty dollars. Their two selections ("Tennessee Waltz" and "Chattanoogie Shoe Shine Boy"), which had been recorded by various artists, were popular tunes of the day.[51] In 1953, the festival was held on Friday, March 27. W. C. Handy's 1944 comment that performers played "without the influence of radio and records" clearly no longer held truth. The augmented Freeman String Band from Monticello played "[Worried] Blues—Freeman Arrangement" and "Down Yonder," made famous by Del Wood (also known as Polly Adelaide Hendricks Hazelwood), a white pianist whose recording was released in 1951.[52] Other titles on Freeman's performance list for the 1953 festival included two old-time fiddle tunes ("Leather Britches" and "Sally Goodwin"), but there is no indication they were played (Bastin 1975a, 16; 1986, 83).

Burrison's field notes,[53] documenting his visit to Monticello during the late 1960s, provide greater insight about Freeman's life, his musicking, and the community in which he lived:

> By the time we had reached the sleepy town of Monticello . . . , it was early afternoon. . . . As we had parked . . . by a downtown auto repair shop, I asked the mechanic if there was anyone in the area who played any old-time instruments. He directed us to the Middle Georgia Music Store and told me to ask Franklin Lynch, the proprietor. . . . [When I met him], he immediately thought of a Negro blues fiddler who lived in town, Elbert Freeman, who worked as a carpenter. . . . It took a while to locate Elbert and his usual guitar accompanist, Nathaniel "Natty" Ford. Meanwhile, Mr. Lynch agreed to record the music in his own studio. . . . After a recording session lasting from 2 pm - 3 pm and taping seven tunes,[54] Elbert seemed eager to continue . . . but we kept our promise to his daughter and got him back home in time to get in some good fishing.[55]
>
> Both men are approximately in their early sixties. . . . Evidently, they had both lived in Monticello all their lives, playing at dances for the Negro community. . . .

Photo 9.5. Elbert J. Freeman holding fiddle. Jasper County, Georgia, 1967. Courtesy of John A. Burrison.

Elbert plays a raggedy blues fiddle, intentionally bouncing the bow on the strings to produce a squealing effect and sliding into the higher notes, as well as striking disharmonious chords. To one unfamiliar with this type of Negro fiddling it might sound like poor playing, but actually Elbert has a good sense of pitch and control over his instrument. (Bastin 1978, 10–11)

Although collected more than a decade after his performances at Fort Valley, the songs Freeman played for Burrison in 1967 suggest that his repertoire continued to be diverse.[56] About half were created during the nineteenth century ("John Henry," "Leather Britches," "Old Hen Cackled," and "Sally Goodwin") and are now considered to be common stock, while others are popular songs composed and recorded during the early twentieth century ("Tennessee Waltz," "Chattanoogie Shoe Shine Boy," and Worried Blues") that he had probably heard on the radio. In terms of sound sources, Freeman combined instruments popular in rural areas (fiddle and acoustic guitar) with those identified with the city (such as bass, piano, and electric guitar). Together, the repertoire and instrumentation demonstrate Freeman's attempts to satisfy a majority Black audience whose tastes were in flux. While some were probably satisfied with the old, others may have preferred sounds that were new and different. These indicators also suggest why members of Freeman's community knew him as a carpenter who played blues, a modern genre for those times, and not someone who only played the fiddle, a mainstay identified with the past. When compared to other fiddlers in this study, Freeman's repertoire is closer, although on a much smaller scale, to that of Livers in Kentucky than rural Black fiddlers in other parts of Appalachia.[57]

Photo 9.6. Elbert J. Freeman (fiddle) and Nathaniel Ford (guitar). Jasper County, Georgia, 1967. Courtesy of John A. Burrison.

Due to the lack of data, we do not know when Freeman started playing the fiddle nor who taught him how to perform the instrument. For example, did he have a role model (perhaps a family member) whom he emulated, or did he learn on his own and acquire his repertoire from listening to recordings available to him? During his youth, was fiddling an activity encouraged or discouraged by family members? This is significant because, in his later years (when he was in his fifties and sixties), the musicians who performed in his different music groups were not kin. This suggests that his performance style, which is unique but similar to others discussed in this study (particularly Bill Livers), is one he developed on this own from listening to the media. To understand his performance style better, an analysis of one his tunes is presented below.

Bastin (1986, 84) indicates that the rough alley fiddling Freeman uses in "Worried Blues" is closer to Atlanta-based blues fiddler Eddie Anthony's playing than Freeman's "John Henry" and his version of Fiddlin' John Carson's "The Old Hen Cackled and the Rooster Is Going to Crow." However, my analysis of Freeman's fiddling suggests that the so-called "rough alley" performance style is characteristic of his musicking generally. His playing is percussive with greater emphasis on rhythm through the use of off-beat phrasing and additive rhythms. In terms of tonality, not only does Freeman regularly slide into notes when attacking them, the squealing effects and disharmonious chords that result from his fiddling are probably features admired by his audience because these characteristics appear in all his performances.

To demonstrate how Freeman integrates these features into his performance style, let us begin with an analysis of "Old Hen Cackled," one of the most popular songs performed by Black fiddlers in this study.[58] The tune's first commercial recording was made in Atlanta on June 14, 1923, by white country musician John Carson, who informed researchers that he had played the song at fiddlers' contests for years before recording it (Wolfe 1997, xvi). Now categorized as a common stock tune (Russell 1970, 9, 28), "Old Hen Cackled," with its varied song titles, most likely grew out of the shared culture of Blacks and whites during the nineteenth century. In fact, Carson's lyrics are similar to those that Talley (1922, 50–51) collected from African Americans in rural Tennessee during the early twentieth century.[59] Although "Old Hen Cackled" was developed in a shared culture environment, the fact that all prewar commercial recordings of the tune were made by white musicians—except for a version by Black harmonica player DeFord Bailey and the unissued recording by Taylor's Kentucky Boys with Jim Booker and "Doc" Roberts on fiddle and John Booker on guitar that were both recorded in 1927—is another example of the misrepresentation of fiddling in the United States.

The manner in which fiddlers performed "Old Hen Cackled" was often a benchmark of their skill in playing the fiddle (Kuntz 1996–2010). Carson's performance is organized around two themes. While the A theme is played in a high register with emphasis on sustained notes to produce a smooth sound, the B theme, which includes intermittent singing and speaking, tends to be performed in a lower register with rhythmic variation in emulation of the sound of a hen clucking. Unlike most old-time songs in which the A and B themes are alternated after playing each twice, the B theme dominates in the performance of "Old Hen Cackled" because of the extensive variation (double-stops, off-beat phrasing, additive rhythms, and increases in tempo) used in this part of the song. In Carson's roughly three-minute performance, about 78 seconds are devoted to performing the A theme, while the remaining time is spent in variations on B.[60]

Freeman's performance of "Old Hen Cackled" differs from Carson's in at least two ways.[61] One, he begins his version with the rhythmically complex B theme before moving to A. Similar to Carson's performance, however, the B theme dominates in Freeman's version. During the one minute, twenty-four seconds that Freeman performs "Old Hen Cackled," the A theme is played twenty-four seconds, while B takes up the remaining part of the performance. Of the Black fiddlers in this study who include the tune in their repertoire, two begin with the B theme: James "Butch" Cage from Mississippi/Louisiana and William Adams from Maryland.[62] In fact, Adams does not perform the A theme at all; rather, he plays the B theme throughout the entire song.

Two, the melody Freeman uses for his A theme is different from that employed by Carson and other fiddlers. Although the A theme in both Carson's and Freeman's versions extend over a one-octave range, the repetition of several short notes in Freeman's A theme, probably using a short-bow technique, gives it a rhythmic quality, rather than a melodic, lyrical quality that makes versions by Carson and other fiddlers distinctive.[63] Freeman may have created this specific a theme for "Old Hen Cackled" because, as noted above, the use of a short jiggly bow results in a performance style that is rhythmic and rough as opposed to a long-bow technique that produces a smooth clearer tone (Wolfe 1981, 115). The fact that a similar percussive-oriented performance is used in Freeman's fiddling of "John Henry" suggests these are features that characterize his fiddling. Linford (2013b) states: "He's using a lot of the same elements in both his blues and old-time repertoire. The real rough attack contrasted with some sweeter notes—a combination of rhythmically oriented bowing with longer melodic bow strokes."

Another interesting feature about Freeman's playing is that he supplements his fiddling with parts that suggest other instruments. Although the guitar provides accompaniment, it seems that Freeman desires more. Wilson (2013) explains: "It's interesting, he is playing multiple parts all the time. With 'Worried Blues,'[64] he's going back and forth between the solo and back-up line. Whereas with the other tunes, he kept it [the back-up part] low. The songs are from different generations. So, the approach to the song is different; the blues is post [trumpeter Louis] Armstrong. So, you're thinking of the wailing sax or a clarinet of New Orleans music, which has that high, soloist concept as opposed to the functional concept for dancing. It was a break with tradition. Now you're taking it into a recital. You have to dampen down that street enthusiasm to call people and turn it into an arrangement."

Joe Kinney Rakestraw (ca. 1911–2000)

Material on Joe Kinney Rakestraw (see photo 9.7), a fiddler and guitarist who continued to be active through the late twentieth century, was collected by Art Rosenbaum and his wife Margo Newmark Rosenbaum during the 1970s and 1980s as part of a larger study on vernacular culture in north Georgia. Findings from their fieldwork were incorporated in a book (Rosenbaum 1983) and two recordings (Rosenbaum 1984a, 1984b). At the start of their research, the Rosenbaums questioned whether secular and sacred musical traditions in the mountain and piedmont regions of the state had survived changes in communications and the social and economic order. In other words, to what extent had the interstate highways, the sprawl of shopping-centers and condominium development, as well as the pervasive influence of gospel, pop, and country music via radio and television affected the musicking? Were musical traditions from earlier years still being performed or had they been obliterated or changed beyond recognition as distinctive regional forms? To their surprise, they learned that older traditions had not vanished; however, "with a few exceptions, . . . they were no longer central to community life. The people who [had] chosen to remember and continue to perform them emerge[d] as extraordinary folk, usually older, individualistic and at times even eccentric, possessed of keen memories, authentic and exemplary performing styles, and a commitment to

Photo 9.7. Joe Kinney Rakestraw, holding fiddle. Athens, Georgia. 1980. Margo Newmark Rosenbaum.

the 'old-time way,' not out of antiquarianism or nostalgia, but for reasons of personal and artistic choice" (Rosenbaum 1983, xi).

Rakestraw was born in the town of Jefferson, the seat of Jackson County, about twenty miles northwest of Athens (the largest city in northeast Georgia) and seventy miles northeast of Atlanta. He was raised by his family in several small communities (Red Stone and Arcade) located about three miles southeast of Jefferson and twenty miles northwest of Athens.[65] It was not until his return from serving in the army during World War II that he settled in Athens, which became his permanent home until his death in 2000. There is no evidence that Rakestraw and his wife, Alberta Lee (1908–1996), who was born in Athens, had any children (Rosenbaum 1983, Rakestraw 1987).[66]

Although longtime residents of the rural South, the Rakestraws[67] were never sharecroppers. Rather, all worked on a farm "that had been handed down in the family from a grandfather who had been a bootmaker as a slave and eventually bought his freedom and land" (Rosenbaum 1983, 184). In an interview with Rosenbaum, Rakestraw (1987) explained: "I grew up on the farm. It was hard; we worked from sun up to sun down. It was probably three or four hundred acres when it was [first purchased]. But it's now seventy-five acres, [because] it has been divided up so many times. That district was owned by Black people; they were well-to-do. And when the boll weevils come, [most farms were] wiped out, sold, [or] was foreclosed on." Rakestraw's eldest brother, Anderson Jr., gave up farming sometime in the teens and became the proprietor and mechanic of a car garage in Athens. Around 1920, he and two of his brothers (Delmar and

Dupree) migrated to Detroit to work in the auto industry. After World War II, Rakestraw (1983) indicated that he worked in various occupations: "I moved to Athens . . . [in] '45. I came out of the army in '45. I had been married about four years in '45. My first job, I was an insurance agent. And I done that for maybe five years. Then I turned to carpentry. And I've been a carpenter ever since."

Music was the chief form of recreation in the Rakestraw family. In fact, three brothers (Anderson, Delmar, and Dupree) formed a Black string band that was active in Arcade, a small community in southern Jackson County, before World War I. In describing the family's musicking, Rakestraw (1983) stated:

> Their repertoire included breakdowns, transitional pieces, and early blues. They played different instruments—bass violin, violin, and guitar. [There] was . . . [a] man in the community that played with them. I forget his name. But he played five-string banjo—a small banjo, [it] didn't have no ornament around the edge. People would come in buggies to pick them up to play for them, and they would be gone practically all night. They played for square dances and the old-time fiddling tunes. After they went off to . . . World War I. . . . they came back and played for a little while, but they left. . . . They went to Detroit, worked at Ford Motor Company, and done pretty good. One of them sent back and got the violin, that was my oldest brother, Anderson Jr. I heard that he played for some church before he died in Detroit.

Interestingly, Rakestraw (1983) indicated that it was not until after his brothers' move to Detroit that he became involved in music: "That was the beginning of my music, just listening to them. I guess [when] I was 10 or 12 years old, I didn't go in for it. But since the instruments [were] there, I begin to fool around with them until I . . . got up and know that I could play pretty good." Although his primary interest was the guitar, he started playing both fiddle and guitar around the same time: "I played in the style of my brothers. They played the old-time square dance tunes. I don't remember them playing any modern tunes. I had brothers [Charlie and Richard] that came along with me [who] picked up what was available. The bass violin and the guitar was there. Some people heard us play and then they started to come and pick us up, and carried us out to play for them." Rosenbaum (1983, 184) writes that "after the younger Rakestraws had organized their string band, they played at country dances and also at school commencements. . . . One of the pieces they played for commencement processions was . . . 'Railroad Bill,' because they discovered that their version had a good march tempo" (184). In explaining his involvement, Rakestraw (1983) stated: "At school closin' time I was very busy goin' from one vicinity to another. They would have plays and speeches, and I was very popular, 'cause it wasn't but very few that made music."

Rakestraw (1983) indicated that performances at home frolics did not occur immediately: "After I got to be a grown man, you'd go to a party in the homes.

They would take the beds out of one room. And that would be the room where they would dance. In the dancing room, there wasn't nothing there but just that room. They had sometime just me and my brother—guitar and fiddle. Other times, it would be three pieces—bass fiddle, guitar, and violin." After settling in Athens, Rakestraw (1983) stated that he continued with his musicking: "I did play bass with a[n] orchestra in spare times. I've played at all the [University of Georgia's fraternity and sorority] chapter houses . . . at the Hilton Club and the Moose Club [Lodge]. I was playing with a dance band . . . the Honey Drippers. They played more modern music. That's where I picked up some of the more modern songs that I play."[68] Instead of learning tunes from recordings, Rakestraw indicated that he "learned mostly from listenin' to the people—what the people was singing, is what I learned" (Rosenbaum 1983, 184).

Although their father had issues with his sons performing secular genres, he never stopped them from continuing with their music. When Rosenbaum asked if he was ever scorned by church members for playing worldly music, Rakestraw laughed and stated: "Never was. I like church music and I like that [secular music]. Never did make no difference with me, but I tried to conform with the community. I didn't play them on Sunday. Music was music, regardless of what kind it was. My father was very strict, yet and still, he liked both kinds, but I remember my brothers, if they were playin' church song, he didn't want them to pat their foot, he'd come up behind them [and put his foot on theirs]."[69]

Like other Black fiddlers, Rakestraw's repertoire is diverse.[70] Included are religious songs ("Amazing Grace," "How Great Thou Art," "Rock of Ages," and "When the World's on Fire"); tunes from the nineteenth century ("John Henry" and "Shortnin' Bread"); musicking with lyrics reflecting life experiences in the early twentieth century ("Boll Weevil" and "Leavin' Here, Don't Know Where I'm Goin'"); and certain blues tunes ("Corinna, Corinna" and "Saint Louis Blues") that were especially popular during that time.[71] Although he performed fiddle on only three songs ("John Henry," "Leavin' Here, Don't Know Where I'm Goin'," and a tune with no name) during his interviews with Rosenbaum, his repertoire is similar to that of other fiddlers in this study. Regardless of the circumstances, Rakestraw continued to appreciate old-time music. "For him the old songs have a similar function: 'They have a value, a meaning. If you could go back to the author and search his life, you would readily feel, see what he's tryin' to express'" (Rosenbaum 1983, 187).

Other Black Fiddlers in Georgia

Little information can be found on the two remaining Black musicians (Alfred Thomas and George Hollis) known to have played the fiddle in rural Georgia during the early twentieth century. All we know is that Thomas was born and active in the Black music community of Hancock County near the eastern portion of the Georgia piedmont. On visits to his family home, which was close to

Thomas's residence, blues researcher Gene Wiggins (1977) states that he personally observed how Thomas would "lay the fiddle down on his lap and play it" (6). Those who have heard performances by Hollis and lived in Talbot County near the western portion of Georgia's piedmont region indicate that he played in the style of Elbert Freeman, which is not surprising considering that both fiddlers lived in similar social environments (Bastin 1986, 125, 153).[72]

In summary, the available evidence indicates that Georgia was similar to other areas during the early twentieth century in that much variation existed in the Black fiddle tradition. In the mountain region, supporters of the tradition on the local level were whites, particularly in places like Gordon County. While Black fiddlers were active in both white and Black communities in the piedmont regions, it is noteworthy that the tradition continued to be supported by African Americans in majority-Black communities. Most significant is the greater prominence of blues in the repertoire of fiddlers, demonstrating changes in the tastes of African American audiences during this period. Thus, musicians like the Baxters had two different personas—one in which they were known locally among whites for their performance of old-time music, and another from songs released on race records, which tended to be blues or genres identified with African American culture.

Alabama

Similar to other areas of the South, minimal research has been done on the secular music of African Americans in Alabama. Reporting on fieldwork conducted during the 1950s, Frederic Ramsey (1956b) states: "The southern county seat no longer burgeons with guitar players and small instrumental groups as it did on Saturday nights some thirty to forty years ago. The groups known as 'skiffle' and 'string bands' have all but disappeared" (30). While works by Harold Courlander (1951–1956, 1960) and Frederic Ramsey (1956a) focus on cries, calls, play party songs, ballads, and the blues, Maggie Holtzberg-Call (1989) discusses the role of music in the work of Black railroad gangs. Thomas W. Talley, Joyce Cauthen, and Burgin Mathews are the only researchers to examine Black fiddling in any detail. While Talley (1922, 235–39) provides excellent information on the creativity and structure of fiddle tunes used by African Americans, Cauthen (1989a) includes data on Black Alabama fiddlers, primarily from the pre–twentieth century era. Mathews (2008, 2023) is the only researcher to focus on a Black fiddler, John Earnest Mostella, who was active during the early twentieth century.

John Earnest Mostella (ca. 1908–2003)

Black fiddling was widespread in all parts of Alabama during the nineteenth century.[73] However, the only evidence of the tradition in twentieth-century rural

Photo 9.8a. Earnest Mostella playing fiddle he constructed. St. Clair County, Alabama. February 22, 2000. Courtesy of Joe Songer.

Alabama is the musical life of John Earnest (Ernest) Mostella, the grandson of Augustus "Gus" Cochran (ca. 1865–1927) who was a well-known Alabama Black fiddler during the late nineteenth and early twentieth centuries.[74] As Mathews (2023, 7) writes: "what had once been a flourishing tradition had largely faded by the time Earnest Mostella entered adulthood; by the time he reached old age, Mostella was a unique living link to a legacy that appeared to have vanished."

Like many fiddlers in rural areas, Mostella spent much of his life in the community where he was born, which was located near Ashville, St. Clair County, Alabama.[75] In addition to working as a coal miner, the US census indicates that he was a farmer, laborer, and was occasionally employed by the county road industry. His life, like that of his family members, who were sharecroppers and blacksmiths, was defined by music and work: "we worked on a farm and played in a family band. Our daddy would always give us the Fourth of July off from field work and we were so glad; we'd eat cookies and cakes at picnics and play our music" (Mathews 2023, 8).

Unlike other fiddlers in this study who continued to be involved in the tradition through performance, Mostella was unique in that he constructed fiddles, which had been a tradition among his ancestors. Using a power saw to carve musical instruments out of raw trees (see photos 9.8a and 9.8b), his skill in constructing them made him something of a celebrity in his community.[76] Not only has he been featured in Alabama regional newspaper articles, his instruments were showcased

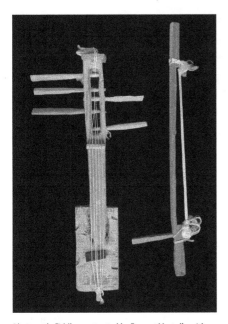

Photo 9.8b. Fiddle constructed by Earnest Mostella with rectangular hole in resonator. St. Clair County, Alabama. Photograph by M. Sean Pathasema, Birmingham, Alabama. September 9, 2021. Courtesy of Burgin Mathews.

in exhibitions in Montgomery (the state capital) and displayed in local museums (Evans 1984; Wilkerson 1994; Mathews 2023). Mathews (2023, 7) explains:

> Mostella was prolifically, endlessly creative. He was a musician, a heavy laborer, a lay preacher, and a craftsman; a bearer of long family tradition; a prodigious, animated talker and singer; and a beloved presence in his native community of Ashville, Alabama. He was a rare practitioner, too, of southern Black fiddle traditions—both fiddle-playing and fiddle-making—surviving into the twenty-first century. "The fiddle was just handed down, and it's a gift that a man has got," he said, explaining his family's history with the instrument. "We're just gifted to music." His great uncle was a fiddle maker, he explained, and his grandfather a legendary local musician. Mostella himself made his first fiddle around the age of eight, with wood he cut from a black gum tree. Many more would follow.

Mostella stated that he "learned to play [the fiddle] by watching his grandfather. One of his favorite tunes was the novelty number 'Mockingbird'" (Mathews 2008).[77] "No one gave us music. We just sat down (on grandfather's knees) and looked [at] his fingers. Oh, he was a fiddling man" (Evans 1984, 1c). Although he rarely played the fiddle, Mostella sang tunes he remembered from his early days, providing evidence of some of the songs included his repertoire.[78] Mostella's "repertoire included spirituals, shape note and gospel hymns, 'frolic' tunes, patriotic songs, topical ballads, and his own, often improvised compositions" (Mathews 2023, 12). Known in his community as a preacher, "sermonizing and story-telling came naturally to him." Whether these varying activities resulted in conflicts between him and members of his family or community during his early years as a musician is unknown (Mathews 2008).

No one really knows why, but it appears that fiddling by African Americans in Alabama began to wane during the early decades of the twentieth century. Cultural memory, especially when it is negative, may provide an explanation. African Americans who had experienced the horrors of slavery at the hands of whites did whatever they could to be independent. In many cases, this was done by creating an identity and environment with cultural patterns they defined as nonwhite (Evans 1978a, 5). Did the fiddle, for some Blacks, become a symbol of the old ways of thinking or a performance tradition that reminded them of enslavement—and thus had to be discarded? To what degree did views on religion and the fiddle's association with the devil play a role in its decline?

With many changes occurring during the economic upheaval of the Great Depression, the instrument may have become less prominent among Alabama Blacks when blues and jazz, with roots that are more African-derived, came into vogue (Cauthen 1989b, 16). As in North Carolina, the performance of new genres became an act of defiance against repression in the social environment (Lornell 1975; Hinson 1978). Regardless of the reasons, the fact that Black fiddling seems to have declined more quickly in Alabama than it did in other parts of Central and Southern Appalachia is a topic that needs further investigation, particularly since the one jug band based in Birmingham (the Birmingham Jug Band) during the early twentieth century also rarely, if ever, included the fiddle. Yet, fiddlers played major roles in jug bands in Louisville and Memphis, cities located in regions where Black fiddling continued to be popular in rural communities through the 1940s.[79] Nonetheless, Cauthen (1989c, 41) believes Black fiddlers left an important legacy among Euro-Americans. White Alabama musicians who continued playing the instrument show influence from Black culture, specifically in the performance of "hot" or "hoedown" fiddling, which is distinct from traditions in New England, the Midwest, and the British Isles.

Mississippi

Although Mississippi historically has been a state of great contrasts, this is not reflected in the literature on Black musicking.[80] Just as researchers in other areas of the United States focused almost entirely on religious music, just the opposite occurred in Mississippi, where the emphasis has been on secular music, specifically the blues, a broad category of dance music identified with the largest number of Black people in the state.[81] David Evans, who has conducted much research on musicking in Mississippi, believes it was the intense individual styles and personalities of Mississippi's blues artists that impressed both commercial talent scouts and researchers. In their efforts to document the entire range of African American musicking, which involved searching for vestiges of nineteenth-century forms, early investigators such as John and Alan Lomax "couldn't help but notice the prominence of the blues among the people they encountered" (Evans 1999b). Paul Oliver (1972, 34) writes that the social environment's impact on musical creativity was the most important factor that affected him:

> The sheer crudity of segregation in Mississippi, the barbarity of the measures to enforce it, the rich and yet despairing landscape with its low, red clay hills and the monotony of the flat bottomlands combine to give the state a perverse fascination. It is occasionally beautiful, but mostly it is elemental, cruel even, stifling in its feudalism. That a folk music of such stature and dignity took root and thrived in this soil continues to thrill and astonish, and for this reason perhaps, the view of Mississippi as the birthplace of the blues and the epitome of the whole music is seldom questioned. . . . But blues is not a music of state and county lines or river boundaries, but of a people.

In spite of the emphasis on blues, some information has been published on Black fiddling. Several print publications and sound recordings exist for all five regions of Mississippi. The most significant for this study is Sylvester Oliver's dissertation (1996) on sacred and secular music in the eastern Hills counties, which includes a detailed analyses of the social environment, performance contexts, repertoire, and performance style of Black fiddlers in the region.[82] Sound material documenting Black fiddling in the western Hills counties can be found in field and commercial recordings produced by Alan Lomax, with liner notes by various researchers.[83] Although the information is in no way comparable to what is presented on white fiddlers, publications by Bolick and Austin (2015) and Bolick and Russell (2021) are noteworthy for providing the names, biographies, and repertoire of Black fiddlers active in various regions of the state during the early twentieth century[84] (see figure 9.1). Not only do these findings demonstrate that Black fiddling continued to be popular in communities that had majority Black populations in Mississippi, the repertoire of some musicians was comparable to that of Black and white fiddlers in other parts of the South. In addition to tunes reflecting the shared music culture that developed among the races between the nineteenth and early twentieth centuries, song titles also display the ingenuity of Black musicians in Mississippi;[85] fiddlers were innovative in creating songs that document old and new cultural experiences.[86] The findings also confirm that Mississippi Black fiddlers were not passive observers but active participants who employed resources available to them to protest racism and oppression (Evans 1978a, 4; 1999a).[87]

Mississippi Black Fiddlers

Legend for Demographics

This list of names and information about Mississippi Black fiddlers comes from Taylor (2001), Bolick and Austin (2015), as well as Bolick and Russell (2021). The legend provides information on the demographics for counties between 1900 and 1940. The (+) indicates that the county was majority Black, while (–) indicates that it was majority white. A (?) indicates that no information is available.

Majority black—1900, 1910, 1920, 1930, 1940 [+++++]
Majority white—1900, 1910, 1920, 1930, 1940 [-----]

Hills Region
• Marshall County [+++++]   1. Ernest "Boose" Taylor

• Panola County [+++++]
  1. Sidney Hemphill
  2. Robert Pratcher

• Tate County [+++++]   1. Henry McClatching

Pines Region
• Webster County [-----]   1. Thomas Jefferson Dumas

Delta Region
• Carroll County [+++++]   1. Allen Alsop
• Sharkey County [+++++]   1. Henry Simms

• Tallahatchie County [+++++]
  1. Jim Gooch
  2. Thomas Jefferson Dumas

• Washington County [+++++]   1. Prince Albert McCoy

Capital/River Region

• Copiah County [+++–+]
  1. Willis Taylor
  2. Mott Willis

• Hinds County [+++++]
  1. Annie Lee
  2. Frank Wharton
  3. Armenter Chatmon [Bo Chatmon, Bo Carter]
  4. Harry Chatmon
  5. Lonnie Chatmon

• Madison County [+++++]   1. Theodore Harris
• Pike County [-----]   1. Charles Addison
• Walthall [??---]   1. Herb Quinn

Coastal Region

• Harrison County [-----]
  1. Josephine Compton
  2. E. Thomas

Figure 9.1. Selected list of Mississippi Black fiddlers who were active, 1900–1950. Based on information in Taylor (2001); Bolick and Austin (2015); and Bolick and Russell (2021).

The following discussion on Mississippi Black fiddling addresses two issues: (1) it helps explain why the fiddle continued to be performed by Black musicians in the state, even in areas with majority Black populations, and (2) it demonstrates how the fusion of African- and European-derived elements provided source material to create a performance style in Mississippi that was distinct but also similar to that in other parts of the United States. As Bolick (2015a, xi) indicates, "this propensity for reshaping tunes is the defining trait of Mississippi old-time fiddling." But this is also one of the prominent features of African-derived musicking. Only findings about Black fiddling in the Hills and Pines regions[88] are presented below because, geographically and culturally, the counties in these regions are similar to the state's Appalachian hills. Black fiddling in other regions (Delta, Capital/River, and Coastal) is discussed later (see chapter 11), for it is more similar, in my opinion, to the musicking of African Americans who lived along the Gulf Coast.

The Mississippi Hills Region: Eastern Counties

Sylvester Oliver believes the development of African American music in the eastern Hills counties (Alcorn, Benton, Marshall, Prentiss, Tippah, and Tishomingo) was greatly affected by geography and the rural isolated lifestyle that Black and white people experienced. In Alcorn, Prentiss, Tippah, and Tishomingo counties where African Americans were smaller in population, self-sufficient, and more scattered among the larger white communities, the close contact between the races allowed Black and poor white people to share similar song materials. Cultural patterns and traditions identified with Africa and the larger mid-south Black Belt were more often preserved in counties (such as Benton and Marshall) with larger numbers of Black people (Oliver 1996, 62, 340–41). For these reasons, Oliver indicates that four African American secular music traditions have been prominent in the Mississippi Hills: fiddle and banjo music, fife and drum band music, string band music, and blues. While fiddle and banjo music dates to the early nineteenth century, fife and drum music became popular during and after the Civil War. String band music did not come into vogue until the late nineteenth and early twentieth centuries after other types of string instruments became available to rural settlers. Blues developed after the introduction of the guitar in the late nineteenth century and matured in the early twentieth century (Oliver 1996, 334–37).[89] For this discussion, greater attention is given to fiddle and banjo and string band music with a brief discussion of blues.

Fiddle and Banjo Music. Prior to 1930, African Americans in the eastern Hills communities had close affinities with Appalachian mountain music (such as fiddle and banjo tunes, reels, jigs, hillbilly, or early country and western music) that had developed from the Black and white shared culture of the nineteenth century, but in the early twentieth century was identified primarily with European Americans. The performance of fiddle and banjo music by Black people in the eastern counties reached its peak during the second decade of the twentieth century and waned as an active form in the 1950s, well past the time it disappeared in other parts of the state. By the turn of the century, the banjo had all but faded but was still used in many circles as late as the 1940s. Although some musicians were mentioned in local newspapers, the great majority remained obscure outside their immediate communities because record company executives ignored them when recordings of Black musicking began to appear in various parts of the South during the early twentieth century (Oliver 1996, 350, 355–56).

Most Black fiddlers were self-taught or learned from other Black musicians in the region. In performances, they either played alone or with another fiddler or banjo player. Just as their lifestyle had not changed drastically since the nineteenth century, their repertoire also was not different from earlier days.[90] Similar to other mountain regions of the United States, the repertoire of Black Mississippi fiddlers was broad, including tunes that originated or were performed by the enslaved, as well as those of white origin ("The Arkansas Traveler," "The Eighth of January," "Little Liza Jane," "The Old Hen Cackle," "Old Zip Coon," and "Turkey in the Straw") that are now regarded as common stock. A few songs (including "Tishomingo County Blues" and "Boll Weevil Blues") related specifically to Mississippi or the southern United States. Although Black Mississippi fiddlers used one repertoire for both Black and white dance audiences, they tended to experiment with tunes performed for African American audiences, who were also more critical of their music[91] (Oliver 1996, 351, 357).

During the early twentieth century, Black fiddlers were highly regarded because both the fiddle and banjo were closely tied to an old southern agricultural lifestyle enjoyed primarily by an older generation of Black and white people who had grown up dancing and listening to this type of music. Dozens of African American fiddlers in small eastern county communities played for family, friends, and neighbors at socials of the affluent and the not so affluent audiences. Most accompanied dancing at barbecues, fish fries, frolics, house parties, and country dances for both races. Born in 1909, Marshall County resident and blues singer-guitarist Monroe "Guy" Jackson recalls the house parties he attended in his youth: "We didn't have no cars back then. They went to dances at one another's houses by the wagon loads, just like you see cotton going to the gin. They carried children and all; they put the children in a back room, and you didn't have to worry about them. The old folk were in the other room. Them women dances all night in those $1.98 slippers. When they left the dance that night, there wouldn't be any bottoms left on the slippers. They would be cakewalking, ring dancing, and two-stepping all night long!" (Oliver 1996, 423). Jackson states that several Black fiddlers were active during the 1920s and 1930s: Nute Wilkins, who "would put his fiddle down and do it with his mouth," and

Uncle Ruff Lucas. While Charlie Wilkerson and Abraham and Joe Mosley were popular at country dances and frolics in Tippah and Union counties, Henry "Legg" Simmons, a farmer before he began his performance career as a fiddler, was regarded by many in Ripley [Tippah County] to be the most competent member of the Ripley String Band (Oliver 1996, 355). A group popular during the 1930s was Uncle Dick and Uncle Nell from Marshall County. In a WPA interview, Uncle Dick's daughter states that the group played throughout the community at Black and white social functions, and one of their more popular tunes was "Eighth of January." Since there were no clubs or dance halls for Black people at that time, most dances took place at a home or farm. In another WPA interview, Bill Holt and Jones Snipes indicate that they sometimes played old-time dances with other African Americans at the white Masonic Hall in Chulahoma, a small community in Marshall County (Oliver 1996, 354–55).

Starting in the 1930s, Black fiddlers had more competition from their white fiddle counterparts for performances at dances that were once their exclusive province. When entertainment at white dances declined, this led to a change in repertoire. More of the music was aimed at African American audiences after the 1930s. So, tunes popular during the nineteenth and early twentieth centuries, by the late 1930s, were replaced by more modern songs such as blues. The change in audience also resulted in fiddling becoming a player's art form. In the 1940s and 1950s, fiddlers in some counties had showdowns by competing with one another during performances. Bluesman Junior Kimbrough and his former bass player, George Scales, stated that old fiddle players used to gather and have playing duels at the section house (waiting station for train passengers) and in front of the four or five stores in Hudsonville near the border of Marshall and Benton counties.[92] As fiddlers performed, onlookers and passengers waiting for the train danced and cheered for their favorite fiddler. Informal and spontaneous, the sessions were not organized or set up by anyone. Kimbrough states that "If one could not play the song they called off, another one came right in there, picked it up and played it like a champ. I can't remember all the songs they used to play now, but they played that old-time music on those fiddles, including a lot of blues songs too" (Oliver 1996, 352–53). Interestingly, fiddlers' repertoire at the waiting station was the same as that of blues musicians. In addition to original compositions, songs that had been recorded on race record and hillbilly labels were performed. Some of the favorites included "Honeydripper Blues," "Shake 'Em on Down," "Coal Black Mattie," "Joe Turner Blues," "Pop Wide Open," "Big Foot N----r," "The Old Hen Cackle," and "Turkey in the Pea Patch" (Oliver 1996, 342, 347, 353).

When African Americans who had lived in outlying rural communities in the early decades settled in larger nearby towns and cities (Memphis, Tupelo, Corinth, Booneville, and Ripley) to improve their economic status,[93] the audience and contexts for performing the fiddle in the eastern counties became more limited. Whereas guitarists were able to find audiences both in Mississippi and Memphis where some often moved, fiddlers did most of their performing in the Hills. Thus, the changing demographics became another factor that caused fiddle and banjo music to decline in popularity (Oliver 1996, 343).

String Band Music. The string band tradition is an expansion or outgrowth of the performance of fiddle and banjo music. Thus, group playing with a variety of string instruments did not become popular until the turn of the twentieth century, when the sale of instruments through mail catalogs had decreased the price, and individuals had more income to purchase instruments. Although little research has been done on Black string band music in the state, Oliver states that African American string bands were everywhere and played for everyone. "Nearly every sizable African American community in the region had one or two string bands that played together as a group or, with flexible instrumentation or personnel as a fife and drum band, brass band, fiddle duet or fiddle and banjo team" (Oliver 1996, 382–83).

While most string bands in eastern counties were formed in the 1890s, Oliver (1996) indicates that they did not reach their peak of popularity until the late 1930s, and had disappeared by the late 1950s. In Mississippi, the instrumentation for string bands varied. Occasionally, the harmonica, Jew's harps, and drums were performed. Drums, generally not included in string bands in other parts of the South, were used in Mississippi because of the popularity of fife and drum music in the region.[94] Monroe Jackson states that "the string band he played with sometimes used a bass drum, a washtub bass and the kazoo as part of the instrumentation" (Oliver 1996, 382). Older people who spoke with Oliver "said the purpose of these instruments was to accompany words of a song and provide secondary melodic and rhythmic parts, but seldom to create just purely instrumental music" (382). But instruments were sometimes used for a strictly instrumental performance.

Like other traditions in the South, few string band performers had formal training. Most learned from older community musicians who passed on their knowledge orally. Many performers could play several instruments and often did at dances. Blues performer Ellen Jeffries (1910–1991), who lived in Marshall, one of the eastern Hills counties, remembered how her uncles often displayed great dexterity and ability as soloists on the banjo, fiddle, mandolin, and guitar in the 1920s. "Many of their musical styles and techniques and songs possessed lingering influences of minstrelsy and often featured fiddle and banjo tunes, hillbilly music, folk ballads, variations of patting juba, pre-blues, and other folk songs [sic] traditions of the South" (Oliver 1996, 384). In later years, the band also played blues on old Sears and Roebuck guitars, mandolin, and fiddles (398).

String bands played for a variety of social occasions, but most provided entertainment at Friday and Saturday night country dances that took place at a musician's home or neighbor's house similar to fiddle and banjo performances (see foregoing). Because of their location between the foothills of Southern

Appalachia and the Mississippi Delta, string bands drew heavily from both Black and white southern music. During the 1930s, musicians started incorporating popular tunes and secular songs from the radio as part of their repertoire. Bands combined old rural and new traditions, including some ragtime music, hokum songs, blues, hillbilly music, and western songs. The degree to which one style dominated depended on the audience. For example, blues in the Mississippi Hills was different from that performed in the Delta (Oliver 1996, 404); see further discussion below.

Most bands did not have formal names but were called by the names of men who led them or the community in which they lived. "Jim Chief's String Band near Chulahoma was a popular group that regularly played at house parties in the western part of Marshall County in the late twenties and thirties. Another popular band was Jim Mosley's string band near Ripley in Tippah County. Mosley played fiddle and owned nearly all the instruments the band performed. His band was a family band, and the members of the group consisted of his sons and brothers" (Oliver 1996, 386).

The Ripley String Band (RSB), one of the more popular bands in the region during the 1930s, took its name from Ripley, Tippah's county seat. With a flexible roster of about ten players and singers, RSB included fiddle, banjo, guitar, mandolin, bass viol, and sometimes harmonica. Willie Grey, the leader of the group and a native of Ripley, did most of the singing; he was also the only person who had musical training. Unlike other local groups, RSB was semi-professional in that band members performed in a variety of contexts other than community events and house parties. Between 1924 and 1941, the band made regular tours in towns and cities in west Tennessee, north Mississippi, and west Alabama. They played at hotels on Beale Street in Memphis and at different events in Ripley, including dances, school houses, picnics, jamborees, and old-fashioned music contests. At the movie theater in Ripley on Saturday afternoons, the group provided background music for silent movies playing there. Payment for performances was modest but significant for the time. Leggs Simmons, the fiddle player, recalled receiving five dollars a night (Oliver 1996, 388).

RSB's repertoire, a synthesis of lower Appalachian mountain music and blues from the Hills, was similar to that of fiddle musicians in the area.[95] Because of their repertoire, Legg Simmons and Willie Grey indicate that the majority of their audiences were white. In addition to relying on head arrangements carefully worked out in rehearsals, they specialized in what Grey called western music (country or bluegrass), jigs, reels, and blues. The group's repertoire was eclectic with tunes such as "Texas Bell," "Cindy," "Grub Springs," "Turkey in the Straw," "Eighth of January," "Tom and Jerry," "Uncle Ned," "Lonesome Widow," "Arkansas Travelers" [sic]. The fox trot dance rhythms and arpeggio-chord[96] variation on pop standards and country tunes of the day were also popular. Songs identified with African American culture included songs and homespun humor common to minstrel and medicine shows as well as popular music heard on radio and records. With most members self-trained, the music was improvisatory and based on what they heard around them, and what members of the group sometimes introduced. Although RSB did not record because Grey believed this would damage their musical image, the string bands heard on recordings from Mississippi in the 1930s characterize what they may have sounded like (Oliver 1996, 387–91).

By the 1960s, many Black fiddlers in the eastern Hills counties were no longer active. Reasons for the decline of fiddle and banjo music as well as the string band tradition in Mississippi are the same: change in music preference, lack of recordings by the media, racism, and urbanization. Similar to other regions of the United States, the emergence of blues, the enticement of more sophisticated music from urban areas such as Memphis, and the desire of musicians to remain current with new music styles and trends heard on records and the radio that satisfied their dance audiences were also reasons for the demise of the Black fiddle tradition.

When World War II began, many young string players were drafted and left the area. While some older band members continued to play, others stopped performing because of changes in their lifestyles; a few decided to join the church and/or spend more time with their families by staying home. Black string bands also represented a communal form of African American musicking that was replaced by the blues, an individualized music-making form. So, changes in the worldview of Black people also led to a decline in the popularity of string bands. The rural string band tradition reminded many of their humble rural origins, while rhythm and blues bands, in contrast, suggested the liberated sounds of urban life. In the 1940s and 1950s the demand for string band music dwindled remarkably, causing many groups to disband, and individual musicians (especially fiddlers) to give up playing altogether. Therefore, although fiddlers existed, they had no occasions to perform their music.

Some changes are specific to Mississippi. When racial tensions increased during the 1930s, white people in the larger mid-South regions refused to hire Black musicians to play at events, resulting in a decrease in the number of African American string bands that played for both races. As the rural electrification program expanded in the late 1950s to include African American communities, the number of string bands declined when audiences demanded the new electric sound of blues musicians. The majority of Black fiddlers who continued to perform focused on furnishing music for their families and neighbors. By 1960, older musicians once prominent in performing fiddle and banjo or string band music had faded from the scene, thus rendering both age-old traditions obsolete (Oliver 1996, 357–58; 390–92).

Blues. Like other regions in Mississippi, African American musicians in the eastern Hills counties developed their own blues style with varied influences.[97]

As Oliver (1996) explains: "Besides the strong influence from the Appalachian Mountain music of reels and fiddle and banjo tunes, it had a powerful African American musical counter influence after the turn of the century. The jug bands, string bands, jazz and ragtime, and blues were all a part of the nearby Memphis musical scene, which affected both the repertoire and style of playing of musicians who lived here" (400). Although most blues singers in the eastern Hills counties sang to the accompaniment of guitars, other instruments (such as drums, fiddles, banjos, jew's harps, harmonicas, mandolins, and string bass) were used from the earliest days (Oliver 1996, 404). Most interesting for this study is that many of the old blues singers consciously or unconsciously integrated fiddle and banjo tunes and techniques into the new musicking they were playing.

Of the Black fiddlers who specialized in blues and were active in the eastern Hills counties during the early twentieth century, extensive information, to my knowledge, is available on only one—Ernest "Boose" Taylor who was born and raised in Marshall County.[98] Taylor was living in Collierville, a small town in Shelby County, Tennessee, about thirty miles east of Memphis when Frederic Hay (2001) interviewed him in 1972. US census records indicate that Taylor moved to Tennessee sometime between 1920 and 1930 when he was in his early twenties.

Although the fiddle was his primary instrument, Taylor also played the fife (his first instrument) as well as the guitar, like his father and younger brothers.[99] As Hay (2001, 113, 121) explains, all were probably participants in the regional style described by Oliver (1996). Yet, it is noteworthy that Taylor did not begin playing the fiddle until he was in his late teens:[100]

> I heard another fellow play and I told that fellow, "I sure want me one of them things." And [it was] the first time I'd ever had seen one. . . . I was just about a grown man. And this fellow played it. . . . I was wanting to put it in my hand but he wouldn't let me look at it. . . . I reckon he thought it was too precious. And I told him, "I'm going to get me one." He said, "Well, if you get one . . . you got to go to school and learn how to play it." I said, "Well, I may have to do that but I'm going to get me one if I have to study so hard where I got a song." . . . He didn't let me sees his and so I was working, I was working wages for a fellow. (Hay 2001, 115–16)

The way Taylor acquired and learned to play the fiddle is also interesting because it provides more detailed insight on how musicians received training from others:

> [When Taylor told the wife of the person he was working for that he wanted a fiddle], she say, "Alright, I order you one." After it come, I didn't know how to tune it up. So, my brother [Richard], he could play a guitar. . . . He tuned it up and played the first piece on it. And handed it to me and told me, "If I had to play this thing, I'd leave my home. I wouldn't stay here." And so . . . he didn't never play it

no more. So, I sawed around, . . . tried to play it. And some fellows came to my house that could play guitar. They were old fellows. So, I get my fiddle. I say, "I going to try to do something with y'all." So, I try a little piece along with them, . . . and done pretty good. Then, they finally left; then I just took it on my own. I don't play no fiddle like people play 'em. I learned another way to play. I play with a guitar all the time. I play the song like I sing a song. . . . Sometimes my brother would sing a verse. Then I would sing a verse. That's the way we played. People would be glad to hear us anytime. They'd say, "The Taylor boys are going to play at such and such place." So, I just picked it up by myself. (Hay 2001, 116–17, 147)

After learning, Taylor states that he and his family members walked to the houses of neighbors and friends at different locations in the community and played for dances. Most activities occurred in Marshall County, where nearly two-thirds of the African Americans in the entire region lived.[101] His repertoire included various types of blues songs: "Drop Down Mama and Let Your Daddy See," "Too Many Mornings," "Run Here, Baby, Let Me Smell Your Hand," "Got to the Bottom Up and Go," and "Tease Me Over Blues." In addition to songs they created on their own, Taylor indicates that they performed religious songs, "Give Me That Old Time Religion," for church people when they passed their house on Sunday mornings.[102] But they did not go to church themselves (Hay 2001, 150). Taylor's life experiences are interesting because he, like some fiddlers in this study (for example, Freeman and Baxter), began to experiment with new traditions because of the interests of those in his community. However, Taylor's innovations appear to have been modest because of the region where he lived. Blues in the eastern Hills counties were noted for the inclusion of fiddle and banjo tunes and techniques from old-time music into their musicking.

The Mississippi Hills Region: Western Counties

The fiddling of Black people in the western Hills counties is noteworthy in several ways. Similar to eastern counties, the western Hills counties reflected the musicking of a shared culture. Performing tunes identified with European Americans ("Buffalo Girls" and "Turkey in the Straw") and African Americans ("I'm Alabama Bound," "Stagolee," and "Shoo Shoo Mama") was common practice. In addition, some fiddlers in the Hills were just as well-known as those from the Delta, where musicking was strongly African American (Evans 1999b).

Due to the research of Alan Lomax and others between the 1930 and 1960, we know that the performance of fiddle music in the Hills western counties continued through the mid-twentieth century, but its development differed from fiddling in eastern counties because of its close proximity to the Delta. On the one hand, musicking in the Delta was constantly changing partly due to the interactions of its residents with traveling musicians (on the Mississippi River, the railroad, and state highways) as well as the media (radio and television), all of which provided opportunities to be introduced to new musical ideas. Not only did a fresh style of music develop every ten or fifteen years, each style, typical of the self-renewing flow of the African American tradition, more or less obliterated the one before it. On the other hand, the Hills was a backwater in which various types of older music lived on as farmland was turned over to Black people. In towns such as Como in Panola County, musicians continued to play music from nineteenth-century country picnics (Southern Journey 1997). Yet, the situation was not as straightforward as it appears. As will be demonstrated in the material below, older traditions continued to be performed in the Delta in new and interesting ways, and musicians in the western Hills counties occasionally embraced the new in their own manner.

To understand the dynamics and features of Black fiddling in Southern Appalachia's neighboring Mississippi regions, the lives and musicking of several fiddlers are examined. Sidney Hemphill and Robert Pratcher are from the western Mississippi Hills counties. Thomas Jefferson Dumas is from the Pines region, but moved to the Delta region later in life. No doubt, other Black fiddlers were active, but details on them are almost nonexistent. For example, the only information on Henry McClatching, a fiddler identified by WPA researchers during the 1930s, is the fact that he lived in Wyatte, a small community in Tate County (among the western Hills counties), and is known to have performed two songs—"N----r in the Tater House" and "Possum Up the Simmon Tree"— that WPA collectors transcribed for their study (Bolick and Austin 2015, 140–41).

Sidney Hemphill (1876–1961)[103]

On August 15, 1942, Alan Lomax traveled to Sledge, a small town in Quitman County, to meet Sid Hemphill, a Black fiddler who had been recommended to him by a musician in Clarksdale.[104] Hemphill was a blind musician who had lived his entire life in Panola County, which is one county east of Quitman. For more than fifty years, he had earned a living entertaining both white and Black audiences at house dances, picnics, circuses, churches, and other events in rural communities from Memphis through the Delta and the Hills (Lomax 1993, 334). Like many fiddlers in rural areas, Hemphill was a multi-instrumentalist. In addition to the fiddle (see photo 9.10a), he played guitar, drums, mandolin, banjo, harmonica, fife, and quills (panpipes).[105] His group, which included three other musicians (Lucius Smith on banjo, Alec Askew on guitar, and Will Head on bass drum), could alternately be a fife and drum band consisting of cane fife, two snare drums and bass drum, which by 1942 had become a substitute for the bass fiddle,[106] or a string band including fiddle, banjo, guitar, bass fiddle, and the kazoo (or jazz horn). The group's repertoire consisted mainly of fiddle

Photo 9.10a. Sidney Hemphill (fiddle) and Lucius Smith (banjo). Senatobia, Tate County, Mississippi. September 22, 1959. From the Alan Lomax Collection at the American Folklife Center, Library of Congress. Courtesy of the Association for Cultural Equity.

tunes, blues ballads (used for dancing), and spirituals. Hemphill's father, Dock, also a fiddler born around 1840 in Choctaw County in the Mississippi Pines region, learned how to play the fiddle from his first cousin. Hemphill's brothers were musicians, as were his three daughters, and granddaughter, the blues singer-guitarist, Jessie Mae Hemphill (1923–2006).[107] Therefore, playing the fiddle was a family tradition. In his 1942 interview with Lomax (1993), Hemphill explained: My father "played fiddle and farmed. It was six of us boys played music. And one didn't. Seven. We had a whole family band, before the boys all married and their wives stopped them" (333–34).[108] Lucius Smith indicated that when they played string music with the drum, the "fiddle would go louder than the drum. . . . A fiddle is the leading music of the whole world, outa all the music. The fiddle leads all the music and the banjo's the next" (338).

For Alan Lomax, the 1942 recording session in Sledge was historic because it confirmed that fiddle tunes ("Arkansas Traveller," "The Eighth of January," and "Leather Britches") Hemphill and his group performed, which researchers previously identified solely with European Americans, were, in fact, part of Mississippi's Black and white shared music culture. As Evans (1978a) explains, "When one also considers the rarity of recordings of black string bands, it becomes apparent that this 1942 session is one of the most important of all time in the documentation of black folk music" (3). Although Hemphill performed both church songs and reels, which varied in content and performance, but had remained unchanged since the early 1900s,[109] "most of the session was devoted to local ballads he had himself composed early in the century. Two of the songs had more than twenty-five verses and all commemorated local characters and events: train wrecks, bad men, and jail breaks" (Wade 1999).

"The Carrier Line" ["The Carrier Railroad"], a blues ballad that combines the narrative quality of balladry with the loose, shifting, and subjective approach of blues singing,[110] was performed by Hemphill singing and playing the fiddle, accompanied by musicians in his group performing banjo, guitar, and bass drum. Hemphill wrote "The Carrier Line" in 1903 when a white section foreman on the Sardis and Delta Railroad Line asked him to compose it.[111] The fact that the song was commissioned by a white male, the main characters of the story are white, and Hemphill often performed this tune for white audiences could be the reason a string band was used in performance instead of another ensemble of instruments (Evans 1978a, 11, 1999a).

In terms of fiddling, however, the musical characteristics Hemphill used demonstrate that his musicking is similar to but also different from that of other musicians. Roughly six minutes in length, Hemphill's performance of "The Carrier Line" can be divided into three sections: opening, middle, and closing with solo fiddling serving as markers of different sections. In this performance and on other tunes (see discussion below), the fiddle part is not the lead, but serves as an accompaniment to Hemphill's half singing/half speaking twenty-four verses of text.[112] The main melody for each verse comprises twenty-two quarter note beats of music, and the fiddle plays the melody in its entirety only three times: once during the opening (0:12–0:20), and twice during the middle (1:05–1:12 and 4:48–4:55). During the remaining part of the performance, Hemphill plays an off-beat melodic pattern on the fiddle using double stops and a bowing style that produces a shuffling percussive sound, a characteristic feature of his fiddling and common to other Black fiddlers in this study.

In "Arkansas Traveller," a ballad that has become common stock, Hemphill's musicking begins with the shuffling of the fiddle and a sung introduction. Like "The Carrier Line," the rest of the performance includes him half-singing/half-speaking and the occasional playing on the fiddle in a continuous shuffling style. The musicking in "Hog Hunt," performed by Hemphill (voice and fiddle) and his accompanying musicians, suggests the sound of hounds and mounted hunters pursuing a wild hog. Although this type of music is typical of models in the British Isles, African American musicians have often modified performances by varying the tempo, including percussive sounds, bent notes, and other vocal effects. Hemphill's performances are particularly noteworthy because of his blindness and sensitivity to the sounds of dogs, roosters, trains, horse races, and crying babies (Evans 1999a). "Skillet Good and Greasy" ["Keep My Skillet Greasy If I Can"] is another common stock song known to have been performed by European Americans (Uncle Dave Macon's 1924 recording and Ozark singer Almeda Riddle's text of "Mandy") and African Americans (Henry Thomas's

Photo 9.11. Bob Pratcher (fiddle). Como, Panola County, Mississippi. September 21, 1959. From the Alan Lomax Collection at the American Folklife Center, Library of Congress. Courtesy of the Association for Cultural Equity.

"Shanty Blues" in 1927 and the Mississippi Sheiks' "Bootlegger's Blues" in 1930). In 1940, Work III printed a version of the tune in his *American Negro Songs* "that incorporates a 'rabbit in the log' verse that Hemphill also employs. An aspect of the song's meaning emerges in the Work text when it says: 'O de rabbit's in de log, / I ain't got no rabbit dog / Goin' to keep my baby eatin' if I can'" (Wade 1999).

Because Hemphill performs with little melodic and rhythmic improvisation, some may think his music is derived or influenced solely by elements from Anglo-American culture, not realizing that Hemphill's music reflects the experiences and aesthetics of African American musicians in the early twentieth century. By linking antebellum musicking to genres (blues) that evolved in later years, Hemphill's music continued to be a living tradition among African Americans. When Lomax returned to Mississippi in 1959, "he revisited Sid Hemphill and another surviving member of his band.[113] Recordings of a guitar and fiddle combination, the nucleus of a string band, as well as another outstanding fife and drum band, some singers of children's songs, and several excellent singers of spiritual were made at this time" (Evans 1978a, 3). Therefore, Black fiddling in the Mississippi Hills was still somewhat intact, although almost twenty years had passed.[114] Commenting on the importance of Hemphill's music, Wade (1999) writes: "If Tennessee is the 'center of gravity' [for Appalachian music] . . . then Hemphill symbolizes its unifying force. He brings together the string band music of the old-time repertoire. . . . At the same time, his performances at local

Photo 9.12. Bob Pratcher (fiddle) and Miles Pratcher (guitar) on Ed Young's porch. Como, Panola County, Mississippi. September 21, 1959. From the Alan Lomax Collection at the American Folklife Center, Library of Congress. Courtesy of the Association for Cultural Equity.

picnics connect to the experiences of the street musicians.... His approach to balladry anticipates the blues..., while it links to the songster repertoire that opens it.... Hemphill... is continuity."

Robert "Bob" Pratcher (1892–1968)

When Lomax conducted research in the western Hills counties in September 1959, he made recordings of two brothers, Bob Pratcher (fiddle) and Miles Pratcher (guitar), who both lived in the small community of Como in Panola County (see photos 9.11 and 9.12).[115] Of the six tunes the Pratchers recorded with fiddle and guitar, three—"All Night Long" ["If It's All Night Long"], "Buttermilk" and "I'm Gonna Live Anyhow till I Die"—have been released on several recordings produced by Lomax.[116] On all recordings, both men sing but only Bob performs the fiddle.[117] Lomax provides no biographical information about the artists in his liner notes, because "there appears to have been no interview recorded" (Bolick 2021b). Yet, he does include a discussion of the uniqueness and similarities of the Pratchers' performances to musicking in Mississippi. Lomax (1960) states that "they played the old reels for square dancing and they played rags like 'Bully of the Town' and many raggy blues.... Their music represents an early, important, but little known stage in the development of the blues, for the fiddle and banjo were the common instruments of country Negroes before the guitar and piano became dominant. Note the heavily-bowed, swinging fiddle style and the relatively unornamented melodic line. Here the blues are still happy." For the tunes "Buttermilk" and "I'm Gonna Live Anyhow till I Die," Lomax (1977) writes: "There is a distinctively African approach to the solo-string accompanied type, heard in these recordings and common elsewhere only in Africa. A rather open voice with playful vocal quality, often employing rasp, falsetto, and glissando, performs a simple repetitive melody (often one phrase with variation, in descending cadence) in rich antiphonal and cross-rhythmed interplay with the instrument, which sustains a driving rhythm in a simple ostinato pattern under the voice and then breaks out between vocal phrases" (2).

Regarding "Buttermilk's" similarity to other Appalachian tunes, Lomax explains: "This is a black string band playing more old-time square-dance music of the type once common to the whole frontier, white and black, yet with many traits linking it to the blues—a driving ostinato figure; the instrumental part in complementary and overlapped antiphony with the voice; the voice changeful and playful; polyrhythms among vocal part, handclapping, and orchestra; and finally a plethora of blued notes in both vocal and instrumental parts" (7). Concerning "I'm Gonna Live Anyhow till I Die," he states that "[It is] one of a family of tunes lying between black square-dance music, like 'Buttermilk,' and the first true instrumental blues. . . . The strophic form, standard in frontier balladry, appears in a new and sophisticated guise, graced with blue notes and backed up by a catchy dance beat. In this text, the dancing, drinking crowd defies the hellfire—intimidated churchly folk, who disapprove of their sinful ways, saying 'What you say about me don't worry me none; I'm gonna live how I please, and when I die I'll just be dead, that's all'" (8). "All Night Long"[118] is noteworthy for features identified with the blues: a repetitive ten-bar blues melody using the I, IV, V, I chord progression and the prominence of flatted thirds and sevenths in both the vocal and fiddle melody. As Scott Linford (2013b) explains: "Whereas old-time music tends to be dance tunes that have words, singing is much more important here. And the fiddle's role in the music is different. It is more of a supporting instrument; it's going along in the background, playing along with the voice at certain times." When compared to other Black fiddlers in the study, Linford indicates that Pratcher's fiddling sounds more like Freeman in Georgia. "The two fiddlers are not that far part. They play different roles in the mix [Freeman performs the lead part in his group, while Pratcher takes on the supporting role in his performances]. But the actual style is not that different. Pratcher has a similar rough attack mixed with sweeter notes. He also performs some nice rhythmic patterns. A lot of the rhythmic figures are the same even though he doesn't use them in the same way. But there is a similar rhythmic approach to the bowing, and the loose approach to pitch is pretty similar to it."

The Mississippi Pines Region

Thomas Jefferson Dumas (1888–1980)

Information about Black fiddling in the Mississippi Pines region is limited, especially when compared to data that exists on fiddlers in other regions of the state (see figure 9.1). It is unknown if this is because there were no Black fiddlers, or the fact that this is an area that has been overlooked in terms of research. From the available evidence, Thomas Dumas, who was born in Bellefontaine, a small community in Webster County in the Pines region, is one of the few Black fiddlers who was active in the region during the early twentieth century.[119] Dumas's life history is interesting because, in 1924 (when he was thirty-six years told), he moved from his birthplace and permanently settled in Tallahatchie County in the Mississippi Delta region. Although the actual move does not differ from that of other fiddlers in this study, it is significant that Dumas did not relocate to another state (similar to Bertram and Rice) or settle in a larger town or city within the state like other Black Mississippi fiddlers.[120] Rather, Dumas took up residence in a small community not very different in terms of size from the area he was born.[121] The primary difference is that from the 1900s through the 1960s, Webster County (his birthplace) had a majority white population, while the population in Tallahatchie County (where he relocated) was majority Black (see figure 9.1). The degree to which these factors affected musicking and, more specifically Black fiddling, are issues that will be addressed in the following. In many ways, Dumas's life history[122] will help us understand why some Black fiddlers continued to perform the fiddle when it was rejected by many within African American culture. In Dumas's case, it was members of the majority Black community where he lived during the latter part of life who gave him little support.

In interviews with journalists during the 1970s, Dumas, who worked as a farmer the majority of his life, indicated that he started playing the fiddle as well as other instruments when he was a child; also, he learned to play them on his own: "When I was about nine years old, they [the family] went to church. Me and my other brother, the one next to me, didn't want to [go to] church one Sunday, and I picked up the fiddle—it was left there in good tune—I picked up the fiddle and commenced playing. I commenced playing the fiddle just as good as if I'd been playing it fifty years, while my brother never did learn, ain't never learned yet, never did learn nothing. I commenced playing. And when my daddy come home, my sister, the third child, told my daddy. . . . [She] said 'Pa, Tom and Fulton playing your old fiddle'" (Brown 1976).

After being reprimanded by his father for "messing with the fiddle," this did not stop Dumas's interest in wanting to play the instrument. In fact, when his sister spoke to the father again about Dumas and the fiddle, she stated: "Thomas

Photo 9.13. Tom Dumas with his fiddle at his home in Tutwiler, Mississippi, 1968. Courtesy of William Ferris.

'can play the fiddle just as good as you can.' With that, his father handed him the instrument, and he began to play that thing in the best rhythm possible since he was too young at the time to pat his foot on the floor. His father was so proud of his clever son that he took him to play for the white folks at Bellefontaine and Walthall. Pretty soon, he started carrying his son around all the time to play the fiddle" (quoted in Moore 2021b, 148). Therefore, when reporters asked how he learned to play the instrument, he often responded by stating: "Nobody taught me how to play the fiddle, I taught myself. I picked it up and went to playing and played just as good when I picked it up as I could. . . . I picked up a banjo done the same thing, picked up a guitar done the same thing, jew's harp done the same thing, tried to blow the French harp for ten years and never could blow a tune on it" (Brown 1976).

Playing the fiddle had been a tradition in the Dumas family for years; their family history indicates that the fiddle Dumas played most of his life was one that belonged to Andrew Jackson, the ninth president of the United States (see photo 9.13). In interviews, Dumas explained: "After he [Andrew Jackson] died, he gave it [the fiddle] to one of his slaves. Well, that [person] was some relation to my daddy, I reckon some way or another. And when he died then, well my daddy got it. Daddy died in 1941. Daddy had the fiddle when I was born. . . . My daddy played it every night" (Brown 1976).[123]

Dumas's life as a fiddler started when he was a youth and organized a string band. Explaining how his performance career began, Dumas stated:

In 1897, we got us up a little bitty band. We got a banjo, a guitar, a mandolin and fiddle. We played music then from 1897 on up until 1905. I finally just quit the fiddling business and we just stowed away our music.

I played fiddle at dances all night long and all day. In the wintertime, why we'd have dances every night. We had dances over there at Eupora [largest city in Webster County in the Pines region], have dances over there at Kilmichael [town in Montgomery County in the Pines region], and up there at Houston [one of the seats for Chickasaw County in the Pines region], and Calhoun City [town in Calhoun County in the Hills region]. We'd just go out and play for everybody then. We'd get in a wagon and stay there all night long, just make music all night. I've played a fiddle many a night all night long, what we call the old square dance, one fellow calling the act, letting the people know what to do.

Quit the first music in 1905 and we started back the second music in 1930. We stayed up there in Vance [community in Quitman/Tallahatchie counties in the Delta region], play out here on the Cagles Crossing [community in Coahoma County in the Delta region], play over there at Shelby [town in Bolivar County in the Delta region]—out all where white folks was, we never did play for no colored folks because they in the Delta didn't like it. (Brown 1976)

When he started playing the fiddle again in 1930 after relocating, Dumas indicated that only a few in the Delta appreciated his musicking: "Yessir, we used to have music. But there ain't been a colored fellow since I been here fifty-two years that ever have enjoyed music. In that café, some of the women would get me to bring my fiddle out there and play for them some night. Well, I'd drink a little whisky then, I'd go out here and tune up my fiddle and commence playing a little. They'd have Seeburgs [jukeboxes] in there and they'd turn them on just as loud as they could, dada-dump dada-dump dada-dump, and I'd just pick my fiddle up and walk on out. You see these white folks still got the old-timey music in them yet, but these other folks hasn't; they done made a change. I have never changed yet" (Brown 1976).

Although Dumas was well known in his community for being a musician, and received much recognition in local newspaper articles for his musicking, he was actually misrepresented. Interestingly, this misleading representation was noted in one of the publications: "He was reported to be last of the blues players of Tutwiler, but one of his granddaughters said that was not true. 'No, he didn't play the blues. He played mostly country and western. He played the banjo and the fiddle.' The confusion apparently derived from the fact Dumas played his music in the Tutwiler area back when W. C. Handy was playing in the same area and giving birth to the blues. Dumas did know Handy, but he never played with him" (Brown 1976). This discrepancy also suggests that Dumas's lack of popularity was not because he performed the fiddle. Rather, community members were not pleased that his musical preference was old-time music. If he had performed the blues, a genre not only known but also admired by some members of the Black community, the disconnect probably would not have occurred, because other Black fiddlers in the Delta region during this period performed blues on the fiddle (see discussion below).

Like most musicians, Dumas succeeded as a fiddler by playing for audiences that appreciated his musicking—both the instrument and the type of music he performed. While his supporters in the Pines region included both Blacks and whites, those in the Delta region were all-white. For this study, Dumas's life history raises another interesting issue in considering reasons Black fiddling is not appreciated by some in the Black community. Both the instrument and the type of music performed on the instrument must be taken into consideration.

Summary

In separating the Appalachians into two distinct regions (Central and Southern), it becomes apparent that slight variations existed. The evidence indicates that demographics was an important, but not the sole criterion for the continued interest in old-time music among some Blacks during the early twentieth century. Similar to the misconception that scholars (Southern 1997 and Epstein 1977) made regarding the prominence of fiddling among Blacks before the 1900s—that is, African Americans performed the fiddle solely because of its association with whites—other factors seem to have caused the continued popularity of the instrument among rural Blacks in Southern Appalachia during the early twentieth century. One of the most important is the fact that pressure to adopt new genres, particularly those identified with the city, did not appear to be as great in small towns, where change tended to be slow. Therefore, fiddlers continued to be active in small rural communities that had majority Black populations because this is the music that some community members enjoyed, especially when fiddlers used a performance style that was African-derived. Commenting on the musicking and repertoire of rural Black fiddlers in the early twentieth century, Wiggins (1977) writes: "There were some fiddle tunes of British origin, no doubt. There probably was stuff of minstrel-show origin. Whatever we might guess *a priori*, the evidence is that such stuff was heartily accepted by blacks. Collections of black songs are full of it, and are the easiest place to find verses which have racial derogation as their very essence. There would, no doubt, have been some vagrant 'heart songs.' But the most interesting possibility is that there would have remained some African influence, in style, if not in substance" (6–7).

By the same token, demographics may have played a role in other aspects of the tradition. For example, not only was the sharing of musical ideas between the Blacks and whites in Southern Appalachia not as extensive as in Central Appalachia and even the Ozarks, where fewer African Americans lived, differences existed in the repertoire and ensemble organization of Black and white fiddlers. While some rural Black southern Appalachians preferred old-time music, others were interested in new genres that were becoming popular among many African Americans during the early twentieth century. What is significant is that some were satisfied in hearing the new genres performed on the fiddle. In such situations, blues may have been appreciated because it was new, but also it served as an act of protest against whites and European-derived culture where social conditions were the most repressive. Although the banjo continued to be performed, it was used less in performing the blues, resulting in greater prominence of the guitar within African American musicking. Because the amount of information on Black fiddling in the southern Appalachians is uneven, with fewer examples for each state, making conclusions is difficult. The above should be regarded as tendencies until more data becomes available and analyzed.

fiddlingismyjoycompanion.net

Notes

1. 🎻 See Map 9.1, Map 9.2, Land Regions 9.1, and History 9.1.
2. Most research on Black secular music in South Carolina has been conducted in the Low Country, where the large number of Blacks on the coast helped stimulate interest in Gullah Geechee culture on the Sea Islands rather than musicking in the piedmont and mountain areas. The Sea Islands are also where African practices are dominant; see Guy and Candie Carawan (1994, 1995); Guy Johnson (1930); George Starks (1973, 1985, 1991); and John Szwed (1970).
3. Walker was interviewed by researchers documenting the cultural history of African Americans who lived near the Savannah River (Kane and Keeton 1994). US census records indicate that Henry Bryant was the second eldest of six children born to Hal Bryant Sr. (1858–1926) and Julia Williams Bryant (1861–1951). Henry and his wife, Minerva Thompson Bryant (1878–1940), gave birth to one daughter, Louella Bryant Walker (1900–2000). All family members were born and lived in Abbeville County.
4. 🎻 See Demographics 9.1.
5. 🎻 See Demographics 9.2.
6. 🎻 See Map 9.3, Map 9.4, Land Regions 9.2, and History 9.2.
7. For a select list of sources (print and audio) on religious music, see Parish (1942); Cogdell (1972); DjeDje (1978c, 1983); Georgia Sea Island Songs (1977), Rosenbaum (1984c); Reagon (1994); Georgia Sea Islands (1998); and Rosenbaum and Buis (1998).
8. Sources (print and audio) on secular music include Lowry and Bastin (1974/75); Bastin and Lowry (1975a, 1975b); Bastin (1978, 1986); Rosenbaum (1983, 1984a, 1984b, 1984c); Jones and Hawes (1987); Bastin and Green (1989); and Cureau (1989).
9. See Lowry (1977); Nemerov (1987, 2008); Wiggins and Russell (1977); and *Now What a Time* (2000).
10. 🎻 See Repertoire 9.2. (for Freeman) and Repertoire 9.3 (for Rakestraw) to view details about the songs that were collected.
11. 🎻 See Demographics 9.3.
12. In 1898, *Strand Magazine* published six pages on Georgia barbecues (Watkins 1898, 463–68), including details about the preparation and type of food eaten. In 1902, *Wide World Magazine* reprinted the article but added a photograph with the caption "A Barbecue Orchestra at Work," which provided visual representation of four Black instrumentalists (one fiddler, two guitarists, and what looks like a jug player) entertaining the white guests (Wiley 1902, 190).
13. This photograph may also be the earliest visual evidence of the jug being used as a wind instrument in the context of African American culture. In North Carolina, Hinson (1978, 1) indicates that the "thumping of the washtub bass and jug" provided a percussive sound to accompany reels and other dance tunes performed at recreational activities attended by Blacks, but little evidence exists of the jug being used as a wind instrument to accompany string band music; the exception includes a discussion of Black string bands in Kentucky by Ware (1981, 33).
14. As noted earlier, Eddie Anthony, a Black fiddler based in Atlanta, made commercial recordings with several musicians during the late 1920s and early 1930s (Dixon and Godrich 1982, 343–44). Because the focus of this study is rural-based Black fiddlers, a discussion of Anthony is limited here.

15. US census records indicate that Andrew's parents, father Willis Baxter (b. ca. 1827) and mother Jane Baxter (b. ca. 1837), had nine children: six females and three males. Andrew was the sixth child and second oldest male. Andrew had two wives: Nancy Hogan Baxter (1874–1930) and Leola Hamer Baxter (1901–1976). With his first wife, Andrew had two daughters (Irene and Laura) and one son, James, who was the youngest of the three. Andrew had no children with his second wife.

16. 🎵 See Demographics 9.4 and 9.5.

17. Pre-1945 recordings of "Katy Hill" are limited. The first recording was by Allen Sisson (fiddle) and John Burckhardt (piano) on Edison Records in New York City on February 26, 1925. Bill Monroe and His Blue Grass Boys recorded the tune in Atlanta in October 1940 (Russell and Pinson 2004, 631, 836).

18. Although a native of Cherokee County, Alabama, Shores spent much of his adult life in Rome, Georgia (Wolfe 1977a, 4). There is no way of knowing if Shores is referring to the Rakestraw family, Black fiddlers who lived in northeast Georgia near Athens, and were noted for playing old-time music in their community during the early twentieth century.

19. Established in 1924, the fiddle convention celebrating north Georgia's string band tradition continues in Calhoun in present day. For online comments about the festival by Paul Shoffner, an organizer of the Calhoun festival, see Gadaya (2010).

20. Jim Booker's April 1927 recording with Taylor's Kentucky Boys is the only documented evidence of an earlier recording of old-time music by a racially mixed group. Although Black and white people played music together in a variety of other settings locally, a practice that began before the Civil War, the integrated recording session was rare for the 1920s (Wyatt 1999).

21. 🎵 See Repertoire 9.1.

22. "'G Rag' uses a tune generally associated with Alabama fiddler Wyzee Hamilton, who recorded it in 1926 as 'Hamilton's Special Breakdown'" (Wyatt 2001, 23).

23. Songs by Blacks referring to trains with the phrase, "Thought I heard that K. C. whistle blow," date to the early 1900s (Odum 1911a, 287; 1911b, 360–61). See chapter 12 for a discussion of Butch Cage's use of the phrase in his performance of "44 Blues."

24. The two blues songs by the Baxters ("Bamalong Blues" and "K. C. Railroad Blues") were issued together, while "The Moore Song" was paired with "Never Let the Same Bee Sting You Twice," a song from an earlier (March 1927) session that Victor recorded with New Orleans blues guitarist and composer Richard "Rabbit" Brown (Bastin 1986, 39).

25. These individuals were identified as managers for recording purposes only. Most often they were record or music store owners who acted as talent scouts for record companies.

26. 🎵 See Repertoire 6.1.

27. See discussion of this issue in chapter 6.

28. 🎵 See Repertoire 9.1.

29. Odum (1911, 261) confirms that train songs, which are derived from their imitation of the running train, were popular among African Americans. Yet, the train and travel were themes used in the lyrics of all types of songs during the late nineteenth and early twentieth centuries, including musicians who performed old-time music, blues, and jazz. Trains were easy metaphors for popular songs, signifying arrivals, departures, and other key stops on the long journey of life (Leggett 1998).

30. During the early twentieth century, blues was not appealing to many white people, especially those in Appalachia; it was a new musical form identified primarily with Black culture.

31. Also, see discussion in Record Fiend 2010.

32. 🎵 Go to Audio Examples to listen to a performance of "Hamilton's Special Breakdown." Although Wyatt (2001, 23) gives 1926 as the date of Hamilton's recording with Victor, other sources indicate January 1927 (Russell and Pinson 2004, 393). The first names of Hamilton's accompanying musicians are unknown, but the surnames are Tucker (banjo) and Lecroy (guitar).

33. 🎵 Go to Audio Examples to listen to a performance of "G Rag" by Andrew Baxter and the Georgia Yellow Hammers.

34. 🎵 See Form 9.1.

35. Regarding the provenance of this tune, George Walburn and Emmett Hethcox write: "This simple country tune, recorded by OKeh in Atlanta, Georgia, in June of 1925, is performed by the guys who also wrote the classic 'Kansas City Railroad Blues' (recorded by Bill Monroe in the mid-50's, and dozens of others since)—despite the similarity in the titles, one tune is very different from the other." http://machine-whisperer.com/music/kcrail.html. Accessed July 29, 2023.

36. ♪ See Lyrics 9.1.

37. ♪ See Lyrics 9.1. Unfortunately, only the text to "Thought I Heard That K. C. Blow" appears in publications (Odum 1911b, 360–61; Odum and Johnson 1925, 225–26). To my knowledge, no sound versions of the tune are available.

38. Regarding train songs, Odum (1911a, 261) provides a detailed description on how a string instrument (fiddle or guitar) is performed to imitate the sound of a moving train.

39. ♪ Go to Audio Examples to listen to a performance of "K. C. [Kansas City] Railroad Blues" by Andrew and James Baxter.

40. ♪ See Form 9.2.

41. ♪ See Map 9.3 and Map 9.4, and Demographics 9.6.

42. Fort Valley State College (now known as Fort Valley State University) began as the Fort Valley High and Industrial School in 1895. In 1939, the school merged with the State Teachers and Agricultural College of Forsyth (founded in 1902) to become Fort Valley State College; for details, see "Fort Valley State University" (2012).

43. Although many faculty and students at Black colleges during the late nineteenth and early twentieth centuries performed and promoted the concert spiritual, which included performance practices similar to European art music, only a few, if any, performed or were involved in traditions that related to vernacular culture. Therefore, the participation of Black faculty in the Fort Valley College festival was innovative. Also see discussion in chapter 7.

44. ♪ Also see History 7.2. In January 1941, Horace Mann Bond invited Alan Lomax to attend and document the college's second annual festival. When Lomax discovered he could not make it, he arranged for Work III to attend in his place; Work III's recordings were donated to the Library of Congress at the same time he deposited his Nashville material. Some recordings have been released on LP (*Fort Valley Blues* 1973) and discussed in Lowry and Bastin (1974/75). In 1943, the Library of Congress had activities at the festival documented again. Lewis Wade Jones, a graduate and sociology professor at Fisk, and Willis Laurence James, the Fort Valley festival director and music professor at Spelman College, recorded several performances between March 5 and 7, 1943. James was also a member of the summer faculty at Fort Valley from 1941 to 1949 (Maher 2000, *Now What a Time* 2000, Jacobs 2009).

45. By the 1940s and 1950s, most record companies were promoting primarily urban genres such as rhythm and blues, jazz, and some religious music.

46. Monticello, the seat for Jasper County, is located about sixty-five miles north of Fort Valley, thirty-seven miles north of Macon, and sixty-one miles southeast of Atlanta.

47. US census records indicate that Freeman's paternal grandfather, Henry Freeman (ca. 1840–1915), lived in Walton County, about thirty miles north of Jasper County, as a youth and moved to Jasper County after emancipation. While Freeman's father, Elbert Sr. (1866–1910), had lived most of his life in Jasper County, Elbert Jr.'s mother, Florine Johnson Freeman (b. ca. 1888), was from Clarke County, also located in the piedmont about sixty miles northeast of Jasper. Elbert Sr. and Florine had two children: Elbert Jr. and a daughter, Della (b. ca. 1904). Elbert Jr. and his wife Lucy Hancock Freeman (ca. 1902–1995), who, like her husband, had been born and raised in Jasper County, had one daughter, Mattie Lou Freeman Gordon (1918–1989).

48. ♪ See Demographics 9.7.

49. ♪ See History 9.3.

50. ♪ See Repertoire 9.2.

51. Two pre-1945 recordings (for instruments only) were made of "Tennessee Waltz" (all by white artists): one by Paul Warmack and His Gully Jumpers on September 28, 1928, and another by the Roane County Ramblers on October 15, 1928. The lyrics for "Tennessee Waltz" were written by Redd Stewart and Pee Wee King in 1946 and released in 1948. The recording of

"Tennessee Waltz" by white pop singer Patti Page resulted in a big hit for her in 1950 (Russell and Pinson 2004, 751, 939). "Chattanoogie Shoe Shine Boy," written by Harry Stone and Jack Stapp in 1950, was the signature song for white country musician Red Foley who recorded it in 1950 (Leggett n.d.a).

52. ♪ See History 9.4.

53. In addition to Burrison's field notes, the recording compiled by Bastin (1978) contains three field recordings—"Worried Blues," "John Henry," and "Old Hen Cackled"—performed by Elbert Freeman (fiddle) and Nathaniel Ford (guitar).

54. ♪ See Repertoire 9.2.

55. Burrison indicates that he limited the recording session to a few tunes because of "the unnatural surroundings of the studios," but added: "One of (my) students returned several weeks later to conduct an interview with Elbert but simply could not locate him" (Bastin 1978, 10–11).

56. ♪ See Repertoire 9.2.

57. Livers was an entertainer and performer known for his diverse repertoire because he learned many of his tunes from listening to the media; most likely, this was also the case with Freeman. Whereas white listeners in the late twentieth and early twenty-first centuries appreciate Black fiddlers performing old-time music, Black audiences do not. For example, Joe Thompson, in North Carolina, received acclaim primarily from white people because of his maintenance of the old rather than any attempt on his part to be innovative in experimenting with new genres.

58. ♪ See Repertoire 2.2 for a list of songs included in the repertoire of fiddlers that are being investigated in this study. "Old Hen Cackled" (or a song that has a similar name) has the largest number of names listed.

59. ♪ See Lyrics 9.2a and 9.2b.

60. ♪ Go to Audio Examples to listen to "The Old Hen Cackled and the Rooster's Going to Crow" by John Carson and "Cacklin Hen" by Howard Armstrong. The tune's introduction and A theme (0:00 to 0:19) is much shorter than the B theme, which is performed several times with singing (0:20–0:50) before Carson returns to the A melody. Howard Armstrong's 1985 performance provides an example of the form and improvisation used by some fiddlers.

61. ♪ Go to Audio Examples to listen "Old Hen Cackled" by Freeman.

62. ♪ Go to Audio Examples to listen to versions of "Old Hen Cackled" by William Adams and "Butch" Cage.

63. The lyrical quality of the A theme is especially distinctive in performances of "Cacklin' Hen" by Howard Armstrong (1985) and other performers such as the Foggy Mountain Boys (1962).

64. ♪ Go to Audio Examples to listen to Freeman perform "Worried Blues."

65. ♪ See Demographics 9.8.

66. Details about Rakestraw's family and musical life are based on Rosenbaum's interviews with the musician, except for demographic and historical information obtained from the US census and other historical records. Rosenbaum's materials have been deposited in the Digital Library of Georgia. The year 1911 for Rakestraw's birth date presented here is based on army and US Social Security records, and differs from the year 1910 Rosenbaum gives in his accounts.

67. ♪ See Biography 9.1.

68. Moose Lodge is the local name for the Loyal Order of Moose, a fraternal and service organization founded in Louisville, Kentucky, in 1888, with members in the United States, Canada, and Bermuda (Ferre 2017). Led by Joseph Christopher "Joe" Liggins Jr. (1916–1987), the Honeydrippers was an African American music group, popular during the 1940s and 1950s, that played blues, jazz, and rhythm and blues. Although he was born in Oklahoma, Liggins's family moved to California during the 1930s where, as an adult, he spent the majority of his music career. It is doubtful that Rakestraw played with the California-based Honeydrippers. Perhaps there was a music group in the Athens area with the same name.

69. It is unclear from the interview if Rakestraw's father was critical of secular music generally or specifically songs that included fiddling (Rosenbaum 1983, 184).

70. ♪ See Repertoire 9.3.

71. The number of blues in Rakestraw's repertoire is significant, particularly since some musicians in Appalachia (for example, Cuje Bertram) preferred not to perform these songs (see chapter 7).

72. 🎵 See Demographics 9.9.

73. 🎵 See Map 9.5, Map 9.6, Land Regions 9.3, and History 9.5.

74. US census records indicate that Mostella's father, Marion Mostella (1870–1952), married twice. With his first wife, Lilla May Cochran (1886–1917), who was Mostella's mother and the daughter of the fiddler Gus Cochran, the couple had six children (four males and two females), and Mostella was the third eldest. US census records also indicate that Mostella was married three times and had eleven children.

75. 🎵 See Demographics 9.10.

76. 🎵 See Photo 9.9a, Photo 9.9b, and Photo 9.9c.

77. 🎵 See Repertoires 9.4 and 11.1 as well as earlier discussion about fiddling at the 1951 Fort Valley music festival. "Listen to the Mocking Bird," the complete title, dates to the mid-nineteenth century. Composed in 1855, a Euro-American Philadelphia songwriter Septimus Winner, "wrote the song using a tune he heard an African American street musician whistle. Richard Milburn, known as 'Whistling Dick,' played guitar and whistled on Philadelphia streets for money in the mid-nineteenth century. One of his entertainments was to imitate a mockingbird by whistling a particular melody. Winner took this melody and wrote lyrics to it. With its catchy 'listen to the mockingbird' refrain, the song became hugely popular." During the nineteenth century, "the song sold millions copies of sheet music and was sung (and whistled) throughout the United States and parts of Europe" (McCarthy 2017). For information on the recording history of the tune, see Discography of American Historical Recordings (n.d.b).

78. 🎵 See Repertoire 9.4.

79. Clifford Hayes, Jess Ferguson, and Henry Miles are among the Black fiddlers who were members of jug bands in Louisville, while Will Batts, Charlie Pierce, and Milton Robie were Black fiddlers who performed in jug bands in Memphis. Jug bands were active in Louisville as early as 1905 with many attracting musicians from rural areas to perform during Derby week. During the 1920s and 1930s, several fiddlers made recordings with bands (Ware 1981; Wolfe 1982; Wright and Cox 1993; Jones 2014).

80. 🎵 See Map 9.7, Map 9.8, Land Regions 9.4, and History 9.6.

81. While blues is one of the most important musical forms to be created in the United States because of its prominence and influence on other genres, it has not been supported by all Black people in Mississippi. Since its beginnings, blues was most popular among groups from the lower rungs of society; African Americans who disassociated themselves from this social class did not patronize the genre (Oliver 1996, 414–15).

82. 🎵 See Demographics 9.11a and 9.11b.

83. 🎵 See Repertoire 9.5 for field recordings of fiddling by Hemphill and Pratcher that come from Lomax's field research in Mississippi in 1942 and 1959. Also, see Evans (1978a, 1999a 1999b); Lomax (1960, 1977, 1997); Wade (1999); and Work III, Jones, and Adams (2005).

84. Bolick (2015a, x) indicates that field workers employed by the Works Progress Administration (WPA) in 1936 were given "no direction to collect fiddle tunes from African American sources. And yet, there seem to have been eight 1936 African American sources for fiddle tunes." In 1939, no fiddle music by African Americans was recorded, although many performances by African Americans performing other styles of music were documented.

85. 🎵 See Repertoire 9.5.

86. Of the roughly eighteen Black fiddlers listed and/or discussed in Bolick and Austin (2015) and Bolick and Russell (2021), the large majority lived in majority Black communities. Only transcriptions are provided for tunes in the fiddlers' repertoire, making it difficult to address the issue of performance style and the degree to which African-derived features were retained. However, sound recordings by the Mississippi Sheiks, Hemphill, and Pratcher suggest that African performance practices continued to be prominent (see below).

87. Evans (1978a, 4; 1999a) states that pitch tolerance (bent notes), the use of polyrhythms, additive rhythms, call and response, and instruments of African origin are just some of the features that reflect the maintenance of African practices among African Americans in Mississippi.

88. 🎵 See Map 3.2d. Probably because of influence and contact, several counties in the Mississippi Hills and Pines regions have musical and cultural elements that are similar to those in other parts of Southern Appalachia.

89. Genres identified with the city, including music for brass bands and dance orchestras, vaudeville blues, jazz, Broadway music, and minstrels, rarely had a strong impact on musicking in the Hills (Oliver 1996, 334–37).

90. 🎵 See Repertoire 9.5A.

91. The fact that several tunes in the repertoire of Black fiddlers are similar to those performed by white musicians during the 1930s also provides evidence that sharing and musical interchange among the races continued through the first decades of the twentieth century (see Bolick and Austin 2015; Bolick and Russell 2021, 4).

92. 🎵 See Repertoire 9.5B.

93. By the 1980s and 1990s, few community-oriented secular music activities for African Americans took place in the eastern counties. Similar to other parts of the United States, most Blacks became consumers of commercial popular music and its related activities.

94. 🎵 See Video 1.7 to view West African fiddle ensembles with drums and other percussive instruments. What was performed in Mississippi in the early twentieth century demonstrates performance aesthetics that combined features from several cultural traditions including elements from West Africa, Southern Appalachia, and the Delta.

95. 🎵 See Repertoire 9.5C.

96. Arpeggio is the sounding of the notes of a chord in succession rather than simultaneously (Arpeggio 2001).

97. As noted above, the eastern Hills counties are locked between two cultural regions: (1) the predominantly white, lower Southern Appalachia mountain region and (2) the predominantly Black Mississippi Delta region. Of the six eastern counties, Marshall is the only one that was majority Black between 1900 and 1960 (Oliver 1996, 400).

98. Hay (2001, 114) indicates that he decided to focus on Taylor because he was part of the generation of musicians from the Hills region that reworked country fiddle and banjo tunes into blues.

99. Taylor's parents—William Henry Taylor (b. ca. 1875) and Lula Moody Taylor (1874–1975)—were both born in Marshall County. US census records indicate that they had fifteen children (nine females and six males). Ernest was the sixth child but eldest male.

100. The following is a condensed and edited version of information included in Taylor's interview (Hay 2001, 115–17).

101. For a discussion of performance contexts, see Oliver (1996, 419–49).

102. When church people passed by their home, Taylor indicated that he and family members would play religious songs for them (Hay 2001, 120).

103. Although many sources indicate that Hemphill died in 1963, his tombstone at the New Salem Baptist Church Cemetery in Senatobia, Tate County, Mississippi, indicates 1961 (Moore 2021c).

104. 🎵 See Map 9.8 and Demographics 9.12. While conducting research in Clarksdale (Coahoma County, Delta region) for the Library of Congress Fisk University Project, Alan Lomax met Turner Junior Johnson, a blind street singer from the Hills region, who suggested that he go and record Sid Hemphill (Wade 1999). Lomax recorded Hemphill near Sledge in Quitman County, where he was performing at a country picnic. For a list of songs recorded during the session, see Dixon, Godrich, and Rye (1997, 377).

105. 🎵 See Photo 9.10b for an image of Hemphill playing quills.

106. The bass drum in Hemphill's string band was included when no string bass was available. The player would use one stick to play the drum and hold a tambourine in the other hand and beat it against the knee. Thus, drumming in string bands was not as complex as that for the fife (Evans 1978a, 12).

107. US census records indicate that Sid and his wife, Maggie Buck (b. 1882), had three daughters: Virden L. (b. 1907), Rosa Lee (b. 1909), and Sidney L. (b. 1911); also see Evans (1978a, 1999a); Wade (1999); and Moore (2021c).

108. 🎵 Go to Audio Examples to listen to Lomax's interview with Hemphill, in which he provides additional information about his family, his life as a musician, and the circumstances surrounding him composing the song "The Carrier Line."

109. 🎵 See Repertoire 9.5E. To view musical transcriptions of select tunes by Hemphill as well as further discussion of his musicking, see Moore (2021c).

110. The performer of a blues ballad often assumes that the audience has a prior knowledge of the underlying events of the story (Evans 1999a). In the literature, at least two titles are used for this song: "The Carrier Line" and "The Carrier Railroad." I have decided to use the former, which is referenced in Lomax Digital Archive; also see Dixon, Godrich, and Rye (1997, 377).

111. 🎵 Go to Audio Examples to listen to "The Carrier Line" by Hemphill and his group. "The Carrier Line" concerns lumber magnate, John Carrier, and his engineers Dave Cowart and Mr. Bailey, and the wreck on the road at Malone's Trestle. For the history of this song, see Moore (2021c, 205).

112. 🎵 See Lyrics 9.3.

113. 🎵 See Map 9.8. In 1959, US census records indicate that Hemphill was living in Senatobia, the seat for Tate County, which is located one county north of Panola County.

114. 🎵 Go to Audio Examples to listen to recordings from Lomax's 1959 session with Hemphill.

115. US census records indicate that their parents, Joseph Pratcher (b. ca. 1850) and Sarah Pratcher (b. ca. 1859), had eleven children (seven females and four males) with Bob as the eighth and Miles (1895–1964) as the tenth born. Bob was married twice, but there is no evidence that he had children. Miles was married once and had eleven children. Unfortunately, no information is available to indicate if other members of the Pratcher family (parents, siblings, or children) were involved in musicking.

116. 🎵 See Repertoire 9.5G for a list of recordings of Pratcher's musicking produced by Lomax.

117. 🎵 Go to Audio Examples to listen to songs performed by the Pratchers. Although the liner notes indicate that both Bob and Miles perform the fiddle, Bob is the sole fiddler on these recordings (Lomax 1977; Bolick 2021b).

118. 🎵 Go to Audio Examples to listen to the Pratchers perform "All Night Long."

119. 🎵 See Repertoire 9.5H. For additional information, see Present from a President (1974), Brown (1976), Wheeler (1976), Burtt (1980), Kynerd and Echols (1980), Ferris (2018), and Moore (2021b).

120. See chapter 7 for a discussion of Bertram and Rice. In the information below, we will learn that several other Black fiddlers in Mississippi relocated, but to areas that tended to be distinct from the places they were born and raised.

121. According to Moore (2021b, 149), Dumas had lived in Tallahatchie County for a short time in 1918 when he was called to serve in the military at Camp Grant in Illinois. He also lived for a short time in Cairo, Illinois, in 1923 (Wheeler 1976). After discovering he did not like living in the North, he learned about Roy Flowers, who owned a farm around Tutwiler in the Delta region. When he contacted Flowers about working for him and the two men agreed on the arrangements, Dumas moved to Tutwiler in 1924 and lived there and surrounding communities for the rest of his life. Typical of many Black fiddlers in this study, Dumas preferred living in communities (including Bellefontaine, Walthall, Tutwiler, and Dublin) with a small number of people (Moore 2021b). In fact, information about the population of these communities is not known because the US census does not include data for locations with less than 2,500 people (1920 and earlier) and 1,000 people (1930 and later).

122. US census records indicate that Tom Dumas's parents—James Dumas (1851–1941) and Cornelia B. Marshall Dumas (1859–1932)—were both born and raised in Webster County. The couple had ten children, and Thomas was the second eldest. For other details about Dumas's life history, see Moore (2021b).

123. After playing the fiddle for eighty years, Dumas sold the instrument in 1974 "for $250, fearing that it might not be preserved by his heirs. It was said to have once had a label inside saying 'Italy 1792' but mice ate it away." A Memphis couple who bought the fiddle "had the fiddle evaluated, but say any value was lost when mice chewed away the label. They do believe, however, that it very probably did belong to Andrew Jackson" (Brown 1976).

The Ozark Mountains

CHAPTER 10

Missouri

Although Missouri's rural Black population was small during the early twentieth century, aspects of African American culture could be found in some areas due to transplants and the maintenance of a southern way of life.[1] For example, Little Dixie, located in the central portion of the state, included cultural traditions from the South that some believed to be "more Dixie than Dixie," especially in terms of language, architecture, food, music, agriculture, and politics (Bergey 1984a, 2). During this period, the fiddle was the most popular instrument, partly because it was easy for migrants to transport, but also because musicians performed music their audiences preferred. Its popularity is somewhat paradoxical because many musicians believe the fiddle was difficult to play. But Howard Wight Marshall indicates that "almost every town [in rural Missouri] had fiddlers, and every family had someone who could play fiddle music" (Historically Black 2016). This was a period when African American fiddlers were influential and respected in Missouri; Blacks and whites shared tunes and often performed with each other (Marshall 2008, 17; 2012, 116–18).[2]

Unfortunately, minimal research has been done on the fiddle as it relates to African Americans in Missouri. Most of the data on Missouri Black fiddling[3] comes from newspaper articles, incidental publications, and the findings of several researchers.[4] While Barry Bergey and Marshall provide excellent historical and cultural information, R. P. Christeson's song books (1973, 1984) and field recordings (1976, 2011) of old-time fiddle music, which date from the 1940s through the 1960s, include both biographical and musical information about several Black fiddlers. The recordings are particularly important for details about performance style, for no Missouri Black fiddlers were commercially recorded during the early twentieth century (Carter 1980).

Contexts for Black fiddling in Missouri varied during the early twentieth century. Black fiddlers were welcomed and provided entertainment at emancipation picnics, family reunions and celebrations, as well as other events (fish fries, church picnics, platform dances, and house parties that included baseball, footraces, and other games). It was not uncommon for "white acquaintances and musicians" to frequent such events, a practice that continued through the early twentieth century. Marshall (2012, 116) indicates that when Blacks in southern Callaway County held large outdoor dances during the early twentieth century, white neighbors from the area would sit in parked cars along the road to listen to the music.[5] Dancing to string bands that included a fiddle with banjo, piano, guitar, and other instruments was a favorite pastime for Blacks and whites.[6] A 1913 document describing Boone County taverns reveals that the barroom was the social center of the community,[7] for it was there that "people danced the minuet and Virginia reel, and afterwards were disciplined for it in their respective religious denominations. The music on such occasions of frivolity was furnished by two negroes, experts in the use of the fiddle and the banjo, who needed no bandmaster to wield the baton, for they marked time as they called the figures with a footfall heavy enough to give an emphatic accent" (Bergey 1984a, 6–7).

Performing on the radio was another opportunity for Black and white fiddlers to share their talents, especially when the Missouri State Marketing Bureau established the WOS (Watch Our State) radio station in 1922, with broadcasts from Jefferson City that could be heard in all forty-eight states, Canada, and Mexico.[8] Although the broadcast's primary function was to provide market reports and agricultural information to "take the city to the farmer," the opposite occurred. In response to the unwanted urbanization and perceived "erosion of traditional values exhibited by the flaunting of prohibition laws and the proliferation of jazz, the most popular programming was . . . the Friday night fiddle shows. Fiddle contests were also wildly popular. . . . The fiddle frenzy would reach its peak during the 1926 Interstate Old Fiddlers Contest, when an estimated 1,000,000 listeners tuned in and over 250,000 votes were cast. The winner, who received the majority of the votes . . . took home a $500 prize and a silver loving cup" (Christeson 2009, 44).

Unlike radio stations in many parts of the United States during the early 1900s, which did not allow Blacks to perform or participate in fiddle contests, race was not an issue in Missouri. Marshall (2012) explains: "It was natural for the WOS programmers to bring in the best old-time fiddlers from the neighboring counties, and this included prominent white contest champions [as well as] the regions' best-known black players. . . . While many listeners thought they were hearing white performers . . . people in nearby counties could easily recognize the tunes and playing styles of [local Black fiddlers]. Ironically, although black performers could in certain instances be successful on radio, they typically were snubbed by recording companies and promoters if they were playing 'old-time fiddle music'" (120). Fiddlers from central Missouri (such as William

Katon and Bill Burdick) figured prominently in WOS programming and their success in state and inter-state fiddle contests were indicators of the musical richness of the Little Dixie traditions. Because WOS was broadcast over a large area of the Midwest, the early exposure on radio may explain why the style and repertoire of mid-Missouri fiddling had a widespread influence in the Ozarks (Bergey 1984a, 6–7).

Profiles of Black Missouri Fiddlers

Several Black Missouri fiddlers were active during the early twentieth century.[9] John Banks, a fiddler and mandolin player who lived in Arrow Rock (a village in Saline County that borders the southern part of the Missouri River),[10] impressed many in his community not only for his ability to play fox-trots, rags and other dances popular during the 1920s and 1930s, but also old-time square-dance tunes he had absorbed while growing up in the community. Walt Dougherty from Highbee, a small town in southern Randolph County, was well known for performing with whites as well as creating songs that other fiddlers learned and passed on to others, sometimes with alternate titles (Marshall et al. 1989, 17).[11] Born in 1851, Filmore Taylor Hancock (known as "Uncle Fil") was popular in his home town of Rolla-Salem in Phelps County (located approximately sixty miles south of the Missouri River) for storytelling and performing a variety of instruments. He gave up fiddling in his later years but continued to perform the tambourine and "liked to say he could play as well as any of 'those Georgia minstrels . . . 'fore the Civil War'" (Marshall 2012, 117–18). In addition to operating a horse livery stable, Cal Jefferson was a multi-instrumentalist who performed piano, mandolin, and the fiddle at venues in Neosho (Newton County), a railroad boom town and popular entertainment spot for Black musicians who played for local workers. Jefferson attended school with George Washington Carver (1864–1943), the well-known Tuskegee scientist and professor whose home was also in Newton County. As a youth, Carver "played the violin and guitar and was a good singer" (117–19). John Henry "Bud" Summers, who was born during slavery and learned to play fiddle music as a youngster, became a well-known dance fiddler in the Monroe City area of Monroe County during the late nineteenth and early twentieth century. In his later years, Summers taught white children the rudiments of fiddling (132–33).[12] Along with William Katon (see below), Bill Burdick was one of the better-known Black fiddlers to perform on live radio programs on WOS during the 1920s; both were also favorites at fox hunts, picnics, and barbecues in different parts of Little Dixie (112, 120, 125).[13] The three Black Missouri fiddlers—Ace Donell Sr., William "Bill" Katon, and William "Bill" Driver—for which some detailed information is available are examined below and discussed chronologically according to their birth dates.

Ace Donell Sr. (ca. 1849–1927)

As an adult, Ace Donell (also spelled Donnell) lived in Monroe City in central Missouri, about ninety miles northeast of Jefferson City and the Missouri River.[14] Marie, Donell's daughter, states that her father had been enslaved in Kentucky before emancipation. After the war, he and his family moved to Missouri with their slave owners (the Judys) and settled there. He "grew up near Florida, Missouri, and eventually purchased his own eighty-acre farm. He loved to play the violin and often played while she [Marie] and her younger brother, Eddie, tap-danced in front of Hawkin's Grocery when they were small. 'People would throw money at us . . . and sometimes we would make a whole fistful of money in one night'"[15] (Monroe City 1976, 53). What is noteworthy about Donell is the fact that inserting rattles from the tails of rattlesnakes inside his fiddle resonator was commonplace for him, which suggests that some African performance practices had been maintained even in the Midwest.[16]

William "Bill" Katon (1864–1934)

Bill Katon/Caton, a Black fiddler born in Callaway County, Missouri, was an important figure in Missouri fiddling, but little is known about his life.[17] Marshall (2012, 121) states that Katon's slave owners, a white family that migrated from Kentucky in 1816 and established a farm with nine enslaved Blacks near Columbia, were fiddlers, which may account for Katon learning to play the instrument. Blacks and whites in his community continued to participate in musicking together, even after emancipation. To encourage neighbors to volunteer and help with the corn shuckings, hog killings, and "sugaring" that took place during the fall and winter of each year, community members announced that the occasions would feature dancing and fiddle music, and dinner would be served to everyone when the work was completed.

Katon was well known for playing the fiddle at dances with his partner, fiddler-guitarist Ola Gathright (1879–1966), in white and Black communities throughout the region. The duo also achieved fame during the 1920s when they performed over WOS on several occasions (Marshall 2012, 121–25).[18] Although remembered by many Little Dixie residents as a fine musician, with neighbors describing musicking by the duo as "tops," Katon appeared to be special. Christeson (1973, xi) recalls listening to them when he joined others on Main Street in front of the community's grocery store, which had the only radio with a loudspeaker. Unfortunately, he died before Christeson started documenting fiddling in the region. In describing Katon's fiddling in an interview, Christeson states: "Bill Katon played a lot, and his music is a little different. It has got a distinctive air of its own—the pattern, or whatever it is. One in particular was an old Irish tune called 'Beaux of Oak Hill.' He was fabulous. I've heard enough of his tunes, and I know of two or three people that play a few that they learned from him. I've gotten the impression that he made up quite a number of tunes on his own. I'm sure of that, because I just can't trace 'em to any of the literature" (Lance 1998, 27).

Of the 245 melodies in Christeson's 1973 collection, five are by Katon as played by others, and in Christeson's 1984 volume of 212 tunes, twelve are attributed to Katon.[19] Christeson (1973) states that when he located Katon's son, John, in Jefferson City, in 1952, John recorded several numbers. Because he did not play the fiddle regularly, he could recall only a portion of his dad's tunes. However, "he described one evening at home when Bill got out the fiddle and asked John's mother to keep a record of the tunes, which she did by making tally marks on the wall with a nail. John said his dad played 165 tunes before midnight" (xi).

William "Bill" Alexander Driver Jr. (1881–1986)

William Driver Jr. was born in Eldridge, a small town in Laclede County in south-central Missouri.[20] In 1907, he married Violet Mae Williams (1886–1957), and the couple had eight children—seven daughters and one son (Watson 1995, Hake 2007b). During the late teens, the family moved to Iberia, a rural community in Miller County, Missouri, where Driver worked as a farmer and spent most of his fiddling career (see photos 10.1 and 10.2).[21] In the early 1940s, the family moved to western Cole County. In this location, he worked on a farm near Centertown for more than a decade before retiring to a daughter's home in Jefferson City.[22] Wherever he lived, according to local journalist, Bob Watson (1995), Driver "generally was accepted and respected as a member of the community—in spite of his race—in an era when a majority of Americans considered blacks inferior to whites."[23] Driver was residing in Jefferson City when he died. According to Hake (2007a), "his last years were spent in darkness when he lost his eyesight but . . . he could still play his beloved fiddle."

Family members indicate that Driver played several instruments (piano, harmonica, and guitar), but he was best known for his fiddling. In the podcast *Historically Black* (2016) that recounts the history of the Driver family, Darleen Goldston explained: "Bill Driver's father [William Driver Sr.] played the fiddle and taught his son some tunes. No one is sure whether Driver [Jr.] had any formal training. But what people do know is that Bill Driver was a fiddle playing sensation in central Missouri. He played live on radio station WOS in Jefferson City. . . . At night, the station signal was so powerful that Driver's fiddle could be heard from Canada to Cuba." The fact that Driver's father, a Baptist minister, performed the fiddle and the drum, and shared what he knew with his son is significant, because it suggests that the popularity of the fiddle among members of the community offset the negative views of fiddling.[24] Driver's community

Photo 10.1. William Driver Jr. (portrait view) as a young man. Around 1910 in Richwoods, Missouri. Courtesy of Darleen Goldston and Raffeal A. Sears.

Photo 10.2. William Driver Jr. with wife Violet. Jefferson City, Missouri. Early 1950s. Courtesy of Darleen Goldston and Raffeal A. Sears.

regarded him highly and his music was "the best example . . . of a repertory strictly indigenous to local area" (Voices 1983, 13). Christeson (1973), who writes about his professional and personal interactions with Driver, provides details:

> He was gifted with talent, had a keen ear, steady time, and played vigorously. My first contact with Bill's music was at one of the annual summer encampments at Iberia, Missouri, in the late 1920s. This was a six-day picnic and celebration that was first organized to honor Civil War veterans. Bill played for the outdoor dance floor at the encampment and had a large repertory of breakdowns suitable for square dances. This was one of the sections of Missouri where both men and women would jig dance throughout the figures. This required steady, peppy fiddle music, which Bill could provide in abundance. He won many local contests but was never sponsored for any of the state contests. On one occasion, local townspeople arranged for him to play a program over WOS at Jefferson City. This one appearance brought mail from listeners in several states and Canada. . . . Bill represented the best example I encountered of a repertory strictly indigenous to a local area. In contrast to fiddlers in the Boone County area, for example, Bill's repertory was largely undiluted with hornpipes, jigs, or reels, which obviously came from the phonograph, or from the printed page shipped in by mail, or from an itinerant fiddler. (xi–xii)

In describing her encounters with Driver, Hake (2007a) writes: "I was just a small child when I last saw Bill Driver, who was a wonderful musician. Many people say he was the best musician in our part of the country. . . . He was very well-learned on the old country fiddle and during his lifetime he won many fiddling contests across the countryside. Often his first-place prize was $25 in cash. . . ."[25] He was much in demand at Saturday night dances where he played to the delight of his many admirers."[26] Recalling the times when he participated in contests, Driver's daughter, Minnie Driver Fulcher, stated: "When he would go to those contests, he did good. Most of the time he would always win—either first or second prize. He enjoyed it. We would have these 'house parties,' as they called them in those days, and he would play music. He did a lot of that" (Watson 1995). Family and community members also remembered him "sitting out on the porch playing the fiddle and then getting comments from people from miles away, who would say, 'Late at night, we could hear him playing. You're talking 11, 12 o'clock at night, after working all day on the farm' near Centertown" (Watson 1995).

The cultural environment in central Missouri also helped his popularity in that "whites and blacks often mixed freely at social gatherings. This was especially [the case] at events where Bill Driver ruled the dance floor with his fiddle" (Historically Black 2016). On the podcast, Marshall indicated that Driver's performances at community dances were special because of his "rock solid rhythm, which is the hallmark of a successful and seasoned dance fiddler. If you don't have that rhythm and that ability, you won't be invited back to play the next dance. They'll find somebody else." He was also noted for "playing with a heavy bow and using a type of sawing action at the low end. While playing a melody at the high end, it soared and wandered, almost like a sailor's hornpipe. It was a recipe that enabled Driver to win money at fiddle competitions" (Historically Black 2016).

In terms of Driver's repertoire[27] and performance style, what we know is limited to material collected by Christeson (see photo 10.3), who provides few details about the provenance of Driver's songs.[28] However, his comments about the fiddler's performance style are useful in understanding the aesthetic preferences of fiddlers in the Midwest.[29] When Driver is compared to Bob Walters, a white fiddler from Nebraska who is the "spotlighted musician" on the recording, with twenty-nine of the forty-one cuts (T. Carter 1980, 65), Christeson (1976) states: "We're going to hear Bill Driver playing an un-named breakdown also in the key of C. As a fiddler, Bill was characterized by some of his rivals as rough but good. So, we have the smooth fiddler [Walters] and the vigorous fiddler [Driver]. Both are fine players, but neither resembling some of the commercial fiddling that we've begun to hear in the mid-1970s. When he was asked the name of this tune, Bill Driver replied, 'It's just one of those old Iberia tunes.'" While he does not elaborate further, it appears that vigorous means a fast tempo and highly energetic rhythm that was probably preferred by dancers.

Photo 10.3. William Driver Jr. holding book and recording by R. P. Christeson. Jefferson City, Missouri, May 10, 1976. Courtesy of Darleen Goldston and Raffeal A. Sears.

In addition to Driver's fiddling, the context in which he made his recordings with Christeson appeared to be special. The recording sessions began in the summer of 1948 when Driver was living in Cole County. Others took place in Christeson's home in Callaway County where he provided the accompaniment: "I would second on the piano. My parents enjoyed listening to him play" (Christeson 1998, 37). After Driver moved to Jefferson City in 1952, Christeson (1998) indicates that the "last recording session was at Driver's daughter's home one evening with a large audience of listeners in the front yard. [Driver] was in his late sixties but was playing near his fiddling prime when these recordings were made" (37).

Like many old-time tunes that date to the early twentieth century and possibly earlier, songs performed by Driver[30] are generally based on two themes (AB), which are repeated alternately in a high- and low-pitched range.[31] The A and B themes of both songs consist of a four-beat, four bar melody: "Iberia Breakdown," a tune common to the region and town where he lived, and "Scott Number One," a tune composed by Driver (1976). Regarding "Scott Number One," Christeson (1976) states: "Apparently, this tune, 'Scott Number One,' is quite rare. A folklorist in Arkansas spent many years searching for a version, and he did not come across one. This one is by Bill Driver."

Because of his social environment, it is also not surprising that Driver's performance style is distinct from the fiddling of Black fiddlers in other parts of the United States both in the instrumentation (fiddle accompanied by piano played by Christeson) as well as melody and rhythm. Linford (2013b) explains: "It sounds like what I would expect from a white fiddler from that area to play. The emphasis is on melody and rhythmic drive. The piano accompaniment is chord heavy and there are no harmonic cadences or anything like that. All of this tends to be identified with white fiddling and not something I associate with an African American fiddle style. 'Scott Number 1' is very harmonically structured. Very quick, very clean melody and articulation of melodic notes. It's a pretty straight style of fiddling." Wilson (2013) states that Driver's music sounds like "a Black fiddler playing with a white band. They may have played together, but they are not playing together. Driver's fiddling had a lot of energy. So, it sounds like the piano player is trying to keep up with the fiddler. Also, it sounds like the fiddler is trying to go one way and the piano player is trying to go another way. He was trying to pull away from the piano, but he had to stay with his accompanist. In addition, they did not use single notes or long, sustained notes. They used staccato, triplet notes to perform the melody. That sounds like a northern style of old-time music."

In the essay that accompanies the recording *Now That's a Good Tune: Masters of Traditional Missouri Fiddling*, Marshall (1989) explains that Missouri fiddling consists of three regional styles, which Goertzen (1993, 467) summarizes as follows: (1) Ozark, which includes short bow strokes, heavy rhythm, double stops, with melodies that are comparatively simple, fastest, and the least healthy of the three styles); (2) Little Dixie, which is performed with hard-driving, more intricate melodies, short and long strokes that are mixed to produce a rolling rhythm, and more harmonically complex accompaniments; and (3) North Missouri,[32] which includes complex melodies that are performed slowly. Based on these descriptions, Driver's fiddling reflects musicking in the areas (Ozark and Little Dixie) where he lived, and provides an example of the Black-white interchange and aesthetic preferences of Black fiddlers in Missouri during the first half of the twentieth century.

To summarize, the fiddle continued to be identified with Blacks and whites in parts of rural Missouri during the early twentieth century primarily because of isolation and limited contact or influence from emerging musical genres that were becoming popular in urban black communities of the United States. The maintenance of southern traditions as well as demographics (small number of Blacks with extensive interaction with whites) were also factors. Although some differences exist (because of varied population trends and social environment), Black fiddling in both mountain regions—the Ozarks and the Appalachians—was comparable. Black musicians continued to perform the fiddle because this is what their audiences (Black and white) preferred and supported.

fiddlingismyjoycompanion.net

Notes

1. 🎻 See Map 10.1, Map 10.2, Land Regions 10.1, and History 10.1.

2. To listen to the fiddling of both Black and white fiddlers from Missouri, go to: https://mofiddledance.org/profiles/bill-driver/. Please note that the publication by Marshall, Williams, and Williams (2008) is a revised and updated version of the recording and notes originally published in 1989.

3. With a few exceptions, most findings on Black fiddling focus on two regions in the central part of Missouri: (1) the Ozark Highlands and (2) the southern portion of the Dissected Till Plain that extends eastward to the Mississippi River.

4. See Christeson (1973, 1976, 1984, 1998, 2011), Bergey (1984a, 1984b), Marshall et al. (1989, 2008), and Marshall (2012).

5. 🎻 See Demographics 10.1.

6. Because string bands were organized with dancing in mind, Marshall (2012) states that "choices of instruments were geared to providing volume and danceable rhythm behind the fiddler's melody" (121).

7. 🎻 See Demographics 10.2.

8. 🎻 See Demographics 10.3.

9. Although unevenness exists in details about the fiddlers, I believe it is important to present whatever information is available not only to note their contributions but also so comparisons can be made with fiddlers in Missouri and other parts of the United States.

10. 🎻 See Demographics 10.4

11. Marshall (2012, 126) mentions Walt Dougherty briefly in his discussion of song titles that were culturally offensive to Blacks, but were appropriated by white fiddlers who performed them with alternate titles.

12. Marshall (2012, 119, 125–26) provides names of several other Missouri Black fiddlers who were active during the early twentieth century; they are not discussed here because little is known about them. It is noteworthy that, except for Cal Jefferson, who lived in southwest Missouri about two hundred miles from Jefferson City, most Black fiddlers active in the early twentieth century continued to reside in (or near) counties in Little Dixie. However, Black presence in these counties varied.

13. 🎻 See Demographics 10.5.

14. 🎻 See Demographics 10.6.

15. Donell married twice. He had five children with his first wife and several children with his second wife, Carrie Mitchell. It is unknown if family members were fiddlers or musicians. For details, see Monroe City (1976); Ace Donell (2002–2007); Lanham (1976); and Marie Donell (1976).

16. As noted in the foregoing, fiddlers in many parts of West Africa inserted pebbles and other objects inside their resonators (see photo 1.7) to produce a percussive sound quality in performance (DjeDje 2008a, 2020; Soileau and Bellard 1993; Tisserand 1998, 74).

17. The spellings for both surnames—Caton and Katon—appear in the literature. However, the family prefers Katon, which is the way it is written on Katon's gravestone in southern Callaway

County (Marshall 2012, 119). US census records indicate that Bill Katon and his wife, Lizzie Kemp (b. ca. 1874), had four children: Addie, Charlie Elwood, John Henry, and Fred. Katon was probably most active as a fiddler between 1890 and 1930 when, as noted above, the population of the Black community in Callaway County was substantial.

18. For details, see Lance (1998, 27, 35).

19. According to Marshall (2012, 125), "the best-known tune attributed to Katon is 'Old Jeff City' (a.k.a. 'Jefferson City Blues,' 'Jefferson City,' 'Katon's Hornpipe,' and 'Katon's Reel')." Christeson (1976) published the tune with the generic title "Breakdown" ("Another Bill Caton [*sic*] tune"). Several tunes by Katon—"Bill Katon Breakdown in D," "Bill Katon Breakdown in G #2," and "Bill Katon's Tune/Reel"—can also be found in the Folk Music Index: http://www.ibiblio.org/folk index/. Accessed January 15, 2020.

20. Driver's father, William A. Driver Sr. (ca. 1858–1934), and mother, Susan Catherine Shipley (1867–1935), were born in Jefferson City. The couple had eight children, but only two—William Jr. and a younger daughter, Grace (1892–1957)—survived into adulthood (Watson 1995). Eldridge is located a little less than eight miles northeast of Springfield, the third largest city in Missouri.

21. In the *Historically Black* (2016) podcast, Darleen Goldston, one of Driver's grandchildren, states: "Iberia was predominantly white [in terms of population]. While Missouri had harsh segregation laws and customs, the Driver family enjoyed easy relations with whites in their community." But the couple encountered problems when they decided to marry. Because Violet's father was white (and her physical appearance reflected that she was also white), she and Driver "needed help from the local justice of the peace" to obtain a marriage license. "They had to get permission [from marriage license officials] because they weren't sure if she was colored."

22. 🎵 See Demographics 10.7 and History 10.2.

23. Minnie Driver Fulcher (1921–2006), one of the Driver Jr.'s younger daughters, stated that although she and her family experienced racism and separation because she was Black, "we didn't have any big problems with the people" (Watson 1995).

24. 🎵 See Photo 10.4 and Photo 10.5.

25. 🎵 See Figure 10.1.

26. Driver was sometimes accompanied by the Howser sisters (Sadie and Sylvia) as they picked their flat-top guitars for dances. He and the Howsers (including Sadie and Sylvia's blind brother) also played at local picnics. In addition, it was not uncommon for Driver to meet community members at the Adams and Casey Store in Iberia, and they would sit for hours playing their fiddles in double harmony (Hake 2007a).

27. 🎵 See Repertoire 10.1.

28. Tom Carter (1980, 64) states that Christeson sees himself as a collector and compiler and rejects the roles of analyst or interpreter. Consequently, the recordings reflect little internal cohesion save that the tunes are "Midwestern and come to us through the collector's early interest in old-time fiddling." Also see the Fiddle Hangout Discussion Forum 10.

29. Before the listener hears the music, Christeson provides commentary on the tunes, describing what he believes is unique about the performance.

30. 🎵 Go to Audio Examples to listen to Driver's fiddling.

31. 🎵 See Form 10.1 and Form 10.2.

32. While Goertzen (1993) concurs with Marshall's descriptions for Ozark and Little Dixie, he believes features identified with North Missouri are the least convincing because they exist in pockets in the upper Midwest where fiddlers were strongly influenced by intricate playing broadcast from Ontario.

South Atlantic and Gulf Coasts and Neighboring Regions

CHAPTER 11

Virginia and North Carolina, South Carolina and Georgia, Florida, Alabama, Mississippi, Arkansas

This is the first of two chapters that covers states along or near the South Atlantic and Gulf coasts. Unfortunately, the amount of information on Black fiddling in each varies. In spite of the unevenness, each state will be examined for whatever is available, thereby providing material for comparison with other parts of the United States.[1]

Virginia and North Carolina

Because evidence of Black fiddling is scant along Virginia's and North Carolina's coast, particularly when compared to research conducted in the states' piedmont regions, it is difficult to assess the prominence of the tradition in the region during the early twentieth century.[2] What is available suggests that while Black fiddling may have been widespread in several Virginia counties and some piedmont communities during the pre-1900s, it was not a favorite pastime among coastal Blacks during the early twentieth century.[3] The only fiddler identified with Virginia's coastal region for whom I have found information is William Moore, who played fiddle and guitar around Richmond County for local dances (Bastin 1986, 300).

For North Carolina, Gates County in the northeast is one of the few locations where Black fiddling and string band music has been documented. A Black fiddler known only as Alvin is believed to have taught most of Gates

County's white players who lived on the edge of the Dismal Swamp; at one time fiddlers traveled from all over the county to meet and play on Christmas Day (Bastin 1986, 281, 286). Bastin's interviews with Jack Jordan, born 1908 in Pitt County, North Carolina, indicate that a Black string band tradition existed in his home area during the 1920s, but interaction with whites was not the norm (283). Guitarist Joe Black, a member of the Pitt County string band, states that "the band generally comprised fiddle, mandolin, and guitar, and [Jordon] played guitar whenever he was present" (285). Although Black was unable to remember the names of tunes the group played, Bastin believes "there seems to be little doubt that it was similar to that played by other black string bands in the period before and during the 1950s" (285).[4]

Unlike Virginia, demographics may have played a major role in the prominence of fiddling in select communities in North Carolina. Not only was the population of North Carolina's piedmont communities where Black fiddlers resided smaller, the ratio of Blacks to whites in the piedmont was different from what existed on the coast. In other words, coastal Black populations tended to be larger than those in the piedmont.[5] In the early twentieth century new musical forms, such as the blues, better reflected the musical tastes and social identities evolving in coastal areas as well as nearby North Carolina towns and cities, instead of old-time music that continued to be popular in North Carolina's piedmont and mountain communities.

South Carolina and Georgia

Culturally, the coastal areas of South Carolina and Georgia are similar[6] primarily because of the enslaved Africans who lived on the Sea Islands with little contact with outsiders, "coupled with the fact that Blacks outnumbered Whites for most of the time after the permanent settlement of Europeans" (Starks 1985, 60). Referred to as Gullah in South Carolina and Geechee in Georgia, "the descendants of cotton plantation slaves retained many aspects of the old slave culture with some African retentions: a regional dialect, Gullah, still marked by distinctly African traits; a large body of folktales, cures, and supernatural beliefs; and a folk version of Christianity with a 'shouting' style of singing spirituals and hymns in a local praise house" (Carawan and Carawan 1995, 19).

Because of the resilience of African culture on the coasts of South Carolina and Georgia, most of the data collected by researchers has been concerned with the maintenance of Africanisms and sacred music.[7] Secular music idioms may have existed, but they were only briefly investigated. For example, much of the material in the first book-length work on African American music, *Slave Songs of the United States* (1867), edited by William Francis Allen, Charles Pickard Ware, and Lucy McKim Garrison, focuses on musicking in South Carolina.

Although the editors note that Blacks performed secular music (work songs, dance songs, fiddle-sings, devil-songs, and more) before the Civil War, this type of musicking was rarely heard after emancipation, which is the reason their book focused primarily on religious music.[8] When Sierra Leone–born Nicholas George Julius Ballanta conducted research on the Sea Islands during the 1920s, the primary focus of his pioneering study, *Saint Helena Island Spirituals* (1925), was also religious music. Ballanta writes: "There are several other classes of songs known as fiddle-songs, coon-songs,[9] jig-tunes and devil songs but all these taken together are smaller in number than the spiritual" (Starks 1985, 63). Results from federal and university-funded projects conducted by researchers during the twenties and thirties also make no mention of fiddling because none of the blues, dance pieces, breakdowns, two-steps, and guitars, referred to as "jooking," included the fiddle (Bastin 1986, 57). If fiddling had been observed, most likely the tradition would have been disregarded because researchers did not associate this type of music with African American culture nor considered it to be African-derived.[10] In small towns in southeast Georgia (for example, in Wayne, Ware, and Camden counties), most community members entertained themselves by going to house parties. Those who worked in turpentine camps often went to jukes in shanty houses near their homes. In such contexts, the guitar, washboard, and Jew's or "lip" harp were the dominant instruments. Fiddle music was never performed (Cogdell 1998).

Florida

Unlike other states along the Atlantic and Gulf coasts, Florida did not have large plantations during the nineteenth century.[11] Because fewer Blacks lived and worked in rural areas, the settlement patterns and migration trends of African Americans in Florida in the early twentieth century differed from those in other parts of the South. Bastin (1986) writes: "During the period of significant rural depopulation in the early 1920s, Black Florida farmers were fewer than one-tenth of those in Georgia, while the ravages of the boll weevil elsewhere had little impact on the state outside the very north. Migration to northern cities like New York was less from Florida than from the states to the north. In the forty years between 1890 and 1930 Florida shifted from a sparsely populated, almost entirely rural-dwelling state to one with three times the population, the bulk of whom lived in urban centers: Jacksonville, Miami, and Tampa had populations in excess of 100,000" (31). Florida was also the destination for African Americans who relocated there from other southern areas. Favorable reports from neighbors and kin who had migrated earlier, the popular image of the state as a land of sunshine, bountiful harvests, and place of potential economic prosperity were all reasons the state was attractive to

Blacks. Between 1930 and 1940, Florida's in-migration was only surpassed by the state of New York (DeVane 1981, 2).

Since few studies have been done on Black secular music in Florida during the early twentieth century, it is not surprising that limited material exists on Black fiddling.[12] DeVane (1987) stated that twentieth century Black music in Florida, particularly areas in northern Florida, was no different from that found in neighboring states: "In terms of regions, Florida is an extension of the Lower South Black music tradition; there was no special development outside of the genres other Black people performed. However, there may be more country blues traditions." Many musicians imitated blues songs popularized by Black recording artists of the time (DeVane 1981, 2).

The only documented evidence of fiddling in Florida during the early twentieth century comes from a Library of Congress recording made in the late 1930s by John A. Lomax and Ruby Terrill Lomax. In summer 1939, the fiddle-guitar duet of Fred Perry and Glenn Carver cut half a dozen titles at Raiford State Farm, a Florida prison (Bastin 1986, 64) in Bradford County, Florida, located about sixty miles from the Atlantic Coast.[13] Since no biographical information is available on either artist, it is unknown if they were longtime Florida residents or out-of-state migrants who had been imprisoned in Florida.[14] However, the music they recorded is revealing[15] because the repertoire and performance style are characteristic of fiddling by Black and white string band musicians in mountain states.[16] In terms of repertoire, Perry and Carver performed songs that had been popular among the enslaved ("Sally Gordon," also known as "Sally Goodin") as well as tunes recorded by old-time musicians during the 1920s and 1930s: "Lost Train Blues," "The Mocking Bird," "Pretty Girl Don't Pay Me No Mind," "Walking in My Sleep"); see Russell and Pinson (2004) and discussion of J. D. Smith's performance at the 1951 Fort Valley music festival as well as Mostella's repertoire in chapter 9.

"Lost Train Blues" is noteworthy because the title references trains and travel, two topics musicians during the early twentieth century used as themes for songs to comment on issues important to their audience. Although "blues" is included in the title, the musicians perform the tune using characteristics identified with old-time music. Only when Perry performs the fiddle so that it emulates the sound of a train—for example, the wailing of the horn (0:13–0:23) or the musical interplay between the fiddle and the guitar to emulate the fast movement of the wheels on the railroad tracks (0:24–0:45)—does he include slurs and slides used by both Black and white fiddlers to demonstrate showmanship—many of which are features identified with African American culture. However, other characteristics associated with Black music—such as off-beat phrasing or extensive variations of the form—are not prominent.

While we do not know how long Perry and Carter had been imprisoned, their performances demonstrate the type of musicking Black fiddlers performed before twentieth-century innovations became prominent in African American culture. Like most Black fiddling, the tunes were probably learned through oral tradition and performed for audiences when requested or they were favorites of the musicians, because few commercial recordings had been made of them.[17] In summary, this brief analysis indicates that both the repertoire and performance style from the nineteenth and early twentieth centuries continued to be played by Black fiddlers through the late 1930s, even in areas near the Atlantic Coast. From this evidence, which is minimal, there does not appear to be any rejection of the tradition.

Alabama

Similar to Florida, Black musicians in Alabama were influenced by music from neighboring states, especially recording artists who were well liked by the public. For the Alabama Sheiks, a duo that included Eddie West (fiddle) and Ad Fox (guitar),[18] African American musicians performing the blues became the target of their attention. The Mississippi Sheiks, one of the most commercially successful string bands of the 1930s, was the most influential (see discussion below). Not only did the two groups have similar names, but on January 20, 1931, the Alabama Sheiks recorded one of the Mississippi Sheiks' most marketable tunes, "Sittin' on Top of the World," as well as covers of songs made popular by other blues musicians.[19] Although they used the same instrumentation as the Mississippi Sheiks, the Alabama Sheiks' version of "Sittin' on Top of the World" appeared to be less interesting to record buyers.[20] After this initial recording session, the duo never returned to the studio, which is significant because this was not the first Black fiddle-guitar group that Victor recorded. Between 1927 and 1929, Victor released several recordings by Andrew and James Baxter, a father-son duo from north Georgia, who were among the first African Americans in the United States to make commercial recordings (see chapter 9).

To my knowledge, the only information available on the Alabama Sheiks is that written by record reviewers. Burgin Mathews (n.d.) refers to music by the group as "fair duets . . . obviously influenced by the great Mississippi Sheiks, whose 'Sittin' on Top of the World' they imitate reasonably well." Marshall Wyatt (1999) writes: "In January 1931, guitarist Ad Fox and fiddler Eddie West, known as 'The Fox and the Rabbit,' traveled to Camden, New Jersey, where they waxed four titles for Victor under the name Alabama Sheiks. . . . Afterward, the Alabama Sheiks returned to obscurity, our knowledge of them limited to the scant information provided by the records themselves." While no one knows why recordings by the Alabama Sheiks did not attract sales, several reasons can be proposed: (1) they were unable to establish an identity distinct from the Mississippi Sheiks; (2) the quality of their music was lacking when compared to that of other artists from that period; and (3) the worldwide depression of the 1930s threw the recording industry into serious decline (Development of Musical Recording 2020). In spite of these issues, I believe that an analysis of musicking by the Alabama Sheiks will help us understand how the group is both similar to and different from other musicians experimenting with new sounds emanating from African American culture during the first half of the twentieth century.

Of the four tunes West and Fox recorded on January 20, 1931, "Travelin' Railroad Man Blues" is the most distinctive due to the fact that it is not simply a cover, but a unique arrangement of the common stock tune "Traveling Man" (also known as "Traveling Coon").[21] Although no author or composer has been attributed to "Traveling Man," researchers believe it was created and played by musicians in a variety of contexts and performance styles during the early twentieth century. One of the earliest performers was Pinkney "Pink" Anderson, an African American who used it during the 1920s as his theme song in medicine shows in different parts of the Southeast (White, Belden, and Hudson 1952; Traveling Man 2019).

After Henry Whitter, a white musician singing with guitar accompaniment, released the first commercial recording of "Traveling Man" on OKeh in 1924 (Whitter 1924), the tune became a hit. At least ten recordings, almost equally divided among all-Black and all-white groups, were made before the Alabama Sheiks released their version in January 1931;[22] see Dixon, Godrich, and Rye (1997) and Russell and Pinson (2004) for details. The lyrics of the different recordings portray the protagonist (the traveling man) as a trickster (suggesting that he is a Black man because descriptions often refer to him to as a coon) who makes his living stealing chickens and sometimes money. In most versions, he is shot by the police because he would not stop stealing (Whitter 1924).[23] In addition to both Black and white artists probably receiving enormous profits from the creation and performance of coon songs, the lyrics helped to perpetuate negative views about African Americans, which may have been one of the major reasons such songs were so popular. Historian James Dormon (1988) writes that coon songs were "a necessary socio-psychological mechanism for justifying segregation and subordination.... [For whites], blacks were not only the simple-minded comic buffoons of the minstrel tradition; they were also potentially dangerous. They constituted a threat to the American social order ... [and] had to be controlled and subordinated by whatever means. The songs also argued, implicitly at least, for coercion, for lynching if necessary, to maintain control and the domination of white over black" (466).

The Alabama Sheiks' (1931) version departed from the original version by Whitter (1924) and its covers in several ways.[24] One, no other performers, to my knowledge, used the Sheiks' title, "Travelin' Railroad Man Blues." Including the words, "traveling," "railroad," and "blues" in the title provided commentary on activities important to Black people during the early twentieth century. As noted above, migration to different parts of the country had become commonplace, and people of various ethnicities often made these trips by railway. Incorporating "blues" in the title also lets Black record buyers know this was a song contemporary for its time. Two, the lyrics as well as their underlying meanings were different from previous recordings. In the Alabama Sheiks' version, Fox performs the song in the first person. In other words, the singer talks about his personal experiences and not those of someone else or a distant person who is foreign to the singer's everyday life. Also, whereas all or most of the pre-1931 versions fall into the category of coon songs, the Alabama Sheiks' version transforms the usual braggadocio of "traveling man" into a wistful love song, rendered with a gentle touch. The male singer is sad and disappointed that the relationship with his female loved one is not working out. Not only does he express his feelings openly, but he indicates how the relationship will most likely end (Wyatt 1999).

Three, what is most unique about the Alabama Sheiks' performance is the organization formally, harmonically, and lyrically. Divided into two parts—A (main melody) and B (refrain melody)—the song opens with part A (0:00), which includes an elaborate instrumental performance of the main melody by the fiddle and guitar, and a repeat of this instrumental melody with singing in verse 1 (0:18) and verse 2 (0:37). Part B or the refrain (0:55) includes a melody performed by the singer similar to versions of "Traveling Man" recorded by other artists; however, the lyrics and harmonies are unlike those used by other musicians. Instead of mentioning the coon theme, the singer describes his travels, using a modified twelve-bar structure (thirteen bars) with I-IV-V harmonies. After repeating the refrain a second time with different lyrics (1:15), West and Fox perform the instrumental interlude (1:36) as well as verse 3 (1:55) and verse 4 (2:13), which are lyrically and harmonically the same as musicking performed at the beginning of the song. The song's ending (2:32–2:50) is a repeat of the refrain (part B) that was played earlier.

In terms of the fiddler's performance style, there is nothing outstanding. Throughout the song, Perry plays the fiddle, with some off-beat phrasing and bent notes, in unison with the singing, and inserts a few additional melodies or short motives when no singing occurs in the fill-in sections. A similar fiddling style is used when he performs the instrumental interlude. Thus, it appears that more emphasis was given to the lyrics, perhaps because the words and meaning differed from other versions of the song. Since the Alabama Sheiks may be one of the first groups to make major changes to the original version recorded by Whitter, it would be interesting to compare sales of "Travelin' Railroad Man Blues" with that of the other songs the group recorded in January 1931. Did the listening public respond positively or negatively to their innovations? Or could this have been one of several reasons their sales were low, resulting in the duo not returning to the studio?

Mississippi

Unlike rural Black fiddlers in the mountain regions who tended to remain in one area for much of their lives, just the opposite was the case for African American fiddlers in the Mississippi Delta and southern regions of the state.[25] Although Mississippi was one of the most rural states (with no large industrial cities) and had one of the most rigid caste systems in the United States, the Mississippi River and Delta region's rich soil were attractive to those who needed work. Black farmers from counties in the Hills and other parts of the state made the area an important economic sector in the Black Belt during the early twentieth century.[26] Despite its rural character, the Delta was also not isolated: "the highly-intensified plantation and sharecropping system made the region somewhat like a rural factory, sharing to a certain degree some of the characteristics of an urban environment. Like many American cities with their immigrant communities, the Delta served as a center of innovation, opportunity, and cross-fertilization of ideas as well as for the retention of old ways and patterns uprooted from their former homes" (Evans 2018b, 208–9). As a result of these factors, the setting was unique musically; it was a place where new musical ideas were introduced and musicians could be nurtured so they could use these skills and talents to make additional money. While some migrated to Memphis, St. Louis, Chicago, and other parts of the United States, others returned to their homes in Mississippi.[27] The river and the railroads that intersected the Delta served as arteries for entry, internal movement, and escape for artists and their creations (Evans 2018b, 208–09; 2021, 23).

Due to these extensive cultural interactions, various regions in the Mississippi Delta produced not only guitarists, but also fiddlers who performed a variety of songs and musical genres, especially the blues. As music researcher Julie Lyonn Lieberman (2002) explains, "The violin actually played an important role in the evolution of the blues. The recording industry caught only the tail end of this tradition. By the early 1930s, there were over fifty recorded blues fiddlers. We can assume that there were actually hundreds in existence throughout the South" (78). In fact, several Black fiddlers born and raised in or near the Delta between the 1880s and early 1900s made commercial recordings and achieved recognition for their talents, while others became well known because of their links to more established musicians. What is presented here, which is taken almost entirely from the liner notes of recordings as well as articles by journalists and music critics, provides some details about fiddling in the Capital/River and Delta regions. The discussion of fiddlers is organized chronologically according to their birth dates, with special attention given to family and community, learning, Black/white interactions, performance contexts, repertoire, performance style, and the media. The only exception is that the Chatmons are discussed together because they are members of the same family.

Profiles of Mississippi Black Fiddlers

The Chatmon Family: Lonnie Chatmon (ca. 1887–1950), Armenter "Bo" Chatmon [Bo Carter] (1893–1964), and Harry Chatmon (b. ca. 1903)

Although members of the Chatmon family performed in various configurations with different names (the Carter Brothers, the Chatmon Brothers, the Jackson Blue Boys, the Mississippi Hot Footers, and the Mississippi Mud Steppers), it was musicking by the Mississippi Sheiks, featuring Lonnie Chatmon on fiddle and Walter Vinson (1901–1975)[28] on guitar, that resulted in the group's broad appeal among both Black and white listeners. Bo Chatmon (also known as Bo Carter)[29] is best known as a solo guitarist, but he was the first member of the Chatmon family to make a recording performing the fiddle (see photo 11.1). In addition, Bo recorded with the Sheiks on guitar and as a vocalist and sometimes second fiddler (Palmer 1975; Russell 1997, 99–100; Briggs 2002; Mississippi Sheiks Tribute 2010; Mississippi Blues Trail 2014). Yet, recent research by DeWayne Moore (2021d, 381) suggests that it was Harry, not Bo, who performed the fiddle on several recordings made during the late 1920s and early 1930s.

Compared to other musicians in this study, the Mississippi Sheiks are known not only for the large number of recordings they made, but also their impact on the development of US popular music. Writing in 1975, journalist Robert Palmer states: "Forty-five years later the music of these Mississippi Sheiks, who became one of the best-selling black recording groups of the 1930s, has lost little of its immediacy and none of its charm. Reissues of Sheiks music and recordings of surviving Sheiks and Sheik relatives are proliferating, and catching the fancy of listeners to whom most of the rural popular music of the Depression years has seemed forbiddingly obscure or austere." Comments by producers of a 2010 concert tribute in honor of the Mississippi Sheiks are also revealing: "Though they only were together for five years, by the time they called it quits the Mississippi Sheiks had left a body of work behind that still resonates in today's world. This is music that sounds as ancient as a Dead Sea Scroll and like it could have been written yesterday" (Mississippi Sheiks Tribute 2010).

Because of their popularity and influence, much has been written about the Chatmons by researchers who have interviewed family members or used secondary sources and the music itself to document, interpret, and establish an appreciation for their contributions. So, unlike other Black fiddlers for which little information is available, just the opposite is the case with the Chatmon family.[30] The challenge in writing about the Mississippi Sheiks and their associates is being able to synthesize the wealth of material to both resolve contradictions and address issues important to this study. However, recent research by Moore (2021d) has helped clarify some issues.

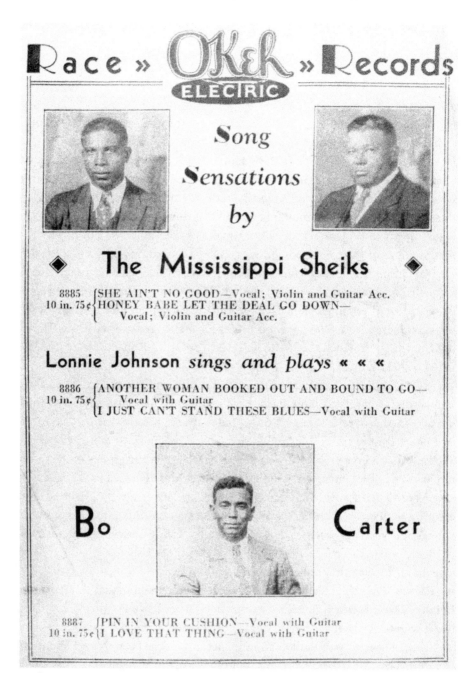

Photo 11.1. OKeh race records advertisement for the Mississippi Sheiks and Bo Carter, July 1931. John Edwards Memorial Foundation Records (20001), Southern Folklife Collection at Wilson Special Collections Library, University of North Carolina at Chapel Hill.

While their father, Miles Henderson Chatmon (ca. 1848–1934),[31] was born in Terry, Lonnie, Bo, and Harry were born and raised in Bolton. Both are small towns in Hinds County, located near Jackson, the seat and state capital, in the Capital/River region just south of the Delta.[32] According to Evans (2018a), the Capital/River region was a haven for upwardly mobile Blacks and families of mixed racial heritage: "The large Chatmon family of musicians . . . certainly had such a heritage. Utica Institute, a black college,[33] was located nearby and no doubt raised the educational level of the area. . . . It is interesting to note how many prominent early blues artists came from this general area a few miles to the south and west of the city of Jackson. In addition to Charley Patton [ca. 1886–1934] and the Chatmons, there were . . . Walter Vinson . . . and Charlie McCoy [1909–1950],[34] and many others who moved north to the Delta" (43). When members of the Chatmon family relocated to the Delta region in the late teens, they lived in various locations (Moore 2021d, 390–92; Calt, Stewart, and Kent 1974; Mississippi Blues Trail 2014).

After emancipation, the Chatmons worked as farmers; Henderson "rented land from Gaddis and McLaurin Farms and raised crops with his sons at various locations south and west of Bolton" (Mississippi Blues Trail 2014). However, this changed in the early twentieth century. Although Harry, in 1925, lists "laborer" as his occupation in the Memphis city directory, his profession in the Jackson directory is registered as "musician" for 1929, 1932, and 1939 and "porter" in 1945.[35] According to the US census, Lonnie pursued a variety of occupations as an adult. In the 1920 census, working as wagon driver for a coal company is indicated as his employment, and in 1930, he lists his occupation and industry as "musician [in] hotel orchestra."[36] In 1936, Lonnie opened a cafe in Glen Allan, an unincorporated area in Washington County in the Delta region. When he returned to the Bolton vicinity in 1937, he worked in assorted enterprises, including the management of a fishing spot until his death (Calt, Stewart, and Kent 1974; Mississippi Blues Trail 2014). Regarding the impact of work on Lonnie's musicking, Moore (2021d) writes: "Even though Lonnie Chatmon devoted his energies to music making, he also started to devote more and more of his time inside, and sometimes operating, the rural barrelhouses or 'jook' houses. The jook was the place that . . . provided the foundations on which he built his performance and recording career" (390).

The Chatmons' residences are significant because of the impact that context can have on musicking. It is unknown why some members of the family moved to the Delta, the region where the Sheiks lived when they made most of their recordings. But, like other state residents, it may have been for greater opportunities economically.[37] In doing so, their social environment and audiences for performances changed from their birthplaces. Commenting on this issue, Palmer (1975) writes: "Seven of the Chatmon brothers played in a family string band which performed for white square dances and black socials from the early years of World War I until the departure of four of the brothers for the Delta.... The family group's 'music for all occasions' approach was probably a result of the Bolton area's demographics; black musicians in northern Mississippi [Hills] often chose a similarly eclectic approach, while in the predominately black Delta region, string bands concentrated on the blues." Evans (2018b) also makes the point that relocation to the Delta may have caused the Sheiks to come in closer contact with musical features from the Hills "because many of the famed 'Delta' bluesmen were actually born or grew up in the hill country" (208–9).

Like many Black fiddlers, Lonnie, Bo, and Harry were members of a large family that played multiple instruments. Sam Chatmon (2010) has reported in interviews that his father "owned fiddles, guitars, a banjo, mandolin, clarinet, piano, and bass viol, and his sons banded together to play white square dances and black parties. 'All of us nine brothers played together. Lonnie and Edgar would play the violins. Harry would play the guitar, piano, or violin. Willie and Bert played the guitar. Bo would play the guitar or banjo, and brother Laurie [Larry] beat the drums. I'd usually play bass violin for them.'" In an interview with Oliver (1972, 49–50), Sam provided even more details: "My brothers were Lonnie, Edgar, Bo, Willie, Lamar and me, Sam Chatman . . . and Laurie [Larry], and Harry Chatman, and Charlie Chatman.... I played bass viol for them, and Lonnie, he played violin and Harry he played second violin. And my Brother Bo, he played clarinet and my brother Bert played guitar and my brother Larry, he beat the drums. And my brother Harry, he played piano.... And my brother Bo he played guitar too and he even used to play tenor banjo. And I played guitar. We just pick and play any instrument and play one to another."

In such contexts, children learned from elders and each other. When Henderson played the fiddle during enslavement, performing tunes such as "Little Liza Jane" and "Can't Get the Saddle on the Grey Mule," his wife, Eliza, probably sang; most likely she did not start playing the guitar until after slavery (Chatmon 1978). Recalling his early learning experiences, Sam explained: "My father, he played in slavery time, when the white folks wan' it, he *had* to play. And when I was big enough to remember when he used to be playing round the house at times, I'd ask him, 'Let me try!' He say, 'No, you too small yet to play, too little, so you wait.'... So, when I did get big enough to play, I go to playin' a piece, and I'd make a mistake. I was playing a guitar. He said, 'Bring me a fiddle here, let me show you how that go.' And then me and him would sit down and play for maybe two hours" (Oakley 1997, 52). Moore (2021d, 389) believes Henderson provided Lonnie with his earliest musical lessons, but it is likely that he also learned from Milton Bracey, a family friend who was a Black fiddler.[38] In interviews, Josie Williams, Lonnie's sister, has stated: "I believe it was Lonnie who got the first fiddle and papa know a heap of old-time songs.... And that's what Lonnie learned by him and then he began to take lessons from my brother-in-law" (Moore 2021d, 389; also see below).

Although several siblings were multi-instrumentalists, Lonnie, Bo, and possibly Harry were the only ones who made commercial recordings playing the fiddle. Lonnie was considered to be the better fiddler because of his ability to generate what some critics refer to as swing (Kent 1972). Critics also indicate that Lonnie had excellent technique: "he could play in position, he had superior bowing ability, he played in tune, and he had a nice rolling vibrato" (Lieberman 1986, 37). To enhance his appeal to local whites, Lonnie learned to read sheet music from a fiddling brother-in-law, Neil Winston (1872–1944), around World War I, and began "purchasing sheet music in nearby Jackson and teaching popular tunes to his brothers" (Big Road Blues Show 2010). According to Sam, Lonnie soon surpassed Winston at these efforts, which were practically unparalleled in country blues (Calt, Stewart, and Kent 1974).[39] Both Lonnie and the fiddle were admired by his peers. "Other than learning Lonnie's elementary sight reading, [Vinson's] idealization of the violin as 'the king of string instruments' led him to conceive of his role [in the group] as purely secondary. Thus, he felt obliged to strum most of his accompaniments, and never hazard a back-up on mandolin, an instrument he played proficiently . . . but regarded as a redundant lead" (Calt, Stewart, and Kent 1974; also, see Moore 2021d, 391).

As noted in the above, early in their careers (from around 1910 until 1928) several brothers performed in a string band, known as the Chatmon Brothers, that played for white audiences at country dances, suppers, parties, and picnics (Big Road Blues Show 2010). When Sam was asked, "Did you meet any bluesmen when you were young?" he responded: "No, I never did go out that way. I didn't start out till I was seven years old, and I was with my brothers. And we didn't play no blues hardly because we's playin' for white folks" (Obrecht 2009, 71; Chatmon 2010). In another interview, Sam added: "Mighty seldom I ever play for coloured, they didn't have nothing to hire you with. I used to serenade for 'em [whites], right here in Hollandale. He [the white man I worked for] give me 60 cents a day for plowin', and give me five dollars for playin' three or four pieces at his house" (Oakley 1997, 52; Obrecht 2009, 71). Even writers for the Mississippi Blues Trail (2014) report that "Various Chatmon ensembles entertained black and white audiences for several decades in Mississippi. . . . On record, they were best known for blues, but they also played waltzes, reels, Tin Pan Alley songs, ballads, and minstrel show tunes to cater to both their white and black audiences. Muddy Waters, who then played in a similar string band, said he 'walked ten miles to hear them play.'" In addition to local performances, the Sheiks toured throughout the South, and traveled to Chicago and New York. Providing details about the family's travels, Sam (1978) stated: "All of us played, the whole family. When we'd get through with us crops . . . in June or July, we'd all get together and take a tour all up through Memphis, Chicago, and diff'rent places like that."

Although commercial recordings by Black fiddlers/violinists began during the 1910s with James Reese Europe and others,[40] the larger majority were made in the 1920s by African Americans based in the urban South, Midwest, and Northeast who specialized in performing blues, novelty songs, and some pop tunes. The Chatmon brothers, whose fiddle recordings were released between the late 1920s and mid-1930s, are among the few Black fiddlers based in the rural South to record commercially, except for Jim Booker from Kentucky and Andrew Baxter from Georgia, who both recorded in 1927 (see above). So, it is significant that the Chatmons made as many recordings as they did when media executives during the early twentieth century tended to shun Black musicians or musicking associated with rural Black culture. According to music critic Marty Pahls (1985),[41] record companies drew a strict color line in producing their commercial releases. "Black players and singers had their own segregated 'race music' catalogs, almost exclusively jazz, blues, and gospel. The 'hillbilly' catalog was the exclusive province for white string and fiddle band music. (The few and distinguished exceptions to this include the Memphis and Louisville jug bands, the Mississippi Sheiks, and [Howard] Armstrong's own Tennessee Chocolate Drops)." Even when hillbilly and race records began to wane in popularity during the early thirties due to the economic upheaval of the Great Depression, the Sheiks' recordings sold surprisingly well. John Tefteller of Tefteller's World's Rarest Records explains:

> The Mississippi Sheiks literally sold millions of records for OKeh, particularly with their big hit, "Sitting on Top of the World," but the group's contract went dormant in 1932. At that same time, Paramount was in severe financial trouble, just hanging on by the skin of its teeth.... They were desperate to find something that would sell. Everything they were putting out, as good as it was, was just not selling, because in 1932, very few people had money to buy records, let alone poor African-Americans.... Well, Paramount, ... from what I can speculate, snapped them up and said, "Come to Grafton we'd like you to come here, we'll give you some money and put some more records out on you and keep your legacy and keep your ability to keep jobs at juke joints."
>
> The Sheiks headed to Wisconsin for a July 1932 recording session that produced six records.... The collaboration between The Sheiks and Paramount proved to be the end of the line for the record label. [These songs were] the last official Paramount release that resembles its previous blues recordings.[42] (Sliwicki 2011, 98)

Although the Sheiks' recordings did not help the label escape financial ruin, the fact that Paramount contacted the artists with a record deal (and not musicians with whom they had previously worked) demonstrates the group's high regard by the media (Big Road Blues Show 2010).

Most researchers believe it was the sound that accounted for the Sheiks' popularity; the fact that some recordings were considered to be musically colorless[43] encouraged OKeh to issue them in their regular (or hillbilly) series instead of solely the race record series[44] (Lornell 1974; Lowry 1977; Pahls 1985; Laird and Rust 2004; Waterman 2000). In other words, the Sheiks' appeal to a diverse demographic base assured the media that their recordings would have a wide distribution and positively affect sales. Even if this generalization is accurate, this raises several questions. To what degree did the issue of race affect Lonnie's and Bo's fiddling or influence their identification with African American music? Could their success have also been the result of good business sense or did other factors—repertoire, lyrics, or performance style—mark them as distinct from other Black string bands? As the most successful fiddler in the Chatmon family, was there anything special about Lonnie's life that affected his fiddling? In addressing these questions, my attention will be given first to Bo and, to a limited extent, to Harry, followed by a more extensive discussion of Lonnie.

Bo Chatmon. Unlike Lonnie, who made all of his recordings during the 1930s, Bo's recording career extended from 1928 to 1940; however, the thirty-three songs in which he is listed as playing the fiddle were released between 1928 and 1930.[45] Bo's success, according to some music critics, had as much to do with his professionalism as his musicking. Oliver (1972) writes: "Of all the family and the Mississippi Sheiks, Bo Carter had been the most successful. . . . [H]e was one of the youngest of the brothers but his business head and general reliability—he was less inclined than many blues singers to get drunk on the royalty advance and the whiskey that was usually provided to loosen up the sessions—ensured him a regular retainer from the Bluebird company. Moreover, he had a successful formula for double-entendre blues which were more amusing than profound. Even when he was singing at his most sexually exuberant, his voice had a melancholy touch, and his gently swinging guitar playing was always sensitively executed" (123).

Bo began making recordings during the last two months in 1928, when he participated in several sessions with Columbia and Brunswick. The name listed on recordings is noteworthy because, of the thirty-four tunes he recorded playing the fiddle during his career, the name Bo Carter is used only once (at the December 19, 1930, session with Charlie McCoy); however, Bo Chatmon appears several times. This evidence also raises other questions. One, why did Bo use the group's name, Mississippi Hot Footers, on the majority of the recordings he is listed as playing the fiddle? Was this to ensure that record buyers did not confuse his name (Bo Chatmon) and the group (Mississippi Hot Footers) with Lonnie Chatmon and the Mississippi Sheiks or another reason?[46] However, recent findings by Moore (2021d) suggest that it was not Bo, but rather Harry, who performed the fiddle on several recordings made during the late 1920s and early 1930s:

> Drawing on previously undiscovered interviews with Lonnie Chatmon's older sister and younger brother, Josie and Larry Chatmon, we now know that McCoy and Vinson developed their talents initially under the tutelage of fiddler and

pianist Harry Chatmon, the youngest son of Henderson and Eliza Chatmon, whom the duo backed in a string band in the late 1920s. Moreover, we conclude that the fiddler heard in the recording of Alec Johnson and Chatmon's Mississippi Hot Footers is not Bo Carter, as previously believed, but rather Harry Chatmon, who remained employed as a musician in a hotel orchestra in Jackson throughout the Great Depression. (380-381)

Two, were the recordings released on different labels[47] evidence of exploitation on the part of the media or a decision made by both the Chatmons and record company executives to generate greater interest and exposure for the different groups with which family members and associates were affiliated? In the article, "How 'Race Records' Turned Black Music into Big Business," journalist Erin Blakemore (2019) explains: "Many artists were put on records that gave them pseudonyms or left out their names entirely, which meant they weren't able to parlay their recording careers into successful performing careers." However, Lieberman (2002, 79) suggests this was a decision on the part of musicians "to get around their record contract." An interview between Oliver and Bo in 1960 suggests that Lieberman's argument may be a more accurate interpretation of the relationship between the Chatmons and the media. In the interview, Bo makes clear his feelings when record company executives attempted to control one of the Sheiks' recording sessions: "We was the Mississippi Sheiks and when we went to make the records in Jackson, Mississippi, the feller wanted to show us how to stop and start the records. Try to tell us when we got to begin and how we got to end. And you know, I started *not* to make 'em! I started *not* to make 'em 'cause he wasn't no musicianer, so how could he tell *me* to stop and start the song? We was the Sheiks, Mississippi Sheiks and you know we was famous" (quoted in Big Road Blues Show 2010).

In terms of repertoire and performance style, fiddling by the brothers differed. Bo (or possibly Harry) was less versatile both in the types of songs performed and the manner in which they were played. While Bo may have performed some pop or novelty tunes, the majority of his (or Harry's) recordings on fiddle, like those by many Black fiddlers in urban areas during the mid-1920s, were twelve-bar blues, with some organized as eight- or sixteen-bar blues. By the late 1920s, the length and arrangement of blues recordings had become standardized. As Lieberman (2002) explains, "Because 78 records allowed for only a little more than three minutes per side, most groups developed a standard arrangement to fit into that time. Groups using fiddle tended to open with a fiddle intro, go on to a sung verse or two, a fiddle solo, a few more sung verses, and then a tag usually played by the fiddler.... Classical techniques [meaning features identified with European art music] like vibrato and tremolo[48] were adapted to play the blues: the width and speed of the vibrato became more varied, and tremolo became a blues shimmer. Various slide techniques developed, and, of course, each player had to learn how to improvise" (79).[49] Using arpeggios in playing melodies also became a characteristic improvisatory technique.[50]

With some noted exceptions, Bo placed greater emphasis on African-derived features such as bent notes and off-beat phrasing (syncopation) when improvising, such as in the 1930 recording, "It's Hot Like That," which is his version of "It's Tight Like That" that had been recorded earlier by blues artists Tampa Red (Hudson Whittaker, 1903–1981) and Georgia Tom (Thomas A. Dorsey, 1899–1993) in 1928[51] as well as Clara Smith in 1929. In addition, he did not take great liberties (or make any grand statements) when performing the fiddle, probably because he was an expert on the guitar and not the fiddle. Therefore, typical of fiddlers who accompanied blues singers during the early 1920s, Bo tended to follow the singing style and melody of the lead vocalist with minimal variations. For example, in three ("Mysterious Coon," "Sister Maud Mule," and "Toodle Doo") of the four tunes in which he (or Harry) accompanies Alec Johnson, Bo (or Harry) merely plays in unison with the singer without including any melodic variations to demonstrate some of the unique sound qualities of the fiddle. Even on "Miss Meal Cramp Blues," which is based on a twelve-bar blues, Bo (Harry) does not respond by playing during bars 3–4, 7–8, and 11–12, after the singer performs the main melody or the call.[52] Rather, the mandolin performs most of the response while Bo (Harry) inserts a few slurs and slides during his unison accompaniment with Johnson. However, Bo uses a different performance style in the three twelve-bar blues songs he performed with Mary Butler. Including arpeggios and vibrato during the response and interlude, when the fiddle performs the main AAB melody, differs from the unison accompaniment he played in his session with Johnson.[53]

Bo's most memorable recording session on fiddle, in my opinion, took place in November 1928 when he served as leader of the group.[54] The session is also noteworthy because of its inclusion of two twelve-bar blues songs that became important in Bo's career—"Corrine Corrina," one of his biggest hits that is now a common stock tune, and "East Jackson Blues," which has been included on several record compilations.[55] On "Corrine Corrina," in which he performs a vocal duet with mandolin player Charlie McCoy while also playing the fiddle, Bo's fiddling (in unison) and singing the main melody (in harmony) with McCoy serves as the call. The response consists of him playing a florid melodic passage on the fiddle with brief arpeggios. Instead of continuing to perform only the main melody later in the performance, however, Bo occasionally plays tremolos lightly on the fiddle -- during the fifth (1:44), sixth (2:08), and seventh (2:30) repeats of the AAB verse—as a response to the calls.

On "East Jackson Blues," in which Bo sings the vocal lead and plays the fiddle, his fiddling includes more melodic variation, inspiring a similar performance style by the mandolin player. In addition to performing arpeggios during the response (break), Bo incorporates extensive pitch-bending and off-beat phrasing. Also noteworthy is the vibrato and movement up two or more octaves in pitch on the fiddle during his singing of verse 3 (1:05-1:12). He performs vibrato on double stops (1:58–2:05) during verse 5, which is an interesting way of improvising that provides him time to concentrate on singing the lyrics. When Bo plays arpeggios and vibrato during and after each call to contrast with the main AAB melody, his fiddle melodies are more florid and performed in the style of blues fiddlers Clifford Hayes and Lonnie Johnson. Commenting on Bo's performance, Wyatt (2001) states: "'East Jackson Blues' is notable for Bo's sultry vocals and a tremulous fiddle that often races up the neck."[56]

The lyrics to "East Jackson Blues" are interesting because they reflect the dilemma of Blacks living in the South during the early twentieth century.[57] When African Americans migrated north or to another part of the South (in this case Tennessee) for a better life and work opportunities,[58] oftentimes they discovered that the situation or conditions in their new home were no different or sometimes worse than the place they left.[59] After migrating, most Blacks remained in their new location and attempted to make the best of the circumstances. Yet those who could obtain the money returned to their old homes. In fact, Odum (1911b, 361) indicates that some of the more interesting stories are told by Blacks who describe their experiences in returning home. In this song by Bo, the singer returns to his home in East Jackson.[60] A similar theme is expressed in "The Northern Starvers Are Returning Home," a song Bo (on fiddle) and Charlie McCoy (on guitar) recorded on December 19, 1930, a year after the release of "East Jackson Blues."[61]

Lonnie Chatmon. As noted above, the Mississippi Sheiks grew out of a collaboration between Lonnie Chatmon (fiddle) and Walter Vinson (guitar and vocal during the late 1920s). The Sheiks' big break took place in 1930 in the small Delta town of Itta Bena in Leflore County.[62] Calt, Stewart, and Kent (1974) explain: "It was at an engagement for a white square dance in Itta Bena that they were discovered by the local record dealer, Ralph Lembo, who arranged for them to record in Shreveport for OKeh. When the recording director of their session (Polk Brockman, who became their 'manager') solicited a 'fancy' name for their anonymous group, Vinson suggested 'The Mississippi Sheiks' in tribute to the pop hit 'Sheik of Araby.'"[63] Sam Chatmon attributes several factors to the demise of the Mississippi Sheiks: "Unable to get proper medical treatment for a stroke that paralyzed his left arm, he [Vinson] moved to Chicago, where he boarded with a sister and worked for a Swift's packing plant. . . . Over the last years of Lonnie's life, he suffered from heart trouble. True to the blues tradition, he blamed his ill-health upon blues-playing. When I'd go out to see him, he says: 'Whenever I get up, if I live to get up, me and you gonna put out nothin' but gospel music . . . I done joined the church and I don't wanna play no more blues.' I told him 'Okay' but I wasn't lookin' for him to get up."[64]

Between 1930 and 1936, Lonnie recorded 107 songs as a member of the Sheiks and other groups on several labels: OKeh, Columbia, Paramount, Champion,

Broadway, Crown, Varsity, and Bluebird.[65] Besides the large number of songs recorded, what most distinguished Lonnie from Bo and other Black fiddlers was his versatility. As Lieberman (2002, 79) explains, "Popular groups such as the Mississippi Sheiks placed the fiddle in a central position, and for good reason; fiddler Lonnie Chatman [sic] had a solid command of the instrument. In fact, under the guiding influence of Lonnie Chatman, the Mississippi Sheiks were one of the few professional string bands in the Mississippi area." Commenting on Lonnie's contributions to the Mississippi Sheiks, Moore (2021d) writes, "His fiddle playing shaped their sound while his opportunism paved the way for their success. [In later interviews, Vinson stated] 'He didn't make no mistakes; he didn't play no discords . . . he was just a violin player. Got the record all the way through Mississippi . . . as the best violin-player'" (378). In many ways, Lonnie's fiddling is more similar to musicians in urban areas (because of his incorporation of so many new ideas and his ability to fuse the old with the new) than Black fiddlers in rural communities who tended to be more reserved and restrained in playing the fiddle and creating new songs.

To understand more clearly the multifaceted nature of Lonnie's contributions, I will focus on three topics: lyrics, repertoire, and performance style. The Sheiks' incorporation of a variety of themes in the lyrics of their songs—gender ("She's a Bad Girl"); sex ("Bed Spring Poker"); politics ("Sales Tax"); economics ("Times Done Got Hard"); religion ("He Calls That Religion"), and other topics—made their musicking appealing to both Black and white audiences.[66] The Sheiks' repertoire was also diverse. Palmer (1975) explains: "Lonnie Chatmon does seem to have been responsible for the broad range of the Sheiks' repertoire. . . . But . . . if Vinson's guitar was often pedestrian, his voice, with its regional peculiarities of diction and its quavering resonance, contributed to the uniqueness of the Sheiks' sound. The result was a hybrid representative of the entire spectrum of American popular music, and the Sheiks demonstrated their awareness of its possibilities by recording it." Interestingly, the breadth of Lonnie's repertoire is apparent in the Sheiks' first recording session in Shreveport on February 17, 1930. The five blues songs—"Driving That Thing," "Alberta Blues," "Winter Time Blues," "Sitting on Top of the World," "Stop and Listen Blues"—are performed using elements (bent notes and extensive melodic variation) identified with African American musicking. However, the song types and limited melodic and rhythmic improvisation in the three pop tunes—"The Sheik Waltz," "The Jazz Fiddler," and "Lonely One in This Town"—display a greater fusion of African American and Euro-American features.

It is also significant that three songs from the Sheiks' first recording session—"Alberta Blues," "Sitting on Top of the World," and "Stop and Listen Blues"—became hits in country blues. Like Bo who used the same melody for several song titles, the Sheiks made multiple recordings of "Sitting on Top of the World" and "Stop and Listen Blues," with similar tunes and/or different song titles and texts (Evans 1982, 124). Although Vinson credits himself with composing "Sitting on Top of the World," some researchers indicate differently. Calt, Stewart, and Kent (1974) state: "While the composition of the song is problematic (the melody is almost certainly Tampa Red's), there seems little doubt that the Sheiks' subsequent recordings were generally based on Lonnie's arrangements." In addition, the Sheiks' "Stop and Listen Blues" is derived from "Big Road Blues" by blues guitarist Tommy Johnson (1896–1956), but the mood of the former "is in total contrast to that of Johnson's record" (Evans 1982, 285).[67]

Lonnie's performance style is particularly noteworthy because of the many ways he used the fiddle to produce interesting sounds. To demonstrate this diversity, I present an in-depth analysis of two songs: "Sitting on Top of the World" and "Stop and Listen Blues No. 2."[68] "Sitting on Top of the World," recorded on February 17, 1930, at the Sheiks' first recording session, in my opinion, is not Lonnie's most outstanding performance but useful for comparing an early recording with those released in later years. Based on a nine-bar blues, the fiddle plays in unison with the singer in a medium pitch range with some off-beat phrasing and vibrato. While some may consider the song to be a nine-bar blues, actually the verses performed by the singer consist of eight bars; the ninth bar after each verse (0:18–0:22; 0:42–0:45; 1:06–1:10, and so on) is used as an opportunity for the fiddle to improvise (using arpeggios) and provide a segue or connecting phrase to the main melody of the next verse. This is evident because when Lonnie performs the verse on fiddle during the interlude (1:34–1:52), his melody consists of eight bars with no segue to the main melody. Due to the lack of unique features in the performance of "Sitting on Top of the World" by the instrumentalists, some may question why it became so popular. Jazz researcher Eddie Meadows (2020) believes the essence of the song is in the lyrics: "'Sitting on Top of the World' was a modern concept for that time. Most early blues songs focused on the negative, 'not hope.' Therefore, this was the appropriate song for troubled people in troubled times; this is why it was recorded so many times." Others have stated the lyrics "convey a stoic optimism in the face of emotional setbacks . . . [it is] 'a simple, elegant distillation of the blues'" (Sitting on Top of the World 2020).

However, "Stop and Listen Blues No. 2," recorded on December 19, 1930, is one of the Sheiks' most memorable recordings because of the central role of the fiddler in the performance and the interaction (polyphony) that occurs between the fiddle and guitar. As Oliver (1987) states, "the blending of Vinson and Lonnie on this piece represents Sheikdom at its heights." The importance of the fiddle is reflected in the song's structure. As noted above, blues recordings that included the fiddle during the 1920s normally opened with a brief fiddle introduction, followed by sung verses, a fiddle solo during the interlude, more sung verses, and a closing by the fiddle (Lieberman 2002, 79). A similar song structure is used in "Stop and Listen Blues No. 2," but the role of the performers differs, which from the outset affects the power dynamics in the group.[69] Departing from the form normally used on 78 recordings that included fiddling (Lieberman 2002, 79), the main AAB melody in "Stop and Listen Blues No. 2" is performed six times, or one could say that the song consists of six verses.

After the instrumental introduction (0:00–0:10) with fiddle and guitar, the fiddler continues to lead by performing the first verse (0:10–0:40) with guitar accompaniment but no singing, while the remaining five verses are performed by the singer with accompaniment by the fiddle and guitar. In addition, the song includes no interludes. The fact that Lonnie performs the introduction and the first verse without a vocalist are important markers, indicating that he is central to the performance and not merely a supporting accompanist. Several other features in Lonnie's performance of "Stop and Listen Blues No. 2" demonstrate his uniqueness as a fiddler. One, the introduction and verses are performed in a high-pitched range, which is a technique some fiddlers used to bring attention to the instrument, for it was a sound quality that could not be produced by most instrumentalists.[70] Two, his use of vibrato, tremolos, and bent notes during the first four bars of the AAB melody, followed by a florid and intricate rendition of the remaining eight bars, are features that fuse elements from both Africa and Europe. Three, features identified with African American musicking (bent notes, off-beat phrasing, melodic variation, polyphonic interplay between parts, call and response, and so on) can also be heard in this piece, making it an excellent example (in one song) of Lonnie's incorporation of these elements in his fiddling. Finally, he introduces interesting melodic and rhythmic patterns to bring both unity and interest to the piece. For example, the arpeggio off-beat melodic phrase[71] used as the response to the second statement of A is one that Lonnie repeats when verses two through six are performed by the singer. Also, the musical interplay that takes place between the fiddle and guitar during the A portion of the main melody in verses two through six is striking for the polyphonic sound quality it produces. Instead of playing repeated notes or strumming back and forth as he did in verse one, the guitarist plays a repetitive four-note pattern in octaves while the singer and the fiddle perform the main melody.[72]

The fact that the Sheiks became well known for including characteristics from a variety of cultures into their musicking may account for the "colorless" label often used to describe their recordings. For example, Oliver (1987) suggests that the Sheiks' "Yodeling Fiddling Blues" was influenced by white country musician Jimmie Rodgers's (1897–1933) blue yodeling songs, while their "Lazy Lazy River" is believed to have been inspired by white songwriter Hoagy Carmichael's (1899–1981) "Lazy River."[73] "The Sheik Waltz" and "Fingering with Your Fingers" (an example of old-time music) can also be identified with Euro-Americans. However, "The Jazz Fiddler" demonstrates his skills in performing jazz and jug band music that had become popularized by Black fiddlers Armand Piron and Clifford Hayes during the twenties and thirties (Cox 1976). In addition, "The Jazz Fiddler" is another example in which the fiddler serves as the featured artist in the performance, and not merely the singer's accompanist. Although the music is not improvisatory with extensive melodic variation, the fiddle dominates in the opening, the interludes, and the closing. In this case, the lack of melodic variation is intentional, so Lonnie could emulate the sounds of horns that were becoming popular in jazz performances in urban settings such as New Orleans, Chicago, and New York.

The session on June 10, 1930, is noteworthy for the four sides featuring Lonnie on fiddle with guitar accompaniment but no vocalists. Each song has a distinctive style that allows him to demonstrate his versatility on the fiddle. "Dear Girl" begins as a ballad waltz with the fiddle replacing the smooth and lyrical sound that would normally be performed by the vocalist. Then, in the middle of the song (1:50), the guitarist changes to a 2/4 rhythm with Lonnie playing double stops, off-beat phrasing, and movement into a higher register. "Mississippi Low Down" is typical of nineteenth-century old-time music, while "Sheiks Special" is another ballad-type waltz in which Lonnie demonstrates how the lyrical qualities of the fiddle can easily replace the voice. "That's It" and "Loose Like That" are performed in the style of the off-beat, syncopated rough sound of blues songs like "It's Tight Like That" made popular by Tampa Red and Georgia Tom (1928), Clara Smith (1929), and Bo's "It's Hot Like That" (1930).

The Sheiks also varied the pace and delivery of their performances, from the lively dance tempo of "Please Don't Wake It Up" to the sentimental "Please Baby" and hard blues ("Cracking Them Things" and "Stir It Now"). On some tunes, Lonnie performed melodies that included features identified with Euro-American classical music (arpeggios, tremolos, vibrato, etc.) that had become commonplace during the mid-1920s with Black fiddlers accompanying female and male blues singers. Other times he accompanied the vocalist by performing a melody using a limited pitch range and little improvisation. During his last recording sessions in the 1930s, probably when audiences had become enamored with bands that included brass instruments over those with fiddles or violins, Lonnie performed riffs with the fiddle to suggest the sound of brass instruments.

There is no doubt that the Sheiks' ability to creatively perform a variety of music traditions contributed to their success. As Adam Gussow (2010b) explains, "The Chatmons didn't just embody the transition from the pre-blues world of fiddle-driven string bands to the guitar-driven blues, but they fused the two styles in a distinctive way" (187). When most Black musicians during the early 1930s turned away from the old-time music of earlier decades toward a harder, harsher blues sound, the Sheiks combined the two traditions. Expanding on this point, Palmer (1975) states:

> The sedately lilting guitar strumming of lead vocalist Walter Vinson and the propulsive vinegary violin of Lonnie Chatmon blended into an immediately identifiable whole which fused the "high lonesome sound" of white mountain music,

the gritty directness of blues, and the off-color humor and ragtime chord changes of vaudeville music. The result was a hybrid representative of the entire spectrum of American popular music, and the Sheiks demonstrated their awareness of its possibilities by recording rags, reels, folk ballads, minstrel tunes, waltzes, pop songs, and hoedown numbers, as well as such Mississippi blues classics as "Stop and Listen Blues" and their original "Sittin' on Top of the World."

Lonnie was unique and different from other rural Black fiddlers who were active during the time that he lived and recorded. While he may have learned much from family members, he expanded his knowledge and technique through formal training (learning how to read music) and listening to the media. His musicking and actions suggest that he preferred the life of an urban musician, one in which he would be introduced to ideas that he could nurture and develop into something new. Close proximity to the Mississippi River, urban spaces and different audiences became an escape for him to enhance his talents. Lonnie existed in a liminal space. While he may have lived, and interacted with people in the rural, his lifestyle and musicking reflected the urban.

Henry "Son" Simms (1890-1958)

Henry Simms (also spelled Sims)[74] is well known primarily because he recorded with two of the most influential blues musicians from Mississippi: Charley (also spelled Charlie) Patton and Muddy Waters (birth name McKinley Morganfield) (see photo 11.2). Henry "Son" Simms. Simms was born in Anguilla, a small town in Sharkey County in the western portion of the Delta region, and died in Memphis.[75] Family members believe his maternal grandfather, Warren Scott, a formerly enslaved person who played the fiddle for his personal enjoyment, is the person who encouraged his grandson to play the fiddle. Lillie Hester, one of Simms's younger sisters, explains: "'Son' started out playing hisself. He'd sit outside on the porch and play. He had done played the guitar first. . . . He learned the fiddle from mother's daddy [Scott]. We was all kids when he started playing (around 1910). We lived at Renova[76] there" (Wardlow 1994, 13).

Yet, John W. Work III, who interviewed Simms during his 1941 field research in Mississippi,[77] believes Simms's decision to concentrate on the fiddle was influenced by his contact with Lonnie Chatmon. Work III (2005) explains: "As a boy, the 'string bands' strongly attracted him. It was only natural that he should hanker to play one of the stringed instruments. The first instrument he learned to play was the guitar. There being several guitar players around to whom he could listen and from whom he could receive instruction, he eventually developed considerable skill in playing the instrument. Two fiddlers, who formerly lived in the Friars Point Section [of Coahoma County], Lonnie Chapman [Chatmon] and Rand Smith, taught him [how] to play the fiddle, which fascinated him so strongly that he forsook the guitar for it" (118). When Simms returned from his army service in World War I, he became leader of a string band known as the Mississippi Corn Shuckers that played at local dances, fish-fries and parties (Wyatt 1999; Big Road Blues Show 2014; Henry "Son" Sims n.d.; Layne n.d.). In the end, Simms became a multi-instrumentalist. In addition to the fiddle, he played piano, bass, viola, mandolin, and guitar (Wardlow 1994, 13).

Because information about Simms's life is sketchy, I believe we can learn more about him and his musicking by focusing on the musicians (Patton and Waters) with whom he recorded. An examination of the repertoire and performance style Simms uses when playing with others will also help in demonstrating the distinctiveness of his fiddling. As noted above, Patton was born in Edwards, a small town in Hinds County in the Mississippi Capital/River region, but died in Sunflower County in the Delta region (Oliver 1972, 31; Evans 2018a, 25–26). To improve their economic prospects, the Patton family moved one hundred miles north to Dockery,[78] a cotton farm in Sunflower County founded in 1895 by William Alfred "Will" Dockery (1865–1936). The relocation was a turning point in Patton's musical career because it was at Dockery that he befriended and was tutored by local Delta bluesmen. By 1912, Patton had become a dominant musical force on Dockery (Evans 1977a, 1977b; Dicaire 1999). Whatever music he and others performed was disseminated quickly by the annual migration of Blacks who traveled to large plantations like Dockery to pick cotton but also to play with, as well as learn from musicians such as Patton (Kent 1977).

After Patton left Dockery around 1920, he lived near the small community of Merigold, outside the town of Mound Bayou in Bolivar County. But when he started recording with Paramount Records in June 1929, he moved near Clarksdale in Coahoma County where he joined a country fiddler, Son Simms (Oliver 1972, 31).[79] When Patton had the opportunity to record again in early 1930, Simms joined him in the Paramount studios in Grafton, Wisconsin, where he cut four sides under his own name and backed Patton on several numbers (Big Road Blues 2014). After making these memorable sides with Patton, Simms's musical partnership ended. Wardlow (1994) writes: "After the 1930 session, Sims never saw Patton again, nor did he actually hear either of his Paramount releases. Lillie [Simms's sister] said: 'We never heard his records, and he said he never heard 'em either.' The March 1930 issue of Paramount 12912 'Farrell Blues/Come Back Corrina' was not advertised in *The Chicago Defender*, and it sold poorly" (16).

Patton's recording session with Simms in winter 1930 is the only time the guitarist recorded with a fiddler (Dixon, Godrich, and Rye 1997, 708),[80] but performing with fiddlers was not new. "In playing country breakdowns for black dancers, a fiddle player gave Patton an opportunity to rest his voice" (Wardlow 1994, 16). Although Patton is known primarily as a blues musician, his repertoire

Photo 11.2. Henry "Son" Simms and Muddy Waters. From the John Wesley Work III Collection, Center for Popular Music, Middle Tennessee State University.

on recordings is diverse, which is not surprising considering he began his musical career during the late nineteenth and early twentieth centuries, when Black musicians were expected to perform all types of music for varied audiences. Patton "recorded many examples of spirituals, ballads, popular songs, and non-blues lyric songs" (Evans 1977a). Like other fiddlers in the twenties and thirties, Simms's repertoire was also varied.[81] For example, Simms's fiddling on "Running Wild Blues" sounds like an eight-bar vernacular (folk) song. His fiddle part, with little variation, is performed almost in unison with Patton's singing. Off-beat phrasing, bent notes, and other features normally associated with the blues are not performed.

The four tunes on which Simms served as leader of the duo are: "Farrell Blues," "Come Back Corrina," "Tell Me Man Blues," and "Be True Be True Blues." The first three are twelve-bar blues, while "Be True Be True" is Simms's version of "Careless Love," a sixteen-bar blues ballad that had been rarely recorded, probably because of its unique melody and structure (Calt et al. 1971).[82] In describing the performance of the two musicians on the recording, Evans (1977a) states:

"Patton's accompaniment to Henry Sims' 'Be True Be True Blues' is fortunately unique for him. Patton is content to strum chords, often inappropriate ones, and play an occasional bass note behind Sims' singing. The song itself seems related to the well-known 'Careless Love.'" Comments by Kent (1977) about the musical collaboration provide insight about Simms as a fiddler:

> Sims . . . possessed a singular aptitude coupled with a singular fiddle to play the correct phrases behind Patton. One feels a smoother fiddler, such as Lonnie Chatman, would not fit half as well. The acrid tones of Sims' fiddle, unduplicated anywhere, is probably due to his instrument being home-made or exceedingly cheap. As a singer, Sims possesses a distinctly mournful quality, which goes well with his playing. Patton's accompaniment on these tracks are among the simplest he ever did, largely "Boom-chang" strumming, with a few bass runs in E natural. This may have been to showcase Sims' talents rather his own, or perhaps laziness.

With Simms as leader and Patton accompanying him on the guitar, Simms's fiddling tends to be straightforward with little variation, except for the occasional off-beat phrasing, use of double stops, or bending and sliding into notes at the beginning a melody, which in this case, produces a percussive sound. Regarding the issue of sound quality, Simms's family members provide an interesting perspective: "One of Sims' sisters described his fiddle playing as '. . . kinda like a saw. He didn't put any resin [sic] on it. I'd be listenin' at the music. I didn't take time to ask him about the roughness. I'd be enjoyin' the music" (Wardlow 1994, 16). The fact that Simms's rough sound quality did not prevent his sister from appreciating his musicking indicates that there was nothing inappropriate or negative about his fiddling; only outsiders to the tradition seem to be concerned about this issue rather than those within the culture.[83]

The limited variation on the fiddle is probably due to the fact that Simms placed more emphasis on his singing and the lyrics.[84] The four songs are structurally similar: each consists of three parts (opening, middle, and closing); also, the twelve- or sixteen-bar pattern, on which each song is based, is performed nine times. While the opening and closing are always performed with lead fiddle, guitar accompaniment, and no singing, the middle includes singing with guitar accompaniment and sometimes one or two interludes in which the fiddle is accompanied by the guitar.

As a side musician accompanying Patton on guitar, Simms's fiddling is mixed. He goes from one extreme of performing with the guitarist so closely without variation that the sound of the fiddle is barely heard; see "Circle Round the Moon." Other times, his variations are extensive with double stops, contrasting melodic passages, and off-beat phrasing during the response or fill-in; see "Joe Kirby." In other cases, Simms plays a contrasting melody while Patton sings, and inserts varied melodic passages as a fiddle response when Patton is not singing; see "Elder Greene Blues." One of the more interesting performances is when Simms and Patton insert a four-bar instrumental pattern, distinct in character from the four-bar phrase normally performed, during the A-part of a twelve-bar blues form; see "Going to Move to Alabama."[85] After the pattern is introduced by Patton on guitar without singing (0:00–0:07) at the beginning of the piece, it is repeated by the two musicians together with singing by Patton at the same point during the remaining portion of the performance.

Although Simms's recording with Waters took place in 1942, the research began in 1941.[86] Like Simms, Waters (ca. 1913–1983) was born in Sharkey County, the second son of Ollie Morganfield and Berta Jones, who were sharecroppers. When he was three years old, Waters's mother died and his father sent him to live with his grandmother, who moved to the Stovall Plantation near Clarksdale in Coahoma County "where his interest in the region's traditional music was kindled and nurtured. He took up the harmonica when he was thirteen, and guitar about four years later" (Welding 1966). Around the age of fifteen, Waters was performing with a small group—Scott Bowhandle (or Bohanna) on guitar, Sonny Simms (Henry Simms) on violin, and Lewis Fuller on mandolin—that played music typical of the country, old-time string band style of the period (Charters 1975, 246; Oliver 1968, 14, 1972, 149; Mississippi Blues Trail 2008b).[87]

At the recording sessions scheduled for July 20–24, 1942, Lomax first went to Clarksdale where he recorded Waters (vocal and guitar) and Charles Berry, who accompanied Waters on guitar. It was not until July 24, at Stovall, that Lomax recorded the Son Simms Four,[88] which included Simms (violin), Waters (guitar and vocal), Percy Thomas (guitar and vocal), and Louis Ford (mandolin and vocal). Simms also performed guitar with Waters on several tunes (Dixon and Godrich 1982, 550). Regarding the group's performance, Welding (1966) states: "The wry, pungent charm and ragged, exuberant spontaneity of the music created by this rough string band is most likely typical of that played by countless such groups in that and other areas of the rural south, a brand of raw, exciting music that all too seldom found its way onto record."

The four songs performed by the Son Simms Four are all twelve-bar blues. With the exception of "Joe Turner Blues," performed in the style of early country blues (or even a late nineteenth- or early twentieth-century vernacular song), the remaining three—"Pearlie May Blues," "Ramblin' Kid Blues," and "Rosalie"—have a harsher, down-home sound typical of blues in the late 1930s. Probably because the latter three songs are performed in a slower tempo, Simms's fiddling is more involved with bent notes, off-beat phrasing, and contrasting melodies. In "Rosalie,"[89] for example, a polyphonic sound dominates throughout, with each performer contributing to the overall sound aesthetic. In the first verse, Simms performs a contrasting melody in a higher pitch range as the singer performs the main melody and the mandolin inserts repeated notes at various points. What occurs during the first four bars of the second (0:48–0:58), third

(1:21–1:31), and fifth (2:27–2:37) verses is also distinct. A call-and-response dialogue takes place between the vocal and fiddle parts with the fiddler playing a single arpeggio pattern in response to the half-sung/half-spoken statements the singer performs as the call. The fourth verse (1:55–2:26) is an instrumental interlude in which all performers independently improvise on their instruments. While the fiddle plays a high-pitched contrasting melody, similar to musicking in the first verse, the mandolin plays repeated notes and the guitarist performs a boogie-woogie walking bass ostinato pattern.

It can be concluded that Simms, as a fiddler, was influenced both by the times in which he lived as well as the performers with whom he recorded. As the leader of the duo on the four songs he recorded with Patton (on guitar) in the late 1920s (and his first time recording in the studio), Simms did not vary from what was expected of him as a singer and side musician (on the fiddle); he followed the guitarist's lead—performing conservatively to such a degree that the fiddle was sometimes inaudible; occasionally he responded creatively to what Patton introduced. When performing with the Son Simms Four (as an older and more mature musician) during the early 1940s, Simms's fiddling was more varied. While he did not sing the lead, he freely performed his fiddle without concern about outshining the leader. The assessment by Work III (2005) is fairly accurate when he indicates that the fiddler's musicality is due essentially to his lack of exposure to musicking outside his community: "There are few fiddlers now in the Delta, and phonograph records of folk fiddlers are extremely rare. As a result, Sims, not having playing models to listen to, has developed an individual style of performance. His style consists largely of bowed tremolos, trills, and counterpoints to the melodies of the instruments which he may be supporting. Although he might be expected to use it because of its rhythmic possibilities, he makes no use of the pizzicato. The fiddle in 'Son' Sims hand is not a solo instrument and rarely carries the melody as is usually the fiddlers' function in folk music" (118).

In analyzing Simms's musicking, Work III also provides an explanation for the decline in interest in Black fiddling among Black listeners in some rural areas during the 1940s. As stated elsewhere, the emerging trends were gaining ground, which is the reason many young Blacks were not interested in learning the tradition. According to Work III (2005), "Sims would like to teach some youngster to play the fiddle as he taught several to play the guitar in former days, but can interest none in it. He deplores the loss of interest in playing instruments today among the plantation youth. Recently, an admirer of his playing presented him with a new, handsome violin which is his great pride and his constant companion. Today he is a share-cropper on a Delta plantation" (118). Work III's statements indicate that in spite of lack of interest on the part of some in the community, a few listeners continued to appreciate Black fiddling, which is the reason an admirer presented Simms with a new instrument. Could this have been the case with Black fiddling generally? Although members of the larger community were not supportive or receptive, there were a few who appreciated Black fiddle music. For this reason, the tradition continued to survive in spite of the fact that some Black people did not relate to it.

Arkansas

Although territorial boundaries separate Arkansas, Mississippi, and west Tennessee, the history and cultural patterns of Blacks in the tristate region have historically been similar.[90] Yet, the number of investigations that have been done on Black fiddling in Arkansas is miniscule when compared to research that has been conducted on traditions in Mississippi and Tennessee. Except for brief details about the early life of Bill Broonzy (ca.1893–1958) when he played the fiddle,[91] John Lomax's recording of "two street-corner" musicians in Little Rock on September 27, 1934, is the only documentation of Black fiddling in the state during the early twentieth century.[92] In total, Lomax recorded eight tunes by a Black fiddler named Blind Pete[93] and his guitar partner, George Ryan, but only six included the fiddle.[94] Although the musicians' repertoire comprised commercially recorded blues performed in the style of Charley Patton and other Mississippi Delta musicians, they "also played music from the proto-blues and country string band traditions" (Wade 1999). The melodies for "Cacklin' Hen"—the tune most often mentioned in the repertoires of fiddlers in this study—and "Black Bayou Ain't Got No Bottom" are similar in structure, just as those used for "Stagolee" and "Booker" are similar. In fact, the first version of "Banty Rooster" sounds the same as "Cacklin' Hen."[95] Reviewers indicate that it was Blind Pete's performance of old-time music that demonstrated his prowess on the fiddle. Regarding "Black Bayou Ain't Got No Bottom," Wade (1999) states that Blind Pete "gallops through the fiddle show piece," while Alan Lomax (1999) describes the performance as "an Arkansas black mountaineer tune performed in Western ragtime fiddle style" (9). Steve Leggett (n.d.b) refers to "Blind Pete's fiddle style [as] wonderfully loose and wild."

Since this may be the first field recording of Black fiddling to be made by a researcher, the musicking by Blind Pete is important. And the fact that he decided to perform both old-time music and blues is also significant. Not only does this inform us of the type of music patrons in Little Rock preferred, but also the musicking that Blind Pete (like Dumas in Mississippi) felt more comfortable performing because these were his favorite tunes from earlier years. In any case, this evidence confirms that fiddling from the nineteenth century continued to be performed by African Americans in Arkansas through the 1930s.

fiddlingismyjoycompanion.net

Notes

1. 🎻 See Map 11.1, South Atlantic Coast states; and Map 11.2, Gulf Coast states.
2. 🎻 See Land Regions 11.1, Map 11.3, and Map 11.4.
3. 🎻 See Demographics 11.1.
4. 🎻 See Demographics 11.2.
5. 🎻 See Demographics 11.3.
6. 🎻 See Land Regions 11.2, Map 11.5, and Map 11.6.
7. In addition to print publications and recordings—for example, DjeDje (1978a, 1983), Floyd (2002), and Rosenbaum (1984c)—the film *The Language You Cry In* (1998) is an excellent source for documenting the maintenance of African musicking by enslaved people on the Atlantic Coast.
8. Commenting on the musicking of formerly enslaved people in Port Royal, a town in Beaufort County on the coast of South Carolina, Allen indicates that he "never saw a musical instrument among them. The last violin owned by a 'worldly man' disappeared from Coffin's Point de year gun shoot at Bay Point" (Govenar and Lornell 2019, 51; also quoted in Epstein 1977, 175). "Gunshoot at Bay Point" refers to a battle in South Carolina that started the Civil War.
9. Coon songs, which present a stereotype of Black people, date to the nineteenth century with the beginnings of minstrelsy; they continued to be popular through the early twentieth century (Dormon 1988, 455; Southern 1997, 93; Evans 2018a, 39).
10. Several research projects have focused on the musicking of South Carolina and Georgia coastal Blacks: Library of Congress archivist Robert Gordon recorded around Darien, Georgia, in 1926; folklorist Guy Johnson worked on St. Helena Island in the 1920s; and the Federal Writers Project closely documented African retentions around Savannah in the 1930s. With a research team that included John Lomax, Alan Lomax, and Black folklorist Zora Neale Hurston, much secular music was also collected off the coast of Georgia for the Library of Congress in the 1930s. To view information about these projects, search for them on the Library of Congress website (www.loc.gov).
11. 🎻 See Map 11.7, Map 11.8, and Land Regions 11.3.
12. Material on Black jug bands in Florida includes no mention of the fiddle; see Florida Jug Band (1904–1905) and Bastin and Green (1989).
13. 🎻 See Demographics 11.4.
14. In John Lomax's work for the Library of Congress, particularly in his home state of Texas, his basic methodology was to visit prisons to collect vernacular materials, for he believed this is where older Black songs survived with minimum innovations. With some exceptions, he used the same research methods in other states (Bastin 1986, 53).
15. 🎻 See Repertoire 11.1.
16. 🎻 Go to Audio Examples to listen to all songs recorded by Perry and Carver.
17. Before Perry's and Carver's 1939 field recording of "Lost Train Blues" for the Library of Congress, only two commercial recordings had been made of this tune: a May 1927 release by Gennett of Price Goodson playing the harmonica, and a 1935 release by Bluebird of Arthur Smith (fiddle), Alton Delmore (guitar), and Rabon Delmore (tenor guitar) performing as a group; see Russell and Pinson (2004).
18. Because West's and Fox's birthplace and residence are unknown, the Alabama Sheiks are discussed in this section because the group's performance style is closer to musicking along the Gulf Coast and the Mississippi Delta than fiddling in the mountains and piedmonts. My review of

the literature indicates that much of the research on Alabama Black music focuses on the sacred. The few studies on secular music—Courlander (1960), Cauthen (1989a), Holtzberg-Call (1989), and Baklanoff (1991)—make no mention of Black fiddling in the early twentieth century. For this reason, limited discussion of Alabama's African American music culture is presented here.

19. 🎻 See Repertoire 11.2. Covers by the Alabama Sheiks include "Lawdy Lawdy Blues," a Bessie Smith tune she recorded on Columbia on January 10, 1924, but was unissued. Charlie Jackson's "Papa's Lawdy Lawdy Blues" (his first commercial release) was recorded on Paramount in August 1924, but reviewers indicate that the Alabama Sheiks' version "belongs to the same family as Papa Charlie Jackson's 'Cat's Got the Measles'" that he recorded in January 1925 (Record Fiend 2010). "The New Talkin' 'Bout You" by the Alabama Sheiks is a cover of Memphis Minnie's and Kansas Joe's "I'm Talking About You," which was released by Vocalion in collaboration with several other labels on February 21, 1930 (Dixon, Godrich, and Rye 1997).

20. 🎻 Go to Audio Examples to listen to "Sitting on Top of the World" by Lonnie Chatmon (Mississippi Sheiks) and Eddie West (Alabama Sheiks).

21. In many coon songs, Black men were described as "not only ignorant and indolent, but also devoid of honesty or personal honor.... [most were] portrayed as making money through gambling, theft, and hustling rather than working to earn a living" (Dormon 1988, 455).

22. 🎻 Go to Audio Examples to listen to "Traveling Man" by Henry Whitter and "Travelin' Railroad Man Blues" by Eddie West (Alabama Sheiks).

23. Different versions by various artists also indicate that he is "arrested, shot, and sent home for burial, but escapes his coffin; he sails on the Titanic, but when it sinks he's found shooting dice in Liverpool. Carrying water ten miles from a spring, he stumbles, but runs home for another bucket and catches the water before it hits the ground" (Traveling Man 2019).

24. My analysis is based on listening to recordings by Henry Whitter (1924), Luke Jordan (1927), Coley Jones (1927), Prince Albert Hunt (1928), Jim Jackson (1928), the Alabama Sheiks (1931), and Washboard Sam [Robert Brown] (1941). Releases by the following were unavailable to me for examination: Dock Walsh (1926), Sid Harkreader (1928), Charlie and Bud Newman (1930), and Phineas Flat Foot Rockmore (1940). As noted in the foregoing, see Dixon, Godrich, and Rye (1997) and Russell and Pinson (2004) for discographical details about each recording.

25. As noted above, I have divided the discussion of Black Mississippi fiddling into two parts. Because of their location with physical and cultural elements that are similar to Southern Appalachia, Black fiddlers in the Hills and Pines regions were discussed in chapter 9. Black fiddling in the remaining regions (Delta, Capital/River, and Coastal) are discussed here in chapter 11 because it is more similar, in my opinion, to the musicking of African Americans who lived along the Gulf Coast.

26. 🎻 See Map 11.9, Map 11.10, and Map 11.11 to view the Mississippi River's connection with peoples both inside and outside the state of Mississippi.

27. Evans (2021, 527) reports that Herb Quinn (1917–1972), a Black fiddler who lived in Walthall County (Capital/River region) in the southern part of the state, sometimes traveled to the Delta region in the north during the fall harvest season, mainly for agricultural work, but also to make a little money from his musicking.

28. In the literature, Walter Vinson, who was recruited to play in the family band in the late teens/early 1920s, is known as Walter Vincson, Walter Vincent, as well as Walter Jacobs.

29. Although Armenter Chatmon is his birth name, Bo Chatmon will be used in this discussion because it is the name used early in his career when he performed the fiddle (see Calt, Stewart, and Kent 1974; Obrecht 2009, 68; Moore 2018, 2021d).

30. See works by Calt, Perls, and Stewart (1970); Oliver (1972); Palmer (1975); Evans (1977a, 1977b); Lieberman (1986); Wyatt (2001), Huber (2013), and others. Because little data are available, discussion about Harry is minimal.

31. The number of children and female partners Henderson (ca. 1848–1934) had during his lifetime has been a topic of much discussion. My review of US census records for 1900, 1910, and 1920, at which time Eliza Jackson Chatmon is listed as Henderson's wife, provides the following information about his children: Elese (daughter, born 1881); Ferdinand (son, born 1885); Mollie (daughter, born 1885); Mary (daughter, born 1887); Lonnie (son, ca. 1888–1942); Fred (son, born

1890); Hends (son, born 1890); Irene (daughter, ca. 1892–1951); Armenter (son, 1893–1964); Willie Edgar (son, born 1895); Nellie (daughter, born 1895); Lamar (son, born 1897); Berton (son, born ca. 1899); Sam Vivian (son, 1899–1983); Larry (son, born 1901); Lorin (son, born 1902); and Harry (son, born 1903); also see the Chatmon Family (Mississippi Blues Trail 2014) and Moore (2021d).

32. 🎵 See Map 9.7, Map 9.8, and Demographics 11.5.

33. Utica Normal and Industrial Institute, a Black educational institution founded in 1903 as a small agricultural high school, began as a small college in 1917; it started offering college-level academic courses in 1922 and was accredited by the Southern Association of College and Schools in 1926 (Evans 2018a, 43). Utica is located about thirty-two miles southwest of Jackson.

34. Similar to Vinson, Charlie McCoy began performing in bands with the Chatmons during the early 1920s (Obrecht 2009, 71).

35. This information was obtained from the US city directories (1822–1995) for Memphis (1925) and Jackson, Mississippi (1929, 1932, 1939, 1945). For 1947, Harry's name is listed in the directory, but no profession is indicated.

36. Moore (2021d) indicates that "in 1930, when Henderson and Eliza lived in Jackson, the city directory listed his occupation as 'musician.' [Also] in 1930, several members of the Chatmon family played together in a hotel orchestra in Jackson" (387).

37. In explaining why some Mississippi families moved to the Delta, Evans (2018a) states: "Despite the relative degree of freedom and opportunity that may have been found . . . east of Vicksburg and south and west of Jackson, there appeared to be even greater opportunities in the Delta to the north. . . . For people living . . . to the South on farms that were eroded and threatened by the advancing boll weevil infestation, the Delta must have seemed like a dream come true, a frontier paradise with plenty of opportunities for work, where a man's labor might earn him a real sense of freedom and dignity" (43).

38. Milton Bracey is someone with whom Henderson probably interacted during the late nineteenth century in the Bolton area (Moore 2021d, 386, 389).

39. US census records indicate that Neil Winston (or Cornelius Winston) was the husband to Mollie Chatmon, one of Henderson's eldest daughters.

40. Some of the first commercial recordings by Black musicians were made during the late nineteenth century (Brooks 2004).

41. Pahls wrote the liner notes for the soundtrack recording that accompanied *Louie Bluie*, the documentary film about the life of African American fiddler Howard Armstrong, who was one of the founders of the Tennessee Chocolate Drops, a Black string band that gained popularity during the thirties.

42. Some of the most important records in the history of African American music were made at Paramount studios on the grounds of Wisconsin Chair Company factory, which is responsible for the founding of the record label in 1917. Although known for recording a wide range of music, Paramount's most famous blues and jazz recordings were made by Ma Rainey, Ida Cox, Blind Lemon Jefferson, Jelly Roll Morton, the Mississippi Sheiks, as well as others (Mississippi Blues Trail 2010). It is significant that the majority of the artists were associated with urban Black culture.

43. In this case, "musically colorless" refers to songs that included fewer elements identified with Black music in terms of melody, rhythm, repertoire, and vocal inflections.

44. OKeh was an independent record company that began issuing records in 1918. When its recording of African American blues singer Mamie Smith in 1920 became a surprise hit, OKeh became a pioneer and leader in cultivating the US public's interest in race records. To increase sales, the label used advertisements in Black newspapers in US cities where large communities of African Americans resided (including Chicago, Atlanta, and New York) (Lornell 1989).

45. 🎵 See Repertoire 11.3. In total, Bo recorded thirty-four songs on fiddle. However, one song, "Yellow Coon Has No Race," was unissued, making thirty-three releases on fiddle.

46. 🎵 See Repertoire 11.3 and Repertoire 11.4. On February 17, 1930, Bo Chatmon is listed as second fiddle to Lonnie's lead on the "Lonely One in This Town" at the Mississippi Sheiks' first recording session in Shreveport, Louisiana. On June 9, 1930, only Bo Chatmon (on fiddle), his brother Sam (on guitar), and an unknown person (on second guitar) are listed as the Mississippi

Sheiks accompanying vocalist Texas Alexander; interestingly, neither Lonnie nor Vinson is included on this recording. At the sessions when Bo plays fiddle with the Mississippi Hot Footers, the instrumentation of the performers is generally listed as Bo Chatmon (fiddle), Charlie McCoy (guitar or mandolin), and Walter Vinson (guitar). A review of the tunes Lonnie recorded indicates that he rarely performed the fiddle on recordings with Bo. The only exception is when a second fiddle is included in the February 1930 session with the Mississippi Hot Footers. Since the artist's name is listed as unknown, Harry may have been the fiddler on this recording.

47. 🎵 See Repertoire 11.3 and Repertoire 11.4.

48. When performing stringed instruments, vibrato and tremolo are not the same. Vibrato is "a slight fluctuation of pitch produced on sustained notes by an oscillating motion of the left hand" (Vibrato 1970, 900). Tremolo is "the quick reiteration of the same tone, produced by a rapid up-and-down movement of the bow" (Tremolo 1970, 861).

49. The use of classical techniques in urban blues fiddling became commonplace during the mid-1920s with Black fiddlers accompanying female and male blues singers, particularly Robert Robbins (with Bessie Smith in 1924); Clifford Hayes (with Sarah Martin in 1924), and Lonnie Johnson (with Cora Perkins, George Hannah, and Luella Miller in 1926).

50. As noted in the foregoing, arpeggio is the playing of notes in a chord in succession rather than simultaneously; an arpeggio may also span more than one octave (Arpeggio 2001).

51. Hudson Whittaker is a guitarist and singer who became well known during the 1920s when he was based in Chicago. Early in his career, he and pianist Thomas Dorsey recorded more than sixty sides together.

52. In a twelve-bar blues that includes lyrics based on an AAB form, the main melody performed by the singer or lead instrumentalist during bars 1–2, 5–6, and 9–10 serves as the call, while musicking performed in bars 3–4, 7–8, and 11–12 is the response. For this discussion, the bars where the response occurs is referred to as the break. It is during the response (break) that accompanying musicians and the leader generally comment on the call by performing melodic, textual, or even rhythmic variations. For a full discussion of the AAB form, see Guide to Song Forms (2000–2022).

53. Perhaps, the fiddle accompaniment used during Alec Johnson's sessions (in Atlanta, on November 2, 1928), which is extremely subdued when compared with the fiddling performed on Mary Butler's recording (in New Orleans in November 1928), is another indicator that the person performing the fiddle during these different recording sessions is uncertain.

54. Sources vary regarding the month this recording session took place. While some indicate December 1928 (Dixon and Godrich 1982, 150), others note November 1928 (Dixon, Godrich, and Rye 1997, 150; *Discography of American Historical Recordings* n.d.a). Because they are more recent publications, with information that is more up to date, I decided to use the latter.

55. 🎵 Go to Audio Examples to listen to "Corrine Corrina" and "East Jackson Blues" by Bo Chatmon.

56. Bo's November 1928 session on Brunswick and its affiliates is the first recording of "Corrine Corrina," but the melody was later recorded with other titles. The Jackson Blue Boys, including Bo (vocal), McCoy (mandolin and vocal), and Vinson (guitar and vocal) but no fiddle, used the "Corrine Corrina" melody for "Sweet Alberta" on a recording made by Columbia on December 17, 1928. The "Corrine Corrina" melody was used by the Mississippi Sheiks for the tune, "Alberta Blues," at their first OKeh session on February 17, 1930. Several months later (December 19, 1930), Bo and McCoy used the "Corrine" melody for "The Northern Starvers Are Returning Home." And in 1934, "the Sheiks recycled 'Corrine Corrina' in the song 'Sweet Maggie,' replacing the name of the woman and keeping the melody" (Moore 2021d, 385). As a common stock tune, "Corrine Corrina" has been recorded by many artists in a variety of styles, including blues, jazz, rock, Cajun, and western swing. Also, see "Corrine, Corrina" (2020), Waterman (2000), and discussion below.

57. 🎵 See Lyrics 11.1.

58. 🎵 See Lyrics 11.1, verse 2.

59. During the early twentieth century, some white businessmen offered attractive inducements to encourage Blacks to migrate to other locations in the South and the North for work.

Many Blacks believed they would become wealthy and prosperous if they migrated. Unfortunately, once they arrived in their new environment, they were not treated fairly and the living conditions were poor. With little money, many did not always have enough to eat. Therefore, all who could obtain funds returned to their old homes (Odum 1911b, 360–61).

60. ✍ See Lyrics 11.1, verse 6.

61. The lyrics and melody for "West Jackson Blues," recorded by the Mississippi Sheiks on June 30, 1930, with Bo singing the lead vocal, are similar to that of "East Jackson Blues." However, the former is one of the few songs by the Sheiks that remained unissued until its release by a modern company: *Roots 'N' Blues: The Retrospective (1925–1950)*. Legacy, Columbia, 1992.

62. ✍ See Demographics 11.6.

63. Popularity of the term *sheik* during the 1920s and 1930s evolved from the best-selling book *The Sheik*, by English writer Edith Maude Hull (1919); the 1921 silent movie of the same name; and the hit song, "The Sheik of Araby," by white composers Harry B. Smith, Francis Wheeler, and Ted Snyder that was also written in 1921 (Palmer 1975). During the mid-1920s, two Black guitarists (Frank Stokes and Dan Sane) performed on Beale Street as the Beale Street Sheiks, and they recorded with this name on Paramount Records in August 1927 (Dixon and Godrich 1982, 64, 707–8; Russell 1997, 169). By 1928, the Mississippi Sheiks were known nationally; see ✍ Figures 11.1a, 11.1b, and 11.2.

64. Comments by Lonnie about giving up fiddling and performing only religious songs indicate that negative attitudes about the fiddle, which began during eighteenth and nineteenth centuries when many Blacks adopted Protestant Christianity, continued to be important among some Mississippi Blacks in the early twentieth century.

65. ✍ See Repertoire 11.4. Lonnie recorded 107 songs but twelve were unissued, making his total releases ninety-five. Besides the Sheiks, artists and groups that Lonnie recorded with included Bo Carter, the Carter Brothers, the Chatmon Brothers, and the Mississippi Mud Steppers. While the majority (65 percent) of the recordings were made by OKeh/Columbia, Bluebird made 29 percent and Paramount and its affiliates made 6 percent. Although the same musicians performed in different group configurations, only in rare instances did the same labels record Lonnie and Bo on fiddle together.

66. The song, "He Calls That Religion," is noteworthy because it is the Sheiks' response to criticism from Black ministers who condemned blues as devil's music (Gussow 2010b, 187–88). See Oliver (1987) for examples of other themes in songs.

67. The Mississippi Sheiks made five recordings of "Sitting on Top of the World" and four of "Stop and Listen Blues." After their first recording of "Sitting on Top of the World" (OKeh) on February 17, 1930, subsequent recordings were made on December 15, 1930 ("Sitting on Top of the World, Number 2," OKeh); October 24, 1931 ("Things About Comin My Way," OKeh); July 1932 ("The New Sittin' on Top of the World," Paramount and affiliates); and March 26, 1934 ("Hitting the Numbers," Bluebird). The Sheiks' first recording of "Stop and Listen Blues" (OKeh) on February 17, 1930, was followed by covers on December 19, 1930 ("Stop and Listen Blues, Number 2," OKeh); July 1932 ("The New Stop and Listen," Paramount and affiliates); and March 27, 1934 ("Lonesome Grave Took My Baby," Bluebird). Victor made a recording of "Big Road Blues" by Tommy Johnson on February 3, 1928 (Calt, Stewart, and Kent 1974; Dixon and Godrich 1982, 401).

68. ✍ Go to Audio Examples to listen to "Sitting on Top of the World" and "Stop and Listen Blues No. 2" by Lonnie Chatmon (Mississippi Sheiks).

69. From my experience, most listeners assume that the person (singer or instrumentalist) being featured in a blues song is also the person who performs the first verse.

70. In later years, however, musicians included the clarinet or the harmonica into the ensemble to reproduce the sound quality of the violin.

71. ✍ Go to Audio Examples and listen to "Stop and Listen Blues No. 2" by Lonnie Chatmon (Mississippi Sheiks). The arpeggio phrase that starts in the introduction (0:06–0:08) serves as fill-in material for each verse of the song: verse 1 (0:26–0:28, 0:36–0:38); verse 2 (0:56–0:58, 1:06–1:08); verse 3 (1:26–1:28, 1:35–1:38); verse 4 (1:55–1:57, 2:04–2:06); verse 5 (2:23–2:25, 2:33–2:35); and verse 6 (2:52–2:54, 3:02–3:04). Note: Because of differences in equipment used, the time

counter numbers may not be exact when played. Therefore, these time counts should be regarded as rough estimates of when the melodic motives appear in the song.

72. 🎵 Go to Audio Examples and listen to "Stop and Listen Blues No. 2" by Lonnie Chatmon (Mississippi Sheiks). Using time counter numbers, the polyphonic interplay between the fiddle and guitar occurs in the following verses: verse 2 (0:40–0:50), verse 3 (1:11–1:21), verse 4 (1:40–1:50), verse 5 (2:09–2:20), and verse 6 (2:38–2:48).

73. For further discussion of the Sheiks' use of country music, see Charters (1967, 139) and Moore (2021d, 383). Jimmie Rodgers is widely regarded as the "father of country music" and probably best known for performing blue yodeling songs. When Rodgers sang a "Blue Yodel," he combined blues verses with a yodeled refrain, which became a formula he repeated many times. Rodgers is also well known for his recordings with Black artists, including jazz fiddler Clifford Hayes (1893–1941), jazz trumpeter Louis Armstrong (1901–1971), and blues singer Mae Glover (1907–1985).

74. The spelling of the surname on his headstone is Simms, which is the reason this spelling is used in this discussion (Moore 2014, 74).

75. 🎵 See Map 9.7 and Map 9.8. Although born in Sharkey County, US census records indicate that Simms resided in various parts of the Delta region. As a child, he lived with his parents in Bolivar County. After serving in the army (1918–19), he lived and worked as a laborer in the saw mill industry in Quitman County. By his mid-twenties, he had married and settled in Coahoma County, where he worked as a farmer.

76. Renova, a small community in Bolivar County in the Delta Region, is located south of the larger towns—Mound Bayou and Merigold (see discussion below).

77. During the 1940s, professors from Fisk University collaborated with the Library of Congress in conducting fieldwork in various parts of the South (Maher 2000, 4).

78. US census records indicate that Patton was one of twelve children of William H. Patton (1864–1927) and Anna Martin (1862–1934). As a young person, his regular partners were members of the Chatmon family who also lived in Hinds County. Located in the heart of the Delta, Sunflower County and Dockery Farms are two important locations in Mississippi blues history because this is where musicians such as Willie Brown, Tommy Johnson, and Howlin' Wolf lived and learned from Charley Patton. Dockery was a self-sufficient town with an elementary school, churches, post and telegraph offices, its own currency, resident doctor, railroad depot, ferry, blacksmith shop, cotton gin, cemeteries, picnic grounds for the workers, and a commissary that sold dry goods, furniture, and groceries. In the early twentieth century, Dockery housed roughly four hundred tenant families, most of whom were African Americans who migrated to the region for work (Mississippi Blues Trail 2008a).

79. Mound Bayou, in Bolivar County, was founded in 1887 as an independent Black community by the formerly enslaved. Clarksdale, a large town where several blues musicians (including Robert Johnson, Muddy Waters, and B. B. King) started their musical careers, is located in Coahoma County, just north of Sunflower. For more details, see Oliver (1972, 33), Charters (1975, 247), and Mississippi Blues Trail (2008a).

80. While some sources (Wardlow 1994, 11; Moore 2014, 77; Evans 2018a, 81) indicate that Simms's recordings with Patton took place in winter 1930, other sources (Dixon, Godrich, and Rye 1997, 708) indicate fall 1929.

81. 🎵 See Repertoire 11.5.

82. Go to Audio Examples to listen to "Come Back Corrina" by Simms and Patton. The earliest recordings of "Careless Love" took place in 1925 and 1926 by Bessie Smith and Papa Celestin and his Tuxedo Dixieland Jazz Band, respectively (Dixon and Godrich 1982).

83. When Wyatt (1999) states that Simms "often neglected to rosin his bow," resulting in a "raw, blistering tone," it seems that he is suggesting that the sound was unpleasant to the ear. As noted in the foregoing, it is possible that Simms's abrasive sound may have been intentional to produce a percussive sound aesthetic that is preferred by some African and African American musicians. Similar sounds can be heard in fiddling by Bill Livers (Kentucky), Elbert Freeman (Georgia), and Butch Cage (Louisiana/Mississippi); see Brown (1992, 129), Kubik (1999, 117), and DjeDje (2008a).

84. As noted above, one of the reasons Lonnie Chatmon excelled as fiddler is because he focused on fiddling and never performed as a lead vocalist.

85. 🎵 Go to Audio Examples to listen to "Going to Move to Alabama" by Simms and Patton.

86. During the summer of 1941, Lomax and Work conducted fieldwork in Mississippi together. But on subsequent visits, Work did not travel to Mississippi; Lomax did all of the recording himself (Nemerov 1987; Work, Jones, and Adams 2005).

87. Although raised in Clarksdale, Waters occasionally returned to live with his father who played blues guitar. But "he was taught the basic rudiments of the instrument by a close friend, Scott Bowhandle (or Bohanna) who was only a year or two older than Waters" (Welding 1966). It should also be noted that the 1941–42 Library of Congress recordings are among Waters's first; thus, they foreshadow the type of artist he would become as well as the music that most influenced him when he was a young musician in Mississippi.

88. See Moore (2014) for the history of the Son Simms Four.

89. 🎵 Go to Audio Examples to listen to Simms perform "Rosalie" with the Son Simms Four.

90. 🎵 See Map 11.12, Map 11.13, Map 11.14, Land Regions 11.4, and History 11.1.

91. Most writings about Broonzy mention that he began playing the fiddle during his youth while living in Arkansas. The guitar did not become his primary instrument until his move to Chicago (Fry 2019). During the 1930s, he played the fiddle on recordings with a few groups (see Wyatt 2001 for details).

92. 🎵 See Demographics 11.7.

93. Lomax met Blind Pete, whose full name is unknown, through the efforts of Huddie Ledbetter, a Black musician professionally known as Lead Belly. After his release from Louisiana's Angola Prison in August 1934, Lomax engaged Lead Belly as his driver and assistant, and the pair traveled the South together for the next three months collecting songs (Harold and Fleming n.d.; John Avery Lomax 2021). Lead Belly was familiar with the area because he was born in Mooringsport, Louisiana, about 200 miles southwest of Little Rock. During the three days they stayed at a tourist camp just outside of Little Rock, Ledbetter would go into Black sections of the city on his own and to look for possible song sources by demonstrating his own playing and singing what Lomax wanted (Wade 1999).

94. 🎵 See Repertoire 11.6.

95. 🎵 See Repertoire 2.2. "Cacklin Hen," which dates to the nineteenth century and is cited in narratives of formerly enslaved Africans as one of the most popular tunes (Winans 1990, 51–52), was one of the first tunes to be commercially recorded by white fiddler John Carson (see chapter 9).

CHAPTER 12

Louisiana and Texas

Louisiana

Louisiana's unique history and culture have had an interesting impact on musicking, and more specifically Black fiddling.[1] Located in the southeastern portion of the state, New Orleans was considered to be the capital for violin playing during the nineteenth century. As a result, it was not uncommon for Blacks and whites from different parts of the United States to visit the city to learn how to play the instrument (Wolfe 1989; Wyatt 1999; Henry 2018a, 2024). Although most scholars identify early New Orleans musicking (especially ragtime and jazz) with piano, brass, and reed instruments, the violin also played a seminal role in the city's music scene in the late nineteenth and early twentieth centuries. While information about the contributions of violinists is not as extensive as performers who played other instruments, a directory of New Orleans Black musicians indicates that the earliest jazz bands contained more violinists than non-violinists because it was a nineteenth-century custom to have violins in dance bands. The violinist was usually the leader and almost always the front man,[2] which continued through the 1920s in both Black and white bands (Friedwald 1961; Oliver 1972, 49; Pelote 1983; Rose and Souchon 1984; Wyatt 1999).[3]

Although Black fiddlers were popular in Louisiana's rural areas of the state around the same time violinists were active in cities in the early twentieth century, the amount of information on the former is in no way comparable to that of the latter. Yet, documentation of rural Black fiddling has not been completely ignored, due to the investigations of researchers who began collecting materials in the mid-twentieth century. Since the majority of their findings focuses on rural Black fiddlers in southeast and southwest Louisiana, the following discussion is concerned with these two regions.[4]

Profiles of Louisiana Black Fiddlers

Southeast Louisiana

James "Butch" Cage (1894–1973), a Black fiddler born in southwest Mississippi, moved to southeast Louisiana when he was in his early thirties.[5] Like most Black fiddlers of his generation, Cage lived and worked in the rural South his entire life. When he moved to Zachary (East Baton Rouge Parish), Louisiana, about eighty miles south of his birthplace, Meadville (Franklin County), Mississippi, both towns were similar culturally and in terms of population,[6] making it easy for him to continue performing the music he had learned during his youth. After meeting Cage in the late 1950s, folklorist Harry Oster (1960) stated: "As soon as I heard Butch dig into his cracked and scarred fiddle, I knew that he was a . . . great representative of the now virtually extinct nineteenth century . . . fiddle tradition. I gave him a decent fiddle and we began a series of all-day recording sessions at his house." Regarding Cage's background, Oster (1960) provides a detailed account of his early family life and musical training:

> Butch (James) Cage was born . . . where his parents were sharecroppers.[7] . . . When Butch was ten years old his father died; his widow had to take care of the thirteen children. . . . They moved about every year or two to another unproductive farm. Their living quarters were crude board shacks without inside sealing and without a loft. Butch says, "We could look out through the holes in the roof at the stars." During these years, Butch went to school a total of three weeks.
>
> Though almost everything else was lacking, there was plenty of music. . . . "I had sisters play accordeen, an' another brother play the fife. My mother was a good songster, an' she was the best dancer in Franklin County." Butch remembers hearing two old [Black] fiddlers, Frank Felters and Ole Man Carol Williams; he sat at their feet listening and watching until he too could scrape away on their favorites: "Dixie," "Arkansas Traveller," "Hell Broke Loose in Georgia," "Old Wagoner," "Hen Cackle," "Old Mule," and many breakdowns, square dances and buck dances. He took part in the moaning and shouting at the local church. He danced the blues and he also heard popular hits like "Oh You Beautiful Doll" and "If You Like Me Like I Like You." He fell under the fascination of phonograph records when he heard a cylinder played in 1907. He also played the fife in "an old field band," which consisted of fifes, kettle, snare, and bass drums. The fifes were often handmade out of cane reed.

Although Cage earned extra money as a professional musician in Mississippi, it was not enough to take care of his basic needs, which is the reason he moved to Louisiana. Oster (1960) explains:

Although Butch was picking up some money playing at both white and colored dances on weekends, he felt he wasn't getting anywhere. In 1927, the year of the worst flood disaster on the Mississippi,[8] he made only four bales of cotton. That year he left to join his brother who was farming a patch of land in Louisiana on shares. He later also worked on cane and strawberry farms, and from 1941 to 1945 did odd jobs for the railroad. In the '50s he got a steady job for the city of Baton Rouge, cleaning out ditches, picking up trash, and putting in pipes. Two years before these records were made he retired to live on Social Security and his city pension. (Also, see Oster 1969, 8)

Through the mid-1950s, Cage performed "at suppers and house parties for four or five dollars a night and also for the fun of it at all-night jam sessions" (Oster 1969, 8). Although he played for Louisiana whites, jam sessions, similar to the all-Black frolics described by other Black fiddlers in this study, were the contexts in which his most innovative musicking was performed. Oster (1969) describes a typical jam session in southern Louisiana where much of Cage's musicking was recorded:

> Even though the texts of many of the songs are sad, the style of performance is gay and spirited. As the performers begin to pick up steam, to become possessed by the spirit, the excitement of the music draws a crowd into the tiny building; the walls seem to bulge. A field hand seizes a partner and they gyrate wildly. Members of the crowd exuberantly laugh and shout encouragement. Some of the guests chip in to buy more wine, whiskey or beer. Before long the whole rickety shack begins to rock and the floor to heave under their stomping feet. Often the swingy infectious music and dance sweep on until a new day calls for shuffling off to the back-breaking toil of farm work, or drearier jobs as janitors and laborers in nearby towns. (7)

Although documentation exists for the instruments (fife and guitar) Cage performed before moving to Louisiana, no information is available on the instruments used to accompany his fiddling in Mississippi. However, his music partner in Louisiana, Willie B. Thomas,[9] started playing the kazoo with Cage in 1928, and the guitar in 1939. Thomas also played a tenor banjo at Saturday suppers (see photos 12.1 and 12.2).

Except for field recordings collected and published by various researchers (see below), Cage's fiddling was never recorded commercially.[10] While Oster's recordings took place between the late fifties and early sixties, material collected by others occurred on the following dates: Moses Asch (July 3, 1960) at the Newport Folk Festival in Rhode Island;[11] Paul Oliver (summer 1960)[12] in Zachary; and Chris Strachwitz (August 7, 1960) in Zachary.[13] In addition to recordings in different locations and performance contexts, Cage was

Photo 12.1. Butch Cage (fiddle) and Willie Thomas (guitar) standing and playing instruments in yard. Baton Rouge, Louisiana, 1960. Photo by Chris Strachwitz. Chris Strachwitz Collection, Arhoolie Foundation.

documented performing in a variety of ensembles. About half the songs feature Cage playing the fiddle and singing, with Thomas accompanying him on guitar and singing. In other cases, Cage provides fiddle accompaniment for musicians who sing and/or perform the guitar; Thomas joins Cage by singing and/or playing the guitar on these examples as well.

From the material collected by various researchers, Cage's repertoire is extensive, including songs that are both sacred and secular. While some are traditional spirituals[14] created by Blacks, others are songs that suggest the maintenance of African spiritual practices in the Americas.[15] Among the secular songs are old-time tunes Cage learned as a youth and later in life ("Hen Cackle," "It Ain't Gonna Rain No More," and "Raise a Ruckus Tonight"), which he probably performed for audiences that requested them. Besides a few original songs, such as "Butch's Blues," the vast majority of Cage's repertoire consists of his versions (or covers) of blues from the early twentieth century that he probably learned from listening to the media. Most are songs originally recorded by urban-based musicians whose instrumental accompaniment varied, but almost all included the guitar or piano as the primary instrument. For this discussion, two songs, "44 Blues" and "Jelly Roll," are analyzed to demonstrate how Cage introduces

Photo 12.2. Butch Cage (fiddle) and Willie Thomas (guitar) standing and playing instruments in yard with two women and young boy listening. Baton Rouge, Louisiana, 1960. Photo by Chris Strachwitz. Chris Strachwitz Collection, Arhoolie Foundation.

different features into the music to make it his own, and to examine how his fiddling compares with other musicians in this study.

Not only is "44 Blues" the first song recorded by Roosevelt Sykes (1906–1983), an African American piano player also known as "The Honeydripper,"[16] it is his signature composition. Because of its popularity, "44 Blues" has also become a blues standard with a history that helps explain how some songs in African American culture are created, adapted by others, and become hits. The song's origins date to the early 1920s in Louisiana, but its development involves musicians, who, like Cage, have roots in various parts of the South. Eurreal Wilford "Little Brother" Montgomery (1906–1985), who was born in Louisiana, is credited with developing the piano-based blues theme title, "The Forty-Fours," that serves as the basis for "44 Blues."[17] Montgomery later taught the song to a Mississippi born piano player, Leothus "Les" Green (ca 1900–1945), in Vicksburg, Mississippi, who in 1925, taught it to Sykes (Hall 2006; Lee Green 2019). Sykes has stated that Green was the first person he ever heard play the song; nobody had recorded it, and no one had added words or lyrics to it.[18]

Cage made his version of "44 Blues" different from Sykes's by modifying the lyrics, form, and music.[19] Oster (1969) explains: "The Cage and Thomas variant follows closely in tune and text (except for their first and fifth stanzas which do not occur in the Sykes recording).... However, their style of performance is different" (395). In addition to creating new lyrics, Cage and Thomas alter the order in which they are presented.[20] Whereas Sykes only alludes to the lyrics of the early twentieth-century song, "Thought I Heard That K. C. Whistle Blow,"[21] by stating: "Like my baby said, she heard the Forty-four whistle blow" (Sykes verse 3), Cage and Thomas integrate two lines from the original song into their performance:

Well, I thought I heard 44 whistle blow,
Well, it blowed just like ain't gonna blow that whistle no mo' (Cage and Thomas verse 8).

In making these innovations, some researchers suggest the performers changed the meaning of the song. For example, Oliver (1968) believes Cage's and Thomas's repetition of lyrics out of sequence not only "affected the sense ... but it was clear ... that this was essentially blues for dancing and the playing of the fiddle by Butch Cage ... was the music of the reel. Meaning was less important than function and the excitement of the dance tune accelerated as ... the musicians got under way.... This was an excellent example of absorption and adaptation of more sophisticated, recorded material by members of an essentially folk community" (116–17). The importance that Oliver gives to the text and the role of the fiddle in affecting the behavior of those in attendance is noteworthy, particularly in specifying the features of a song that he identifies as sophisticated (urban) and folk (vernacular/traditional).

Cage's "Jelly Roll" (1960) is based on the song "Original Jelly Roll Blues" composed by jazz pianist Jelly Roll Morton, which was first recorded in 1924. However, Cage's version of "Jelly Roll" is his cover of a tune known as "New Jelly Roll Blues," recorded by Peg Leg Howell and His Gang in 1927, with Eddie Anthony on fiddle and Howell on guitar.[22] Although both versions employ a twelve-bar blues form, the two performances differ in several ways. One, the lyrics used in the two songs are completely different except in one instance. Verse four in Cage's and Thomas's version (see below) is similar to verse three performed by Howell and Anthony[23]:

Reason why I like my best gal so,
Same sweet jelly she had a hundred years ago. (Oster 1969, 354)

Two, Anthony and Howell's version consists of seven verses of singing (with fiddle and guitar accompaniment) and one instrumental interlude (with no singing). Although Anthony sings briefly on two verses, his primary role in the performance is playing the fiddle, which is what he does in a downhome style that Oster (1969, 355) describes as "the rough syncopated style characteristic of folk Negro fiddlers." Although Anthony performs countermelodies during the singing of the verse, as well as during the fill-in sections of the twelve-bar blues, in many cases he merely accompanies Howell's singing by playing in unison.

Cage makes "Jelly Roll" his own in several ways. In allowing Thomas to do all of the singing, the organization of the piece differs slightly from the version performed by Anthony and Howell. In Cage and Thomas's version, there are six verses of singing (with fiddle and guitar accompaniment) and two instrumental interludes. In other words, Cage's role as fiddler is not merely to accompany the singing; the two instrumental interludes give him the opportunity to improvise more extensively. Although his fiddling has the same downhome feel as Anthony's, the melodic content is more developed. Like Mississippi fiddler Lonnie Chatmon, Cage uses this freedom (in not singing) to improvise by playing arpeggios and using other techniques that make the sound of the fiddle distinctive. Even when he accompanies Thomas's singing, he varies his fiddling by integrating short melodic motives and double-stops, performing in different pitch registers, and alternating between eighth and dotted sixteenth notes. In summary, Cage is a creative fiddler in the vein of Lonnie Chatmon; he is not satisfied with merely repeating what someone has done without creating his own version. Probably because he was the only fiddler in his community, he had to be flexible in terms of repertoire and performance style to cater to the diverse audiences interested in his musicking.

Southwest Louisiana

During the early twentieth century, Black Creoles' contacts with different ethnicities and cultural groups in southwest Louisiana were substantial.[24] For this reason, many often prided themselves on being distinct from people of African descent in other parts of the United States, for, like other Creoles and Cajuns in the region, they promoted diversity.[25] In addition to the commingling of enslaved and free Black French speakers and their descendants with the heirs of French and Spanish colonialists, Black Creoles intermingled with European migrants (Germans, Italians, and Irish); Scots and Irish Americans who arrived with enslaved Blacks from the deep and upper South after the Louisiana Purchase; as well as the offspring of the region's Indigenous peoples. Yet, their most numerous and influential neighbors were Cajuns, the French colonists expelled from Acadia (now Nova Scotia) by the British during the French and Indian War (Minton 1996b, 489).

During slavery, free Black Creoles who settled in the bayous, marshlands, and prairies west of New Orleans subsisted as small farmers, fishermen, ranchers, trappers, or slave-owning planters; most were Catholic and spoke French (Mattern 1997, 159; Broussard 2012, 7). Since the majority, like many Cajuns, worked as tenant farmers after emancipation, both groups shared an economic background that led to competition and an emphasis on hard work (Menestrel 2007, 100). In spite of similar values regarding work, both groups were ostracized, persecuted, and attacked by urban upper-class Cajuns and French Creoles who, having met with monetary success and genteel status, had become embarrassed by their rural and unrefined neighbors (Elliott 1992, 146). In fact, stereotypes used to distinguish white Appalachians from the landed British elite in the upper South were similar to those employed by whites in southwest Louisiana. Acadians were considered to be "lazy vagabonds, with neither education nor ambition, who rejected American values . . . spending much of their time at church or at balls, or the gaming-table." Cajuns' participation in dance, or the *fais do-do*,[26] caused some to state that they "seemed possessed by a devil." Shortly after the Civil War, for example, an article in *Harper's Weekly* portrayed Cajuns as "good representatives of the white trash"[27] (Elliott 1992, 17–20).

Not surprisingly, the abuses and attacks that Black Creoles and Cajuns experienced led to much cultural exchange between the two groups (Mattern 1997). In an interview, Cajun fiddler Dewey Balfa (1987)[28] explained: "The Cajun people and the Black people felt very, very close. They felt very looked down upon by the rest of America. The Blacks because they were Black. The Acadians were sent away from one country because they rebelled against their government. They were people that was in prisons; they were deported; they were exiled. Also, the Blacks and the Acadians were very, very close in their music, and one music influenced the other. To us people down here in this area, to be a Creole has nothing to do with your color, it is nothing other than you were born in America. You could have been a German or an Italian or Black or Cajun or of French descent. But if you were born of these areas, you are a Creole."

Not only did the racism and discrimination lead to physical isolation, it encouraged both groups to maintain their distinctiveness from US mainstream culture, which affected their musicking in interesting ways (Ancelet 1989, 16–17). Folklorist Barry Ancelet (1984) states that "in the days before modern transportation, . . . people tended to be fiercely provincial. Eventually, music proved to be one of the great compromisers. . . . People from different settlements were brought together at house dances and dance halls for their earliest lessons in social interaction" (83). Among Black Creoles, skin color played an important role in both isolation and musicking. Black accordionist Alphonse "Bois Sec" Ardoin[29] explains:

> In those days, you stayed in your own neighborhood. People didn't mix very easily. It was like they were jealous of each other or something. . . . Take, for example, the people from La Pinière. You see, those people didn't want to mix with us. They were lighter-skinned.[30] They were mulattoes. And we couldn't go to their dances. I was able to go because I played music for them, but I couldn't bring a friend. They didn't allow that. It was just like trying to go to a white dance in those days. Then,

when they began to go out to other dances, they saw that they didn't know how to dance. So, to have a good time, they eventually started going out with us. Then, later, when people started behaving like people, we all got to be like brothers and sisters. Other places didn't have the music that we had, so they had to come and meet us. That's what started the change. (quoted in Ancelet 1984, 84–85)

Information on Black fiddling in southwest Louisiana, as noted in the foregoing, is substantial. In addition to print publications with details on the lives of musicians, their repertoire, and the social environment, a number of recordings by Black fiddlers have been released. Interviews with musicians are especially noteworthy for documenting, in their own voice, their personal life histories and perspectives about the tradition.[31] Not surprisingly, the wealth of material is not due to a strong interest in Black fiddling or rural Black culture. Rather, when researchers learned that the musicking of rural Black Creole musicians during the late nineteenth and early twentieth centuries provided the foundation for the creation of zydeco,[32] an urban Black Creole genre that evolved around the 1940s, much attention was given to those who performed this early music. Another factor is the close relationship that exists between the musicking of Cajuns and Black Creoles. As a result of the close intermingling, much of the music performed by Black Creoles has been adaptations of European genres (ballads and love lyrics, game songs, lullabies), historically sung in French, and Africanized versions of fiddle tunes from the British Isles imported via Acadia and the American South. Music idioms that paralleled the traditions of African Americans in other parts of the United States included work songs, hollers, topical satires, as well as dance songs known as *juré*.[33] "Percussive traditions . . . were also important, as Louisiana blacks were generally free from the prohibition on drumming imposed through much of the South" (Minton 1996b, 489–90).

Although Acadians' interactions with Indigenous and other European groups transformed their musicking in several ways,[34] contacts with African-derived cultures were the most influential. From Black Creoles, Cajuns adopted off-beat (syncopated) rhythms, bent notes, various percussion techniques, and improvisational singing. Most Europeans, prior to their arrival in the Americas, performed songs and instrumental music separately. Dance music was almost exclusively instrumental, and ballads were sung for content, traditionally unaccompanied. Since African singing and dancing were all inextricably linked, this influence resulted in the development of new songs that combined the two traditions. A new body of material was created when instrumental parts were added to old European ballads and words were composed for fiddle tunes. Not only did this provide greater opportunity for ensemble playing, it accelerated the exchange and blending of styles. Music that had been performed largely by audiences could now be played by semi-professional musicians who entertained listeners for food or were paid by passing the hat (Ancelet 1989, 19; Elliott 1992, 97–98).

In spite of this complementary history, tensions arose among late twentieth-century community organizers in documenting the diverse musical traditions in the region. The fact that festivals, publications, and recordings[35] as well as legislative initiatives, public documents, and pronouncements routinely subsumed Black Creole traditions under the label Cajun partially erased features identified with Black people. Although Black Creole musicians were featured in several works and projects,[36] many were not always recognized despite their demographic importance and significant contributions (Mattern 1997). Interestingly, the representation that music promoters used was not very different from that of earlier researchers who often portrayed Black and white communities as monolithic groups, ignoring the class and cultural cleavages that had sometimes fragmented them. Therefore, the task here is to demonstrate how and why Black Creole and Cajun fiddle traditions influenced each other, but also remained distinct. To understand these distinctions, the contributions of both groups need to be equally highlighted. In documenting the fiddle tradition among Black Creoles, at least two questions will be addressed. What factors helped the tradition maintain its popularity through the mid-twentieth century? What are some of the elements that made fiddling in southwest Louisiana distinct from fiddle music in other parts of the United States?

Similar to African American music ensembles in mountain and piedmont regions, fiddling continued to be important to the musicking of Black Creoles in southwest Louisiana through the mid-twentieth century.[37] Factors that contributed to the maintenance and popularity of the fiddle among Blacks during the early twentieth century—isolation from mainstream culture, religious tolerance, community support, and interaction with whites—are similar to those in other parts of the United States. However, most secular ensembles in Black Creole and Cajun communities in rural southwest Louisiana included two fiddles (one fiddler played the melody while the second fiddler did the bassing), an accordion, and a triangle.[38] Therefore, the most important distinguishable feature of fiddle groups in this part of the country was instrumentation—specifically, the adoption of the diatonic button accordion after its invention in Austria in the early nineteenth century and the use of percussion—the triangle and later the *vest frottoir* (also spelled *frattoir*).

Most researchers believe the accordion was introduced into Louisiana by German immigrants during the 1880s, but other data reveal that it was already current among Black Creoles (and possibly Cajuns) before 1850 (Dole 1978, 1). "By the early twentieth century the accordion had come to dominate both [Black] Creole and Cajun tradition, replacing the fiddle as lead instrument in most rural dance bands" (Minton 1996b, 490).[39] Agreeing with this history, Balfa (1987) explained further: "It is believed that the Black people used the diatonically-tuned accordion before the white people. I mean it sounds logical to me because the first person that ever recorded was this man called Amédé Ardoin who was a Black man, and he played accordion like nobody has been able to copy. Everybody tries to copy what he did but nobody can. He had a voice and he could cry out what his problems were."

The rough-edged, whiney sounds that listeners associate with Cajun and Black Creole fiddling are the features that "give the music its depth of expression, its raw quality uncluttered with musical polish" (Elliott 1992, 102–3). And most people agree that the music of Black accordionist Amédé Ardoin and white fiddler Dennis McGee reflects this sound.[40] Not only did McGee use different tunings and complicated rhythms and grace notes, Balfa states that he had a "unique way of making a drone from one string to another. When I say 'drone,' that is a crying style. It's like a lonesome, hurting sound. Like the Cajun blues sound" (quoted in Elliott 1992, 101–2).[41] According to Black Creole fiddler Canray Fontenot, "only Cajun and Creole fiddlers can do that. We do it by coming back on the high string and sort of choking it as the bow rubs over it gently. I can't say exactly how you do it, but I can do it. So can . . . Dennis McGee and a few other old-time fiddlers" (102–3). Balfa believes this type of music is a reflection of their environment, but younger musicians do not appreciate it because they haven't "lived [in] the periods we lived. Music reflects one's life. There were hard times when I was a young man, but I'm sure not half as hard as in McGee's day" (102–3).

As stylistic changes began to occur in Black musicking in other parts of the United States around the mid-twentieth century, comparable transformations took place in southwest Louisiana. This is when Black Creole artists became interested in blues as well as rhythm and blues,[42] and many Cajuns began listening to country and western music. Although Cajuns generally performed songs with more lyrics in French, the primary factor that distinguished Cajun and Black Creole music during this period was again instrumentation. In Black ensembles, the *vest frottoir* started to be used along with the triangle for percussion (Minton 1996b, 489; Savoy 1984, 316–27, 328). Balfa (1987) states: "Blacks played fiddle, triangle, and rubboard. The rubboard, that's a Black man's music. That's not the white man's music."[43]

Most researchers agree that although the performance style of nineteenth- and early twentieth-century ensembles foreshadowed postwar urban dance music, "the merging of styles into a music called 'zydeco' *outside* the Cajun/Black Creole areas of southwest Louisiana can be pinpointed with reasonable certainty in both time and space: the best evidence indicates that all this occurred in southeast Texas after 1940" (Minton 1996b, 504). Furthermore, zydeco's initial spread back to southwest Louisiana and subsequent dispersion can be "attributable in part to Creole return migration and in part to recording and touring by musicians operating from East Texas—and especially Houston—or even southern California" (489).

Musicians in southwest Louisiana entertained their audiences in various contexts. When Black Creole musicians performed for whites (similar to what had occurred during slavery), audiences were rarely integrated.[44] Mattern (1997, 162) explains: "Clifton Chenier,[45] popular with white as well as black audiences, regularly played white clubs, and whites sometimes braved racial segregation to hear him perform at black Creole clubs." Because there were no clubs in rural areas during the early twentieth century, the *fais do-do* was the primary context for Cajun fiddling, while house dances were generally the settings for fiddling in Black Creole communities.

Some Black Creole musicians who performed in rural contexts in earlier times indicate that there was no special name for such events. In an interview with Tisserand (1998, 27), Black accordion player Boozoo Chavis stated: "I heard about *la-la*, but we never used that. In them days they'd call it a house dance. They didn't have no clubs, they'd go to a house dance. That's the name for it, right there, a house dance." However, Mama Lena Pitre, a Black Creole female who attended many dances, states: "They can call it *la-la*. We are going to *la-la*. Oh, are you going to the *la-la* tonight? Oh yeah, we're going to go to the *la-la*. They're going to the *la-la* au soir. Ou nous allons bal au soir" (Tisserand 1998, 27). According to Carl Brasseaux (2010), "*La-la* [is] a Francophone Catholic tradition closely tied melodically and in instrumentation to early Cajun music. *La-la* twentieth-century instrumentation and styling became dominant in Creole music over the course of the early mid-twentieth century, and house dances, the typical venue for Creole music during this era, usually featured single or twin fiddles. Bébé Carrière, Calvin Carrière, and Canray Fontenot were perhaps the most notable *la-la* performers of their respective generations" (4). While he does not give a specific term for house dance, Fontenot (1988) describes how they came about and what transpired at such events:

> If they had some musicians in the neighborhood, they would get together and play house dances. So, they was gonna pick one of the biggest houses they had in the neighborhood to make the dance. They had the old ladies and the young ladies inside. Some musicians would be in there too. The young and old mans would stay outside, because they only allow so many men to come in and dance a few tunes.[46] Whoever was in charge of that would give them so many numbers. They go and dance, and put whatever they could in the collection. They played French music. Most Black men in my age would call that Creole. And the dance, most of the time, would last from Saturday night after sundown to sun up.

Bois Sec Ardoin recalls that "if the house was small, we'd make a platform of boards all around the outside of the house for a dance floor. The musicians would sit outside. There would be an accordion and a *bastringue* [*bastrange*] (triangle), or . . . [the musicians] would play just two fiddles, old dances like they used to do. They'd play all night. If the dance was inside, we'd take all the furniture out of the rooms and put planks around the walls, like benches After the dance, we'd have to sweep and put all the furniture back" (Savoy 1984, 305). When house dances started to lose their popularity during the 1940s, clubs (honky-tonks) in the area began booking national rhythm and blues bands as well as zydeco acts like Clifton Chenier. "Every Saturday they had [something at] . . . Richard's Club there, so the people wouldn't hardly make no more house dances," remembers Bébé Carrière. "They'd go to the Club. People came from different places and visit. That's how the thing went on there, until the house dance expired" (Tisserand 1998, 37–38). Another context was the church, but during certain seasons in the church calendar, fiddling was not allowed. Fontenot explains: "I remember after Mardi Gras people had this idea that it was bad luck to play music during Lent. I couldn't touch my fiddle during Lent as long as my mama was living. Some of them old people, in the month of May, they wouldn't go to no dances 'cause that was the month of Mary" (Savoy 1984, 329).

The repertoire of Black Creole musicians during the early decades of the twentieth century was similar to that of Black fiddlers in the mountain and piedmont regions in that both groups continued to perform tunes popular among Euro-Americans but with African influences. In certain contexts, they also performed genres created by African Americans. Bois Sec Ardoin states: "We used to have two-steps, one-steps, waltzes, jigs, reels, contradances. . . . The violin played all that. That's what people wanted" (Savoy 1984, 311). Canray Fontenot (1988) indicated that while French music was regularly performed at house parties, blues was not accepted: "You could play a two-step, one-step, or whatever you wanted. But no blues. You was supposed to be playing that at a saloon, not in a house where they respect the people that was in there. And we wanted to play the blues so bad. I guess it's in our system to play blues. So, we would work on something like 'Prison Bars'[47] that was close to the blues, but they thought it was some new waltz."[48] Regarding the performance of blues, Freemont Fontenot (b. 1900), also a well-known Black Creole accordion player, states: "If there was a dancehall on the side, a dive or something, people would go there to play the blues. But one wouldn't go play a blues in the house. . . . It's not respectable. . . . And the little girls . . . if they weren't married, they couldn't go in certain places" (Savoy 1984, 313).

Although many residents of southwest Louisiana during the early twentieth century participated in musicking as members of an audience with community musicians performing, choosing music as a profession was not encouraged. Unlike areas of the United States where Protestantism dominated, Catholicism had greater tolerance for recreational activities such as music and dancing. Thus, religion was not the culprit that discouraged individuals from becoming musicians. In this case, the primary issue was that families of both Black Creole and Cajun musicians did not consider musicking to be a serious endeavor. Many believed musicking represented the crudest elements of society and the height of vulgarity because of its association with drinking and dancing.[49] While some

Black Creoles and whites called blues "the devil's music," they regarded Cajun music as "nothing but chanky-chank" (Elliott 1992, 146).

Southwest Louisiana had several generations of Black Creole fiddlers during the twentieth century who regularly provided entertainment for the local community. Douglas Bellard was probably the most well known during the first decades of the twentieth century, while fiddlers active from the 1930s through the 1960s included Joseph "Bébé" Carrière, Canray Fontenot, Calvin Calise Carrière, and Morris K. Chenier. Although the performance of the fiddle began to decline with the growing popularity of zydeco after the forties and fifties, some Black fiddlers found audiences in later years at local, state, and national festivals as well as other public arts events. Interestingly, those who decided to become fiddlers during the late twentieth and early twenty-first centuries tended to be multi-instrumentalists,[50] which may have been a factor in the continuation of the tradition through the years.[51] Angel Romero (2016) explains: "Jeffery Broussard . . . is commonly referred to as . . . the best accordion player around, although he is not limited to just the accordion. Jeffery plays every instrument. He is an awesome fiddler which he also uses in his performance . . . and there is a point in his performance where he does the old 'switch-a-roo' with D'Jalma Garnier III who is the bass player, and in the midst of a song D'Jalma will take over fiddle and Jeffery will play bass, the crowd goes wild."

The primary focus here will be on fiddlers active during the early twentieth century for which information is available (see names listed above). For this reason, Morris Chenier (1916–1978) (see photo 12.3), Clifton Chenier's uncle who sometimes recorded with him, will not be extensively discussed because little data has been found on his involvement in fiddling.[52] However, we know that he was a multi-instrumentalist. In addition to the fiddle that he learned to play from a local musician (Antoine Valet) while working in Lake Charles, Louisiana, he was a guitarist and owner/manager of a club in Lake Charles. Some sources indicate that he also played accordion (Tisserand 1998, 111; Govenar and Lornell 2019, 275). For the remaining fiddlers, the discussion is organized chronologically according to the fiddlers' birth dates, with special attention given to family and community, learning, Black/white interactions, performance contexts, repertoire, performance style, and the media.

Douglas Bellard (b. ca. 1905)

Information about Douglas Bellard is limited except for the fact that he was the first Black Creole, along with Kirby Riley (1904–1992) on accordion,[53] to make a commercial recording. Whereas Bellard's recording session with Brunswick/Vocalion Records took place in October 1929, accordionist Amédé Ardoin, to whom most people give this credit, made his recording debut on Columbia

Photo 12.3. Morris Chenier (fiddle) and Clifton Chenier (accordion). Houston, Texas, May 1966. Photo by Chris Strachwitz. Chris Strachwitz Collection, Arhoolie Foundation.

Records two months later (December 1929) with white fiddler Dennis McGee.[54] Although Bellard and Ardoin did not make the first recording together, it is believed they collaborated early in their careers. Pomea (2002–2016) explains: "Douglas Bellard, a black fiddler, was the playing partner of the great Amédé Ardoin before Ardoin decided to go with fiddler Dennis McGee, a white man who could offer him more protection when playing before crowds in those racially segregated days." Yet, comments by Canray Fontenot suggest that Bellard and Ardoin were also competitors, which may have been another factor for their break-up: "They played together; they played good music together, but they never could get along together. They both wanted to start the tune and if one would start the other one couldn't catch up. And they both like to sing; they were always in a big brawl about that" (Savoy 1984, 331).

Bellard was born in Evangeline Parish near the town of Ville Platte.[55] His brother (David) and a family friend (Murph Soileau) indicate that Bellard "was well known in Ville Platte for playing [the fiddle], and he played just about every weekend at Coreil Saloon, which was on the main street. Old man Coreil had a big saloon and a big hardware store. He was a big wheel in Ville Platte. He had ... two bars—one for the colored people in the back and one [for whites] in the front. But Douglas [on fiddle with no accompaniment] would play both sides in one night" (Soileau and Bellard 1993).

Musically, Bellard is greatly respected among musicians in southwest Louisiana not only because he was the first Black Creole to record, which has led some who refer to him as the "spiritual father of zydeco music," but also because of his performance style and creativity. One admirer states that "his records are rarely heard, but for all their roughness, they are deep American roots music of the highest order" (DiverseRecords 2011). Savoy (1984, 305) indicates that "Bellard's free, bluesy style had a large influence on many fiddlers of the 1920s–1930s era."[56] Of the four tunes recorded in 1929,[57] the two most popular were: "La Valse De La Prison" ("Prison Waltz") and "Mon Camon le Case Que Je Sui Cordane" ("My Gun Is the Reason I Am Convicted," also known as "Les Flammes d'Enfer" ("The Flames of Hell").[58] However, the song by Bellard that has been most often recorded and used as a basis for re-creation is "La Valse de la Prison"; see Savoy (1984, 335) and discussion in the blog Early Cajun Music (2014, 2016).

The Carrière Family: Joseph "Bébé" Carrière (1908–2001) and Calvin Calise Carrière (1921–2002)

Joseph "Bébé" Carrière. While several members of the Carrière family performed the accordion,[59] Bébé and his nephew, Calvin, were among the few who played the fiddle. Bébé was born in Lawtell, a small unincorporated community in St. Landry Parish.[60] Like most children in his community, Bébé received only a fifth-grade education because "his parents were pressured by the landlord for whom they were sharecropping to take him out of the classroom and put him in the fields" (Stanford and Stanford 1974). Reflecting on his early life in an interview, Bébé indicated that he sharecropped cotton, corn, and sweet potatoes; raised hogs and cattle; and bootlegged white mule moonshine. "If I had got more schooling, I could of got on some good job maybe. Instead I had to work all my days in the doggone fields mostly for nothing. Hell, I didn't earn nothing like that. You couldn't sell your crop. They'd give you so little for it you'd come out with nothing. You had to make a little credick (credit) account through the years, and it would take mostly all your cotton to pay the doggone thing. You'd come out maybe with a twenty, maybe twenty-five dollars at the end of the year. Oh, I'm gonna tell you, it was really tough" (Stanford and Stanford 1974). During World War II, Bébé worked in army camps (defense plant) in the cities of Lake Charles (in Calcasieu Parish) and Leesville (in Vernon Parish), which are located west of his home residence (Spitzer 1979, 5; Savoy 1984, 343, 345; Tisserand 1998, 72) (see photo 12.4).

Unlike many in their community, Bébé's father supported his children's interest in music, probably because he was also a musician. When Bébé made his first fiddle out of a cigar box, which he strung up with wires from an old screen, the

Photo 12.4. Joseph "Bébé" Carrière (fiddle) and Eraste Carrière (accordion). Lawtell, Louisiana, 1974. Photo by Chris Strachwitz. Chris Strachwitz Collection, Arhoolie Foundation.

screen wire didn't give the sound he wanted. So, his father bought him a pack of fiddle strings to improve the sound. After Bébé was able to play a tune on his cigar box fiddle, "his father got him a real fiddle and at the age of thirteen or fourteen he was playing his music" (Savoy 1983a). Similar to other Black Creole fiddlers, Bébé never had formal lessons. "Older players in the area taught young Carrière the secrets of playing, telling him that he needed to find rattlesnake tails to put inside the fiddle. Friends in the town of Washington [in St. Landry Parish] killed some snakes and gave him the rattles. The sound was better"[61] (quoted in Tisserand 1998, 74). He also indicates that he learned by listening to recordings: "I used to play . . . a good many Jimmy [sic] Rodgers' songs. . . . I used to sing them, too. . . . Sometime I'd copy the song if I'd like it. I'd keep it up and I'd play it over and over. And I'd write the words down" (Savoy 1984, 344).

Similar to those of other Black Creole musicians in southwest Louisiana, the Carrières' repertoire[62] and performance style indicate that although they maintained the traditions of their parents, they also adopted new songs and performed in a manner that was popular during the early twentieth century. In 1974, Stanford and Stanford write:

> The Carrière brothers' repertoire reflects the music of their ancestors, as well as the popular genres which have come and gone in their own lifetimes. "La Robe à

Parasol"... is an old-time dance tune called mázulka (mazurka)... a dance originating in central Europe. Eraste says that the tune is even older than his father and was probably popular in the time of his grandfather's youth. The lyrics describe a style of dress apparently called the 'parasol,' which... is a full, hoop skirt.

In addition to a large number of standard Cajun waltzes and two-steps, many of which they have learned over the years from radio broadcasts, Bébé and Eraste know a curious potpourri of tunes including: "Baby, Please Don't Go," a blues first recorded by Big Joe Williams; "Kentucky Waltz," a sentimental piece by Bill Monroe; "Waiting for a Train," a yodeling song by Jimmie Rodgers; and "Home Sweet Home," with which they, as many other old-time musicians, ended every dance.

"Bébé's Blues"... is a fiddle number which Bébé learned from a record long ago; he can't remember either the original title or the lyrics, which he recalls were in English. The song, both men say, was extremely popular when Bébé played it at the old dances. "I made many people dance off of that song," he reminisces. "When I played that tune they cut up the floor. Many time I had to play it twice."

Savoy (1983a) states that the Carrières' repertoire "could be described as a mixture of blues, traditional Cajun, and French-American... tunes. 'Bébé' invented some fine fiddle tunes of his own such as 'Madame Faielle' and 'Blue Runner' which are blends of all the above musical influences, especially inspired by blues." And it was Bébé's ability to perform various types of music that helped him and the Lawtell Playboys[63] maintain their popularity. In an interview, he explained: "I could tune up a violin three kind of ways.[64] I could tune my violin to play the blues, and that's why the people were attached to me so much.... And I liked some of them hillbillies, and Jimmie Rodgers's song; I could play 'I'm going to California where they sleep out every night.'[65] I'd sing all that, and people would find that funny that I could sing in English and French—you know, they thought I could just sing in French" (quoted in Tisserand 1998, 74–75). It is also significant that Bébé often included African-derived elements in his musicking. Savoy (1983a) writes that Bébé played "his fiddle in a raw, driving way, often double tuning his fiddle to EAEA, making it possible to repeat a tune in a low bass tone on the re-tuned lower strings." Stanford and Stanford (1974) indicate that both Bébé and Calvin performed the fiddle as if it was a "strong rhythm instrument, as well as [an instrument] for carrying the melodic line when the music demands."

The context for Bébé's fiddling varied. During his early years as a performer, he played in small communities (Lawtell, Eunice, and Basile) in St. Landry Parish with Amédé Ardoin (Spitzer 1979, 5). When Amédé began making commercial recordings during the 1930s, "a talent scout for a national record label heard Bébé playing at a store and was impressed enough to invite him to come to New Orleans with a band to make 78s. Bébé remembers sadly, 'I was a young fella, near 18, and it just kinda slip my mind'" (Spitzer 1977). However,

Bébé made several recordings with family members in later years.[66] In addition to performing with family at house parties locally, Bébé often went outside his community, "sometimes as far away as Lake Charles (sixty miles), to play with other groups. He also played with Cajun musicians at a time when hillbilly and popular music was coming into favor among Louisiana French people" (Spitzer 1979, 5). In addition to the "Kentucky Waltz," tunes such as "Blue Yodel #1" and "Marie" were among his favorites. Musically, Eraste was more conservative, but together they played "South of the Border" and "The Ballad of Jed Clampett," which they learned from TV and called "Deux Pas à Granny (Granny's Two Step)" (Spitzer 1979, 5).

When Eraste's son, Calvin, on fiddle, and his daughter, Beatrice, on rhythm guitar, began performing with them, the type of music the group played was updated. During the 1970s, for example, the sound of the Lawtell Playboys could best be described as modern rural zydeco. Unlike urban zydeco bands from Lafayette or Lake Charles, however, the Lawtell Playboys included a fiddle and the one-row button accordion. "Urban groups usually use two- or three-row button accordions and occasionally a chromatic scale piano accordion. They also play more blues and soul and less of the old time highly syncopated zydeco. Delton Broussard [1927–1994] generally calls the music played by such groups, French rock 'n' roll" (Spitzer 1977).

Calvin Calise Carrière. Calvin, the son of Eraste and Elizabeth Carrière, was also born and raised in Lawtell where he and his wife, Valentine Guillory, were living when I interviewed them in 1987. He had been a farmer all of his life until he became ill and, in 1979, began working as a trucker. Similar to many musicians in southwest Louisiana, Calvin did not tell his family he wanted to play the fiddle. He stated that he hid his interest until he started experimenting with the fiddle when he was around eight years old: "My uncle, Bébé, he used to live at our house. And he'd leave and put his violin on top of a big dresser or *armoire*. And I'd make me a ladder with two chairs and I'd climb up there. Sometime when he needs to go to work, I'd play on this fiddle. Then I asked Daddy, 'Make me a violin with [a] cigar box.' Then I let his violin alone and I started to learn to play" (C. Carrière 1987). To master the fiddle, Calvin stated that one must first learn the fingering and bowing:

> The most important part is the fingering. That's where you get your notes, from those four strings. A good violin player gonna make some good strong notes. I scratched when I was small until I pick it up right. I call it scratch music.[67] You ain't gonna play the fiddle easy like accordion. There's some notes that's kind of hard for you to make on the fiddle. I guess that's why these guys tried [referring to his children who were sitting on the porch during the interview], but they never could get the right thing to go in.[68] I got two fiddles that I keep all the time. They don't want to learn it. I can't get to them play. They try to learn

guitar. But I don't find the fiddle hard. I showed a young man from Beaumont, Edward Poullard. He would come to the house twice a month and I guaranteed he's gonna learn. He learns fast, and he play good. (C. Carrière 1987)

Calvin believed fiddling continued in his family for such a long time because it was a family pastime: "I was small and I used to hear the people get together and sit down on Sunday and make a little music, drink a little White Mule [an alcoholic beverage]." His sister played the guitar. So, the three of them—father, son, and daughter—used to play a lot.

Although he was sometimes referred as the "king of zydeco fiddle" (Feintuch 2022, 32), Calvin also played the guitar. And when his father (Eraste) died, he started performing the accordion, his father's instrument. During the 1940s, Calvin stated that he had a string band that included fiddle, guitar, and banjo. The fiddler would play the lead, while the other parts would "do the basic." Before World War II, "they played just French music." He did not remember all of the songs he played, but recalled such tunes as "La Robe à Parasol," "Jambalaya," and "Baseball." As a young man, Carrière (1987) indicated that he often played with Cajun musicians: "At one time, they don't see accordion, just fiddling and string music.[69] So, when they started on accordion, that's when my daddy opened his band. I played with him. There would be two accordions for people to dance to it. The fiddler would play his part of the song on the fiddle and the two accordions would play the other parts. One would play the song, the other the basic."

Calvin did not think of himself as a composer but indicated that he wrote some songs when he was younger. Having access to the radio and record player helped him with ideas; so, he normally started with the words before adding the music: "You just got to think of something and try to complete the words. Say whatever you gonna sing and try to get a beat to them words to match them. After I whistle it, then I could play it on the violin. Sometime I listen to the radio. The radio at that time pick up some sounds from Baton Rouge. We never did make no recordings at that time. But we had a record player that you have to wind. I used to have to listen just about one or two times. Then I'd play it. We had country and western; we got Amédé Ardoin records. I learned it listening to that record. I play blues on my fiddle that I learn from Bébé. I think he learned his from Jimmie Rodgers because he listened to the radio" (C. Carrière 1987).

When asked how his playing style differed from other fiddlers, such as Canray Fontenot, Calvin stated: "Canray might play a little double fiddle more than I do; he got notes he make I never did on the fiddle. He plays more notes at the same time. When you double, you gonna play more than the big string and play two or three at the time, and the single just carry one tune. It's just gonna be like a little bird sing. That's why you get the right sound" (C. Carrière 1987). In terms of the sound that he preferred, he related that it "depended on what the song you played. Some songs call for double. Some songs you got to play single behind the accordion. The accordion is the lead. The violins do the bassing" (C. Carrière 1987).

Calvin indicated that people in his community liked that he played the fiddle. He had performed at his church, Holy Family Catholic Church, but not on a regular basis because he was too tired after his late Saturday-night performances. In 1986, one of the nuns at his church invited him to perform: "She wanted me to play the violin behind the organ. I went one time. But it looked like the young people didn't like it. She didn't ask me back to practice with her. But I still got the record that they play violin behind some hymns" (C. Carrière 1987). Valentine, Calvin's wife, who also took pleasure in his fiddling, explained that they met each other at a house party: "We used to live close together. He used to work with my daddy in the field. But I never thought that we would have got married. Then after that we started dating, I started going with my mother to dances. His sister, his momma, and I'd go to house parties with him at the school house. We had an old house we called the Green Thumb. We just dance. And at that time, he was playing. It was okay. When I met him, he was playing the fiddle; we been married for forty-one years" (V. Carrière 1987).

Like other members of his family, Calvin did not regard fiddling as a profession. Most performances took place around his home but on occasion he would go to Houston: "We'd leave from here around two o'clock to three. I'd get off of my tractor around twelve, eat dinner, rest a while, get ready and go to Houston and come back the same night. I played at the Church Hall, the Fifth Hall. The Catholic church, they always got halls, and that's where they make them big dances in the hall. They like French music anytime you go play there" (C. Carrière 1987). When researchers started taking an interest in the music of southwest Louisiana during the 1970s and 1980s, Calvin stated that he began traveling and performing at festivals in New York and other parts of the country: "We went to New York last year and we stayed there a week. And we played music at a concert one night. That same night we changed to get ready to come home, but they wanted us to stay and play at another party. They had a back room in that place where we played. That's in one day. Some people in Washington, DC, came up that year" (C. Carrière 1987). In addition to several recordings with the Lawtell Playboys (see photo 12.5), Calvin released *Les Miseres dans le Coeur* (2000) with Goldman Thibodeaux, who played accordion and sang.[70]

Calvin acknowledged the decline in use of the fiddle among young Black Creoles, and explained why the accordion had become popular: "The people in the community just think fiddling is out of style. You can drive I don't know how many miles, you won't find nobody that plays violin—just guitar, piano accordion, triple note. If I can play a dance, I'd rather have a fine accordion. They play French accordion now with rubbing board, guitar, and drums—everything. Accordion is more popular and exciting if you've got a dance; you have more

Photo 12.5. Calvin Carrière and the Lawtell Playboys (L-R): Linton Broussard, Delton Broussard, Calvin Carriére, and J. C. Gallow. Near Eunice, Louisiana, 1983. Photo by Chris Strachwitz. Chris Strachwitz Collection, Arhoolie Foundation.

volume to back up the music with a French accordion. I like it. The two music that's been made to match: French accordion and the fiddle" (C. Carrière 1987).

Canray Adam Fontenot (1922–1995)

Similar to the Carrières, the Fontenots were a family of musicians who had been popular in southwest Louisiana since the early twentieth century. Most were accordion players, with only a few learning to perform the fiddle (Tisserand 1998, 69–70). Canray Fontenot was probably the most well-known fiddler in

Photos 12.6. Canray Fontenot playing fiddle with group. New Orleans Jazz & Heritage Festival, 1974. Photo by Chris Strachwitz. Chris Strachwitz Collection, Arhoolie Foundation.

the region during the 1940s and 1950s, but his reputation expanded nationally during the 1960s and later years (see photo 12.6). With his music partner, accordionist Bois Sec Ardoin, Fontenot performed at the Newport Folk Festival in 1966[71] and received the National Heritage Award from the National Endowment for the Arts (NEA) in 1986. Both performed at New York's Carnegie Hall as well as concerts and festivals in Louisiana, different parts of the United States, and Europe. In addition to being featured in several documentary films, his music has been released on a number of recordings,[72] and his image has appeared on countless festival posters, Louisiana travel brochures, and even in *Newsweek* magazine (Speal n.d.; Savoy 1983a; Tisserand 1998, 68; Fortieth Anniversary 2000). Commenting on Fontenot's impact, Black fiddler and music historian D'Jalma Garnier III (2015, 16) writes: "Canray Fontenot's influence is unsurpassed as a Louisiana Black Creole fiddler, who taught and had contact with many fiddlers. His original repertoire has often been recorded and played by Cajuns and Black Creoles alike.... A few are Creole standards; a few tunes he learned from his father. A funky feel is a priority in Louisiana Black French music, and humor is always present. But a lot of grief, sorrow and tears are channeled into the music. Canray Fontenot epitomized Louisiana Black Creole history and music; many of us had the 'blessed' opportunity to experience it."

When I met Fontenot in 1988,[73] he lived in Welsh, the seat for Jefferson Davis Parish, with his wife, Artile, and worked in a hardware store (Savoy 1984, 326). Before this job, he had been a farmer like most Black Creoles in the region. Born in a small community called L'Anse aux Vaches, near Basile in Evangeline Parish, Canray is the son of Adam J. Fontenot (1898–1939) and Ozémie Victorien (1899–1940).[74] Canray decided to become a fiddler partly because most musicians in his family played the accordion. Not only did two uncles (Freeman Fontenot and Rayde Fontenot) perform the instrument, both parents were accordionists:

> My mama could play the accordion. She wouldn't play in public; she played at the house sometimes.[75] My grandfather, he played like that. And my daddy, he was all the time going playing here and there. But he never was like Amédé [Ardoin]. Cause my daddy always did farming.[76] And Amédé, he never did get married and didn't want to work. He was a lazy man, which set a bad example for us young people who wanted to learn how to play. But they would hire my daddy all the time. And I remember whenever him and Amédé would play [music] for work, they would charge two dollars and a half. When I started playing with them, I would get fifty cents and they'd get two dollars. When it got to where people didn't have no money in them time, he always thought about something he needed in the house. Cause in those days, people would go and slaughter a whole calf or whatever and they would have some meat. So, if you was running short of meat, my daddy would tell them. "Well, I play the dance. So, give me a little bit of meat and pass the hat." Sometimes they wouldn't get much out of the hat, but you knew you was gonna get that meat. (Fontenot 1988)

Displaying pride in his father's musical abilities and accomplishments, Canray stated: "Any person over sixty years old in the black race or the white race, they heard about him [in our community]. He was a great man on the accordion" (Savoy 1984, 326). Although just as well known as Amédé Ardoin, Adam never made any recordings. Canray indicated that "all type of people came to the house and asked him and offered him a lot of money to make some record. 'No,' he said. He never did want to make no record cause he had this idea, he says, 'I don't care how it goes'" (Fontenot 1988). Canray recalled his father also saying, "When I die, I want Adam to be dead. And that's it. Me and my music, we're going to both be dead"[77] (quoted in Tisserand 1998, 88).

Unlike his family members, Canray stated that he chose the fiddle because he wanted to perform something different: "I was born and raised with an accordion in the house, but I never did want to play the accordion. I'm gonna put it straight. I had no idea. In them days I'd hear them records, classical and all, and I'd say, 'You can't do that with an accordion. I wanna play something that you can change. I wanna play something that I want, or I won't play at all'" (Savoy 1984, 326). Providing more details on why he chose the violin over the accordion, he stated:

> I don't know why nobody played no guitar or nothing like that, and the only thing I ever heard beside accordion was a fiddle.[78] And one time, I'll never forget that, I saw a white guy. God dang! He was playing on an accordion and the fiddle. And he came one day with his guitar. Wow! I thought it was some good music. That was something extra.
>
> Where I was born and raised, it never was no Black people playing the fiddle too much. There was two old Black men who picked cotton; they could play the fiddle, but only one tune. They had a waltz they would play, and it was named "The Carpenter Waltz." That was all they could play. But I didn't want to play only one tune. So, I started playing and I says, "If ever I get to a position where I can play what they play, I'm going to be able to play anything I want." (Fontenot 1988)

Yet, choosing the fiddle over the accordion, at that time, was not completely extraordinary. Canray's maternal uncle, Joel [Jules] Victorian (1917–1935), learned to play the fiddle when he was fourteen, and regularly performed with Amédé Ardoin and Adam Fontenot (Savoy 1984, 328; Yule 2009, 107). Canray stated: "There was four or five girls [in the family] and he [Joel] was the only boy. And he was the baby of the family and as usual he would get what he wanted" (Fontenot 1988).

Playing the fiddle also relates to the fact that Canray wanted to be more than a farmer. Since education was important to him, he believed fiddling was a way of demonstrating his interest in learning: "I had this idea. I don't have hardly no education. My education was a fifth-grade education. When I was going to school, we didn't have but three months of school. People used to say, 'Canray's a smart little boy.' I made my fifth-grade education in less time than some of them other people. And when they started having school, I had to go to work. My daddy was dead, and then they didn't have no work or nothing. I knew how to do all kinds of work on the farm. So, I had a hard life. But, in them time, you didn't realize that you were having a hard life" (Fontenot 1988).

Fontenot began playing the fiddle when he was seven or eight years old and his first instrument was made from a cigar box; the person who introduced him to the gramophone also taught him how to make a fiddle: "He [Joel] had started playing the fiddle, too. He invented those cigar box fiddles.... And his cousin, Douglas Bellard, played the fiddle. Whenever he [Douglas] wasn't there, we'd go play his fiddle. And we'd put it right back where it was. So, Joel said, 'We could make us some fiddles out of cigar boxes.' So, we made the boxes and we got the strings off his mama's brand new screen door. We made our bows from branches off the peach trees and sewing thread. And for the rosin we got that off the pine trees, pine sap" (Savoy 1984, 328; also see Doucet 1995; Tisserand 1998, 69; Harris 2008; and Yule 2009, 108).

Comments by Fontenot (1988) indicate that Black Creoles in southwest Louisiana had mixed views about children pursuing music as a career. On the one hand, some family members encouraged his interest in fiddling, while others did not (see foregoing and discussion below): "I had an uncle that could handle his self pretty well, and he wanted to play the fiddle. He wasn't much more than three to four years older than I am. He say, 'I'm gonna get you this little fiddle.' He had a few head of cattle and we used to have some Indians around our area.[79] So, my uncle went and bought a fiddle for two dozen eggs and a pack of rice from them Indians. And so, he played his little fiddle and he was good too. Then, finally, he had a new one; he could get him a real fiddle for ten dollars, cash."

Early in their musical careers, Fontenot indicated that both he and Bois Sec Ardoin played triangle for Amédé Ardoin: "When I was young I was watching how he was playing and listening to his tune and learning the words" (quoted in Tisserand 1998, 65). In 1937, Amédé invited Fontenot "to travel to New York and play on his recording of 'Les Portes de la Prison.' [His mother], however, refused to let him go, telling him he was too young to go to New York" (Harris 1995). Reflecting on this missed opportunity, he stated: "Most of them old people, they didn't care for you to learn how to play music when you was young. Amédé was a good example and a bad example. Because they figure if you learn how to play music you was going to wind up like he was" (quoted in Tisserand 1998, 65). Many of the views people in the community held about the music profession was based on what they observed from local musicians: "They didn't want us to be musicians until we learned how to do this and had a profession, until you was eighteen or twenty years old. Cause a small kid, if he learn how to play music, he was born to be a lazy little kid. They wanted you to learn how to work. Then, when you was gonna be on you own, you can do what you wanted" (Fontenot 1988).

When Fontenot began playing with family and other musicians, he indicated that his role in the group was limited:

> When I first learned, you had to be right with the accordion. I would play the fiddle and my daddy or Amédé or anybody would play the accordion. But I couldn't play the lead. In other words, when I first started, I couldn't play every key my

daddy or the other man played. But I could second, because I knew I had [to] learn how to do it perfectly.

When I first learned, the accordion player in them days, they was gonna sit there and they have to do it. They can't play a tune all the way through. Cause when they learned how to play, they start the tune and they make a break. Then the guitar take his break. The violin take a break. When it's time for them to play again, the tune is all weak. Actually, I've heard them play this way.

Then I decided I'm going to do it the way I do it cause they keep telling me I'm unusual. I was teaching them too. When I heard the way Dewey [Balfa] play it, he says, "But your sound is different." I says, "Well, any type of musician or gospel singer is gonna be different. Black or white man, he gonna do his fiddle his way." (Fontenot 1988)

In 1948, Fontenot and Bois Sec Ardoin organized their first band, the Duralde Ramblers,[80] which included accordion, fiddle, rhythm guitar, drums, and a triangle. For about forty years, the two performed at various events: house parties, community dances, night clubs, festivals, live radio broadcasts on Sundays on KEUN in Eunice, as well as other occasions (Reed 1966; Tisserand 1998, 70). Fontenot explained:

At first, them young people didn't care too much about accordion music; I had a string band going on. . . . And we kept that up for a long time. Then some of the boys started acting kind of coo-coo. So, I said, "I'm gonna' go and play with Bois Sec." But I always would play with him if he didn't have a band. And Bois Sec learned his music through my daddy and Amédée. Bois Sec used to beat the triangle with Amédée a lot of times, and he started playing the accordion. . . . In them times, most of the old people, whether they was white or black, they didn't care too much about string music. They wanted to hear an accordion and a fiddle. So Bois Sec and I would play like that. (Savoy 1984, 330).

When musicking in southwest Louisiana began changing during the 1940s and 1950s, "Ardoin and Fontenot moved from house dances to clubs, and when the rhythm and blues-influenced zydeco bands crowded them from the local clubs, they began to appear on international festival stages" (Tisserand 1998, 68).

Fontenot composed extensively; thus, many of the songs he recorded were his compositions (Garnier III 2015, 17; Tisserand 1998, 32). When asked about the method he used to compose, Fontenot (1988) stated: "It must be just a God gift. Most of my best songs that I ever got on the record is one that took me by surprise. But it's kind of hard to put everything down. But you always get a little bit from here and there from talking to people. That's my personality. Like we are talking here. We're talking about this; we're talking about that. If they gave me a little while to think about a song or something like that, I might come up with something we had talked about and make a song out of that. Or I might take something from that joke. I got to hear the music first. If I think that's the right lyric for it, I'm gonna get some words."

In addition to his interest in creating new music, Fontenot took pleasure in revising old songs (Tisserand 1998, 32). "La Valse de la Prison," originally recorded by Douglas Bellard in 1929, is a blues waltz that several fiddlers—Dewey Balfa, the Carrière Brothers, among others—have used to create their own recordings. In his interview, Fontenot (1988) explained how his version was distinct from the recording by Bellard:[81]

> Douglas was a fiddle player. He was a good one, but he had a habit of playing the fiddle in a way where . . .[82] Cause my main purpose is to play a song in a way where, if people want to dance, they can dance and be comfortable on it. But Douglas, he was the type of man, he would play his fiddle the way he felt. He only made one record that was a big thing in those times. "Barres de Prison," it went like this [Fontenot performed excerpts on the fiddle]. Well, the way he would sing it, it would sound nice. But whenever he would play that, they didn't have nobody on the floor. I was a small boy. So, I said to myself, "I'm gonna record that cause that's one of the first tunes I ever learned how to play." You know, in them time, you didn't have too much music. So, I took mine [he played his version to demonstrate differences]. So, in this way, you can dance and relax—no problems. It's the same tune, but you give it some pep and a little different idea [he played excerpts from tune again].[83]

In addition to the music, the lyrics of songs helped to make it distinctive. In comparing the lyrics of "Les Barres de la Prison" by the Carrière Brothers to those performed by Canray Fontenot, differences are apparent, as noted by Ancelet (2014): "The melody of the Carrières' version of 'Barres de la prison' is similar to Canray Fontenot's version with the same title, and both versions share similar lyrical references to the narrator pleading with his mother to pray for him to save him from the flames of hell. The Carrières' version preserves the lyric 'mon . . . canon . . . la cause' from the 1929 recording by Douglas Bellard and Kirby Riley that clearly inspired both, though the earlier version is 2/4 time, while both the Carrière and Fontenot versions became bluesy waltzes in 3/4 time. Interestingly, despite the title, the Carrière lyrics do not mention 'les barres de la prison' (the prison bars)" (Ancelet 2014).[84]

Also interesting is the manner in which Fontenot's musicking combines features that are both African- and European-derived. In addition to emphasizing the triplet rhythmic pattern, which is common in both European and African music, his use of off-beat phrasing in performing the text of "Barres de la Prison" creates a different feel from merely stating lyrics without giving attention to how they impact the overall organization and character of the tune. In addition, Fontenot occasionally performs the fiddle in a high-pitched range so the sound not only complements his singing, but the fiddle's variations are not drowned out by the sound of the accordion.

The form of "Canray's One Step" is noteworthy for features that are African-derived.[85] In the same way that some West African and African American fiddlers use a single theme (melodic ostinato) as the basis for a song upon which variations are created (DjeDje 2008a, 221; 2020, 91–92), Fontenot uses one sixteen-beat (four-bar) melody, which is repeated throughout the performance with variations, as the basis for "Canray's One Step."[86] Although his performance includes less variation, structurally it is similar to "Smokey Hole" by William Adams and "Georgia Buck" by Joe Thompson.[87] With the fiddle, accordion, and triangle all using a triplet rhythm pattern, the rhythm of the tune is comparable to that of other dance songs he performs.

Fontenot believed fiddlers have distinctive sounds, making it difficult for them to duplicate the playing style of others. For example, he stated that the Carrières' performance style is different from his. "We got the same soul feeling, but the rhythm is a little different." To explain further about the differences in fiddling, he recalled a conversation he had with Balfa.

> Dewey Balfa, he got caught in a jam, and he talked to me about it. Well, he says, "Canray, I've been trying and trying to play your music." Cause I also went some place and they ask me to play some of Balfa's tunes. Well, I say to the folks, "It's not going to be exactly like what Dewey plays, but I can play it the best way I can." And then Dewey went to some places, and they started raising hell with him. They wanted to hear my song and he said, "I can't play it." And they got mad and say. "Oh yeah. How come he play your stuff?" So, he felt very bad about it. So, I told him, "Dewey, all I can tell you. The best way for you to do. Play something close to it the best way you can and you tell them that's the way Dewey Balfa will play the same song." (Fontenot 1988)

Because of the distinctive sound of Black Creole fiddling,[88] much has been written about Fontenot's performance style and influence (Mattern 1997, 162; Tisserand 1998, 71, 282–83, 295). Nick Spitzer (1979), one of the first researchers to document his fiddling, states: "His violin style is unique in mingling blues tonalities and jazz improvisation with modal Acadian scales. One number of this sort in Canray's huge repertoire of songs and instrumentals is a blues waltz called 'Les Barres de la Prison'" (10). Upon his death, Michael Doucet, founder of BeauSoleil,[89] a music group noted for its performance of Cajun music, wrote: "Canray's unique style was bluesy, yet melodic. [He performed with] wild slides and gravelly vocals. . . . Canray originals such as 'Joe Pitre a Deux Femmes,' 'Les Barres de la Prison' and 'Bonsoir Moreau' have become standards in the Cajun and Zydeco repertoires"[90] (Yule 2009, 110). For his obituary for the *New*

York Times, Peter Watrous (1995) reported: "Mr. Fontenot played music that took many of its cues from the French settlers of the area. In his hands, an early French folk song was made bluesy, with bent notes and embellishments, riffs and copious amounts of improvisations. He could be a striking improviser, with the ability to change profoundly the material he scrutinized. He was a synthesizer of cultural identities."

Commenting candidly about the decline of Black Creole fiddling, Fontenot (1988) stated that the fiddle "was always a popular instrument" in southwest Louisiana, but there never have been many people who played it. After the 1950s, the situation became more desperate in rural areas. "Oh, they may have fiddlers but they are not around here. Some young Black men play the fiddle, but their fiddle style is like white people's style. All them play with the wrong type of rhythm. I like them boys just like if they would be my sons. But they can't get the fiddling style; they learned more from the white culture." Like other fiddlers,[91] Fontenot (1988) believed the primary reason for the fiddle's lack of popularity had to do with the difficulty in playing the instrument.

As Black Creole music became more urban and groups began experimenting with different instrumentation, the fiddle was the instrument that was singled out to be retained or discarded. In other words, use of the fiddle marked a group as rural or urban—old or modern (Tisserand 1998, 17). As Delton Broussard, who became the leader of the Lawtell Playboys after the Carrière Brothers retired, explained: "I believe a fiddle is nice for Cajun music, but if I was trying to make my driving sound with the fiddle dragging me down, I'd probably catch a headache" (quoted in Tisserand 1998, 265).

Texas

Because much of the music literature on African Americans in Texas[92] focuses on the blues, many researchers are unaware of the fact that several Texas Black musicians grew up in families with fathers who were fiddlers.[93] Not only was fiddling widespread among rural Blacks in the state during the early twentieth century, musicking by whites (such as contest fiddling and western swing) show a distinct African American influence. Govenar and Brakefield (1998) explain: "Texas style fiddling is characterized by intricately fingered and rhythmically varied interpretations of traditional tunes, which sometimes include the slurring of notes to produce a bluesy or swing sound. About this, Bob Wills said, 'I slurred my fiddle in order to play the blues,' and, referring to his vocal style with his band, commented, 'I have always been a blues singer'" (153). Similar to other parts of the United States, fiddling by Texas Blacks was not documented by researchers or record companies when it was most prominent because fiddle and string band music was identified with Anglo-Americans. In fact, Bill

C. Malone (1979, 81) indicates that white Texas musicians constitute the largest group in the country music idiom, but rarely is it noted that their contributions were oftentimes derived from what they learned from other music cultures, including African Americans, Cajuns, Mexicans, and Central Europeans.

Except for publications by John Minton (1996a), Dan Foster (2020), and Suzy Thompson (2021), no written works, to my knowledge, have been published on Black Texas fiddling. The first focuses on aspects of the tradition during the slave era, while the second and third examine the musicking of Teodar Jackson, one of the few Black fiddlers for which sound material exists. However, a publication that contains more substantial information on the subject is *Blues Come to Texas*, the unfinished book by Paul Oliver and Mack McCormick that has been compiled by Alan B. Govenar and Kip Lornell (2019). With research beginning in 1959, Oliver and McCormick placed special importance on the narratives and recollections of musicians who played a creative part in the development of blues, as well as the relatives, friends, acquaintances and members of the Black communities who listened, enjoyed, or shared the music (Govenar and Lornell 2019, 46). Not only does the work contain names with brief biographical data about several fiddlers, details about performance contexts and repertoire make the material extremely valuable. Therefore, almost all of the following discussion is based on material presented in this work.

During the early twentieth century, the fiddle continued to be the most popular instrument among Blacks in Texas, particularly in rural communities where social conditions had not changed. Although African Americans were no longer enslaved, "they still depended on the 'Big House,' still worked on the large plantations and entertained themselves in a manner already established in long custom. The 'fiddle songs,' the 'devil songs,' the 'corn songs,' and the 'Jim Crow songs' had their counterparts in the songs and dances of the Blacklands,[94] and, with a stable economy, no mass media to influence a dramatic change in the music, the traditions persisted, perpetuated to no small degree by the entertainments and dances of the minstrel show which fed back into the tradition the elements it had borrowed" (Govenar and Lornell 2019, 51). Opportunities for musicking were numerous. Dances on Saturday evenings, when the week's work was over and the Sunday religious worship yet to begin, were held in barns or buildings that remained vacant during the week to be used for entertainment at the end of it. When the weather was warm, play-parties were held in the open, under a grove of trees or by the river. The Saturday night fish-fry "at which many families gathered to cook in the open the fish caught by the children for the occasion . . . , was as popular in Texas as elsewhere in the South. So too was the 'crawdad brunch' where large quantities of live fresh-water crayfish were boiled in huge vats over open fires, to be peeled and eaten with lemon in intervals in the dancing. Little excuse was required for the holding of the barbecues and picnics which were an essential part of community life" (51). Work activities, such as corn-husking or corn-shucking, also provided opportunities for dancing to fiddle music. Rural Blacks traveled for many miles by horse and buggy, wagon and team along the dirt roads to the site for such events. "A yard, carefully swept down and hard-packed, served as a dance-floor and the swirling skirts and stomping feet kicked up the dust before the kerosene lamps. No one minded the dust clouds as they joined in the square dances. . . . The fiddler sawed at 'Ticonderoga,' 'Sally Goodin,' 'Lost Girl in Dallas,' or 'Cotton-Eyed Joe'—traditional pieces were some, minstrel show items others, still others square dances and jigs for which new tunes and new themes had developed locally" (51).

In addition, Juneteenth celebrations[95] and country suppers in Texas, like frolics in rural Black communities in other parts of the South, provided opportunities for recreation that included fiddling. As Mance Lipscomb explained, [If] "we were givin' a supper Saturday night, I would put it out that I was givin' a supper; well I'd barbecue a hawg probably, and my wife'd cook up some cakes, chicken, and then we'd have a supper, and they come in and dance all night; and buy, until they'd buy us out. . . . That's how we were trained up, playing Saturday night suppers" (Govenar and Lornell 2019, 52). According to Susie Sansom Piper (1921–2019), the principal of Aycock High School in Rockdale, a small town in Milam County,[96] Saturday-night country suppers were sometimes called country balls with musicking that varied: "When the fiddler, the guitarist, banjo and piano players struck up a sad blues tune, or jazz number, those who wanted to dance did the 'barrelhouse,' Charleston, tap dance, buck dance, two-step or wopsy. . . . Music was more or less a natural, for many of these musicians were self-trained and played by ear, or according to their feelings, cares, and woes" (Foster 2020).

Although the physical environment and history of groups in different regions of the state limited the extensive sharing of culture that occurred in other parts of the South, some intermixing did take place. Researchers explain: "Though the Negro population was to a considerable extent obliged to be segregated from that of the white, the music of the fiddlers and their accompanists was shared by both, and the dances had much in common" (Govenar and Lornell 2019, 52). It was also not uncommon for white Texans to invite Mexican as well as African American string bands to provide entertainment, with each group performing at different occasions (53). During the early twentieth century, Black fiddling continued to be popular on ranches in Texas while blues was less appealing, probably because of demographics, which was similar to that of some mountain states in other parts of the South. "[W]hen the noose of discrimination tightened, and the black culture was forced to find its own identity in its own terms, the blues developed. But on the range, where black cowboys worked beside white, where the fiddle remained as a folk instrument because there was no need for the popularization of a new instrument to suit a new music; where the cowboy culture—and the cowboy myth—rose above any affiliation to an essentially black culture, the blues did not appear because it served no purpose" (262).

In terms of ensemble organization, the fiddle in Texas, like other parts of the United States, could be accompanied by any one of the following instruments—banjo, bones, accordion, or sticks that were beaten on the back of a chair. Only with the rise in popularity of the guitar, which, in Texas, coincided with emergence of the blues, did changes begin to occur. So, the decline in fiddling varied in different parts of the state. According to Oliver and McCormick, "The appearance of the guitarists indicated the ultimate direction of the traditions, presaged their decline and heralded a new idiom. An old town with a large Mexican population provided opportunities to exchange tunes with the Mexican musicians and to learn a number of tunes and waltzes from them" (Govenar and Lornell 2019, 53). It was in this way that some Black musicians learned to play guitar.

Therefore, several factors led to the decline in the fiddle around the turn of the twentieth century in Texas. In addition to the influx of more Mexicans, escaping the troubled political climate in their home country, the ceding of sovereignty of Hawaii to the United States and the subsequent immigration of Hawaiians with their bands that became especially popular in western states, all affected the use of the fiddle. Once the guitar was introduced and Black musicians discovered that one instrument could provide both the fiddle's melody and the banjo rhythm, this also caused the fiddle to become less popular. For young Black men who were beginning to learn to play and accompany their fathers, the guitar also presented an irresistible attraction and break with the traditions of their ancestors; replacing fiddles and banjos with guitars was the most dramatic element to bring about a change in Black musicking (Govenar and Lornell 2019, 57). Although Oliver and McCormick identify the names of several Black fiddlers in rural communities in East Texas (Govenar and Lornell 2019),[97] little is known about their lives. For this reason, the discussion here will focus only on fiddlers—Charlie Thomas, Oscar Nelson, and Teodar Jackson—for which substantial information exists.

Profiles of Texas Black Fiddlers

Charlie Thomas (b. 1892)

Charlie Thomas, a celebrated Texas fiddler with a more than fifty-year tradition of performing, was born in Fayetteville, a small community in Fayette County, Texas, that had a total population of 269 people in 1890, which was less than 1 percent of the county's total population.[98] Professionally known as Fiddling Charlie Thomas, his career is important "not only for the esteem with which he was generally held, but for the light it sheds on the kind of work that was available to a good musician, and the variety of kinds of entertainment for which a fiddler and a string band could play. He continued to work in string bands for many years"

(Govenar and Lornell 2019, 345). Although Thomas played both guitar and fiddle, his admirers in 1952 said that he's "the best fiddle player there is in Texas.... He'd sing and play violin right at the same time. He played a big variety—blues, boogie-woogies, sentimental.... He's dangerous on that fiddle" (344).[99]

Thomas did not become interested in musicking until 1908 (around the age of sixteen) when he started playing on the family pump organ with his sister. It is unknown why he was drawn to fiddling, but there were many Black string musicians in East Texas who may have stimulated his interest and desire to emulate, particularly musicians he had seen in earlier years. In 1905, Frank Justice and Young Douglas were the two best known fiddlers in the Temple (Bell County) area. In fact, Thomas learned "Frankie and Albert" from Douglas, whom many regarded as a violin-playing songster. Tonk Grady, a fiddler Thomas heard in 1910 and a resident of Granger (Williamson County), Texas, taught him "Cocaine Done Killed My Baby," a widely known non-blues song (Thomas 1962).[100] Closer to home, Thomas was listening to fiddler Pink Johnson when he decided that he wanted to learn how to play the fiddle. He took a few lessons from Della Tanner from Brazoria County, Texas, who taught school in Fayetteville; from her, he learned the rudiments of playing and how to read a little music. By the time he was twenty-two or twenty-three years old, he was playing at country suppers and dances in small towns in southeast Texas—New Ulm and Sealy in Austin County, Brookshire in Waller County, and Fayetteville in Fayette County (344).[101]

During his career, Thomas most often performed with guitarists; in fact, there is no mention of him being accompanied by a banjoist. Although he worked for some years with the celebrated violinist/guitarist Lonnie Johnson (see below), he had strong recollections about Monroe Stephenson, who died during the 1930s, but, in his view, was "an outstanding guitar man" even though he did not have an opportunity to record (Thomas 1962). Hugo Martin, who owned a small farm not far from Thomas's home in Fayetteville,[102] sometimes played guitar as "second" to Thomas, but because he had a "regular place to get back to," he preferred not to travel far from home for performances. Researchers indicate that Thomas "was an extrovert entertainer who needed no encouragement to explore further afield, playing in San Antonio, Houston and Dallas, and eventually, in St. Louis and Oklahoma" (Govenar and Lornell 2019, 71). In the late teens, Thomas partnered with Henry Thomas (no relation to Charlie), a well-known Texas guitarist:[103] "I played with him for some time but he was pretty much his own man and not one for playing in time, though he was a straight country music player. He had a lot of breakdowns and square dance pieces on guitar. I'd say he was five, six years older than me, but that's just a guess. He had real old time stuff even then when I got to hear him around 1917, 1918" (Thomas 1962).

One of Thomas's most interesting work experiences was performing with a medicine show. Enjoyed by Blacks and whites in many parts of the rural South, particularly when theaters as well as traveling vaudeville and burlesque entertainment became popular, medicine shows were an important context for Black fiddling. In describing his performance experiences in this context during the mid-1920s,[104] Thomas (1962) stated:

> In 1925, I got with Dr. Tate's Medicine Show.[105] He was a white man who traveled about with us to warm up the crowd and give entertainment while he did a spiel for his TateLay Medicine. I had a 1925 Buick that I carried my men in and he had a truck that had the stage right on the back. When he got to a place he'd get permission to set up right in the courthouse square. The band I had was me on fiddle, Leon Green guitar, Fenn Pose on bass and Simon Williams—he played trumpet and trombone. There were several boys—one named Warren—that did the singing and clowning. That way the show . . . start with a big hullabaloo and gather a crowd with a few pieces of music—one guy'd do a buck dance, or we'd all sing "Sittin' on Top of the World" or "Elder Green" or have a thing like "Mama Don't Want No Guitar Playing in Here" or go on with "Match Box Blues" or maybe a sentimental [ballad], if it was a lot of whites in the crowd. Then there'd be a comedy thing—a dialogue between me and the Doctor or between two of the singers. (345)

After leaving the medicine show, Thomas started performing at marriage parties as well as dances for Blacks and whites on Saturday nights. He even played at dances on the Harlem State Farm (a prison) for the guards and their families who lived on a compound (Govenar and Lornell 2019, 344). During the 1930s, Thomas, along with musicians who accompanied him during the medicine show, performed with guitarist Lonnie Johnson and other musicians in various cities (Guthrie and Oklahoma City) in Oklahoma. According to Thomas, Johnson "was a big star and we played all kinds of white dances, theaters and everything. I met Lonnie in St. Louis the first time, and after I got him from St. Louis, I worked around country suppers for a while with two girls from Industry, Texas, they was both guitar players and singers; they was Alberta Perkins, and Eddie Perkins, sisters. Both were good but Eddie might have the edge there. Both sang blues with real big, full, heavy voices. Lots of them songs about how men had mistreated them and gone off in the army. Some of them was 'France Blues,' 'Gambling Man' and 'Lying Blues'" (Thomas 1962).

After performances with Johnson ended, Thomas continued his musicking in various parts of the state:

> After I split from Lonnie Johnson in 1940, the band split up but I stayed around Waller County [near Houston] and then I got together with a group that played all over Houston and all over the [state] round Fulshear, Brookshire and in there.[106] We'd play on the streets, go out on 75th Street into the bars there by the ship channel and play blues and country stuff for the sailors from all over

the world—France, England, Brazil, Africa, Japan. That was just before the war when the Japanese ships were coming to pick up scrap iron out of Houston. We went serenading out to picnics and outdoor parties. Sometimes into the white hotels for parties. We got a reputation and they'd come out to 75th Street . . . and get us and carry us off to something they needed music for. Now that was a regular string band, playing a little of everything: breakdown blues, sentimentals, with two or three different ones singing. We had Freddie Chase; he played the "Original Blues," which Monroe Stephenson used to play. . . . Then there was Benny Jones; he came from the Fort Bend County bottoms, good guitar man. Fenn Pose on bass, only later it was Dave Grimes, and Wop Williams mandolin. I played fiddle. (345)

The manner in which they played during a performance, called serenading, is significant because it reflects contact and influence from Mexicans. Thomas (1962) explained: "We always worked standing up, walking around while we played, just like you see the Mexican musicians go from place to place out at beer gardens and such. That was the way a string band worked—in a bar or out on the streets" (345). In fact, Oliver and McCormick believe the tradition of serenading by string bands in the area was probably derived from Mexico (345).

Later in life, Thomas continued traveling and performing. In 1952, Buster Pickens, one of his fans who had kept up with his career over the years, stated: He "played around Brookshire, Bellville, Sealy, Hempstead, Brenham, Navasota.[107] He's still at playing, one of Texas' oldest musicians. He and . . . old man Williams [another Black fiddler known as Fiddling Charlie Williams] used to play over at the Buzzard Roost on Cleveland and Tennessee Streets in the Fourth Ward, Houston. . . . Every Friday evening they'd saw on down there" (344). When the roadhouses that catered to blues ousted the musicians who played country breakdowns, many of the fiddlers ceased playing. A few Black fiddlers, like Gus Stuart who was born in 1882, retired; they had spent a lifetime playing in minstrel shows and jazz bands and did not want to make the change. Other Black fiddlers who remained active either joined guitarists and played at various functions or string band musicians who could compete and accept playing the blues. Because he was flexible and open to new ideas, Thomas maintained an active performing career. He also had established a strong enough reputation that allowed him to compete on equal terms with any other musician (344).

Oscar William Nelson (1901–1984)

Oscar Nelson, also known as "Preacher" Nelson, was born into a musical family.[108] His ancestors were transported from Alabama to Milam County, Texas, sometime during the mid-nineteenth century; his grandfather was five years old when family members were freed in 1865. Nelson's grandfather "was well known for banjo playing," which may account for two of his grandsons—Charlie and Oscar—becoming musicians.[109] Starting in 1915, Oscar played fiddle and guitar with the family string band for forty years. Regarding the manner in which the family learned and developed their repertoire, Oscar explained how it was related to his fiddling:

> We just learned music through ear. My daddy played five-string banjo and I got on it when I was small, and then went to violin. One of the first songs I learned was "Eat on the table, eat on the floor; see anyone coming, a hit the door." I learned that on banjo when I was about ten or eleven. That was the time before the blues come up, back in 1910 or so, and the songs you'd hear was "Alabama Bound," and "Ella Speed" and ones about "If the train don't run I got a big black mule to ride" and "Brown skin woman make a bull dog break his chain." . . . Now those was fiddle and banjo pieces and later them songs got the blues,[110] but I learned them as fiddle and banjo songs and played in a different style just as you'd expect from fiddle and banjo. We was going in the country in those days, around Milam County playing that music and pure fiddle tunes and reels and breakdowns. There was a lot of others doing the same thing, older men than we was, so we just carrying on with the ordinary way of music. (Nelson 1962, 69)

With his brothers—Ira J. (on French harp), Richard Bailey (on mandolin), and John Daniel (on guitar)—the Nelson family band was one of many string bands popular in the hilly country between Waco and Austin during the early twentieth century. Because they performed primarily fiddle tunes, little information is available on them.[111] But researchers indicate that the Nelsons played half of the time for Blacks and half for whites (346). In fact, when Tary Owens, a University of Texas student, inquired about performance contexts, they indicated that "they played square dances and parties in communities like Griffin Chapel and white folk dances in Rockdale and Cameron."[112] When asked if they played different music for white and Black audiences, Oscar Nelson answered, 'No, we played about the same thing'" (Foster 2020).

Teodar Jackson (1903–1966)

Although documented evidence indicates that fiddling by African Americans in Texas continued through the mid-twentieth century, sound material is lacking, except for the 1965 field recordings of Teodar Jackson made in Austin by Tary Owens.[113] By examining Jackson's material, as Foster (2020) states, "we have our best chance to listen back across time to the music of distant generations, to hear some of the signal concepts of the core of country fiddling, black and white, here in Texas."

Teodar Jackson was born in Gonzales County, which is located in southeast Texas.[114] Sometime between 1910 and 1920, the family moved north to Travis County in the Austin area.[115] It is unknown where or when Jackson began playing the fiddle. However, Foster (2020) suggests that this may have occurred at an early age because "Gonzales County and the surrounding area in South Texas had been home to African American musicians since before the 1850s. Tommie D. Wright, a noted member of what has been described as 'an enormous clan of Texas fiddlers,' learned the music from his father as well as from his grandfather, Jack Wright, who was born in Gonzales County in 1845. . . . Jack Wright used to fiddle and call sets for eight men and women all 'out on the floor dancing squares.' He fiddled tunes like 'Sally Goodin,' 'Old Hen Cackle,' 'Pick the Meat Off the Devil's Backbone,' 'Sally in the Wildwood,' 'Green Corn,' and others."

After World War II, sources indicate that Jackson played music with musicians—Alfred Johnson (a guitarist) and Ammie Deaver (a harmonica player)—in the Austin area. But it is doubtful that this continued for any length of time because of the rapidly changing musical environment taking place in most parts of the United States during the mid-twentieth century. It was not until Owens approached Jackson in 1965 that he agreed to have a recording made of him playing the fiddle accompanied by his son T. J. Jackson on guitar. "Owens also encouraged . . . Jackson to perform at local student hang-outs like the Id Coffee House and the Eleventh Door" (Foster 2020). Similar to what transpired with other Black fiddlers during the 1960s and 1970s in other parts of the country, who were encouraged to come out of retirement and make recordings,[116] Jackson's performances were well-received. As Foster (2020) explains: "Jackson was embraced by the young crowd at the heart of the nascent Austin music scene in the mid-1960s. . . . Like his friend the Navasota songster Mance Lipscomb, he was idolized, playing for many rapt, largely white audiences in venues . . . , where he was recorded by another young student named George Lyon. Teodar and T. J. were featured at the KHFI-FM Summer Music Festival in Zilker Park in July 1965. . . . [He] was expected to be featured in the upcoming Newport Folk Festival up in Rhode Island. Unfortunately, a heart attack would intervene and send him off for a stay in the hospital instead."

Musically, Jackson's fiddling is similar to other musicians discussed in this study. His repertoire includes a mix of old-time tunes developed from a shared culture of Anglo-Americans and African Americans, as well as songs that relate geographically to his home region.[117] In creating and performing music for his audiences, he obviously spent a lot of time listening to the media and/or the musicking of other musicians. Except for a few,[118] all songs appear to be his versions of tunes recorded by others. Of those that are derived from African American culture, the breadth of his repertoire—traditional sacred and secular songs, such as "Golden Slippers," originally recorded by the Fisk Jubilee Quartet in 1909, "See See Rider Blues," first recorded in 1924 by Ma Rainey with Her

Georgia Band with later versions recorded by Big Bill Broonzy and Huddie Ledbetter during the 1930s—is noteworthy. Old-time tunes originally recorded by white fiddlers during the 1920s—including "Whoa, Mule, Whoa" by the Dixie String Band, "Drunkard's Hiccups" by John Carson, and "Lost John" by Henry Whitter (on harmonica)—also demonstrate his knowledge of the tradition. In terms of performance style, Jackson includes elements identified with African American musicking generally. Creating his own versions of songs melodically, rhythmically, and in terms of form, using elements from African American culture that had been maintained from earlier times, but fusing these features with the blues, made his fiddling both similar to and distinct from that in other parts of the South.

Summary

Because of their unique history, Louisiana and Texas are important for Black fiddling during the early twentieth century because, unlike other states, they encompassed the totality—excellence in both the rural and the urban.[119] Fiddlers in both states remained popular primarily because they embraced new styles that were emerging in African American culture in the early 1900s. They discovered creative ways to combine the old with the new that appealed to their listeners. Whereas Black fiddlers in southeast Louisiana performed tunes that reflected the fusion of old-time music with local and emerging genres in African American music, Black Creole fiddlers in the southwest combined features that included Cajun, local styles, and new genres. In both Louisiana and Texas Black fiddling, elements from Africa served as the basis for innovations.

fiddlingismyjoycompanion.net

Notes

1. 🎻 See History 12.1.

2. Unlike the band's leader, who is responsible solely for the music, the front man can be the star soloist and/or the person responsible for business arrangements. Occasionally, the band's leader performs both functions (Meadows 2023).

3. Information on Black fiddlers/violinists who were active in the New Orleans jazz scene during the early twentieth century—for example, John Robichaux (1866–1939), Peter Bocage (1887–1967), and Armand Piron (1888–1943)—is in no way comparable to the amount of material

that exists on other jazz instrumentalists—such as cornet/trumpet players Joe "King" Oliver (1881–1938), Freddie Keppard (1890–1933), and Louis Armstrong (1901–1971); trombonist Edward "Kid" Ory (1886–1973); pianist Jelly Roll Morton (1890–1941); clarinetist Johnny Dodds (1892–1940); or drummer Warren "Baby Dodds (1898–1959). For details on early Black New Orleans violinists, see Rose and Souchon (1984).

4. ❦ See Map 12.1, Map 12.2, and Land Regions 12.1.

5. The only information on African American fiddling in southeast Louisiana is that provided by folklorist Harry Oster, who conducted interviews and made field recordings of Cage in Louisiana between 1959 and 1962. As result of Oster's research, other researchers (Paul Oliver and Chris Strachwitz) became interested in Cage's fiddling. Therefore, Cage's life as a musician is important because it gives evidence of fiddling during the first half of the twentieth century in a region of the southern United States for which little information exists.

6. ❦ See Demographics 12.1.

7. US census records indicate that both parents, John Jr. (1864–1904) and Lethea Cage (1861–1920), were born in Franklin County, Mississippi, and Butch was their sixth child.

8. In 1927, the Great Mississippi Flood was the most destructive river flood in the United States on record; the uninflated cost of the damage has been estimated to be between $246 million and $1 billion. Economic woes from the Mississippi flood, the infestation of the boll weevil, and the Great Depression are all factors that started the migration of Black southerners to various parts of the United States between the twenties and sixties (Watkins 1997; Hornbeck and Neidu 2014).

9. Willie Thomas was born 1912 in Lobdell, Louisiana, an unincorporated community in West Baton Rouge Parish, which is about sixteen miles southwest of Zachary and fourteen miles south of Baton Rouge. Thomas's family moved to Zachary around 1925, when he was thirteen years old (Oster 1960). Thus, Thomas and Cage both settled in Zachary around the same time.

10. ❦ See Repertoire 12.1. Selections of Cage's fiddling appear on more than twenty different audio recordings and films. In 1960, Cage and Thomas were among the first Black musicians from rural parts of the southern United States to perform at the Newport Folk Festival in Rhode Island.

11. Only two songs, "44 Blues" and "Stranger Blues (I'm a Stranger Here)," from and Thomas's performance at the Newport Folk Festival were issued on a recording. Irwin Silber (1961, 2) believes the musicians were in the wrong place at the wrong time—vainly trying to communicate to an audience that had no basis for understanding their music.

12. At his initial meeting with Cage, Oliver (1965) reports that he recorded an all-day session with "a fair proportion" of the community present, and states that Cage "plays wild exciting fiddle music in a raw country tradition, holding the instrument against his chest" (178).

13. According to Oster (1960), these materials represent the high points of jam sessions recorded in several country sections of Louisiana: Zachary, Scotlandville, the State Penitentiary at Angola, and the State Mental Hospital in Jackson (all in north Baton Rouge); Napoleonville (fifty miles south of Baton Rouge); and Kilona (thirty miles south of New Orleans).

14. Although Cage was an active member of the church (Oster 1969, 8), there is no indication that he performed the fiddle during worship services. Of the songs collected by researchers, "It's the Sign of Judgement" and "Since I Layed My Burden Down" are the only spirituals on which Cage sings and performs the fiddle. On other religious songs, he merely provides fiddle accompaniment.

15. Although some titles ("Hoodoo Blues" or "Black Cat Bone") relate to spiritual practices that are African-derived, the lyrics suggest they may be secular love songs in which the singer describes how to use special potions or charms to sway or control the feelings of a lover (Hoodoo of Black Cat Bone 2012).

16. Roosevelt Sykes created the lyrics and recorded "'44' Blues" on OKeh Records in New York City on June 14, 1929; on the recording, he sings and plays piano with no accompaniment (Dixon and Godrich 1982, 714). Sykes was born in Elmar (Phillips County), Arkansas, but moved (around 1909) with his family to St. Louis. As a youth, he often visited his grandfather's farm near West Helena (Phillips County), Arkansas. Since his grandfather was a preacher who had an organ, Sykes used it to practice and, by the age of ten, had learned how to play the instrument. When he was

twelve years old (around 1918), Sykes was playing blues piano, and, by age fifteen was performing in barrelhouses and juke joints (bars and saloons) in Helena, Arkansas (Metrailer 2013).

17. Montgomery does not claim exclusive credit for composing the song, but states that several pianists contributed to its creation (Oliver 1968, 94).

18. 🎵 See Lyrics 12.1. Green recorded his version, titled "Number 44 Blues" on Vocalion Records, two months (August 16, 1929) after Sykes, and about one year later (September 1930), Montgomery recorded his version, titled "Vicksburg Blues" on Paramount Records. Neither version became popular. Oliver (1968) believes Sykes's lyrics, with the double meanings for the phrase forty-four—"the train number 44, the .44 caliber revolver, and the 'little cabin' on which was the number 44 that presumably referred to a prison cell"—accounted for the popularity of his version to singers. The lyrics to verse 6 in Thomas and Cage's performance of "44 Blues" at the Newport Folk Festival indicate that the number 44 refers to a cabin that the singer purchased: "I bought a little cabin, cabin number, number forty-four [twice] / When I wake up in the morning / Blues is hollering around my door" (Silber 1961, 5).

19. 🎵 Go to Audio Examples to listen to "44 Blues" by Sykes and Cage; also see Analysis 12.1.

20. To view the complete lyrics for Cage and Thomas's version of "44 Blues," see Oster 1969, 393–95).

21. "Thought I Heard That K. C. Whistle Blow" is a song title with lyrics from the early twentieth century or earlier. Odum (1911a, 256) describes the collection that includes "Thought I Heard That K. C. Whistle Blow" as "negro folk-songs." Although identified with African American culture, the lyrics have been used in songs by both Black and white musicians. Also see discussion in chapter 9.

22. 🎵 Go to Audio Examples to listen to "New Jelly Roll Blues" by Eddie Anthony with Peg Leg Howell and His Gang and "Jelly Roll" by Cage and Thomas.

23. 🎵 See Lyrics 12.2.

24. 🎵 See Demographics 12.2.

25. In this discussion, the term "Black Creole" will be used instead of "African American" because most Black residents of southwest Louisiana prefer the former (Mattern 1997, 159). For many African Americans, the term *Creole* refers to Black people who are light in skin color or a person whose racial background is of French or Spanish ancestry. In southwest Louisiana, however, Creole refers to French-speakers of mixed ancestry including enslaved Blacks from the Caribbean and American South, *gens libres de couleur* (free people of color), Spanish, French and German planters and mercantilists, local Indian tribes, Anglo-Americans and Cajuns (Spitzer 1979, 2). Cajun, an Anglicized version of the word Cadien (and shortened variant of Acadien), refers to rural, French-speaking whites of southwest Louisiana whose ancestors are from Canada (Elliott 1992, 25). Thus, Cajuns regard their forebears to be different from French Creoles (French-speaking whites born in North America) and Anglo-Americans (whites who trace their ancestry to the British Isles).

26. In Louisiana, Cajuns held private dances in their homes as well as the public county dance that they called the *fais do-do*. A similar tradition existed in Black Creole communities, but there does not appear to be one special term used for this event (Post 1962, 152; Elliott 1992, 26–27).

27. Some researchers believe class distinctions often outweighed racial ones for poor whites in the Upper South during the slave era (Farmelo 2001, 182).

28. Dewey Balfa (1927–1992), a Cajun fiddler and singer who contributed significantly to the popularity of Cajun music, was born near Mamou (Evangeline Parish), the heart of Cajun country. Balfa is probably best known for his performance at the Newport Folk Festival in 1964 and different arts events in Louisiana and other parts of the United States.

29. Alphonse Ardoin (1915–2007), a well-known Black accordion player who began his career during the early twentieth century, and Black Creole fiddler Canray Fontenot were musical partners for more than forty years (see discussion below).

30. Menestrel (2007, 97) states that "after slavery, the descendants of free people of color chose to designate themselves Creoles of color in order to differentiate themselves from former slaves."

31. For information, see works by Barry Ancelet, Sharon Arms Doucet, J. Gary Elliott, D'Jamal Garnier III, Paul Harris, Mark Mattern, John Minton, Ann Allen Savoy, Nick Spitzer, Fay and Ron Stanford, Chris Strachwitz, Michael Tisserand, Ron Yule, and others. In October 1987 and summer 1988, I conducted interviews with several people who lived in southwest Louisiana: Barry Ancelet, Dewey Balfa, Calvin Carrière, Canray Fontenot, and Dennis McGee. Therefore, much of what is included in this discussion comes from my conversations with these individuals as well as information from other researchers. Because Cajun and Black Creole fiddling are closely intertwined (Garnier III 2015, 8–9), data about both are presented here but the primary focus is on the contributions of Black Creoles.

32. Much has been written about the history of zydeco; see Tisserand (1998), Minton (1996b), and Garnier III (2012). Early twentieth-century Black Creole performers who provided the foundation for zydeco music—including Douglas Bellard (fiddle), Amédé Ardoin (accordion), Alphonse "Bois Sec" Ardoin (accordion), Bébé Carriere (fiddle), Claude Faulk (accordion), Canray Fontenot (fiddle), and Freeman Fontenot (accordion)—are some of the same musicians cited as early influences for Cajun music (Mattern 1997, 161). The spelling of the term *zydeco* was first established in 1960 by Mack McCormick, a music researcher in Houston who was attempting to phonetically re-create the word Black Creole musicians used for the phrase, *les haricots sont pas salés* (the snap beans are not salted). Variant spellings for the term include *zarico, zodico, zordico, zologo* (Spitzer 1977, 1979, 3; Savoy 1984, 305; Ancelet 1989, 1; Mattern 1997, 165), but the most common is zydeco.

33. In Louisiana, *juré* refers to a local form of the African American ring shout, consisting of a counterclockwise procession accompanied by antiphonal singing and the shuffling, stamping, and clapping of the dancers, occasionally supplemented by simple percussion, such as the metal-on-jawbone scraper or the washboard (Minton 1996b, 490; also see DeWitt 2020).

34. While some songs of European origin survived, new ones were created or new lyrics were added to old songs. Indigenous groups contributed "a terraced singing style and new dance rhythms," while the Spaniards furnished new tunes and certain melodic elements. Since instruments were not always available or were forbidden, dance music was produced with voices, clapping hands, and stamping feet, which enhanced the percussive and rhythmic development of the music. When instruments became available, the fiddle predominated, and tunes originally performed on brass or reed instruments were transferred to strings (Ancelet 1989, 17; Elliott 1992, 96–97)

35. In 1981, KEUN radio in Eunice (St. Landry Parish) "began broadcasting a full hour of zydeco music each Saturday morning from eleven to noon. According to the station 'zydeco, traditional black Cajun music, has been neglected by Southwest Louisiana radio stations for years'" (Broven 1983, 116). John Broven (1983, 101) described zydeco as music sung by "black Cajuns." Chris Strachwitz, owner of the California-based Arhoolie record label, which helped introduce the music of southwest Louisiana to a national and international audience, used *Amédé Ardoin: The First Black Cajun Recording Artist* (1991) as the title of a collection of recordings by Ardoin (1898–1942) and *Cajun Fiddle Styles: The Creole Tradition* (1983) as the title of a release by the Carrière Brothers, a duo that included Black Creole musicians Joseph "Bébé" Carrière and Eraste Carrière. Strachwitz's title is also inaccurate because the October 1929 recording by Black Creole fiddler Douglas Bellard predates Amédé Ardoin's December 1929 recording by two months (Tisserand 1998, 69).

36. ♪ See Repertoire 12.4 (Carrière family) and Repertoire 12.5 (Fontenot) for compilations of recordings. Although her pioneering investigations are appreciated, Savoy (1984, xi) made statements that misinterpret the contributions of Black Creoles and Cajuns (Mattern 1997). Other works that focus on Black Creole traditions include Spitzer (1977, 1979, 1986), Minton (1996b), Garnier III (2007, 2009, 2012, 2015), Garnier III and Wiley (2010), and Tisserand (1998).

37. Only with the rise in popularity of zydeco during the 1940s did the fiddle begin to lose its prominence (see discussion below).

38. In addition to *bastringue*, sometimes the triangle is called *'tit fer*, which literally means "little iron" (Minton 1996b, 493–94; Menestrel 2007, 89).

39. Spitzer (1979) indicates that "the accordion in both *zodico* and Cajun music is generally thought to be a German introduction to the area in the 1870s" (3–4).

40. Amédé Ardoin (1898–1942) and Dennis McGee (1893–1989) became legends in southwest Louisiana for the unique ways in which they performed. For a discussion of these two musicians, see Elliott (1992) and Savoy (1983b, 1984). Writers have used different spellings for Ardoin's first name: Amade, Amadie, Amédé, Amédée, etc. I have decided to use Amédé, the spelling employed by most researchers in southwest Louisiana.

41. The drone is derived from the ancient French Celtic tradition wherein the music was accompanied by wind instruments (*biniou* or *cabrette*) from the bagpipe family. When these instruments were abandoned in the Americas, the tunes and sounds were transferred to string instruments. Therefore, the drone was retained and became the lonesome, crying sound in Cajun music, and blues influence transformed the gay, lilting melodies to soulful, plaintive tunes (Ancelet 1989, 15; Elliott 1992, 102).

42. Researchers believe the blues that filtered into the area from New Orleans and the Mississippi Delta may have been introduced by accordionists Adam Fontenot (Canray's father) and Amédé Ardoin (Ancelet 1989, 19; Stewart, Shapiro, and Romaine 1982, 15).

43. While the Cajun triangle is often used by Black Creole musicians, the rubboard (*frottoir*), played with spoons, bottle openers, or thimbles, is rarely included in Cajun bands. *Frottoirs*, which are made of corrugated metal and worn hanging from the shoulders like a backless vest, have antecedents in Africa and the Caribbean as scraped gourds, notched sticks, and washboards. Models made in Louisiana by tinsmiths became popular after the introduction of sheet metal for roofing and barn siding to the area in the 1930s. Along with the bass, drums, eclectic guitar, and horns, *frottoirs* comprise the basic configuration for zydeco bands (Spitzer 1979, 3).

44. In spite of the borrowings and close contacts among musicians, racism, similar to what existed in other parts of the United States, continued to plague musicking in southwest Louisiana. Musicians sometimes crossed racial barriers, but nonmusicians found it much more difficult. Everyday social life, including music venues, remained segregated even though workplaces and schools were desegregated (Mattern 1997, 162; Tisserand 1998, 5, 33–35).

45. Born in a small community near Opelousas, the seat of St. Landry Parish, Clifton Chenier (1925–1987) was an accordion player known as the king of zydeco. He began his recording career during the mid-1950s, and won a Grammy award in 1983 for his album *I'm Here*.

46. Musicians describe the performance contexts in different ways. In an interview with Tisserand (1998), Fontenot also stated: "They would set some bench all around the house . . . and one part was for the old ladies to sit. And them old men, they'd head to the barn and play cards and drink . . . , while the young people was dancing" (5). In an interview with Spitzer (1979), Bébé Carrière recalled: "They'd clear out the furniture from the front rooms and pack in the people." Bébé's brother, Eraste (a Black Creole accordion player), added: "I would be sittin' in one corner, me, and playin' loud keeping good time so's people could dance" (5).

47. This song title is also known in English as "Prison Waltz."

48. In interviews with other researchers, Canray has stated: "In my time, [blues] was something nasty. . . . If you played blues in a house, they'd throw you out" (Savoy 1984, 328). "They [community members] didn't want no blues, because they [audience members] would dance too close to one another, they didn't want that at all" (quoted in Tisserand 1998, 33–34).

49. Interestingly, rural dwellers' attitudes toward jazz musicians were positive. Menestrel (2007, 97, 99) indicates that the social background of jazzmen around rural areas of Lafayette was typical of Creoles of color during the early twentieth century. Most were either tradesmen (barbers, carpenters) or teachers who could afford to send their children to school. They valued formal musical studies in both theory and practice. The families of jazzmen in rural areas were typically able to read music. Jazz was considered high on the social ladder and associated with elite status.

50. Fiddlers (listed alphabetically) active during the late twentieth century and early twenty-first century include: Jeffery Broussard (b. 1967), John Delafose (1939–1994), Carlton Frank

(1930–2005), D'Jalma Garnier III (b. 1954), Edward Poullard (b. 1952), and Cedric Watson (b. 1983); see Garnier III (2015) for names of other Black fiddlers.

51. Willging (2005) provides an interesting historical overview of the developments that occurred between musicians in Louisiana and Texas, which helped make Black fiddling continue to be an important component of musicking among Black Creoles in the twenty-first century.

52. 🎵 See Repertoire 12.2.

53. Information about Kirby Riley is also limited, except for the following indicating that he "was [born in] Opelousas, St. Landry Parish" https://www.ancientfaces.com/person/kirby-riley-birth-1904-death-1992/63663149#obituary. Accessed October 20, 2022.

54. 🎵 See Figure 12.1 and Figure 12.2. These two newspaper articles provide evidence that Bellard and Riley were the first Black Creole musicians to make commercial recordings. Figure 12.1 confirms that the first recording took place in October 1929, while Figure 12.2 indicates that Dennis McGee and Amédé Ardoin made their recordings in December 1929.

55. 🎵 See Demographics 12.3. Three musicians important to this study were born or lived in Evangeline Parish: Dewey Balfa, Douglas Bellard, and Canray Fontenot.

56. Beyond Black Creole fiddler Canray Fontenot and Cajun fiddler Wade Frugé (1916–1992), Bellard's crying blues tunes also influenced other instrumentalists such as accordionist Bois Sec Ardoin (Pomea 2002–2016).

57. 🎵 See Repertoire 12.3.

58. 🎵 Go to Audio Examples to listen to "La Valse De La Prison" and "Les Flammes d'Enfer" by Bellard and Riley.

59. In addition to several of his children, Bébé's father (Ernest) and older brother (Eraste) both played accordion. In performances and on recordings, Eraste was the person who accompanied Bébé.

60. US census records indicate that Bébé's paternal grandparents (Cyprien Joseph Carrière Sr. and Natalie Boureaux) were born during the 1840s and died in 1919 and 1918, respectively, while his parents (Ernest Carrière and Edmonia Young) were both born during the 1870s and died in 1957 and 1937, respectively. Bébé's parents had seven children; Eraste and Bébé were the two eldest. When Bébé and Eraste performed together, they were called the Carrière Brothers, but when family members and others became a part of the group in later years, the name was changed to the Lawtell Playboys (see below). For photos of the Carrière Brothers and their home in Lawtell, see website created by Ron Stanford (2020). Because of its small size, the US census has no demographic data for Lawtell.

61. Soileau and Bellard (1993) indicate that placing parts of a rattlesnake inside the fiddle's resonator was common practice when they were youngsters. Black fiddlers in other parts of the United States are also noted for doing this (see earlier discussion in this chapter as well as chapters 1, 8, and 10).

62. 🎵 See Repertoire 12.4.

63. The group became known as the Lawtell Playboys because most were born or lived in Lawtell. After Bébé and Eraste retired in 1966, the group included Calvin, as well as several non-family members: J. C. Gallow (rubboard) and Delton Broussard (accordion), who served as leader. When the Lawtell Playboys became the house band at the famed Black Creole club Slim's Y-Ki-Ki in Opelousas, their ranks grew to include four of Delton Broussard's eleven children. Over time the influence of the younger generation helped push the group toward a more contemporary sound. After Delton's death in 1994, his son, John, became the leader, ensuring that the combo's lengthy existence would continue to keep pace with the times. In addition, the San Francisco–based Andrew Carrier (Bébé's son), who plays accordion and rubboard, carries on the family tradition in bands such as the Cajun Orchestra (Ankeny n.d.b).

64. The phrase, "three kinds of ways," refers to the fact that his repertoire included songs identified with three musical genres: blues, country and western, and Cajun tunes.

65. This sentence is part of the lyrics of the song, "Blue Yodel Number 4 (California Blues)," released in 1929 by Jimmie Rodgers.

66. 🎵 See Repertoire 12.4.

67. Placing extra pressure on the bow to change the tone of the sound on a fiddle is referred to as scratching. According to Garnier III and Wiley (2010, 9), "The best place to bear down is from the middle of the bow to the frog [because] this is the part of the bow where you can play precise accentuated zydeco rhythms. A little scratching sound is good!"

68. One of Calvin's sons was interested in music, but he preferred the drums. The son stated that the fiddle is "old fashioned. Young people like to play guitar" (quoted in C. Carrière 1987).

69. Calvin is referring to earlier times when Cajuns did not include the accordion in their music ensembles; also see foregoing.

70. 🎵 See Repertoire 12.4. Accompanied by drummer Russell Deville and guitarists Jimmy Latiolais and Lisa McCauley, Carrière indicated that they included a variety of French Louisiana songs on the disk that had not been recorded in twenty or thirty years.

71. 🎵 See Video 12.1. Also go to Audio Examples to listen to "Barres de la Prison" and "Bonsoir Moreau I" performed by Fontenot at the Newport Folk Festival.

72. 🎵 See Repertoire 12.5.

73. 🎵 See Photo 12.7. After talking with Fontenot, I discovered, from reading other publications, that there were slight differences in the stories he told me about his family, the construction of his first instrument, his learning to play to the fiddle, and so on. From reviewing these interviews, I realized that although the gist of his stories was the same, details varied as he talked with different people, which is not uncommon when recounting events orally. For this reason, I sometimes include various versions of the same story in this discussion to ensure all points are presented (Fontenot 1988; Savoy 1984; National Endowment for the Arts 2011; Speal n.d.).

74. US census records indicate that Ozemie was born in St. Landry Parish, while her husband, Adam, was from Duralde, "an unincorporated village [in Evangeline Parish] situated between the towns of Mamou and Basile" (Spitzer 1979, 10).

75. In another interview, Canray stated: "In those days, women didn't play in public, but she would play for us children for birthdays and [things] like that" (Doucet 1995, 14).

76. Instead of performing music professionally, Adam Fontenot stayed at home, raised his children, and worked as a farmer, growing rice, potatoes, corn, and watermelons. It was only at the weekend *bals de maison* (house parties) that he played for family, friends, and neighbors, including whites (Savoy 1984, 327).

77. In his interview with Tisserand (1998, 88), Fontenot also explained that his father didn't like the idea of his music "still going while he was dead, and that's why he never made a record." But since he knew almost all his father's songs, he decided to "put some of them on record" so they would live on.

78. In another interview, Fontenot stated that he did not see anyone playing the guitar until he was around sixteen or seventeen years old. "Mostly white people played the fiddle back then. I never understood why not too many black guys played the fiddle" (Savoy 1984, 328).

79. In his interview with Doucet (1995), Fontenot states: "he got himself a fiddle from Déo Langley, he's an Indian from Elton and he played the fiddle" (14).

80. See Doucet (1995, 15) and Harris (2002) for different stories about early groups Fontenot formed or played with.

81. 🎵 Go to Audio Examples to listen to performances of "La Valse de la Prison" by Bellard and "Les Barres de la Prison" by the Carrière Brothers as well as Fontenot and Ardoin.

82. Here, Fontenot did not complete his thoughts. But in his interview with Tisserand (1998, 71), he explained: "If you were to hear the real 'Barres de la Prison' that he made, you can't dance [to] that, it's out of beat.... I learned how to play it when it first came out, and I thought, if ever I make a record, I'm going to set it in my own way, and they're going to be able to dance it. My daddy always was talking about, 'Whenever you're going to play a tune, play a tune that the people can dance.' And that's what I did." In another interview, Fontenot stated: "I listened a lot to musicians from different parts. They got some musicians that when you get on the floor to dance you keep losing your step. Amédée was like that. He'd change or something" (Savoy 1984, 329).

83. 🎵 See Video 12.2. Also go to Audio Examples to listen to "Barres de la Prison" performed by Fontenot.

84. 🎵 See Lyrics 12.3 and Lyrics 12.4.

85. 🎵 See Repertoire 12.5.

86. 🎵 Go to Audio Examples to listen to Fontenot's performance of "Canray's One Step."

87. For discussion of Adams's and Thompson's musicking, see chapters 5 and 8.

88. Some researchers have described Black Creole fiddling as "rootsier" and "having a scratchy edge (versus slick, as in Cajun)" (Willging 1999, 28–29).

89. Michael Doucet is a multi-instrumentalist who cofounded BeauSoleil in 1975 with Kenneth Richard and Sterling Richard. Noted for playing an eclectic combination of traditional Cajun music, blues, country, jazz, and zydeco, Doucet as well as BeauSoleil performed and recorded with Canray Fontenot (Erlewine 2021).

90. 🎵 See Videos 12.2 and 12.3. Also go to Audio Examples to listen to musicking by Fontenot.

91. Similar to Calvin Carrière (1987), Balfa (1987) stated that difficulty in playing the instrument was the primary issue: "The fiddle is dying out because it is so difficult to play. It is the most difficult instrument to master or to play, where you can be accepted as a good musician because it's so sensitive. It's much easier to get a guitar, get an accordion or get some other, a mandolin, a piano that's already tuned."

92. 🎵 See Map 12.3, Map 12.4, Map 12.5, Land Regions 12.2, History 12.2, and Demographics 12.4.

93. The fathers of jazz guitarist Eddie Durham, country bluesman Mance Lipscomb, and rhythm and blues singer Clarence "Gatemouth" Brown were all fiddlers. Brown also performed the fiddle and made several recordings using the instrument.

94. 🎵 See Map 12.5. Named for the rich dark soil in the area, the Texas Blackland Prairies are a temperate grassland ecoregion that runs roughly three hundred miles from the Red River in North Texas to San Antonio in the south.

95. 🎵 See Photo 12.8. It was not uncommon for the fiddle to be used for entertainment at Juneteenth celebrations in Texas (Cherelus 2020).

96. See Demographics 12.5.

97. Black fiddlers and string band musicians mentioned in the research by Oliver and McCormick (Govenar and Lornell 2019) include the following: Holly Benefield, Curtis Johnson, Pink Johnson, Dennis Jones, Jess Morris of Coley Jones String Band, Rowdy Morris, Oscar Nelson, Sam Norman, O. Z. Steen, Charlie Thomas, as well as Jack, Horace, and Tommie Wright.

98. 🎵 See Demographics 12.6. Thomas's grandfather, Peter Thomas, was born during slavery. During enslavement, he worked and purchased two hundred acres of land in the Fayetteville area. After freedom, he stayed in the woods, raised hogs, and sold them to earn a living. Although Charlie Thomas was born on the farm, he sold much of the property later in life and used the proceeds to purchase a house in Houston. When Charlie was in his sixties, he occasionally worked at a grocery store in La Grange, the seat for Fayette County, and continued his grandfather's business of raising hogs (Govenar and Lornell 2019, 344–45). Thomas's death date is unknown.

99. "Sentimental" is the term Black performers used to refer to ballads that were especially popular among white audiences in Texas (Govenar and Lornell 2019, 332).

100. 🎵 See Demographics 12.7.

101. It is noteworthy that Austin, Waller, and Brazoria are counties located along the Gulf Coast or the Texas coastal bend where Black populations were relatively large (and sometimes majority Black) around the turn of the twentieth century. By the mid-1920s, when Thomas was active as musician in the area, the Black populations had decreased in size but were still substantial enough to generate audiences that preferred a certain repertoire and performance style from fiddlers.

102. Hugo Martin indicated that "he was not much of a guitarist himself, but that he kept active as a singer and musician and with the small groups with whom he worked" (Govenar and Lornell 2019, 70).

103. Regarding his relationship with Henry Thomas, Charlie Thomas explained: Henry Thomas "got on records calling himself Ragtime Thomas and a lot of people had his name mixed

up with me because I played a lot of fiddle rags and people'd think I was Ragtime Thomas or something" (Govenar and Lornell 2019, 70).

104. Because this is a first-person narrative by Thomas, who was an actual participant, I quote at length.

105. During his time with the medicine show, Thomas (1962) indicated that he traveled to various cities and towns in Texas (Wichita Falls, Quanah, Lake Pauline, Seymour, Haskell) and Oklahoma (Atlas and Tipton); he made about $25 to $35 a week from the owner of the medicine show and then in most towns he found a place to play for dances at night.

106. While Fulshear, a city in Fort Bend County, Texas, is located on the western edge of Houston, Brookshire is a rural town in Waller County.

107. While it is unknown if Thomas was playing for Black or white audiences or both, it is noteworthy that several of the towns are located in southeast Texas where large Black populations continued to live after enslavement. Black populations did not begin to decrease substantially until the Great Migration, which started in the 1920s and 1930s.

108. Nelson's parents, Oscar William Nelson Sr. (1872–1942) and Livie Riley Nelson (1870–1935), as well as their children, were born in Milam County, Texas. Oscar Jr. (1901–1984) is the fourth eldest, and Nelson (1907–1965) is the seventh eldest of the couple's sixteen children.

109. See Demographics 12.8.

110. The first blues Nelson learned to play were "Brown Skin Woman" (derived from the fiddle tune "West Texas Blues") and "Boll Weevil." His "Brown Skin Woman" consisted of a succession of short lines half-shouted, half-sung over the fiddle tune that were repeated sometimes three, sometimes four times (Govenar and Lornell 2019, 70).

111. The majority of the information about the Nelsons in *Blues Come to Texas* (Govenar and Lornell 2019) concerns Charlie Nelson (their uncle), a blues musician who made a recording in Chicago, spent some time in Detroit, and finally settled in Cleveland, Ohio (70).

112. Since population data indicate that a relatively substantial number of Blacks were living in Milam County where these towns are located, we can only surmise that some Blacks continued to support their performances during this period.

113. Foster (2020) indicates that the only other recorded material of a Black Texas fiddler is that of Elijah Cox (1842–1941), who was recorded at the age of ninety-three by John Lomax in San Angelo for the Library of Congress. To see photo of Cox, go to Foster (2020, 10).

114. US census records indicate that Teodar was the eldest son of Caldwell Jackson (1879–1956) and Ella Harris Jackson (1883–1947), who were both born in Texas. While some records indicate that Caldwell's father, Neptune Griffith Jackson (ca. 1851), was born in Mississippi, others indicate Alabama.

115. See Demographics 12.9.

116. See foregoing discussions about Cage in Louisiana, Thompson in North Carolina, Bowles in Virginia, and Livers in Kentucky.

117. See Repertoire 12.6.

118. While recordings may exist, I was unable to find information about the following songs—"Old Aunt Jessie," "Blood Red Rose," "Out and Down," "Poor Rabbit," "Train Tune," "Silver Spoons"—in sources available to me (Dixon, Godrich, and Rye 1997; Russell and Pinson 2004).

119. Although it is not discussed here, I am referring primarily to jazz performed by Black fiddlers/violins in New Orleans during the early twentieth century; for details, see Chilton (1979, 103), Rose and Souchon (1984), or most recent works that have been published on the subject.

Epilogue

When I began investigating Black fiddling many years ago, my initial goal was to create a comprehensive study on the role and contributions of African American musicians to the tradition—from the earliest forced arrival of Africans into North America (in the seventeenth century) through the present day (early twenty-first century). However, it was not until I delved into the subject matter that I discovered the overwhelming amount of research required to produce a scholarly study on this topic. What became even more revealing was that the fiddle/violin may be one of the oldest (if not the oldest) uninterrupted instrumental traditions performed by Black people in the United States. Thus, a work that examines Black fiddling over time would provide a more accurate history of African American secular music, one that includes the old and new as well as the rural and urban. With the exception of religious music, a few studies on traditions identified with specific states,[1] and blues in both rural and urban areas, most research on the musical history of Blacks during the early twentieth century have focused on musicians who are identified with cities. Overall, the confluence of these issues led me to question, rhetorically, what about Blacks who did not move outside the South, and did not live along the coasts or in urban areas? Hence, an in-depth examination of African American fiddling was needed to provide a more accurate history of Black musicking in the United States.

From songs and dance tunes performed during enslavement[2] to musical genres Black musicians developed or helped develop over the centuries (old-time music, blues, jazz, various styles of popular music), the fiddle/violin has been used as a medium of expression. In addition to a distinct repertoire, performance style, and sound quality that reflect influences from Africa (greater use of percussion, inclusion of bent notes, additive rhythms, shuffling fiddling style, simpler formal structure), the organization of ensembles used by Black fiddlers tended to be different. Instead of large ensembles with more than one person playing the fiddle,[3] most Black string bands included just one fiddler. Geography and demographics also played a role in what was performed. The fiddle-guitar combination started earlier and became more prominent in the

South-Central and Southern Appalachian regions than in Central Appalachia. Furthermore, Black fiddlers in the mountains tended to maintain performance traditions identified with Euro-American culture longer than those who lived closer to coastal regions where larger numbers of Blacks resided.

After reviewing the literature and considering the many contributions of Black fiddlers, I thought that the two questions raised in the prologue—(1) why is the fiddle/violin not identified with African American musicking? and (2) why did Black musicians continue to perform the fiddle/violin when it had been rejected (or regarded as a novelty) by many within African American culture?—required deeper analysis. My response to these two questions, which is limited to the time period of this study (seventeenth century to the mid-twentieth century), will serve as my final remarks on the topic, followed by a profile on Howard Armstrong, an African American fiddler from the early twentieth century who became an icon for the tradition in the late twentieth century. Therefore, greater insight on these issues will be provided by someone who experienced and lived the life of a Black fiddler.

Why is the fiddle/violin not identified with African American music?

Throughout much of world culture, the fiddle/violin is identified with Europe, and most people in the United States accept this as the norm (Smith 2009). Therefore, to expect musicking connected to Europe and whiteness to be also associated with Africa and Blackness would be not only inconceivable, but also extraordinary. Furthermore, many people do not know or realize that bowed lutes or string instruments played with a bow are not indigenous to Europe.[4] But this historical fact does not matter, especially when the fiddle/violin in its current configuration is a European invention.

The fact that the fiddle/violin is used to perform musical genres (for example, old-time music as well as European art or classical music) that are identified with whiteness, even though some of these forms developed from a shared culture, is another reason the instrument is not associated with African Americans. In fact, some slave owners did not believe Black fiddlers could play music for European dances, such as cotillions, quadrilles, minuets, or waltzes. Rather, their function was to provide musicking for square dances or occasions of this sort. Basically, the low-art versus high-art division was a factor in distinguishing performance contexts and what Black fiddlers were expected to perform (Chamberlain 1892; Harrower 1963; Cauthen 1989a).

In addition, there was the issue of perception. Dwight DeVane (1987) indicates that white researchers during the early twentieth century questioned why Blacks would want to participate in old-time music due to its association with enslavement, injustice, mockery, and ill will against them just because of their skin color. And they were correct, because this was the attitude of many African Americans during the early twentieth century. Also, some Black intellectuals did not believe fiddle music was "as rich and distinctive in melodic content as spirituals or the blues" (Work III 1940, 45); therefore, why give attention to its study?

Oftentimes the instrument itself was conflated with the music performed on it, which led to conflicting views and bias about the tradition. In addition to its association with ill cultural memories (injustice, enslavement, Jim Crow, and so on), some African Americans regarded the instrument as ungodly because they believed the music and contexts in which it was performed led to behavior that was not respectable. Louisiana-born Canray Fontenot indicated that he "couldn't touch the fiddle during Lent" because people believed it was bad luck (Savoy 1984, 329). Perhaps this explains why Cuje Bertram (1980), from Tennessee/Kentucky, would not perform blues on the fiddle because he regarded the lyrics as distasteful. When Thomas Dumas moved from the Mississippi Pines region to the Delta, the audience for his performances were primarily white people because he only performed old-time music on the fiddle—not other genres such as blues, that were associated with Black people (Brown 1976).

Along the Atlantic, coastal Blacks were among the earliest to disassociate the fiddle with African American culture. Any number of reasons could have been factors for the decline in the performance of the instrument by Black musicians: the instrument's association with Europeans (elitism or art/classical music), its identification with mountain culture which suggested whiteness and a country lifestyle, or the difficulty in learning to play the fiddle as opposed to other instruments. Discarding the fiddle may have also been an act of defiance to what was happening socially. Hinson (1978) believes that laws further restricting Black political and social rights during the early twentieth centuries were partly responsible for the rise in popularity of the guitar and the blues over the fiddle and playing old-time music in North Carolina. The lack of representation in the media, the increasing urbanization of Black people, and the use of other instruments to replace the sound of the fiddle were all factors that affected the instrument's prominence as well as its association with Black culture.

Why did musicians continue to perform the fiddle?

Although many reasons exist for Black musicians continuing to perform the fiddle, which are noted throughout this study, I believe most can be summarized as follows: personal satisfaction, nostalgia or tradition, support, and versatility.

When Virginia fiddler Leonard Bowles (1987) stated that he performed the fiddle because of the way it affected him personally, I believe, as noted in the foregoing, he spoke for the majority: "That's my joy. It's a song dedicated to me, nobody can take it away. That was my pride." On a human level, playing the instrument gave him pleasure. The act of performing and the response he received from those who experienced the music were reasons he continued to perform the fiddle. Fiddlers such as Joe Thompson (1987) from North Carolina continued to perform not only because of family heritage, but memories of the past allowed him to share the traditions of his ancestors with others so they would not be forgotten. Just as Black fiddlers during enslavement recognized the importance of passing on fiddle tunes to a new generation to encourage community (Cimbala 1995, 18), Thompson was attempting to do the same.

For Tennessee fiddler Joel Rice and his father Jake, fiddling represented the "turning of age" period in a young person's life. As DeVane (1987) explains, "Regardless of race, there seemed to be patterns of times in which musicians played the fiddle; times when musicians are just becoming an adult. Fiddling and fiddlers have been lumped together with all of these activities."[5] Regardless of race, the support and appreciation that Black fiddlers received for their talents were also reasons many continued to perform. When an admirer presented Mississippi fiddler Henry Simms "with a new, handsome violin" that became his pride and constant companion, he bemoaned "the loss of interest in playing instruments among the plantation youth" (Work III 2005).

Finally, the fiddle continues to be used because of its versatility. Other instruments, such as the banjo, which was introduced into the Americas by Black people and is identified with Black culture, seem not to be as versatile. At least, listeners are not as accepting of the banjo and its sound being used in as many contexts as the fiddle. Charlie Thomas, a fiddler from Texas, continued to have an active career during the mid-twentieth century because he was flexible, versatile, open to new ideas, and as a fiddler he could more easily contribute to what others were performing. In addition, it was his strong reputation as a fiddler that allowed him to compete on equal terms with any other musician (Govenar and Lornell 2019, 344). In spite of its limitations, the fiddle's versatility helped it to be accepted even when it was not the most popular. Now let us look at Howard Armstrong to see how he maneuvered his life and his performance of the instrument at a time when the tradition or fiddling was in decline.

Profile of Howard Armstrong

William Howard Taft Armstrong (1909–2003)

Because of his many talents, versatility is a term that describes Howard Armstrong, which was the case with many Black fiddlers during the early twentieth century. In addition to his ability to perform the fiddle, mandolin, and a variety of other instruments, he was a storyteller, painter, and craftsman. His repertoire included secular and sacred old-time tunes, blues, vaudeville, jazz, novelty and popular songs, as well as different types of dance tunes. Because of changes in the way people experienced music during the mid-twentieth century, his live music performances declined. However, when he returned to fiddling in the late twentieth century, he became even more well known. An article in the *New York Times* referred to Armstrong[6] as "the last of the Black string band musicians" (Holden 1989); see photo 13.1.[7] Not only was he the subject of several film documentaries, including *Louie Bluie* (1985), *Sweet Old Song* (2002), *Remembering Howard "Louie Bluie" Armstrong* (2009),[8] he was the recipient of a number of awards—the National Heritage Fellowship awarded by the Folk Arts Programs of the National Endowment for the Arts (1995), the Lifetime Achievement Award from the Detroit Blues Society; and W. C. Handy Award nominee for the recording *Louie Bluie* (1995) on Blue Suit Records. When I interviewed him, he was especially proud that he had been invited to serve as a consultant for the movie *The Color Purple* (1985). Armstrong is important to this study because of his varied talents, but also, he was a master musician and one of the few Black fiddlers whose life and career bridge the rural with the urban. Much of the information that follows is presented in Armstrong's voice, which is rare for Black fiddling because many of the performers active during the early twentieth century were not interviewed. The few who were did not always feel comfortable giving their views on certain issues.[9]

Although born in Dayton, a small town in Rhea County, East Tennessee, Armstrong (1987) was "brought up closer to Knoxville in a little town they call LaFollette" in Campbell County in the northern part of East Tennessee.[10] His parents had nine children—six boys and three girls; and he was the middle child—with four older and four younger siblings. "My mama wanted to name me after a very important person. So, she named me William Howard Taft. The very day that he took his seat as president of the United States was the day I was born."[11] Armstrong's grandfather, James Armstrong (1830–1896), was a blacksmith. In fact, working with iron was a profession that had been passed down through the family, for Armstrong's father was a blacksmith before he became a preacher. "My dad worked at a blast furnace; that's all he knew until he retired from that. He knew if he had been white, he would have been the superintendent or something, 'cause that's how much he knew about metals. After that, he worked at a hotel as a waiter. When he started preaching, he was in his late forties or early fifties. He was one of those preachers who believed in what he was doing. He didn't preach for a lot of glamour or anything because I don't ever remember him ever taking up ten dollars in collection the whole time that he preached all those years."

In terms of musicking, several members of the Armstrong family were musicians, but no one played the fiddle except Howard.[12] Because mandolins were so much a part of his upbringing, it is not surprising that Armstrong's

Photo 13.1. Howard Armstrong onstage at the New Orleans Jazz and Heritage Festival, 1998, by Elijah Wald. Licensed under CC BY-SA 4.0.

first instrument was the mandolin, which he learned to play at age nine: "My dad played mandolin, my brother played mandolin, and some of the neighbors played mandolin. I don't know where they learned the music, but I can tell you they got the mandolins from Sears and Roebuck. Also, you could get a violin, case, bow, and all for five dollars." Armstrong was introduced to the fiddle around the same time he began playing the mandolin, and an older sister started teaching him how to perform guitar:

> I never saw a fiddle until I was about nine or ten years old. Now the first man that ever really whetted my appetite for wanting to play a violin was a blind man, Roland Martin. Carl Martin's half-brother, Roland Martin, was blind.[13] He was older than Carl's mother, and they came out to LaFollette. LaFollette was a little

iron mining town. It had coal mines, and rock quarries. They would come over there when the payday was. And they would play on the street corners and pass the hat. So, anybody with a good free will would drop what they want into the hat.

When I heard this blind man playing the fiddle, I said, "Daddy, I got to have me a violin."

"Well, where you going to get a violin?"

I said, "Can't you buy me one?"

"I'd do well to get you some corn-pone and some grits and some gravy."

After my dad quit playing music, he gave me his old mandolin and then made me the first fiddle I ever had. He said, "I'll tell you what. You go up in the woods and find some dry dogwood." And finally, he told me what kind of old goods' box to get and everything. He made a nice violin out of these old pine box and things he carved. He cut the neck out of poplar wood with a pocket knife, and made a beautiful little instrument. I had to run a little old nag [a horse that is third or fourth rate] a half a day before I could get close enough with a pair of scissors to cut a bunch of hair, a hank of hair, as they say, to make the bow. Horse's tail. Stallion hair. The violin had four strings. It was modern. Heck, it worked. I thought it was wonderful.

In two days, I was sawing on it. I mean sawing on it. First song I learned was by this great Black blues singer, Bessie Smith, "Down Home Blues," in the key of A. I never will forget that. I learned to play that violin. It was just a small thing; it wasn't a full size.

When Armstrong was about twelve years old, his father bought him a real violin: "One day, I went to carry his dinner down at the blast furnace. He says, 'Son, I got a present for you. Look in the dog house[14] over where my jumper is.' There was a shelf in there. I couldn't imagine what it was. But no sooner than I saw that coffin-looking case. I said, 'Oh! I know what it is.' He had won that violin for one quarter, and it was a full-sized violin. It was only half a mile from that furnace to my house, and I almost never got home. I'd walk a few steps and sit down on a log and suddenly start sawing on that fiddle. It sounded so sweet."

After learning to play the fiddle, Armstrong came in contact with other fiddlers, but few regularly performed in the area where he lived. However, members of his community told him about several fiddlers from earlier times: "There was a legendary Black fiddle player in LaFollette where I was raised. It was a guy called Steve Tarter,[15] and he was a Black man. He was king. When I first started playing the fiddle, everybody said, 'Man, you play like Steve Tarter! But, there's nobody in the world who could beat that man playing.'"[16]

Although Armstrong considered himself to be a self-taught musician, he credited others for helping him learn how to play the fiddle, particularly musicians he met when he left LaFollette:

After I left LaFollette and started playing the fiddle, I left the family band. One of my brothers came over to Knoxville. That's where I got my baptism of musical fire. I met hard fiddle players in Knoxville—Black ones, well educated, musically.[17] I started myself reading, but this guy John Garrett gave me some real nice pointers on my positions on the violin. He was a professor of music at the university in Cincinnati. He played real classical fiddle. Of course, he was a teacher, but he still played what we played.

In Knoxville, there was Fred McDade, Dave McDade, a guy they called Gabe, Henry Alexander, and a guy named Frank Nelson.[18] There were violin players and guitar players. There's just so many of them. Now the one who taught us the chromatic scale was George Eskridge, the one that I met in Bluefield, West Virginia, before I met John Garrett. It was also in West Virginia where I saw the first fierce fiddle player. He was a barber and his companion also played violin and guitar; his name was Steve. Then right there in Bluefield, another guy ran what they called the Clifford Street Tea Room. Uncle [David] Runyon, we called him. He'd sit and fiddle all day long. He wasn't connected with anybody.

When asked how he learned new songs for his repertoire, Armstrong explained:

But when I first started playing, I would hear other musicians playing a song on a record, over the radio, or something, and I would learn it. But if it's a popular song, now I go get a piano score and play it two or three times until I have it. Then we make our own arrangement. Cause even in big bands, when a song comes out, they have to arrange for a fifteen- or twenty-piece band. We had more piano scores under our arms than any other string band. We'd go down to the music store before the pop song came out, buy the piano score. And we would get the lead off of that, and we would arrange it to suit the group. The singer's melody and the lyrics are right under the notes. So, I play that on my fiddle. Usually we played it in first position. And then if I want to vary from that, I play it to the third position. The novelty songs were tunes I composed myself; I wrote them.

The special playing techniques that made Armstrong's fiddling distinctive were both self-taught and learned from observing other musicians. He indicated that his ability to play double and triple stops on the violin was something he taught himself: "My dad gave me his old mandolin, and I transferred techniques in playing the mandolin to the violin. That's how I learned double stops. That's like two people singing. It puts more color on it. When I'm playing with musicians behind me, I don't have to rely too much on double stops. I play the solo, but I make improvisations, the little things that a lot of fiddle players don't make." In addition to double stops, smottling was another technique he used to make his playing distinct. Holding the instrument in a playing position, Armstrong explained:

This is what you call smottling the strings. We play some fast things. [He plays the violin.] See that's my stuff that I put in there. You don't see many fiddle players play that old crazy stuff. When I'm playing a real fast song—that's one reason I like to have it amplified—you can sound like a drum and there's a whole lot more crazy things you'd be doing. And when you play these old hymns, you get a certain tone out of the fiddle, like "Come on Jesus, Walk with Me." That's when I jazz it up a little with double stops. There's a type of tremolo that we make with the bow. In the high [European art or classical] music, they call it agitato or agitation. But we call it tremolo. That's when you do that glissando, sliding and stuff with your fingers.

Although Armstrong acknowledged that the violin and fiddle were the same instrument, he believed there is a big difference in playing each:

The violin and fiddle is the same instrument, and it is correct to call it either one. But when it comes to a violinist and a fiddler, they play two different instruments. Many violinists who have been taught classical violin become bored with it because nobody wants to hear a half-way violinist. If you can't play Paganini—play it with verve and gumption and project yourself—you haven't done anything. You don't get in a symphony orchestra, if you can't cut it. Whenever you do play classical, you're stepping in somebody else's footprints. There's just not the freedom—like if I just ad lib and play my fiddle or grab the bow in the middle of it, instead of the back or the end like I'm supposed to do, it's alright.

Most of the fiddle players, they call 'em just fiddle players. Some are really just what the word implies. They're monotonous. They fiddle the same d over and over. No variation. Fiddle-diddle-dee, fiddle-diddle-dee. Same monotone more or less. Most of them make a litany out of it. Most fiddle players play where they can hit a lot of open strings; they play G, A, and D. That's what most of the country fiddle players play in. And then sometimes they cross notes, run the string up or either down the bass string. But now, most blues players, they play in G, C, or F.

But now what they call hot fiddle players are violinists who have orchestra training. They can play in local symphonies, but get bored with that jive. So, what do they want to do? They want to play something that gives them more freedom of expression. So, they get out there and start whipping up a popular number like "I'm in the Money." They love that. They call them hot fiddle players, like a lot of Black fiddle players, and some white ones too.

During slavery, they were fiddlers. That's what they called them because the white man didn't take time to send them to musical schools. They had natural talent. It was unique and beautiful because they did their thing, their way. It's like today. You notice now—when the white people are getting into the blues, they even try to sing and talk like the Black blues people. They want all of it.

In discussing the different ways fiddlers held their instrument in performance, Armstrong explained:

> Holding it under the chin is the classic way. Sometimes they'd play it on the shoulder, sometimes on the chest. You'd catch the bow about a third way up toward the middle. If I don't want to stick it under my chin, I'll put it here on my shoulder. That's where a lot of fiddle players put their instruments. Tom Jarrell [1901–1985], this white fiddle player, used to play like that. When I first started, that's where I played 'cause the first fiddle players I heard were white. That's where they played the fiddle, down there. But then I saw this blind Black man [Roland Martin]. He had it under his chin. He was playing, and had that derby hat swinging. I liked that. So, that's when I started getting the right position.

During his early career, Armstrong performed with a variety of artists throughout the South. As a youngster, he played with the family band in LaFollette: "Most of my early years were in my hometown playing with the family band for locals—for Blacks and the whites, school functions, and things like that." When he was in his early teens, Armstrong joined Roland and Carl Martin in their performances in Knoxville and surrounding communities during the summers, before returning to school in the fall.[19] Armstrong indicated that it was his contact with members of the Martin family that gave him the inspiration to become a professional musician. "I finally went to Knoxville because they wanted me to go. I slipped out of school, so to speak, and went over there and stayed with Carl's mother and their family." When Armstrong became older, he began traveling with the Martins throughout Appalachia and the Midwest.

> I played with Roland Martin on the street corners where we travelled. We'd go to different places all through Virginia—Big Stone Gap, Pennington Gap, and King's Point. Then Martin and all of us formed into a group. First, they called us Tennessee Chocolate Drops. Then we made a group, four of us, the Four Keys. We did that in Huntington, West Virginia. So, when we came to Chicago for the World's Fair, we were the Four Keys. And my brother, Roland Armstrong; my brother's name was Roland, too. He was with the group. We split up from Roland Martin, Carl's half-brother; he went back to his hometown, Spartanburg. We added more people to the group while we were playing around Knoxville. But when we recorded in 1930, it was only the three on that first recording. We did a stupid thing on later recordings. We called ourselves Martin, Bogan, and the Armstrongs. I don't know why. They just wanted their names to shine out. So, I said, OK.[20] Bill Billanger is the one that broke up the Four Keys. He was a string bass player. He fell in love with one of these girls.[21]
>
> And we would go pulling doors. You know what "pulling doors" is? Well, I'll break it down. You don't have a gig, you don't have a regular group. You see a guy,

"Man where your action?" Maybe he played a guitar. This guy over here plays a fiddle. The other guy plays a trumpet or clarinet, anything, cornet. Now we were going by this little place. They didn't have jukeboxes—canned music and records and things—in there like you do now. We'd pull straws to decide who would go up and pull the door. You have to pull the door to get in the saloon or the club. You don't know whether they're going to throw a cuspidor, one of these spittoons. That's one of these brass things or vessels that they used to have round in bars that men chewed tobacco and spit in them. They're liable to throw one of those in your face at you.

We'd see if they want music. If it's my turn, I say, "Hey man, you want some music in here?"

They say, "Aw, go away, you guys are dangerous. Go."

Well, very seldom they ever said that. 'Cause once or twice we played in the area they heard about us. And they would say, "Oh let 'em play. Come on in and play." And so that's what "pulling doors" is.

I started with Martin and Ted Bogan[22] when I was an early teenager. I left Bogan and Martin when we were in Chicago. I think I was in my early twenties."

In the mid-1930s, Armstrong returned to Tennessee and stayed there until he went to Pearl Harbor. When asked why he left Martin and Bogan, Armstrong stated: "I just decided I'd leave and go back to see my mother and dad in Tennessee. I had intended to come back to Chicago. But this boy Steve, who went to school with me, needed a bass player, and he wanted my brother to come down to Sparta.[23] My dad said, 'Son, why don't you go?' It was Halloween. They had to play for Halloween. When I was coming back to go to Chicago, the guy persuaded me to stay. I messed around, love bug bit me,[24] and I didn't get out for several years. I stayed in Sparta about six years." Concerning his stay in Sparta during the 1930s, Armstrong stated:

Steve's Rhythm Boys had several musicians, and I played bass fiddle. The groups had the kind of instruments that was popular at that time for just a dance band—piano, percussion, drums (Steve played a set of drums), and bass fiddle. They also had trumpet, clarinet, and saxophone, but a couple of them doubled. Like I doubled on the violin sometimes. But it was seven pieces in all. We played clubs and dances and things like that. The man who was the head of the band, Crockett Officer—his daddy for years had used the band for the Ringling Brothers Circus. They had a whole Black band who played wind instruments and percussion. But in the interim, Crockett nosed around Sparta. That's how I met my first wife.[25] I spent several years around there playing music.

During the early 1940s (before the bombing of Pearl Harbor), Armstrong traveled to the Pacific Islands and worked as a civilian: "When I left Sparta, I went overseas. I was a painter. That was in 1941. I worked in the art department with the painters and riggers in Pearl Harbor. That was before the war started, before they bombed it. I came back to Tennessee in '43, and came to Detroit in '44. The war was over in '45. I got married in '44.[26] I stayed with my sisters for maybe a month. Then I started painting signs. I'd get a job at a factory but was always the first to be laid off. I couldn't accumulate much seniority. So, I started painting for churches, clubs, and these supermarkets."

When he lived in Detroit during the forties and the sixties, Armstrong indicated that he did not perform regularly: "I played sporadically because my wife's sister was a pianist, Ruth Gordon. And every once in a while, she would say, 'C'mon man, why don't you come sit in and do something?'" Armstrong also worked at a Chrysler plant but retired in the late sixties due to a work injury. This is around the time he heard from his old music partners, Martin and Bogan, which made him to decide to focus on music again in a professional way: "The guys called me and said, 'Come to Chicago.' They had a good agent. I said, 'Shoot, why not?' Sometimes I made more money playing music in one night than I did working at Chrysler in a week. Seeing the country. Traveling to different places—out of the country. I played mostly for white audiences. There was also money with festivals. A few colored people would come, but just a few. So, I didn't really get into the business of playing music again until the 1970s, after my second wife and I split up."

Armstrong had an opportunity to perform in a variety of contexts during his career. During the 1920s and 1930s, performances tended to be local and in geographical areas where the fiddle had been popular during the late nineteenth and early twentieth centuries. It was not uncommon for musicians to travel with carnivals, minstrel and medicine shows, as well as perform at juke joints[27] on the outskirts of small towns. According to Armstrong,

> Black string bands were the vogue before they got the types they got now. Many of them were left over from the gay nineties. They used to play on steamboats and excursions, when trains were going everywhere. You'd see three- and four-piece string bands, sometimes two of them would be on there. And street musicians would play on a street corner anywhere. That's what I was doing all of my younger days. I'd play on the street. Of course, we'd get gigs and play in clubs. I also played for a number of radio stations: Station WROL, WNOX, Knoxville;[28] WOPI, Bristol, Tennessee; WSAZ Huntington, West Virginia; and Charleston, West Virginia; I forget what the station call letters was. I played in so many stations. We also played at what we called meeting paydays. We would go up on a winding gulf all over West Virginia.[29] We played all over Ohio where there were mining towns or places that had that kind of industry—not a great big city like Detroit. In the thirties, the places were Columbus, Ohio, and Huntington, West Virginia.

In addition to rural areas, Armstrong stated that fiddlers were popular in urban areas such as New Orleans: "They had fiddles in New Orleans. But usually the fiddle was a parlor instrument. They had the fiddle in symphonies. They had so many of them in the symphony." But he noted that the contexts for his performances changed when he returned to performing during the 1970s. In later years, festivals and related events were most popular:

> In the 1970s, we played all over New York. I don't know how many times we played in this BAM (Brooklyn Academy of Music). That's where they gave classical [European art music] performances. Played all up in Greenwich Village. Even played down in the Bottom Line, downtown at Fourth Street. That's where we went on tour from Chicago to the West Coast with Mike Seeger. We played all up in Upper Hudson, New York, with Pete Seeger and that group. Kenny's Castaways Club. We played all over Brooklyn. Last year, in 1986, Bogan and I played way up at Blue Mountain Lake, way up in New York. And we played all over California. Gardensville and all up through there. We played for concerts and festivals.

Over the course of his performing career, Armstrong indicated that he had played and recorded in ensembles both as a leader and an accompanist: "I played the lead melody and sometimes would have clarinets and trumpets as accompaniment. Also, we played in a jazz band later on. I would have piano, drums, and all that, but I was featured on the violin. I know when I first went to Knoxville, they used to sit me on top of the piano, till I got to play my violin." Although he had done solo work on guitar and violin, he stated that "it's better to have a little accompaniment for the violin to fill in the spaces. It's like when you string a necklace; you don't want all the beads jammed up close together. You put little spaces in between—bead here, space there, bead here. Sometimes people would come and join. Somebody play the piano, somebody can play some other instrument. Some of them clap their hands." Interestingly, many of the groups he played with did not include percussion.

> During the twenties and thirties, we didn't have a percussionist because we played in the tradition of old string bands. They had a fiddle; that usually was the main instrument. Also, most Black string bands were trios. They had a fiddle, guitar, and a bass—or fiddle, guitar, and another guitar. Sometimes they put a capo[30] on the first guitar to make it an octave higher. Then, the other guitar would act as a bass instrument.
>
> When I first went to the city, Blacks were playing the washboard. In the string bands, the one percussion that we had was washboard. I played with Amos Easton; he was a way-out blues writer who wrote a lot of hits, but he played washboard. I never saw a white musician play washboard. I saw Blacks play tub, sticks, broom handles, jugs. Memphis Minnie (1897–1973)—they called her Kid

Douglas—had a whole jug band.[31] A jug band was basically a string band. But they called it a jug band because they used jugs to play the bass on. Some of them even played baritone on the jugs. An old-time crock jug. They used to have gin in it, vinegar, and stuff.

During the early twentieth century, Armstrong often "played the fiddle cold turkey," a euphemism indicating that fiddlers "didn't have any amplification because the music was performed in acoustic buildings." After World War II, however, fiddlers began amplifying their instruments to adapt to the new instruments and sounds that were being introduced. Comments by Armstrong on the use of amplification and its impact on sound are important for understanding factors that affected Black fiddling during the mid-twentieth century:

> How you gonna be heard when it's a whole bunch of guys playing? They amplified electric guitar and electric bass. Now, you look like a fool not having a violin amplified. So, electric violins—that's what Jean-Luc [Ponty][32] plays. He has two or three of them. It's like having power steering and not having it; I don't have to sweat and push to make the fiddle say what I want it to. With amplification, I don't try to burst your eardrums. But the person in the back of the room or anywhere can hear good. I can do a lot of things with the violin when it's amplified that I can't do to project myself.
>
> The violin was one of the last main instruments that was amplified. After all, the trumpet was louder than a fiddle anyhow. The trombone was louder than a fiddle, amplified or not. But now, if you amplify a fiddle, you can make it as loud as any instrument in the band. You can't carry an amplified violin around with you. So, that's why these school marching bands don't use fiddles. You see instruments that can produce the sound of the violin, which are the clarinets and flutes and piccolos. 'Cause they're loud. A lot of violin jazz players like amplified instruments 'cause they get a much stronger tone. Just like you could with a trumpet or clarinet.

Armstrong explained that the fiddle is popular because it has a sound that is unique from other instruments:

> First of all, the violin is the only instrument that all the human expressions can be expressed upon, at least more easily than any others. It can laugh, it can sob, it can cry, it can make happy sounds. It really is the imitation, the duplication of the human voice. That's what a violin really is. I play twenty-three different instruments; I counted them one time—strings mostly. But the one that will say what's inside me the best is the violin. And if it's tuned right, got the right strings on it, and I got the right volume to it, I don't back up on it. It does what I want it to do. But now, we've gotten electric fiddles and some of them don't even sound

like a violin. I try to let mine, the channel, be open, no treble, no bass. I just like to amplify the strength of the violin. But the violin is the instrument. It can be played in a whisper, and it can be played pretty loud even without amplifying it. You can get up to a microphone and play a violin; the sound will come through very nicely and go through the sound system in the house. If you're playing country or blues, they can be played so you get the fullest tone. The violin is the shrillest when you start going up on the strings. But most violin players, or fiddlers as we call ourselves, we like good strong solid tones. When I play blues, it'll be whining; it'll be crying; it'll be sobbing.

Armstrong believed his fiddling was distinctive because he performed various types of music from different cultures. In his opinion, this was partly due to the places he had lived and traveled[33] and the fact that he was comfortable interacting with people from different ethnic and cultural backgrounds. Armstrong's gift of languages gave him the opportunity to perform for diverse groups. In Chicago, for example, the trio played whatever was necessary (blues, jazz, pop, country, and various non-English favorites) to satisfy the tastes of varying neighborhood groups. Being able to "sing anything with the drop of a dime" helped them to both earn tips and expand their repertoire. Armstrong explained further:

We played a variety of music. Most people can't pinpoint us to one specific type of music such as country, western swing, or what? When we play in nightclubs, I don't just play blues, I don't just play jazz. I don't just play this. I play mix-it-up, a little bit of everything. And usually we get good ovations. We're liable to jump out and sing a song in Chinese. And I have done it. Played songs in Hebrew, Chinese, foreign songs. Versatility is what I would put the accent on more than anything else. I know guys that played fiddle—white fiddle players and Black—but they play just that one style. If they play blues, that's all they play. But very few play blues on the fiddle. It seems to be a lost art.

I played lots of classical music. But who wants to play something that somebody's not going to listen to? Unless you are playing with a symphony orchestra or giving an all-around classical concert, nobody'll listen. They'll figure it's phony anyway. So, I found out that every dog barks loudest in his own backyard. That's why I never copied other fiddle players. I picked up little things here and there, little sounds and cut-offs and things. But as far as copy the style, never.

Armstrong indicated that he composed many of the songs he performed.[34] In describing his compositional process, he stated: "I get the idea in my head, and then write the words. Then I put the tune to it. I get some manuscript paper, put the little black boys on the fence, knock 'em off.[35] I wrote songs for the mandolin, guitar, and fiddle. One song I wrote we recorded, 'You'll Never

Find Another Kanaka Like Me.' In Polynesian, the word *kanaka* means man, male gender. I wrote 'Nana Hawaii,' which means 'Beautiful Hawaii.' I like South Sea Island songs. I wrote 'Mo Anna Lu' about a Hawaiian *wahine* or girl. Then I wrote 'The Streets of Old Chicago.' We recorded that on *That Old Gang of Mine*. Then I wrote 'You Never Get Fat Like That'—it's a comic song—and 'Run, Rover, Run.' That's a kid's song about a little old dog named Rover. It's in a Tennessee vernacular." In addition to live performances, Armstrong indicated that he had made recordings:

> During the 1930s, we made several records.[36] Some of them we never got to hear before they were released. Just like this movie documentary, *Louie Bluie*, from one of the records that we made. Some of them I've even forgotten the names. "Sail On, Little Girl, Sail On," "Ain't It a Crying Shame," "Stepchild Blues." And the vocalist was the blues great, Bumblebee Slim. His name was Amos Easton. When we went to Chicago [in the early 1930s, it] was just Ted Bogan and I who recorded down in the Merchandise Mart and made the song "State Street Rag" and "Knox County Stomp" ["Ted's Stomp"] under the title *Louie Bluie*. "Knox County Stomp" ["Ted's Stomp"] was just a fast, blue up-kick number. Some of the songs we recorded were composed. I don't know where I learned that one. Just something we played.[37]

It is noteworthy that many of the fiddlers Armstrong observed or worked with early in his career also lived in the mountain and piedmont regions. Armstrong's comments about musicians and towns suggest that central Appalachia was a lively music scene during the twenties and thirties.

> There used to be just down-hard scuffling fiddle players like Salty, who used to play "See You in My Dreams." Steve Tarter, Harry Gay, and John Garrett and all those guys. Not all were from Tennessee. I met and performed with Gay in Tennessee. But Salty lived in Big Stone Gap, Virginia. He was an all-around musician, but the fiddle was his best hope. We played up in Wise [Virginia], Coeburn [Virginia], Big Stone Gap [Virginia], over Black Mountain. All that's my territory. George Eskridge was from Bluefield, West Virginia. And Steve, another Steve, I forgot his last name. I know another guy named Runyon that played fiddle too. This was during the thirties and forties. West Virginia, Virginia, Tennessee, and Kentucky. That was the territory we were in mostly. Claude Williams—Fiddling Claude—was in St. Louis.[38]
>
> I remember Ray Nance.[39] Old Dublin was a real outstanding fiddle player in Huntington, West Virginia. A mulatto guy named Old [Ray] Emerson, he used to beat to that song about "Fit as a Fiddle and Ready for Love" on the fiddle. And "Tiger Rag." We used to do that "Tiger Rag" together. He was a way-out fiddle player. I can't think of his first name.

Gatemouth Brown.⁴⁰ That's a way-out fiddle player. He plays guitar, but he's a real fiddle player. He's from Texas. He's the only Black fiddle player I know that played with the Grand Ole Opry. He played there with Roy Clark. I don't know how long, but I saw him on TV there. Eddie South.⁴¹ He didn't stay on this continent here very long. They called him the "Dark Angel of the Violin." He was a way-out musician. But his music leaned toward the classic more than the stuff we played.

When asked why the fiddle was more popular in mountain states, Armstrong stated: "I wouldn't say it was more popular. That's just where you meet violin players and fiddlers. Most of them were raised around there."

Regarding the issues of social class and race and their impact on Black fiddling, Armstrong's comments were extensive:

During the early years, when whites had proms, and graduating exercises, we played popular songs, like "Dinah," "Tiptoe Through the Tulips," and "Looking Over a Four-Leaf Clover." There were two kinds of blues you could play. And if you played anything else, you better start running—"St. Louis Blues" by old [W. C.] Handy and "Memphis Blues." Then we played all the other popular songs that was current songs of the day. Some white people would hire some Negroes to call figures. "Do si do, cross the ball," and all that. We just played the same way, but usually Black people called it different.

Mostly when we played for Blacks, we'd give a little shindig or dance and charge admission at the door. The "seditty" [snobbish] Black people would like for you to play the same songs that white people like. They'd call them two-steps, fox-trots. That's the popular music we played for upper class whites and upper Blacks. Now when we'd go on the Chitlin' Circuit⁴² or one of those things they call a sociable, there would be just common Blacks that wasn't so "high up on the hog." They would even want us to play music for square dances, and then play some old slow, low-down dirty blues. The seditty Blacks didn't care that much for the blues. They didn't care for the guys playing them either. If you played it, the seditty Blacks didn't like it. But now, it's a different story. They realize that the blues are a part of our heritage.

I played for the "seditty" Blacks too in Knoxville. There was a woman who was a mulatto, and her husband was a mulatto. They were blue blood, but they liked Black music. Dr. Green was a city doctor and his wife did charity work. She would give these exhibitions they called cakewalks. Blacks did it during slavery for white people on big celebration days. But the cakewalk was strictly African, Black. The women would be dressed in fine gowns with the bustles.⁴³ And the men would have tails on. And the one who could cut the most capers got the cake. And we used to have a song that we played: "Buck up to me, I'll buck up to you. Way down in Georgia, da-da-da-da-da." [Armstrong sings the melody to the song.] You can just imagine hearing a band playing that. And sometimes we had brass, trombones doing the slurs, similar to that old New Orleans style. And the dancers would turn some curlicues. It was really something.

We had violins, guitars, string bass, sometimes clarinet, trumpet. This was early, long about the latter twenties into the thirties. And this Mrs. Green, Dr. Green's wife, would do that and give the proceeds to charity. She's the first person to give me a studio down in what they call downtown, an apartment in the Black part of Knoxville. Alderman Bard Brader gave me a big easel. Just because of my painting.

Armstrong indicated that when he was young, it was not uncommon for some Black people to have ambivalent feelings about fiddle music. While some accepted the music, others did not tolerate it under any circumstances:

Right there in my own town. When I learned to play, all the young Blacks wanted us to play. We played in schools and places like that. We played one Easter Sunday for church where my daddy was preaching. And these old foggy ex-slaves, when we brought the fiddles in there, someone said: "My brothers, my brothers. We ain't gonna." They said, "We ain't gwine to hear that or listen to that. That's the devil's instrument." And you know those old sisters and brothers walked out of that church. The young ones didn't. I told my mother, "Mama, that's the last time I'll ever play for any kind of doggone church." That's the Negro church. They hurt me till I cried? Honest to goodness.

When asked why the fiddle is called the devil's instrument and if he knew of other instruments that were not accepted, Armstrong exclaimed: "Ignorant! Ignorant! You know what they had sitting in the church? One of these pipe organs, and that was alright. And they squawked when they put pianos in church. You better start running by the church if they saw you with a guitar. Dad loved the violin. He was more intelligent to go for that crap. Ex-slavery time people were just like some of the Amish. They don't believe in anything—modern tractors. But they work the heck out of everybody, including horses and mules."

When asked if he had performed for many Black audiences, Armstrong stated: "Well, not in the later years. You might not like what I'm going to say. I found it was harder for me to play for Black people. They seem to be more critical than whites. I've also played for a lot of Black people. And after playing, they say, 'I am so proud of you.'" He indicated that he had also experienced racism and rejection from whites:

We played all over the United States, and I noticed anywhere there was a white element, they went for the fiddle. Especially Black guys playing it. We played for auction sales and all that. The only sad part about it is when they had a fiddler's contest, they would never let us participate. And that was a slur as far as I'm concerned. I didn't care for that. Well, we also ran into some places where they didn't even allow Black people. They had signs up. Some of them said: "N----r, read as you run. If you can't read, run anyhow." In Jamestown, Tennessee, we went up there on James River. And they didn't even allow a Black cat to go down the street. But that was when I was playing bass in a seven-piece band. Steve's Rhythm Boys.

When I asked Armstrong if Black fiddling had changed over the years, particularly from slavery to the early twentieth century, he stated:

Not the fiddle playing. It's just the material they have to work with. The songs that they played were Virginia reels. Most of the Black fiddle players played to suit the white man's taste. Many of them were very polished. And they played even gavottes, minuets, and all those classic things. A lot of them couldn't read a note, and played beautifully.

The instruments are a little different now. We got electric violins, electric guitars. But there's one thing in the fiddle family that has changed quite a lot. As a matter of fact, they've just about thrown the bow away because there is a lot of pizzicato, plucking the strings. When I started, guys used to saw on the bow, saw on the big bass fiddle.

While some researchers indicate that "by the end of the decade [1930s], the popularity of the radio and emergence of the jukebox brought Armstrong's professional playing days to a halt," (Ankeny n.d.a), I wanted to know his thoughts on the matter. Therefore, on the subject of the decline in fiddling by Black people and possible reasons the fiddle no longer seemed to be a popular instrument in Black culture, Armstrong provided several reasons:

First of all, it takes more schooling to play the fiddle and to play what they want to hear on it now. Most Black fiddle players can't play blues even on the fiddle. And those that go to school now play classics because the big orchestras are gone. When you see a blues combination, it's usually this guy with a lead guitar, bass guitar, all amplified, with drums. There is no fiddle because it's hard to find fiddle players who can play blues or anything secular like that. You have to go to school, whether you go to a conservatory or not; you got to apply yourself. People play for years and can't get a decent tone out of a violin. But you can hit one string on a guitar, and, if it's amplified, it'll sound good.

I've had white people to come to me, not once, not twice, but ten times: "Mr. Armstrong, why don't Black people come to these festivals? It isn't just all just country music or western. Why don't they come up?" I don't know. What can I tell them? Perhaps they're holding a prayer meeting somewhere or the preacher is preaching some stuff to them. At festivals, we had more Black performers on stage than we did in the audience. The whites in the audience even were huge. White people who wouldn't listen to blues years ago when I was coming up were now my students—like my pupils I taught at Davis and Elkins College a few weeks ago.[44] Whites like it because it's a new vista open up to them. Why? I can't answer for them, but I think they like change. I played four times at the World's Fair in Knoxville, and we got ovation after ovation after ovation.

Some Blacks won't give you a chance. They don't want to be identified with it. But usually when they do, it's a revelation to them. And most Negroes won't even listen to the banjo. I think it is stereotypes They always show Negroes with a banjo on these big bills and in minstrel shows. That's what you saw. Brother Bones playing a banjo. Fiddles and banjos. So, when they see a banjo, that's a minstrel show, that's back in the sticks. That reminds them of where they came from. That's what they heard back there, the hoedown. But when they hear what you can really play on a violin, they can't believe it. Prejudice means, if you break the word down, "pre-judge without giving a person a chance." If you don't know, why don't you try it. You might like it. But most people say, "Oh, I know all about that."

Black string bands are mostly nonexistent too. That's why our band was so unique. How many Blacks do you see playing a fiddle and have group now? Whenever you do see these groups, they have a drum, a piano; they'll have an electric guitar, electric bass and maybe a harmonica. So that's the sound they have, because it's hard to find guys who can play that stuff on fiddles anyway, to get the real blues sound on the fiddle. Most of the old fiddle players that could do that are gone.

fiddlingismyjoycompanion.net

Notes

1. See Holtzberg-Call (1989), Baklanoff (1991), Evans (1994), and select publications on the Sea Islands (chapter 9).

2. When musicking for the big house (that is, white people) was performed in the slave quarters, oftentimes the enslaved would add bow shuffles and off-beat phrasing to the same tunes to stimulate or accompany the intensely rhythmic dances done there. Researchers indicate that terms such as hoedown and breakdown were used to describe vigorous dancing and soon these words were applied to the type of tunes that inspired such dancing. Less emphasis was placed on melody and more on rhythm and repetition of short phrases when performing breakdowns. Hoedown-style fiddling was eventually adopted by whites who visited slave gatherings (Cauthen 1989c, 40–41; Milnes 1999, 97; Wig and Ward 2002–2011).

3. The Mississippi Sheiks included two fiddlers on one of their first recordings. Also, early Black Creole groups in southwest Louisiana may have included two fiddlers, but this was not norm for Black fiddle groups in most rural areas of the South. Including more than one fiddler appeared to be more commonplace in white string bands (Russell and Pinson 2004).

4. Most music scholars agree that the bowed lute originated in Asia and was introduced to peoples on the European continent by West Asians or peoples from the Arab world (Remnant 2001; Wachsmann et al. 2001; Kjemtrup 2010; Beisswenger 2011, xix).

5. Because of its association with deviance and defiance, perhaps this is the reason the fiddle more than other musical instruments has taken on negative connotations (Wimbush 2010).

6. When I visited Detroit in August 1987, I had the opportunity to spend an entire day with Howard Armstrong, who was extremely generous with his time. The importance of history to Armstrong can be seen in the way he intertwines national historical facts into his family and local history. Not only was he well read, he had traveled extensively and spoke several languages. Because all quoted material by Armstrong comes from the 1987 interview, this source will not be cited throughout the discussion.

7. 🎼 See Photos 13.2–13.6 for additional photos of Armstrong and his family.

8. 🎼 See Repertoire 13.1 to see a list with details about Armstrong's recordings, compositions, and films that document his life.

9. Some may consider Armstrong's quotes to be too long and in need of paraphrasing, which has already been done for clarity and length. Yet, I believe it is important to hear (or read) the voice of the performer instead of filtering the material through the lens of an outsider to the tradition, particularly since the latter approach has already been used in other parts of this study. Of the many interviews researchers have conducted with Armstrong, I found the following to be most useful for this study: Feld (1998), Brisbin (2003a, 2003b, 2004).

10. 🎼 See Map 13.1 and Demographics 13.1.

11. Armstrong's parents—Thomas Franklin Armstrong (1871–1944) and Daisy Ann Milam Armstrong (1875–1945)—were both born in Middle Tennessee; his mother in Stewart County near Clarksville and his father in a place called Dover Furnace or Dover. US census records indicate that after their marriage in 1901 in Stewart County, they moved to East Tennessee where they started their family. The couple's nine children were all born in East Tennessee in either Rhea or Campbell County; their names are: Edward (1901–1950), Ella Mae (1901–1923), Clara Portia (1906–1980), Robbie Elaine (1907–1995), William Howard Taft (1909–2003), Thomas A. (1911–1924), Roland H. (1914–1980), Lee Crockett (1916–1987), and Francis Lee (1919–2000).

12. 🎼 See Photo 13.2 to view the Armstrong Family Band.

13. As noted earlier, Frank Martin, Roland and Carl Martin's father, was originally from Spartanburg, South Carolina. When family members left South Carolina during the late nineteenth and early twentieth centuries, Frank settled in Big Stone Gap, Virginia, where Carl was born, while Roland moved to Knoxville. The Martin family reunited when Frank relocated to Knoxville during the early twentieth century (see chapter 5).

14. According to Armstrong, "The dog house was a place where all the men ate their dinner at twelve o'clock. Nobody carried lunch in a paper sack; they had aluminum dinner pails. One for the steak or whatever, and then on the bottom was coffee or whatever liquid. Then next one was for dessert and it went like that. The pail was hanging on a peg where this big old cast iron stove was. And it'd stay warm."

15. Stephen Tarter was a Virginia-born Black multi-instrumentalist who played fiddle, guitar, banjo, and mandolin. When he died, he was living in Gate City in Scott County, Virginia (see chapter 5).

16. Other musicians active in East Tennessee at the time included Andy Kline, Clarence Venerable, and John Dye. Concerning Dye, Armstrong stated: "John Dye was the guy who played the guitar and would sit and cry. He played the piece about 'Careless Love.' He was always in and out of love. And then there was Willie Osmond, who we called Pete Osmond. He was in my age group. He played fiddle and he played mandolin too. His daddy, old man Jim Osmond, he also played."

17. Because Armstrong has a distinctive playing style, I include much of what he stated about performance technique and other details about musicking.

18. Armstrong (2002) indicates that the musicians played a variety of instruments: Fred McDade (a little of everything), Dave McDade (violin), Gabe Alexander (violin), Henry Alexander (guitar), and Frank Nelson (guitar).

19. While in Knoxville, they played for dances, fish fries, picnics, and radio broadcasts. For a while, Carl and Howard played for a medicine show; then they returned to Knoxville and met Ted Bogan.

20. In Dixon and Godrich (1982, 97–98; 745), Howard Armstrong is listed twice. In 1930, he is listed as an accompanist in the group, Tennessee Chocolate Drops, with Carl Martin (string bass), Roland Martin (guitar), and Howard Armstrong (violin). In 1934, Armstrong, as leader, recorded under the name Louie Bluie (violin and mandolin) with Ted Bogan (guitar and vocal); see Repertoire 13.1.

21. As the Tennessee Chocolate Drops, their music was marketed to consumers whom the record companies believed would purchase race records. But when the music was marketed to white consumers, the group was known as the Tennessee Trio (Danser 2018, 55; Everett 2016).

22. Born in Spartanburg, South Carolina, Theodore R. Bogan (1909–1990) was a guitarist, singer, and songwriter. Bogan became an important figure in the Knoxville music scene during the 1930s as a music partner with Carl Martin and Armstrong (Chadbourne n.d.; Martin, Bogan, and Armstrong 1974).

23. See Map 13.1. Sparta is the county seat for White County, which is located southwest of Armstrong's family home in Campbell County.

24. It was during this period that Armstrong met and married his first wife, Celestine Crook (1918–2004).

25. Armstrong was married three times: first to Celestine Crook (1918–2004), who was born and raised in Sparta (White County), Tennessee; second to Anna Gordon (1925–1997), who was born and raised in Detroit; and finally, to Barbara Ann Ward (1940–2013) from Boston. His marriage to Crook produced one son, Thomas Lee Armstrong (1936–1996). With Gordon, he had three sons: William Jr., Robert, and Ralphe Alan.

26. Armstrong is referring to his second marriage to Anna Gordon (1925–1997).

27. See discussion in the foregoing for the meaning of juke joint and its role in rural Black culture.

28. During the 1920s and 1930s, the city of Knoxville had several radio stations. The city's first, WNOX, began broadcasting in 1921, while WROL, its rival, began in 1927. By the early 1930s, WFBC had been started (Smyth 1987, 36–41).

29. Locations along the Tug Fork River in West Virginia included several small towns (Gary, Sawmill Hollow, and Keystone) in McDowell County. Keystone, founded in 1892 by the Keystone Coal and Coke Company, and incorporated in 1909, is a majority Black community; its history involves major protests by local Black miners (see Lewis 2009, 137–38; Deaner 2004).

30. A *capo*, which is short for the Italian word *capodastro*, is a device musicians use on the neck of a string instrument to shorten the playable length of the strings and raise the pitch. It is a common tool for players of guitars, mandolins, banjos, and ukuleles.

31. Although she stated that she was born in New Orleans, researchers indicate that Memphis Minnie (real name Lizzie Douglas), was a blues guitarist, vocalist, and songwriter born in Mississippi.

32. Born in 1942 in France, Jean-Luc Ponty is a white violinist known for pioneering the electric violin in jazz-rock during the 1970s (Ginell n.d.).

33. In addition to residing in Tennessee and the Midwest, his participation in state and national festivals as well as tours, sponsored by the United States State Department, allowed him to travel throughout the United States, various parts of Central and South America (Costa Rica, Colombia, Brazil, Bolivia, Chile, Peru, Panama, Nicaragua) and Southeast Asia (Bali).

34. See Repertoire 13.1.

35. Armstrong is referring to the process of composing or notating music—placing notes (black boys) on the staff (fence).

36. Go to Audio Examples to listen to Armstrong's early recordings from the 1930s.

37. When Armstrong began performing professionally again in the 1970s, he made several other records with Carl Martin, Ted Bogan, and family members. His first record, *Barnyard Dance* (1972) on Rounder Records, included his younger brother, L. C. [Lee Crockett], who played guitar and bass.

38. Actually, Claude Williams (1908–2004) was born in Muskogee, Oklahoma, near the Ozark Mountains; he moved to Kansas City during the late 1920s and remained there and established a professional career performing jazz. But it is significant that Armstrong assumed that Williams was born in the mountain region, probably because he played the fiddle. Thus, in the minds of some musicians, instrumental traditions are associated with specific geographical regions, and the fiddle is identified with the mountains.

39. Born in Chicago, Ray Nance (1913–1976) is an urban-based musician most noted for his performance of violin and trumpet in different jazz groups. In addition to leading his own band and performing with jazz pianist Earl Hines during the 1930s, he is probably best remembered for his long association with Duke Ellington from the early 1940s through the early 1960s.

40. Clarence "Gatemouth" Brown (1924–2005) was born in Vinton, Louisiana, and raised in Orange, Texas. Known for playing the fiddle and guitar, he became a well-known and established urban-based musician during the 1960s known for performing various styles of popular music.

41. Eddie South (1904–1962) was born in Louisiana, Missouri, in Pike County. Formally trained in European art music, he had hoped to become a concert artist specializing in performing classical music. When he was unsuccessful in doing this, primarily because of racism, he spent much of his career performing jazz and was based in Chicago with travels throughout Europe and the United States.

42. "Chitlin Circuit" refers to the network of Black-centered entertainment venues popular in the United States during the early twentieth century.

43. The bustle was a pad or framework expanding and supporting the fullness and drapery of the back of a woman's skirt.

44. Davis and Elkins College, located in Elkins, a small town in the mountains of central West Virginia, was the site for the Augusta Heritage Arts Workshops held each summer at the Augusta Heritage Center (Augusta Heritage Arts 1989, 4). During the 1980s, and perhaps even later, Armstrong regularly taught fiddle and mandolin during Blues Week.

References Cited

Print Sources, Interviews, Personal/Email Communication

Abbott, Lynn, and Doug Seroff. 2002. *Out of Sight: The Rise of African American Popular Music 1889–1895*. Jackson: University Press of Mississippi.
Abernethy, Francis Edward. 1996. "African American Folklore in Texas and in the Texas Folklore Society." In *Juneteenth Texas: Essays in African-American Folklore*, edited by Patrick B. Mullen and Alan B. Govenar, 1–13. Denton: University of North Texas Press.
Abrahams, Roger D. 1992. *Singing the Master: The Emergence of African American Culture in the Plantation South*. New York: Penguin Books.
"Ace Donell." 2002–2007. Personal Narratives. African Americans in Monroe County: Their History and Heritage. http://sites.rootsweb.com/~momonroe/aa_narrative6.htm. Accessed November 13, 2019.
Adams, Edward Clarkson Leverett. 1928. *Nigger to Nigger*. New York: Charles Scribner's Sons.
"African American Old-time String Band Music: A Selective Discography." n.d. The Free Library by Farlex. https://www.thefreelibrary.com/African+American+old-time+string+band+music%3a+a+selective+discography.-a0179615963. Accessed September 4, 2021.
Agawu, Kofi. 2003. *Representing African Music: Postcolonial Notes, Queries, Positions*. New York: Routledge.
Allen, James Lane. 1887. "Mrs. Stowe's 'Uncle Tom' at Home in Kentucky." *Century Illustrated Magazine* 34(6): 852–67, October.
Allen, William Francis, Charles Pickard Ware, and Lucy McKim Garrison, eds. 1867. *Slave Songs of the United States*. New York: A. Simpson.
Allison, Robert J. 1999. Book review. *Exchanging Our Country Marks: The Transformation of African Identities in the Colonial and Antebellum South, 1526–1830*, by Michael A. Gomez. *Journal of Interdisciplinary History* 30(3): 475–81.
Ames, David W. 1973. "A Sociocultural View of Hausa Musical Activity." In *The Traditional Artist in African Societies*, edited by Warren D. d'Azevedo, 128–61. Bloomington: Indiana University Press.
"An Artist Selecting an Instrument." 1871. *Frank Leslie's Illustrated Newspaper* 32(818): 192, June 3.
Ancelet, Barry Jean. 1984. *The Makers of Cajun Music*. Austin: University of Texas Press.
Ancelet, Barry Jean. 1989. *Cajun Music: Its Origins and Development*. Lafayette: Center for Louisiana Studies.
Ancelet, Barry Jean. 2014. Email communication to the author. June 14.
Andrews, Nathalie, and Eric Larson. 1978. "Child of the Lord: Interview with Bill Livers by Nathalie Andrews and Eric Larson." *Southern Exposure: A Journal of Politics and Culture* 6(1): 14–19, April 1.
Ankeny, Jason. n.d.a. "Howard Armstrong—Biography." *AllMusic.com*. https://www.allmusic.com/artist/howard-armstrong-mn0000272591/biography. Accessed March 16, 2022.

Ankeny, Jason. n.d.b. "The Lawtell Playboys." *AllMusic.com*. https://www.allmusic.com/artist/the-lawtell-playboys-mn0002143143/biography. Accessed September 20, 2021.

Apel, Willi. 1970. *Harvard Dictionary of Music*. Cambridge, MA: Belknap Press of Harvard University Press.

Apel, Willi. 1970. "Tremolo." In *Harvard Dictionary of Music*, 2nd ed., revised and enlarged, edited by Willi Apel, 861–62. Cambridge, MA: Belknap Press of Harvard University Press.

Apel, Willi. 1970. "Vibrato." In *Harvard Dictionary of Music*, 2nd ed., revised and enlarged, edited by Willi Apel, 900. Cambridge, MA: Belknap Press of Harvard University Press.

"Appalachian Regional Commission." 2016. *Encyclopaedia Britannica*, September 28. https://www.britannica.com/topic/Appalachian-Regional-Commission. Accessed June 11, 2022.

Armstrong, Howard. 1987. Personal interview with the author. Detroit, Michigan. November 5.

Armstrong, Howard. 2002. Mail communication to the author, February 21.

"Arpeggio." 2001. In *Oxford Music Online*. https://www.oxfordmusiconline.com/grovemusic/view/10.1093/gmo/9781561592630.001.0001/omo-9781561592630-e-0000001327?print=pdf. Accessed November 23, 2022.

Astley, Thomas, ed. 1968 [1745–47]. *A New General Collection of Voyages and Travels Consisting of the most esteemed Relations which have been hitherto published in any Language. Comprehending Everything Remarkable in Its Kind in Europe, Asia, Africa, and America*. 4 volumes. London: Frank Cass and Company, Travels and Narratives No. 47.

Augusta Heritage Arts Workshop. 1989. "Schedule of Classes." Elkins, WV: Davis and Elkins College.

Austin, Allan D. 1984. *African Muslims in Antebellum America: A Sourcebook*. New York: Garland Publishing.

Austin, Allan D. 1997. *African Muslims in Antebellum America: Transatlantic Stories and Spiritual Struggles*. New York: Routledge.

Avirett, James Battle. 1901. *The Old Plantation: How We Lived in Great House and Cabin Before the War*. New York: F. Tennyson Neely Co.

Baker, Bruce E. n.d. "Black Fiddlers in Upstate South Carolina, by County." http://personal.rhul.ac.uk/unra/373/music/Black_Fiddlers_in_Upstate_South_Carolina.html. Accessed May 30, 2011.

Baker, Etta Reid. 1987. Personal interview with the author. Morganton, North Carolina. August 22.

Baklanoff, Joy Driskell. 1991. "Traditional Black Musical Events in West Alabama and Northeast Mississippi, 1940–60: A Classificatory-Descriptive Perspective." In *Discourse in Ethnomusicology III. Essays in Honor of Frank J. Gillis*, edited by Nancy Cassell McEntire et al., 127–50. Bloomington: Ethnomusicology Publication Group, Indiana University.

Baldwin, Peggy. 2021. "Louis Southworth (1829–1917)." Oregon Encyclopedia. https://www.oregonencyclopedia.org/articles/southworth_louis_1829_1917_/. Accessed July 20, 2021.

Balfa, Dewey. 1987. Personal interview with the author. Basile, Louisiana. October 19.

Ball, Charles. 1837. *Slavery in the United States: A Narrative of the Life and Adventures of Charles Ball, A Black Man, Who Lived Forty Years in Maryland, South Carolina, and Georgia, as a Slave, Under Various Masters, and Was One Year in the Navy with Commodore Barney, During the Late War. Containing an Account of the Manners and Usages of the Planters and Slaveholders of the South—a Description of the Condition and Treatment of the Slaves, with Observations Upon the State of Morals Amongst the Cotton Planters, and the Perils and Sufferings of a Fugitive Slave, Who Twice Escaped from the Cotton Country*. New York: John S. Taylor, Brick Church Chapel.

Ballanta, Nicholas George Julius. 1925. *Saint Helena Island Spirituals*. New York: G. Schirmer.

Banjo Ray. 2012. "Obituary: Joe Thompson, Old-Time Fiddler 1918–2012." Mudcat Café. Posted February 12, 2012. 4:10 AM.

Banks, David. 2002. "The Sound of 1930s Florida Folk Life." National Public Radio. February 28.

Barnett, Anthony. 1995. *Desert Sands. The Recordings and Performances of Stuff Smith: An Annotated Discography and Biographical Source Book*. East Sussex, UK: Allardyce, Barnett.

Barnett, Anthony. 1998. *Up Jumped the Devil. The Supplement to Desert Sands. The Recordings and Performances of Stuff Smith: An Annotated Discography and Biographical Source Book*. East Sussex, UK: Allardyce, Barnett.

Barnett, Anthony. 1999. *Black Gypsy: The Recordings of Eddie South: An Annotated Discography and Itinerary*, including cassette with broadcasts and with foreword by Leroy Jenkins. East Sussex, UK: Allardyce, Barnett.

Barlow, William. 1989. *"Looking Up at Down": The Emergence of Blues Culture*. Philadelphia: Temple University Press.

Barrett, Mary Tess. 2014. "What Race Sounds Like: Perceiving American Music through the Carolina Chocolate Drops." M.A. thesis, Wesleyan University.

Barrow, David Crenshaw. 1882. "A Georgia Corn-Shucking." *Century Magazine* 24: 873–78, October.

Barry, Boubacar. 1997. *Senegambia and the Atlantic Slave Trade*. Cambridge: Cambridge University Press.

Bass, Robert Duncan. 1931. "Negro Songs from the Pedee Country." *Journal of American Folklore* 44(174): 418–36, October-December.

Bastin, Bruce. 1975. "'Back before the Blues Were Blues . . .': Pre-Blues Secular Music in North Carolina." *Sing Out: The Folk Song Magazine* 24(3): 13–16, July-August.

Bastin, Bruce. 1978. Liner notes. Various artists. *Another Man Done Gone*. Flyright Records LP 528.

Bastin, Bruce. 1986. *Red River Blues: The Blues Tradition in the Southeast*. Urbana: University of Illinois Press.

Bastin, Bruce. 1990 [1978]. "An Overview of Black History in North Carolina: Black Music in North Carolina." In *The Heritage of Blacks in North Carolina, Volume 1, 1990*, edited by Philip N. Henry and Carol M. Speas. Project Director, Linda Simmons-Henry. Charlotte: North Carolina African American Heritage Foundation in cooperation with The Delmar Co., 70–75. Reprint from *The Black Presence in North Carolina*, edited by Jeffrey Crow and Robert E. Winters Jr. Raleigh: North Carolina Museum of History.

Bastin, Bruce, and Jeffrey Green. 1989. "Turn-of-the-Century Jug Bands in the Southeastern United States." *Black Music Research Bulletin* 11(1): 1–3, spring.

Bastin, Bruce, and Pete Lowry. 1975a. "Fort Valley Blues: Part 2." *Blues Unlimited* 112: 13–16, March.

Bastin, Bruce, and Pete Lowry. 1975b. "Fort Valley Blues: Part 3." *Blues Unlimited* 114: 20–21, May.

Bedasse, Monique. 2017. "Revising the Gomez Imperative: Exchanging Our Country Marks and the Africana Studies Tradition, ASWAD, 2017." *Black Scholar* 48(4): 19–27.

Beisswenger, Drew. 2011. *North American Fiddle Music: A Research and Information Guide*. New York: Routledge.

Benners, Alfred H. 1923. *Slavery and Its Results*. Macon, GA: J. W. Burke.

Bergey, Barry. 1984a. "City Sounds/Rural Rhythms: 'Little Dixie Music Comes to Kansas City.'" Festival Program Booklet. Columbia: Missouri Arts Council/Missouri Cultural Heritage Center, University of Missouri.

Bergey, Barry. 1984b. "City Sounds: Urban Music of Kansas City and St. Louis." Festival Program Booklet. Columbia: Missouri Arts Council/Missouri Cultural Heritage Center, University of Missouri.

Berlin, Edward A. 2001. "Ragtime." In *Oxford Music Online*. https://doi.org/10.1093/gmo/978156 1592630.article. Accessed December 24, 2023.

Berquin-Duvallon, Pierre-Louis. 1806. *Travels in Louisiana and the Floridas, in the Year 1802, Giving a Correct Picture of Those Countries*. Translated from the French by John Davis. New York: I. Riley and Co.

Bertram, Cuje. 1980. Personal interview with Bobby Fulcher. Indianapolis, Indiana. February 27.

Besmer, Fremont B. 1983. *Horses, Musicians, and Gods: The Hausa Cult of Possession-Trance*. Zaria, Nigeria: Ahmadu Bello University Press.

"Black Belt." 2017. *Encyclopaedia Britannica*, September 5. https://www.britannica.com/place/Black-Belt. Accessed September 18, 2022.

Blake Jr., John. 2001. "Jazz and the Violin." Lecture demonstration with Billy Taylor and the Billy Taylor Trio, John F. Kennedy Center Performing Arts Series, *Billy Taylor's Jazz at The Kennedy Center*. Washington, DC, February 7.

Blake Jr., John. 2011. Telephone interview with the author, May 30.

Blakemore, Erin. 2019. "How 'Race Records' Turned Black Music into Big Business." *History*, February 22. Originally published August 7, 2018. https://www.history.com/news/race-records-bessie-smith-big-bill-broonzy-music-business. Accessed May 15, 2020.

Blassingame, John W. 1979. *The Slave Community: Plantation Life in the Antebellum South*. Revised and enlarged edition. New York: Oxford University Press.

Blaustein, Richard. 1972. "More on Slave Fiddling." *The Devil's Box, Newsletter* 16: 11–15.

Bogert, Pen. 1995 [1994]. "The Booker Orchestra." *Blues and Rhythm* 99: 18–19, May. Originally published in *Blues News: A Publication of the KYANA Blues Society*, July/August 1994.

Bolick, Harry. 2015a. "Introduction." In *Mississippi Fiddle Tunes and Songs from the 1930s*, edited by Harry Bolick and Stephen T. Austin, ix–xi. Jackson: University Press of Mississippi.

Bolick, Harry. 2015b. "Collecting Folk Music in 1936 and 1939." In *Mississippi Fiddle Tunes and Songs from the 1930s*, edited by Harry Bolick and Stephen T. Austin, 3–27. Jackson: University Press of Mississippi.

Bolick, Harry. 2021a. "Introduction." In *Fiddle Tunes from Mississippi: Commercial and Informal Recordings, 1920–2018*, by Harry Bolick and Tony Russell, 3–9. Jackson: University Press of Mississippi.

Bolick, Harry. 2021b. "Bob Pratcher." In *Fiddle Tunes from Mississippi: Commercial and Informal Recordings, 1920–2018*, by Harry Bolick and Tony Russell, 507–11. Jackson: University Press of Mississippi.

Bolick, Harry, and Stephen T. Austin. 2015. *Mississippi Fiddle Tunes and Songs from the 1930s*. Jackson: University Press of Mississippi.

Bolick, Harry, and Tony Russell. 2021. *Fiddle Tunes from Mississippi: Commercial and Informal Recordings, 1920–2018*. Jackson: University Press of Mississippi.

Born in Slavery: Slave Narratives from the Federal Writers' Project 1936–1938. 2001. Library of Congress. Updated March 31, 2001. http://memory.loc.gov/ammem/snhtml/snhome.html. Accessed June 22, 2014.

Bouton, Nathaniel. 1856. *The History of Concord, from Its First Grant in 1725, to the Organization of the City Government in 1853, with a History of the Ancient Penacooks*. Concord, MA: Benning W. Sanborn.

Bower, David. 2009. "Joe Thompson at 90." *Old-Time Herald: A Magazine Dedicated to Old-Time Music* 11(9): 22–26.

Bowles, George Leonard. 1976. Personal interview with Kip Lornell. October 10.

Bowles, George Leonard. 1987. Personal interview with the author. Martinsville, Virginia. August 25.

"Bowles, George L." 2004. Obituary. *Martinsville Bulletin*, December 13. http://www.martinsvillebulletin.com/obituaries/bowles-george-l/article_20132b4b-a874-5e63-b825-952919dd0089.html. Accessed August 4, 2015.

Bowles, Naomi. 1987. Personal communication with the author. Martinsville, Virginia. August 25.

Brady, Erika. 2013. "Contested Origins: Arnold Shultz and the Music of Western Kentucky." In *Hidden in the Mix: The African American Presence in Country Music*, edited by Diane Pecknold. Durham, NC: Duke University Press, 100–118.

Brasseaux, Carl A. 2010. "Foreword." In *Louisiana Creole Fiddle Method: The Music and Technique for Fiddlers and Guitarists* by D'Jamal Garnier III and Robert Wiley. Pacific, MO: Mel Bay Publications, 4.

Brice, Andy. 1936–38 [2001]. "Ex-slave 81 Years Old. Project #1655. W. W. Dixon, Winnsboro, South Carolina." In *Born in Slavery: Slave Narratives from the Federal Writers' Project 1936–1938*, 75–78. Library of Congress. Updated March 31, 2001. http://memory.loc.gov/ammem/snhtml/snhome.html. Accessed June 22, 2014.

Briggs, Keith. 2002. Liner notes. *Bo Carter: The Essential*. Classic Blues CBL 200028.

Brisbin, John Anthony. 2003a. "Howard Armstrong: The Interview." Part 1. *Living Blues* 169: 42–47.

Brisbin, John Anthony. 2003b. "Howard Armstrong: The Interview." Part 2. *Living Blues* 170: 44–49.

Brisbin, John Anthony. 2004. "Howard Armstrong: The Interview." Part 3. *Living Blues* 171: 34–39.

Bronner, Simon J. 1987. *Old-Time Music Makers of New York State*. Syracuse, NY: Syracuse University Press.

Brooks, Tim. 2004. *Lost Sounds: Blacks and the Birth of the Recording Industry, 1890–1919*. Urbana: University of Illinois Press.

Broussard, Sherry T. 2012. *African Americans in Lafayette and Southwest Louisiana*. Charleston, SC: Arcadia Publishing.

Broven, John. 1983. *South to Louisiana: The Music of the Cajun Bayous*. Gretna, LA: Pelican Publishing.

Brower, David. 2012. "Fiddler Joe Thompson Dies at 93." North Carolina Public Radio WUNC.

Brown, Danielle. 2021. "An Open Letter on Racism in Music Studies, Especially Ethnomusicology and Music Education," June 12. https://www.mypeopletellstories.com/blog/open-letter. Accessed March 7, 2022.

Brown, David. 1976. "The Man Who Played Jackson's Fiddle." *Charleston [Mississippi] Sun-Sentinel*, July 8, 12.

Brown, Ernest D. 1990. "Something from Nothing and More from Something: The Making and Playing of Music Instruments in African American Cultures." In *Issues in Organology: Selected Reports in Ethnomusicology, Volume 8*, edited by Sue Carole DeVale, 275–91. Los Angeles: UCLA Department of Ethnomusicology and Systematic Musicology.

Brown, Ernest D. 1992. "The African/African American Idiom in Music: Family Resemblances in Black Music." In *African Musicology: Current Trends, Volume II*, edited by Jacqueline Cogdell DjeDje, 115–34. Los Angeles and Atlanta: UCLA International Studies and Overseas Program (ISOP)/The James S. Coleman African Studies Center; Crossroads Press/African Studies Association.

Brown, Karen McCarthy. 2005. "Vodou." In *Encyclopedia of Religion, Volume 14*, 2nd ed., edited by Lindsay Jones. Detroit: Macmillan. Reference 9634–9635.

Brown, Karida. 2018. *Gone Home: Race and Roots through Appalachia*. Chapel Hill, NC: University of North Carolina Press.

Brown, William Wells. 1880. *My Southern Home or The South and Its People*. Boston: A. G. Brown and Co.

Browne, Kimasi Lionel John. 1995. "Variation in the Vocal Style of Brenda Holloway: Soul Singer and 1960s Motown Recording Artist." Master's thesis, University of California, Los Angeles.

Browne, Kimasi Lionel John. 1998. "Brenda Holloway: Los Angeles's Contribution to Motown." In *California Soul: Music of African Americans in the West*, edited by Jacqueline Cogdell DjeDje and Eddie S. Meadows, 321–51. Berkeley: University of California Press.

Browne, Kimasi Lionel John. 2005. "Soul or Nothing: The Formation of Cultural Identity on the British Northern Soul Scene." PhD dissertation, University of California, Los Angeles.

Browne, Kimasi Lionel John. 2019. "Soul Music." In *The Sage International Encyclopedia of Music and Culture*, Volume 4, edited by Janet Sturman. Los Angeles: Sage.

Bruce, Philip Alexander. 1907 [1964]. *Social Life of Virginia in the Seventeenth Century*. New York: Frederick Ungar Publishing.

Bucuvalas, Tina, Peggy A. Bulger, and Stetson Kennedy. 1987. *South Florida Folklife*. Jackson: University Press of Mississippi.

Burtt, Steve. 1980. "Folk Musician Tom Dumas of Tutwiler dies at 94." *Charleston [Mississippi] Sun Sentinel*, December 11.

Buster, Charlie. 1979. Personal interview with Bobby Fulcher. Lexington, Kentucky. April 14.

Cable, George Washington. 1886a. "The Dance in Place Congo." *Century Illustrated Magazine* 31(4): 517–32, February.

Cable, George Washington. 1886b. "Creole Slave Songs." *Century Illustrated Magazine* 31(6): 807–28, April.

Calt, Stephen, Nick Perls, and Michael Stewart. 1970. Liner notes. *Bo Carter: Greatest Hits 1930–1940*. Yazoo L 1014.

Calt, Stephen, Jerry Epstein, John Fahey, Don Kent, Nick Perls, Michael Stewart, and Alan Wilson. 1971. Liner notes. *Charley Patton: Founder of the Delta Blues, 1929–1934*. Yazoo Records L 1020.

Calt, Stephen, Michael Stewart, and Don Kent. 1974. Liner notes. Mississippi Sheiks. *Stop and Listen*. Mamlish S3804.

Cantwell, Robert. 2003. *Bluegrass Breakdown: The Making of the Old Southern Sound*. University of Illinois Press.

Carawan, Guy, and Candie Carawan. 1994 [1989]. *"Ain't You Got a Right to the Tree of Life?" The People of Johns Island, South Carolina: Their Faces, Their Words, and Their Songs*. Athens: University of Georgia Press.

Carawan, Guy, and Candie Carawan. 1995. "Singing and Shouting in Moving Star Hall." *Black Music Research Journal* 15(1): 17–28, spring.

Carleton, George Washington. 1864a. *The Suppressed Book About Slavery! Prepared for Publication in 1857—Never Published until the Present Time*. New York: Carleton Publisher.

Carleton, George Washington. 1864b. "The Coffle Gang" (image title). In *The Suppressed Book About Slavery! Prepared for Publication in 1857—Never Published Until the Present Time*. New York: Carleton Publisher. Image located between pages 96 and 97.

Carlin, Bob. 1994. "Odell Thompson, 1911–1994." *Old-Time Herald: A Magazine Dedicated to Old-Time Music*, fall.

Carlin, Bob. 1999. Liner notes. *Joe Thompson: Family Tradition*. Rounder 2161.

Carlin, Bob. 2004. *String Bands in the North Carolina Piedmont*. Jefferson, NC: McFarland.

Carlin, Bob. 2016. "African-American String Band, Fiddle and Banjo Traditions." Interview with Paul Brown, *Across the Blue Ridge Weekly*. Episode 8 Audio Story, Radio WFDD, Winston Salem, North Carolina. February. https://beta.prx.org/stories/171765?play=true. Accessed May 18, 2018. Posted by Sysop on Monday, 21 August 2017. https://www.africanbluegrass.com/blogs/sysop/episode-8-african-american-string-band-fiddle-banjo-traditions-1097. Accessed May 18, 2018.

"Carl Martin." 1979. *Living Blues* 43, summer. Reprinted in *Bluesmandolin: Mandolins and Blues*, March 9, 2015. https://bluesmandolin.wordpress.com/2015/03/09/carl-martin-living-blues-no-43-summer-1979/. Accessed July 31, 2015.

Carney, George O. 1994. *The Sounds of People and Places: A Geography of American Folk and Popular Music*. 3rd ed. Lanham, MD: Rowman & Littlefield.

Carrière, Calvin. 1987. Personal interview with the author. Lawtell, Louisiana. October 19.

Carrière, Valentine. 1987. Personal interview with the author. Lawtell, Louisiana. October 19.

Carter, Regina. 2011. Personal interview with the author. San Francisco, California. March 21.

Carter, Tom. 1980. Record review. R. P. Christeson, *Old-Time Fiddler's Repertory: Historic Field Recordings of Forty-One Traditional Tunes*. *Folklore Forum* 13(l): 64–66.

Casey, Michael. 1983. "Joe and Odell Thompson: Examples of the Black Fiddle and Banjo Tradition." Unpublished paper.

Cauthen, Joyce H. 1989a. *With Fiddle and Well-Rosined Bow: Old-Time Fiddling in Alabama*. Tuscaloosa and London: University of Alabama Press.

Cauthen, Joyce H. 1989b. ". . . And Bring Your Fiddle! The Fiddler in Alabama Community Life." *Alabama Heritage* 13: 3–21, summer.

Cauthen, Joyce H. 1989c. "A 'Peculiar Wiggling of the Bow': Old-time Fiddling in Alabama." In *Alabama Folklife: Collected Essays*, edited by Stephen H. Martin, 37–44. Tuscaloosa: University of Alabama Press.

Chadbourne, Eugene. n.d. "Ted Bogan: Biography." *AllMusic.com*. https://www.allmusic.com/artist/ted-bogan-mn0000028752/biography. Accessed November 7, 2022.

Chamberlain, Mary E. 1892. "Folk-Lore Scrap-Book: Negro Superstition Concerning the Violin." *Journal of American Folk-Lore* 5: 329–30, October-December.

Chambers, Ephraim. 1728. *Cyclopaedia*. London: James and John Knapton.

Chapman, Iris Thompson. 2011. Personal interview with the author. Midlothian, Virginia. March 8.

Charters, Samuel B. 1966. Liner notes. *The Great Jug Bands*. Origin Jazz Library OJL 4.

Charters, Samuel B. 1967. *The Bluesmen*. New York: Oak Publications.

Charters, Samuel B. 1975 [1959]. *The Country Blues*. New York: Da Capo Press.

Chatmon, Sam. 1978. "Sam Chatmon Interview." Interview with Alan Lomax. https://www.youtube.com/watch?v=96NwV6g-3PE&t=28s. Accessed April 22, 2020. Recorded by Alan Lomax, John Bishop, and Worth Long, August 1978, at Chatmon's home in Hollandale, Mississippi.

Chatmon, Sam. 2010. *Sam Chatmon, Mississippi Sheiks: The Complete 1980 Interview.* Jas Obrecht Music Archive.

Cherelus, Gina. 2020. "This Is How We Juneteenth." *New York Times,* June 18.

Chilton, John. 1979 [1978]. *Who's Who of Jazz: Storyville to Swing Street.* New York: Time-Life Records.

Christeson, Mike. 2009. "Robert Perry Christeson: 'Dean of Missouri Fiddle Music.'" *Old Settlers Gazette* (Old Stagecoach Stop Foundation, Waynesville, MO) 27: 42–49. http://oldstagecoach stop.org/webgeezer/Gazette09/pages%2042-49%20R.%20P.%20Christeson.pdf. Accessed September 15, 2019.

Christeson, R. P. [Robert Perry]. 1973. *The Old-Time Fiddler's Repertory,* vol. 1. Columbia: University of Missouri Press.

Christeson, R. P. [Robert Perry]. 1984. *The Old-Time Fiddler's Repertory,* vol. 2. Columbia: University of Missouri Press.

Christeson, R. P. [Robert Perry]. 1998. "A Tribute to William A. (Bill) Driver." *Missouri Folklore Society Journal* 20: 37–38.

Cimbala, Paul A. 1995. "Black Musicians from Slavery to Freedom: An Exploration of an African American Folk Elite and Cultural Continuity in the Nineteenth-Century Rural South." *Journal of Negro History* 80(1): 15–29, winter.

Claiborne, John Francis H. 1906. "A Trip Through the Piney Woods." *Mississippi Historical Society Publications* 9: 483–536.

Clay, Henry. 1937 [1996]. Interview with Ethel Wolfe Garrison. In *The WPA Oklahoma Slave Narratives,* edited by T. Lindsay Baker and Julie P. Baker, 79–86. Norman and London: University of Oklahoma Press.

Clinkscales, John George. 1969 [1916]. *On the Old Plantation: Reminisces of His Childhood.* New York: Negro Universities Press.

Coffey [Coffee], Shell. 1979. Personal interview with Bobby Fulcher. Monticello, Kentucky. March 24.

Cogdell, Jacqueline. 1972. "An Analytical Study of the Similarities and Differences in the American Black Spiritual and Gospel Song from the Southeast Region of Georgia." Master's thesis, University of California, Los Angeles.

Cogdell, Leslie C. 1998. Telephone conversation with the author, September 22.

Conway, Cecelia. 1990. "Hands Up Eight and Don't Be Late: The Frolic Music of Joe and Odell Thompson." *North Carolina Folklore Journal* 37(2): 73–80, summer-fall.

Conway, Cecelia. 1995. *African Banjo Echoes in Appalachia: A Study of Folk Traditions.* Knoxville: University of Tennessee Press.

Conway, Cecelia. 1998. Liner notes. *Black Banjo Songsters of North Carolina and Virginia.* Smithsonian Folkways SF CD 40079.

Cook, Irvin. 1976. Personal interview with Kip Lornell. October 10.

Coolen, Michael T. 1982. "The Fodet: A Senegambia Origin for the Blues." *Black Perspective in Music* 10(1): 69–84, spring.

Coolen, Michael T. 1984. "Senegambia Archetypes for the American Folk Banjo." *Western Folklore* 43(2): 177–32, April.

Coolen, Michael T. 1991. "Senegambia Influences on Afro-American Musical Culture." *Black Music Research Journal* 11(1): 1–18, spring.

Coppin, Levi Jenkins. 1919 [1968]. *Unwritten History.* New York: Negro Universities Press.

Corbin, David A. 1985. "Class over Caste: Interracial Solidarity in the Company Town." In *Blacks in Appalachia,* edited by William H. Turner and Edward J. Cabbell, 93–113. Lexington: University Press of Kentucky.

"Country Music: Crowder Gives Foundation His 'Paper' on Negroes' Influence." 1969. *Billboard* 81(16): 65, April 19. https://www.worldradiohistory.com/Archive-All-Music/Billboard/60s /1969/Billboard%201969-04-19.pdf. Accessed November 27, 2023.

Courlander, Harold. 1951–56. Liner notes. *Negro Folk Music of Alabama.* Folkways FE 4417.

Courlander, Harold. 1960. *Negro Songs from Alabama.* New York: Published on a grant by the Wenner Gren Foundation for Anthropological Research.

Courlander, Harold. 1963. *Negro Folk Music, USA*. New York: Columbia University Press.

Cox, Fred E. 1976. Liner notes. *Clifford Hayes and the Dixieland Jug Blowers*. Yazoo 1054.

Coxe, Elizabeth Allen. 1912. *Memories of a South Carolina Plantation during the War*. Privately printed.

Creecy, James R. 1860. *Scenes in the South and Other Miscellaneous Pieces*. Philadelphia: J. B. Lippincott.

Creel, Margaret Washington. 1988. *"A Peculiar People": Slave Religion and Community-Culture among the Gullahs*. New York: New York University Press.

Cresswell, Nicholas. 1924. *The Journal of Nicholas Cresswell, 1774–1777*. New York: Lincoln MacVeagh, Dial Press.

Crèvecoeur, Michel Guillaume Jean de. [J. Hector St. John, pseud.]. 1925. *Sketches of Eighteenth Century America: More "Letters from an American Farmer."* New Haven, CT: Yale University Press.

Crowder, Russelltaze. 1969. "The Influence of the Negro in Country, Hillbilly, and Allied Folk Music." Master's thesis, Tennessee State University.

Cuming, Fortescue. 1810. *Sketches of a Tour to the Western Country Through the States of Ohio and Kentucky: A Voyage Down the Ohio and Mississippi Rivers, and a Trip Through the Mississippi Territory, and Part of West Florida, Commenced at Philadelphia in the Winter of 1807, and Concluded in 1809*. Pittsburgh: Cramer, Spear, and Eichbaum.

Cureau, Rebecca T. 1989. "Kemper Harreld and Willis James: Music at Atlanta University, Morehouse College, and Spelman College." *Black Music Research Bulletin* 11(1): 5–7, spring.

Curtin, Philip D. 1969. *The Atlantic Slave Trade: A Census*. Madison: University of Wisconsin Press.

Curtin, Philip D. 1975. *Economic Change in Precolonial Africa: Senegambia in the Era of the Slave Trade*. Madison: University of Wisconsin Press.

"Cylinder Recording." 2023. *Encyclopaedia Britannica*. https://www.britannica.com/technology/cylinder-recording. Accessed July 14, 2023.

Danser, Kathleen A. 2018. "Strings Attached: Black Musicians in String-bands in the American South, 1920–1950." PhD dissertation, University of Alberta.

Davis, Charles Henry Stanley. 1870. *History of Wallingford, Connecticut, from Its Settlement in 1670 to the Present Time. . . .* Meriden, CT: Author.

Deaner, Larry Scott. 2004. "Home in the McDowell County Coalfields: The African American Population of Keystone, West Virginia." Master's thesis. Ohio University.

Dean-Smith, Margaret. 2001a. "Hornpipe." In *Grove Music Online*, January 20. https://doi.org/10.1093/gmo/9781561592630.article.13367. Accessed June 24, 2022.

Dean-Smith, Margaret. 2001b. "Jig." In *Grove Music Online*, January 20. https://doi.org/10.1093/gmo/9781561592630.article.14307. Accessed June 24, 2022.

de Barros, Philip. 2009. "How Far Inland Did the Arm of the Slave Trade Reach? An Overview of the Slave Trade in Togo." Excavating the Past: Archaeological Perspectives on Black Atlantic Regional Networks. Conference in Honor of UCLA Emeritus Professor Merrick Posnansky, April 3–4, 1–46. Unpublished manuscript.

DeVane, Dwight. 1979. "Fiddle-Playing Tradition in Afro-America." Term paper presented to Burt Feintuch, Western Kentucky University, December.

DeVane, Dwight. 1981. Liner notes. *Drop on Down in Florida: Recent Field Recordings of Afro-American Traditional Music*. White Springs: Florida Folklife Program.

DeVane, Dwight. 1987. Personal interview with the author. Polk City, Florida. August 10.

"The Development of Musical Recording." 2020. *Encyclopaedia Britannica*, October 9. https://www.britannica.com/topic/music-recording/The-development-of-musical-recording. Accessed August 6, 2023.

DeWitt, Mark F. 2020. "Zydeco." In *Grove Music Online*, July 30. https://www.oxfordmusiconline.com/grovemusic/view/10.1093/gmo/9781561592630.001.0001/omo-9781561592630-e-1002225932?print=pdf. Accessed September 9, 2021.

Dicaire, David. 1999. "Charley Patton (1891–1934): Pony Blues." In *Blues Singers: Biographies of 50 Legendary Artists of the Early 20th Century*. Jefferson, NC, and London: McFarland, 6–10.

Dickens, Charles. 1842. *American Notes for the General Circulation*. Volume 1. London: Chapman and Hall.

Dickens, Charles. 1913. *American Notes for General Circulation and Pictures from Italy*. London: Chapman and Hall, Ltd. Online edition [Chapter VI, New York, 67]. http://www.gutenberg.org/files/675/675-h/675-h.htm#page67. Accessed May 16, 2014.

Dickey, James H. 1835. "How Slavery Honors Our Country's Flag: From Rankin's Letters." Visual image. *The Anti-Slavery Record* 1(2): 13, February.

Diderot, Denis, ed. 1751–1765. *Encyclopédie, ou Dictionnaire Raisonné des Sciences, des Arts et des Métiers*. Paris: Briasson.

Diouf, Sylviane A. 1998. *Servants of Allah: African Muslims Enslaved in the Americas*. New York: New York University Press.

Discography of American Historical Recordings. 2008–2024. Santa Barbara: University of California Santa Barbara Library. https://adp.library.ucsb.edu/index.php. Accessed September 7, 2024.

Dixon, Robert M. W., and John Godrich. 1982. *Blues and Gospel Records, 1902–1943*. 3rd ed. Chigwell, UK: Storyville Publications.

Dixon, Robert M. W., John Godrich, and Howard Rye. 1997. *Blues and Gospel Records, 1890–1943*. 4th ed. Oxford: Clarendon Press.

DjeDje, Jacqueline Cogdell. 1978a. "The One String Fiddle in West Africa: A Comparison of Hausa and Dagomba Traditions." PhD dissertation, University of California, Los Angeles.

DjeDje, Jacqueline Cogdell. 1978b. Liner notes. *Music of the Dagomba from Ghana*. Recorded and produced by Verna Gillis with David Moises Perez Martinez. Ethnic Folkways Records 4324.

DjeDje, Jacqueline Cogdell. 1978c. *American Black Spiritual and Gospel Songs from Southeast Georgia: A Comparative Study*. Los Angeles: Center for Afro-American Studies, University of California.

DjeDje, Jacqueline Cogdell. 1980. *Distribution of the One String Fiddle in West Africa*. Los Angeles: UCLA Program in Ethnomusicology, Department of Music.

DjeDje, Jacqueline Cogdell. 1982. "The Concept of Patronage: An Examination of Hausa and Dagomba One String Fiddle Traditions." *Journal of African Studies* 9(3, fall):116–27.

DjeDje, Jacqueline Cogdell. 1983. *Black American Religious Music from Southeast Georgia*. Folkways Record FS 34010.

DjeDje, Jacqueline Cogdell. 1984. "The Interplay of Melodic Phrases: An Analysis of Hausa and Dagomba One String Fiddle Music." In *Selected Reports in Ethnomusicology*, edited by J. H. Kwabena Nketia and Jacqueline Cogdell DjeDje. Los Angeles: UCLA Program in Ethnomusicology, Department of Music, 5:81–118.

DjeDje, Jacqueline Cogdell. 1992. "Music and History: An Analysis of Hausa and Dagbamba Fiddle Traditions." In *African Musicology: Current Trends. Vol. 2. A Festschrift Presented to J.H. Kwabena Nketia*, edited by Jacqueline Cogdell DjeDje. Los Angeles and Atlanta: UCLA International Studies and Overseas Program (ISOP)/James S. Coleman African Studies Center and African Studies Association Press, 151–79.

DjeDje, Jacqueline Cogdell. 1998a. "African American Music to 1900." In *The Cambridge History of American Music*, edited by David Nicholls, 103–34, 577–80. Cambridge: Cambridge University Press.

DjeDje, Jacqueline Cogdell. 1998b. "West Africa: An Introduction." In *Africa: The Garland Encyclopedia of World Music, Volume 1*, edited by Ruth M. Stone, 442–70. New York and London: Garland.

DjeDje, Jacqueline Cogdell. 1999. "The Fulbe Fiddle in The Gambia: A Symbol of Ethnic Identity." In *Turn Up the Volume! A Celebration of African Music*, edited by Jacqueline Cogdell DjeDje, 98–113. Los Angeles: UCLA Fowler Museum of Cultural History.

DjeDje, Jacqueline Cogdell. 2007. *Fiddling in West Africa (1950s–1990s): The CD Recording*. Los Angeles: UCLA Ethnomusicology Publications.

DjeDje, Jacqueline Cogdell. 2008a. *Fiddling in West Africa: Touching the Spirit in Fulbe, Hausa, and Dagbamba Cultures*. Bloomington: Indiana University Press.

DjeDje, Jacqueline Cogdell. 2008b. *Fiddling in West Africa (1950s–1990s): The Songbook*. Los Angeles: UCLA Ethnomusicology Publications.

DjeDje, Jacqueline Cogdell. 2010. "The Fiddle in West African and African-American Cultures . . . The Devil's Instrument?" Invited lecture presented at the Institute for Signifying Scriptures, School of Religion, Claremont Graduate University. Claremont, California, October 7.

DjeDje, Jacqueline Cogdell. 2016. "The (Mis)Representation of African American Music: The Role of the Fiddle." *Journal of the Society for American Music* 10(1): 1–32, February.

DjeDje, Jacqueline Cogdell. 2020. "Appalachian Black Fiddling: History and Creativity." *African Music: Journal of the International Library of African Music* 11(2): 77–101.

DjeDje, Jacqueline Cogdell. 2024. "African Music in the Global African Diaspora." In *Oxford Research Encyclopedia of African History*. Oxford University Press, May 22. https://doi.org/10.1093/acrefore/9780190277734.013.924. Accessed September 14, 2024.

DjeDje, Jacqueline Cogdell. n.d. "Salisu Mahama: A Fiddler's Role in the Cultural Development of Modern Dagbon." Unpublished manuscript.

DjeDje, Jacqueline Cogdell, and Eddie S. Meadows. 1998. "Introduction." In *California Soul: Music of African Americans in the West*, edited by Jacqueline Cogdell DjeDje and Eddie S. Meadows, 1–19. Berkeley: University of California Press.

Dole, Gerard. 1978. Liner notes. *Louisiana Creole Music*. Folkways Records FA 2622.

Dormon, James H. 1988. "Shaping the Popular Image of Post-Reconstruction American Blacks: The 'Coon Song' Phenomenon of the Gilded Age." *American Quarterly* 40(4): 450–71, December.

Doucet, Sharon Arms. 1995. "'If You Remember My Song, You'll Remember Me': An Interview with Canray Fontenot." *Fiddler Magazine* 2(3): 14–20.

Drago, Edmund L. 1998. *Hurrah for Hampton! Black Red Shirts in South Carolina during Reconstruction*. Fayetteville: University of Arkansas Press.

Dresser, Amos. 1836. "How Slavery Honors Our Country's Flag." Wood engraving. In *The Narrative of Amos Dresser*. New York: American Anti-Slavery Tract Society.

Dunaway, Wilma A. 2003a. *Slavery in the American Mountain South*. Cambridge: Cambridge University Press.

Dunaway, Wilma A. 2003b. *Slavery and Emancipation in the American Mountain South: Evidence, Sources, and Methods*. Virginia Tech, Online Archives. http://scholar.lib.vt.edu/vtpubs/mountain_slavery/where.htm. Accessed June 22, 2014.

Durman, Chris. 2008. "African American Old-Time String Band Music: A Selective Discography." *Notes* 64(4): 797–810.

Duvelle, Charles. 1961. Liner notes. *Musique Bisa de Haute-Volta*. Ocora OCR 58.

Elliott, J. Gary. 1992. "The Partnership of Amédé Ardoin and Dennis McGee: Folk Music and Cultural Determination in Southwestern Louisiana." Master's thesis, University of Southwestern Louisiana.

Ellis, Edward Robb. 1966. *The Epic of New York City: A Narrative History*. New York: Old Town Books.

Eltis, David. 2001. "The Volume and Structure of the Transatlantic Slave Trade: A Reassessment." *William and Mary Quarterly* Third Series 58(1): 17–46, January.

Eltis, David, and David Richardson. 2002. "The Achievements of the 'Numbers Game.'" In The Atlantic Slave Trade. 2nd ed., edited by David Northrup, 95. Boston: Houghton Mifflin.

Eltis, David, and David Richardson. 2010. *Atlas of the Transatlantic Slave Trade*. New Haven, CT: Yale University Press.

Emery, Lynne Fauley. 1972. *Black Dance in the United States from 1619 to 1970*. Palo Alto, CA: National Press Books.

Epstein, Dena. 1973. "African Music in British and French America." *Musical Quarterly* 59: 61–91.

Epstein, Dena. 1975. "The Folk Banjo: A Documentary History." *Ethnomusicology* 19(3): 347–71, September.

Epstein, Dena. 1977. *Sinful Tunes and Spirituals: Black Folk Music to the Civil War.* Urbana: University of Illinois Press.

Erlewine, Stephen Thomas. 2021. "Michael Doucet." *AllMusic.com*, January 5. https://www.allmusic.com/artist/michael-doucet-mn0000886101/biography. Accessed October 6, 2021.

Erlmann, Veit. 1986. *Music and the Islamic Reform in the Early Sokoto Empire: Sources, Ideology, Effects.* Stuttgart: Kommissionsverlag F. Steiner Wiesbaden.

Evans, David. 1977a [1961]. Liner notes. *The Immortal Charlie Patton, No. 1 (1929–32).* Origin Jazz Library OJL 1.

Evans, David. 1977b [1964]. Liner notes. *The Immortal Charlie Patton, No. 1.* Origin Jazz Library OJL 7.

Evans, David. 1978a. Liner notes. *Afro-American Folk Music from Tate and Panola Counties, Mississippi.* Library of Congress AFS L67.

Evans, David. 1978b. Liner notes. *Let's Get Loose: Folk and Popular Blues Styles from the Beginnings to the Early 1940s.* New World Records NW 290.

Evans, David. 1982. *Big Road Blues: Tradition and Creativity in the Folk Blues.* Berkeley: University of California Press.

Evans, David. 1994. "The Music of Eli Owens: African Music in Transition in Southern Mississippi." In *For Gerhard Kubik: Festschrift on the Occasion of His 60th Birthday*, edited by August Schmidhofer and Dietrich Schüller, 329–59. Berlin: Peter Lang.

Evans, David. 1999a. Liner notes. *Deep River of Song. Mississippi: Saints and Sinners from before Blues and Gospel.* Alan Lomax Collection. Rounder 1824.

Evans, David. 1999b. Liner notes. *Deep River of Song. Mississippi: The Blues Lineage. Musical Geniuses of the Fields, Levees, and Jukes.* Alan Lomax Collection. Rounder 1825.

Evans, David. 2018a. "Charley Patton: The Conscience of the Delta." In *Charley Patton: Voice of the Mississippi Delta*, edited by Robert Sacré and William Ferris, 23–138. Jackson: University Press of Mississippi.

Evans, David. 2018b. "Mississippi Blues Today and Its Future." In *Charley Patton: Voice of the Mississippi Delta*, edited by Robert Sacré and William Ferris, 207–20. Jackson: University Press of Mississippi.

Evans, David. 2021. "Herb Quinn." In *Fiddle Tunes from Mississippi: Commercial and Informal Recordings, 1920–2018*, by Harry Bolick and Tony Russell, 524–33. Jackson: University Press of Mississippi.

Evans, Murphy. 1984. "He's a Fiddlin' Man." *The Anniston [Alabama] Star.* September 30, 1C and 2C. Photos by Ken Elkins.

Everett, Matthew. 2016. "The Knoxville Sessions: An Introduction to the St. James Hotel Recordings of 1929–30." *Knoxville Mercury.* An archive brought to you by Knoxville History Project. May 4, 2016. https://www.knoxmercury.com/2016/05/04/knoxville-sessions-introduction-st-james-hotel-recordings-1929-30/. Accessed September 15, 2023.

Fancourt, Les, and Bob McGrath, compilers and producers. 2006. *The Blues Discography 1943–1970.* West Vancouver: Eyeball Productions.

Farmelo, Allen. 2001. "Another History of Bluegrass: The Segregation of Popular Music in the United States, 1820–1900." *Popular Music and Society* 25 (1–2): 179–203.

Farmer, Henry George. 1929. *A History of Arabian Music to the XIIIth Century.* London: Luzac and Co.

Federal Writers' Project. 1941. *Slave Narratives: A Folk History of Slavery in the United States from Interviews with Former Slaves.* 17 volumes. Washington: Federal Writers' Project.

"Fee Memorial Institute Notes." 1928. *Lexington [Kentucky] Herald.* Sunday, May 6, 2.

Feintuch, Burt. 1983. "The Fiddle in the United States: An Historical Overview." *Kentucky Folklore Record* 39(1): 30–38, January.

Feintuch, Burt. 2022. *Creole Soul: Zydeco Lives.* Jackson: University Press of Mississippi.

Feld, David. 1998. "A Conversation with the Erstwhile Minstrel Singer Howard Armstrong." *Blues Access* 35, Fall. https://bluesmandolin.wordpress.com/2015/03/16/howard-armstrong-blues-access-no-35-fall-1998/. Accessed September 10, 2015.

Ferre, Lux. 2017. "Moose (Loyal Order of Moose)." *Occult World*, July 30.

Ferris, William. 2018. *Voices of Mississippi: Artists and Musicians Documented by William Ferris.* Atlanta: Dust-to-Digital. Disc 1: Blues.

"Fiddler Joe Thompson Dies at 93: Was Master of African-American Country Music Style." 2012. *Variety.* Posted February 21.

Field Trip South: Exploring the Southern Folklife Collection. 2012. "In Tribute to Joe Thompson: 1918–2012." University of North Carolina Southern Folklife Collection. Posted February 23. http://www.lib.unc.edu/blogs/sfc/index.php/2012/02/23/in-tribute-to-joe-thompson-1918-2012/. Accessed March 4, 2012.

Fithian, Philip Vickers. 1957. *Journal and Letters of Philip Vickers Fithian, 1773–1774: A Plantation Tutor of the Old Dominion*, edited, with an introduction by Hunter Dickinson Farish. Charlottesville: University Press of Virginia.

Flemons, Dominique "Dom." 2011a. Personal interview with the author. Charlottesville, Virginia. February 25.

Flemons, Dominique "Dom." 2011b. Personal interview with the author. Philadelphia, Pennsylvania. March 3.

Flemons, Dominique "Dom." 2011c. "'Po' Black Sheep/Gwine Dig a Hole.'" *Folk Life Center News* 33(1–2): 12–13, winter/spring.

Flemons, Dominique "Dom." 2012. "Carolina Chocolate Drops Mentor, Joe Thompson, Passes Away." Music Maker Relief Foundation Newsletter. February 23. http://www.bmansbluesreport.com/2012/02/carolina-chocolate-drops-mentor-joe.html. Accessed October 19, 2017.

Flemons, Dominique "Dom." 2015. "'Po' Black Sheep': My Introduction to Black String Bands." *Ecotone Magazine: Reimagining Place* 20. https://ecotonemagazine.org/one-track-mind/po-black-sheep-my-introduction-to-black-string-bands/. Accessed June 16, 2017

Flint, Timothy. 1826. *Recollections of the Last Ten Years, Passed in Occasional Residences and Journeyings in the Valley of the Mississippi, from Pittsburg and the Missouri to the Gulf of Mexico, and from Florida to the Spanish Frontier.* Boston: Cummings, Hilliard, and Company.

"A Florida Jug Band." 1904–1905. *Wide World Magazine* 14, October-March, 414.

Floyd Jr., Samuel. 2002. "Ring Shout! Literary Studies, Historical Studies, and Black Music Inquiry." *Black Music Research Journal* 22: 49–70.

"Folklorist, Writer, and Activist Stetson Kennedy Dies at 94." 2011. *Folklife Center News* 33(3–4): 10–11, summer/fall.

Fontenot, Canray. 1988. Personal interview with the author. Welsh, Louisiana. August 15.

Fortieth Anniversary Collection, 1960–2000: The Journey of *Chris* Strachwitz. 2000. Liner notes. El Cerrito, CA: Arhoolie Records.

"Fort Valley State College Music Festival Announcement." 1940. *Atlanta Constitution.* April 6, 17.

"Fort Valley State University." 2012. *The New Georgia Encyclopedia.* https://web.archive.org/web/20121011185622/http://www.georgiaencyclopedia.org/nge/Article.jsp?id=h-1424. Accessed September 15, 2022.

Foster, Dan. 2020. "Teodar Jackson and African-American Fiddling from Texas: Lost Music from the Rural." *The Old-Time Herald: A Magazine Dedicated to Old-Time Music* 15(1), October 10.

Foster, George G. 1848. "Philadelphia in Slices: Slice IV, Dandy Hall." *New-York Tribune* 8(190): 1, November 17.

Foster, George G. 1850. *New York by Gas-Light: With Here and There a Streak of Sunshine.* New York: Dewitt and Davenport.

Foster, Pamela E. 1998. *My Country: The African Diaspora's County Music Heritage.* Nashville: My Country.

Fowler, William Chauncey. 1872. *Local Law in Massachusetts and Connecticut, Historically Considered.* Albany: Joel Munsell.

Franklin, John Hope. 1980. *From Slavery to Freedom: A History of Negro Americans,* 5th ed. New York: Knopf.

Franklin, John Hope, and Alfred A. Moss Jr. 1994. *From Slavery to Freedom: A History of African Americans,* 7th ed. New York: McGraw-Hill.

Friedwald, Herb. 1961. Liner notes. *New Orleans. The Living Legends. Peter Bocage with His Creole Serenaders with the Love-Jiles Ragtime Orchestra*. Riverside RLP 379 or RLP 9379.

Friskics-Warren, Bill. 2007. "Adding Notes to a Folklorist's Tunes." Review of *Recording Black Culture*. *New York Times*, December 2.

Fry, Robbie. 2019. "'Big Bill' Broonzy." In *CALS Encyclopedia of Arkansas*, April 23. https://encyclopediaofarkansas.net/entries/big-bill-broonzy-2489/. Accessed February 8, 2021.

Fryer, Peter. 1998. "The 'Discovery' and Appropriation of African Music and Dance." *Race and Class* 39(3): 1–20, January.

Fulcher, Bobby J. 1987. "Cuje Bertram: Excerpts from an Interview." *Tennessee Folklore Society Bulletin* 53(2): 58–70, summer.

Fulcher, Bobby J. 1988a. Liner notes. *Gettin' Up the Stairs: Traditional Music from the Cumberland Plateau*. County Records C-786.

Fulcher, Bobby J. 1988b. Liner notes. *Five Miles Out of Town: Traditional Music from the Cumberland Plateau, Volume 2*. County Records C-787.

Fulmer, Douglas. 1995. "String Band Traditions." *American Visions* 10(2): 46, April-May.

Gadaya. 2010. "32 'Georgia Stomp' by Andrew and Jim Baxter: Andrew and Jim Baxter's World." My Old Weird America: An Exploration of Harry Smith's Anthology of American Folk Music. Blog, January 22. https://oldweirdamerica.wordpress.com/2010/01/22/32-georgia-stomp-by-andrew-jim-baxter/. Accessed April 24, 2018.

Gaddy, Kristina R. 2020. "William Adams and the Sounds of KenGar." June 16. https://www.kristinagaddy.com/blog/william-adams-kengar Accessed December 11, 2023.

Garnier III, D'Jamal. 2007. "The Musical and Cultural Roots of Louisiana Black Creole and Zydeco Fiddle Tradition." *Routes to Roots* 2.

Garnier III, D'Jamal. 2009 [2007]. "The Musical and Cultural Roots of Louisiana Creole and Zydeco Fiddle Tradition." *Folklife in Louisiana: Louisiana's Living Traditions*. Originally published in *Routes to Roots*, Volume 2 in 2007. http://www.louisianafolklife.org/LT/Articles_Essays/creoleroots.html. Accessed December 25, 2014.

Garnier III, D'Jamal. 2012. "The Genesis of Zydeco and Black Creole Music." *Kreol International Magazine*, October 20.

Garnier III, D'Jamal. 2015. "The Musical and Cultural Roots of Louisiana Creole and Zydeco Fiddle Tradition through Canray Fontenot." *Louisiana Folklore Miscellany* 25: 8–21. http://www.louisianafolklife.org/LT/Articles_Essays/creoleroots.html Accessed May 30, 2021.

Garnier III, D'Jamal, and Robert Wiley. 2010. *Louisiana Creole Fiddle Method: The Music and Technique for Fiddlers and Guitarists*. Pacific, MO: Mel Bay Publications.

Gibson, George R. 2018. "Black Banjo, Fiddle, and Dance in Kentucky and the Amalgamation of African American and Anglo-American Folk Music." In *Banjo Roots and Branches*, edited by Robert Winans, 223–55. Urbana: University of Illinois Press.

Giddens, Rhiannon. 2011a. Personal interview with the author. Charlottesville, Virginia. February 25.

Giddens, Rhiannon. 2011b. Personal interview with the author. Philadelphia, Pennsylvania. March 3.

Gifford, Paul M. 2010. "Henry Ford's Dance Revival and Fiddle Contests: Myth and Reality." *Journal of the Society for American Music* 4(3): 307–38.

Gilman, Caroline Howard. 1838. *Recollections of a Southern Matron*. New York: Harper and Brothers.

Ginell, Richard S. n.d. "Jean-Luc Ponty Biography." *AllMusic.com*. https://www.allmusic.com/artist/jean-luc-ponty-mn0000228299/biography. Accessed December 11, 2022.

Givens, Bill. 1982. Liner notes. *Peg Leg Powell and His Gang, 1927–1930*. Origin Jazz Library OJL 22.

Goertzen, Chris. 1993. Review of *Now That's a Good Tune: Masters of Traditional Missouri Fiddling* by Howard Wight Marshall, Amy E. Skillman, Charles Walden, C. Ray Brassieur, Spencer Galloway, and Julie Youmans. *Ethnomusicology* 37(3): 467–69, Autumn.

Goertzen, Chris. 2008. *Southern Fiddlers and Fiddle Contests*. Jackson: University Press of Mississippi.

Goertzen, Chris. 2020. *American Antebellum Fiddling*. Jackson: University Press of Mississippi.

Gomez, Michael A. 1998. *Exchanging Our Country Marks: The Transformation of African Identities in the Colonial and Antebellum South, 1526–1830*. Chapel Hill: University of North Carolina Press.

Gordon, Robert, and Bruce Nemerov, eds. 2005. *Lost Delta Found: Rediscovering the Fisk University-Library of Congress Coahoma County Study, 1941–1942* by John W. Work III, Lewis Wade Jones, and Samuel C. Adams Jr. Nashville: Vanderbilt University Press.

Govenar, Alan. 1985. *Living Texas Blues*. Dallas: Dallas Museum of Art.

Govenar, Alan B., and Jay F. Brakefield. 1998. *Deep Ellum and Central Track: Where the Black and White Worlds of Dallas Converged*. Denton, TX: University of North Texas Press.

Govenar, Alan B., and Kip Lornell. 2019. *The Blues Come to Texas: Paul Oliver and Mack McCormick's Unfinished Book*. College Station: Texas A&M University Press.

Graham, Sandra Jean. 2013. "Jubilee Singers [Fisk Jubilee Singers]." In *Grove Music Online*. https://doi.org/10.1093/gmo/9781561592630.article.A2249936. Accessed April 19, 2023.

"Great Migration." 2024. *Encyclopaedia Britannica*, August 19. https://www.britannica.com/print/article/973069. Accessed September 23, 2024.

Green, Archie. 1971. "A Discography/Biography Journey: The Martin-Roberts-Martin 'Aggregation.'" *Western Folklore* 30(3): 194–201, July.

Greene, Lorenzo Johnston. 1942 [1966]. *The Negro in Colonial New England 1620–1776*. New York: Columbia University Press.

Greer, Walter, and Robert Cogswell. 1975. *Walter Greer: African American Fiddler*. Nashville: Center for Popular Music, Middle Tennessee State University.

Greer, Walter, and Robert Cogswell. 2022. *Uncovering the Voice of Walter Greer: The 1975 Nashville Recording*. Spring Fed Records SFR 120. Interview conducted by Robert Cogswell. Liner notes and reissue production by Tiffany Minton. Audio engineering by Martin Fisher. https://www.youtube.com/watch?v=x0OkGw8110E&t=9s. Accessed September 11, 2023.

". . . A Groundhog Is Good Eatin.'" 1986. *Courier-Journal*. February 2, 380.

"A Guide to Song Forms—AAB Song Form." 2000–2022. Songstuff. https://www.songstuff.com/songwriting/article/aab-song-form/. Accessed November 23, 2022.

Gurda, John. 1999 [2018]. *The Making of Milwaukee*. Milwaukee: Milwaukee County Historical Society.

Gussow, Adam. 2010a. "Ain't No Burnin' Hell: Southern Religion and the Devil's Music." *Arkansas Review: A Journal of Delta Studies* 41(2): 83–98, Summer/August.

Gussow, Adam. 2010b. "Heaven and Hell Parties: Ministers, Bluesmen, and Black Youth in the Mississippi Delta, 1920–1942." *Arkansas Review: A Journal of Delta Studies* 41(3): 186–203, December.

Hake, Peggy Smith. 2007a [1985, 2005]. "Though Sparse Here Today, Negroes Helped Settle Area." Biographical Sketches: Biographies from Black Families of Miller County. Miller Historical Society. 1–3. http://www.millercountymuseum.org/bios/bio_black.html. Accessed September 15, 2019.

Hake, Peggy Smith. 2007b. "William Driver, Sr. and His Son, William 'Bill' Driver, Jr." 2007. Biographical Sketches: Biographies from Black Families of Miller County. Miller Historical Society. 7–9. http://www.millercountymuseum.org/bios/bio_black.html. Accessed September 15, 2019.

Hale, John P. 1886. *Trans-Allegheny pioneers: Historical sketches of the first white settlements west of the Alleghenies, 1748 and after, wonderful experiences of hardship and heroism of those who first braved the dangers of the inhospitable wilderness, and the savage tribes that then inhabited it*. Cincinnati: Graphic Press.

Hall, Bob. 2006. "Vicksburg Blues." In *Encyclopedia of the Blues*, edited by Edward Komara. New York City: Routledge.

Halpert, Herbert. 1995. "The Devil, the Fiddle, and Dancing." In *Fields of Folklore: Essays in Honor of Kenneth S. Goldstein*, edited by Roger D. Abrahams, 44–54. Bloomington: Trickster Press.

Hanchett, Tom. 1985. "Recording in Charlotte 1926–1945." History South. https://www.historysouth.org/recordingclthanchett/. Accessed January 17, 2022.

Hanchett, Tom. 2014. Liner notes. *Charlotte Blues*. Nehi Records [Frog Records] CD NEH06. History South. https://www.historysouth.org/charlotte-blues/. Accessed January 17, 2022.

Handy, William Christopher. 1941. *Father of the Blues: An Autobiography*. New York: Macmillan, Da Capo.

Hanna, Judith Lynne. 1974. Book review. *Black Dance in the United States from 1619 to 1970* by Lynne Fauley Emery. *Ethnomusicology* 18(1): 155–57, January.

Hannah-Jones, Nikole, Caitlin Roper, Ilena Silver, and Jake Silverstein, eds. 2021. *The 1619 Project*. New York: One World.

Harlow, John. 2021. "Marilyn Raphael on Climate and Justice." *UCLA Magazine*, November 16. https://newsroom.ucla.edu/magazine/marilyn-raphael-geography-climate-justice-sustainability?utm_source=january-issue-email2&utm_medium=email&utm_content=marilyn-raphael&utm_campaign=ucla-magazine-newsletter-2022. Accessed January 24, 2022.

Harold, Ellen, and Don Fleming. n.d. "Huddie Ledbetter (Lead Belly)." Association for Cultural Equity. https://www.culturalequity.org/alan-lomax/friends/ledbetter. Accessed November 22, 2022.

Harris, Craig. 1995. "Biography: Canray Fontenot." *AllMusic.com*, July 29. https://www.allmusic.com/artist/canray-fontenot-mn0000946810/biography. Accessed October 1, 2021.

Harris, Joel Chandler. 1881. *Uncle Remus, or, Mr. Fox, Mr. Rabbit, and Mr. Terrapin*. London and New York: G. Routledge and Sons.

Harris, Michael W. 1992a. "Conflict and Resolution in the Life of Thomas Andrew Dorsey." In *We'll Understand It Better By and By*, edited by Bernice Johnson Reagon, 165–82. Washington: Smithsonian Institution Press.

Harris, Michael W. 1992b. *The Rise of Gospel Blues: The Music of Thomas Andrew Dorsey in the Urban Church*. New York: Oxford University Press.

Harris, Paul. 2002. "The Carrière Brothers." *Juke Box* 50: 26–28.

Harris, Paul. 2008. "Canray Fontenot: The Greatest Black Louisiana French Fiddler of Our Time." *Juke Box* 65: 22–26, spring.

Harrison, Daphne Duval. 1993. *Blues Queens of the 1920s: Black Pearls*. New Brunswick, NJ: Rutgers University Press.

Harrod, John. 1987. Personal interview with the author. Owenton, Kentucky. August 6.

Harrod, John. 1997. Liner notes. *Traditional Fiddle Music of Kentucky: Along the Kentucky River, Volume 2*. Rounder CD 0377.

Harrod, John. 2002. Personal communication with the author. January 10.

Harrower, John. 1963. *The Journal of John Harrower: An Indentured Servant in the Colony of Virginia, 1773–1776*, edited by Edward Miles Riley. Williamsburg, VA: Colonial Williamsburg.

Hay, Fred J. 2001. *Goin' Back to Sweet Memphis: Conversations with the Blues*. Athens and London: University of Georgia Press.

Hay, Fred J. 2003. "Black Musicians in Appalachia: An Introduction." *Black Music Research Journal* 23(1/2): 1–19, spring/autumn.

Hazeldine, Mike. 2003. "Original Creole Band [Original Creole Orchestra]." In *Oxford Music Online*. https://doi.org/10.1093/gmo/9781561592630.article.J339200. Accessed August 8, 2022.

Hazzard-Gordon, Katrina. 1990. *Jookin': The Rise of Social Dance Formations in African-American Culture*. Philadelphia: Temple University Press.

Henry, Linda L. 2018a. "'Some Real American Music': John Lusk and His Rural Black String Band." Master's project, American Studies, University of Massachusetts, Boston.

Henry, Linda L. 2018b. "'Some Real American Music': The Gribble, Lusk, and York Black String Band of Warren County." Presentation at the Tennessee Folklore Society. https://www.youtube.com/watch?v=X5sWa9t2BiM. Accessed July 21, 2022.

Henry, Linda L. 2020. "The Saturday Fish Fry and Square Dance in Dogtown." June. GribbleLuskandYork.org. Accessed May 21, 2024.

Henry, Linda L. 2024. "'Some Real American Music': John Lusk and His Rural Black String Band." GribbleLuskandYork.org. Accessed May 21, 2024.

"Henry 'Son' Simms." n.d. *All About Blues Music*. https://www.allaboutbluesmusic.com/henry-son-simms/. Accessed January 4, 2021.

Herbemont, N. 1836. "On the Moral Discipline and Treatment of Slaves—Read before the Society for the Advancement of Education, at Columbia." *Southern Agriculturist and Register of Rural Affairs* 9(2): 70–75, February.

Higginson, Thomas Wentworth. 1870. *Army Life in a Black Regiment*. Boston: Fields, Osgood.

Hildreth, Richard. 1836. *The Slave: or Memoirs of Archy Moore. Volume 1*. Boston: John H. Eastburn.

Hildebrand, Lee. 1998. "Oakland Blues." In *California Soul: Music of African Americans in the West*, edited by Jacqueline Cogdell DjeDje and Eddie S. Meadows, 104–12. Berkeley: University of California Press.

Himmelman, Isaac. 2019. "Why Is Country Music Considered So White?" HuffPost Entertainment, July 17. https://www.huffpost.com/entry/country-music-black-artists_n_5d2de760e4b085eda5a25516?ncid=newsltushpmgnews__TheMorningEmail__071819. Accessed July 18, 2019.

Hinson, Glenn. 1978. Liner notes. *Eight-Hand Sets and Holy Steps: Traditional Black Music of North Carolina*. North Carolina Department of Cultural Resources. Crossroad C-101.

"Historically Black: The Black Fiddler Who Charmed Missouri." 2016. A podcast published by APM [American Public Media] Reports and the *Washington Post*, October 10.

"History of the Boll Weevil in the United States." n.d. Mississippi Boll Weevil Management Corporation. http://bollweevil.ext.msstate.edu/history.html#. Accessed November 12, 2022.

Hobbs, Margaret. 2018. "Lost History: Effort Underway to Preserve Memory of John Martin Lusk." *Southern Standard*. McMinnville, Tennessee, March 21, 3C.

Hoffheimer, Michael H. 2002. "Playing the Blues." *Strad* 113(1351): 1184–188, November.

Hoffman, Frank. 2004. *The Encyclopedia of Recorded Sound*. New York: Taylor and Francis.

Holden, Stephen. 1989. "The Pop Life: Folk-Violin Masters." *New York Times*, March 8, C16.

Holland, Annie Jefferson. 1892. *Refugees: A Sequel to Uncle Tom's Cabin*. Reprint edition. Austin, TX: Published for the Author. Charleston, SC: BiblioLife Publishers, 2009.

Holtzberg-Call, Maggie. 1989. "The Gandy Dancer Speaks: Voices from Southern Black Railroad Gangs." In *Alabama Folklife: Collected Essays*, edited by Stephen H. Martin, 64–71. Tuscaloosa: University of Alabama Press.

"The Hoodoo of Black Cat Bone." 2012. KUNC Community Radio for Northern Colorado, October 13. https://www.kunc.org/music/2012-10-13/the-hoodoo-of-black-cat-bone. Accessed July 23, 2021.

Hornbeck, Richard, and Suresh Naidu. 2014. "When the Levee Breaks: Black Migration and Economic Development in the American South." *American Economic Review* 104(3): 963–90.

Horne, David L. 2017. "Practical Politics: The Politics of Never Downplaying Black Folk." *Our Weekly* 13(30): 6, July 27–August 2.

Huber, Patrick. 2013. "Black Hillbillies: African American Musicians on Old-Time Records, 1924–1932." In *Hidden in the Mix: The African American Presence in Country Music*, edited by Diane Pecknold, 19–81. Durham, NC: Duke University Press.

Hulan, Richard. 1969. "Fiddling among the Slaves in Louisiana." *Devil's Box* 8: 14, July.

Hull, Edith Maude. 1919. *The Sheik: A Novel*. London: Eveleigh Nash.

Hundley, Daniel R. 1860 [1979]. *Social Relations in Our Southern States*. Baton Rouge and London: Louisiana State University.

Hunter, Robert. 1943. *Quebec to Carolina in 1786–1786: Being the Travel Diary and Observations of Robert Hunter Jr*. Edited by Louis B. Wright and Marion Tinling. San Marion, CA: Huntington Library.

Hurley, F. Jack, and David Evans. 1981. "Bukka White." In *Tom Ashley. Sam McGee. Bukka White: Tennessee Traditional Singers*, edited by Thomas G. Burton, 143–203. Knoxville: University of Tennessee Press.

Hurston, Zora Neale. 1994. "Characteristics of Negro Expression." In *Within the Circle: An Anthology of African American Literary Criticism from the Harlem Renaissance to the Present*, edited by Angelyn Mitchell. Durham, NC: Duke University Press.

Hutchinson, John, and Anthony D. Smith. 1996. "Introduction." In *Ethnicity*, 3–16. Oxford and New York: Oxford University Press.

Ingersoll, Ernest. 1879. "The City of Atlanta." *Harper's New Monthly Magazine* 60: 30–43, December.

"In Memoriam." 1874. *The Anderson Intelligencer* (Anderson Court House, SC), January 8. *Chronicling America: Historic American Newspapers*. Library of Congress. https://chroniclingamerica.loc.gov/lccn/sn84026965/1874-01-08/ed-1/seq-2/. Accessed June 11, 2022.

Irving, Washington. 1891. *Knickerbocker's History of New York*. London: Cassell.

Jabbour, Alan. 1966a. Notes. Alan Jabbour, and Henry Reed. *Forked Deer*. Retrieved from Library of Congress. https://www.loc.gov/item/afcreed000131/. Accessed May 12, 2017.

Jabbour, Alan. 1966b. Notes. Alan Jabbour, and Henry Reed. *Old Joe Clark*. Retrieved from Library of Congress, https://www.loc.gov/item/afcreed000130/. Accessed October 09, 2017.

Jabbour, Alan. 1985. "Fiddle Tunes of the Old Frontier: In Search of a Better Historical Model." Unpublished paper.

Jabbour, Alan. 1996. "Fiddle Music." In *American Folklore: An Encyclopedia*, edited by Jan Harold Brunvand, 253–56. New York: Garland.

Jabbour, Alan. 2002. "In Search of the Source of American Syncopation." *Strings* 16(8): 46–56, May–June.

Jackson, George Pullen. 1944. *White and Negro Spirituals: Their Life Span and Kinship*. New York: J. J. Augustan.

Jackson, Stevan R. 2006. "Peoples of Appalachia: Cultural Diversity within the Mountain Region." In *A Handbook to Appalachia: An Introduction to the Region*, edited by Grace Toney Edwards, JoAnn Aust Asbury, and Ricky L. Cox, 27–50. Knoxville: University of Tennessee Press.

Jackson, Carlton, and Nancy Richey. 2016. *Mose Rager: Kentucky's Incomparable Guitar Master*. Morley, MO: Acclaim Press.

Jacobs, Jake. 2009. "Folk Music Festival Once Was a Mainstay at Fort Valley State Show." *Macon [Georgia] Telegraph*, April 19.

Jamieson, Robert S. 1987. "Gribble, Lusk, and York: Recording a Black Tennessee Stringband." *Tennessee Folklore Society Bulletin* 53(2): 43–57, summer.

Jamison, Phil. 2015. *Hoedowns, Reels, and Frolics: Roots and Branches of Southern Appalachian Dance*. Urbana: University of Illinois Press.

JDZ. 2013. "Andrew Baxter with the Georgia Yellow Hammers (1927): 'G Rag.'" *Never Yet Melted*. Blog, March 14.

Jefferson, Thomas. 1781 [1995]. *Notes on State of Virginia*, edited by William Harwood. Chapel Hill: University of North Carolina Press.

Jenoure, Theresa. 1981. "The Afro-American Fiddler." *Contributions in Black Studies: A Journal of African and Afro-American Studies* 5(1): 68–81. Special Joint Issue with *New England Journal of Black Studies*.

Jobson, Richard. 1932 [1623]. *The Golden Trade or A Discovery of the River Gambra, and the Golden Trade of the Aethiopians. Set down as they were collected in traveling part of the yeares 1620 and 1621*. London: Penguin Press.

"John Avery Lomax." 2021. Wikipedia, May 6. https://en.wikipedia.org/wiki/John_Lomax. Accessed July 14, 2021.

Johnson, Guy Benton. 1930. *Folk Culture of St. Helena Island, South Carolina*. Chapel Hill: University of North Carolina Press.

Johnson, James Weldon, and J. Rosamond Johnson. 1969 [1925, 1926, 1953, 1954]. *The Books of American Negro Spirituals*. New York: Viking.

Jones, Bessie, and Bessie Lomax Hawes. 1987. *Step it Down: Games, Plays, Songs, and Stories from the Afro-American Heritage*. Athens: University of Georgia Press.

Jones, Charles Colcock. 1842. *The Religious Instruction of the Negroes in the United States*. Savannah: Thomas Purse.

Jones, LeRoi (Amiri Baraka). 1963. *Blues People: Negro Music in White America*. New York: William Morrow.

Jones, Michael L. 2014. *Louisville Jug Music: From Earl McDonald to the National Jubilee.* Charleston, SC: History Press.

Joyce, Mike, and Bob Rusch. 1977. "Carl Martin: An Interview." *Cadence: The American Review of Jazz and Blues* 3(1 and 2), August. Reprinted March 2015. https://bluesmandolin.wordpress.com/2015/03/09/carl-martin-cadence-the-american-review-of-jazz-blues-vol-3-nos-12-august-1977/. Accessed September 10, 2015.

"Juke Joint." 2019. Wikipedia, December 17. https://en.wikipedia.org/wiki/Juke_joint.

Kalra, Ajay. 2006a. "Report on 2006 Appalachian Music Fellowship: Berea's Celebration of Traditional Music Archives Offer a Window into the History of African American Experience(s) in Appalachia," August 1. Unpublished. http://libraryguides.berea.edu/ld.php?content_id=19031500. Accessed May 31, 2017.

Kalra, Ajay. 2006b. "Appalachian Music Fellowship Program: Report Excerpts, Performer Profiles." Unpublished.

Kane, Sharyn, and Richard Keeton. 1994. *In Those Days: African-American Life Near the Savannah River.* Atlanta: US Army Corps of Engineers, Savannah District.

Kaplan, Bruce. 1979. "Carl Martin." *Living Blues* 43, summer. Reprinted in *Bluesmandolin: Mandolins and Blues*, March 9, 2015.

Keith, Jeffrey A. 2013. "Fiddling with Race Relations in Rural Kentucky: The Life, Times, and Contested Identity of Fiddlin' Bill Livers." In *Hidden in the Mix: The African American Presence in Country Music*, edited by Diane Pecknold, 119–39. Durham, NC: Duke University Press.

Keller, Mark. 1976. "Alabama Plantation Life in 1860: Governor Benjamin Fitzpatrick's 'Oak Grove.'" *Alabama Historical Quarterly* 38(3): 218–27, fall.

Kennedy, Stetson. 2011. "A Two-Way Street: Folklore and Cultural Well-Being." *Folklife Center News* 33(3–4): 12–19, summer/fall.

Kensington History Society. 2022. "Historic Kensington Maryland." https://www.kensingtonhistory.org/. Accessed July 26, 2022.

Kent, Don. 1972. Liner notes. *Mississippi and Beale Street Sheiks, 1927–1932.* Biograph Records BLP 12041.

Kent, Don. 1977. Liner notes. *Patton, Sims, and Bertha Lee, 1929–1934.* Herwin 213.

Kent, Don. 1998. Liner notes. *Ruckus Juice and Chitlins: The Great Jug Bands. Classic Recordings of the 1920's and 30's, Volume 2.* Yazoo Records 2033.

Kent, Dot. 1997. "Frolics: African American House Dance Traditions of the North Carolina Piedmont." *Old-Time Herald: A Magazine Dedicated to Old-Time Music* 5(7): 9–11, 32.

"The Kidnapping Case: Narrative of the Seizure and Recovery of Solomon Northrup. Interesting Disclosures." 1853. *New York Daily Times*, January 20, 1.

Kiely, Denis. 2018. "African American String Music in the Roberts Family of Overton County." Paper presented at the meeting of the Tennessee Folklore Society. https://www.youtube.com/watch?v=XNB1Bn6-A44. Accessed August 27, 2022.

Killian, Joe. 2004. "Joe Thompson: Documentary. Showcases Fiddler." *News and Record* Rockington County (Reidsville, North Carolina), October 7. https://www.greensboro.com/joe-thompson-documentary-showcases-fiddler/article_006980d5-8fd5-5c4c-9ce6-9d348077155c.html. Accessed February 28, 2019.

Kjemtrup, Inge. 2010. "The Bow Project: Daniel Hope Searches for Violin's Roots." *Strings* 25(4): 16, November.

Kloosterman, Robert C., and Chris Quispel. 1990. "Not Just the Same Old Show on My Radio: An Analysis of the Role of Radio in the Diffusion of Black Music among Whites in the South of the United States of America, 1920 to 1960." *Popular Music* 9(2): 151–64, April.

Knauff, George P. 1839. *Virginia Reels: Selected and Arranged for the Piano Forte.* Four volumes. Baltimore: Geo. Willig.

Koster, Rick. 2018. "Melding Classical and Hip Hop: Black Violin Brings Their Unique Sound to the Kate." *The Day.* https://www.theday.com/article/20180122/ENT10/180129869. Accessed December 29, 2018.

Krehbiel, Henry Edward. 1962 [1914]. *Afro-American Folksongs: A Study in Racial and National Music*. New York: Frederick Ungar Publishing.

Kubik, Gerhard. 1999. *Africa and the Blues*. Jackson: University Press of Mississippi.

Kubik, Gerhard. 2010. *Theory of African Music, Volume II*. Chicago: University of Chicago Press.

Kuntz, Andrew. 1996–2010. "The Fiddler's Companion." http://www.ibiblio.org/fiddlers/EIB_EMY.htm. Accessed July 12, 2017.

Kynerd, Bryle A., and Eddie Echols. 1980. Liner Notes. *Mississippi Sawyers: A Collection of Old-Time Mississippi Fiddling*. Sawyer Records 101.

Labat, Jean-Baptiste. 1728. *Nouvelle relation de l'Afrique occidentale: Contenant une description exacte du Senegal & des païs situés entre le Cap-Blanc & la riviere de Serrelionne. Avec l'etat ancien et present des compagnies qui y font le commerce*. Volume 4. Paris: G. Cavelier.

LaBrew, Arthur R. 1977 [1976]. *Black Musicians of the Colonial Period*. Detroit: Arthur R. LaBrew.

Laing, Alexander Gordon. 1825. *Travels in the Timannee, Kooranko, and Soolima Countries, in Western Africa*. London: J. Murray.

Laing, James T. 1985. "The Negro Miner in West Virginia." In *Blacks in Appalachia*, edited by William H. Turner and Edward J. Cabbell, 71–78. Lexington: University Press of Kentucky.

Laird, Ross, and Brian Rust. 2004. *Discography of OKeh Records, 1918–1934*. Westport, CT: Praeger.

Lamb, Andrew. 2001. "Quadrille." In *Oxford Music Online*. https://www.oxfordmusiconline.com/grovemusic/display/10.1093/gmo/9781561592630.001.0001/omo-9781561592630-e-0000022622. Accessed December 16, 2023.

Lance, Donald M. 1998. "Reminiscences of R. P. Christeson." *Missouri Folklore Society Journal* 20: 25–36.

Lange, Fabian, Alan L. Olmstead, and Paul W. Rhode. 2009. "The Impact of the Boll Weevil, 1892–1932." *Journal of Economic History* 69(3): 685–718, September 1.

Lanham, Nellie Ann. 1976. "History Notes Her Father Was Slave." *Monroe City News*, October 7, A12.

Lavender, Chris. 2012. "Famed Mebane Fiddler Dead at 93." *Burlington Times News*, February 21.

Lawrence, Keith. 1980. "Arnold Schultz: The Greatest (?) Guitar Picker's Life Ended Before Promise Realized." *Messenger-Inquirer* (Owensboro, KY), March 2, E1-E2.

Lawrence, Keith. 1981. "Arnold Schultz: The Greatest (?) Guitar Picker's Life Ended before Promise Realized." *JEMF* [John Edwards Memorial Foundation] *Quarterly* 1(61): 3–8, spring.

Lawrence, Keith. 2020a. "Shultz Finally Getting Long Deserved Recognition." *Messenger-Inquirer* (Owensboro, KY), June 25, Updated August 4.

Lawrence, Keith. 2020b. "Arnold Schultz: The Greatest (?) Guitar Picker's Life Ended Before Promise Realized." The IBMA Foundation, October 22. https://bluegrassfoundation.org/2020/10/22/arnold-shultz-the-greatest-guitar-pickers-life-ended-before-promise-realized/. [This article, which originally appeared in the *Messenger-Inquirer* (Owensboro, KY), March 2, 1980, has been lightly edited by Nancy Cardwell.]

Layne, Joslyn. n.d. "Henry 'Son' Sims Biography." AllMusic.com. https://www.allmusic.com/artist/henry-son-sims-mn0000676004/biography. Accessed November 22, 2022.

Lee Green. 2019. Wikipedia, December 10. https://de.zxc.wiki/wiki/Lee_Green. Accessed August 4, 2021.

Lacy, Travis. 2014. "African American Violinists: Old Presence New Genres." Just Soul You Know (blog), February 8. https://justsoulyouknow.wordpress.com/2014/02/08/african-american-violinists-old-presence-new-genres/. Accessed January 8, 2019.

Leggett, Steve. 1998. Record review. *Train 45: Railroad Songs of the Early 1900s*. Rounder Records 1143. https://www.allmusic.com/album/train-45-railroad-songs-of-the-early-1900s-mw0000043585. Accessed April 17, 2018.

Leggett, Steve. n.d.a. Record review. "Red Foley Hillbilly Fever." AllMusic.com. https://www.allmusic.com/album/hillbilly-fever-mw0000427460. Accessed September 15, 2022.

Leggett, Steve. n.d.b. Record review. "Blind Pete and Partner." Blind Dog Radio. Mississippi Delta and Country Blues. https://blinddogradio.blogspot.com/2019/02/blind-pete-and-partner.html. Accessed November 28, 2023.

Leggett, Steve. n.d. Record review. "Boll Weevil Here, Boll Weevil Everywhere: Field Recordings, Volume 16 (1934-1940)." AllMusic.com. https://www.allmusic.com/album/boll-weevil-here-boll-weevil-everywhere-field-recordings-vol-16-1934-1940-mw0000404133. Accessed July 27, 2023.

Lewis, Ronald L. 2009. *Black Coal Miners in America: Race, Class, and Community Conflict, 1780–1980*. Lexington: University Press of Kentucky.

Lieberman, Julie Lyonn. 1986. *Blues Fiddle*. New York: Oak.

Lieberman, Julie Lyonn. 2000. *Rockin' Out with Blues Fiddle*. New York: Huiksi Music.

Lieberman, Julie Lyonn. 2002. "A Brief History of Jazz Violin." *American String Teacher* 52(4): 78–85, November.

Lightfoot, William E. 1988. "It All Goes Back to Arnold Shultz." *Merle Travis Newsletter* 2: 67.

Lightfoot, William E. 1990. "A Regional Musical Style: The Legacy of Arnold Shultz." In *Sense of Place: American Regional Cultures*, edited by Barbara Allen and Thomas J. Schlereth, 127–37. Lexington: University Press of Kentucky.

Linford, Scott. 2013a. Personal interview with the author. Los Angeles, California. May 1.

Linford, Scott. 2013b. Personal interview with the author. Los Angeles, California. September 4.

Lingold, Mary Caton. 2013. "Fiddling with Freedom: Solomon Northup's Musical Trade in 12 Years a Slave." *Sounding Out! The Sound Studies Blog*, December 16. https://soundstudiesblog.com/?s=solomon+northrup. Accessed October 9, 2018.

Livers, Hattie. 1987. Personal interview with the author. Owenton, Kentucky. August 6.

Livers, William "Bill." 1987. Personal interview with the author. Owenton, Kentucky. August 6.

Lofgren, Lyle. 2001. "Remembering the Old Songs: I Truly Understand You Love Another Man." *Inside Bluegrass*, July. http://www.lizlyle.lofgrens.org/RmOlSngs/RTOS-TrulyUnderstand.html. Accessed September 3, 2015.

Lomax, Alan. 1960. Liner notes. *Roots of the Blues*. Atlantic SD 1348.

Lomax, Alan. 1977. Liner notes. *Roots of the Blues*. New World NW 80252-2.

Lomax, Alan. 1993. *The Land Where the Blues Began*. New York: Pantheon.

Lomax, Alan. 1999. "Introduction." *Deep River of Song. Black Appalachia: String Bands, Songsters and Hoedowns*. Alan Lomax Collection. Rounder 1823.

Long, Edward. 1774. *The History of Jamaica, Or, General Survey of the Ancient and Modern State of that Island: With Reflections on Its Situation, Settlements, Inhabitants, Climate, Produce, Commerce, Laws, and Government*, 3 volumes. London: T. Lowndes.

Lornell, Christopher "Kip." 1973. "Albany Blues." *Living Blues* 14: 25–26, autumn.

Lornell, Christopher "Kip." 1974. "North Carolina Pre-Blues Banjo and Fiddle." *Living Blues* 18: 25–27, autumn.

Lornell, Christopher "Kip." 1975. "Pre-Blues Black Music in Piedmont North Carolina." *North Carolina Folklore Journal* 23(1): 26–32, February.

Lornell, Christopher "Kip." 1976. "A Study of the Sociological Reasons Why Blacks Sing Blues: An Examination of the Secular Black Music found in Two North Carolina Communities." Master's thesis, University of North Carolina at Chapel Hill.

Lornell, Christopher "Kip." 1978. Liner notes. *Virginia Traditions: Non-Blues Secular Black Music*. Blue Ridge Institute Records BRI-001.

Lornell, Christopher "Kip." 1981. "Why Blacks Sing Blues: Cedar Grove and Durham, North Carolina in the 1930s." *Jazzforschung* 13: 117–27.

Lornell, Christopher "Kip." 1987. Personal interview with the author. Ferrum, Virginia. August 24.

Lornell, Christopher "Kip." 1989. *Virginia's Blues, Country, and Gospel Records, 1902–1943: An Annotated Discography*. Lexington: University Press of Kentucky.

Lornell, Christopher "Kip." 1990. "Banjos and Blues." In *Arts in Earnest: North Carolina Folklife*, edited by Daniel W. Patterson and Charles G. Zug III, 216–31. Durham, NC: Duke University Press.

Lornell, Christopher "Kip." 1996. Book review. *The Sounds of People and Places: Readings in the Geography of American Folk and Popular Music*, 3rd ed., edited by George O. Carney. *Notes* 52(3): 827–28, March.

Lornell, Christopher "Kip." 2000. Liner notes. *Virginia and the Piedmont: Minstrelsy, Work Songs and Blues*. Alan Lomax Collection. Rounder 1827.

Lornell, Christopher "Kip." 2013. "Old-Time Country Music in North Carolina and Virginia: The 1970s and 1980s." In *Hidden in the Mix: The African American Presence in Country Music*, edited by Diane Pecknold, 171–90. Durham, NC: Duke University Press.

Lovell Jr., John. 1939. "The Social Implications of Negro Spiritual." *Journal of Negro Education* 8(4): 634–42, October.

Lowry, Pete. 1977. "Atlanta Black Sound: A Survey of Black Music from Atlanta During the Twentieth Century." *Atlanta Historical Society Bulletin* 21(2): 88–113, summer.

Lowry, Pete, and Bruce Bastin. 1974/75. "Fort Valley Blues: The Music." [Part 1]. *Blues Unlimited* 111: 11–13, December/January.

Maher, Christa. 2000. "Three Pioneering Folk Music Collectors." *Folklife Center News* 22(3): 3–5, summer.

Malet, William Wyndham. 1863. *An Errand to the South in the Summer of 1862*. London: Richard Bentley.

Mallard, Robert Quarterman. 1892. *Plantation Life Before Emancipation*. Richmond, VA: Whittel and Shepperson.

Malone, Bill C. 1979. *Southern Music. American Music*. Lexington: University Press of Kentucky.

Malone, Bill C., and Travis D. Stimeling. 2012. "Grand Ole Opry." In *Oxford Music Online*. https://www.oxfordmusiconline.com/grovemusic/view/10.1093/gmo/9781561592630.001.0001/omo-9781561592630-e-1002224530. Accessed November 30, 2022.

Mangin, Julianna. 2022. "Will Adam, Fiddler of Ken-Gar." February 3. https://juliannemangin.com/category/music/ Accessed December 13, 2023.

Mapoma, Mwesa. 2009. Personal communication with the author. August.

Mapoma, Mwesa. 2014. Email communication to the author. March 26.

Mapoma, Mwesa. 2016. Email communication to the author. September 17.

Marcus, George E. 1995. "Ethnography in/of the World System: The Emergence of Multi-Sited Ethnography." *Annual Review of Anthropology* 24: 95–117.

Marcuse, Sibyl. 1975 [1964]. *Musical Instruments Comprehensive Dictionary*. New York: W. W. Norton.

"Marie Donell." 1976. In *Monroe City, Missouri: "Queen of the Prairie,"* 52–53. Monroe City, MO: Monroe City Bicentennial Commission.

Marks III, Joseph E. 1957. *America Learns to Dance: A Historical Study of Dance Education in America Before 1900*. New York: Exposition Press.

Marquez-Frees, Linda, and Jim Sumner. 1982. "White Furniture Company." National Register of Historic Places—Nomination and Inventory. North Carolina State Historic Preservation Office. https://files.nc.gov/ncdcr/nr/AM0466.pdf. Accessed September 9, 2022.

Marshall, Erynn. 2006. *Music in the Air Somewhere: The Shifting Borders of West Virginia's Fiddle and Song Traditions*. Morganton: West Virginia University Press.

Marshall, Howard Wight. 1989. "An Introduction to Traditional Violin Playing in Missouri." In *Now That's a Good Tune: Masters of Traditional Missouri Fiddling*. Accompanied by two CD Recordings. Grey Eagle Records 101.

Marshall, Howard Wight. 2008 [1989]. "An Introduction to Traditional Violin Playing in Missouri." In *Now That's a Good Tune: Masters of Traditional Missouri Fiddling*. Accompanied by two CD Recordings. Seattle: Voyager Recordings and Publications.

Marshall, Howard Wight. 2012. *"Play Me Something Quick and Devilish": Old-Time Fiddlers in Missouri*. Columbia: Curators of the University of Missouri, University of Missouri Press.

"Martin, Bogan and Armstrong at the 36th National Folk Festival, 1974." 2014. National Council for the Traditional Arts. March 20. http://ncta-usa.org/the-36th-national-folk-festival-1974/. Accessed November 7, 2022.

Martin, Douglas. 2012. "Joe Thompson Dies at 93; Helped Preserved the Black String Band." *New York Times*, March 1.

Martin, Wayne. 1987. Personal interview with the author. Chapel Hill, NC. August 20.

Martin, Wayne. 1989. "Joe and Odell Thompson." *Old-Time Herald: A Magazine Dedicated to Old-Time Music* 1(8): 4–7, May–July.

Mathews, Burgin. n.d. Record review. *String Bands (1926–1929)*. Various artists. Document DOCD-5167.

Mathews, Burgin. 2008. "Ernest Mostella." Posted December 24. http://ladymuleskinnerpress.com/2008/12/ernest-mostella/. Accessed August 7, 2014.

Mathews, Burgin. 2023. "The Fiddles of Earnest Mostella." *Tributaries: Journal of the Alabama Folklife Association* 17: 7–15, November.

Mattern, Mark. 1997. "Let the Good Times Unroll: Music and Race Relations in Southwest Louisiana." *Black Music Research Journal* 17(2): 159–68, autumn.

Matteson Jr., Richard L. 2008. "Lily May Ledford and White Oak Mountain." Bluegrass Music and Artwork Blog, November 1. http://richardmattesonsblog.blogspot.com/2008/11/lily-may-ledford-and-white-oak-mountain.html. Accessed September 5, 2015.

Mayo, Margot, Robert Stuart Jamieson, and Freyda Simon. 1946. Margot Mayo Collection. Library of Congress. https://lccn.loc.gov/2008700402. Accessed August 23, 2024.

McArdle, Terence. 2012. "Joe Thompson, 93, Well-respected fiddler." *Washington Post*, February 29.

McCarthy, Jack. 2017. "Listen to the Mocking Bird." *The Encyclopedia of Greater Philadelphia*. https://philadelphiaencyclopedia.org/essays/listen-to-the-mockingbird/#:~:text=Written%20in%201855%20by%20a%20Philadelphia%20songwriter%20who,throughout%20the%20United%20States%20and%20parts%20of%20Europe. Accessed September 14, 2024.

McCartney, Martha W. 2003. *A Study of the Africans and African Americans on Jamestown Island and at Green Spring, 1619–1803*. Williamsburg, VA: Colonial National Historical Park, National Park Service, US Department of Interior.

McCormick, Fred. 1998. Liner notes. *The Hammons Family: The Traditions of a West Virginia Family and Their Friends*. Rounder 1504/1505, http://www.mustrad.org.uk/articles/hammons.htm. Accessed July 11, 2015.

McCormick, Fred. 2002. Record review. *The Hammons Family: The Traditions of a West Virginia Family and Their Friends. Magazine for Traditional Music Throughout the World*, October 20, Item 023.

McCray, Michael. 2012. "Influential N.C. Fiddler Joe Thompson Dies at 93." *Fayetteville Observer*. February 22.

McDonald, Roderick A. 1999. Book review. *Exchanging Our Country Marks: The Transformation of African Identities in the Colonial and Antebellum South, 1526–1830*, by Michael A. Gomez. *American Historical Review* 104(5): 1660–1661, December.

McLagan, Elizabeth. 2009. "Lou Southworth (ca. 1830–1917)." BlackPast.org. https://www.blackpast.org/african-american-history/southworth-lou-ca-1830-1917/. Accessed July 20, 2021.

Meade, Guthrie T. 1980. Liner notes. *Old Time Fiddle Band Music from Kentucky*. Morning Star 45003, 45004, 45005.

Meade Jr., Guthrie T., with Dick Spottswood, and Douglas S. Meade. 2002. *Country Music Sources: A Biblio-Discography of Commercially Recorded Traditional Music*. Chapel Hill: Southern Folklife Collection, University of North Carolina.

Meadows, Eddie S. 2017. Personal conversation with the author, May 11, 26. Los Angeles.

Meadows, Eddie S. 2020. Personal conversation with the author, April 20. Los Angeles.

Meadows, Eddie S. 2023. Personal conversation with the author, December 14. Los Angeles.

Meiner, Hannah. 2021. "Juneteenth: The Life and Legacy of Louis Southworth." *Corvallis [Oregon] Advocate*. June 19. https://www.corvallisadvocate.com/2021/juneteenth-the-life-and-legacy-of-louis-southworth/. Accessed July 20, 2021.

Menconi, David. 2012. "Joe Thompson, Rest in Peace." *News and Observer*, Raleigh, NC. Blog, February 21. http://blogs.newsobserver.com/beat/joe-thompson-rest-in-peace. Accessed March 4, 2012.

Menestrel, Sara Le. 2007. "The Color of Music: Social Boundaries and Stereotypes in Southwest Louisiana French Music." *Southern Cultures* 13(3): 87–105, fall.

Menius, Art. 1992. "The Marrow of Tradition: Joe and Odell Thompson." *Bluegrass Unlimited* 27(2): 33–35, September.

Merriam, Alan P. 1959. "African Music." In *Continuity and Change in African Cultures*, edited by William R. Bascom and Melville J. Herskovits, 49–86. Chicago: University of Chicago Press.

Merriam-Webster: An Encyclopaedia Britannica Company. 2014. np: Merriam-Webster. http://www.merriam-webster.com/dictionary/. Accessed June 26, 2014.

Metrailer, Jamie. 2013. "Roosevelt 'The Honeydripper' Sykes." *Encyclopedia of Arkansas*, September 19. https://encyclopediaofarkansas.net/entries/roosevelt-the-honeydripper-sykes-5881/. Accessed August 6, 2021.

Miller, Joseph C. 1999. Book review. *Exchanging Our Country Marks: The Transformation of African Identities in the Colonial and Antebellum South, 1526–1830*, by Michael A. Gomez. *The Journal of Southern History* 65(4): 845–46, November.

Miller, Lewis. 1853. "Lynchburg Negro Dance, August 18th, 1853." Watercolor. Virginia, 1853–1867. Colonial Williamsburg Foundation.

Milnes, Gerald. 1999. *Play of a Fiddle: Traditional Music, Dance, and Folklore in West Virginia*. Lexington: University Press of Kentucky.

Minton, John. 1996a. "West African Fiddles in Deep East Texas." In *Juneteenth Texas: Essays in African-American Folklore*, edited by Patrick B. Mullen and Alan B. Govenar, 291–313. Denton: University of North Texas Press.

Minton, John. 1996b. "Houston Creoles and Zydeco: The Emergence of an African American Urban Popular Style." *American Music* 14(4): 480–526, winter.

Minton, Tiffany. 2022. Liner notes. *Uncovering the Voice of Walter Greer: The 1975 Nashville Recording*. Spring Fed Records. SFR 120.

Mississippi Blues Trail. 2008a. "Birthplace of the Blues? Dockery." Mississippi Blues Commission. http://msbluestrail.org/blues-trail-markers/birthplace-of-the-blues. Accessed January 2, 2021.

Mississippi Blues Trail. 2008b. "Muddy Waters Birthplace." Mississippi Blues Commission. http://msbluestrail.org/blues-trail-markers/muddy-waters-birthplace. Accessed January 2, 2021.

Mississippi Blues Trail. 2010. "Paramount Records—Grafton." Mississippi Blues Commission. http://www.msbluestrail.org/blues-trail-markers/paramount-records. Accessed May 15, 2020.

Mississippi Blues Trail. 2014. "The Chatmon Family—Mississippi Sheiks." Mississippi Blues Commission. http://msbluestrail.org/blues-trail-markers/the-chatmon-family. Accessed April 4, 2020.

Mississippi Genealogical Web Slave Narrative Project. 2006–2008. *Mississippi Slave Narratives from the WPA Records*. http://msgw.org/slaves/mack-xslave.htm. Accessed June 9, 2014.

A Mississippi Planter. 1851. "Article III.—Management of Negroes Upon Southern Estates." *DeBow's Review* 10: 621–27, June.

Miyake, Mark Y. 2009. "The Discourse on Race within the Bluegrass Music Community." PhD dissertation, Indiana University.

Monge, Luigi. 2022. *Wasn't That a Mighty Day: African American Blues and Gospel Songs on Disaster*. Jackson: University Press of Mississippi.

"Monroe City, Missouri, 1857–1976: 'Queen of the Prairie' 'Gateway to Cannon Dam.'" 1976. No publisher, 52–53.

Moore, T. DeWayne. 2014. "Uncovering Henry 'Son' Simms: Mt. Zion Memorial Fund Locates Headstone of Blues Fiddler Henry 'Son' Simms." *Living Blues* 45(3): 74–77, June.

Moore, T. DeWayne. 2018. "Bo Carter: The Genius of the Country Blues." *Blues and Rhythm* 330: 14–24, May.

Moore, T. DeWayne. 2021a. "The Segregation of Sound: Unheard African American Fiddlers." In *Fiddle Tunes from Mississippi: Commercial and Informal Recordings, 1920–2018*, by Harry Bolick and Tony Russell, 23–32. Jackson: University Press of Mississippi.

Moore, T. DeWayne. 2021b. "Thomas Jefferson Dumas." In *Fiddle Tunes from Mississippi: Commercial and Informal Recordings, 1920–2018*, by Harry Bolick and Tony Russell, 147–60. Jackson: University Press of Mississippi.

Moore, T. DeWayne. 2021c. "Sidney Hemphill Sr." In *Fiddle Tunes from Mississippi: Commercial and Informal Recordings, 1920–2018*, by Harry Bolick and Tony Russell, 202–22. Jackson: University Press of Mississippi.

Moore, T. DeWayne. 2021d. "The Mississippi Sheiks." In *Fiddle Tunes from Mississippi: Commercial and Informal Recordings, 1920–2018*, by Harry Bolick and Tony Russell, 378–415. Jackson: University Press of Mississippi.

Mordecai, Samuel. 1856. *Richmond in By-Gone Days Being Reminiscences of an Old Citizen*. Richmond, VA: George M. West.

Moreau de Saint-Méry, Médéric Louis Élie. 1797. *Déscription Topographique, Physique, Civile, Politique et Historique de la Partie Francaise de l'Isle Saint-Domingue.* . . . Philadelphia: Chez l'Auteur.

Morton, Jelly Roll, and Alan Lomax. 1938. Library of Congress Narrative. Transcribed by Michael Hill, Roger Richard, and Mike Meddings. Washington: Library of Congress. http://www.doctorjazz.co.uk/locspeech1.html#locaafs1. Accessed May 10, 2017.

Mott, Abigail Field. 1875. *Narratives of Colored Americans*. New York: William Wood.

Myers, Helen. 1992. "Introduction." In *Ethnomusicology*, edited by Helen Myers, 3–18. New York: W. W. Norton.

National Endowment for the Arts. 2011. "Canray Fontenot." *64 Parishes*. https://64parishes.org/entry/canray-fontenot. Accessed September 24, 2021.

Nelson, Oscar William. 1962. Interview with Mack McCormick. Cameron, Texas. April 27. In *The Blues Come to Texas: Paul Oliver and Mack McCormick's Unfinished Book*, edited by Alan B. Govenar and Kip Lornell, 69–70. College Station: Texas A&M University Press.

Nemerov, Bruce. 1987. "John Wesley Work III: Field Recordings of Southern Black Folk Music, 1935–1942." *Tennessee Folklore Society Bulletin* 53(3): 82–103, fall.

Nemerov, Bruce. 2008. Liner notes. *John Work, III: Recording Black Culture*. Spring Fed SFR 104.

Nevins, Richard. 2003. Liner notes. *Kentucky Mountain Music: Classic Recordings of the 1920s and 1930s*. Yazoo 2200.

Nketia, J. H. Kwabena. 1972. "The Present State and Potential of Music Research in Africa." In *Perspectives in Musicology: The Inaugural Lectures of the Ph.D. Program in Music at the City University of New York*, edited by. Barry S. Brook, Edward O. D. Downes, and Sherman van Solkema. New York: W. W. Norton.

Nketia, J. H. Kwabena. 1974. *The Music of Africa*. New York: W. W. Norton.

Northup, Solomon. 1968 [1853]. *Twelve Years a Slave: Narrative of Solomon Northup, a Citizen of New-York; Kidnapped in Washington City in 1841, and Rescued in 1853*, edited by Sue Eakin and Joseph Logsdon. Baton Rouge: Louisiana State University Press.

Norton, Pauline. 2001. "Breakdown." In *Grove Music Online*. https://doi.org/10.1093/gmo/9781561592630.article.03898. Accessed April 28, 2018.

Norton, Pauline. 2014. "Cotillion." In *Oxford Music Online*. https://www.oxfordmusiconline.com/grovemusic/view/10.1093/gmo/9781561592630.001.0001/omo-9781561592630-e-1002256236?print=pdf. Accessed December 6, 2022.

Now What a Time: Blues, Gospel, and the Fort Valley Music Festivals, 1938 to 1943. 2000. Washington, DC: American Folklife Center. Library of Congress. https://www.loc.gov/collections/blues-gospel-and-the-fort-valley-music-festivals/articles-and-essays/noncommercial-recordings-the-1940s/1950-to-1955/. Accessed July 5, 2019.

Oakley, Giles. 1997 [1976, 1983]. *The Devil's Music: A History of the Blues*. London: Da Capo Press.

Obrecht, Jas. 2009. "Sam Chatmon: The Last of the Mississippi Sheiks." *Living Blues* 40(1): 68–73, February.

Odell, Jay Scott, and Robert B. Winans. 2014. "The Banjo." In *Oxford Music Online*, January 31. https://doi.org/10.1093/gmo/9781561592630.article.A2256043. Accessed December 25, 2023.

Odum, Howard Washington. 1911a. "Folk-Song and Folk-Poetry as Found in the Secular Songs of the Southern Negroes." *Journal of American Folklore* 24(93): 255–94, July–September.

Odum, Howard Washington. 1911b. "Folk-Song and Folk-Poetry as Found in the Secular Songs of the Southern Negroes (Concluded)." *Journal of American Folklore* 24(94): 351–96, October–December.

Odum, Howard Washington, and Guy Benson Johnson. 1925 [1972]. *The Negro and His Songs: A Study of Typical Negro Songs in the South.* Westport, CT: Negro Universities Press.

Odum, Howard Washington, and Guy Benson Johnson. 1926 [1969]. *Negro Workaday Songs.* New York: Negro Universities Press.

"Old Fiddlers' Convention, Galax, Virginia." 2015. http://www.oldfiddlersconvention.com/history.htm. Accessed August 5, 2015.

Oliver, Paul. 1965. *Conversation with the Blues.* Cambridge: Cambridge University Press.

Oliver, Paul. 1968. *Screening the Blues: Aspects of the Blues Tradition.* New York City: Da Capo Press.

Oliver, Paul. 1970. *Savannah Syncopators: African Retentions in the Blues.* New York: Stein and Day.

Oliver, Paul. 1972 [1969]. *The Story of the Blues.* Middlesex, UK: Penguin Books.

Oliver, Paul. 1984a. *Songsters and Saints: Vocal Traditions on Race Records.* Cambridge: Cambridge University Press.

Oliver, Paul. 1984b. Liner notes. *Songsters and Saints: Vocal Traditions on Race Records, Volume 1.* Matchbox MSEX 2001/2002.

Oliver, Paul. 1987. Liner notes. *Mississippi Sheiks. Volume 2, 1930–1934.* Matchbox Bluesmaster Series MSE 1012.

Oliver, Paul. 2003a. "Hokum." In *Grove Music Online.* https://doi.org/10.1093/gmo/9781561592630.article.J205000. Accessed February 2, 2022.

Oliver, Paul. 2003b. "Jug Band (Jazz)." In *Grove Music Online.* https://doi.org/10.1093/gmo/9781561592630.article.J239700. Accessed June 3, 2022.

Oliver, Roland, and J. D. Fage. 1990. *A Short History of Africa*, 6th ed. Middlesex, UK: Penguin Books.

Oliver Jr., Sylvester W. 1996. "African-American Music Traditions in Northeast Mississippi." PhD dissertation, University of Memphis.

Olmsted, Frederick Law. 1860. *A Journey in the Back Country.* New York: Mason Brothers.

Olmsted, Frederick Law. 1861. *The Cotton Kingdom: A Traveller's Observations on Cotton and Slavery in the American Slave States*, 2 volumes. New York: Mason Brothers.

Oster, Harry. 1960. Liner notes. *Country Negro Jam Session.* Arhoolie Records 2018. Originally issued as Folklyric LP 111.

Oster, Harry. 1969. *Living Country Blues.* Detroit: Folklore Associates.

Otto, John S., and Augustus M. Burns. 1974. "Black and White Cultural Interaction in the Early Twentieth Century South: Race and Hillbilly Music." *Phylon* 35(4): 407–17.

Page, John W. 1853. *Uncle Robin, in His Cabin in Virginia, and Tom without One in Boston.* Richmond, VA: J. W. Randolph.

Pahls, Marty. 1985. Liner notes. *Louie Bluie.* Soundtrack from the film. Arhoolie 1095.

Paine, Lewis W. 1851. *Six Years in a Georgia Prison: Narrative of Lewis W. Paine, Who Suffered Imprisonment Six Years in Georgia, for the Crime of Aiding the Escape of a Fellowman from That State, After He Had Fled from Slavery.* New York: Author.

Palmer, Colin A. 1995. "From Africa to the Americas: Ethnicity in the Early Black Communities of the Americas." *Journal of World History* 6(2): 223–36, fall.

Palmer, Robert. 1975. "When the Sheiks Sang the Depression Blues." *New York Times*, September 28.

Parish [Parrish], Lydia. 1942. *Slave Songs of the Georgia Sea Islands.* New York: Creative Age Press.

Parks, Gordon. 1984. *Solomon Northup's Odyssey.* Television movie on series *American Playhouse.*

Parramore, Tom. 1988. "Cabin Point Fagan and the Catgut Scampers." *The State*, 18–21, September.

Parramore, Tom. 1989. "Old Frank Johnson—And the Day the Music Died." *The State*, 8–9, April.

Patterson, Karin, 2000. Personal conversation with the author, Los Angeles, spring.

Pecknold, Diane, ed. 2013. *Hidden in the Mix: The African American Presence in Country Music.* Durham, NC: Duke University Press.

Pelote, Vincent. 1983. Liner notes. *Jazz Strings: The Great Jazz Recordings of All Time.* Franklin Mint Record Society FM Jazz 029, 030, 031, 032. Rutgers, NJ: Institute of Jazz Studies Office Archive Collection.

Perbi, Akosua Adoma. 2004. *A History of Indigenous Slavery in Ghana from the 15th to the 19th Century.* Legon-Accra, Ghana: Sub-Saharan Publishers.

Perryman, Charles W. 2013. "Africa, Appalachia, and Acculturation: The History of Bluegrass Music." PhD dissertation, West Virginia University.

Pestcoe, Shlomo. 2011. Personal email communication with the author. January 13.

Pestcoe, Shlomo, and Greg C. Adams. 2018. "Banjo Roots Research: Changing Perspectives on the Banjo's African American Origins and West African Heritage." In *Banjo Roots and Branches*, edited by Robert B. Winans, 3–18. Urbana: University of Illinois Press.

Phillips, Cora Geneva Reid. 1987. Personal interview with the author. Morganton, NC. August 22.

"Pictures of the South—Marriage of a Colored Soldier." 1866. *Harper's Weekly: A Journal of Civilization* 10(496): 411–12, June 30.

Pierpont, John. 1816. *The Airs of Palestine: A Poem*. Np: B Edes, printer.

Platt, Orville H. 1900. "Negro Governors." *Papers of the New Haven Colony Historical Society* 6: 315–35.

Playfair, Robert. 1856. *Recollections of a Visit to the United States and British Provinces of North America, in the Years 1847, 1848, and 1849*. Edinburgh: Thomas Constable.

Poche, Christian. 2001. "Rabab: Spike Fiddles." In *Oxford Music Online*. https://doi.org/10.1093/gmo/9781561592630.article.22763. Accessed August 12, 2022.

Pointer, Noel. 1981. "Jazz on Electric Violin." Interview by Penny Williams, Channel 10 TV Station. Norwalk, Virginia. WAVY Archive 1981. WAVY.com | Nexstar Broadcasting, Inc. https://www.youtube.com/watch?v=iOQxLoA3ZDs. Accessed December 14, 2018.

Post, Laren. 1962. *Cajun Sketches*. Baton Rouge: Louisiana State University Press.

"Present from a President: Legendary Violin Offered for Sale." 1974. *Clarksdale [Mississippi] Press Register*, December 11, 3A.

Purdue, Theda. 1985. "Red and Black in the Southern Appalachians." In *Blacks in Appalachia*, edited by William H. Turner and Edward J. Cabbell, 23–29. Lexington: University Press of Kentucky.

Puryear, Mark. 2023. "African Americans and the Blues in Texas." Liner notes. *Playing for the Man at the Door: Field Recordings from the Collection of Mack McCormick, 1958–1975*. Smithsonian Folkways SFW 40260, 13–17.

Quigley, Colin. 1986. Notes on "Library of Congress Fiddle Tunes by Ford Britten, Frank Patterson, and John Lusk." Unpublished document submitted to Jacqueline Cogdell DjeDje as part of the research project, "A Study of the Black Fiddle Tradition in the United States," funded by the UCLA Academic Senate, Spring.

Rakestraw, Joe Kenny. 1983. Personal interview with Art Rosenbaum. Athens, GA. May 7.

Rakestraw, Joe Kenny. 1987. Personal interview with Art Rosenbaum. Athens, GA. July 31.

Ramsey, Frederic. 1956a. Liner notes. *Music from the South, Volume 5: Song, Play, and Dance*. Folkways 2654. Field recordings taken in Alabama, Louisiana, and Mississippi under a grant from the John Simon Guggenheim Memorial Foundation.

Ramsey, Frederic. 1956b. "A Study of the Afro-American Music of Alabama, Louisiana and Mississippi, 1860–1900." *Ethno-Musicology Newsletter* 1(8): 28–31, September.

Rankin, John. 1823–1839. *Letters on American Slavery, Addressed to Mr. Thomas Rankin, Merchant at Middlebrook, Augusta County, Virginia*. Ohio: Np; Boston: Garrison and Knapp; Newburyport, MA: Charles Whipple; Np: Isaac Knapp.

Rath, Richard Cullen. 2000. "Drums and Power: Ways of Creolizing Music in Coastal South Carolina and Georgia, 1730–1790." In *Creolization in the Americas: Cultural Adaptations to the New World*, edited by David Buisseret and Steven G. Reinhardt, 99–130. College Station: University of Texas at Arlington.

Ratliff, Martha Ann. 1937 [1996]. Interview with J. S. Thomas in *The WPA Oklahoma Slave Narratives*, edited by T. Lindsay Baker and Julie P. Baker, 338–39. Norman and London: University of Oklahoma Press.

Ravitz, Abe C. 1960. "John Pierpont and the Slaves' Christmas." *Phylon* 21(4): 383–86.

Rawick, George P., ed. 1977–1979. *Mississippi Slave Narratives*. 5 volumes. Westport, CT: Greenwood Press.

Record Fiend. 2010. Record review. *String Bands 1926–1929*. Document DOCD 5167. Blog, October 13.

Reed, Revon. 1966. Liner notes. *Les Blues du Bayou*. Melodeon MLP 7330.

Remnant, Mary. 2001. "Fiddle." In *Oxford Music Online*, 8th edition, January 20. Oxford University Press. https://doi.org/10.1093/gmo/9781561592630.article.09596. Accessed April 12, 2023.

"Rhiannon Giddens." 2024. Wikipedia. July 19. https://en.wikipedia.org/w/index.php?title=Rhiannon_Giddens&oldid=1235508913. Accessed August 30, 2024.

Riley, Doris. 2010. "Livers, William 'Bill.'" In *The Encyclopedia of Northern Kentucky*, edited by Paul A. Tenkotte and James C. Claypool, 558–59. Lexington: University Press of Kentucky.

Riley, Edward Miles. 1963. "Introduction." In *The Journal of John Harrower: An Indentured Servant in the Colony of Virginia, 1773–1776*, edited by Edward Miles Riley, xiii–xxi. Williamsburg, VA: Colonial Williamsburg.

Roberts, John Storm. 1998 [1972]. *Black Music of Two Worlds: African, Caribbean, Latin, and African-American Traditions*. 2nd ed. New York: Schirmer Books.

Romero, Angel. 2016. "Interview with Zydeco Accordion Virtuoso Jeffery Broussard." World Music Central.org, August 19. https://worldmusiccentral.org/2016/08/19/interview-with-zydeco-accordion-virtuoso-jeffery-broussard/. Accessed September 21, 2021.

Rose, Al, and Edmond Souchon. 1984. *New Orleans Jazz: A Family Album*. 3rd ed., revised and enlarged. Baton Rouge: Louisiana State University Press.

Rosenbaum, Art. 1983. *Folk Visions and Voices: Traditional Music and Song in Northern Georgia*. Athens: University of Georgia Press.

Rosenbaum, Art, and Johann S. Buis. 1998. *Shout Because You're Free: The African American Ring Shout Tradition in Coastal Georgia*. Athens: University of Georgia Press.

Rowser, Yvette. 2018. Email communication with the author. May 21.

Russell, Tony. 1970. *Blacks, Whites and Blues*. New York: Stein and Day.

Russell, Tony. 1997. *The Blues: From Robert Johnson to Robert Cray*. Dubai: Carlton Books Limited. 169, 171–72; 99–100, 119.

Russell, Tony. 1999. Liner notes. *Black Fiddlers: The Remaining Titles of Andrew and Jim Baxter, Nathan Frazier and Frank Patterson. The Complete Recorded Works of Cuje Bertram 1929—c. 1970*. Document Records DOCD 5631.

Russell, Tony. 2021. *Rural Rhythm: The Story of Old-Time Country Music in 78 Records*. New York: Oxford University Press.

Russell, Tony, and Bob Pinson. 2004. *Country Music Records: A Discography, 1921–1942*. Oxford and New York: Oxford University Press.

Russell, William Howard. 1861. *Pictures of Southern Life: Social, Political, and Military. Written for the London Times*. New York: James G. Gregory.

Rust, Brian. 1978. *Jazz Records 1897–1942*. 2 volumes, 4th ed. New Rochelle, NY: Arlington House.

Rye, Howard. 2010. "Chronology of the Southern Syncopated Orchestra: 1919–1922." *Black Music Research Journal* 30(1): 4–18, spring.

Sacks, Howard L., and Judith Rose Sacks. 1988. "Way Up North in Dixie: Black-White Musical Interaction in Knox County, Ohio." *American Music* 64: 409–27, winter.

Sacks, Howard L., and Judith Rose Sacks. 1993. *Way Up North in Dixie: A Black Family's Claim to the Confederate Anthem*. Washington: Smithsonian Institution Press.

Sacks, Howard L., and Judith Rose Sacks. 2003. "From the Barn to the Bowery and Back Again: Musical Routes in Rural Ohio, 1800–1929." Phillips Barry Lecture, October 2000. *Journal of American Folklore* 116: 314–38, summer.

Salsburg, Nathan. 2017. "Camp Nelson Blues." *Oxford American: A Magazine of the South*. 99, winter, November 21. https://www.oxfordamerican.org/magazine/item/1378-camp-nelson-blues. Accessed May 17, 2018.

Savoy, Ann Allen. 1983a. Liner notes. *Cajun Fiddle Styles, Volume 1: The Creole Tradition*. Arhoolie Records 5031.

Savoy, Ann Allen. 1983b. "Cajun-Creole Columbia Releases—Amedé Ardoin and Dennis McGee (1929)." Library of Congress. Essay by Ann Savoy (guest post). https://www.loc.gov/static/programs/national-recording-preservation-board/documents/CajunCreoleColumbiaReleases_ArdoinMcGee.pdf. Accessed September 24, 2021.

Savoy, Ann Allen. 1984. *Cajun Music: A Reflection of a People, Volume 1*. Eunice, LA: Bluebird Press.

Schoenbaum, David. 2013. *The Violin: A Social History of the World's Most Versatile Instrument*. New York: W. W. Norton.

Schweninger, Loren. 1984. "Introduction." In *From Tennessee Slave to St. Louis Entrepreneur: The Autobiography of James Thomas by James Thomas*, 1–19. Columbia: University of Missouri Press.

Sears, Richard. 1992. "Camp Nelson." In *The Kentucky Encyclopedia*, edited by J. E. Kleber. Lexington: University Press of Kentucky.

Seeger, Mike. 1997. Liner notes. *Close to Home: Old Time Music from Mike Seeger's Collection, 1952–1967*. Smithsonian Folkways Recordings LC9628.

Sewall, Samuel. 1878. *The Diary of Samuel Sewall, 1674–1729*. Boston: Massachusetts Historical Society.

Silber, Irwin. 1961. Liner notes. *The Folk Music of the Newport Folk Festival 1959–60, Volume 1*. Folkways FA 2431.

"Sitting on Top of the World." 2020. Wikipedia, March 4. https://en.wikipedia.org/wiki/Sitting_on_Top_of_the_World. Accessed May 29, 2020.

Slade, Daniel Denison. 1890. "A New England Country Gentleman in the Last Century." *New England Magazine* New Series 8(1): 3–21, March.

Sliwicki, Susan. 2011. "Flashback: The Death of a Record Label." *Goldmine* 37(6): 98, May.

Small, Christopher. 1998. *Musicking: The Meanings of Performing and Listening*. Middletown, CT: Wesleyan University Press.

Smalley, Eugene V. 1887. "Sugar-making in Louisiana." *Century Illustrated Magazine* 35(1): 100–120, November.

A Small Farmer. 1851. "Article III.—Management of Negroes." *DeBow's Review* 11: 369–72, October.

Smith, Dale. 2009. "Missouri's Finest Fiddlers: Howard Marshall Traces Missouri's Fiddling History." *Mizzou: The Magazine of Mizzou Alumni Association*, University of Missouri, Summer. http://mizzoumag.missouri.edu/2009-summer/features/fiddle/index.php. Accessed September 1, 2010.

Smith, Ignatius. 1910. "Jean-Baptiste Labat." In *The Catholic Encyclopedia*. New York: Robert Appleton. Accessed February 1, 2015, from New Advent: http://www.newadvent.org/cathen/08718a.htm.

Smith, Mark M. 2001. "Remembering Mary, Shaping Revolt: Reconsidering the Stono Rebellion." *Journal of Southern History* 67(3): 513–34, August.

Smith, Mark M, ed. 2005. *Stono: Documenting and Interpreting a Southern Slave Revolt*. Columbia: University of South Carolina Press.

Smith, Richard D. 2000. *Can't You Hear Me Callin': The Life of Bill Monroe, Father of Bluegrass*. New York: Little, Brown.

Smyth, William Jense. 1987. "Traditional Humor on Knoxville Country Radio Entertainment Shows." PhD dissertation, University of California, Los Angeles.

Soileau, Murph, and David Bellard. 1993. Interview conducted by Ann Savoy, March 18. Ann Savoy Collection on Douglas Bellard. Arhoolie Foundation. https://arhoolie.org/ann-savoy-collection-douglas-bellard/. Accessed August 25, 2021.

A Soldier's Journal, Containing a Particular Description of the Several Descents on the Coast of France Last War; with an Entertaining Account of the Islands of Guadeloupe, Dominique, and also of the Isles of Wight and Jersey. 1770. London: Printed for E. and C. Dilly.

"Solomon Northup." 2021. *Encyclopaedia Britannica*, July 6. https://www.britannica.com/biography/Solomon-Northup. Accessed September 2, 2021.

"A Southern Barbecue." 1887. *Harper's Weekly: A Journal of Civilization* 31(1594): 487, July 9.

Southern, Eileen. 1971a. *The Music of Black Americans: A History*. New York: W. W. Norton.

Southern, Eileen. 1971b. *Readings in Black American Music*. New York: W. W. Norton.

Southern, Eileen. 1983a. *The Music of Black Americans: A History*. 2nd ed. New York: W. W. Norton.

Southern, Eileen. 1983b. *Readings in Black American Music*. 2nd ed. New York: W. W. Norton.

Southern, Eileen. 1989. "The Georgia Minstrels: The Early Years." *Inter-American Music Review* 10: 157–67, spring–summer.

Southern, Eileen. 1997. *The Music of Black Americans: A History*. 3rd ed. New York: W. W. Norton.

Southern, Eileen, and Josephine Wright. 1990. *African-American Traditions in Song, Sermon, Tale, and Dance, 1600s-1920: An Annotated Bibliography of Literature, Collections, and Artworks*. New York: Greenwood Press.

Southern Journey, Volume 3: 61 Highway Mississippi: Delta Country Blues, Spirituals, Work Songs and Dance Music. 1997. Liner notes. Alan Lomax Collection. Rounder CD 1703.

Speal, Shane. n.d. "Canray Fontenot: From Cigar Box Fiddle to Creole Legend." https://www.cigarboxguitar.com/knowledge-base/canray-fontenot-from-cigar-box-fiddle-to-cajun-legend/. Accessed September 30, 2021.

Spitzer, Nick. 1977. Liner notes. *La La: Louisiana Black French Music*. Maison de Soul Records LP 1004.

Spitzer, Nick. 1979. Liner notes. *Zodico: Louisiana Créole Music*. Rounder 6009.

Spitzer, Nick. 1986. "Zydeco and Mardi Gras: Creole Identity and Performance Genres in Rural French Louisiana." PhD dissertation, University of Texas.

Stanfield, John H. 1985. "The Sociohistorical Roots of White/Black Inequality in Urban Appalachia: Knoxville and East Tennessee." In *Blacks in Appalachia*, edited by William H. Turner and Edward J. Cabbell, 133–44. Lexington: University Press of Kentucky.

Stanford, Ron, and Fay Stanford. 1974. Liner notes. *J'Étais au Bal: Music from French Louisiana*. Swallow Records LP 6020. https://www.bigfrenchdance.com/carriere-brothers. Accessed November 20, 2022.

Stanton, Gary. 1980. "'All Counties Have Blues': County Blues as an Emergent Genre of Fiddle Tunes in Eastern Mississippi." *North Carolina Folklore Journal* 28(2): 79–88, November.

Starks Jr., George L. 1973. "Black Music in the Sea Islands of South Carolina: Its Cultural Context, Continuity, and Change." PhD dissertation, Wesleyan University.

Starks Jr., George L. 1985. "Salt and Pepper in Your Shoe: Afro-American Song Tradition on the South Carolina Sea Islands." In *More Than Dancing: Essays on Afro-American Music and Musicians*, edited by Irene V. Jackson, 59–80. Westport, CT: Greenwood Press.

Starks Jr., George L. 1991. "Singing 'bout a Good Time: Religious Music on the Sea Islands." In *Sea Island Roots: African Presence in the Carolinas and Georgia*, edited by Mary A. Twining and Keith E. Baird. Trenton, NJ: Africa World Press.

Stearns, Marshall, and Jean Stearns. 1994 [1968]. *Jazz Dance: The Story of American Vernacular Dance*. New York: Da Capo Press.

"Stetson Kennedy." 1988. Florida Folk Heritage Award. https://dos.myflorida.com/historical/preservation/florida-folklife-program/folk-heritage-awards/list-of-past-recipients/stetson-kennedy/. Accessed March 7, 2022.

"Steve Tarter." 1935. Obituary. *Roanoke [Virginia] Times*, March 20, 2.

Stewart, Bruce, Linn Shapiro, and Anne Romaine. 1982. "Oh, What a Time." *The Southern Grassroots Music Tour*. Nashville: The Southern Folk Cultural Revival Project. [Booklet accompanies the recording, *Oh, What a Time! Southern Grassroots Music*. Southern Grassroots Revival Project SGR 1101, 1980.]

Stewart, Helen Booker. 1994. Personal interview conducted by Kim McBride, September 6. University of Kentucky, History of Hall, Kentucky, Oral History Project. https://kentuckyoralhistory.org/ark:/16417/xt7sbc3sxq44. Accessed October 9, 2023.

Stowe, Harriet Beecher. 1852. *Uncle Tom's Cabin; or Life Among the Lowly*. Boston: John P. Jewett; Cleveland: Jewett, Proctor & Worthington.

Strachwitz, Chris. 1964. Liner notes. *The Jug, Jook, and Washboard Bands*. Blues Classics BC 2.

Straw, Richard. 2006. "Appalachian History." In *A Handbook to Appalachia: An Introduction to the Region*, edited by Grace Toney Edwards, JoAnn Aust Asbury, and Ricky L. Cox, 1–26. Knoxville: University of Tennessee Press.

Stuart, Isaac William. 1853. *Hartford in the Olden Times: Its First Thirty Years*, edited by William B. Hartley. Hartford CT: F. A. Brown.

Stuckey, Sterling. 1987. *Slave Culture: Nationalist Theory and the Foundations of Black America*. New York: Oxford University Press.

Summers, Keith. 2000. Record review. *Joe Thompson: Family Tradition*. Rounder 2161. *Musical Traditions Internet Magazine: The Magazine for Traditional Music Throughout the World.* http://www.mustrad.org.uk/reviews/thompson.htm. Accessed November 3, 2019.

Szwed, John F. 1970. "Africa Lies Just Off Georgia: Sea Islands Preserve Origins of Afro-American Culture." *Africa Report* 15: 29–31, October 1.

Talley, Thomas Washington. 1922. *Negro Folk Rhymes (Wise and Otherwise)*. New York: Macmillan.

Talley, Thomas Washington. 1942/43. "The Origin of Negro Traditions." *Phylon* 3(4): 371–76; *Phylon* 4(1): 30–38.

Talley, Thomas Washington. 1991 [1922]. *Thomas W. Talley's Negro Folk Rhymes*. A new, expanded edition, with music; edited, with an introduction and notes, by Charles K. Wolfe and music transcriptions by Bill Ferreira. Knoxville: University of Tennessee Press.

Talley, Thomas Washington. 1993 [1922]. *The Negro Traditions*, edited, with an introduction by Charles K. Wolfe and Laura C. Jarmon. Knoxville: University of Tennessee Press.

Taylor, Fiddler Ernest "Boose." 2001. "It Don't 'Bide a Good Man Well for You to Play Them Things." In *Goin' Back to Sweet Memphis: Conversations with the Blues*, edited by Fred J. Hay, 113–55. Athens and London: University of Georgia Press.

"Television in the United States: Rural Humour." n.d. *Encyclopaedia Britannica*. https://www.britannica.com/art/television-in-the-United-States/Rural-humour#ref1057336. Accessed July 28, 2022.

Thomas, Charlie. 1962 [2019]. Interview with Mack McCormick. La Grange, Texas, April 24. In *The Blues Come to Texas: Paul Oliver and Mack McCormick's Unfinished Book*, edited by Alan B. Govenar and Kip Lornell, 69, 344–45. College Station: Texas A&M University Press.

Thomas, Tony. 2007. "Why Black Folks Don't Fiddle." https://www.bluegrasswest.com/ideas/why_black.htm. Accessed June 6, 2022.

Thompson, Deborah J., and Darrin Hacquard. 2009. "Region, Race, Representation: Observations from Interviews with African American Musicians in Appalachia." *Journal of Appalachian Studies* 15(1/2): 126–39, spring/fall.

Thompson, Joe. 1987. Personal interview with the author. Mebane, NC. August 21.

Thompson, Johnson. 1937 [1996]. Interview with Ethel Wolfe Garrison. In *The WPA Oklahoma Slave Narratives*, edited by T. Lindsay Baker and Julie P. Baker, 420–22. Norman and London: University of Oklahoma Press.

Thompson, Katrina Dyonne. 2014. *Ring Shout, Wheel About: The Racial Politics of Music and Dance in North American Slavery*. Urbana: University of Illinois Press.

Thompson, Maurice. 1884. "Plantation Music." *The Critic* 4: 20, January 12.

Thompson, Odell. 1987. Personal interview with the author. Mebane, NC. August 21.

Thompson, Suzy. 2021. Music review. "African-American Fiddling from Texas." *Teodar Jackson: African-American Fiddling from Texas*. *Old-Time Herald: A Magazine Dedicated to Old-Time Music*, December 6.

Tisserand, Michael. 1998. *The Kingdom of Zydeco*. New York: Arcade.

Titon, Jeff Todd. 2001. *Old-Time Kentucky Fiddle Tunes*. Lexington: University Press of Kentucky.

"Traveling Man (Traveling Coon)." 2019. In *The Traditional Ballad Index*, edited by Robert B. Waltz and David G. Engle. California State University, Fresno.

Trotter, James M. 1881. *Music and Some Highly Musical People*. Boston: Lee and Shepard, Publishers; New York: Charles T. Dillingham.

Tucker, George. 1816. *Letters from Virginia*. Baltimore: Fielding Lucas Jr., J. Robinson, printer.

Turner, Edward. 1911. *The Negro in Pennsylvania: Slavery, Servitude, Freedom, 1639–1861*. Washington, DC: American Historical Association.

Twain, Mark. 1884. *Adventures of Huckleberry Finn*. UK and Canada: Chatto and Windus, Charles L. Webster.

Vann, Lucinda. 1937 [1996]. Interview with Annie L. Faulton. In *The WPA Oklahoma Slave Narratives*, edited by T. Lindsay Baker and Julie P. Baker, 435–41. Norman and London: University of Oklahoma Press.

"Voices." 1983. *Missouri Life*. July–August, 12–14.

Wachsmann, Klaus, James W. McKinnon, Robert Anderson, Ian Harwood, Diana Poulson, David van Edwards, Lynda Sayce, and Tim Crawford. 2001. "Lute." In *Grove Music Online*. https://doi.org/10.1093/gmo/9781561592630.article.40074. Accessed July 2, 2020.

Wade, Stephen. 1999. Liner notes. *Deep River of Song. Black Appalachia: String Bands, Songsters and Hoedowns*. Alan Lomax Collection. Rounder 1823.

Walsh, Lorena S. 2001. "The Chesapeake Slave Trade: Regional Patterns, African Origins, and Some Implications." *William and Mary Quarterly* Third Series 58(1): 139–70, January.

Wardlow, Gayle Dean. 1994. "Henry 'Son' Sims." *78 Quarterly* 1(9): 11–20.

Ware, Burnham. 1981 [1978]. "Bill Livers: Tenant Farmer and Rural Musician." *Living Blues* 51: 31–33, summer. Also available as "Kentucky Blues: Bill Livers Interview, Owenton, Ky., 1978."

Ware, Burnham. 1987. Personal interview with the author. Frankfort, KY. August 7.

Ware, Burnham, and Jim O'Neal. 1981. "Henry Miles and the Louisville Jug Bands." *Living Blues* 51: 34–36, summer.

Waterman, Christopher. 2000. "Race Music: Bo Chatmon, 'Corrine Corrina,' and the Excluded Middle." In *Music and the Racial Imagination*, edited by Ronald Radano and Philip V. Bohlman, 167–205. Chicago: University of Chicago Press.

Watkins, John R. 1898. "Barbecues." *Strand Magazine: An Illustrated Monthly* 16: 463–68, October.

Watkins, T. H. 1997. "Boiling Over." *New York Times*, April 13.

Watrous, Peter. 1995. "Canray Fontenot, 72, a Singer and Violinist in Creole Style." *New York Times*, August 2.

Watson, Bob. 1995. "Driving Forces in Area History Inspired Harmony." *Jefferson City [Missouri] News Tribune*, February 19.

Watson, John F. 1846. *Annals and Occurrences of New York City and State, in Olden Time; Being a Collection of Memoirs, Anecdotes, and Incidents Concerning the City, County, and Inhabitants from the Days of the Founders*. Philadelphia: Henry F. Anners.

"Watts, Cato." n.d. *Notable Kentucky African Americans Database*. https://nkaa.uky.edu/nkaa/items/show/356. Accessed December 13, 2021.

Wax, Darold D. 1973. "Preferences for Slaves in Colonial America." *Journal of Negro History* 58(4): 371–401, October 1.

Webster's New Collegiate Dictionary. 1974. Springfield, MA: G. & C. Merriam.

Welding, Pete. 1966. Liner notes. *Muddy Waters: Down on Stovall's Plantation. The Historic 1941–42 Library of Congress Recordings*. Testament Records T 2210.

Welding, Pete. 1979. "Carl Martin (1906–1979): Multi-instrumentalist with Very Cool Blues Mandolin!" *Living Blues* 43, summer.

Welding, Pete. 1992. "An Interview with Carl Martin." *78 Quarterly* 1–2: 96–100. https://s3.amazonaws.com/DinosaurDiscs/78+Quarterly+No.+1+%26+2.pdf. Accessed April 17, 2018.

Wells, Paul F. 1993. Book review. *Thomas W. Talley's Negro Folk Rhymes*, edited by Charles K. Wolfe. *Ethnomusicology* 37(1): 127–30, winter.

Wells, Paul F. 2003. "Fiddling as an Avenue of Black-White Musical Interchange." *Black Music Research Journal* 23(1–2): 135–47, spring/fall.

Wheeler, Lonnie. 1976. "Honest Man: Tom Dumas Has 'a Good Name,' and He's Got Everything He Needs." *Clarion-Ledger* [Jackson, MS], November 12, 33.

White, Newman Ivey, Henry M. Belden, and Arthur Palmer Hudson, eds. 1952. *The Frank C. Brown Collection of North Carolina Folklore, Volume Three: Folk Songs from North Carolina*. Durham, NC: Duke University Press.

Wig, Christian, and Mark Ward. 2002–2011. *Come Back Boys and Feed the Horses: Fiddling on the Frontier*. http://www.chriswig.com/cds/cbbafth/tracklist.html; http://www.chriswig.com/cds/cbbafth/notes/21.html. Accessed June 16, 2017.

Wiggins, Gene. 1977. "Not Very Aristocratic." *Old Time Music* 26: 5–7, autumn.

Wiggins, Gene, with Tony Russell. 1977. "Hell Broke Loose in Gordon County Georgia." *Old Time Music* 25: 9–21, summer.

Wilder, Mike. 2012. "Thompson Remembered as a Man as well as a Musician." *Burlington Times News*. Posted February 23, 2012.

Wiley, Day Allen. 1902. "Barbecues, and How They Are Conducted." *Wide World Magazine: An Illustrated Monthly of True Narrative—Adventure, Travel, Custom, and Sport* 9: 189–94, April–September.

Wilkerson, Isabel. 2010. *The Warmth of Other Suns: The Epic Story of America's Great Migration*. New York: Vintage Books.

Wilkerson, M. P. 1994. "Gallery Showcases Alabama-Made Instruments, Their Makers." *The Montgomery [Alabama] Advertiser*. December 11, 7H and 12H.

Willging, Dan. 1999. "D'Jalma Garnier of Filé: Digging at the Roots of Creole Music." *Dirty Linen*, 28–30, February.

Willging, Dan. 2005. "Louisiana's Prodigal Son: Creole Fiddling." *Dirty Linen*, 44–48, April.

"William Driver, Sr. and His Son, William 'Bill' Driver, Jr." 2007. Biographical Sketches: Biographies from Black Families of Miller County. Miller Historical Society, 7–9. http://www.millercountymuseum.org/bios/bio_black.html. Accessed September 15, 2019.

Williams, Charley. 1937. Interview with unidentified WPA field worker. In *The WPA Oklahoma Slave Narratives*, edited by T. Lindsay Baker and Julie P. Baker, 472–84. Norman and London: University of Oklahoma Press.

Williams, Isaac D. 1885. *Sunshine and Shadow of Slave Life: Reminiscences as Told by Isaac D. Williams to "Tege."* East Saginaw, MI: Evening News Printing and Binding House.

Williams, Vivian T. 2009. "Lou Southworth, Pioneer Oregon Fiddler." *Old-Time Herald: A Magazine Dedicated to Old-Time Music* 11(10): 10–12, April–May.

Willis, Charles. 1937 [1996]. Interview with Ida Belle Hunter in *The WPA Oklahoma Slave Narratives*, edited by T. Lindsay Baker and Julie P. Baker, 435–41. Norman and London: University of Oklahoma Press.

Wills, David W. 1997. "The Central Themes of American Religious History: Pluralism, Puritanism, and the Encounter of Black and Whites." In *African-American Religion: Interpretive Essays in History and Culture*, edited by Timothy E. Fulop and Albert J. Raboteau, 7–20. New York: Routledge.

Wilson, Sule Greg. 2013. Personal interview with the author. San Diego, California. October 3–4.

Wimbush, Vincent L. 2010. Comments and response to a lecture presented by the author, at the Institute for Signifying Scriptures, School of Religion, Claremont Graduate University, Claremont, California, October 7.

Winans, Robert B. 1979. "The Black Banjo-Playing Tradition in Tradition in Virginia and West Virginia." *Folklore and Folklife in Virginia: Journal of the Virginia Folklore Society* 1: 7–30.

Winans, Robert B. 1982. "Black Instrumental Music Traditions in the Ex-Slave Narratives." *Black Music Research Newsletter* 5(2): 2–4, spring.

Winans, Robert B. 1990. "Black Instrumental Music Traditions in the Ex-Slave Narratives." *Black Music Research Journal* 10(1): 43–53, spring.

Winans, Robert B., ed. 2018a. *Banjo Roots and Branches*. Urbana: University of Illinois Press.

Winans, Robert B. 2018b. "Black Musicians in Eighteenth-Century America: Evidence from Runaway Slave Advertisements." In *Banjo Roots and Branches*, edited by Robert B. Winans, 194–213. Urbana: University of Illinois Press.

Wise, Jennings Cropper. 1967 [1911]. *Ye Kingdome of Accawmacke, or the Eastern Shore of Virginia in the Seventeenth Century*. Baltimore: Regional Publishing Company.

Wolfe, Charles K. 1973. "Man of Constant Sorrow: Richard Burnett's Story, Part 2." *Old Time Music*, 5–9, autumn.

Wolfe, Charles K. 1977a. "Five Years with the Best: Bill Shores and North Georgia Fiddling." *Old Time Music* 25: 4–8, summer.

Wolfe, Charles K. 1977b. *Tennessee Strings: The Story of Country Music in Tennessee*. Knoxville: University of Tennessee Press.

Wolfe, Charles K. 1981. "Sam McGee." In *Tom Ashley. Sam McGee. Bukka White: Tennessee Traditional Singers*, edited by Thomas G. Burton, 61–141. Knoxville: University of Tennessee Press.

Wolfe, Charles K. 1982. *Kentucky Country: Folk and Country Music of Kentucky*. Lexington, KY: University of Press of Kentucky.

Wolfe, Charles K. 1987a. "Black String Bands: A Few Notes on a Lost Cause." *Old-Time Herald: A Magazine Dedicated to Old-Time Music*. 1(1): 15–18.
Wolfe, Charles K. 1987b. "Editor's Introduction." *Tennessee Folklore Society Bulletin* 53(2): 42, Summer.
Wolfe, Charles K. 1987c. "Thomas Talley's Negro Folk Rhymes." *Tennessee Folklore Society Bulletin* 53(3): 104–11, fall.
Wolfe, Charles K. 1989. Liner notes. *Altamont: Black Stringband Music from the Library of Congress*. Rounder 0238.
Wolfe, Charles K. 1990. "Rural Black String Band Music." *Black Music Research Journal* 10(1): 32–35.
Wolfe, Charles K. 1991. "Introduction." In *Thomas W. Talley's Negro Folk Rhymes*, vii–xxvii. Knoxville: University of Tennessee Press.
Wolfe, Charles K. 1997. *The Devil's Box: Masters of Southern Fiddling*. Nashville: Country Music Foundation Press and Vanderbilt University Press.
Wolfe, Charles K. 2002. "The Lost Tradition of Black String Bands." *No Depression: The Journal of Roots Music* 38, February 28.
Wooding, G. I., III. 1987. "Black Fiddle Player Recalls Heyday." *Martinsville [Virginia] Bulletin* 98(207): 1A-2A, August 30.
Wooley, Amy Suzanne. 2003. "Conjuring Utopia: The Appalachian String Band Revival." PhD dissertation, University of California, Los Angeles.
Work III, John W. 1940. *American Negro Songs and Spirituals: A Comprehensive Collection of 230 Songs, Religious and Secular*. New York: Bonanza Books.
Work III, John W. 2005. "Untitled Manuscript." In *Lost Delta Found: Rediscovering the Fisk University-Library of Congress Coahoma County Study, 1941–1942*, edited by Robert Gordon and Bruce Nemerov, 53–124. Nashville: Vanderbilt University Press.
Work III, John W., Lewis Wade Jones, and Samuel C. Adams Jr. 2005. *Lost Delta Found: Rediscovering the Fisk University-Library of Congress Coahoma County Study, 1941–1942*, edited by Robert Gordon and Bruce Nemerov. Nashville: Vanderbilt University Press.
Work Projects Administration. 2006 [1941]. *Slave Narratives: A Folk History of Slavery in the United States from Interviews with Former Slaves Georgia Narratives, Part 4*. Np: Project Gutenberg ebook. http://www.gutenberg.org/files/18485/18485-h/18485-h.htm. Accessed June 9, 2014.
"Works Progress Administration." 2020. *Encyclopaedia Britannica*, July 7. https://www.britannica.com/topic/Works-Progress-Administration. Accessed June 27, 2022.
Wright, Henry. 1941. "Slavery as Seen Through the Eyes of Henry Wright—Ex-Slave, Age 99." In *Slave Narratives: A Folk History of Slavery in the United States from Interviews with Former Slaves Georgia Narratives, Part 4*, edited by Work Projects Administration, 194–204. Np: Project Gutenberg ebook. http://www.gutenberg.org/files/18485/18485-h/18485-h.htm. Accessed June 9, 2014.
Wright, Laurie, and Fred Cox, compilers. 1993. *The Jug Bands of Louisville*. Essex, UK: Storyville Publications.
Writers' Program (Virginia). 1940. *The Negro in Virginia: Compiled by Workers of the Writers' Program of the Work Projects Administration in the State of Virginia*. New York: Hastings House.
Wyatt, Marshall. 1999. Liner notes. *Violin, Sing the Blues for Me: African-American Fiddlers 1926–1949*. Old Hat CD 1002.
Wyatt, Marshall. 2001. Liner notes. *Folks, He Sure Do Pull Some Bow*. Old Hat CD 1003.
Wyatt, Marshall. 2005. Liner notes. *Good for What Ails You: Music of the Medicine Shows, 1926–1937*. Old Hat CD 1005.
Wyatt, Marshall. 2018. Liner notes. *Fiddle Noir: African American Fiddlers on Early Phonograph Records 1925–1949*. Old Hat LP 5001.
Wyatt, Marshall. 2021. Email communication to the author. August 28.
Yarnell, Susan L. 1998. *The Southern Appalachians: A History of the Landscape*. US Department of Agriculture Forest Service. Asheville, NC: Southern Research Station.
Yetman, Norman R., ed. 1970. *Voices from Slavery*. New York: Holt, Rinehart and Winston.

Young, Sir William. 1801. *A Tour through the Several Islands of Barbadoes, St. Vincent, Antigua, Tobago, and Grenada, in the Years 1791 and 1792*. N.p. Also found in *The History, Civil and Commercial, of the British West Indies*, edited by Bryan Edwards III, 261–301. London: Printed for J. Stockdale, 1793–1801.

Yule, Ron. 2009. *Louisiana Fiddlers*. Jackson: University Press of Mississippi.

References Cited

Discography, Radio, Videography, Websites

Discography

The Arhoolie Records Fortieth Anniversary Box Set: 1960–2000: The Journey of Chris Strachwitz. 2000. Arhoolie CD 491.

Christeson, R. P. [Robert Perry]. 1976. *The Old-Time Fiddler's Repertory: Historic Field Recordings of Forty-One Traditional Tunes.* Columbia: University of Missouri Press.

Christeson, R. P. [Robert Perry]. 2011. *The Old-Time Fiddler's Repertory: Historic Field Recordings of Forty-One Traditional Tunes.* Columbia: University of Missouri Press.

Fort Valley Blues. 1973. Flyright-Matchbox SDM 250.

Georgia Sea Island Songs. 1977. New World Records NW 278.

Georgia Sea Islands: Biblical Songs and Spirituals. 1998. Rounder CD 1712.

Hamilton, Diana, Liam Clancy, and Paul Clayton, compilers. 1956. *Instrumental Music of the Southern Appalachians.* Tradition Records TLP 1007. Notes by Paul Clayton. http://clancy brothersandtommymakem.com/trad_1007_appalachians.htm. Accessed August 16, 2017.

Les Miseres dans le Coeur. 2000. Louisiana Radio.

Lomax, Alan. 1960. *Roots of the Blues.* Atlantic SD 1348.

Lomax, Alan. 1977. *Roots of the Blues.* New World NW 80252.

Lomax, Alan. 1997. *Southern Journey, Volume 3: 61 Highway Mississippi: Delta Country Blues, Spirituals, Work Songs and Dance Music.* Alan Lomax Collection. Rounder Records CD 1703.

Marshall, Howard Wight, Amy E. Skillman, Charles Walden, C. Ray Brassieur, Spencer Galloway and Julie Youmans, producers and editors. 1989. *"Now That's a Good Tune": Masters of Traditional Missouri Fiddling.* Grey Eagle Records 101.

Marshall, Howard Wight, Vivian Williams, and Phil Williams, producers. 2008. *"Now That's a Good Tune": Masters of Traditional Missouri Fiddling*, revised ed. Seattle: Voyager Recordings and Publications.

Martin, Carl. 1966. *The Chicago String Band.* Testament Records T 2220. Notes by Pete Welding.

Martin, Carl. 1972. *The New Mississippi Sheiks.* Rounder Records 2004. Notes by Frank Proschan and Bruce Kaplan.

Meade, Guthrie T., John Harrod, and Mark Wilson, compilers. 1997a. *Traditional Fiddle Music of Kentucky, Volume 1: Up the Ohio and Licking Rivers.* Rounder 0376.

Meade, Guthrie T., John Harrod, and Mark Wilson, compilers. 1997b. *Traditional Fiddle Music of Kentucky, Volume 2: Along the Kentucky River.* Rounder 0377.

The Mississippi Sheiks Tribute Concert: Live in Vancouver. 2010. Vancouver: Black Hen Music (DVD Recording of a Live Concert).

Music from the Hills of Caldwell County. 1975. Physical Records PR 12–001. http://michaelmesser .proboards.com/thread/9042/music-hills-caldwell-county. Accessed August 16, 2017.

Reagon, Bernice Johnson. 1994. *African American Congregational Singing Nineteenth-Century Roots*. Washington, DC: Smithsonian/Folkways.

Roots N' Blues: The Retrospective (1925–1950). 1992. Columbia, Legacy C4K 47911.

Rosenbaum, Art. 1984a. *Folk Visions and Voices: Traditional Music and Song in Northern Georgia, Volume 1*. Ethnic Folkways Records FE 34161.

Rosenbaum, Art. 1984b. *Folk Visions and Voices: Traditional Music and Song in Northern Georgia, Volume 2*. Ethnic Folkways Records FE 34162.

Rosenbaum, Art. 1984c. *The McIntosh County Shouters: Slave Shout Songs from the Coast of Georgia*. Ethnic Folkways Records FE 4344.

Ward, Fields, Uncle Alec Dunford, Crockett Ward, and John Avery Lomax. 1937. *Long, Lonesome Road*. Galax, VA. Library of Congress.

Radio

Eyre, Banning. 2023 [2000]. *The African-American String Tradition*. Afropop Worldwide. Produced by Banning Eyre. https://afropop.org/audio-programs/the-african-american-string-music-tradition-2?utm_source=main_mail_list&utm_campaign=fcc5b3ea7b-EMAIL_CAMPAIGN_2023_02_03_03_54&utm_medium=email&utm_term=0_-fcc5b3ea7b-%5BLIST_EMAIL_ID%5D. Accessed February 11, 2023.

Big Road Blues Show. 2010. *Sitting on Top of the World—Mississippi Sheiks and Associates*. Big Road Blues Radio, August 1. https://sundayblues.org/?p=2250. Accessed May 26, 2020.

Big Road Blues Show. 2014. *Raise a Ruckus Tonight—Post-War Black String Bands*. Big Road Blues Radio, October 19. https://sundayblues.org/?tag=new-mississippi-sheiks. Accessed January 1, 2021.

Sublette, Ned, and Georges Collinet. 2012. "Hip Deep Angola, Part 3: A Spiritual Journey to Mbanza-Kongo." Afropop Worldwide. https://soundcloud.com/afropop-worldwide/hip-deep-angola-part-3-a. Accessed June 29, 2024. Go to 24:30 for discussion of the fiddle.

Videography

Appalachian Journey. 1991. Association for Cultural Equity. American Patchwork Series, PBS Video (58 minutes). Film by Alan Lomax. Joe and Odell Thompson perform "Old Joe Clark" and "Going Downtown." One of five films made from footage that Alan Lomax shot between 1978 and 1985 for the 1991 PBS American Patchwork series. Subtitles in film misidentify Joe Thompson (as James Thomas) and Odell Thompson (as Odell Thomas).

Black Fiddlers. 2021. A Film by Eduardo Montes-Bradley. Eduardo and Soledad. Heritage Film Project.

Chapman, Iris Thompson, producer. 2004. *The Life and Times of Joe Thompson*. 27 minutes. https://www.youtube.com/watch?v=LiiEiJqq-Tw&t=6s. Accessed September 10, 2024.

DiverseRecords. 2011. "Douglas Bellard and Kirby Riley: Les Flammes D'Enfer." Uploaded September 15. https://www.youtube.com/watch?v=adsMeLmBfwo&t=30s. Accessed October 20, 2021.

Ferris, William, David Evans, and Judy Peiser. 1971. *Gravel Springs Fife and Drum*. 16mm color film. Center for Southern Folklore and Indiana University Audio-Visual Center.

The Language You Cry In. 1998. Documentary film produced and directed by Angel Serrano and Alvaro Toepke, with Tazieff Koroma, Joseph Opala, Cynthia Schmidt. 52 minutes.

McQueen, Steve. 2013. *Twelve Years a Slave*. 2013. Summit Entertainment, Regency Enterprises, River Road Entertainment, Film 4, and Plan B.

Palmer, Robert, and Robert Mugge. 1991. *Deep Blues: A Musical Pilgrimage to the Crossroads*. Radio Active Films.

Parks, Gordon. 1984. *Solomon Northup's Odyssey*. A television movie on PBS series *American Playhouse*.

Websites

Banjo Hangout. https://www.banjohangout.org/. Accessed September 2, 2023.

Digital Library of Appalachia. Appalachian College Association. https://dla.contentdm.oclc.org/. Accessed September 2, 2023.

Discography of American Historical Recordings. n.d.a. "Corrine Corrina / Bo Carter; Chas. McCoy." University of California, Santa Barbara Library. https://adp.library.ucsb.edu/index.php/matrix/detail/2000246006/NOR761-Corrine_Corrina. Accessed September 8, 2024.

Discography of American Historical Recordings. n.d.b. "Mockingbird." University of California, Santa Barbara Library. https://adp.library.ucsb.edu/index.php/matrix/index?Matrix_page=2&yt2=Next&Matrix_page=3&yt5=Next&yt0=First&Matrix_page=1. Accessed September 14, 2024.

Early Cajun Music. 2014. "'Mon Camon La Case Que Je Suis': Douglas Bellard." Blog, October 13. https://earlycajunmusic.blogspot.com/2014/10/. Accessed September 24, 2021.

Early Cajun Music. 2016. "'La Valse la Prison': Douglas Bellard and Kirby Riley." Blog, July 9. https://earlycajunmusic.blogspot.com/search/label/Douglas%20Bellard%20%26%20Kirby%20Riley. Accessed December 15, 2022.

Geni: American Slave Owners. n.d. https://www.geni.com/projects/American-slave-owners/11457. Accessed June 28, 2022.

Henry, Linda L. n.d. *Gribble, Lusk, and York: Rural Black String Band Music from Warren County, Tennessee.* https://www.gribbleluskandyork.org/. Accessed August 23, 2024.

Lacy, Travis. 2014. "African American Violinists: Old Presence New Genres." Just Soul You Know. Blog, February 8. https://justsoulyouknow.wordpress.com/2014/02/08/african-american-violinists-old-presence-new-genres/. Accessed January 8, 2019.

The Mudcat Café. n.d. Mudcat Café Music Foundation. https://mudcat.org/@displaysong.cfm?SongID=7943. Accessed July 30, 2022.

Pomea (Pommier), Neal. 2022–2016. *Cajun Mus mp3: Hadacol It Something!* http://npmusic.org/artists.html. Accessed October 9, 2021.

Stanford, Ron. 2020. *Big French Dance Music: Cajun and Zydeco Music, 1972–1974.* New Digital Liner Notes with Lots of Photographs. Includes liner notes. *J'Étais au Bal: Music from French Louisiana: The Carrière Bros.* Swallow Records LP 6020. https://www.bigfrenchdance.com/carriere-brothers. Accessed November 20, 2022.

Index of Subjects and Names

Legend:
bf – Black fiddler
rbf – rural Black fiddler
ubv – urban Black violinist

Page numbers in *italics* indicate illustrations.

Abbott, Lynn, 296
abolitionists, anti-slavery movement, *80*, 83, 92–93, 109
Abrahams, Roger, 38n27, 44, 89
Acadia (Acadians), 16, 399, 400, 401, 422
Accomack (Accomac, Acomorack) County (Virginia), 5–6, 174n16
accordion, xix, 45, 108, 114, 120n48, 136, 172, 174n18, 200, 237, 258, 289, 394, 402–6, *407*, 408, *409*, 411–14, 416–19, 421, 425, 433n29, 434n32, 435n39, 436n59, 437n69, 438n91
Adams, Edward C. L., 65–66
Adams, Greg, xxvin9, 38n19
Adams, Samuel C., Jr., 338n83, 392n86
Adams, William, Jr. (Maryland-rbf), 53–55, 57, 60–63, 139–40, 151–54, 174n3, 174n7; performance style, 153–54, 304, 337n62, 421, 438n87; repertoire, 53–63, 139–40, 152–53, 174n10, 174n13, 186–87; *Will Adam, Fiddler of Ken-Gar*, 174n4, 174n7
Addison, Charles (Mississippi-rbf), 54, 59, 314
Africa, xv, xvi, xviii, xxiv, 3–4, 8–15, 428, 435n43. *See also specific countries, ethnic groups, and regions*
African influences, xxviiin29, 35, 42, 50, 85, 121n51, 168, 242, 234, 249, 277, 328, 333, 338nn86–87, 378, 381, 387n43, 391n83, 398–99, 405, 420–21, 422, 430, 435n43;

Africanisms, 116, 358; dance, 41–42; derivations, xvii, xxii, 21, 23, 29, 45, 66, 69n5, 73, 76, 99, 105–7, 117, 151, 153, 166, 214, 220, 250n9, 296, 312, 359, 373, 401, 410, 432n15; performance practices (off-beat phrasing/syncopation, slurs, slides, bent notes, rhythm), 140, 166, 171, 172, 191, 212, 213, 218n51, 229, 232, 234, 249, 277, 297, 299, 303, 304, 325, 328, 360, 363, 373, 376–78, 381–83, 401, 420, 459n2; retentions, 386n10
Agawu, Kofi, 76. *See also* representation
Alabama Sheiks, 361–63, 386n18, 387nn19–20, 387n22, 387n24
Allen, William Francis, 358–59, 386n8
Allen Brothers, The, 189, 190, 217n42
Alexander, Edward (ubv), 141
Alexander, Henry (Tennessee-rbf), 447
Allison, Robert J., xxiv
Almack's (Dicken's Place), 73
Alsop, Allen (Mississippi-rbf), 54, 56, 57, 63, 314
Alvin (North Carolina-rbf), 357–58
Americas, the, xv–xvii, xxiv, xxvin8, xxvin10, xxviiin34, 3, 4, 5–7, 14, 15–36, 37n4, 39, 41, 49, 50, 73, 107, 121n51, 401, 435n41, 443. *See also individual countries and regions*
Ancelet, Barry, 400, 401, 420, 434n31, 434n34, 435n42
Anderson, Gabe (Tennessee-rbf), 447, 460n18

Anderson, Pinkney "Pink," 362
Anderson, Virgil, 239, 240, 252n49
Andrews, Nathalie, 205, 206, 208–10, 219n78
Angola, 16
Anglo-Americans. *See* European Americans
antebellum period, 39, 42, 44, 65, 71, 83, 102, 103, 326
Anthony, Eddie (Georgia-ubv), 63, 64, 118n16, 303, 334n14, 398–99, 433n22
appropriation, xx, 121n51, 249
Arab world. *See under* Asia: West
Ardoin, Alphonse "Bois Sec" (Louisiana), 400, 404, 405, 415, 418, 419, 433n29, 437n81. *See also* Fontenot, Canray
Ardoin, Amédé (Louisiana), 402–3, 406–7, 410, 412, 416, 417, 419, 434n32, 434n35, 435n40, 435n42, 436n54
Armstrong, Howard (Tennessee-bf), xxv, xxviin18, 55, 169, 170, 176n45, 212, 220n91, 221, 234, 263, 337n60, 370, 441, 443–62, *445*; Carl Martin, 176nn44–45, 460n13, 461n20; Four Keys, 170, 449; media, 176n45, 370, 387n41, 388n41, 444, 455, 461n28, 461n37; performance style and techniques, 403, 447–48; repertoire, 454–55; Roland Martin, 169, 176nn44–45, 445, 449, 460n13; Steve's Rhythm Boys, 450, 458; Ted Bogan, 169, 170, 221, 449–52, 455, 461nn19–21; Tennessee Chocolate Drops, 176n45, 212, 370, 388n41, 449, 461nn20–22; Tennessee Trio, 461n21
Armstrong, Louis, 305, 391n73, 432n3
arpeggio. *See under* fiddle performance style: practices and techniques
art music (classical music), xvii, xxi, xxvn1, 17, 24, 96, 101, 104, 114, 116, 146n29, 217n32, 336n43, 372, 378, 389n49, 417, 441, 442, 447, 448, 452, 454, 462n41
Asch, Moses, 395
Asia: South, xviii; West (Arab world, Middle East), 9, 14, 15, 33, 34, 36, 37, 120n47, 374, 390n63, 460n4
Athens, Georgia, *306*, 307, 308, 335n18, 337n68
Atlanta, Georgia, xviii, 70n19, 83, 118n16, 129, 222, 252n53, 290, 294, 303, 304, 306, 334n14, 335n17, 336n35, 388n44, 389n53
attitudes of slave owners, 22, 110–11
Atwater, Rufe (North Carolina-rbf), 259
Austin, Allan, 16, 33–34
Austin, Gene, 188, 217nn37–38
Austin, Stephen T., xxviin21, 313, 314, 323, 338n86, 339n91
Austin, Texas, 429, 430

autoharp, 258, 262
avant-garde music, xviii

Bailes, George (West Virginia-rbf), 172
Bailey, DeFord, 221, 304
Baker, Etta Reid, 255, 260–63, 280n5, 281n16. *See also* Phillips, Cora Reid
Baklanoff, Joy Driskell, 70n14, 386n18, 459n1
balafon (*balafo*, xylophone), 18, 26
Balfa, Dewey, xix, 400, 402, 403, 419–21, 433n28, 434n31, 436n55, 438n91
ballads, 136, 138, 139, 238, 241, 248, 309, 312, 318, 324, 325, 327, 328, 340n110, 369, 378–81, 401, 410, 411, 426, 427
Ballanta, Nicholas George Julius, 359
ballroom dances, 204
Baltimore, Maryland, 26, 173n2, 260
Bang, Billy (ubv), xviii, xxviin18
banjo, xvii, xxvin9, 20, 21, 26, 33, 34, 36, 37n3, 38n19, 40, 41, 46, 50, 66, 68, 70n12, 76, 78, 79, 81, 82, 90, 92–95, 97, 100, 101, 103–5, 107, 109, 110, 112, 115, 117, 120n42, 131–33, 135–39, 144, 155, 157, 159–61, *163*, *164*, 165–68, 170–72, 175n29, 178, *184*, 188, 191, 193–95, 199–202, 204, 206, 210, 211, 215n6, 216n23, 218n54, 219n71, 221, 223–29, 231–34, 236, 237, 239, 241, 243, 246, 251n19, 254, 255, 257–63, *265*, 266–68, 271, 273–80n4, 282n36, 296, 297, 307, 315, 316, 318–23, *324*, 325, 327, 331–33, 335n32, 339n98, 344, 368, 395, 412, 424–26, 429, 443, 459, 460n15
Banjo Hangout, 215n6
Baptists, 161, 200, 244, 245, 261, 266, 282n33, 339n103, 347
Baraka, Amiri (LeRoi Jones), 66
barbecue, 26, 44, 45, 76, 96, 208, 290, 316, 334n12, 345, 423, 424
Barnett, Anthony, xxviin20
Barrett, May Tess, xxviin20. *See also* Carolina Chocolate Drops
barrelhouse dance, 424
bass (string bass), 50, 134, 136, 168, 169, 176n45, 192, 194, *206*, 211, 218n54, 263, 267, 302, 307, 308, 317, 319, 321, 323, 368, 380, 406, 427, 428, 435n43, 449, 450, 452, 457, 458, 461n20
Bastin, Bruce, xviii, 129, 133, 136, 142, 143, 147n36, 169, 171, 172, 176n50, 176n53, 223, 255, 258–60, 262, 265, 279, 282n48, 289, 290, 293, 294, 299, 300, 301, 334n8, 336n12, 337n53, 337n55, 357–60, 386n12, 386n14
Baton Rouge, Louisiana, 395, *396*, *397*, 412, 432n9, 432n13
Batts, Will (ubv), 338n79

Baxter, Andrew (Georgia-rbf), 181, 291–99, *292*, *293*, 322, 335n15, 336n39; Georgia Yellow Hammers, 181, 293–95, 297, 335n33; performance style, 295, 296–99; recordings, 292–95, 361, 370; Wyzee Hamilton, 297–98, 335n22

Baxter, James (Georgia). *See* Baxter, Andrew

Beale Street Sheiks, 390n63

beating bones, 172

beating straws (straws, straw-beating), 82, 83, 91, 102, 114, 118n15, 246

bebop, xviii, xix

Beisswenger, Drew, xx, xxviin16, xxviin19, 460

Bellard, Douglas (Louisiana-rbf), 406–8, 420, 434n35, 436n54

Berber (Amazigh), 15; Bisa, 70n11

Bergey, Barry, 343–45, 352n4

Bertram, Bennie "Cuje" (Tennessee-rbf), 179, 197, 201, 215n2, 218n62, 221, 222, 234–38, *235*, 252n41, 329; lyrics, 442; performance style, 236, 239; race, 236, 239–41; repertoire, 54–57, 59–60, 63, 203, 238–39, 338n71, 442

Bertram, Dock (Tennessee-rbf), 53, 54, 57, 59, 61, 62, 235–37, 251n40

big band (swing) music, xix, 160

Big Road Blues Show, 369, 370, 372, 380

Birmingham, Alabama, 46, *311*, 312

Black Belt, 119n35, 145n14, 315, 364

Black colleges and universities. *See individual institutions*

Black Creole, xix, xxviin20, 33, 399–422, 431, 433nn25–26, 434n31, 434n36, 435n43, 435n46, 435–36n50, 436n51, 436n54, 436n56, 438n88, 459n3

Black George (West Virginia-rbf), 77, 177n56

Black string band, xxviin19, 185, 195, 221, 227, 242, 243, 258, 273, 307, 318, 328, 352n6, 358, 388n41, 444

Black Violin (ubv), xxviin18

Black violinists (ubv). *See individual names*

Blake, John, Jr. (ubv), xvi, xviii, xxviin18

Blakemore, Erin, 372

Blassingame, John, 84

Blind James Campbell's Nashville Washboard Band, 252n60

Blind Pete (Arkansas-rbf), 55, 62, 385, 392n93

blue yodel, 377, 391n73, 411, 436n65

blues music, xvii, xviii, xx–xxii, xxv, xxvin14, xxviin18, 49, 51, 55, 61, 63, 64, 66, 90, 93, 114, 128, 132–38, 141–45n15, 146nn20–21, 147n33, 147n35, 155, 169–72, 180, 181, 185–87, 188–190, 194, 195, 203–5, 207, 209–10, 211–13, 215n3, 217nn41–42, 218n48, 219n83, 220nn86–87, 222, 225, 227, 239, 240, 243, 246, 248, 250n10, 250n13, 252n48, 252n53, 254, 255, 258, 261, 263, 266, 271, 273–76, 279, 281n20, 289–91, 293–96, 298–99, 301–3, 305, 307–9, 312, 313, 315–22, 324–28, 332, 333, 335, 336n35, 336n39, 336n44, 337n53, 337n64, 338n71, 338n81, 339nn89–98, 340n110, 353n19, 358–85, 386n14, 387n19, 387n22, 387n44, 389n49, 389n52, 389nn55–56, 390n61, 390nn66–69, 390n71, 391nn72–73, 391nn78–79, 392n87, 394–99, 403, 405, 406, 408, 410, 412, 420–31, 432n11, 432–33n16, 433nn18–19, 433n22, 435nn41–42, 435n48, 436n56, 438n89, 438n93, 439nn110–11, 440, 442, 444, 446, 448, 452, 454–59, 461n31, 462n44

blues singers, 49, 289, 321, 373, 378, 389n49. *See also individual names*

Bocage, Peter (ubv), 431n3

Bolick, Harry, xx–xxi, xxiv, xxviin21, 313–15, 323, 327, 338n84, 338n86, 339n91

boll weevil, 55, 145n14, 308, 316, 359, 388n37, 432n8

bones (jaw bones), 40, 45, 46, 50, 78, 79, 90, 94, 95, 98, 100, 103, 105, 117, 172, 425

boogie-woogie, 160, 384, 426

Booker, James, Sr. (Kentucky-rbf), 87

Booker, James "Jim," Jr. (Kentucky-rbf), 179–93, 214, 242, 294, 295, 370; media, 183–85, 187–89, 215n9, 217n38, 370; performance style, 188, 212, 294–95, 298, 299; recordings, 295; repertoire, 55, 57, 61–63, 186–88; Taylor's Kentucky Boys, *184*, 295, 298, 304, 335n20. *See also* Booker Orchestra

Booker, Joe (Kentucky-rbf), 54, 214

Booker, John (Kentucky-rbf), 53–56, 62, *182*, 214, 215n11, 304

Booker Orchestra (Kentucky-rbf), 181, 185, 186, 188–91, 217n40, 218n48, 296

Boston, Massachusetts, 5, 32, 84, 118n21, 461n25

Bouton, Nathaniel, 20

Bowles, George Leonard (Virginia-rbf), xxiv, *163*, *164*, 60, 154–68, 173, 174n21, 174–75n22, 175n23, 175n27, 175n31, 175n33, 176n41, 234, 249n3, 253n64, 278, 439n116, 442; performance style, 157, 165–68, 176n41, 187–88, 234, 278; repertoire, 60, 163–65

Bowles, Naomi Pettie, 160–61

Bracey, Milton (Mississippi-rbf), 368, 388n38

Brady, Erica, 129, 130, 179, 193–96, 215n2. *See also* Shultz, Arnold

Bragger, David, 153

Brakefield, Jay F., 422. *See also* Govenar, Alan

Brazil, 70n21

breakdown and hoedown, 64, 91, 146n24, 203, 250n13, 297, 335n22, 348–50, 353n19, 380, 394, 426, 428, 459n2
Brewer, Christopher (Alabama-rbf), 119n26
Brewer, Whit (Alabama-rbf), 119n26
Brice, Andy (South Carolina-rbf), 87
Briggs, Karen (ubv), xxviin18
Britton, Ford (Tennessee-rbf), 54, 224, 225
Broonzy, "Big Bill" [William Lee Conley] (Arkansas-rbf), 385, 392n91, 431
Broussard, Delton, 411, *414*, 422, 436n63
Broussard, Jeffrey (ubv), 406, 435–36n50
Broussard, Sherry, 399
Broven, John, 434n35
Brown, Clarence "Gatemouth" (ubv), xxviin18, 438n93, 456, 462n40
Brown, Danielle, xxvii–xxviiin26
Brown, Ernest, 51, 220n90, 298, 391n83
Brown, Karida, 132
Browne, Kimasi Lionel John, xxvin13
Bruce, Philip Alexander, xvi, xxviinn8, 5–6
Bryant, Henry J. (South Carolina-rbf), 287–90, *288*, 334n3; repertoire, 287–88
buck dance, 41, 43, 100, 163, 174–75n22, 202, 209, 231, 394, 424, 427
Burkina Faso, 9, 70n11
Burnett, Richard Daniel "Dick," 196, 197, 202, 204, 219n71, 219n76, 234, 238, 240–41, 252nn52–53
Burnham, Charles (ubv), xviii
"Bur Rabbit in the Red Hills Churchyard" (folktale), 65–66
Burns, Augustus M. *See* Otto, John S.
Burrison, John, 290, 300, *302*, *303*, 337n53, 337n55
Burt, Thomas (North Carolina-rbf), 258
Buster, Charlie (Kentucky-rbf). *See* Coffey Family, The

Cable, George Washington, 69n5, 105, *106*, *107*, 120nn46–47
Caesar (Connecticut-rbf), 19
Caesar (New York-rbf), 72
Cage, James "Butch" (Louisiana/Mississippi-rbf), 394–99; family and community, 394–95, *396*, *397*, 432n5, 432n9, 432n14; learning, 394, 396; lyrics, 395, 397–99, 432n15, 433n18; media, 337n62, 394, 396, 432n5, 432n10; performance contexts, 394–96; performance style, 304, 337n62, 391n83, 395, 397–99; repertoire, 53, 55, 56, 58, 60, 62, 64, 394, 396, 399, 432n10
Cajun, xix, 16, 389n56, 399–406, 408, 410–12, 416, 421–22, 431, 433nn25–26, 434n31, 434n36, 435n39, 436n56, 437n69, 438nn88–89
cakewalk, 41, 85, 100, 316, 456
Caleb (Texas-rbf), 101
Calloway, Cab, 161, 210
Calt, Stephen, 367, 369, 374, 376, 381, 387nn29–30, 390n67
Camp Nelson, Kentucky, *182*, 183, 187, 190, 216n14, 218n48, 295, 296
Canada (Nova Scotia), 16, 76, 103, 337n68, 344, 347, 348, 353n32, 399, 433n25
Carawan, Candie, 334n2, 358
Carawan, Guy, 334n2, 358
Caribbean. *See under* West Indies
Carlin, Bob, xxviin17, 41, 175n25, 255–57, 273, 277, 280n3, 281n27, 282n39
Carnegie Hall, 271, 415
Carmichael, Hoagy, 377
carnivals, 139, 162, 207, 208, 451
Carolina Chocolate Drops, xvi, xxii, xxvin5, 175n30, 266, 271, 273, 281n30, 282n42
Carrière, Calvin (Louisiana-rbf), 406, *414*; creativity, 412; family and community, 411–14, 437n68; learning, 411–12; performance contexts, 413; performance style, 412; recordings, 412–13
Carrière, Eraste (Louisiana), 409, 410, 411, 434n35. *See also* Carrière, Joseph "Bébé"; Carrière, Calvin
Carrière, Joseph "Bébé" (Louisiana-rbf), 406, *409*; creativity, 410, 420; family and community, 408–9, 436n60; learning, 409; lyrics, 420; performance contexts, 410–11; performance style, 409–10; recordings, 410–11, 434n35; repertoire, 409
Carson, John, 70n19, 217n35, 303, 304, 337n60, 392n95, 431
Carter, Bo. *See* Chatmon, Armenter "Bo"; Mississippi Sheiks
Carter, Regina (ubv), xv–xvi, xviii, xxvin6, xxviin18
Carter Brothers, 365, 367–70, 390n65. *See also* Chatmon, Armenter "Bo"; Mississippi Sheiks
Carter Family, The, 176n50
Carver, Glenn (Florida), 360–61; performance style, 360, 386n14; repertoire, 60, 61, 360
Casey, Michael, 268, 280n3
Catholics, 66, 109, 116, 120n45, 399, 404, 405, 413
Cato (Connecticut-rbf), 19–20
Caton, William "Bill." *See* Katon, William "Bill"
Cauthen, Joyce H., xxviin21, 64, 91, 92, 97, 99–103, 109, 112, 114, 309, 312, 386–87n18, 441, 459n2

Celtics. *See under* Europe
Central Africa, 9, 16, 37n4, 120n45
Chamberlain, Mary E., 68–69
Chapman, Iris Thompson, 264, 265, 268, 270–72, 275, 279, 280n3, 281n27, 282n35
Charleston (dance), 424
Charleston, South Carolina, 88, 118n21
Charleston, West Virginia, 205, 266, 451
Charlotte, North Carolina, 181, 293, 295, 297, 298
Charters, Samuel, xxviin17, 51, 383, 391n73
Chatmon, Armenter "Bo" ["Bo" Carter] (Mississippi-bf), 371–74; Carter Brothers, 365, 390n65; family and community, 314, 365, *366*, 367, 369, 371–74, 387n29; Jackson Blue Boys, 365, 389n56; learning, 368; lyrics, 374; media, 369, 371–73, 388n45, 388–89n46; performance style, 372, 373; repertoire, 56, 227, 372, 388n45
Chatmon, Harry (Mississippi-bf), 314, 367–69, 371–73, 387n30, 387n35
Chatmon, Lonnie (Mississippi-bf), 374–79; family and community, 314, *366*, 367, 369, 371, 374–79, 390n63; learning, 368, 369; lyrics, 371, 375–76, 378; media, 365, 369, 370, 375–79, 387n20, 389n46, 390n65, 390nn67–68; performance contexts, 374; performance groups, 390n65; performance style, 369, 371, 373, 375–79, 388–89n46, 391n72, 399; race, 369, 371, 374, 375; repertoire, 62, 63, 371, 374–76
Chatmon, Miles Henderson (Mississippi-rbf), 367, 387n31, 388n36
Chatmon, Sam (Mississippi), 368, 369, 388n46
Chatmon Brothers (Mississippi), 367, 369, 370, 390n65
Chatmon Family, The (Mississippi), 364–79, 387nn30–31, 387n33, 388nn34–36, 391n78
Chenier, Clifton, 404, 406, *407*, 435n45
Chenier, Morris (Louisiana-rbf), 406, *407*
Cherokee, 63, 97, 98
Chicago, Illinois, 170, 192, 194, 297, 364, 369, 374, 378, 388n44, 389n51, 392n91, 439n111, 449–52, 454, 455, 462n39, 462n41
Christeson, R. P. [Robert Perry], xxviin17, 344, 346–49, *350*, 351, 352n4, 353n19, 353nn28–29
Christian, Will (Kentucky-rbf), 179
Christianity, 16, 21, 28, 29, 36–37, 39, 65–66, 78, 83, 84, 86, 108, 244, 245, 270, 358
Christmas, 18, 21, 27, 76–78, 85, 87, 103, 113, 159, 202, 246, 289, 358
churches, 5, 21, 23, 43, 49, 66, 83, 84, 87, 94, 104, 110, 111, 135–38, 158, 161–62, 200, 209, 210, 244, 248, 251n40, 261, 266, 269, 270, 288, 291, 299, 307, 308, 320, 322, 324, 329, 339n102, 374, 394, 395, 400, 405, 413, 432n14, 457
Cimbala, Paul A., xxvin11, 42–44, 111, 443
Cincinnati, 93, 116, 146n30, 200, 212, 400, 447
circle whistle dance, 211, 220n89
Civil War, xvi–xvii, 33, 39, 42–43, 65, 66, 81, 82, 87, 93, 96, 98, 99, 119n24, 273, 315, 335n20, 345, 348, 359, 386n8, 400
city (cities), xviii, 19, 30, 51, 68, 83, 88, 101, 104, 137, 144, 155, 176n48, 194, 250n8, 267, 269, 302, 329, 333, 339n89, 393, 452. *See also* urbanization
Clarinda (South Carolina-rbf), 28–29
clarinet, xviii, 50, 88, 117, 191, 305, 368, 390n70, 393, 432n3, 450, 452, 453, 457
Clarksdale, Mississippi, 111, 339n104, 380, 383, 391n79, 392n87
class. *See under* fiddle/fiddling: social class and status
classical music (art music), xvii, xxi, xxvin1, 17, 24, 96, 101, 104, 114, 116, 146n29, 217n32, 336n43, 372, 378, 389n49, 417, 441, 442, 447, 448, 452, 454, 462n41
Clay, Henry (North Carolina/Louisiana/Oklahoma-rbf), 98, 119n32
Clinkscales, John George, 84–85
clubs (nightclubs), 46, 405, 406, 436n63, 450, 452
coal mining, 127–30, 145n6, 145n9, 169, 192, 193, 230, 238, 289, 310, 367, 446, 461n29
Cochran, Augustus "Gus" (Alabama-rbf), 97, 310, 338n74
Coffey Family, The (Kentucky-rbf), 53–59, 61–63, 180, 197–204, *198*, 215n2, 218n63, 219n67, 221, 234, 235
Cogdell, Jacqueline, 154n7
Cogdell, Leslie Clifford, 359
Cogswell, Robert, 242, 250n5, 252nn54–55
Companion (Fiddling Is My Joy Companion), xiii–xiv, xxviiin28, xxviiin32, 124
Compton, Josephine (Mississippi-rbf), 59, 314
congo (dance), 23
Congo Square (Place Congo), 104, 105, 120n41
contra dances, 23–24, 41, 88
Conway, Cecilia, xxvin9, 255, 265, 268, 273, 275, 277, 280n3, 281n27, 282n45
Cook, Irvin (Virginia), *163*, *164*, 165–68, 175n31. *See also* Bowles, George Leonard
coon songs, 64, 103, 210, 316, 359, 362, 363, 373, 386n9, 387n21, 388n45
Copeland, Polk, 227. *See also* Patterson, Frank, Jr.
Corbin, David, 129, 145nn8–9
corn-shucking, 44, 81, 82, 83, 89, 100, 116, 260, 261, 268, 346, 424

cotillion, 41, 69n6, 82, 92
country/western music, xxii, xxvin6, xxviin20, 130, 138, 142, 143, 146n20, 175n28, 183, 187, 192, 194, 196, 209, 215, 217n41, 242, 252n46, 254, 260, 305, 318, 319, 391n73, 403, 411, 412, 423, 426, 458
Courlander, Harold, 33, 70n14, 120n42, 132, 309, 386–87n18
courthouse, 178, 202, 204, 208, 209, 219n76, 221, 237, 238, 241, 291, 292, 427
cowboy (cowboy culture), 131, 424
Cox, Elijah (Texas-rbf), 439n113. *See also* Lomax, John
Creach, "Papa" John Henry (ubv), xxviin18
creativity, xxiii, 35, 39, 115, 197, 203, 313, 408
Creecy, James R., 105
Creole, 17, 18, 33, 105–6, 107, 250n9, 120n48, 399, 400, 433n25
Creole songs, 250n9, 401
Crowder, Russelltaze, 243, 252n54
Cuba, 34, 70n21, 103, 347
Cuffee (New York-bf), 21

Dagbamba, 8, 9, 11, 13, 14, 38n20, 118n19, 153
dance, xx, xxvin4, 5–6, 23–24, 41–42, 211, 349, 351n6, 394, 423, 430; European-derived, 41
dance halls, xxvi, 73, 74, 83, 116, 130, 317, 400, 413
Danser, Kathleen, xxviin20, xxviiin27, 70n14, 118n16, 146n26, 147n34, 461n21
Davis, Charles Henry Stanley, 19–20
Delafose, John (ubv), 435–36n50
Derby (Virginia-rbf), 31
Detroit, Michigan, 200, 307, 439n111, 451, 460n6, 461n25
DeVane, Dwight, 134, 137, 222, 244–48, 250n5, 253n61, 253n66, 360, 441, 443
devil (Satan), xx, 14, 28, 29, 66–68, 79, 118–19n23, 132, 154n15, 203, 212–13, 219n74, 245, 246, 312, 359, 390n66, 400, 423
devil's songs (devil's music), 14–15, 66, 145n15, 146n23, 203, 219n74, 270, 359, 390n66, 423, 457
DeWitt, Mark, 434n33
Dickens, Charles, 73, 118n6; Almack's (Dicken's Place), 73
Dickey, James H., 92–93, 119n27
Diggory (South Carolina-rbf), 88–89
Diouf, Sylviane, 14, 15, 34, 36, 38n23, 43, 70n21
Discography of American Historical Recordings, 174n9, 338n77, 389n54
Dixon, Robert M. W., 118n16, 146–47n30, 153, 171, 174, 176n45, 216n19, 250n17, 298, 334n14, 339n140, 340n110, 362, 380, 383, 387n19, 389n54, 390n63, 391n80, 432n16, 461n20

DjeDje, Jacqueline Cogdell, xv, xxiii, xxvn2, xxvin10, xxviin18, xxviin20, 4, 7–9, 10–13, 14, 15, 17, 18, 35, 36, 50, 65, 67, 70n11, 86, 106, 107, 118n19, 142, 146n27, 153, 175n24, 184, 214, 220n90, 334n7, 386n7, 391n83, 421
Dockery Farms (Mississippi), 380, 391n78
Donell, Ace, Sr. (Missouri-rbf), 345, 346, 352n15
Dormon, James, 362, 386n9, 387n21
Dorsey, Thomas (Georgia Tom), xviii, 220n87, 373, 378, 389n51
Doucet, Michael, 418, 421, 434n31, 437n75, 438n89
Doucet, Sharon Arms, 418, 434n31, 437n75, 437nn79–80
Douglass, Frederick, 141
Douglass, John Thomas (ubv), 46
Douglass, Joseph (ubv), 141
Driver, William "Bill," Jr. (Missouri-rbf), 345, 347–51, 348, 349, 350, 353nn20–21, 353n26; field recordings, 348, 350, 353n28; *Historically Black*, 343, 347, 349, 352n21; performance style and repertoire, 348–51, 353n27; race and racism, 347, 349, 353n21, 353n23
Driver, William "Bill," Sr. (Missouri), 347, 348, 353n20
drone, 166, 168, 403, 435n41
drums/drumming, xvii, 12, 20, 21, 35, 36, 37n3, 49, 50, 67, 70n12, 77–78, 83, 88, 90, 100, 101, 105, 114, 115, 117, 136, 147n37, 172, 174n18, 210, 211, 219n78, 223, 315, 318, 323–26, 339n106, 347, 368, 394, 448, 459
Dublin, Old [Old Dublin] (West Virginia-rbf), 455
Duke Ellington Orchestra, xix, 462n39
dulcimer, 117, 174n18
Dumas, Thomas Jefferson (Mississippi-rbf), 314, 323, 329–32, 330, 385; newspapers, 329, 332; performance contexts, 331; race, 332; repertoire, 55, 56, 58
Dunaway, Wilma, 89, 119n25
Durman, Chris, xxviin20

East Africa, 9
East Tennessee, 221, 229, 249, 250n14, 291, 444, 460n11
Ebony Hillbillies, xxii, 175n30
Edison, Thomas: recordings, 202, 207, 219n70, 261, 335n17; Victrola, 141, 207, 237
electric bass, 219n78, 262, 453, 458, 459
electric guitar, 219n78, 302, 435n32, 453, 458, 459
Ellington, Edward Kennedy "Duke," xix, 462n39
Elliott, J. Gary, xxviin20, 400, 401, 403, 406, 433nn25–26, 434n31, 435n40

emancipation, 39, 40, 44–46, 50, 66, 69n10, 82, 83, 98, 100, 101, 102, 104, 112, 119n36, 153, 180, 216n14, 336n47, 344, 346, 359, 367, 399
Emancipation Proclamation, 119n36
Emerson, Old Ray (West Virginia-rbf), 455
England, xxiv, 4, 16, 17, 22, 23, 27, 30, 37n1, 38n17, 69n6, 73, 86, 104, 178, 390n63, 428
enslaved (enslavement). *See* slavery
Epstein, Dena, xv, xvii, xxvin9, 5–7, 17–19, 21–26, 28–31, 38n18, 40, 51, 69n8, 70n12, 75, 78, 79, 83–88, 90, 92, 101, 103–5, 108, 110, 111, 113, 118n4, 119n27, 120n44, 254, 333, 386n8
eScholarship (*Fiddling Is My Joy Companion*), xiii–xiv, xxviiin28, xxviiin32, 124
Eskridge, George (West Virginia-bf), 447
Estill, Monk (Kentucky-rbf), 179, 180
Europe, xv–xvi, xvii, xx, xxiii, xxiv, xxvn1, xxvin4, xxvin7, xxviiin25, xxviiin29, 3–4, 7, 15, 16, 20, 22–24, 27, 29, 32–38n25, 39, 41, 51–52, 65–67, 69n6, 75, 79, 89, 90, 92, 96, 99–102, 105, 107, 114, 116, 117, 120n47, 121n51, 140, 141, 143–44, 146n26, 166, 171, 172, 217n32, 220n90, 255, 260, 269, 290, 315, 333, 336n43, 358, 372, 399, 401, 410, 415, 420–23, 433n25, 434n34, 441, 442, 448, 452, 460, 462n41; British, 27, 31, 34, 90, 99, 100, 173, 271, 273, 290, 293, 312, 325, 333, 399–401, 433n25; Celtic, 171, 435n41; Scots-Irish, 52, 92, 114, 399. *See also specific countries*
Europe, James Reese, xxvi, 141, 146n28, 186, 369
European Americans, xv, xvii, xxiii, xxvin3, xxvin7, xxviin26, 6–7, 21, 22, 24, 26, 27, 34, 36, 37n2, 39, 41–42, 44, 51, 64–67, 69n6, 81, 84–86, 90–92, 95–99, 101, 104, 107, 112, 115, 116, 128, 137, 168, 189, 191, 196, 289, 202, 212, 236, 237, 245, 249, 251n33, 268, 272, 275, 288, 289, 291, 315–16, 320, 322, 324, 326, 335n20, 337n57, 402, 422, 437n78, 442, 448, 456, 458, 459n2
Evans, David, xxviiin17, 50, 114, 147n35, 147n37, 311–13, 322, 324–26, 338n83, 338n87, 339nn106–7, 340n110, 364, 367, 368, 376, 380, 381, 386n9, 387n27, 388n33, 388n37, 391n80, 459n1

fais do-do, 400, 404, 433n2
Feintuch, Burt, xxvin6, 43, 412
Felters, Frank (Mississippi-rbf), 394. *See also* Cage, James "Butch"
Ferguson, Jess (ubv), 338n79
festivals, xvii, 20, 21, 35, 44, 72, 74, 104, 113, 163, 205, 208, 212, 224, 250n7, 268, 271, 282n36, 290, 299–301, 335n19, 336nn43–44, 338n77, 360, 395, 402, 406, 413, 415, 419, 430, 431, 432nn10–11, 433n18, 437n71, 445, 451, 452, 458, 461n33
fiddle contests and conventions, 41, 102, 155, 158–59, 162, *163*, *164*, 175n25, 188, 195, 207, 222, 239, 249n3, 256, 257, 259, 271, 291, 292, 335n19, 344, 348, 349, 422, 457
fiddle ensembles, xix, xxiii, xxvin10, xxviinn19–20, 3, 36, 41, 50, 51, 70nn11–13, 76–78, 89, 90–91, 94, 99–104, 108, 116, 117, 120n48, 140–41, 167, 194, 205, 210, 219n78, 226, 246, 267, 295, 300, 325, 333, 352n6, 401, 425
fiddle performance style, 153–54, 157, 165–68, 176n41, 187–88, 194, 210–12, 227–29, 232–34, 236, 239, 257, 261, 267, 274–78, 294, 298, 299, 303, 304, 391n83, 337n62, 349–51, 360, 363, 369, 371–73, 382–84, 386n14, 388–89n46, 391n72, 391n83, 395, 397–99, 401, 403, 408–10, 412, 420–21, 430, 438n87; practices and techniques (arpeggio, bent notes, offbeat phrasing, pizzicato, tremolo, vibrato), 319, 339n96, 372–78, 384, 389nn48–50, 390n71, 399, 437n67, 447–48; playing positions, 17, 65, 157, 175n24, 261, 432, 449; races, xxiii, xxiv, xxvin3, xxviiin19, 5, 7, 26, 68, 85, 129, 130, 138–42, 145n10, 147n35, 151–52, 156, 162, 184–85, 187, 191, 194–97, 205, 208, 212, 216n20, 227, 231, 236, 239–41, 243, 247, 255, 256, 268, 269, 271, 272, 289, 291, 294, 295, 309, 317, 332, 344, 347, 349, 353n21, 353n23, 366, 369, 371, 374, 375, 395, 422, 426–28, 430, 438n89, 458
fiddle repertoire, xiii, xiv, xxiii, 41, 53–63, 64, 68, 88, 90, 95, 116, 123, 138–40, 146n24, 147n33, 152–54, 163–66, 168, 173, 174n8, 174n10, 174n13, 175n32, 180, 181, 183, 185–87, 194, 195, 201, 203, 209, 216n21, 216n25, 216nn27–28, 217nn30–31, 217n34, 281n55, 219n72, 220n85, 223, 225, 227, 230, 231, 237–42, 244, 245, 247, 249, 250n16, 251n20, 251n29, 252n44, 252n54, 253n65, 274, 275, 282n38, 282n44, 291, 294, 295, 296, 301–5, 307–9, 311, 313, 316, 317, 319, 321–23, 326, 327, 333, 334n10, 335n21, 337n54, 338n71, 338n78, 339n90, 345, 353n27, 360, 361, 364, 371, 372, 375, 308, 381, 385, 386n15, 387n19, 388n43, 388nn45–47, 390n65, 391n81, 392nn94–95, 396, 399, 401, 405, 409, 410, 416, 421, 429, 430, 436n52, 436n57, 437n70, 437n72, 438n85, 439n117, 440, 444, 447, 454, 460n8, 461n20
fiddle sound quality, xviii, xix, xx, 17, 104, 117, 166, 168, 234, 275, 252n16, 352n16, 353n28, 377, 382, 390n70, 391n83, 440; amplification, xvi, xviii, 453; buzzing, raspy, and rough,

18, 51, 107, 146n27, 166, 409, 436n61; human voice, xix, 18, 103, 453–54
fiddle/fiddling, xv, xvii–xix, xxi, xxvn1, xxviin14; attitude toward, xx, 15–16, 35, 20, 24–27, 29, 35, 43–44, 66, 84, 94, 113, 173, 239, 263, 270, 299, 390n64, 405–6, 435n49, 442, 456–57; construction of, xvi, 3, 11, 36, 38, 76–77, 89, 90, 99–100, 106, 107, 140, 146n27, 264, 310–11, 346, 352n16, 409, 436n61; decline in popularity, xvii, xix, xxi, xxv, xxviin15, 43, 46, 68–69, 101–2, 123, 131, 132, 134, 143, 162–63, 173, 212, 245, 262–63, 266–67, 279, 312, 317–18, 320, 361–62, 384, 406, 413–14, 422, 425, 428, 434n37, 438n91, 442, 443, 458–59; devil's instrument, xx, 14, 28, 29, 67, 68, 79, 118–19n23, 132, 145n15, 203, 212–13, 219n74, 245, 246, 312, 359, 400, 423, 457; novelty, xvi, xxi, xxv, 51, 119n39, 257, 311, 370, 372, 441, 444, 447; social class and status, xxi, 12, 19, 26–27, 29, 31, 32, 35, 38, 42, 43, 66, 68, 71, 72, 74–75, 86–87, 89, 92, 93, 106, 111–13, 115, 124, 143, 145n10, 151, 272, 338n81, 400, 435n49, 441, 456. *See also* lute; melody; musical form; performance contexts; rhythm
Fiddlin' Martin, 169, 176n44, 281n29, 290, 460n13
Fiddling in West Africa, xxiii, 8, 34–35
Fiddling Is My Joy Companion, xiii–xiv, xxviiin28, xxviiin32, 124
fife, 20, 21, 30, 49, 100, 117, 323, 339n106, 394, 395
fife and drum, 21, 136, 147n37, 174n18, 315, 318, 321, 323, 326, 394
film and television, xvii, 146n21, 175n28, 209, 270–72, 275, 282n35, 282n37, 289, 305, 323, 386n7, 388n41, 444
fish fries, 208, 209, 316, 344, 461n19
Fisk University, 36, 134, 221–24, 226, 227, 249n2, 336n44, 339n104, 391n77; Fisk Jubilee Quartet, 146n28, 391n77, 430
Flemons, Dom, 250n18, 273, 281n30. *See also* Carolina Chocolate Drops
Floyd, George, xxviin26
Floyd, Samuel, 386n7
flute (piccolo), 23, 78, 81, 100, 117, 144, 444, 453
Foddrell, Posey (Virginia-rbf), 155, 170–71, 173, 176nn46–47
Foley, Red, 220n87, 337n51
folk music revival, xvii
folklore, xx, 116, 146n19, 205, 221, 243, 250n5, 253n61, 271, 350, 394, 400
Fontenot, Adam J. (Louisiana), 416–17, 435n42
Fontenot, Canray (Louisiana-rbf), xix, 414–22, 415; Black/white interactions, 422, 438n89; creativity (composing), 419–21; Duralde

Ramblers, 419; family and community, 404, 406, 407, 413–17, 433n29, 442; learning, 417–19; lyrics, 420; media, 394, 419; performance contexts, 404–5, 419; performance style, 403, 412, 420, 421; repertoire, 54, 57–59, 64, 405
Fontenot, Freemont (Louisiana), 405, 416
Ford, Henry, 249n3, 271, 307
Ford, Nathaniel (Georgia), 301, 303. *See also* Freeman, Elbert J.
form (musical structure). *See* musical form
Fort Valley College: music festival, 224, 250n7, 299–302, 336n43, 338n77, 360; state college/university, 336nn42–44
Foster, Dan, 128, 423, 424, 429, 430, 439n113
Foster, George G., 73, 74, 117
Four Keys, 170, 449
Fox, Ad (Alabama), 361–63, 386n18. *See also* West, Eddie
fox trot, 319, 345, 456
France, xxiv, 4, 6, 15–17, 19, 22, 30, 31, 34, 35, 70n21, 99, 104, 170, 399, 401, 403–5, 411–13, 422, 428, 433n25, 435n41, 437n70, 461n32
Frank, Carlton (ubv), 435–36n50
Frankfort, Kentucky, 208, 216n14
frattoir/frottoir/vest frottoir (rubboard), 402, 403, 435n43
Frazier, Nathan (Tennessee). *See* Patterson, Frank, Jr.
Freeman, Elbert J. (Georgia-rbf), 250n7, 290, 291, 300–305, *302*, *303*, 322, 336n47, 337n53; performance style, 217n35, 302, 303–5, 309, 328, 391n83; repertoire, 55, 58, 59, 61, 62, 64, 334n10
frolics, 41–44, 46, 49, 76, 102, 116, 135, 138, 155, 158, 162, 165, 167, 268, 282n32, 296, 298, 307, 311, 316, 317, 395, 424
Fulbe, 8–10, 12, 15, 35
Fulcher, Robert, 90, 119n24, 197, *198*, *199*, 202–4, 215n2, 219n67, 219n69, 219nn75–76, 235, 236–41, 250n5, 252nn48–49, 252n52, 349, 353n23
Fulks, Darley, 220n92

Gadaya, 295, 335n19
Gaddy, Kristina, 174n4. *See also* websites
Gaither, Archibald "Baldy" (North Carolina-rbf), 256, 280n10
Gaither, Harvey (North Carolina-rbf), 257, 280n10
Galax, Virginia, 175n25, 176n37
Gambia, The, 9, 10, 12
Gardiner, Polydor (Rhode Island-rbf), 19
Garnier, D'Jamal, III (ubv), xxviin20, 406, 416, 419, 434n31, 435–36n50, 437n67

Garrett, John (ubv), 447, 455
Garrison, Lucy McKim, 358–59
Gate City String Band, 171
Gay, Harry (Tennessee-rbf), 455
Geechee, 146n18, 334n2, 358, 386n10
gender, xxviin11, 12, 30–31, 49, 85, 129, 136, 145n8, 265–66, 389n49, 437n75. *See also* women
Genuine Negro Jig. *See* Carolina Chocolate Drops
Georgia Sea Islands. *See* Sea Islands
Georgia Tom, xviii, 220n87, 373, 378, 389n51
Georgia Yellow Hammers, 181, 293–95, 297, 335n33
Germany, 88, 98, 170, 171, 178, 399, 400, 402, 433n25, 435n39
Ghana, 9, 11, 13, 38n20, 118n19, 153
Gibson, George R., 179, 180, 215n2
Giddens, Rhiannon (North Carolina-bf), 273, 281n30, 282n42. *See also* Carolina Chocolate Drops
Gillespie, John Burks "Dizzy," xiii–xix
Gilliat, Simeon "Sy" (Virginia-rbf), 23, 38n18
Gilliland, Henry, 70n18, 147n32, 217n17
Gilman, Caroline Howard, 88–89, 117, 118n21
Givens, Bill, xxviin17, 147n33
Glover, Mae, 391n73
Godrich, John. *See* Dixon, Robert M. W.
Goertzen, Chris, xxviin21, 90, 351, 353n32
Goldston, Darleen, 347, 348, 350, 352n21
Gomez, Michael A., xxviiin34
Gooch, Jim (Mississippi-rbf), 55, 314
Gordon, Robert, 386n10. *See also* Library of Congress
gospel music, 142, 143, 170, 175n31, 220n87, 305, 311, 370, 374, 419
gourd, xvi, 100, 435n43; banjo, 70n12; fiddle, 11, 36, 76, 90, 99, 100, 116, 200. *See also* fiddle/fiddling: construction of
Govenar, Alan, 66, 102, 114, 121n50, 135, 137, 386n8, 406, 422–27, 438nn97–99, 438–39n103, 443
Grace, Jilly (West Virginia-rbf), 172
Grafton, Lacy, 172–73
Grand Ole Opry, 152, 154, 174n11, 196, 221–23, 456
Great Depression, 312, 362, 365, 370, 372, 432n8
Great Migration. *See* migration
Green, Jeffrey, 290, 334n8, 386n12
Green, Leothus "Les," 397, 433n18
Greene, Lorenzo Johnston, 19, 20, 21
Greer, Walter (Tennessee-bf), 222, 242–43, 250n5, 252nn55–56, 252n60; repertoire, 53, 55, 58, 60, 61, 63, 252n54
Griffin (South Carolina-rbf), 84–85

Griffin, Ella Shultz (Kentucky-rbf), *193*, 194–97. *See also* Shultz, Arnold
Guadeloupe, 17, 35
guitar, xviii, xix, 33, 40, 41, 53, 62, 66, 94, 97, 114, 133, 136–38, 144, 157, 160, 165, 168–72, 176n45, 176n50, 178, 179, *182*, *184*, 186, 191, *192*, 193–97, 200–204, *206*, 208, 210, 211, 216n23, 218n54, 219n69, 219n71, 225, 231–37, 240, 241, 246, 251n29, 256–59, 261, 262, 264, 266, 267, 275, 279, 280n15, 281n20, 289–91, 294, 297, 298, 301, *302*, *303*, 304, 305, 307–9, 315, 318, 319, 321–23, 325, *326*, *327*, 328, 331, 333, 335n32, 336n38, 337n53, 338n77, 344, 345, 347, 357–65, 368, 371, 373–80, 381–85, 386n17, 388–89n46, 391n72, 392n87, 392n91, 395–99, 411–13, 417, 419, 425–30, 437n68, 438n91, 440, 442, 445, 447, 450, 452, 454, 456, 457, 460n16, 460n18, 461n20, 462n40
Gullah, Gullah Geechee, 146n18, 334n2, 358, 386n10
Gussow, Adam, 137, 378, 390n66
Guyton, Ben (Alabama-rbf), 96
Gwari, 70n11

Haiti (Saint-Domingue), 19, 69n5, 104, 120n45
Hake, Peggy Smith, 347, 349, 353n26
Halpert, Herbert, 68
Hamilton, Wyzee, 297–98, 335n22
Hammons, Burl, 172–73
Hampton Institute, 174n17
handclapping, 12, 117, 328
Handy, William Christopher, xviii, xxvin14, 90–91, 119n26, 141, 194, 299, 301, 332, 444, 456
Hannah, George, 389n49
Hannah-Jones, Nikole, 37n2
harmonica (French harp), 78, 136, 138, 144, 159, 161, 174n18, 207, 208, 216n23, 221, 244, 245, 258, 261, 262, 304, 318, 319, 321, 323, 331, 347, 383, 386n17, 390n70, 429, 430, 431, 459
Harper's Weekly, 45, 400. *See also* newspapers and magazines
Harris, Don "Sugar Cane" (ubv), xxviin18
Harris, Theodore (Mississippi-rbf), 314
Harrison, Daphne, 136
Harrod, John, 178–79, 194, 202, 205, 206, 209–15n2, 219n78, 220n86, 220n89, 220n92
Harrower, John, 26–27, 441
Hausa, 8, 9, 11, 12, 14
Hawaii, 425, 455
Hawkins, George, 179, 215n6
Hay, Fred J., xxviin18, 321, 322, 339n98
Hayes, Clifford (ubv), 374, 377, 338n79, 389n49, 391n73

Hee Haw, 175n28, 411. *See also* film and television
Hemphill, Sidney (Mississippi-rbf), 314, 323–27, *324*; repertoire, 53, 55, 57–59, 62
Henry, Linda L., xxviin20, 49, 120n40, 231, 250n5, 251n28, 393
Hicks, Charles B., 46
Hidden in the Mix, xx. *See also* Pecknold, Diane
Higginson, Thomas, 81
Hinson, Glenn, 255, 258, 260, 262, 280n3, 312, 334n13, 442
hip hop, xix, xx
Historically Black, 343, 347, 349, 352n21
hoedown, 64, 112, 312, 379, 459
Hoffheimer, Michael L., xv, xxviin17
hokum, 189, 217n41, 319
holidays, 5, 18, 20, 21, 43, 44, 50, 74, 76–78, 85, 90, 102, 103, 116, 119n36, 202
Hollis, George (Georgia-rbf), 308–9
Holly, Buddy, 196
Holtzberg-Call, Maggie, 309, 386–87n18, 459n1
Howard, Darnell (ubv), 141
Howell, Peg Leg, 118n16, 398–99, 433n22
horn (brass), xviii, 29, 33, 50, 51, 67, 70n12, 98, 139, 202, 266, 318, 323, 339n89, 360, 378, 379, 393, 434n34, 435n43, 450, 457
hornpipes, 23, 64, 70n20, 227, 349, 353n19
house party (house dance), xxiv, 41, 46, 49, 78, 82, 112, 114, 135, 158, 161, 165, 167, 178, 201, 202, 208, 209, 237, 246, 258, 267, 319, 344, 349, 359, 368, 369, 395, 400, 403–5, 411, 413, 419, 423, 435n48, 437n76
Houston, Texas, 331, 403, 413, 426, 427, 428, 438n98
Howard University, 250n9
Huber, Patrick, xxviin22, 139, 183, *184*, 185, 186, 215n11, 216n19, 387n30
Hundley, David R., 108–9
Hunt, Bill (West Virginia-rbf), 172
Hurston, Zora Neale, 69–70n10, 299, 386n10
Hutchison, Frank (West Virginia), 172
hymns/hymnody, xxv, 78, 84, 87, 111, 245, 246, 311, 358, 413, 448

identity, xvii, xxiv, 39, 42, 65, 88–89, 130, 131, 133, 190, 247, 312, 361, 424
improvisation, 50–51, 103, 188, 277, 337n60, 373, 375, 376, 378. *See also* melody; musical form; rhythm
Indians/Indigenous/Native American people, 4, 36, 97, 98, 260, 281n28, 401, 418, 433n25, 434n34, 437n79; Cherokee, 63, 97, 98; Trail of Tears, 128

Ireland, 27, 38n17, 52, 64, 92, 110, 114, 140, 152–54, 173, 178, 187, 260, 346, 399
Islam and Muslims, 14–15, 33, 38n23, 65, 66
Italy, 340n123, 399, 400

Jabbour, Alan, 52, 140, 146n26, 187–88, 274, 276
Jackson, Carlton, 193, 194, 218n59
Jackson, Charlie, 189, 217n40, 217n42, 217n44, 387n19
Jackson, Mississippi, 367, 369, 372–74, 388n33, 388nn35–37, 388n39, 390n6
Jackson, Teodar (Texas-rbf), 57, 60, 64, 423, 425, 429–31, 439n114; family and community, 425–26; learning, 430; media, 430; performance contexts, 430; performance style, 430; repertoire, 430
Jackson Blue Boys, 365, 389n56. *See also* Chatmon, Armenter "Bo" ["Bo" Carter]
Jacksonville, Florida, 359
jam session, 395, 432nn12–13
Jamaica, 18, 21, 22, 70n12
Jamaica (New York-bf), 21–22
Jamieson, Stuart, 229–33, 250n5, 251n34
James, Willis Laurence, 250n9, 299, 336n44
Jarratt, Devereux (Virginia-rbf), 25
jawbones, 40, 70n12, 94, 105, 117, 174n18, 434n33. *See also* bones
jazz, xvi–xix, xxi, xxii, xxvn1, xxviii18, xxvii20, 51, 91, 93, 133, 134, 138, 139, 141–43, 160, 186, 189, 191, 210–12, 217n32, 222, 232, 312, 321, 336n29, 336n45, 337n68, 339n89, 370, 375–78, 388n42, 389n56, 391n73, 393, 398, *415*, 421, 424, 428, 431–32n3, 435n49, 438n89, 439n119, 440, 444, *455*, 452–54, 461n32, 462nn38–39, 462n41
Jefferson, Blind Lemon, 203, 388n42
Jefferson, Randolph. *See* Jefferson, Thomas
Jefferson, Thomas, 24–25, 38n19
Jefferson City, Missouri, 344, 346–48, *349*, 350, 352n12, 353n20
Jenkins, Leroy (ubv), xxviin18
Jenoure, Theresa, xx, xxviin18
jerky, jiggly, jiggety, and jiggy (performance styles), 140, 194, 200, 204, 212, 236, 239, 241–42, 305, 422
Jew's (Jews) harp, 101, 114, 359
jig, xxvin5, 17, 19, 23, 27, 38n17, 41, 51, 68, 70n20, 78, 82, 102, 105, 110, 112, 138, 187, 248, 315, 348, 424
Jim Crow. *See under* racism/segregation
jitterbug, 91
John Canoe, 18
Johnson, Alec, 372, 373, 389n53

Johnson, Charlie (Alabama-rbf), 103
Johnson, Guy B., 133, 299, 334n2, 386n10. *See also* Odum, Howard
Johnson, Lonnie (ubv), 374, 389n49, 426, 427
Johnson, Pink (Texas-bf), 426, 438n97
Johnson, Tommy, 376, 390n67
Johnson, William "Bill" Manuel (Louisiana), 186, 189, 217n32; Original Creole Orchestra, 186, 217n32
Jones, LeRoi (Amiri Baraka), 66
Jones, Lewis Wade, 336n44, 392n86
juba (dance), 25, 41, 93, 318
jug, 51, 70nn13–14, 93, 114, 136, 219n81, 290, 334nn12–13, 377, 452–53. *See also* jug bands
jug bands, 51, 136, 142, 144, 191, 219n81, 290, 312, 321, 334n13, 338n79, 370, 377, 386n12, 453
juke (jook) joint, xxviin4, 69–70n10, 254, 359, 367, 370, 432–33n16, 451, 461n27
juré, 401, 434n33
Juneteenth, 100, 119n36, 424, 438n95

Kalra, Ajay, 210, 219n78
Kandeh, Tamba (The Gambia), *10*
Kansas City, Missouri, xix, 98, 462n38
Kansas Joe, 387n19
Katon, William "Bill" (Missouri-rbf), 344–47, 352–53n17, 353n19
kazoo, 136, 189, 191, 318, 333, 395
Keith, Jeffrey, 181, 206, 208, 212, 219n78
Kemble, Edward Winsor, *106*, *107*, 120n44
Kennedy, Joe, Jr. (ubv), xviii
Kennedy, Stetson, 134, 146n19
Kent, Don, 144, 367, 369, 374, 376, 380, 382, 387n29, 390n67
Keppard, Freddie, 189, 191, 217n42, 432n3
King, Thomas S. (Tennessee-rbf), 224, 225
Kjemtrup, Inge, 460n4
Knoxville, Tennessee, 169, 170, 176n45, 205, 221, 444, 447, 449, 451, 452, 456, 457, 459, 460n13, 461
kora, xxvin6
Koster, Rick, xix–xx
Kubik, Gerhard, 18, 391n83

Labat, Jean-Baptiste, 6, 7, 9, 37n8
Lacey, Travis, xxvin4
Lacy, Grafton [Lacy Grafton] (West Virginia-rbf), 172–73
Laing, Alexander Gordon, *10*, 14
Laing, James T., 129, 145n7, 145n10
la-la (house party), 404
Larson, Eric, 205, 206, 208–10, 219n78

Latin America, xviii
Lawrence, Keith, 192, *193*, 194–97, 218nn54–55, 218n59
Lawson, Sherman (West Virginia), 172
Lawtell Playboys, 410, 411, 413, *414*, 422, 436n63
Lead Belly, 392n93, 430
'Lection Day, 20, 21, 121n51
Ledbetter, Huddie, 392n93, 430
Lee, Annie (Mississippi-rbf), 314
Leggett, Steve, 145n14, 335n29, 336–37n51, 385
Lembo, Ralph, 374. *See also* Chatmon, Lonnie
Lewis, Frederick Elliot (ubv), 46
Lexington, Kentucky, 181, 183, *198*, *199*, 201, 216n14, 218n59, 219n77
Library of Congress, 40, 133, 142, 172–73, 189, 225, 227, 230, *324*, *326*, *327*, 336n44, 339n104, 360, 386n10, 386n14, 391n77, 392n87
Lieberman, Julie Lyonn, xxviin20, 364, 369, 372, 375–77, 387n30
Lindy hop, 160
Linford, Scott, 167–68, 191, 228, 234, 278, 305, 328, 351
Lipscomb, Charles (Texas-rbf), 114, 121n50, 438n93
Lipscomb, Mance (Texas), 121n50, 424, 430, 438n93
Little Dixie (Missouri), 343, 345, 346, 351, 352n12, 353n32
Little Rock, Arkansas, 385, 392n93
Livers, Claude (Kentucky-rbf), 206
Livers, Hattie, 209
Livers, Hood (Kentucky-rbf), 206
Livers, Virge (Kentucky-rbf), 206, 208, 210
Livers, William "Bill" (Kentucky-rbf), xxviin18, 180, 204–13, *205*, *206*, 219nn78–79, 219n81; Bill Livers and the Holbrook Idiots, 208; Bill Livers String Ensemble, 205, 219n78; Owen County Idiots, 208; performance style, 210–12, 257, 302, 303, 337n57, 391n83, 439n116; Progress Red Hot String Band, 205; race, 205, 208; repertoire, 53–55, 57, 59–64, 209–10, 220n86
Lomax, Alan, xxviin17, 133, 137, 138, 145n15, 146n23, 188, 189, 221, 249n4, 271, 313, 322, 323, *324*, *326*, *327*, 328, 336n44, 338n83, 339n104, 340n110, 340nn116–17, 383, 385, 386n10, 392n86
Lomax, John, 133, 176n37, 249n4, 313, 360, 385, 386n10, 386n14, 392n93, 439n113
Lomax, Ruby Terrill, 360
Lornell, "Kip" Christopher, xxii–xxiii, xxviin20, 78, 102, 114, 121n50, 131, 135, 137, 138, 141, 147n32, 147n35, 154, 155, 157, 159, 163–65, 167,

171, 174n17, 175n27, 175n29, 176n38, 251n31, 254, 258, 259, 263, 266, 268, 273, 274, 276, 281n22, 282n46, 289, 312, 371, 386n8, 387n44, 406, 423–27, 438n97, 439n103, 443

Louie Bluie, 388n41, 444, 455, 461n20. *See also* Armstrong, Howard

Louisiana, xix; history, 401–2; performance style, 401, 403; repertoire, 405; songs, 250n9. *See also* Black Creole; Cajun; Creole

Louisville, Kentucky, 51, 70nn13–14, 179, 180, 194, 230, 312, 337n68, 338n79, 370

Lowry, Pete, 136, 138, 142, 143, 300, 334n8, 336n44, 371. *See also* Bastin, Bruce

Lucas, Uncle Ruff (Mississippi-rbf), 316–17

Lusk, Jeff (Tennessee-rbf), 120n40

Lusk, John (Tennessee-rbf), xxviin18, 220n88, 222, 229–32, 251nn28–30; media, 211, 231, 251n34; performance style, 211, 228, 232–34, 251n35–38; repertoire, 53–57, 61–62, 174n10, 231

lute: bowed, early history, xv, xvi, xxiv, 9, 34, 36, 50, 70n11, 100, 107, 120n47, 441, 460n4; plucked, xxvin9, 12, 50, 70n11, 90, 100

lyrics, xiii, xiv, 94, 134, 136, 137, 139, 165, 166, 176nn36–37, 188–90, 209, 215n3, 217nn40–42, 217n44, 223, 239, 248, 252n53, 253n66, 276, 277, 298, 299, 304, 308, 326, 335n29, 336n37, 337n59, 338n77, 340n112, 362–63, 371, 374–76, 389n52, 390nn60–61, 395, 397, 398, 401, 403, 410, 420, 432nn15–16, 433n18, 433nn20–21, 433n23, 434n34, 436n65, 438n84, 442, 447

Mack, Chaney (Georgia), 76–77, 188n11

Macon, Uncle Dave, 223, 227, 230, 325

Mahama, Salisu (Ghana), *11*, 153

Malone, Bill C., 130, 174n11, 423

mandolin, 50, 134, 136, 144, 167, 168, 170, 171, 176n50, 193, 195, 211, 215n2, 218n52, 219n81, 225, 237, 246, 262, 267, 318, 321, 323, 331, 345, 358, 368, 369, 373, 380, 383, 384, 390n46, 428, 429, 438n91, 443–47, 460nn15–16, 461n20, 462n44

Mangin, Julianna, 174n4, 174n7. *See also* websites

Marcus, George E., xxiii

Marrant, John (New York-rbf), 28–29

Marshall, Erynn, 171, 176n53, 177n56

Marshall, Howard Wight, xxviin21, 98, 119n23, 140, 343–46, 349, 351, 352n2, 352n4, 352n6, 352nn11–12, 353n17, 353n19, 353n32

Martin, Carl Choice (Virginia-bf), 58, 155, 168–71, 176n42, 176nn44–45, 212, 221, 281n29, 290, 445, 449–51, 460n13, 461nn20–22

Martin, Christopher Columbus "Uncle Lum" (Kentucky-rbf), 179

Martin, Frank [Fiddlin' Martin] (South Carolina-rbf), 169, 176n44, 281n29, 290, 460n13

Martin, Roland (South Carolina, Tennessee-rbf), 169, 176nn44–45, 445, 449, 460n13, 461n20

Martin, Sarah, 389n49

Martin, Wayne, 204, 263, *265*, 266–68, 274, 275, 280n3, 280n5

Martinique, 6

Martinsville, Virginia, 156, 159, 161, *163*, *164*, 165, 174n19, 257

Mathews, Burgin, 97, 119n30, 309–12, 361

Mattern, Mark, 399, 400, 402, 404, 421, 433n25, 434nn31–32, 434n36, 435n44

Mayo, Margot, 229, 230, 250n5, 251n34

mazurka, 410

McClatching, Henry (Mississippi-rbf), 314, 323

McCormick, Mack, 102, 118n15, 121n50, 423, 425, 428, 434n32

McCoy, Charlie (Mississippi), 367, 371, 373, 374, 387n34, 388–89n46

McCoy, Prince Alpert (Mississippi-rbf), 314

McDade, Dave (Tennessee, rbf), 447, 460n18

McDade, Fred (Tennessee, rbf), 447, 460n18

McGee Brothers, The, 189, 217n42, 250n10

McGee, Dennis (Louisiana), 403, 407, 434n31, 435n40, 436n54

McMichen, Clayton, 238, 252n46

Meade, Guthrie "Gus," 153, 174n9, 180, 182, 187, 215, 219, 283n48

Meadows, Eddie S., 15, 217n32, 376, 431n2

media, xvii, xxi, xxiii, 124, 132, 133, 139, 141, 143, 146n20, 154, 160, 164, 175n33, 180, 183, 184, 186–89, 202, 203, 214, 237, 243, 248, 269, 272, 282n83, 292, 295, 303, 337n57, 364, 370–72, 379, 396, 406, 423, 430, 442

medicine shows, 46, 51, 83, 139, 170, 208, 254, 274, 320, 362, 426–27, 439n105, 451, 461n19

melody, xviii, xix, 13, 19, 64, 94, 118n15, 137, 141, 153, 154, 166–68, 176n39, 178, 189–91, 211, 217, 226–29, 232, 233, 251n24, 252n53, 275–78, 282n47, 297–99, 304, 325, 328, 337n60, 338n77, 349–51, 352n6, 363, 373–78, 381–84, 388n43, 389n52, 390n61, 402, 403, 420, 425, 447, 452, 456, 459; drone, 166, 168, 403, 435n41; heterophony, 167, 168, 228, 233, 278; musical texture, 13, 232, 233, 297; polyphony (polyphonic), 13, 229, 232–34, 249, 277, 297, 376, 377, 383, 391n73; strain, 19, 78, 187, 223

Memphis, Tennessee, xviii, 46, 51, 70n14, 109, 221, 251n39, 312, 317–21, 323, 338n79, 340n123, 364, 367, 369, 370, 388n35

Memphis Minnie, 387n19, 452–53
Menestrel, Sara Le, 400, 433n30, 434n38, 435n49
Menius, Art, 271–72
Mexico, 344, 423–25, 428
Miami, Florida, 359
Middle Tennessee, 36, 120n40, 221–25, 229, 243, 249, 250n5, 251n39, *381*, 460n11
Midwest, xxi, 127, 170, 312, 345, 349, 353n28, 353n32, 370, 449, 461n33
migration, xv, xx, 128–29, 130, 145n3, 236, 241, 260, 261, 296, 298, 335n29, 343, 359–60, 363, 367–69, 374, 380, 387n27, 389–90n59, 394–95, 403, 432n8, 439n107, 451, 461n33
Miles, Henry (ubv), 338n79
Miller, Luella, 389n49
Milnes, Gerald, xxviin21, 64, 91, 96, 119n29, 143, 171–73, 176n53, 213, 223, 459n2
minuet, 17, 18, 23, 42, 89, 344
minstrel songs, 50, 95, 153, 173, 210, 227, 369, 379, 424
minstrelsy, xx, xxviin19, *45*, 46, *47*, *48*, 50, 69n9, 81, 115, 143, 151, 173, 208, 217n41, 238, 274, 318, 320, 333, 339n89, 345, 362, 369, 386n9, 423, 424, 428, 451, 459; Christy's Minstrel's, *46*; G.W. Serenaders, *48*; Original Georgia Minstrels, *48*; Virginia Minstrels, *45*
Minton, John, xxviin18, 76, 90, 99, 100–102, 104, 112, 399, 401–3, 422, 423, 434n31
Minton, Tiffany, 132, 242, 243, 252nn54–57, 252n60
Mississippi Blues Trail, 365, 367, 369, 383, 387–88n31, 391nn78–79
Mississippi Corn Shuckers, 380
Mississippi Delta, 51, 131, 133, 221, 274, 314, 319, 323, 329, 331, 332, 339n97, 340n121, 364, 367, 368, 379, 380, 385, 386n18, 387n27, 387n37, 391nn75–76
Mississippi Hills, 315–28, 339n88, 364, 368; Black fiddlers, 316–17
Mississippi Hot Footers, 365, 371, 372, 388–89n46
Mississippi Mud Steppers, 365, 390n65
Mississippi River, 98, 108, 131, 145n14, 251n39, 258, 323, 352n3, 364, 379, 387n26
Mississippi Sheiks, 361, 365, *366*, 368, 370–72, 374–79, 388n42, 388–89n46, 390n63, 390nn66–68
Miyake, Mark Y., xxviin20
Mobile, Alabama, 102, 109
Monroe, Birch, 194
Monroe, William Smith "Bill," 192, 195, 218n52, 218n56, 218n59, 335n17, 336nn35–56, 410

Montes-Bradley, Eduardo, xxviin18
Montgomery, Alabama, 101, 151, 311
Montgomery, Wilford "Little Brother" (Louisiana), 397, 433n17, 433n18
Moore, T. DeWayne, xxviin18, xxviin22, 142, 331, 339n103, 339n107, 340n109, 365–69, 371–72, 389n56, 391n73
Moore, William (Virginia-rbf), 357
Mordecai, Samuel, 23, 69n8
Morganfield, McKinley (Muddy Waters-Mississippi), 369, 379, *381*, 383–84, 392n87. *See also* Simms, Henry "Son"
Morris, George (West Virginia-rbf), 96
Morton, Jelly Roll, 189, 193–94, 388n42, 398, 432n3
Moses, Bruin (North Carolina-rbf), 259
Mostella, Earnest (Alabama-rbf), 97, 118n11, 309–12, *310*, *311*, 338n74; repertoire, 55, 56, 60, 61, 311, 360
Mott, Abigail Field, 28–29
mouth bow, 114, 118n15
Mudcat Café, 176n35, 176n37, 273
musical form, xiii, xiv, 13, 70n20, 136, 153, 154, 165, 166, 174n14, 174n16, 176n40, 188, 191, 217n45, 224, 228, 230, 232–34, 248, 251nn22–23, 252n48, 276–79, 283n50, 297, 298, 316, 317, 320, 328, 335n30, 336n40, 337n60, 350, 353n31, 360, 363, 372, 376–77, 382–83, 390n71, 397, 421, 431, 434n33; twelve-bar blues, 190, 213, 215n3, 296, 372, 373, 381, 383, 389n52, 398–99
musical genres, xviii, xxi, 134, 136, 142, 190. *See also specific genres*
musical instruments. *See specific instruments*
musical texture, 13, 232, 233, 297
musicking, definition of, xiii, xxvin12
Muslims, 14–15, 33, 38n23, 65, 66

Nance, Ray (ubv), xix, 469n39
Nashville, Tennessee, 95, 109, 143, 174n11, 192, 221, 224, 225, 227, 229, 230, 242, 243, 249n2, 250n8, 252n60, 336n44
Native American people. *See* Indians/Indigenous/Native American people
Nelson, Frank (Tennessee-rbf), 477
Nelson, Oscar William (Texas-rbf), 425, 428–29
Nemerov, Bruce, 224–27, 250n5, 334n9, 392n86
New Orleans, Louisiana, xviii, 30, 38n22, 51, 70n13, 95, 101, 102, 107, 116, 119n39, 120n40, 131, 193, 194, 217n32, 230, 231, 251n31, 305, 335n24, 378, 389n53, 393, 399, 410, *415*, 431–32n3, 435n42, 439n119, *445*, 452, 457, 461n31; and Congo Square, Place Congo, 104–5, 120n41

New York City, 70n18, 73, 74, 83, 116, 120n40, 146n30, 271, 283n48, 335n17, 359, 369, 378, 388n44, 413, 415, 418, 432n16

Newport, Rhode Island, 20, 395, 415, 430, 432nn10–11, 433n18, 437n71

Newport Folk Festival, 395, 415, 430, 432nn10–11, 433n18, 437n71

newspapers and magazines, xxi, 24, 25, 31–34, 39, 45, 69n7, 71–73, 86, 92, 95, 106, 107, 112, 120n44, 176n51, 183, 216n20, 218n59, 219n77, 256, 271–73, 282n35, 300, 310, 316, 332, 334n12, 343, 380, 388n44, 400, 422–23, 436n54, 444

Nickerson, Camille, 250n9

Nigeria, 9, 11, 14, 16, 70n11

Nketia, J. H. Kwabena, xxviiin29, 9, 51

North Africa, 9, 14

North America, xv, xviii, xx, xxvin3, xxvinn8–9, 3, 5, 7, 15–16, 27, 33, 52, 69n6, 73, 102, 154, 174n11, 222, 433n25, 440

Northeast Africa, 107, 120n47

Northup, Solomon (New York/Louisiana-rbf), 75, 79, 113, 114, 118n7, 118n9, 120–21n49

novelty, xvi, xxi, xxv, 51, 119n39, 257, 311, 370, 372, 441, 444, 447

Now What a Time: Blues, Gospel, and the Fort Valley Music Festivals, 1938–1943, 334n9, 336n44. *See also* Fort Valley: music festival

Oakley, Giles, 368, 369

Obrecht, Jas, 369, 387n29, 388n34

Odum, Howard W., 133, 135, 136, 254, 280n2, 298, 299, 335n23, 336n37, 374, 389–90n59, 433n18, 433n21

off-beat phrasing. *See under* African influences: performance practices; fiddle performance style: practices and techniques

Old Dublin (West Virginia-rbf), 455

old-time music, xvi, xvii, xix, xxii, xxvinn5–6, xxviinn18–19, 112, 114, 133, 137, 139, 141–43, 146n20, 153, 154, 158, 164–68, 172, 175n30, 180, 183, 185–87, 189–91, 194, 197, 200, 210, 215n12, 217, 220n86, 228, 233, 234, 238, 239, 242, 243, 248, 250n18, 253n66, 254–56, 258, 259, 263, 266, 268–73, 276, 278, 281n22, 291, 294, 301, 304, 306–9, 315, 317, 322, 326, 328, 333, 335n18, 335n20, 335n29, 337n57, 343–45, 350, 351, 353n28, 358, 360, 368, 377, 378, 383, 385, 396, 403, 410, 430–31, 441, 442, 444

Oliver, Joe "King" (Louisiana), 101, 431–32n3

Oliver, Paul, xxviin17, 33, 38n12, 46, 51, 69–70n10, 93, 142, 174n35, 217n41, 313, 368, 371, 372, 376, 377, 380, 383, 395, 387n30, 390n66, 391n79, 393, 395, 398, 423, 425, 428, 429, 431–32n5, 433nn17–18, 438n97

Oliver, Sylvester, Jr., xxviin20, 49, 99, 103, 109–11, 315–21, 338n81, 339n89, 339n97

one-step dance, 405

oral tradition, 67, 361

orchestra, xxvin4, xxvin14, 6, 23, 50–51, 73, 78, 119n39, 141, 181–91, 217n32, 218nn48–50, 281, 290, 296, 308, 334n12, 367, 372, 338n36, 436n63, 448, 454

Original Creole Orchestra (Louisiana), 186n32, 217n32. *See also* Johnson, William "Bill"

Osmond Family, The [Jim, Willie "Pete"] (ubv), 460n16

Oster, Harry, xxviin17, 394–95, 397–98, 432n5, 432n9, 432n13, 433n20; field recordings, 394–96

Othello (Massachusetts-rbf), 19, 33

Otto, John S., 39, 130, 189, 194, 215n9, 218n56

Owens, Andy (Mississippi-rbf), 114

Owens, Tary, 429, 430

Page, John W., 84

Pahls, Marty, 143, 370, 371, 388n41

Palmer, Robert, 14, 365, 367, 375, 378–79, 387n30, 390n63

Parker, Charlie, xix

Parker, Leroy (ubv), 141

Patterson, Frank, Jr. (Tennessee-bf), 222, 226, 225–29, 242–43, 250nn12–14, 250n18; learning, 226, 243; media, 227; performance style, 227–29, 233–34; repertoire, 54, 57, 59, 60, 62, 227, 251n19, 251n21

Patterson, Karin, xix

Patton, Charley (Mississippi), 367, 379, 380–85, 391n78, 392n85

Pecknold, Diane, xx, xxviin20

Pentecostalism, 162

percussion, xv, xviii, 12, 13, 17, 29, 35, 40, 41, 46, 49, 50, 69n5, 73, 77, 89, 90, 97, 104, 115, 117, 140, 144, 146, 153, 157, 166, 210, 211, 234, 246, 261, 278, 303, 305, 325, 334n13, 339n94, 352n16, 382, 391n83, 401, 402, 434nn33–34, 440, 450, 452

performance contexts, 151–52, 155–58, 160, 183, 193–94, 208–9, 225, 230, 238, 243, 246, 249n3, 260–61, 268, 288–89, 343–44, 348, 352n26, 368, 369, 371, 374, 380, 394–96, 400, 404–5, 410–11, 413, 419, 423–24, 426–28, 430, 435n46, 449–52, 457

Perkins, Cora, 389n49

Perkins, Mert (West Virginia-rbf), 172
Perry, Fred (Florida-rbf), 360–61; performance style, 360, 386n14; repertoire, 60, 61, 360
Perryman, Charles W., xxviin20
Pestcoe, Shlomo, xxvin9, 37n1, 38n19, 70n11
Peter (Pennsylvania-rbf), 22
Peter (Virginia-rbf), 31
Philadelphia, Pennsylvania, 22, 73, 267, 338n77
Phillips, Cora Reid, 260–63, 280n5, 281n20. *See also* Baker, Etta Reid
piano, xviii, xxvin12, 42, 51, 68, 98, 138, 159, 170, 176n50, 193, 207, 210, 211, 218n51, 225, 262, 266, 270, 296, 302, 328, 335n17, 344, 345, 347, 350, 351, 368, 380, 393, 396, 397, 424, 432n16, 433, 438n91, 450, 452, 457, 459
picnics, 51, 94–96, 138, 192, 243, 259, 269, 310, 319, 323, 327, 344, 353n26, 369, 428, 461n19
Pierce, Charlie (ubv), 338n79
pigeon wing (dance), 23, 41, 82
Pinkster Day, 20, 21, 72, 104, 121n51
Pinson, Bob. *See* Russell, Tony
Piron, Armand (ubv), xxviin18, 377, 431n3, 469n39
Pittman, Lucius (Mississippi-rbf), 114
Place Congo. *See* Congo Square
play parties, 135, 276, 423
play party songs, 227, 248, 253n66, 309
podcasts, 343, 347, 349, 353n21
Pointer, Noel (ubv), xix, xxviin18
polka, 238, 241
Pomea, Neal, 407, 436n56
Ponty, Jean-Luc, 453, 461n32
popular music, xvii, xix, xxi, xxii, xxvn1, xxvin13, xxviin18, 364, 375, 379, 380, 451
postbellum period, 39, 71, 296
Poullard, Edward (ubv), 412, 435–36n50
Pratcher, Miles (Mississippi), 327, 340n115, 340n117. *See also* Pratcher, Robert "Bob"
Pratcher, Robert "Bob" (Mississippi-rbf), 314, 323, 326, 327, 327–28, 338n83, 340n115; lyrics, 326; performance style, 328; repertoire, 55, 58
Presley, Elvis, 130, 196, 220n87
Prim, Robert (Connecticut-rbf), 19–20
Prince (South Carolina-rbf), 86–87
Prince, Henrique (ubv), xxii, 175n30
prisons (state farms), 81, 360–61, 386n14, 392n93, 427, 432n13, 433n18
Pritchett, Jim (Alabama-rbf), 103
Protestants, 27–28, 43, 66–67, 74, 78, 83, 108, 109, 116, 131, 244, 245, 247, 269–70, 390n64
Puryear, Mark, 243

quadrille, 41, 69
Quigley, Colin, 227
quills (panpipes, whistles), 36, 40, 49, 57, 100, 114, 174n18, 323, 340n105
Quinn, Herb (Mississippi-rbf), 314, 387n27

rabab, 120n47
race, xx, xxiii–xxvin3, xxviin19, 4, 5, 7, 16, 26, 29, 41, 69, 75, 85, 116, 129, 130, 131, 133, 138, 142, 145n10, 155, 162, 184–87, 191, 196, 197, 203, 212, 236, 247, 255, 256, 269, 271–72, 274, 289–91, 294, 295, 313, 315, 316, 339n91, 352n21, 371, 400–401, 404, 416, 422, 443, 456–58
racism/segregation, xxi, xxvii–xxviiin26, 127, 133, 156, 162, 195, 271–72, 295, 320, 352n11, 353n21, 353n23, 400, 435n44, 444, 457, 462n41; Jim Crow, 127, 133, 212, 268, 271–72, 422, 423
radio, 132, 133, 139, 140, 143, 152, 154, 160, 162, 170, 174n11, 194, 195, 209, 215n12, 237, 243, 266, 272, 279, 292, 301, 302, 305, 319, 320, 323, 344–48, 353n32, 410, 412, 419, 430, 434n35, 447, 451, 458, 461n19, 461n28
ragtime (ragged), xxvin14, 51, 138, 141, 187, 191, 218n51, 222, 296, 319, 321, 379, 383, 385, 393, 438–39n103
railroad/railroad songs, 79, 98, 129, 151, 169, 293, 296, 298, 307, 309, 323, 325, 335, 336n35, 336n39, 340n110, 345, 360, 362–63, 387n22, 391n78, 395. *See also* migration
Rainey, Ma, 388n42, 430
Rakestraw, Joe Kinney (Georgia-rbf), 290, 291, 305–8, *306*, 334n10, 335n18, 337n68; repertoire, 55, 56, 58, 61
Rankin, John, 92, 93
Raphael, Marilyn, xxiv, xxviiin33
rattlesnake, 107, 409, 436n61. *See also* fiddle sound quality; fiddle/fiddling: construction of
Rawick, George P., 40, 103, 111
rebellions and revolts, 21, 29, 104, 118n17; Denmark Vesey, 118n17; Nat Turner, 118n17
recordings: commercial, xxvin14, 96, 118n16, 135, 141, 142, 160, 165, 166, 172, 185, 187–89, 209, 231, 250n17, 290, 294–96, 298, 299, 320, 365, 369, 370, 373, 374, 376, 380, 383, 388n40, 388n42, 390n65, 394, 408, 410, 412, 413, 416, 419, 420, 426, 437n77, 437n82, 447; Edison, 202, 207, 219n70, 261, 335n17; field, 152–53, 163, 165, 175n33, 176n39, 227, 251n34, 252n55, 260–61, 291, 301, 339n104, 343, 350, 385, 386n17, 392n86, 395, 429, 430, 432n5;

hillbilly records, xxvin6, 139–43, 146n20, 184, 185, 189–91, 196, 216n20, 295, 315, 317, 370, 410; race records, 139, 141, 147n35, 184, 191, 309, 317, 366, 370–72, 387n44, 461n21; Victrola, 141, 207, 237

recording industry, xvii, xviii, xx, xxi, xxvin6, xxvin14, xxviin17, xxviin22, xxviin25, 118n16, 133, 139, 141, 143, 147n35, 174n9, 181, 183, 186, 190, 191, 202, 215n11, 216n20, 216–17n29, 224, 279, 281n47, 292, 293, 295, 296, 299, 301–3, 309, 316, 335n25, 346n45, 351, 361–65, 370–79, 380, 388n42, 388n44, 392n95, 422, 434n35, 461n21

reel, 23, 24, 64, 68, 70n20, 100, 315, 348, 369, 398

Reid, Madison Boone (North Carolina-rbf), 259–63, 280–81n16

religion, xx, xxviin25, 4, 12, 14, 16, 21, 25, 27–29, 33–37, 38n15, 40, 43, 49, 65–68, 69n5, 81, 83–86, 90, 91, 106–9, 118n12, 120n45, 131, 137, 142, 161–62, 174n17, 209, 210, 213, 223, 244–46, 251n40, 252n48, 269, 290, 300, 312, 322, 334n7, 336n45, 339n102, 344, 358, 359, 375, 390n64, 390n66, 402, 405, 413, 423, 432nn14–16, 440. *See also specific denominations and religions*

religious/sacred music, xx, xxv, xxviin25, 14, 109, 114, 131, 142, 174n17, 200, 210, 219n67, 223, 245, 261, 290, 299, 300, 305, 311–13, 322, 334n7, 336n45, 339n102, 358, 359, 386–87n18, 390n64, 396, 430, 432n14, 434n33, 440, 444

repertoire. *See* fiddle repertoire

representation, xv, 37n8, 42–44, 96, 120n44, 141–43, 183, 191, 197, 208, 212, 214, 247–48, 270, 304, 332, 334n12, 359, 360, 362, 371, 390n64, 398, 402, 442

Rhea, Jessie (West Virginia-bf), 172

Rhodes, Gus (Alabama-rbf), 114

rhythm, 13, 64, 70n20, 85, 135, 137, 140, 141, 153, 166–68, 191, 211, 212, 226, 228, 232, 233, 246, 275, 276, 294, 297, 298, 303, 328, 331, 349, 351, 352n6, 378, 388, 410, 411, 419, 421, 422, 425, 459n2. *See also* African influences: performance practices

rhythm and blues, xviii, xxvin1, 279, 320, 336n45, 337n68, 403, 419, 438n93

Rice, Jacob "Jake" (Tennessee-rbf), 244, 245

Rice, Joel (Tennessee-rbf), 222, 243–48, 253n61, 253n63; lyrics, 253n66; repertoire, 53–57, 59, 61–62

Richey, Nancy, 193, 194, 218n59

Richmond, Indiana, 181, 216n19, 216n22, 218n47

Richmond, Kentucky, 215n12

Richmond, Virginia, 23, 25, 38n18, 86

Riddle, Lesley, 171, 176n50

Riley, Kirby (Louisiana), 406, 420, 436nn53–54

ring shout, 69n5

Ripley String Band (Mississippi-rbf), 53, 56, 57, 62, 63, 317, 319–20

Robbins, Robert (ubv), 389n49

Robert (Virginia-rbf), 31

Roberts, Dock (Kentucky), 53, 62, 180, 181, 183, 185, 186, 196, 212, 213, 215n9, 215n11, 217n29, 304

Roberts, John Storm, xvii, 15–16, 33, 34, 36

Robertson, Alexander Campbell "Eck," 70n18, 147n32, 217n17

Robichaux, John (ubv), 431n3

Robie, Milton (ubv), 338n79

Robin (South Carolina-rbf), 87–88

Robinson, Justin (North Carolina-bf), 273. *See also* Carolina Chocolate Drops

rock and roll, xviii, 143, 196, 266, 279, 389n56, 411

Rodgers, Jimmie, 203, 250n17, 377, 391n73, 409, 410, 437n65

Romero, Angel, 406

Rosenbaum, Art, 143, 290, 305–8, 334nn7–8, 337n66, 337n69, 386n7

round dance, 211

Runyon, David "Uncle" (West Virginia-rbf), 447, 455

Russell, Tony, xxviin17, xxviin21, 53, 70nn18–19, 138, 139, 146n25, 152, 153, 155, 164, 165, 174n9, 184, 187, 188, 215n2, 216n19, 217n37, 219n73, 240, 250n17, 252n48, 282–83n48, 291–94, 297, 298, 304, 313, 314, 334n9, 335n17, 337n51, 338n86, 339n91, 360, 362, 365, 386n17, 387n24, 390n63, 439n118, 459n3

Rutherford, Leonard, 201, 202, 204, 219n71, 219n76, 239, 240–41, 252nn52–53

Rye, Howard. *See* Dixon, Robert M. W.

sacred. *See* religion

sacred dancing, 69n5

Saint-Domingue (Haiti), 19, 69n5, 104, 120n45

Salsburg, Nathan, 185, 215n2, 216n20

Salty (Virginia-rbf), 455

Sambo (Virginia-rbf), 31

Saminaka, Musa dan Gado (Nigeria), *11*

Sampson (Massachusetts-rbf), 20

Sankofa Strings, xxii, 175n30

Savannah, Georgia, *77*, 386n10; and Savannah River, 334n3

savannah region, 9, 12, 13, 14, 16, 17, 50, 105

Savoy, Ann Allen, 403, 405, 407–10, 416–19, 434nn31–32, 434n36, 434n48, 435n40, 437n73, 437n76, 442

saxophone, xvi, xviii, xix, 51, 191, 305, 450
schottische, 238, 241
Scotland, 27, 38n17, 178, 399
Sea Islands, xxii, 145n13, 146n18, 290, 334n2, 334n7, 358, 359, 386n10, 459n1
Seattle, Washington, 267, 270
Sears, Roebuck and Company, 216n29, 318, 445
secular culture, xvii, xxi, xxv, xxviin25, xxviiin29, 28, 41, 43, 46, 49, 66, 81, 84, 109, 116, 124, 127–47, 155, 163, 165, 196, 210, 219n67, 223, 244, 245, 254, 255, 258, 279, 290, 299, 305, 308, 312, 313, 315, 319, 334n2, 334n8, 337n69, 339n93, 358–60, 386n10, 386–87n18, 396, 402, 430, 432n15, 440, 444, 458
Seeger, Mike, 139–40, 152–54, 174nn5–6, 186, 271, 452. *See also* Adams, William, Jr.
Senegambia, 9, 12, 14–16, 31, 33, 35, 36, 38n24, 105
sentimental songs, 410, 426, 427, 438n99. *See also* ballads
Seroff, Doug, 296
Sewall, Samuel, 5–7
shared culture, xxii, 23, 26, 39, 41, 65, 70n14, 90, 94, 96, 116, 128, 132, 138–43, 146n24, 153, 155, 156, 173, 182, 187, 196, 203, 213, 214, 223, 227, 231, 239–41, 249, 255, 268, 273, 274, 278, 282n48, 295, 296, 304, 313, 315, 322, 324, 339n91, 343, 347, 349, 351, 360, 362, 367, 375, 377, 391n73, 399, 420, 422, 424, 425, 427, 429, 430, 433n21, 441
sheik, 371, 374, 375, 377, 390n63
Shultz, Arnold (Kentucky-rbf), xxviiin18, 180, *192*, 192–97; performance style, 194
shuffle, 41, 104, 108, 110, 111
Sierra Leone, 9, *10*, 16, 359
Simms, Henry "Son" (Mississippi-rbf), 379–85; family and community, 314, 379–80, *381*, 391n74; learning, 379–80; lyrics, 382; media, 380–81, 391n80; Mississippi Corn Shuckers, 380; performance contexts, 380; performance style, 382–84, 391n83; repertoire, 56, 58, 381, 391n81; Son Simms Four, 383–84, 392nn87–89
Simon, Freyda. *See* Jamieson, Stuart; Mayo, Margot
Simmons, Henry "Legg" (Mississippi-rbf), 317, 319
Sims, Henry "Son" (Mississippi-rbf). *See* Simms, Henry "Son"
Skillings, George A. (ubv), 46
Slade, Daniel, 19, 33
slave coffle, 79, 92, 118n14
Slave Songs of the United States, 358–59. *See also* Allen, William Francis

slavery (enslavement), xv, xx, xxi, xxiii, xxiv, xxvin10, xxviiin34, 3, 4, 14, 15, 31, 34, 37n2, 69, 70n21, 70n23, 75, 79, *80*, 83, 84, 93, 94, 97, 98, 100, *101*, 102, 104, 108, 109, 113, 118n12, 118n17, 121n50, 127, 128, 131, 138, 153, 157–58, 215n8, 230, 239, 251n31, 257, 269, 312, 358–60, 368, 386n7, 392n95, 399–400, 404, 423, 433n27, 433n30, 438n98, 448, 456–58
Small, Christopher, xxviin11
Smalley, Eugene V., 108, 120n48
Smith, Bessie, xxvin14, 281n20, 387n19, 389n49, 391n82, 446
Smith, Clara, 189, 317n42, 373, 378
Smith, Dale, xxvin4
Smith, Hezekiah Leroy Gordon "Stuff" (ubv), xviii–xix, xxviin18, xxviin20
Smith, Mamie, xxvin14, 141, 146n30, 388n44
Smithsonian Folkways Records, 174n5
Smithsonian Institution, 77, 282n36
Smock, Virginia "Ginger," (ubv), xxviiin18
Snowden Family Band, The (Ohio-rbf), 94–95
social class and status. *See under* fiddle/fiddling
Son Simms Four, 383–84, 392nn87–89
songs, 38n21. *See also specific genres*
soul music, xviii, xix, 411
South, Eddie (ubv), xxviiin18, xxviin20, 462n41
South Asia, xviii
Southeast Africa, 9
Southern, Eileen, xv, xvii, xxi, xxviin25, 5, 7, 20–23, 26, 27, 29, 31, 38n21, 40, 45, 46, *48*, 50, 51, 70n12, 72, 73, 78, 79, 81, 82, 84, 86, 90, 93, 101, 103, 104, 110, 113, 114, 116, 118n7, 118–19n23, 119n27, 120n41, 121n51, 136, 141, 146n28, 173n2, 186, 224, 250n9, 333, 386n9
Southworth, Lewis Alexander (Oregon-rbf), 118–19n23
Spain, xxiv, 4, 6, 15, 16, 30, 31, 34, 35, 90, 99, 105, 170, 399, 433n25, 434n34
Spartanburg, South Carolina, 169, 449, 461n22
Spelman College, 336n44
spirituals, xx, xxi, xxv, xxviin25, 131, 135, 146n28, 252n50, 311, 324, 326, 336n43, 358, 359, 381, 396, 430, 432n14
Spitzer, Nick, xxviin20, 408, 410–11, 421, 433n25, 434nn31–32, 435n39, 437n74
Spottswood, Dick, 153, 174n9, 180, 182, 187, 215, 219, 283n48
square dance, 41, 50, 69n6, 91, 103, 137, 138, 155, 158, 160, 162, 167, 174–75n22, 185, 188, 194, 195, 206, 208, 209, 211, 227, 230–32, 243, 244, 258, 259, 261, 268, 272, 273, 294, 296, 298, 307, 328, 331, 345, 348, 367, 368, 374, 394, 424, 426, 427, 429, 441, 456

St. Louis, Missouri, 98, 194, 364, 426, 427, 432n16, 455
Stanford, Fay, 408–10, 434n31
Stanford, Ron, 408, 409–10, 434n31, 436n60
Starks, George L., 130, 334n2, 358–59
Steele, Robert, 181, 182, 185, 189
Stewart, Helen Booker, 182–83
Stewart, Michael, 367, 369, 374, 376, 381, 387nn29–30, 390n67
sticks, 49, 78, 83, 91, 117, 118n15, 339n106, 425, 435n43, 452
Stimeling, Travis D., 174n11
Stono Rebellion, 29, 118n17
Strachwitz, Chris, xxviin17, 69–70n10, 395, *396*, *397*, *407*, *409*, *414*, *415*, 432n5, 434n31, 434n35
strain, 19, 78, 187, 223
straws (beating straws, straw-beating), 82, 83, 91, 102, 114, 118n15, 246
string bands, xviii, xxvin5, xxviinn19–20, 43, 49–51, 91, 100, 118n23, 134–36, 139, 141–44, 147n33, 147n37, 154, 155, 159, 165, 168, 169, 171, 175n22, 176n42, 178, 181, 183–86, 189, 195, 196, 200, 201, 205, 208, 210–12, 219n78, 219n81, 221, 222, 227, 229–31, 232, 242, 243, 250n13, 254, 255, 257, 258, 267, 271–73, 281n30, 289, 296, 301, 307, 309, 315, 317, 318–20, 321, 323–26, 328, 331, 334, 335, 344, 352n6, 357–61, 367–72, 375, 379, 380, 383, 385, 388n41, 412, 419, 422, 424, 425, 428, 429, 438n29, 440, 444, 447, 451–53, 458, 459
string bass. *See* bass
string instrument, xvii–xx, 69n7, 336n38, 461n30
Stuart, Ambrose Gaines, 188, 217nn37–38
Stuckey, Sterling, 65–66
sukey jump, 231
Summers, Keith, 263
suppers, 94, 97, 110, 135, 138, 261, 288, 289, 369, 395, 424, 426, 427
swing (swing era), xviii, 91, 160, 210
Sykes, Roosevelt, 397–98, 432n16, 433n18
syncopation. *See under* African influences: performance practices; fiddle performance style: practices and techniques

Talley, Thomas Washington, 36, 38n28, 133, 222–24, 229, 249n4, 250nn5–6, 250n9, 254, 299–300, 304, 309
tambourine, 18, 20, 35, 40, 45, 46, 50, 73, 78, 79, 88, 90, 95, 100, 101, 117, 339n106
Tampa, Florida, 359
Tampa Red. *See* Whittaker, Hudson
Tanner, James Gideon "Gid," 252n46
tap dance, 424
Tarter, Stephen (Virginia-rbf), 155, 171, 173, 176n51, 446, 455, 460n15; Gate City String Band, 171
Taylor, Dennis W., 181, 183, *184*, 215n9, 215n12, 216n22. *See also* Booker, James "Jim"
Taylor, Ernest "Boose" (Mississippi-rbf), 314, 321–22; repertoire, 322
Taylor, Willis (Mississippi-rbf), 314
Taylor's Kentucky Boys, 181, 183, *184*, 185, 187, 188, 216n19, 217n37, 295, 298, 304, 335n20. *See also* Booker, James "Jim"
Teakle, Thomas, 5–6
Tefteller, John, 370
Tennessee: East, 221, 229, 249, 250n14, 291, 444, 460n11; Middle, 36, 120n40, 221–25, 229, 243, 249, 250n5, 251n39, *381*, 460n11; West, 187, 221, 251n39, 320, 385
Tennessee Chocolate Drops, 176n45, 212, 370, 388n41, 449, 461nn20–21. *See also under* Armstrong, Howard
Thibodeaux, Goldman, 413
Thomas, Alfred (Georgia-rbf), 308–9
Thomas, Charlie (Texas-rbf): Black/white interactions, 426–28; family and community, 425–26; learning, 426; performance contexts, 426–28
Thomas, E. (Mississippi-rbf), 314
Thomas, James (Tennessee-rbf), 95–96
Thomas, Willie (Louisiana), 395, *396*, *397*, 398–99, 432n9, 433n18. *See also* Cage, James "Butch"
Thompson, Jake (North Carolina-rbf), 259
Thompson, John Arch (North Carolina-rbf), 259, 263–65, 267, 273–75, 280n15
Thompson, Joseph (North Carolina-rbf), xix, xxviin18, 168, 234, 259, 263–80, *264*, *265*, 280n5, 281n23, 281n25, 281n28, 282n37, 337n57, 439n116, 443; media, 271; performance style, 274–78, 282nn45–47, 337n57, 421; repertoire, 54, 56, 58, 60, 61
Thompson, Katrina, 81
Thompson, Odell (North Carolina), 168, 263, *265*, 265–78, 280n5, 282n34, 282n37, 282nn45–46
Thompson, Suzy, 423
Thompson, Walter (North Carolina-rbf), 259, 267–68, 280n15
Tin Pan Alley, 210, 369
Tisserand, Michael, 140, 352n16, 404–6, 408–10, 414, 416–22, 434n31, 435n44, 437n77
Titon, Jeff Todd, xxiii, xxviin21, 178, 179, 181, 186, 187, 213, 215n2

tom-toms (drums), 105
Trail of Tears, 128
travel. *See* migration
tremolo. *See under* fiddle performance style: practices and techniques
triangle, xix, 36, 49, 78, 81, 88, 94, 95, 100, 103, 105, 108, 117, 120, 174n18, 223, 402–4, 418, 419, 421, 434n38, 435n43
Tri-Cities region, 171, 176n48
Tross, Moses (West Virginia-rbf), 172
Trotter, James M., 116, 121n51
Trumbo, Bill (Kentucky-rbf), 179
trumpet, xvi, xix, 5, 33, 51, 101, 191, 305, 391n73, 427, 432n3, 450, 452, 453, 457, 462n39
Tucker, George, 118n14. *See also* slave coffle
Turner, Edward, 22
twelve-bar blues, 190, 213, 215n3, 296, 372, 373, 381, 383, 389n52, 398–99
two-step dance, 57, 211, 405, 410, 424
Tyler, William (ubv), 141

United States, xxiii, xxvin3. *See also specific cities*
urbanization, xvii, xviii, xx–xxiii, xxvn1, xxviin25, 42, 83, 88, 93, 95, 100, 101, 116, 123, 127, 130, 131, 137, 141, 144n2, 145n3, 147n34, 154, 169, 170, 180, 202, 255, 267, 269, 274, 296, 320, 326n45, 351, 359, 364, 370, 372, 375, 378, 379, 388n42, 389n49, 396, 398, 400, 401, 403, 411, 422, 431, 440, 444, 452, 462nn39–40. *See also* city (cities)
Utica Institute (Utica Normal and Industrial Institute), 367, 387n33

Vandiver, Pendleton (Kentucky), *192*, 195
Vann, Lucinda, 97–98
vaudeville, 146n30, 151, 227, 248, 339n89, 379, 427, 444
vaudeville music, 146, 248, 339n89, 379, 427, 444
vernacular, xvii, xxi, xxvn1, xxvin6, 45, 95, 147n32, 155, 176n50, 223, 224, 226, 242, 249n4, 290, 299–301, 305, 313, 324, 336n43, 353n19, 381, 383, 384, 386n14, 398, 430, 455
vibrato. *See under* fiddle performance style: practices and techniques
Vicksburg, Mississippi, 100, 388n37, 397, 433n18
Victorian, Joel [Jules] (Louisiana-rbf), 417. *See also* Fontenot, Canray
Vinson, Walter (Mississippi), 365, 366, 367, 369, 374–79, 387n28, 387n34, 389n56, 390n61. *See also* Mississippi Sheiks
viola, xix, 380. *See also* fiddle/fiddling
violin. *See* fiddle/fiddling

Violin, Sing the Blues for Me, 189. *See also* Wyatt, Marshall
Virginia breakdown, 174–75n22
Virginia reel, 68, 79, 101, 103, 344
Vodun (Vodou, Vodoun, Voodoo), 69n5, 116, 120n45

Wachsmann, Klaus, 406n4
Wade, Stephen, 325, 326, 338n83, 339n104, 339n107, 385, 392n93
Walker, George (Virginia-rbf), 86
Walker, Louella (South Carolina), *288*. *See also* Bryant, Henry J.
Walker, Owen (Kentucky-bf), 180–81, 183, 187, 213, 214, 215n8, 215nn10–11, 242
waltz, 41, 203, 238, 241, 369, 378, 405, 410, 420, 425
Wardlow, Gayle Dean, 379–80, 382, 391n80
Ware, Burnham, 70n13, 206–11, 219n78, 219n81, 334n13, 338n79
Ware, Charles Pickard, 358–59
washboard (rubboard), 70n13, 136, 208, 252n60, 359, 434n33, 435n43, 452. *See also frattoir/frottoir/vest frottoir*
Washington, DC, 127, 151, 413
washtub bass, 318, 334n13
Waterman, Chris, 371, 389n56
Waters, Ethel, xxvin14
Waters, Muddy, 369, 379, *381*, 383–84, 392n87
Watkins, John, 334n12
Watrous, Peter, 421–22
Watson, Cedric (ubv), 435–36n50
Watson, John F., 72
Watts, Cato (Kentucky-rbf), 179, 180
websites, 153, 176n37, 176n39, 386n10, 436n60; Digital Library of Appalachia, 175n33, 176n39; Digital Library of Georgia, 337n66; *Discography of American Historical Recordings*, 174n9, 333n77, 389n54; Lomax Digital Archive, 340n110
Welding, Pete, xxviin17, 168, 169, 383, 392n87
Wells, Paul F., xxviin18, 251n25, 252n54
West, Eddie (Alabama-rbf), 61, 361–63, 386n18; performance style, 362–63, 387n20, 387n22
West Africa, xv, xvi, xxiii, xxvin6, xxvin10, xxvin15, 8–17, 27, 29, 33–37n4, 38n11, 38n20, 38n26, 44, 50, 51, 67, 70n11, 73, 76, 86, 90, 99, 100, 103, 105, 106, 120n45, 146n27, 153, 175n24, 265, 339n94, 352n16, 421
West Indies, 6, 16, 17–19, 21, 22, 29, 35, 73; Caribbean, xxvin9, 18, 30, 34, 38n25, 433n25, 435n43. *See also specific countries*
West Tennessee, 187, 221, 251n39, 320, 385

western swing music, 389n56, 422, 454
Wharton, Frank (Mississippi-rbf), 314
whistles, 78, 94, 114, 265, 293, 338n77, 412. *See also* quills
whites/white people. *See* Europe; European Americans
Whittaker, Hudson (Tampa Red), 373, 376, 378, 389n51
Whitter, Henry, 362, 387n22, 387n24, 431
Wiggins, Gene, 291–94, 309, 333, 334n9
Wiley, Robert, xxviin20. *See also* Garnier, D'Jamal, III
Williams, Big Joe, 410
Williams, Carol (Mississippi-rbf), 394
Williams, Charley (Louisiana-rbf), 100
Williams, Claude (ubv), xix, 462n38
Williams, Isaac (Virginia/Canada-rbf), 76
Williams, Ole Man Carol (Mississippi-rbf), 394. *See also* Cage, James "Butch"
Willis, Mott (Mississippi-rbf), 314
Wills, Bob, 16, 422
Wilson, Sule Greg, 153, 165–67, 174n5, 228, 276, 282n45, 305, 351
Wimbush, Vincent, 67, 460n5
Winans, Robert, xv, xvii, xxvi, 31–34, 38n23, 40, 41, 46, 51–53, 65, 70n15, 71, 76, 117, 138, 139, 141, 152, 154, 155, 175n29, 217n35, 392n95
Wine, Melvin, 172
Winston, Cornelius "Neil" (Mississippi), 369, 388n39
Wolfe, George K., xxviin17, xxviinn21–22, xxviiin30, 66, 70n16, 101, 132, 138–42, 146n24, 147n35, 175n24, 180, 181, 183, 185, 186, 194–97, 215n2, 216n22, 216–17n29, 218n47, 220n87, 221, 223–28, 230–34, 250n5, 251n31, 251nn33–34, 292, 296, 304, 305, 335n18, 383n79, 393
women, xviii, xxiv, xxvin11, 11, 17, 28, 30–31, 85, 100–101, 109–10, 129, 262, 265–66, 316, 332, 348, 389n49, 430, 437n75, 456. *See also* gender
Wooley, Amy Suzanne, xxviin20
wopsy, 424
Work, Frederick Jerome, 250n8
Work, John W., II, 223, 224, 250n8, 250n9
Work, John W., III, xxviin25, 133, 221–27, 250n5, 250nn7–8, 299–300, 326, 336n44, 338n83, 379–80, 384–85, 392n86, 442, 443
Works Progress Administration (WPA), xvi, xx–xxi, xxviin23, 40, 42, 64, 76, 90, 100, 103, 111, 317, 323, 338n84
world music, xvii, 454–55

World War I, 180, 200, 223, 230, 235, 242, 307, 368, 369, 380
World War II, xxi–xxiii, 131, 132, 143, 168, 174n7, 263, 266, 273, 279, 297, 306, 307, 320, 408, 412, 427–28, 430, 453
Wright, Emp [Imp] (North Carolina-rbf), 259, 281n28
Wright, Henry (Georgia-rbf), 76
Wright, Josephine, 22, 26, 27, 31, 40, 82, 86, 90, 93, 103, 104, 110, 119n27. *See also* Southern, Eileen
Wyatt, Marshall, xviii, xxviin17, 46, 91, 176n45, 189, 216n15, 292, 293, 294, 297, 335n20, 335n22, 361, 363, 374, 380, 387n30, 391n83, 392n91, 393

xylophone, 18, 26

yodel/yodeling, 220n86, 391n73, 410
youth/youth culture, 12, 25, 75, 94, 244, 246, 247, 269, 296, 303, 316, 331, 345, 384, 392n91, 394, 396, 410, 432n16, 443
Yule, Ron, xxviin21, 417, 418, 421, 434n31

zydeco, 108, 403, 405, 406, 408, 411, 412, 419, 421, 434nn32–35, 434n37, 435n43, 435n45, 437n67

Index of Songs and Dance Tunes

To see song titles in the repertoires of fiddlers profiled in this study, go to
🎵 *Fiddling Is My Joy Companion* on eScholarship.

Across the Sea / Going Across the Sea, 53
Ain't Gonna Rain No More. *See* It Ain't Gonna Rain No More
Ain't It a Crying Shame, 455
Ain't Misbehavin', 210
Alabama Bound / I'm Alabama Bound, 322, 429
Alberta Blues, 375, 376
All I Got Is Gone, 181
All Night Long / If It's All Night Long / All Night Long Blues, 139, 241, 252n53, 327, 328, 340n118
All the Good Times Are Past and Gone, 165, 176n37
Altamont, 174n10, 231
Amazing Grace, 52, 308
Apple Blossom, 217n33, 231, 233, 251n35
Are You from Dixie?, 288
Arkansas Traveler(s) / The Arkansas Traveler / Arkansas Traveller, 52, 62, 70n18, 103, 112, 139, 152, 187, 203, 227, 237, 316, 319, 324, 325, 394
As We Parted at the Gate, 203
Away in the Kingdom, 200

Baby Please Don't Go, 53, 410
Ballad of Jed Clampett, The / Deux Pas à Granny (Granny's Two Step), 411
Bamalong Blues, 293, 296, 335n24
Barbara Allen, 238

Barlow Knife, 53, 201, 237
Baseball, 412
Be True Be True Blues, 56, 381–82
Beaux of Oak Hill, 346
Bébé's Blues / Blues à Bébé, 55, 410
Bed Spring Poker, 375
Been to the East, Been to the West, 165
Big Fat Coon, 210
Big Foot N----r, 317
Big Road Blues, 376, 390n67
Big-Eared Mule, 54
Bile Them Cabbage Down / Boil Them Cabbage Down, 54, 139, 207, 227, 251n19
Bill Cheatham, 227
Bill Katon Breakdown in D, 353n19
Bill Katon Breakdown in G #2, 353n19
Bill Katon's Tune/Reel, 353n19
Billy in the Low Ground / Billy on the Low Ground, 52, 54, 152, 187, 201, 225, 231, 237, 241, 252n53, 287–88
Black Bayou Ain't Got No Bottom, 385
Black Cat Bone, 432n15
Black Sheep, 60, 242. *See also* Po' Black Sheep
Black-Eyed Susan / Black Eye Susie / Black Eyed Daisy, 52, 54, 112, 187, 273
Blood Red Rose, 439n118
Blue Runner, 410
Blue Yodel, 391n73
Blue Yodel #1, 411
Blue Yodel #4 / California Blues, 436n65

Blues à Bébé / Bébé's Blues, 55, 410
Boil Them Cabbage Down. *See* Bile Them Cabbage Down
Boll Weevil / Boll Weevil Blues, 55, 308, 316, 439n110
Bonsoir Moreau, 421, 437n71
Booker, 385
Bootlegger's Blues, 326
Breakdown (Another Bill Caton Tune), 353n19
Brickyard Joe, 181
Brother Bill Had a Still on the Hill / Mountain Dew, 164
Brown Skin Woman, 439n110
Brownie Blues, 171
Buck Creek Gal(s) / Rye Straw, 55
Buffalo Gal / Buffalo Gals / Buffalo Girls, 52, 55, 70n17, 139, 322
Bully of the Town, 327
Butch's Blues, 396
Buttermilk, 327, 328

Cacklin' Hen / Cackling Hen / Hen Cackle / Hen Cackled / Hen, She Cackle / Old Hen Cackled / Old Hen Cackled and the Rooster Crowed, 55, 70n19, 139, 152, 169, 185, 187, 217n35, 302–5, 316, 317, 337n53, 337n58, 337nn60–63, 385, 392n95, 394, 396, 430
Camp Nelson Blues, 187, 190, 218n48, 295, 296
Camped in Some Strange Land, 200
Canray's One Step, 421, 438n86
Can't Get the Saddle on the Grey Mule, 368
Careless Love, 56, 273, 282n44, 381, 382, 391n82, 460n16
Carrier Line, The / The Carrier Railroad, 325, 340n108, 340nn110–11
Carroll County Blues, 209, 219n83
Casey Jones, 114, 207
Cat's Got the Measles, 387n19
Chattanoogie Shoe Shine Boy, 301, 302, 336–37n51
Cheathem, 237
Chicken Reel, 201, 207
Chock House Blues, 203
Christmas Eve / Old Joe, 231
Cincinnati, 56, 231
Cincinnati Blues, 240
Cincinnati Dancing Pig, 56
Cindy (Gal), 56, 319
Circle Round the Moon, 382
Coal Black Mattie, 317
Cocaine Done Killed My Baby, 426
Coffee Grows on White Oak Trees, 52
Come on Jesus, Walk with Me, 448

Cooney in De Holler, 74
Corrine Corrina / Come Back Corrina / Corrinne, 56, 139, 227, 251n19, 373, 380, 381, 389nn55–n56, 391n82
Cotton Eyed Joe / Cotton-Eyed Joe, 52, 56, 223, 424
Cracking Them Things, 378
Crazy Blues, 141, 146–47n30
Cripple Creek, 56, 187, 197
Crow Jane, 260
Cumberland Gap, 169, 201, 227, 241

Dan Tucker, 227. *See also* Old Dan Tucker
Dance the Georgia Pos, 296
Dear Girl, 378
Deux Pas à Granny (Granny's Two Step) / The Ballad of Jed Clampett, 411
Devil at the Crossroads, The, 203, 219n74
Devil's Dream, 52, 57, 152, 213
Dinah, 456
Dixie, 52, 394
Dixie Land, 87
Dona's Got a Rambling Mind, 273
Done Wrong Blues, 295, 296
Down Home Blues, 446
Down in the Valley, 63, 185
Down South Rag, 179
Down Yonder, 207, 301
Downfall of Paris, 169, 237
Driving That Thing, 375
Drop Down Mama and Let Your Daddy See, 322
Drunkard's Hiccups, 431
Dying Coon, The, 103

East Jackson Blues, 373–74, 389n55, 390n61
East Ninth Street Blues, 296
Easy Rider, 241
Eggnog, Sugar and Beer, 52, 111
Eighth of January, The, 57, 227–29, 231, 251n21, 316, 317, 319, 324
Elder Greene Blues / Elder Green, 383, 427
Ella Speed, 429
Eunice Two-Step, 57

Fair Ellenor and Lord Thomas, 238
Farrell Blues, 380, 381
Fingering with Your Fingers, 377
Fire on the Mountain, 57, 197, 203, 231, 237
Fisher's Hornpipe, 227
Fit as a Fiddle and Ready for Love, 455
Five Miles Out of Town, 237; Five Miles to Town, 203

Flop-Eared Mule, 54
Flowers for the Fields of Alabama, 204; She's a Flower from the Field of Alabama, 241
Forked Deer / Forki Deer, 57, 103, 187, 188, 191, 201, 217n33, 217nn37–38, 269, 295
Forty Drops, 294, 296
Forty-Four Blues / 44 Blues, 335n23, 396–98, 432n11, 432n16, 433nn18–20
Forty-Fours, The, 397
Fox in the Wall, 287
France Blues, 427
Frankie and Albert, 426

G Rag, 293, 295–98, 335n22, 335n33
Gambling Man, 427
Georgia Buck Is Dead / Georgie Buck Is Dead, 276–78, 282n46, 282–83n48, 421
Georgia Stomp, 294, 296
Give Me That Old Time Religion, 322
God's Gonna Trouble the Water, 200
Going Across the Sea / Across the Sea, 53
Going Around the Mountain, 260
Going Down That Road Feeling Bad, 139; Going Down the Road Feeling Bad, 164, 260
Going to Move to Alabama, 383, 392n85
Golden Slippers, 57, 430; Old Dem Golden Slippers, 210
Goodbye Blues, 295, 296
Got to the Bottom Up and Go, 322
Grand Old Jubilee, The, 179
Gray Eagle / Grey Eagle, 57, 187, 188, 269, 295
Green Corn, 430
Grub Springs, 319

Hamilton's Special Breakdown, 297, 335n22
Have Thine Own Way Lord, 210
He Calls That Religion, 375, 390n66
Heel Up the Hall, 201
Hell Broke Loose in Georgia, 394
Hen Cackle / Hen Cackled / Hen, She Cackle. *See* Cacklin' Hen
Here Rattler Here, 223
Hesitation Blues, 169
Hitting the Numbers, 390n67
Hog Hunt, 325
Hog-Eyed Man, 179
Home Sweet Home, 52, 58, 410
Honey Babe Let the Deal Go Down, 139
Honeydripper, The, 397; Honeydripper Blues, 317
Honeysuckle Rose, 210
Hoodoo Blues, 432n15

Hook and Line, 264
Hop Light Ladies, 52, 64; Miss McLeod's Reel, 64

I Truly Understand, You Love Another Man, 176n37
I Would If I Could / I Would but I Couldn't, 227, 205n17
Iberia Breakdown, 350
I'd Wish to the Lord I'd Never Been Born. *See* Wish to the Lord I'd Never Been Born
Ida Red, 179
If You Like Me Like I Like You, 394
I'm Gonna Live Anyhow till I Die, 327, 328
I'm Gonna Work till My Work on Earth Is Done, 200
I'm in the Money, 448
I'm Talking About You / The New Talkin' 'Bout You, 387n19
In the Evening by the Moonlight, 210
Indian and the Woodchuck, 227
It Ain't Gonna Rain No More / Tain't Gonna Rain No More / Ain't Gonna Rain No More, 52, 58, 139, 273, 396
It Tickles Me, 295, 296
It's Hot Like That, 373, 378
It's Right Here for You, 146–47n30
It's the Sign of Judgement, 432n14
It's Tight Like That, 373, 378

Jack O' Diamonds, 139
Jambalaya, 412
Jane Wallace, 201, 203
Jazz Fiddler, The, 375, 377
Jefferson City Blues / Jefferson City, 353n19
Jelly Roll, 396, 398, 399; New Jelly Roll Blues, 398, 433n22; Original Jelly Roll Blues, 398
Jesus Lover of My Soul, 207, 210
Jimmy Long Josey, 112
Joe Kirby, 382
Joe Pitre à Deux Femmes, 421
Joe Turner, 58, 139; Joe Turner Blues, 317, 383
John Henry, 58, 139, 164, 102, 273, 300, 302, 303, 305, 308, 337n53, 345
Johnny Can't Dance (Johnny Peut Pas Danser), 58
Jolie Catin, 58

Katon's Hornpipe, 353n19
Katon's Reel, 353n19
Katy Hill, 391, 335n17
K.C. [Kansas City] Railroad Blues, 293, 296, 298, 335n24, 336n35, 336n39

Kentucky Waltz, 59, 63, 64, 410, 411
Knox County Stomp, 175n45, 455

La Robe à Parasol, 59, 409–10, 412
La Valse de la Prison (Prison Waltz), 53, 408, 420, 436n58, 437n81
Ladies in the Ballroom, 201, 203
Ladies on the Steamboat, 59, 201, 204, 237, 241
Lawdy Lawdy Blues / Papa's Lawdy Lawdy Blues, 387n19
Lazy Lazy River / Lazy River, 377
Leather Britches, 59, 139, 201, 203, 227, 301, 302, 324
Leonard's March, 164
Les Barres de la Prison, 53–54, 420, 421, 437n71, 437nn81–83
Les Flammes d'Enfer (The Flames of Hell), 408, 436n58
Les Portes de la Prison, 418. *See also* Les Barres de la Prison
Listen to the Mocking Bird, 60, 300, 311, 338n77, 360
Little Old Log Cabin in the Lane, 185
Little Rabbit Hare, 201
Liza Jane / Little Liza Jane / Miss Liza Jane, 52, 59, 223, 316, 368
Lonely One in This Town, 375, 388–89n46
Lonesome Grave Took My Baby, 390n67
Lonesome Widow, 319
Long Lonesome Road, 176n37; Lonesome Road, 239
Longest Train I Ever Saw, 165
Looking Over a Four-Leaf Clover, 456
Loose Like That, 378
Lost Girl in Dallas, 424
Lost John, 201, 431
Lost Train Blues, 360, 386n17
Lying Blues, 427

Madame Faielle, 59, 410
Mama Don't Want No Guitar Playing in Here, 427
Mamma's Return, 203
Mandy, 325
Marie, 411
Martha Campbell, 179, 181, 213
Match Box Blues, 427
Maxwell Girl, 70n17, 295
Memphis Blues, 456
Miss Liza Jane / Liza Jane / Little Liza Jane, 52, 59, 223, 316, 368
Miss McLeod's Reel, 64; Hop Light Ladies, 52, 64
Miss Meal Cramp Blues, 373

Mississippi Low Down, 378
Missouri Waltz, 114
Mo Anna Lu, 455
Mocking Bird, The / Mockingbird. *See* Listen to the Mocking Bird
Molly Put the Kettle [Kittle] On, 52, 112, 273
Momma Don't Allow, 60
Mon Camon le Case Que Je Sui Cordane (My Gun Is the Reason I Am Convicted), 408. *See also* Les Flammes d-Enfer (The Flames of Hell)
Moore Girl, The, 293–94, 296
Mountain Dew / Brother Bill Had a Still on the Hill, 164
My Journey Home, 227
Mysterious Coon, 373

Nana Hawaii (Beautiful Hawaii), 455
Natchez Under the Hill, 52
Nearer My God to Thee, 210
Negro Jig, 27
Nero the Slave, 179
Never Let the Same Bee Sting You Twice, 335n24
New Jelly Roll Blues, 398, 433n22; Jelly Roll, 398, 399; Original Jelly Roll Blues, 398
New Money, 179
New Sittin' on Top of the World, The, 390n67. *See also* Sitting on Top of the World
New Stop and Listen, The, 390n67
New Talkin' 'Bout You, The / I'm Talking About You, 387n19
Nobody Knows the Trouble I See, 252n50
Nobody's Darling but Mine, 210
Northern Starvers Are Returning Home, The, 374, 389n56
Number 44 Blues, 433n18

Oh, You Beautiful Doll, 394; Oh, You Beautiful Doll, You Great Big Beautiful Doll, 207
Oil in My Vessel, 273
Old Aunt Jessie, 439n118
Old Buzzard, 181, 186, 187, 215n11
Old Cow Died, 227
Old Dan Tucker, 52, 112. *See also* Dan Tucker
Old Dem Golden Slippers, 210; Golden Slippers, 57, 210, 430
Old Dubuque, 227
Old Flanagan, 206
Old Hen Cackle, The / Old Hen Cackled / Old Hen Cackled and the Rooster Crowed. *See* Cacklin' Hen

Old Jeff City / Jefferson City Blues / Jefferson City / Katon's Hornpipe / Katon's Reel, 353n19
Old Joe / Christmas Eve, 231
Old Joe Clark, 60, 164, 276–78, 282n46
Old Kentucky Home, 94, 207
Old Master's Horn, 179
Old Mule, 394
Old Rooster Crowed in the Pine Tree Top, 164–65
Old Sage Friend, 231, 233, 251n37
Old Virge, 207, 209
Old Wagoner, 394; Waggoner, 227
Old Zip Coon, 64, 316
Operator Blues, 296
Original Blues, 428
Original Jelly Roll Blues, 398; Jelly Roll, 396, 398, 399; New Jelly Roll Blues, 398, 433n22
Out and Down, 439n118

Papa's Lawdy Lawdy Blues / Lawdy Lawdy Blues, 387n19
Paterroller'll Catch You, 52, 61, 70n16, 82, 112, 210, 231, 251n33
Peace in the Valley / (There'll Be) Peace in the Valley, 63, 210, 220n87
Pearlie May Blues, 383
Pick the Meat Off the Devil's Backbone, 430
Please Baby, 378
Please Don't Wake It Up, 378
Pleasures of Youth, 26
Plenty of Good Room, Away in the Kingdom, 200
Plucking Out the Devil's Eye Ball, 213
Po' Black Sheep / Po Black Sheep / Po Little Black Sheep, 60, 227–29, 234, 242, 250n18, 251n21
Poor Rabbit, 439n118
Pop Goes the Weasel, 60, 257
Possum Up Persimmon Tree, 164
Pretty Girl Don't Pay Me No Mind, 360
Prison Bars. *See* Les Barres de la Prison

Rabbit in the Brush, 60, 61, 231
Rabbit in the Ditch, 61
Rabbit in the Log, 60
Rabbit in the Pea Patch, 60, 61
Ragtime Annie, 187
Railroad Bill, 307
Railroad Blues, 169
Rainbow's End, 209
Raise a Ruckus Tonight, 396

Ramblin' Kid Blues, 383
Rat's Gone to Rest, 179
Red Bird, 201, 203
Red River Valley, 63
Richmond, 164
Rock Creek Girls, 203
Rolling River, 231
Rosalie, 383, 392n89
Run, Rover, Run, 455
Run Here, Baby, Let Me Smell Your Hand, 322
Run N----r Run / Run, N----r, Run. *See* Paterroller'll Catch You
Running Around Blues, 210, 220n86
Running Wild Blues, 381
Rye Straw / Buck Creek Gal(s), 55
Ryro / Ryro's House, 273, 274

Sail on Little Girl, Sail on, 455
Sales Tax, 375
Sallie Goodin / Sally Gooden / Sally Goodman / Sally Goodwin / Sally Gordon, 61, 195, 201, 227, 301, 302, 360, 424, 430
Sally Ann, 52, 91
Sally in the Low Ground, 54, 152. *See also* Billy in the Low Ground
Sally in the Wildwood, 54, 430
Salty Dog Blues / Salty Dog, 139, 187, 188–91, 217n42
Sambo, 57, 231. *See also* Fire on the Mountain
Savage Dance, 26
Scott Number One, 350, 351
See See Rider Blues, 430
See You in My Dreams, 455
Shake 'Em on Down, 317
Shanty Blues, 326
Sheik Waltz, The, 375, 377
Sheiks Special, 378
She's a Bad Girl, 375
She's a Flower from the Field of Alabama, 241; Flowers for the Fields of Alabama, 204
Shippingport, 179
Shoo Shoo Mama, 322
Short Life of Trouble, 238–39
Shortening Bread, 223, 260
Silver Spoons, 439n118
Since I Layed My Burden Down, 432n14
Sister Maud Mule, 373
Sitting on Top of the World / Sittin' on Top of the World, 61, 361, 370, 375, 376, 379, 387n20, 390n67, 427
Skillet Good and Greasy / Keep My Skillet Greasy If I Can, 325

Smoke Behind the Clouds, 231
Smokey Hole, 153–54, 174n13, 421
Soldier's Joy, 61, 112, 187, 237, 276
Sourwood Mountain, 62, 139, 169, 185, 187, 197, 201, 260, 295
South of the Border, 411
St. Louis Blues, 61, 169, 207, 239, 456
St. Paul, 204
Stagolee / Stack O'Lee, 62, 322, 385
State Street Rag, 455
Station House Blues, 240
Steel Guitar Rag, 210
Stepchild Blues, 455
Stir It Now, 378
Stop and Listen Blues, 375, 376, 379, 390n67
Stop and Listen Blues No. 2, 376, 377, 390n71, 391n72
Stormy Weather, 210
Stranger Blues / I'm a Stranger Here, 432n11
Streets of Old Chicago, The, 455
Such a-Getting Upstairs I Never Did See, 153
Sugar in the Gourd, 179
Swanee River, 52
Sweet Alberta, 389n56
Sweet Bunch of Daisies, 210
Sweet Maggie, 389n56
Swing Low, Sweet Chariot, 52

Taft Highway, 209
Taint Gonna Rain No More. *See* It Ain't Gonna Rain No More
Take This Ring I Give You, 164, 175n31
T.B. Blues, 203
Tease Me Over Blues, 322
Ted's Stomp, 455
Tell Me Man Blues, 381
Tennessee Wagoner, 62, 237
Tennessee Waltz, 62, 64, 210, 301, 302, 336–37n51
Texas Bell, 319
Texas Traveler, 62, 227
That Old Corn Liquor, 274
That's It, 378
That's What the Old Bachelor's Made of, 185
There's a Meeting Here Tonight, 95
These Bones Shall Rise Again, 200
Things About Comin My Way, 390n67
This Thing Called Love, 146–47n30
Thought I Heard That K.C. Whistle Blow, 298, 335n23, 336n37, 398, 433n21
Ticonderoga, 424
Tie Your Dog, Sally Gal, 152–54, 174n5
Tiger Rag, 455
Times Done Got Hard, 375

Tippy Get Your Hair Cut, 172
Tiptoe Through the Tulips, 456
Tishomingo County Blues, 316
Tom and Jerry, 319
Too Many Mornings, 322
Toodle Doo, 373
Train Tune, 439n118
Travelin' Railroad Man Blues, 362–63, 387n22
Traveling Coon, 362
Traveling Man, 362, 363, 387nn22–23
Treat Him Right, 295
Trouble, 239, 240
Turkey Buzzard Blues, 63
Turkey in the Pea Patch, 63, 317
Turkey in the Straw, 52, 63, 64, 112, 185, 187, 217n33, 316, 319, 322

Uncle Ned, 319
Under the Double Eagle, 63, 204
Underneath the Harlem Moon, 210
Unknown Blues, 171

Vicksburg Blues, 433n18
Vine Street Drag, 176n45
Virginia Reel, 79, 101

Waggoner, 227; Old Wagoner, 394
Waiting for a Train, 410
Walking in My Sleep, 360
Wang Wang Blues, 169
Waynesborough, 181, 213; Waynesburgh, 213, 215n11
West Jackson Blues, 390n61
West Texas Blues, 439n110
Whoa Mule / Whoa, Mule, Whoa, 64, 431
Wild Goose Chase, 203
Winter Time Blues, 375
Wish to the Lord I'd Never Been Born, 163, 165, 166, 176nn37–38
Worried Blues / Worrying Blues, 64, 172, 301–3, 305, 337n53, 337n64

Yankee Doodle, 52
Yellow Coon Has No Race, 388n45
Yes, We Have No Bananas Today, 207
Yes Sir, That's My Baby, 207, 210
Yodeling Fiddling Blues, 377
You Can't Keep a Good Man Down, 146–47n30
You Never Get Fat Like That, 455
You'll Never Find Another Kanaka Like Me, 454–55

About the Author

Photo by The UCLA Herb Alpert School of Music

Jacqueline Cogdell DjeDje is professor emerita, former chair of the UCLA Department of Ethnomusicology, and former director of the UCLA Ethnomusicology Archive. She is author of numerous articles and books, including *Fiddling in West Africa: Touching the Spirit in Fulbe, Hausa, and Dagbamba Cultures*, which won both the Alan Merriam Prize and the Kwabena Nketia Book Prize from the Society for Ethnomusicology.

www.ingramcontent.com/pod-product-compliance
Lightning Source LLC
Chambersburg PA
CBHW081229300625
27785CB00022B/20